Joseph Barber Lightfoot

Saint Paul's Epistle to the Galatians

Joseph Barber Lightfoot

Saint Paul's Epistle to the Galatians

ISBN/EAN: 9783744661157

Printed in Europe, USA, Canada, Australia, Japan

SAINT PAUL'S

EPISTLE TO THE GALATIANS

A REVISED TEXT

WITH

INTRODUCTION, NOTES, AND DISSERTATIONS

BY THE LATE

J. B. LIGHTFOOT, D.D., D.C.L., LL.D.

BISHOP OF DURHAM,

HONORARY FELLOW OF TRINITY COLLEGE, CAMBRIDGE.

TENTH EDITION

London:

MACMILLAN AND CO.

AND NEW YORK.

1890

ΜΙΜΗΤΑΊ ΜΟΥ ΓΊΝΕΣΘΕ ΚΑΘῺΣ ΚἈΓῺ ΧΡΙΣΤΟΥ͂.

Παῦλος γενόμενος μέγιστος ὑπογραμμός.

CLEMENT.

Οὐχ ὡς Παῦλος διατάσσομαι ὑμῖν· ἐκεῖνος ἀπόστολος, ἐγὼ κατάκριτος· ἐκεῖνος ἐλεύθερος, ἐγὼ δὲ μέχρι νῦν δοῦλος.

IGNATIUS.

Οὔτε ἐγὼ οὔτε ἄλλος ὅμοιος ἐμοὶ δύναται κατακολουθῆσαι τῇ σοφίᾳ τοῦ μακαρίου καὶ ἐνδόξου Παύλου.

POLYCARP.

TO

THE RIGHT REV. E. W. BENSON, D.D.,

LORD BISHOP OF TRURO,

IN AFFECTIONATE AND GRATEFUL RECOGNITION

OF

A LONG, CLOSE, AND UNBROKEN FRIENDSHIP.

THE present work is intended to form part of a complete edition of St Paul's Epistles which, if my plan is ever carried out, will be prefaced by a general introduction and arranged in chronological order. To such an arrangement the half-title of the present work refers, assigning this epistle to the second chronological group and placing it third in this group in accordance with the view maintained in the introduction. Meanwhile, should this design be delayed or abandoned, the present commentary will form a whole in itself.

The general plan and execution of the work will commend or condemn themselves: but a few words may be added on one or two points which require explanation.

It is no longer necessary, I trust, to offer any apology for laying aside the received text. When so much conscientious labour has been expended on textual criticism, it would be unpardonable in an editor to acquiesce in readings which for the most part are recommended neither by intrinsic fitness nor by the sanction of antiquity. But the attempt to construct an independent text in preference to adopting the recension of some well-known editor needs more justification. If I had pursued the latter course, I should certainly have selected either Bentley or Lachmann. These two critics were thorough masters of their craft, bringing to their task extensive knowledge and keen insight. But Bentley's text[1] was constructed

[1] His text of this epistle is given in *Bentleii Critica Sacra*, p. 94 sq., edited by the Rev. A. A. Ellis.

out of very imperfect materials, and Lachmann only professed to give results which were approximate and tentative. Of the services of Tischendorf in collecting and publishing materials it is impossible to speak too highly, but his actual text is the least important and least satisfactory part of his work. Dr Tregelles, to whom we owe the best recension of the Gospels, has not yet reached the Epistles of St Paul[1]. But apart from the difficulty of choosing a fit guide, there is always some awkwardness in writing notes to another's text, and the sacrifice of independent judgment is in itself an evil; nor will it be considered unseemly presumption in a far inferior workman, if with better tools he hopes in some respects to improve upon his model. Moreover I was encouraged by the promise of assistance from my friends the Rev. B. F. Westcott and the Rev. F. J. A. Hort, who are engaged in a joint recension of the Greek Testament and have revised the text of this epistle for my use. Though I have ventured to differ from them in some passages and hold myself finally responsible in all, I am greatly indebted to them for their aid.

The authorities for the various readings are not given except in a few passages, where the variations are important enough to form the subject of a detached note. They may be obtained from Tischendorf or any of the well-known critical editions. Here and there, where the text may be considered fairly doubtful, I have either offered an alternative reading below or enclosed a word possibly interpolated in brackets; but these are for the most part unimportant and do not materially affect the sense.

In the explanatory notes such interpretations only are discussed as seemed at all events possibly right, or are generally received, or possess some historical interest. By confining myself to these, I wished to secure more space for matters of greater importance. For the same reason, in cases of disputed interpretations the authorities ranged on either side are not given, except where, as in the case of the fathers, some interest

[1] The part containing the Epistle to the Galatians has since appeared (1869).

attaches to individual opinions. Nor again have I generally quoted the authorities for the views adopted or for the illustrations and references incorporated in my notes, when these are to be found in previous commentaries or in any common book of reference. I have sometimes however departed from this rule for a special reason, as for instance where it was best to give the exact words of a previous writer.

As the plan of this work thus excludes special acknowledgments in the notes, I am anxious to state generally my obligations to others.

What I owe to the fathers of the fourth and fifth centuries will appear very plainly in the notes and in the appendix on the patristic commentators. After these, my obligations are greatest to English and German writers of the last few years. The period from the fifth century to the Reformation was an entire blank as regards any progress made in the interpretation of this epistle. And from that time to the present century, though single commentators of great merit have appeared at intervals, Calvin for instance in the sixteenth century, Grotius in the seventeenth, and Bengel in the eighteenth, there has been no such marked development of interpretational criticism as we have seen in our own time. The value of Luther's work stands apart from and in some respects higher than its merits as a commentary.

To more recent critics therefore I am chiefly indebted. Among my own countrymen I wish to acknowledge my obligations chiefly to Professor Jowett who has made the habits of thought in the Apostolic age his special study, and to Bishop Ellicott who has subjected the Apostle's language to a minute and careful scrutiny. Besides these I have consulted with advantage the portions relating to this epistle in the general commentaries of Dean Alford and Dr Wordsworth. Among German writers I am indebted especially to the tact and scholarship of Meyer and to the conscientious labours of Wieseler. Ewald is always instructive; but my acknowledgments are due more to the *History* of this truly great biblical scholar than to his edition of St Paul's Epistles. Roman Catholic theology is well represented in the devout and intelligent commentary of Windischmann: and the Tübingen school has furnished an able and learned expositor in Hilgenfeld. I have found both these commentators useful though in a widely different way. Besides the writers already mentioned I have constantly consulted Winer, Olshausen, De Wette, and Schott; and to all of these, to the first especially, I am indebted.

I need scarcely add that my obligations to these various writers differ widely in kind. Nor will it be necessary to guard against the inference that the extent of these obligations is a measure of my general agreement with the opinions of the writers. He who succeeds signally in one branch of biblical criticism or interpretation will often fail as signally in another. I do not feel called upon to point out what seem to me to be the faults of writers to whom I am most largely indebted, and I have certainly no wish to blunt the edge of my acknowledgments by doing so.

Besides commentaries, great use has been made of the common aids to the study of the language of the Greek Testament. The works to which I am most indebted in matters of grammar will appear from the frequent references in the notes. The third English edition of Winer (Edinburgh, 1861) has been used[1]. I have also availed myself constantly of the well-known collections of illustrative parallels by Wetstein, Schöttgen, Grinfield, and others; of indices to the later classical writers and earlier fathers; of the Concordances to the Septuagint and New Testament; and of the more important Greek Lexicons, especially Hase and Dindorf's edition of Stephanus.

My thanks are due for valuable suggestions and corrections to the Rev. F. J. A. Hort, late Fellow of Trinity College, and to W. A. Wright, Esq., Librarian of Trinity College; and also to other personal friends who have kindly assisted me in correcting the proof-sheets.

[1] The references to Winer have since been altered and adapted to Moulton's Translation, Edinburgh, 1870.

Though I have taken pains to be accurate, experience gained in the progress of the work has made me keenly alive to a constant liability to error; and I shall therefore esteem any corrections as a favour. I should wish moreover to adopt the language of a wise theologian, whose tone and temper I would gladly take for my model, and to 'claim a right to retract any opinion which improvement in reasoning and knowledge may at any time show me is groundless' (Hey's *Lectures on the Articles*).

While it has been my object to make this commentary generally complete, I have paid special attention to everything relating to St Paul's personal history and his intercourse with the Apostles and Church of the Circumcision. It is this feature in the Epistle to the Galatians which has given it an overwhelming interest in recent theological controversy. Though circumstances have for the moment concentrated the attention of Englishmen on the Old Testament Scriptures, the questions which have been raised on this Epistle are intrinsically far more important, because they touch the vital parts of Christianity. If the primitive Gospel was, as some have represented it, merely one of many phases of Judaism, if those cherished beliefs which have been the life and light of many generations were afterthoughts, progressive accretions, having no foundation in the Person and Teaching of Christ, then indeed St Paul's preaching was vain and our faith is vain also. I feel very confident that the historical views of the Tübingen school are too extravagant to obtain any wide or lasting hold over the minds of men. But even in extreme cases mere denunciation may be unjust and is certainly unavailing. Moreover, for our own sakes we should try and discover the element of truth which underlies even the greatest exaggerations of able men, and correct our impressions thereby.

'A number there are,' says Hooker, 'who think they cannot admire, as they ought, the power of the Word of God, if in things divine they should attribute any force to man's reason.' The circumstances which called forth this remark contrast strangely with the main controversies of the present day; but the caution is equally needed. The abnegation of reason is not the evidence of faith but the confession of despair. Reason and reverence are natural allies, though untoward circumstances may sometimes interpose and divorce them.

Any one who has attempted to comment on St Paul's Epistles must feel on laying down his task how far he has fallen short even of his own poor ideal. Luther himself expresses his shame that his 'so barren and simple commentaries should be set forth upon so worthy an Apostle and elect vessel of God.' Yet no man had a higher claim to a hearing on such a subject; for no man was better fitted by the sympathy of like experiences to appreciate the character and teaching of St Paul. One who possesses no such qualifications is entitled to feel and to express still deeper misgivings.

TRINITY COLLEGE,
February 18, 1865.

CONTENTS.

THE GALATIAN PEOPLE.

WHEN St Paul carried the Gospel into Galatia, he was thrown for the first time among an alien people differing widely in character and habits from the surrounding nations. A race whose home was in the far West, they had been torn from their parent rock by some great social convulsion, and after drifting over wide tracts of country, had settled down at length on a strange soil in the very heart of Asia Minor. Without attempting here to establish the Celtic affinities of this boulder people by the fossil remains of its language and institutions, or to trace the path of its migration by the scores imprinted on its passage across the continent of Europe, it will yet be useful, by way of introduction to St Paul's Epistle, to sketch as briefly as possible its previous history and actual condition. There is a certain distinctness of feature in the portrait which the Apostle has left of his Galatian converts. It is clear at once that he is dealing with a type of character strongly contrasted for instance with the vicious refinements of the dissolute and polished Corinthians, perhaps the truest surviving representatives of ancient Greece, or again with the dreamy speculative mysticism which disfigured the half-oriental Churches of Ephesus and Colossæ. We may expect to have light thrown upon the broad features of national character which thus confront us, by the circumstances of the descent and previous history of the race, while at the same time such a sketch will prepare the way for the solution

The Galatians an alien race

of some questions of interest, which start up in connexion with this epistle.

The great subdivision of the human family which at the dawn of European history occupied a large portion of the continent west of the Rhine with the outlying islands, and which modern philologers have agreed to call Celtic, was known to the classical writers of antiquity by three several names, *Celtæ*, *Galatæ*, and *Galli*[1]. Of these, *Celtæ*, which is the most ancient, being found in the earliest Greek historians Hecatæus and Herodotus[2], was probably introduced into the Greek language by the colonists of Marseilles[3], who were first brought in contact with this race. The term *Galatæ* is of late introduction, occurring first in Timæus, a writer of the third century B.C.[4] This latter form was generally adopted by the Greeks when their knowledge was extended by more direct and frequent intercourse with these barbarians, whether in their earlier home in the West or in their later settlement in Asia Minor. Either it was intended as a more exact representation of the same barbarian sound, or, as seems more probable, the two are diverging but closely allied forms of the same word, derived by the Greeks from different branches of the Celtic race with which at different times they came in contact[5]. On the other hand, the Romans generally designated

[1] On these terms see Diefenbach *Celtica* II. p. 6 sq., Ukert *Geogr. der Griech. u. Röm.* Th. II. Abth. 2, p. 183 sq., Zeuss *die Deutschen u. die Nachbarstämme* p. 6 sq., Thierry *Histoire des Gaulois* I. p. 28.

[2] Hecat. *Fragm.* 19, 21, 22, ed. Müller; Herod. ii. 33, iv. 49. Both forms Κελτοὶ and Κέλται occur.

[3] Diod. v. 32, quoted in note 5.

[4] Timæus *Fragm.* 37, ed. Müller. Pausanias says (i. 3. 5) *ὀψὲ δέ ποτε αὐτοὺς καλεῖσθαι Γαλάτας ἐξενίκησε· Κελτοὶ γὰρ κατά τε σφᾶς τὸ ἀρχαῖον καὶ παρὰ τοῖς ἄλλοις ὠνομάζοντο.* See also the passages in Diefenbach *Celt.* II. p. 8.

[5] This seems the most probable inference from the confused notices in ancient writers. The most important passage is Diod. v. 32, *τοὺς γὰρ ὑπὲρ Μασσαλίαν κατοικοῦντας ἐν τῷ μεσογείῳ καὶ τοὺς παρὰ τὰς Ἄλπεις ἔτι δὲ τοὺς ἐπὶ τάδε τῶν Πυρηναίων ὀρῶν Κελτοὺς ὀνομάζουσι· τοὺς δ' ὑπὲρ ταύτης τῆς Κελτικῆς εἰς τὰ πρὸς νότον νεύοντα μέρη, παρά τε τὸν ὠκεανὸν καὶ τὸ Ἑρκύνιον ὄρος καθιδρυμένους καὶ πάντας τοὺς ἑξῆς μέχρι τῆς Σκυθίας, Γαλάτας προσαγορεύουσι κ.τ.λ.* See also Strabo iv. p. 189, and other passages cited in Ukert II. 2, p. 197 sq., Diefenbach *Celt.* II. p. 10 sq. At all events it seems certain that the Gauls in the neighbourhood of Marseilles called themselves Celtæ.

this people *Galli*. Whether this word exhibits the same root as Celtæ and Galatæ, omitting however the Celtic suffix[1], or whether some other account of its origin is more probable, it is needless to enquire. The term Galli is sometimes adopted by later Greek writers, but, as a general rule, until some time after the Christian era they prefer Galatæ, whether speaking of the people of Gaul properly so called or of the Asiatic colony[2]. The Romans in turn sometimes borrow Galatæ from

Usage o Greek a Roman writers.

[1] See Zeuss *Gramm. Celt.* p. 758.

[2] Owing to the bearing of this fact, which has not been sufficiently noticed, on such passages as 2 Tim. iv. 10, I have thought it worth while to collect the following particulars. (1) Before the Christian era, and for two centuries afterwards, the form Galatia (Galatæ) is almost universally used by Greek writers to the exclusion of Gallia (Galli), when they do not employ Celtice (Celtæ). It occurs on the Monumentum Ancyranum (Boeckh *Corp. Inscr.* III. pp. 89, 90) erected by Augustus in the capital of Asiatic Gaul, where to avoid confusion the other form would naturally have been preferred, if it had been in use. It is current in Polybius, Diodorus, Strabo, Josephus, Plutarch, Appian, Pausanias, and Dion Cassius. It appears also in Athen. p. 333 D, Clem. Alex. *Strom.* I. p. 359 (Potter), and Origen *c. Cels.* p. 335 B. Even Ælian (*Nat. An.* xvii. 19, referring however to an earlier writer) when speaking of the Asiatic people is obliged to distinguish them as Γαλάτας τοὺς ἑῴους. On the other hand St Basil (*Op.* I. p. 28, Garnier) describes the European Gauls as τοὺς ἑσπερίους Γαλάτας καὶ Κελτούς. In Boeckh *C. I.* no. 9764 the Asiatic country is called μικρὰ Γαλατία, 'Little Gaul.' (2) The first instance of Gallia (Galli) which I have found in any Greek author is in Epictetus (or rather Arrian), *Dissert.* ii. 20. 17, ὥσπερ τοὺς Γαλλοὺς ἡ μανία καὶ ὁ οἶνος (probably not before A.D. 100). It occurs indeed in the present text of Dioscorides (I. 92, ἀπὸ Γαλλίας καὶ Τυρρηνίας), perhaps an earlier writer, but the reading is suspicious, since immediately afterwards he has ἀπὸ Γαλατίας τῆς πρὸς ταῖς Ἄλπεσιν. Later transcribers were sorely tempted to substitute the form with which they were most familiar, as is done in 2 Tim. iv. 10 in several MSS. See below, p. 31, note 1. The substitution is so natural that it is sometimes erroneously made where the eastern country is plainly meant: e.g. Pseudo-Doroth. *Chron. Pasch.* II. p. 136, ed. Dind. The form Γαλλία occurs again in the Ep. of the Churches of Vienne and Lyons (Euseb. v. 1) A.D. 177, and in Theophil. *ad Autol.* ii. 32 τὰς καλουμένας Γαλλίας. It is also common in Herodian. (3) In the 4th and 5th centuries the form 'Gallia' had to a very great extent displaced Galatia. See Agathem. ii. 4, p. 37, τῶν Γαλλιῶν ἃς πρότερον Γαλατίας ἔλεγον, and Theod. Mops. on 2 Tim. iv. 10, τὰς νῦν καλουμένας Γαλλίας· οὕτως γὰρ (i.e. Γαλατίαν) αὐτὰς πάντες ἐκάλουν οἱ παλαιοί. Accordingly Athanasius (*Apol. c. Arian.* § 1, pp. 97, 98) in the same passage uses Γαλατία of Asiatic Gaul, Γαλλίαι of the European provinces. At a much earlier date than this Galen says (XIV. p. 80, Kuhn), καλοῦσι γοῦν αὐτοὺς ἔνιοι μὲν Γαλάτας ἔνιοι δὲ Γαλλούς, συνηθέστερον δὲ τὸ τῶν Κελτῶν ὄνομα, but he must be referring in the first two classes to the usage of the Greek and Roman writers respectively.

the Greeks, but when they do so it is applied exclusively to the Celts of Asia Minor, that is, to the Galatians in the modern sense of the term. The word Celtæ still remains in common use side by side with the Galatæ of the Greek and Galli of the Roman writers, being employed in some cases as coextensive with these, and in others to denote a particular branch of the Celtic race[1].

Celtic migrations.

The rare and fitful glimpses which we obtain of the Celtic peoples in the early twilight of history reveal the same restless, fickle temperament, so familiar to us in St Paul's epistle. They appear in a ferment of busy turmoil and ceaseless migration[2]. They are already in possession of considerable tracts of country to the south and east of their proper limits. They have overflowed the barrier of the Alps and poured into Northern Italy. They have crossed the Rhine and established themselves here and there in that vague and ill-defined region known to the ancients as the Hercynian forest and on the banks of the Danube. It is possible that some of these were fragments sundered from the original mass of the Celtic people, and dropped on the way as they migrated westward from the common home of the Aryan races in central Asia: but more probable and more in accordance with tradition is the view that their course being obstructed by the ocean, they had retraced their steps and turned towards the East again. At all events,

See similar notices in Strabo iv. p. 195, Appian *Bell. Hisp.* § 1. The form Γαλατία of European Gaul still continued to be used occasionally, when Γαλλία had usurped its place. It is found for instance in Julian *Epist.* lxxiii, and in Libanius frequently: comp. Cureton *Corp. Ign.* p. 351. Ammianus (xv. 9) can still say, 'Galatas dictos, ita enim Gallos sermo Graecus appellat.' Even later writers, who use Γαλλίαι of the Roman provinces of Gaul, nevertheless seem to prefer Γαλατία when speaking of the western country as a whole, e.g. Ioann. Lydus *Ostent.* pp. 52, 54 (Wachsmuth), Hierocl. *Synecd.* app. p. 313 (Parthey).

[1] e.g. in Cæsar *Bell. Gall.* i. 1. See on the main subject of the preceding paragraph a good paper by M. D'Arbois de Jubainville, *Les Celtes, Les Galates, Les Gaulois*, from the *Revue Archéologique*, Paris 1875.

[2] For the migrations of the Celts see the well-known work of Thierry *Histoire des Gaulois* (4th ed. 1857), or Contzen *Wanderungen der Kelten* (Leipz. 1861). They are considered more in their philological aspect in Diefenbach's *Celtica*, and in Prichard's *Celtic Nations* edited by Latham. The article 'Galli' by Baumstark in Pauly's *Real-Encyclopädie* is a careful abstract of all that

as history emerges into broad daylight, the tide of Celtic migration is seen rolling ever eastward. In the beginning of the fourth century before Christ a lateral wave sweeps over the Italian peninsula, deluging Rome herself and obliterating the landmarks of her earlier history. Three or four generations later another wave of the advancing tide, again diverted southward, pours into Macedonia and Thessaly, for a time carrying everything before it. The fatal repulse from Delphi, invested by Greek patriotism with a halo of legendary glory, terminated the Celtic invasion of Greece.

Sacking of Rome, B.C. 390.

Attack on Delphi, B.C. 279.

The Gaulish settlement in Asia Minor is directly connected with this invasion[1]. A considerable force had detached themselves from the main body, refusing to take part in the expedition. Afterwards reinforced by a remnant of the repulsed army they advanced under the command of the chiefs Leonnorius and Lutarius, and forcing their way through Thrace arrived at the coast of the Hellespont. They did not long remain here, but gladly availing themselves of the first means of transport that came to hand, crossed over to the opposite shores, whose fertility held out a rich promise of booty. Thence they overran the greater part of Asia Minor. They laid the whole continent west of Taurus under tribute, and even the

The Gauls in Asia Minor.

relates to the subject. See also Le Bas *Asie Mineure* (Paris, 1863).

[1] The chief authorities for the history of the Asiatic Gauls are Polybius v. 77, 78, 111, xxii. 16—24, Livy xxxviii. 12 sq., Strabo xii. p. 566 sq., Memnon (*Geogr. Min.* ed. Müller, III. p. 535 sq.), Justin xxv. 2 sq., Arrian *Syr.* 42, Pausanias i. 4. 5. See other references in Diefenbach *Celt.* II. p. 250. It formed the main subject of several works no longer extant, the most important of which was the Γαλατικὰ of Eratosthenes in forty books. The monograph of Wernsdorff, *De Republica Galatarum* (Noremb. 1743), to which all later writers are largely indebted, is a storehouse of facts relating to early Galatian history. See also Robiou *Histoire des Gaulois d'Orient* (1866). The existing monuments of Galatia are described by Texier, *Asie Mineure* (1839—1849), I. p. 163 sq. An article in the *Revue des Deux Mondes* (1841), IV. p. 574, by the same writer, contains an account of the actual condition of this country with a summary of its history ancient and modern. See also his smaller book, *Asie Mineure* (1862), p. 453 sq. More recent is the important work *Exploration Archéologique de la Galatie et de la Bithynie* etc. by Perrot and Guillaume. The account of the Monumentum Ancyranum in this work is very complete and illustrated by numerous plates. The ancient history of Galatia is also given at length.

Syrian kings, it is said, were forced to submit to these humiliating terms[1]. Alternately, the scourge and the allies of each Asiatic prince in succession, as passion or interest dictated, they for a time indulged their predatory instincts unchecked. At length vengeance overtook them. A series of disasters, B.C. 230. culminating in a total defeat inflicted by the Pergamene prince Attalus the First, effectually curbed their power and insolence[2].

Limits of Galatia.

By these successive checks they were compressed within comparatively narrow limits in the interior of Asia Minor. The country to which they were thus confined, the Galatia of history, is a broad strip of land over two hundred miles in length, stretching from north-east to south-west. It was parcelled out among the three tribes, of which the invading Gauls were composed, in the following way. The Trocmi occupied the easternmost portion, bordering on Cappadocia and Pontus, with Tavium or Tavia as their chief town. The Tolistobogii, who were situated to the west on the frontier of Bithynia and Phrygia Epictetus, fixed upon the ancient Pessinus for their capital. The Tectosages settled in the centre between the other two tribes, adopting Ancyra as their seat of government, regarded also as the metropolis of the whole of Galatia[3].

Galatia conquered by the Romans,

But though their power was greatly crippled by these disasters, the Gauls still continued to play an important part in the feuds of the Asiatic princes. It was while engaged in these mercenary services that they first came into collision with the terrible might of Rome. A body of Galatian troops fighting on the side of Antiochus at the battle of Magnesia attracted the notice of the Romans, and from that moment their doom was sealed. A single campaign of the Consul B.C. 189; Manlius sufficed for the entire subjugation of Galatia.

[1] Livy xxxviii. 16.

[2] The chronology is somewhat uncertain. See Niebuhr *Kl. Schrift.* p. 286. The date given is an approximation.

[3] So Strabo xii. p. 567, Pliny *H. N.* v. 42, in accordance with ancient authorities generally and confirmed by the inscriptions, Boeckh III. nos. 4010, 4011, 4085. Memnon is therefore in error (c. 19), when he assigns the chief towns differently. The names of the three tribes are variously written (see Contzen, p. 221), but the orthography adopted in the text is the best supported.

From that time forward they lived as peaceably as their restless spirit allowed them under Roman patronage. No humiliating conditions however were imposed upon them. They were permitted to retain their independence, and continued to be governed by their own princes. The conquerors even granted accessions of territory from time to time to those Galatian sovereigns who had been faithful to their allegiance. It was not the policy of the Romans to crush a race which had acted and might still act as a powerful check on its neighbours, thus preserving the balance of power or rather of weakness among the peoples of Asia Minor. At length, after more than a century and a half of native rule, on the death of Amyntas one of their princes, Galatia was formed by Augustus into a Roman province.

becomes a province, B.C. 25.

The limits of the province are not unimportant in their bearing on some questions relating to the early history of the Gospel. It corresponded roughly to the kingdom of Amyntas, though some districts of the latter were assigned to a different government. Thus Galatia, as a Roman province, would include, besides the country properly so called, Lycaonia, Isauria, the south-eastern district of Phrygia, and a portion of Pisidia[1]. Lycaonia is especially mentioned as belonging to it, and there is evidence that the cities of Derbe and Lystra in particular[2] were included within its boundaries. When the province was

Extent of the Roman province.

[1] The extent of the kingdom of Amyntas may be gathered from the following passages: Strabo xii. p. 568, Dion Cass. xlix. 32 (Lycaonia), Strabo xii. p. 569 (Isauria), p. 571 (Pisidia), p. 577 (part of Phrygia), xiv. p. 671 (Cilicia Tracheia), Dion Cass. xlix. 32 (part of Pamphylia). See Becker *Röm. Alterth.* III. 1. p. 155, Cellarius *Not. Orb. Ant.* II. p. 182. Of the formation of the Roman province Strabo says, xii. p. 567, *νῦν δ' ἔχουσι Ῥωμαῖοι καὶ ταύτην [τὴν Γαλατίαν] καὶ τὴν ὑπὸ τῷ Ἀμύντᾳ γενομένην πᾶσαν εἰς μίαν συναγαγόντες ἐπαρχίαν*, and similarly p. 569. This sweeping statement however must be qualified. See Dion Cass. liii. 26, *τοῦ δ' Ἀμύντου τελευτήσαντος οὐ τοῖς παισὶν αὐτοῦ τὴν ἀρχὴν ἐπέτρεψεν, ἀλλ' εἰς τὴν ὑπήκοον ἐσήγαγε· καὶ οὕτω καὶ ἡ Γαλατία μετὰ τῆς Λυκαονίας Ῥωμαῖον ἄρχοντα ἔσχε· τὰ δὲ χωρία τὰ ἐκ τῆς Παμφυλίας πρότερον τῷ Ἀμύντᾳ προσνεμηθέντα τῷ ἰδίῳ νόμῳ ἀπεδόθη.* Cilicia Tracheia was also separated and assigned to Archelaus, Strabo xiv. p. 671. On the subject generally see Perrot *de Gal. Prov. Rom.* Paris 1867.

[2] The Lystreni are included by Pliny among the Galatian peoples, *H. N.* v.

formed, the three chief towns of Galatia proper, Ancyra, Pessinus, and Tavium, took the name of Sebaste or Augusta, being distinguished from each other by the surnames of the respective tribes to which they belonged[1].

Ambiguity of the name.

Thus when the writers of the Roman period, St Paul and St Luke for instance, speak of Galatia, the question arises whether they refer to the comparatively limited area of Galatia proper, or to the more extensive Roman province. The former is the popular usage of the term, while the latter has a more formal and official character.

Other elements of the Galatian population.

Attention has hitherto been directed solely to the barbarian settlers in this region. These however did not form by any means the whole population of the district. The Galatians, whom Manlius subdued by the arms of Rome, and St Paul by the sword of the Spirit, were a very mixed race. The substratum of society consisted of the original inhabitants of the invaded country, chiefly Phrygians, of whose language not much is known, but whose strongly marked religious system has a prominent place in ancient history. The upper layer was composed of the Gaulish conquerors: while scattered irregularly through the social mass were Greek settlers, many of whom doubtless had followed the successors of Alexander thither and were already in the country when the Gauls took possession of it[2]. To the country thus peopled the Romans, ignoring the old Phrygian population, gave the name of Gallogræcia. At the time when Manlius invaded it, the victorious Gauls had not amalgamated with their Phrygian subjects; and the Roman consul on opening his campaign was met by a troop of the Phrygian priests of Cybele, who clad in the robes of their order and chanting a wild strain of prophecy declared to him that the goddess approved of the war, and would make him

Phrygians.

Greeks.

42. That Derbe also belonged to Galatia may be inferred from Strabo xii. p. 569. See Böttger *Beiträge, Suppl.* p. 26.

[1] Σεβαστὴ Τεκτοσάγων, Σ. Τολιστοβωγίων, Σ. Τρόκμων. See Becker *Röm. Alterth.* III. 1. p. 156.

[2] It might be inferred from the inscription, Boeckh III. p. 82, Ἰουλίου Σεουήρου τοῦ πρώτου τῶν Ἑλλήνων, that the Greeks in Galatia were recognised as a distinct class even under the Romans.

master of the country[1]. The great work of the Roman conquest was the fusion of the dominant with the conquered race—the result chiefly, it would appear, of that natural process by which all minor distinctions are levelled in the presence of a superior power. From this time forward the amalgamation began, and it was not long before the Gauls adopted even the religion of their Phrygian subjects[2].

Fusion of Gauls and Phrygians.

The Galatia of Manlius then was peopled by a mixed race of Phrygians, Gauls, and Greeks. But before St Paul visited the country two new elements had been added to this already heterogeneous population. The establishment of the province must have drawn thither a considerable number of Romans, not very widely spread in all probability, but gathered about the centres of government, either holding official positions themselves, or connected more or less directly with those who did. From the prominence of the ruling race in the Galatian monuments[3] we might even infer that the whole nation had been romanized. Such an impression however would certainly be incorrect. I cannot find in St Paul's epistle any distinct trace of the influence, or even of the presence, of the masters of the world, though the flaunting inscriptions of the Sebasteum still proclaim the devotion of the Galatian people to the worship of Augustus and Rome.

Romans.

More important is it to remark on the large influx of Jews which must have invaded Galatia in the interval[4]. Antiochus

Jews.

[1] Polyb. xxii. 20, Livy xxxviii. 18.

[2] A Brogitarus is mentioned as priest of the mother of the gods at Pessinus; Cicero *de Arusp. Resp.* 28, *pro Sext.* 26. A Dyteutus son of Adiatorix held the same office in the temple of the goddess worshipped at Comana, Strabo xii. p. 558. Other instances are given in Thierry I. p. 411, Perrot *Expl. Arch.* p. 185.

[3] Boeckh *Corp. Inscr.* III. pp. 73—115.

[4] The direct connexion of the Galatians with Jewish history is very slight. In 2 Macc. viii. 20 there is an obscure allusion to an engagement with them in Babylonia. In 1 Macc. viii. 2 it is said that Judas Maccabæus 'heard of the wars of the Romans and the brave deeds which they did among the Galatians (or Gauls) and how they subdued them and laid them under tribute': but whether we suppose the enumeration of the Roman triumphs to proceed in geographical or chronological order, the reference is probably to the Western Gauls, either chiefly or solely, since the successes of the Romans in Spain are

the Great had settled two thousand Jewish families in Lydia and Phrygia[1]; and even if we suppose that these settlements did not extend to Galatia properly so called, the Jewish colonists must in course of time have overflowed into a neighbouring country which possessed so many attractions for them. Those commercial instincts, which achieved a wide renown in the neighbouring Phœnician race, and which in the Jews themselves made rapid progress during the palmy days of their national life under Solomon, had begun to develope afresh. The innate energy of the race sought this new outlet, now that their national hopes were crushed and their political existence was well-nigh extinct. The country of Galatia afforded great facilities for commercial enterprise. With fertile plains rich in agricultural produce, with extensive pastures for flocks, with a temperate climate and copious rivers, it abounded in all those resources out of which a commerce is created[2]. It was moreover conveniently situated for mercantile transactions, being traversed by a great high road between the East and the shores of the Ægean, along which caravans were constantly passing, and among its towns it numbered not a few which are mentioned as great centres of commerce[3]. We read especially of a considerable traffic in cloth

Their commercial instincts,

attracted by the natural advantages of Galatia.

mentioned in the following verse, their victories over Philip and Perseus in the 5th, and the defeat of Antiochus not till the 6th verse. The same uncertainty hangs over the incident in Joseph. *Ant.* xv. 7. 3, *Bell. Jud.* i. 20. 3, where we read that Augustus gave to Herod as his body-guard 400 Galatians (or Gauls) who had belonged to Cleopatra.

[1] Joseph. *Ant.* xii. 3. 4.

[2] An anonymous geographer (*Geogr. Min.* Müller, II. p. 521) describes Galatia as 'provincia optima, sibi sufficiens.' Other ancient writers also speak of the natural advantages of this country; see Wernsdorff p. 199 sq. A modern traveller writes as follows: 'Malgré tant de ravages et de guerres désastreuses, la Galatie, par la fertilité de son sol et la richesse de ses produits agricoles, est encore une des provinces les plus heureuses de l'Asie Mineure.' And again: 'Malgré tous ses malheurs, la ville moderne d'Angora est une des plus peuplées de l'Asie Mineure. Elle doit la prospérité relative dont elle n'a cessé de jouir à son heureuse situation, à un climat admirablement sain, à un sol fertile, et surtout à ses innombrables troupeaux de chèvres, etc.' Texier, *Revue des Deux Mondes*, l. c. pp. 597, 602.

[3] Strabo, xii. p. 567, especially mentions Tavium and Pessinus, describing the latter as ἐμπορεῖον τῶν ταύτῃ μέγιστον. Livy, xxxviii. 18, calls Gordium 'celebre et frequens emporium.'

goods; but whether these were of home or foreign manufacture we are not expressly told[1]. With these attractions it is not difficult to explain the vast increase of the Jewish population in Galatia, and it is a significant fact that in the generation before St Paul Augustus directed a decree granting especial privileges to the Jews to be inscribed in his temple at Ancyra, the Galatian metropolis[2], doubtless because this was a principal seat of the dispersion in these parts of Asia Minor. Other testimony to the same effect is afforded by the inscriptions found in Galatia, which present here and there Jewish names and symbols[3] amidst a strange confusion of Phrygian and Celtic, Roman and Greek. At the time of St Paul they probably boasted a large number of proselytes and may even have infused a beneficial leaven into the religion of the mass of the heathen population. Some accidental points of resemblance in the Mosaic ritual may perhaps have secured for the inspired teaching of the Old Testament a welcome which would have been denied to its lofty theology and pure code of morals[4].

Their influence.

[1] Müller's *Geogr. Min.* l. c. 'negotiatur plurimam vestem.' It is interesting to find that at the present day a very large trade is carried on at Angora, the ancient Ancyra, in the fabric manufactured from the fine hair of the peculiar breed of goats reared in the neighbourhood. See Hamilton *Asia Minor*, I. p. 418, Texier, l. c. p. 602 sq., and especially Ritter's *Erdkunde* XVIII. p. 505. It is to this probably that the ancient geographer refers.

[2] Joseph. *Antiq.* xvi. 6. 2. The influence of Judaism on St Paul's converts here does not derive the same illustration from the statistics of the existing population as it does in some other places, Thessalonica for instance, where the Jews are said to form at least one half of the inhabitants. In 1836 Hamilton was informed that out of about 11,000 houses in Ancyra only 150 were Jewish, the majority of the population being Turks or Catholic Armenians, *Asia Minor*, I. p. 419.

[3] See Boeckh *Corp. Inscr.* Vol. III. P. xviii. In no. 4129 the name Ἠσαῦος occurs with a symbol which Boeckh conjectures to be the seven-branched candlestick. We have also Ἰωάννου 4045, Σάνβατος 4074, Ματατᾶς 4088, Θαδεὺς 4092. Ἀκίλας or Ἀκύλας a name commonly borne by Jews in these parts occurs several times. It is possible however that some of these may be Christian; nor is it always easy to pronounce on the Hebrew origin of a name in the confusion of nations which these inscriptions exhibit.

[4] Pausanias (vii. 17. 5) mentions that the people of Pessinus abstained from swine's flesh (ὑῶν οὐχ ἁπτόμενοι), a statement which has given rise to much discussion. See Wernsdorff p. 324 sq. Some have attributed this abstinence to Jewish influence, but the aversion to swine's flesh was common to several Eastern peoples. Instances are given

The Celtic type predominates.

Still with all this foreign admixture, it was the Celtic blood which gave its distinctive colour to the Galatian character and separated them by so broad a line even from their near neighbours. To this cause must be attributed that marked contrast in religious temperament which distinguished St Paul's disciples in Galatia from the Christian converts of Colossæ, though educated in the same Phrygian worship and subjected to the same Jewish influences. The tough vitality of the Celtic character maintained itself in Asia comparatively unimpaired among Phrygians and Greeks, as it has done in our own islands among Saxons and Danes and Normans, retaining its individuality of type after the lapse of ages and under conditions the most adverse[1].

The Galatians retain their language

A very striking instance of the permanence of Celtic institutions is the retention of their language by these Gauls of Asia Minor. More than six centuries after their original settlement in this distant land, a language might be heard on the banks of the Sangarius and the Halys, which though slightly corrupted was the same in all essential respects with that spoken in the district watered by the Moselle and the Rhine. St Jerome, who had himself visited both the Gaul of the West and the Gaul of Asia Minor, illustrates the relation of the two forms of speech by the connexion existing between the language of the Phœnicians and their African colonies, or between the different dialects of Latin[2].

in Milman's *Hist. of the Jews* I. p. 177 (3rd ed.).

[1] Modern travellers have seen, or imagined they saw, in the physical features of the modern inhabitants of Galatia traces of their Celtic origin. So Texier, l. c. p. 598, 'Sans chercher à se faire illusion, on reconnaît quelquefois, surtout parmi les pasteurs, des types qui se rapportent merveilleusement à certaines races de nos provinces de France. On voit plus de cheveux blonds en Galatie qu'en aucun autre royaume de l'Asie Mineure; les têtes carrées et les yeux bleux rappellent le caractère des populations de l'ouest de la France.'

[2] Hieron. *in Epist. ad Gal.* lib. II. præf. 'Galatas excepto sermone Graeco, quo omnis Oriens loquitur, propriam linguam eandem pene habere quam Treveros, nec referre si aliqua exinde corruperint, quum et Afri Phoenicum linguam nonnulla ex parte mutaverint, et ipsa Latinitas et regionibus quotidie mutetur et tempore' (VII. P. I. p. 430, ed. Vallarsi). By 'excepto sermone Graeco' he means that they spoke Greek in common with the rest of the

With the knowledge of this remarkable fact, it will not be thought idle to look for traces of the Celtic character in the Galatians of St Paul's Epistle, for in general the character of a nation even outlives its language. No doubt it had undergone many changes. They were no longer that fierce hardy race with which Rome and Greece successively had grappled in a struggle of life and death. After centuries of intercourse with Greeks and Phrygians, with the latter especially who were reputed among the most effeminate and worthless of Asiatics, the ancient valour of the Gauls must have been largely diluted. Like the Celts of Western Europe, they had gradually deteriorated under the enervating influence of a premature or forced civilisation[1]. Nevertheless beneath the surface the Celtic character remains still the same, whether manifested in the rude and fiery barbarians who were crushed by the arms of Cæsar, or the impetuous and fickle converts who call down the indignant rebuke of the Apostle of the Gentiles.

and their character essentially unchanged.

St Paul's language indeed will suggest many coincidences, which perhaps we may be tempted to press unduly. His denunciation of 'drunkenness and revellings[2],' falling in with the taunts of ancient writers, will appear to point to a darling sin of the Celtic people[3]. His condemnation of the niggardly

Minor coincidences in St Paul's epistle.

East, *as well as Celtic*. Thierry (I. p. 415) strangely mistakes the meaning, 'les Galates étaient les seuls, entre tous les peuples asiatiques, qui ne se servissent point de la langue grecque.' It is probable that they understood St Paul's epistle as well as if it had been written in their original tongue. None of the Galatian inscriptions are in the Celtic language. The people of Ancyra were perhaps 'trilingues' like the Celts of Marseilles.

1 Livy, xxxviii. 17, represents Manlius as saying 'Et illis majoribus nostris cum haud dubiis Gallis in terra sua genitis res erat. Hi jam degeneres sunt, mixti et Gallograeci vere, quod appellantur.' This language is probably an anachronism in the mouth of Manlius, but it was doubtless true when Livy wrote and when St Paul preached. On the degeneracy of the Western Gauls, see Cæsar *Bell. Gall.* vi. 24, Tac. *Ann.* xi. 18, *Agric.* 11, *Germ.* 28.

2 Gal. v. 21.

3 Diod. Sic. v. 26 *κάτοινοι δὲ ὄντες καθ' ὑπερβολὴν τὸν εἰσαγόμενον ὑπὸ τῶν ἐμπόρων οἶνον ἄκρατον ἐμφοροῦνται καὶ διὰ τὴν ἐπιθυμίαν λάβρῳ χρώμενοι τῷ ποτῷ καὶ μεθυσθέντες εἰς ὕπνον ἢ μανιώδεις διαθέσεις τρέπονται κ.τ.λ.*; Epictet. *Dissert.* ii. 20. 17, referred to in the note p. 3. Compare also the jest, 'Gallos post haec dilutius esse poturos,' quoted from Cicero by Ammian. Marc. xv. 12, and the account Ammianus himself

spirit with which they had doled out their alms, as a 'mockery of God[1],' will remind us that the race is constantly reproached with its greed of wealth, so that Gaulish avarice passed almost into a proverb[2]. His reiterated warning against strife and vainglory[3] will seem directed against a vice of the old Celtic blood still boiling in their veins and breaking out in fierce and rancorous self-assertion[4]. His very expression, 'if ye bite and devour one another,' will recall the angry gesticulations and menacing tones of this excitable people[5]. But without laying too much stress on these points of resemblance, which however plausible do not afford ground enough for a safe inference, we may confidently appeal to the broader features of the Galatian character, as they appear in this Epistle. In two important points especially, in the general temperament and the religious bias of his converts, light is shed on the language of St Paul by the notices of the Gauls found in classical authors.

Broader features of resemblance.

1. General temperament of the Gauls.

1. The main features of the Gaulish character are traced with great distinctness by the Roman writers. Quickness of apprehension, promptitude in action, great impressibility, an eager craving after knowledge, this is the brighter aspect of the Celtic character. Inconstant and quarrelsome, treacherous in their dealings, incapable of sustained effort, easily disheartened by failure, such they appear when viewed on their darker side. It is curious to note the same eager inquisitive temper revealing itself under widely different circumstances, at opposite limits both of time and space, in their early barbarism in the West and their worn-out civilisation in the East. The great Roman captain relates

gives of the intemperance of the Gauls.

[1] Gal. vi. 6, 7.

[2] Diod. Sic. v. 27 *ὄντων τῶν Κελτῶν φιλαργύρων καθ' ὑπερβολήν*. Livy, xxxviii. 27, calls the Galatians 'avidissima rapiendi gens.' Compare Labb. *Conc.* v. 49 (ed. Colet) *ἐφωράθησαν τινὲς κατὰ τῶν Γαλατῶν ὀλιγωροῦντες καὶ παραβαίνοντες δι' αἰσχροκέρδειαν καὶ φιλαργυρίαν κ.τ.λ.*, in the encyclical letter against simony, A.D. 459.

[3] Gal. v. 15, 26; comp. v. 20, 21, vi. 3.

[4] Ammian. l. c. 'avidi jurgiorum et sublatius insolescentes,' Diod. Sic. v. 28.

[5] Diod. Sic. v. 31 *ἀπειληταὶ δὲ καὶ ἀνατατικοὶ καὶ τετραγῳδημένοι ὑπάρχουσι*, Ammian. l. c. 'Metuendae voces complurium et minaces, placatorum juxta et irascentium.'

how the Gauls would gather about any merchant or traveller who came in their way, detaining him even against his will and eagerly pressing him for news[1]. A late Greek rhetorician commends the Galatians as more keen and quicker of apprehension than the genuine Greeks, adding that the moment they catch sight of a philosopher, they cling to the skirts of his cloak, as the steel does to the magnet[2]. It is chiefly however on the more forbidding features of their character that contemporary writers dwell. Fickleness is the term used to express their temperament[3]. This instability of character was the great difficulty against which Cæsar had to contend in his dealings with the Gaul[4]. He complains that they all with scarcely an exception are impelled by the desire of change[5]. Nor did they show more constancy in the discharge of their religious, than of their social obligations. The hearty zeal with which they embraced the Apostle's teaching followed by their rapid apostasy is only an instance out of many of the reckless facility with which they adopted and discarded one religious system after another. To St Paul, who had had much bitter experience of hollow professions and fickle purposes, this extraordinary levity was yet a matter of unfeigned surprise. 'I marvel,' he says, 'that ye are changing so quickly[6].' He looked upon it as some strange fascination. 'Ye senseless Gauls, who did bewitch you[7]?' The language in which Roman writers speak of the martial courage of the Gauls, impetuous at the first onset but rapidly melting in the heat of the fray[8], well describes the short-lived

Their fickleness.

[1] Cæsar *Bell. Gall.* iv. 5.

[2] Themistius *Or.* xxiii. p. 299 A (referred to by Wetstein on Gal. i. 6) *οἱ δὲ ἄνδρες ἴστε ὅτι ὀξεῖς καὶ ἀγχίνοι καὶ εὐμαθέστεροι τῶν ἄγαν Ἑλλήνων· καὶ τριβωνίου παραφανέντος ἐκκρέμανται εὐθὺς ὥσπερ τῆς λίθου τὰ σιδήρια.*

[3] *Bell. Gall.* ii. 1 'Mobilitate et levitate animi'; comp. Tac. *Germ.* 29.

[4] *Bell. Gall.* iv. 5 'Infirmitatem Gallorum veritus quod sunt in consiliis capiendis mobiles et novis plerumque rebus student, nihil his committendum existimavit.' Comp. Motley *United Netherlands* III. p. 326, 'As has already been depicted in these pages, the Celtic element had been more apt to receive than consistent to retain the generous impression which had once been stamped on all the Netherlands.'

[5] *Ib.* iii. 10 'Quum intelligeret omnes fere Gallos novis rebus studere.'

[6] Gal. i. 6.

[7] Gal. iii. 1 *Ω ἀνόητοι Γαλάται, τίς ὑμᾶς ἐβάσκανεν;*

[8] Livy x. 28 'Gallorum quidem etiam

prowess of these converts in the warfare of the Christian Church.

2. Their religious tendencies

2. Equally important, in its relation to St Paul's epistle, is the type of religious worship which seems to have pervaded the Celtic nations. The Gauls are described as a superstitious people given over to ritual observances[1]. Nor is it perhaps a mere accident that the only Asiatic Gaul of whom history affords more than a passing glimpse, Deiotarus the client of Cicero, in his extravagant devotion to augury fully bears out the character ascribed to the parent race[2].

passionate and ritualistic,

The colours in which contemporary writers have painted the religion of the primitive Gauls are dark and terrible enough. A gross superstition, appealing to the senses and the passions rather than to the heart and mind, enforcing rites of unexampled cruelty and demanding a slavish obedience to priestly authority, such is the picture with which we are familiar. It is unnecessary here to enquire how far the religious philosophy of the Druids involved a more spiritual creed[3]. The Druids were an exclusive caste with an esoteric doctrine, and it is with the popular worship that we are concerned. The point to be observed is that an outward material passionate religion had grown up among the Gauls, as their own creation, answering to some peculiar features of their character. Settled among the Phrygians they with their wonted facility adopted the religion of the subject people. The worship of Cybele with its wild ceremonial and hideous mutilations would naturally be attractive to the Gaulish mind. Its external rites were similar enough in their general character to those of the primitive Celtic religion to commend it to a people who had found satis-

shown in their heathen worship.

corpora intolerantissima laboris atque aestus fluere; primaque eorum praelia plusquam virorum, postrema minus quam feminarum esse.' Comp. Florus ii. 4. To the same effect Cæsar *B. G.* iii. 19, and Polyb. ii. 35.

[1] Cæsar's words are, 'Natio est omnis Gallorum admodum dedita religionibus,' *Bell. Gall.* vi. 16; comp. Diod. Sic. v. 27.

[2] Cicero *de Div.* i. 15, ii. 36, 37.

[3] The nobler aspect of the Druidical system has been exaggerated. See the remarks of M. de Pressensé, *Trois Premiers Siècles*, 2me série, 1. p. 52.

faction in the latter. And though we may suppose that the mystic element in the Phrygian worship, which appealed so powerfully to the Græco-Asiatic, awoke no corresponding echo in the Gaul, still there was enough in the outward ritual with its passionate orgies to allure them. Then the Gospel was offered to them and the energy of the Apostle's preaching took their hearts by storm. But the old leaven still remained. The pure and spiritual teaching of Christianity soon ceased to satisfy them. Their religious temperament, fostered by long habit, prompted them to seek a system more external and ritualistic[1]. 'Having begun in the Spirit, they would be made perfect in the flesh[2].' Such is the language of the Apostle rebuking this unnatural violation of the law of progress. At a later period in the history of the Church we find the Galatians still hankering after new forms of Christianity in the same spirit of ceaseless innovation, still looking for some 'other gospel' which might better satisfy their cravings after a more passionate worship.

and infecting their Christianity.

[1] Compare the language of a modern historian describing the western race in a much later age; Motley *Dutch Republic* III. p. 26 'The stronger infusion of the Celtic element, which from the earliest ages had always been so keenly alive to the more sensuous and splendid manifestations of the devotional principle.'

[2] Gal. iii. 3.

II.

THE CHURCHES OF GALATIA.

IN what sense do the sacred writers use the word Galatia? Has it an ethnographical or a political meaning? In other words, does it signify the comparatively small district occupied by the Gauls, Galatia properly so called, or the much larger territory included in the Roman province of the name? This question must be answered before attempting to give an account of the Galatian Churches.

Important consequences flow from the assumption that the term covers the wider area[1]. In that case it will comprise not only the towns of Derbe and Lystra[2], but also, it would seem, Iconium and the Pisidian Antioch: and we shall then have in the narrative of St Luke[3] a full and detailed account of the founding of the Galatian Churches. Moreover the favourite disciple and most constant companion of the Apostle, Timotheus, was on this showing a Galatian[4]; and through him St Paul's communications with these Churches would be more or less close to the end of his life. It must be confessed too, that this view has much to recommend it at first sight. The Apostle's account of his hearty and enthusiastic welcome by the Galatians, as an angel of God[5], will have its counterpart in the impulsive warmth of the barbarians at Lystra, who would have sacrificed to him, imagining that 'the Gods had come down in the like-

[1] The warmest advocates of this view are Böttger *Beiträge* I. p. 28 sq., III. p. 1 sq., and Renan *Saint Paul* p. 51, etc. See more on this subject in *Colossians* p. 24 sq.

[2] See above, p. 7, note 2.

[3] Acts xiii. 14—xiv. 24.

[4] Acts xvi. 1.

[5] Gal. iv. 14.

ness of men[1].' His references to 'the temptations in the flesh,' and 'the marks of the Lord Jesus' branded on his body[2], are then illustrated, or thought to be illustrated, by the persecutions and sufferings that 'came unto him at Antioch, at Iconium, at Lystra[3].' The progress of Judaizing tendencies among the Galatians is then accounted for by the presence of a large Jewish element such as the history describes in these Churches of Lycaonia and Pisidia[4].

Objections to this view.

Without stopping however to sift these supposed coincidences, or insisting on the chronological and historical difficulties which this view creates, there are many reasons which make it probable that the Galatia of St Paul and St Luke is not the Roman province of that name, but the land of the Gauls[5]. By writers speaking familiarly of the scenes in which they had themselves taken part, the term would naturally be used in its popular rather than in its formal and official sense. It would scarcely be more strange to speak of Pesth and Presburg, of Venice and Verona, as 'the Austrian cities,' than to entitle the Christian brotherhoods of Derbe and Lystra, Iconium and Antioch, 'the Churches of Galatia.' Again, analogy is strongly in favour of the popular use of the term[6]. Mysia, Phrygia, Pisidia, are all 'geographical expressions' destitute of any political significance; and as they occur in the same parts of the narrative with Galatia[7], it seems fair to infer that the latter is similarly used. The direct transition for instance, which we find from Galatia to Phrygia, is only explicable if the two are kindred terms, both alike being used in a popular way. Moreover, St Luke distinctly calls Lystra and Derbe 'cities of

[1] Acts xiv. 11.

[2] Gal. iv. 14, vi. 17.

[3] 2 Tim. iii. 11.

[4] Acts xiii. 14, 43, 45, xiv. 1, xvi. 3.

[5] On the other hand in 1 Peter i. 1, where the enumeration seems to proceed by provinces, Galatia is probably used in its political sense. This is not unnatural in one who was writing from a distance, and perhaps had never visited the district.

[6] The case of 'Asia' however is an exception. The foundation of this province dating very far back, its official name had to a great extent superseded the local designations of the districts which it comprised. Hence Asia in the New Testament is always Proconsular Asia.

[7] Acts xiv. 24, xvi. 6—8, xviii. 23.

Lycaonia[1],' while he no less distinctly assigns Antioch to Pisidia[2]; a convincing proof that in the language of the day they were not regarded as Galatian towns. Lastly, the expression used in the Acts of St Paul's visit to these parts, 'the Phrygian and Galatian country[3],' shows that the district intended was not Lycaonia and Pisidia, but some region which might be said to belong either to Phrygia or Galatia, or the parts of each contiguous to the other.

It is most probable therefore that we should search for the Churches of Galatia within narrower limits. In the absence of all direct testimony, we may conjecture that it was at Ancyra, now the capital of the Roman province as formerly of the Gaulish settlement, 'the most illustrious metropolis,' as it is styled in formal documents[4]; at Pessinus, under the shadow of Mount Dindymus, the cradle of the worship of the great goddess, and one of the principal commercial towns of the district[5]; at Tavium, at once a strong fortress and a great emporium, situated at the point of convergence of several important roads[6]; perhaps also at Juliopolis, the ancient Gordium, formerly the capital of Phrygia, almost equidistant from the three seas, and from its central position a busy mart[7]; at these, or some of these places, that St Paul founded the earliest 'Churches of Galatia.' The ecclesiastical geography of Galatia two or three centuries later is no safe guide in settling questions relating to the apostolic age, but it is worth while to

1 Acts xiv. 6.

2 Acts xiii. 14.

3 Acts xvi. 6. See below, p. 22, note 3.

4 Boeckh *Corp. Inscr.* no. 4015 ἡ βουλὴ καὶ ὁ δῆμος τῆς λαμπροτάτης μητροπόλεως Ἀγκύρας. It is frequently styled the 'metropolis' in inscriptions and on coins.

5 Strabo xii. p. 567.

6 Strabo l. c. See Hamilton's *Asia Minor* p. 395. Perhaps however Tavium lay too much to the eastward of St Paul's route, which would take him more directly to the western parts of Galatia.

7 Pliny v. 42 'Caputque quondam ejus (i.e. Phrygiae) Gordium.' Comp. Livy xxxviii. 18 'Haud magnum quidem oppidum est, sed plusquam mediterraneum, celebre et frequens emporium: tria maria pari ferme distantia intervallo habet.' See Ritter *Erdkunde* XVIII. p. 561. The identity of Gordium and Juliopolis however, though assumed by Ritter, Forbiger, Kiepert, and others, is perhaps a mistake: see Mordtmann in *Sitzungsber. der Königl. bayer. Akad.* 1860, p. 169 sq.

observe that these are among the earliest episcopal sees on record in this country[1].

In Galatia the Gospel would find itself in conflict with two distinct types of worship, which then divided the allegiance of civilised heathendom. At Pessinus the service of Cybele, the most widely revered of all pagan deities, represented, perhaps more adequately than any other service, the genuine spirit of the old popular religion. At Ancyra the pile dedicated to the divinities of Augustus and Rome was one of the earliest and most striking embodiments of the new political worship which imperial statecraft had devised to secure the respect of its subject peoples. We should gladly have learnt how the great Apostle advocated the cause of the truth against either form of error. Our curiosity however is here disappointed. It is strange that while we have more or less acquaintance with all the other important Churches of St Paul's founding, with Corinth and Ephesus, with Philippi and Thessalonica, not a single name of a person or place, scarcely a single incident of any kind, connected with the Apostle's preaching in Galatia, should be preserved in either the history or the epistle. The reticence of the Apostle himself indeed may be partly accounted for by the circumstances of the Galatian Church. The same delicacy, which has concealed from us the name of the Corinthian offender, may have led him to avoid all special allusions in addressing a community to which he wrote in a strain of the severest censure. Yet even the slight knowledge we do possess of the early Galatian Church is gathered from the epistle, with scarcely any aid from the history. Can it be that the historian gladly drew a veil over the infancy of a Church which swerved so soon and so widely from the purity of the Gospel?

Silence of St Paul and St Luke.

St Luke mentions two visits to Galatia, but beyond the bare fact he adds nothing to our knowledge. The first occasion was during the Apostle's second missionary journey, probably in the year 51 or 52[2]. The second visit took place a few years later, perhaps in the year 54, in the course of his third missionary

Two visits to Galatia.

[1] Le Quien *Oriens Christ.* I. p. 456 sq.

[2] Acts xvi. 6.

journey, and immediately before his long residence in Ephesus[1]. The epistle contains allusions, as will be seen, to both visits; and combining these two sources of information, we arrive at the following scanty facts.

irst visit, D. 51 or .

I. After the Apostolic congress St Paul starting from Antioch with Silas revisited the churches he had founded in Syria, Cilicia, and Lycaonia. At Lystra they fell in with Timotheus, who also accompanied them on their journey[2]. Hitherto the Apostle had been travelling over old ground. He now entered upon a new mission-field, 'the region of Phrygia and Galatia[3].' The form of the Greek expression implies that Phrygia and Galatia here are not to be regarded as separate districts. The country which was now evangelized might be called indifferently Phrygia or Galatia. It was in fact the land originally inhabited by Phrygians, but subsequently occupied by Gauls: or so far as he travelled beyond the limits of the Gallic settlement, it was still in the neighbouring parts of Phrygia that he preached, which might fairly be included under one general expression[4].

St Paul does not appear to have had any intention of preaching the Gospel here[5]. He was perhaps anxious at once to bear his message to the more important and promising district of Proconsular Asia[6]. But he was detained by a return

[1] Acts xviii. 23.

[2] Acts xv. 40—xvi. 5.

[3] Acts xvi. 6 διῆλθον δὲ τὴν Φρυγίαν καὶ [τὴν] Γαλατικὴν χώραν. The second τὴν of the received reading ought to be omitted with the best MSS, in which case Φρυγίαν becomes an adjective. This variety of reading has escaped the notice of commentators, though it solves more than one difficulty. On the occasion of the second visit the words are (xviii. 23), διερχόμενος καθεξῆς τὴν Γαλατικὴν χώραν καὶ Φρυγίαν. The general direction of St Paul's route on both occasions was rather westward than eastward, and this is expressed in the second passage by naming Galatia before Phrygia, but it is quite consistent with the expression in the first, where the two districts are not separated. If we retain the received reading, we must suppose that St Paul went from west to east on the first occasion, and from east to west on the second.

[4] Colossæ would thus lie beyond the scene of the Apostle's labours, and the passage correctly read does not present even a seeming contradiction to Col. i. 4, 6, 7, ii. 1. See on the whole subject *Colossians* p. 23 sq.

[5] I see no reason for departing from the strictly grammatical interpretation of Gal. iv. 13, δι' ἀσθένειαν τῆς σαρκός.

[6] Acts xvi. 6.

St Paul's illness and hearty reception in Galatia.

of his old malady, 'the thorn in the flesh, the messenger of Satan sent to buffet him[1],' some sharp and violent attack, it would appear, which humiliated him and prostrated his physical strength. To this the Galatians owed their knowledge of Christ. Though a homeless stricken wanderer might seem but a feeble advocate of a cause so momentous, yet it was the divine order that in the preaching of the Gospel strength should be made perfect in weakness. The zeal of the preacher and the enthusiasm of the hearers triumphed over all impediments. 'They did not despise nor loathe the temptation in his flesh. They received him as an angel of God, even as Christ Jesus. They would have plucked out their very eyes, if they could, and have given them to him[2].' Such was the impression left on his heart by their first affectionate welcome, painfully embittered by contrast with their later apostasy.

Attitude of the Galatians towards the Gospel.

It can scarcely have been any predisposing religious sympathy which attracted them so powerfully, though so transiently, to the Gospel. They may indeed have held the doctrine of the immortality of the soul, which is said to have formed part of the Druidical teaching in European Gaul[3]. It is possible too that there lingered, even in Galatia, the old Celtic conviction, so cruelly expressed in their barbarous sacrifices, that only by man's blood can man be redeemed[4]. But with these doubtful exceptions, the Gospel, as a message of mercy and a spiritual faith, stood in direct contrast to the gross and material religions in which the race had been nurtured, whether the cruel ritualism of their old Celtic creed, or the frightful orgies of their adopted worship of the mother of the gods. Yet though the whole spirit of Christianity was so alien to their habits of thought, we may well imagine how the fervour of the Apostle's preaching may have fired their religious enthusiasm. The very image under which he describes his work brings

[1] 2 Cor. xii. 7.

[2] Gal. iv. 14, 15.

[3] They believed also in its transmigration. See Cæsar *Bell. Gall.* vi. 14, Diod. Sic. v. 28.

[4] *Bell. Gall.* vi. 16 'Pro vita hominis nisi hominis vita reddatur, non posse aliter deorum immortalium numen placari arbitrantur.'

Earnestness of the Apostle's preaching.

vividly before us the energy and force with which he delivered his message. He *placarded* Christ crucified before their eyes[1], arresting the gaze of the spiritual loiterer, and riveting it on this proclamation of his Sovereign. If we picture to ourselves the Apostle as he appeared before the Galatians, a friendless outcast, writhing under the tortures of a painful malady, yet instant in season and out of season, by turns denouncing and entreating, appealing to the agonies of a crucified Saviour, perhaps also, as at Lystra, enforcing this appeal by some striking miracle, we shall be at no loss to conceive how the fervid temperament of the Gaul might have been aroused, while yet only the surface of his spiritual consciousness was ruffled. For the time indeed all seemed to be going on well. 'Ye were running bravely,' says the Apostle[2], alluding to his favourite image of the foot-race. But the very eagerness with which they had embraced the Gospel was in itself a dangerous symptom. A material so easily moulded soon loses the impression it has taken. The passionate current of their Celtic blood, which flowed in this direction now, might only too easily be diverted into a fresh channel by some new religious impulse. Their reception of the Gospel was not built on a deeply-rooted conviction of its truth, or a genuine appreciation of its spiritual power.

His departure.

This visit to Galatia, we may suppose, was not very protracted. Having been detained by illness, he would be anxious to continue his journey as soon as he was convalescent. He was pressing forward under a higher guidance towards a new field of missionary labour in the hitherto unexplored continent of Europe.

Second visit, A.D. 54.

2. An interval of nearly three years must have elapsed before his second visit. He was now on his third missionary journey; and according to his wont, before entering upon a new field of labour, his first care was to revisit and 'confirm' the churches he had already founded. This brought him to 'the Galatian country and Phrygia.' From the language used in

[1] Gal. iii. 1, προεγράφη. See the note. [2] Gal. v. 7.

describing this visit we may infer that not a few congregations had been established in Galatia. 'He went through the district *in order*, confirming *all* the disciples[1].'

Dangerous symptoms.

Of the second visit to Galatia even less is known than of the former. It would seem however that some unhealthy symptoms had already appeared, threatening the purity of the Gospel. At all events certain expressions in the epistle, which are most naturally referred to this visit, imply that cause for uneasiness had even then arisen. He was constrained to address his converts in language of solemn warning[2]. He charged them to hold accursed any one who perverted the Gospel as he had taught it[3]. Writing to them afterwards, he contrasts the hearty welcome of his first visit with his cold reception on this occasion, attributing their estrangement to the freedom with which he denounced their errors. 'Have I become your enemy,' he asks, 'because I told you the truth[4]?'

Subsequent communications.

The epistle was written, as I hope to show, about three or four years after the second visit, but in the meanwhile St Paul doubtless kept up his intercourse with the Galatian Churches by messengers or otherwise. A large portion of the intervening time was spent at Ephesus, whence communication with Galatia would be easily maintained. An incidental allusion in the First Epistle to the Corinthians throws light on this subject. It there appears that St Paul appealed[5] to the Churches of Galatia, as he did also to those of Macedonia and Achaia, to contribute towards the relief of their poorer brethren in Palestine, who were suffering from a severe famine. By communication thus maintained St Paul was made acquainted with the growing corruption of the Galatian Churches from the spread of Judaizing errors.

Collection of alms.

Jewish influence in Galatia.

The avidity with which these errors were caught up implies some previous acquaintance with Jewish history and some habituation to Jewish modes of thought. The same inference

[1] Acts xviii. 23.
[2] Gal. v. 21.
[3] Gal. i. 9.
[4] Gal. iv. 13—16. See the notes.
[5] 1 Cor. xvi. 1—6.

may be drawn from the frequent and minute references in the epistle to the Old Testament, assuming no inconsiderable knowledge of the sacred writings on the part of his converts. It has been shown already that there was in Galatia a large population of Jews to whom this influence may be traced[1].

The Galatian Churches contained a nucleus of Jewish converts,

The Apostle had probably selected as centres of his mission those places especially where he would find a sufficient body of Jewish residents to form the nucleus of a Christian Church. It was almost as much a matter of missionary convenience, as of religious obligation, to offer the Gospel 'to the Jew first and then to the Gentile[2].' They were the keepers of the sacred archives, and the natural referees in all that related to the history and traditions of the race. To them therefore he must of necessity appeal. In almost every instance where a detailed account is given in the Apostolic history of the foundation of a Church, we find St Paul introducing himself to his fellow-countrymen first, the time the sabbath-day, the place the synagogue, or, where there was no synagogue, the humbler proseucha. Thus in the very act of planting a Christian Church, the Apostle himself planted the germs of bigotry and disaffection.

but were composed chiefly of Gentiles.

Not however that the Gospel seems to have spread widely among the Jews in Galatia, for St Paul's own language shows that the great mass at least of his converts were Gentiles[3], and the analogy of other churches points to the same result. But Jewish influences spread far beyond the range of Jewish circles. The dalliance with this 'foreign superstition,' which excited the indignation of the short-sighted moralists of Rome, was certainly

[1] See above, p. 9 sq.

[2] Rom. i. 16, ii. 9, 10.

[3] Gal. iv. 8 'Then not knowing God, ye did service to them which by nature are no gods.' See also Gal. iii. 29, v. 2, vi. 12, and the notes on i. 14 ἐν τῷ γένει μου, ii. 5 πρὸς ὑμᾶς. It has been assumed that St Peter, as the Apostle of the Circumcision, must have written to Jewish Christians, and that therefore, as his epistles are addressed to the Galatians among others, there was a large number of converts from Judaism in the Churches of Galatia. His own language however shows that he is writing chiefly to Gentiles (1 Pet. ii. 9, 10) and that therefore the διασπορά of the opening salutation is the *spiritual* dispersion. Comp. 1 Pet. ii. 11, 12.

not less rife in the provinces than in the metropolis. Many a man, who had not cast off his heathen religion, and perhaps had no intention of casting it off, was yet directly or indirectly acquainted with the customs and creed of the Jews, and possibly had some knowledge of the writings of the lawgiver and the prophets. Still there were doubtless some Jewish converts in the Galatian Church[1]. These would be a link of communication with the brethren of Palestine, and a conducting medium by which Jewish practices were transmitted to their Gentile fellow-Christians.

Violent character of Galatian Judaism.

For whatever reason, the Judaism of the Galatians was much more decided than we find in any other Gentile Church. The infection was both sudden and virulent. They were checked all at once in the gallant race for the prize[2]. Their gaze was averted by some strange fascination from the proclamation of Christ crucified[3]. Such are the images under which the Apostle describes their apostasy. It was a Judaism of the sharp Pharisaic type, unclouded or unrelieved by any haze of Essene mysticism, such as prevailed a few years later in the neighbouring Colossian Church. The necessity of circumcision was strongly insisted upon[4]. Great stress was laid on the observance of 'days and months and seasons and years[5].' In short, nothing less than submission to the whole ceremonial law seems to have been contemplated by the innovators[6]. At all events, this was the logical consequence of the adoption of the initiatory rite[7].

Strict observance of the law.

St Paul's authority impugned.

This position could only be maintained by impugning the credit of St Paul. By some means or other his authority must be set aside, and an easy method suggested itself. They represented him as no true Apostle. He had not been one of the Lord's personal followers, he had derived his knowledge of the Gospel at second hand. It was therefore to the mother

[1] See the note on vi. 13, where the various readings οἱ περιτετμημένοι and οἱ περιτεμνόμενοι have some bearing on this point.

[2] Gal. v. 7.

[3] Gal. iii. 1.

[4] Gal. v. 2, 11, vi. 12, 13.

[5] Gal. iv. 10.

[6] Gal. iii. 3, iv. 21, v. 4, 18.

[7] Gal. v. 3.

Church of Jerusalem that all questions must be referred, to the great Apostles of the Circumcision especially, the 'pillars of the Church,' to James in the forefront as the Lord's brother, to Peter who had received a special commission from his Master, to John the most intimate of His personal friends[1]. This disparaging criticism of his opponents St Paul has in view from first to last in the Epistle to the Galatians. He commences by asserting in the strongest terms his immediate divine commission as an Apostle 'not of men neither by man[2],' and this assertion he emphatically reiterates[3]. He gives in the body of the letter a minute historical account of his intercourse with the Apostles of the Circumcision, showing his entire independence of them[4]. He closes, as he had begun, with a defence of his office and commission. 'Henceforth,' he exclaims indignantly, 'let no man trouble me, for I bear in my body the marks of the Lord Jesus[5].' He felt that there was a heartless mockery in the denial of his Apostleship, when he had been marked as the servant of Christ for ever by the cruel brand of persecution.

His defence.

He is charged with inconsistency.

But the attacks of his enemies did not stop here. They charged him with inconsistency in his own conduct. He too, it was represented, had been known to preach that circumcision which he so strenuously opposed[6]. It was convenient to him, they insinuated, to repudiate his convictions now, in order to ingratiate himself with the Gentiles[7]. There must have been doubtless many passages in the life of one who held it a sacred duty to become all things to all men, especially to become as

[1] The participles *τοῖς δοκοῦσιν* (ii. 2), *τῶν δοκούντων εἶναί τι, οἱ δοκοῦντες* (ii. 6), *οἱ δοκοῦντες στύλοι εἶναι* (ii. 9), ought probably to be translated as *presents*, referring to the exclusive importance which *the Judaizers in Galatia* attached to the Apostles of the Circumcision. See the notes.

[2] Gal. i. 1.

[3] Gal. i. 11, 12.

[4] Gal. i. 15—ii. 21.

[5] Gal. vi. 17.

[6] Gal. v. 11. See Lechler *Apost. u. Nachapost. Zeitalter* (ed. 2), p. 384. The case of Titus (Gal. ii. 3), however we explain it, seems to be introduced in order to meet this charge.

[7] See the notes on Gal. i. 10, 'Do I *now* persuade men?' 'Do I seek to please men?' and on ii. 3, v. 2, 11.

a Jew to the Jews[1], to which bigoted or unscrupulous adversaries might give this colour. Such for instance was the circumcision of Timothy[2]; such again was the sanction given to Jewish usages during his last visit to Jerusalem, when at the instigation of James he defrayed the expenses of those who had taken Nazarite vows[3]. To concessions like these, I imagine, continued throughout his life, and not, as some have thought, to any earlier stage of the Apostle's teaching, when his Christian education was not yet matured, and some remnants of Judaism still hung about him (for of such a stage there is no evidence), are we to look for the grounds on which his opponents charged him with inconsistency.

These errors sown from without.

The instigators of this rebellion against St Paul's authority and teaching seem not to have been Galatian residents. His leading antagonists were most probably emissaries from the mother Church of Jerusalem, either abusing a commission actually received from the Apostles of the Circumcision, or assuming an authority which had never been conferred upon them. The parallel case of the Corinthian Church, where communications between the Judaic party and the Christians of Palestine are more clearly traced, suggests this solution, and it is confirmed by the Epistle to the Galatians itself. When St Paul refers to the dissimulation at Antioch occasioned by the arrival of 'certain who came from James[4],' we can scarcely resist the impression that he is holding up the mirror of the past to the Galatians, and that there was sufficient resemblance between the two cases to point the application. Moreover, the vague allusions to these opponents scattered through the epistle seem to apply rather to disturbances caused by a small and compact body of foreign intruders, than to errors springing up silently and spontaneously within the Galatian Church itself. They are the tares sown designedly by the enemy in the night time, and not the weeds which grow up promiscuously as the natural product of the soil. 'A little leaven leaveneth the

[1] 1 Cor. ix. 20, 22.
[2] Acts xvi. 3.
[3] Acts xxi. 20—26.
[4] Gal. ii. 12.

whole lump[1].' 'There be some that trouble you[2].' It would even seem that there was a ringleader among the Judaizing teachers, marked out either by his superior position or his greater activity: 'He that troubleth you shall bear his judgment, whosoever he be[3].'

The Galatian soil congenial to their growth.

But howsoever they were disseminated, these errors found in Galatia a congenial soil. The corruption took the direction which might have been expected from the religious education of the people. A passionate and striking ritualism expressing itself in bodily mortifications of the most terrible kind had been supplanted by the simple spiritual teaching of the Gospel. For a time the pure morality and lofty sanctions of the new faith appealed not in vain to their higher instincts, but they soon began to yearn after a creed which suited their material cravings better, and was more allied to the system they had abandoned. This end they attained by overlaying the simplicity of the Gospel with Judaic observances. This new phase of their religious life is ascribed by St Paul himself to the temper which their old heathen education had fostered. It was a *return* to the 'weak and beggarly elements' which they had outgrown, a *renewed* subjection to the 'yoke of bondage' which they had thrown off in Christ[4]. They had escaped from one ritualistic system only to bow before another. The innate failing of a race 'excessive in its devotion to external observances[5]' was here reasserting itself.

To check these errors, which were already spreading fast, the Apostle wrote his Epistle to the Galatians. What effect his remonstrance had upon them can only be conjectured, for from this time forward the Galatian Church may be said to disappear from the Apostolic history. If we could be sure that the mission of Crescens, mentioned in the latest of St Paul's

[1] Gal. v. 9.

[2] Gal. i. 7. See also iv. 17, vi. 12.

[3] Gal. v. 10.

[4] Gal. iv. 9 πῶς ἐπιστρέφετε πάλιν ἐπὶ τὰ ἀσθενῆ καὶ πτωχὰ στοιχεῖα οἷς πάλιν ἄνωθεν δουλεύειν θέλετε, and v. 1 μὴ πάλιν ζυγῷ δουλείας ἐνέχεσθε.

[5] Cæsar *Bell. Gall.* vi. 16, quoted p. 16, note 1.

epistles, refers to the Asiatic settlement, there would be some ground for assuming that the Apostle maintained a friendly intercourse with his Galatian converts to the close of his life; but it is at least as likely that the mother country of the Gauls is there meant[1]. Neither from the epistles of St Peter can any facts be elicited; for as they are addressed to all the great Churches of Asia Minor alike, no inference can be drawn as to the condition of the Galatian Church in particular. In the absence of all information, we would gladly believe that here, as at Corinth, the Apostle's rebuke was successful, that his authority was restored, the offenders were denounced, and the whole Church, overwhelmed with shame, returned to its allegiance. The cases however are not parallel. The severity of tone is more sustained in this instance, the personal appeals are fewer, the remonstrances more indignant and less affectionate. One ray of hope indeed seems to break through the dark cloud, but we must not build too much on a single expression of confidence[2], dictated it may be by a generous and politic charity which 'believeth all things.'

Effect of the epistle uncertain.

It is not idle, as it might seem at first sight, to follow the

[1] 2 Tim. iv. 10. 'Galatia' in this passage was traditionally interpreted of European Gaul. It is explained thus by Euseb. *H. E.* iii. 4, Epiphan. *adv. Haeres.* li. 11, p. 433, Jerome (?) *Op.* II. p. 960 (ed. Vallarsi), and by Theodore of Mopsuestia and Theodoret commenting on the passage. It is so taken also by those MSS which read Γαλλίαν for Γαλατίαν, for the former reading may be regarded as a gloss. The Churches of Vienne and Mayence both claimed Crescens as their founder. The passage in the *Apost. Const.* vii. 46 Κρήσκης τῶν κατὰ Γαλατίαν ἐκκλησιῶν perhaps points to Asiatic Gaul, but is ambiguous. Later writers made Crescens visit both the European and the Asiatic country. A curious coincidence of names occurs in Boeckh *Inscr.* no. 3888 Κρήσκεντα ἐπίτροπον Λουγδούνου Γαλλίας. I attribute some weight to the tradition in favour of Western Gaul, because it is not the *prima facie* view. Supposing St Paul to have meant this, he would almost certainly have used Γαλατίαν and not Γαλλίαν; see the note, p. 3; and to the authorities there quoted add Theodoret on 2 Tim. iv. 10, τὰς Γαλλίας οὕτως ἐκάλεσεν· οὕτω γὰρ ἐκαλοῦντο πάλαι· οὕτω δὲ καὶ νῦν αὐτὰς ὀνομάζουσιν οἱ τῆς ἔξω παιδείας μετειληχότες. A passage in the *Monumentum Ancyranum* (Boeckh *Inscr.* no. 4040) presents a coincidence with 2 Tim. iv. 10, in the juxta-position of Galatia (i.e. European Gaul) and Dalmatia, ἐξ Ἱσπανίας καὶ Γαλατίας καὶ παρὰ Δαλματῶν.

[2] Gal. v. 10.

stream of history beyond the horizon of the Apostolic age. The fragmentary notices of its subsequent career reflect some light on the temper and disposition of the Galatian Church in St Paul's day. To Catholic writers of a later date indeed the failings of its infancy seemed to be so faithfully reproduced in its mature age, that they invested the Apostle's rebuke with a prophetic import[1]. Asia Minor was the nursery of heresy, and of all the Asiatic Churches it was nowhere so rife as in Galatia. The Galatian capital was the stronghold of the Montanist revival[2], which lingered on for more than two centuries, splitting into diverse sects, each distinguished by some fantastic gesture or minute ritual observance[3]. Here too were to be found

Later heresies of the Galatian Church.

[1] Euseb. *c. Marcell.* I. p. 7 A ὥσπερ γὰρ θεσπίζων τὸ μέλλον αὐτοῖς Γαλάταις τὴν τοῦ Σωτῆρος ἐξηκρίβου θεολογίαν, κ.τ.λ., Hieron. *ad Gal.* ii. *praef.* (VI. p. 427, ed. Vallarsi) '...quomodo apostolus unamquamqueprovinciam suis proprietatibus denotarit? Usque hodie eadem vel virtutum vestigia permanent vel errorum.'

[2] An anonymous writer quoted by Euseb. *H. E.* v. 16. 3. Comp. Epiphan. *Haer.* xlviii. 14, p. 416.

[3] Hieron. l. c. p. 430 'Scit mecum qui vidit Ancyram metropolim Galatiae civitatem, quot nunc usque schismatibus dilacerata sit, quot dogmatum varietatibus constuprata. Omitto Cataphrygas, Ophitas, Borboritas, et Manichaeos; nota enim jam haec humanae calamitatis vocabula sunt. Quis unquam Passalorynchitas et Ascodrobos et Artotyritas et caetera magis portenta quam nomina in aliqua parte Romani orbis audivit?' The Passalorynchites and Artotyrites were off-shoots of Montanism, the one so called from their placing the forefinger on the nose when praying, the other from their offering bread and cheese at the Eucharist: Epiph. *Haeres.* xlviii. 14 sq., p. 416 sq., Philastr. *Haeres.* lxxiv, lxxvi. In the word Ascodrobi there is perhaps some corruption. Theodoret, *Haeret. Fab.* i. 10, speaks of the Ascodrupi or Ascodrupitae, as a Marcosian (Gnostic) sect. Epiphanius, l.c., mentions Tascodrugitae as a barbarous equivalent to Passalorynchitae. Jerome however seems to have had in view the sect called Ascodrogitae by Philastrius, *Haeres.* lxxv. The account of Philastrius well exhibits the general temper of Galatian heresy: 'Alii sunt Ascodrogitae in Galatia, qui utrem inflatum ponunt et cooperiunt in sua ecclesia et circumeunt eum insanientes potibus et bacchantes, sicut pagani Libero patri...Et cum suis caecitatibus properant inservire, alieni modis omnibus Christianae salutis repperiuntur, cum apostolus dejiciat justificationem illam Judaicam carnalemque vanitatem.' After all allowance made for the exaggerations of orthodox writers, the orgiastic character of the worship of these sects is very apparent. The apostasy of St Paul's converts is still further illustrated by Philastrius' account of the Quartodecimani, lxxxvii; 'Alia est haeresis quae adserit cum Judaeis debere fieri pascha. Isti in Galatia et Syria et Phrygia commorantur, et Hierosolymis; et cum Judaeos sequantur, simili cum eis errore depereunt.'

Ophites, Manichæans, sectarians of all kinds. Hence during the great controversies of the fourth century issued two successive bishops, who disturbed the peace of the Church, swerving or seeming to swerve from Catholic truth in opposite directions, the one on the side of Sabellian, the other of Arian error[1]. A Christian father of this period denounces 'the folly of the Galatians, who abound in many impious denominations[2].' A harsher critic, likewise a contemporary, affirms that whole villages in Galatia were depopulated by the Christians in their intestine quarrels[3].

Final struggle with Paganism.

From these painful scenes of discord it is a relief to turn to a nobler contest in which the Galatian Christians bore their part gallantly. A sketch of their final struggle with and victory over heathendom will fitly close this account of the first preaching of the Gospel among them.

The Galatian Churches furnished their quota to the army of martyrs in the Diocletian persecution, and the oldest existing church in the capital still bears the name of its bishop Clement, who perished during this reign of terror[4]. The struggle over

[1] Marcellus and Basilius; Le Quien *Oriens Christianus* I. p. 458. Eusebius wrote two elaborate treatises against Marcellus, which are extant. On the other hand, his orthodoxy was defended at one time by several of his Catholic contemporaries, but his reputation suffered from the more decided Sabellianism of his pupil the hæresiarch Photinus, likewise a Galatian. Basilius presided at the semi-Arian Synod of Ancyra, held in 358. See Hefele *Conciliengesch.* I. p. 655.

[2] Greg. Naz. *Orat.* xxii. (I. p. 422 A ed. Ben.) ἡ Γαλατῶν ἄνοια πλουτούντων ἐν πολλοῖς τῆς ἀσεβείας ὀνόμασι, doubtless alluding to St Paul's ἀνόητοι Γαλάται. Compare Basil. *Epist.* 237 (III. p. 365, sq. ed. Garnier), Hilar. *de Trin.* vii. 3 (II. p. 176, ed. Ben.).

[3] The Emperor Julian's language (*Epist.* 52, speaking of Galatia and certain neighbouring districts) ἄρδην ἀνατραπῆναι πορθηθείσας κώμας, is a painful comment on St Paul's warning, Gal. v. 15, 'If ye bite and devour one another, take heed ye be not consumed one of another.' Julian, however, at no time an unprejudiced witness, has here a direct interest in exaggerating these horrors, as he is contrasting the mutual intolerance of the Christians with his own forbearance.

[4] Texier *Asie Mineure* i. pp. 195, 200, describes and figures the Church of St Clement at Ancyra. He is wrong however in mentioning the Decian persecution. The legend speaks of that of Diocletian; *Acta Sanct.* Jan. xxiii. In a Syrian martyrology published by Dr W. Wright (in the *Journal of Sacred Literature*, Oct. 1865 and Jan. 1866) the Galatian martyrs mentioned are numerous.

and peace restored, a famous council was held at Ancyra, a court-martial of the Church, for the purpose of restoring discipline and pronouncing upon those who had faltered or deserted in the combat[1]. When the contest was renewed under Julian, the forces of paganism were concentrated upon Galatia, as a key to the heathen position, in one of their last desperate struggles to retrieve the day. The once popular worship of the mother of the gods, which issuing from Pessinus had spread throughout the Greek and Roman world, was a fit rallying point for the broken ranks of heathendom. In this part of the field, as at Antioch, Julian appeared in person. He stimulated the zeal of the heathen worshippers by his own example, visiting the ancient shrine of Cybele, and offering costly gifts and sacrifices there[2]. He distributed special largesses among the poor who attended at the temples. He wrote a scolding letter to the pontiff of Galatia, rebuking the priests for their careless living, and promising aid to Pessinus on condition that they took more pains to propitiate the goddess[3]. The Christians met these measures for the most part in an attitude of fierce defiance. At Ancyra one Basil, a presbyter of the church, fearlessly braving the imperial anger, won for himself a martyr's crown. Going about from place to place, he denounced all participation in the polluting rites of heathen sacrifice, and warned his Christian brethren against bartering their hopes of heaven for such transitory honours as an earthly monarch could confer. At length brought before the provincial governor, he was tortured, condemned, and put to death[4]. At Pessinus

Efforts of Julian

defied by the Christians.

[1] About the year 314; Hefele *Conciliengesch.* I. p. 188. See the note on Gal. v. 20.

[2] Ammian. xxii. 9, Liban. *Or.* xii, I. p. 398, xvii. I. p. 513 (Reiske).

[3] Julian *Epist.* 49 Ἀρσακίῳ ἀρχιερεῖ Γαλατίας, preserved in Sozom. v. 16. The 'high priest' is mentioned in the Galatian inscriptions, Boeckh nos. 4016, 4020, 4026. Julian seems to have taken the worship of the mother of the gods under his special protection. An elaborate oration of his (Orat. 3) is devoted to this subject. Comp. Gregor. Naz. I. p. 109 (ed. Ben.).

[4] Sozom. v. 11. The Acts of the Martyrdom of St Basil of Ancyra (Ruinart *Acta Mart. Sinc.* p. 510) are less exaggerated than most, and perhaps entitled to respect.

another zealous Christian, entering the temple, openly insulted the mother of the gods and tore down the altar. Summoned before Julian, he appeared in the imperial presence with an air of triumph, and even derided the remonstrances which the emperor addressed to him [1]. This attempt to galvanize the expiring form of heathen devotion in Galatia seems to have borne little fruit. With the emperor's departure paganism relapsed into its former torpor. And not long after in the presence of Jovian, the Christian successor of the apostate, who halted at Ancyra on his way to assume the imperial purple [2], the Galatian churches had an assurance of the final triumph of the truth.

[1] Gregor. Naz. *Orat.* v. I. p. 175 A. Gregory at the same time mentions another Christian—apparently in Galatia, though this is not stated—whose bold defiance was visited with extreme tortures. One or other of these may be that Busiris, of whom Sozomen (l.c.) speaks as a Christian confessor at Ancyra under Julian.

[2] Ammian. xxv. 10.

III.

THE DATE OF THE EPISTLE.

Absence of direct evidence.

IT has been already noticed that the epistle itself contains singularly few details of St Paul's intercourse with the Churches of Galatia, and that the narrative of St Luke is confined to the bare statement of the fact of his preaching there. Owing to this twofold silence, there is a paucity of direct evidence bearing on the date of the epistle. A few scattered notices, somewhat vague in themselves and leading only to approximate results, are all that we can collect: and the burden of the proof rests in consequence on an examination of the style of the letter, and of the lines of thought and feeling which may be traced in it. With this wide field open for conjecture, there has naturally been great diversity of opinion. The Epistle to the Galatians has been placed by different critics both the earliest and the latest of St Paul's writings, and almost every intermediate position has at one time or the other been assigned to it. The patristic writers are for the most part divided between two views. Some of these, as Victorinus[1] and Primasius, suppose

Diversity of opinion.

[1] Mai *Script. Vet. Coll.* vol. III. Victorinus, who wrote about A.D. 360, mentions this as an opinion entertained by others, so that it dates farther back. 'Epistola ad Galatas missa dicitur ab apostolo ab Epheso civitate.' I suspect it was first started by Origen. In the Canon of Marcion (Tertull. *adv. Marc.* v. 2, Epiphan. *Haer.* xlii. p. 350) the Epistle to the Galatians stood first, but I cannot think that his order was chronological. At all events, supposing it to be so, the fact of his placing the Epistles to the Thessalonians after the Romans diminishes the respect which would otherwise be felt for the opinion of a writer so ancient. Tertullian's language however clearly points to a different principle of arrangement in Marcion's Canon: 'Principalem adversus Judaismum epistolam nos quoque confitemur, quae Galatas docet.' He placed

it to have been written from Ephesus[1]. Others, among whom are Eusebius of Emesa[2], Jerome[3], Theodoret[4], and Euthalius, date it from Rome, in accordance with the subscription found in some MSS and in the two Syriac and the Coptic versions. Of these two opinions, the former was doubtless a critical inference from the statement in the Acts[5] that St Paul visited Ephesus immediately after leaving Galatia, combined with his own mention of the suddenness of the Galatian apostasy[6]; the latter is founded on some fancied allusions in the epistle to his bonds[7]. The former view has been adopted by the vast majority of recent critics, who agree in dating the epistle during the three years of St Paul's residence in the capital of Asia (A.D. 54—57), differing however in placing it earlier or later in this period, according as they lay greater or less stress on the particular expression 'ye are *so soon* changing.'

View generally adopted.

Before stating my reasons for departing from this view, I shall give a brief summary of the events of the period, which

History of the period.

this epistle in the forefront as the most decided in its antagonism to Judaism. At the same time where no such motive interposed, and where the connexion was obvious, as in the Epistles to the Colossians and Philemon (on the juxtaposition of which Wieseler lays some stress, as establishing the principle of a chronological arrangement in Marcion's Canon *Chron.* p. 230), he would naturally follow the chronological order. Volkmar (Credner *Neutest. Kanon*, p. 399) accepts the interpretation of Tertullian which I have given, but denies the accuracy of his statement. The author of the Muratorian fragment (c. A.D. 170) seems to give as the chronological order, Corinthians, Galatians, Romans (see Tregelles *Can. Murat.* p. 42), which corresponds with the view I have adopted; but his language is very obscure, and his statements, at least on some points, are obviously inaccurate.

[1] So Florus Lugdun. and Claudius Altissiod. who copy the words of Primasius. Chrysostom (*Prooem. ad Rom.*) says merely that the Galatians was written before the Romans, but does not define the time or place of writing. Theophylact (*Argum. ad Rom.*) repeats Chrysostom.

[2] About 350 A.D. Cramer *Caten. ad Gal.* iv. 20; 'He was a prisoner and in confinement at the time.' This comment is ascribed simply to 'Eusebius' in the *Catena*, but the person intended is doubtless the bishop of Emesa, whose commentary on the Galatians is mentioned by Jerome (*Comm. in Ep. ad Gal.* Lib. I. *Praef.*). He naturally represents the tradition of the Syrian Churches.

[3] As may be inferred from his commentary on Gal. iv. 20, vi. 11, 17 (VII. pp. 468, 529, 534), Philem. 1 (VII. p. 747).

[4] *Praef. ad Rom.*

[5] Acts xviii. 23, xix. 1.

[6] Gal. i. 6.

[7] Gal. iv. 20, vi. 17.

it will be necessary to bear in mind, in order to follow the course of the argument.

Sojourn at Ephesus. St Paul's long sojourn at Ephesus is now drawing to a close. His labours there have been crowned with no ordinary success. 'The word of God prevailed and grew mightily[1].' So we read in the historian's narrative. He says nothing of persecutions. But we must draw no hasty conclusions from this silence. For the same historian records how the Apostle, in his farewell to the Ephesian elders a year later, speaking of his labours among them, reminded them of his 'many tears and temptations, which befel him by the lying in wait of the Jews[2].' In his own epistles St Paul speaks in stronger language of the persecutions of this time. He compares his sufferings to those of the condemned slave, thrown to the beasts in the amphitheatre, and struggling for life and death—angels and men witnessing the spectacle[3]. The Apostles, he says, were made as the filth of the world, as the offscouring of all things[4].

It was now the spring of the year fifty-seven, and he contemplated leaving Ephesus after Whitsuntide[5]. Friends had arrived from Corinth and drawn a fearful picture of the feuds and irregularities that prevailed there. He at once despatched

1 Corinthians written A.D. 57 (Spring). a letter to the Corinthians, reprobating their dissensions and exhorting them to acquit themselves of guilt by the punishment of a flagrant offender. But he was not satisfied with merely writing: he sent also trusty messengers, who might smooth difficulties, by explaining by word of mouth much that was necessarily omitted in the letter[6]. Titus was one of these: and he awaited his return in great anxiety, as he had misgivings of the reception of his letter at Corinth. And now a tumult broke out at Ephesus. The opposition to the Gospel came to a head. His companions were seized and violently hurried before the people. He himself was with difficulty persuaded to shelter himself by concealment till the storm was over. The storm

[1] Acts xix. 20.
[2] Acts xx. 19.
[3] 1 Cor. iv. 9, xv. 32.
[4] 1 Cor. iv. 13.
[5] 1 Cor. xvi. 8.
[6] 1 Cor. xvi. 11, 2 Cor. xii. 18.

passed, but the sky was still lowering. It was evident that his presence at Ephesus could now be of little use, and might only exasperate the enemies of the Gospel. Besides the time was near, perhaps had already arrived, when he had intended under any circumstances to turn his steps westward. So he left Ephesus[1]. But Titus had not yet come, and his anxiety for the Church at Corinth pressed heavily upon him. He hastened to Troas, hoping to meet Titus there. 'A door was opened' to him at Troas. But Titus came not. He was oppressed at once with a sense of loneliness and an ever growing anxiety for the Corinthian Church. He could no longer bear the suspense. He left Troas and crossed over to Macedonia. Still Titus came not. Still the agony of suspense, the sense of loneliness remained[2]. Time only increased his suffering. Every day brought fresh troubles; gloomy tidings poured in from all sides; church after church added to his anxiety[3]. Nor had persecution ceased. The marks of violence imprinted on his body about this time remained long after—perhaps never left him[4]. Probably too his constitutional complaint visited him once more—the thorn in the flesh to which he alludes in his letter to the Corinthians—the weakness which years before had detained him in Galatia. He seemed to be spared no suffering either of body or mind. There were fightings without and fears within. At length Titus arrived[5]. This was the first gleam of sunshine. The tidings from Corinth were far more cheerful than he had hoped. His mind was relieved. He wrote off at once to the Corinthians, expressing his joy at their penitence, and recommending mercy towards the offender. The crisis was now over. He breathed freely once more. From this time his troubles seem gradually to have abated. A single verse in the sacred historian conveys all we know beyond this point of his sojourn in Macedonia. 'He went over those parts,' we are told, 'and exhorted the people in many words[6].' From thence he visited Greece, where

St Paul in Macedonia.

2 Corinthians written A.D. 57 (Autumn).

Visit to Greece.

[1] Acts xix. 21—41, xx. 1.
[2] 2 Cor. ii. 12, 13.
[3] 2 Cor. xi. 28.
[4] Gal. vi. 17.
[5] 2 Cor. vii. 5—16.
[6] Acts xx. 2.

he remained three months. While at Corinth he wrote the Epistle to the Romans. These are almost all the particulars known of his movements at this period. Of persecutions and sufferings we read nothing: and so far we are left in the dark. But when we contrast the more tranquil and hopeful tone of the Roman Epistle, interrupted occasionally by an outburst of triumphant thanksgiving, with the tumultuous conflict of feeling which appears in the Second Epistle to the Corinthians, we can scarcely avoid the inference, that the severity of his trials had abated in the interval, and that he was at length enjoying a season of comparative repose.

Romans written A.D. 58 (early).

It will be seen then that according to the generally received opinion, which dates this epistle from Ephesus, the chronological order of the letters of the period will be Galatians, 1 Corinthians, 2 Corinthians, Romans, the Epistle to the Galatians preceding the First Epistle to the Corinthians by an interval of a few months according to some, of nearly three years according to others. On the other hand, I cannot but think that there are weighty reasons, which more than counterbalance any arguments alleged in favour of this opinion, for interposing it between the Second to the Corinthians and the Romans. In this case it will have been written from Macedonia or Achaia, in the winter or spring of the years 57, 58 A.D. I shall proceed to state the successive steps of the argument by which this result is arrived at.

Probable date of Galatians.

I. A few scattered historical notices more or less distinct must be put in evidence first, as fixing the date of the epistle later than the events to which they refer. These notices are twofold, referring partly to St Paul's communications with the Apostles of the circumcision, partly to his intercourse with the Galatian Church.

Direct historical notices.

(i) In the opening chapters St Paul mentions two distinct visits to Jerusalem[1]. For reasons which will be given elsewhere, it seems necessary to identify the second of these with the third recorded in the Acts, during which the Apostolic

Jerusalem and Antioch.

[1] Gal. i. 18, ii. 1.

Council was held. The epistle moreover alludes to an interview with St Peter at Antioch, in language which seems to imply that it took place after, and probably soon after, their conference at Jerusalem[1]. If so, it must have occurred during St Paul's stay at Antioch, recorded in the fifteenth chapter of the Acts[2]. On the most probable system of chronology these events took place in the year 51, before which date therefore the epistle cannot have been written.

(ii) The epistle apparently contains an allusion to two separate visits of St Paul to Galatia. 'Ye know,' says the Apostle, 'that through infirmity of the flesh, I preached to you *before*, and...ye received me as an angel of God...What then... have I become your enemy by telling you the truth[3]?' He is here contrasting his reception on the two occasions, on the second of which he fears he may have incurred their enmity by his plain-speaking. If this interpretation be correct, the two Galatian visits thus alluded to must be the same two which are recorded in the Acts[4]. The epistle therefore must be later than the second of these, which took place in 54 A.D. Galatia.

Thus we have established the earliest possible date of the epistle, as a starting point. On the other hand an incidental expression has been rigorously pressed to show that it cannot have been written much after this date. 'I marvel,' says St Paul, 'that ye are *so soon*, or *so fast*, changing from Him that called you to another Gospel[5].' It is necessary to estimate the exact value of this expression. 'So soon changing,'

The generally received view, which fixes the writing of the epistle at Ephesus, is founded on two assumptions with regard to this expression, both of which seem to me erroneous. *First*, It is supposed that in speaking of the rapidity of the change St Paul dates from his last visit to Galatia, 'so soon after I left you.' This however seems at variance with the context. The Apostle is reproaching his converts with their fickleness. wrongly explained.

[1] Gal. ii. 11.
[2] Acts xv. 30—40.
[3] Gal. iv. 13—16. See the notes.
[4] Acts xvi. 6, xviii. 23.
[5] Gal. i. 6. See the note on οὕτως ταχέως.

'They have so soon deserted their Christian profession, so soon taken up with *another Gospel.*' Here the point of time from which he reckons is obviously the time of their conversion, not the time of his second visit. His surprise is not that they have so lightly forgotten his latest instructions, but that they have so easily tired of their newly obtained liberty in Christ. 'I marvel,' he says, 'that ye are so soon changing *from Him that called you.*' Whatever interval therefore is implied by 'so soon,' it must reckon from their first knowledge of the Gospel, i.e. from A.D. 51. *Secondly,* It is insisted that the period cannot be extended beyond a few months, or at the outside two or three years. But quickness and slowness are relative terms. The rapidity of a change is measured by the importance of the interests at stake. A period of five or ten years would be a brief term of existence for a constitution or a dynasty. A people which threw off its allegiance to either within so short a time might well be called fickle. And if so, I cannot think it strange that the Apostle, speaking of truths destined to outlive the life of kingdoms and of nations, should complain that his converts had *so soon* deserted from the faith, even though a whole decade of years might have passed since they were first brought to the knowledge of Christ. So long a period however is not required on any probable hypothesis as to the date of the epistle; and therefore this expression, which has been so strongly insisted upon, seems to contribute little or nothing towards the solution of the problem[1].

Its real bearing.

This epistle allied to the 2nd chronological group.

2. On the other hand the argument from the style and character of the epistle is one of great importance. It may now be regarded as a generally recognised fact that St Paul's epistles fall chronologically into four groups, separated from

[1] The problem of the date of the Galatian Epistle, as it is generally conceived, may be stated thus: Given on the one hand the expression 'so soon,' tending towards an earlier date, and on the other the resemblance to the Epistle to the Romans tending towards a later, to find the resultant. I think that the former consideration may be eliminated, as will be seen from the text, while at the same time some further conditions which have been overlooked must be taken into account.

one another by an interval of five years roughly speaking, and distinguished also by their internal character. The second of these groups comprises (exclusively of the Galatians) the Epistles to the Corinthians and Romans, written at the close of the third missionary journey, in the years 57 and 58. Now it appears that while the Epistle to the Galatians possesses no special features in common with the epistles of the preceding or succeeding groups, either in style, matter, or general tone and treatment, it is most closely allied in all these respects to the epistles of the third missionary journey. It was a season of severe conflict with St Paul, both mental and bodily, and the traces of this conflict are stamped indelibly on the epistles written during this period. They exhibit an unwonted tension of feeling, a fiery energy of expression, which we do not find in anything like the same degree in either the earlier or the later epistles. They are marked by a vast profusion of quotations from the Old Testament, by a frequent use of interrogation, by great variety and abruptness of expression, by words and images not found elsewhere, or found very rarely, in St Paul. They have also their own doctrinal features distinguishing them from the other groups—due for the most part to the phase which the antagonism to the Gospel assumed at this time. Justification by faith, the contrast of law and grace, the relation of Jew and Gentile, the liberty of the Gospel—these and kindred topics are dwelt upon at greater length and with intense earnestness. All these characteristic features the letter to the Galatians shares in an eminent degree, so much so indeed, that it may be considered the typical epistle of the group; and by those who have made St Paul's style their study the conviction arising from this resemblance will probably be felt so strongly, that nothing but the most direct and positive evidence could overcome it.

Characteristics of this group.

3. It seems to follow then that some place must be found for the Galatian Epistle in the group which comprises the Epistles to the Corinthians and Romans. We have next to enquire whether there is sufficient evidence for determining its

It closely resembles 2 Corinthians and Romans.

exact position in this group. I think this question can be answered with some degree of probability.

Pursuing the examination further we find that the resemblance is closest to the Second Epistle to the Corinthians and the Epistle to the Romans.

2 Corinthians.

In the case of the Second Epistle to the Corinthians, the similarity consists not so much in words and arguments as in tone and feeling.

Resemblance in general tone.

"In both there is the same sensitiveness in the Apostle to the behaviour of his converts to himself, the same earnestness about the points of difference, the same remembrance of his 'infirmity' while he was yet with them, the same consciousness of the precarious basis on which his own authority rested in the existing state of the two Churches. In both there is a greater display of his own feelings than in any other portion of his writings, a deeper contrast of inward exaltation and outward suffering, more of personal entreaty, a greater readiness to impart himself[1]." If it were necessary to add anything to this just and appreciative criticism, the Apostle's tone in dealing with his antagonists would supply an instructive field for comparison. Both epistles exhibit the same combination of protest and concession in combating the exclusive rights claimed for the elder Apostles, the same vehement condemnation of the false teachers guarded by the same careful suppression of names, the same strong assertion of his Apostolic office tempered with the same depreciation of his own personal merits.

Special coincidences.

Besides this general resemblance, which must be felt in order to be appreciated, a few special affinities may be pointed out. For instance the expression 'Christ redeemed us from the curse of the law, being made a curse for us[2],' has a close parallel in the allied epistle, 'He made Him to be sin for us, who knew no sin, that we, etc.[3]' The image, 'Whatsoever a man soweth that shall he also reap[4],' is reproduced in almost the same words.

[1] Jowett, I. p. 196, 1st ed. It is interesting to find that the resemblance between the two epistles was observed by a writer as early as Theodore of Mopsuestia, *Spicil. Solesm.* I. p. 50.

[2] Gal. iii. 13.

[3] 2 Cor. v. 21.

[4] Gal. vi. 7.

'He that soweth sparingly shall reap sparingly[1].' Again, the two epistles have in common the peculiar phrases, 'another gospel,' 'a new creature,' 'zealously affect you,' 'persuade men[2].' And other instances might be brought[3]. On these special coincidences however I do not lay any great stress.

Romans.

The resemblance to the Epistle to the Romans is much more striking and definite. Setting aside the personal matter and the practical lessons, and excepting here and there a digressive illustration, almost every thought and argument in the Epistle to the Galatians may be matched from the other epistle. The following table of parallels will show how remarkable this coincidence is. In the first instance I have taken an almost continuous passage, in order better to exhibit the nature of this resemblance.

Close resemblance in thought and language.

Parallel passages.

GALATIANS.	ROMANS.
(1) iii. 6. Even as Abraham believed God, and it was accounted to him for righteousness.	iv. 3. What saith the Scripture? Abraham believed God, and it was accounted to him for righteousness.
iii. 7. Know ye therefore that they which are of faith, the same are the children of Abraham.	iv. 10, 11. How then was it accounted?...in uncircumcision... that he might be the father of all them that believe.
iii. 8. And the Scripture foreseeing...preached before the Gospel unto Abraham, saying, 'In thee shall all nations be blessed.'	iv. 17. As it is written, 'I have made thee a father of many nations.' iv. 18. 'So shall thy seed be.'
iii. 9. So then they which are of faith, are blessed with faithful Abraham...	iv. 23. It was not written for his sake alone...but for us also to whom it shall be accounted, who believe, etc. Comp. iv. 12.
iii. 10. For as many as are of the works of the law are under a curse.	iv. 15. Because the law worketh wrath.

[1] 2 Cor. ix. 6.

[2] Gal. i. 6, 2 Cor. xi. 4; Gal. vi. 15, 2 Cor. v. 17; Gal. iv. 17, 2 Cor. xi. 2; Gal. i. 10, 2 Cor. v. 11.

[3] Compare Gal. i. 9, v. 21, with 2 Cor. xiii. 2, and Gal. iii. 3 with 2 Cor. viii. 6. Again, the expressions *ἀπορεῖσθαι*, *κανών*, *κυρόω*, *τοὐναντίον*, *φοβοῦμαι μήπως*, and the metaphor *κατεσθίειν*, Gal. v. 15, 2 Cor. xi. 20, are peculiar to these epistles; and this list is probably not complete. On the other hand, the Galatian Epistle presents a few special coincidences with 1 Corinthians, the most remarkable being the proverb, 'A little leaven etc.,' occurring 1 Cor. v. 6, Gal. v. 9.

Parallel passages.

Galatians.	Romans.
iii. 11. But that no man is justified by the law in the sight of God it is evident, for	iii. 21. But now the righteousness of God without the law is manifested, being witnessed by the law and the prophets.
'The just shall live by faith.'	i. 17. As it is written, 'The just shall live by faith.'
iii. 12. And the law is not of faith: but 'The man that doeth them shall live in them.'	x. 5. Moses describeth the righteousness which is of the law: that 'The man that doeth them shall live in them.'
iii. 13, 14. [From this curse Christ ransomed us.]	[iv. 23, 24. The same thought expressed in other language.]
iii. 15—18. [Neither can the law interpose] to make the promise of none effect: for if the inheritance be of the law, it is no more of promise: but God gave it (κεχάρισται) to Abraham by promise.	iv. 13, 14, 16. For the promise that he should be the heir of the world was not made to Abraham...through the law...for if they which are of the law be heirs, faith is made void, and the promise made of none effect... therefore it is of faith, that it might be by grace (χάρις).
iii. 19—21. [But the law was temporary and ineffective: for]	[Comp. Rom. viii. 3, 4.]
iii. 22. The scripture hath concluded all under sin, that the promise by faith of Jesus Christ might be given to them that believe.	xi. 32. God hath concluded them all in unbelief, that he might have mercy upon all. iii. 9, 10. They are all under sin, as it is written. Comp. iii. 25; v. 20, 21.
iii. 23—26. [We are now free from the tutelage of the law and are sons of God through Christ.]	[The same thought illustrated differently. Rom. vii. 1—3.]
iii. 27. For as many of you as have been baptized into Christ have put on Christ.	vi. 3. As many of us as have been baptized into Christ. xiii. 14. Put ye on the Lord Jesus Christ.
iii. 28. [There is no distinction of race or caste or sex.]	
iii. 29. If ye be Christ's, then are ye Abraham's seed, and heirs according to the promise.	ix. 8. The children of the promise are counted for the seed. (See the passage cited next.)
iv. 1—5. [We have been hitherto in the position of an heir still in his minority. Christ's death has recovered us our right.]	
iv. 5, 6, 7. That we might receive the adoption of sons. And because ye are sons, God hath	viii. 14—17. For as many as are led by the Spirit of God, they are the sons of God. For ye have

Parallel passages.

GALATIANS.	ROMANS.
sent forth the Spirit of his Son into your hearts, crying, Abba, Father. Wherefore thou art no more a servant, but a son; and if a son, then an heir of God through Christ.	not received the spirit of bondage again to fear, but ye have received the Spirit of adoption, whereby we cry, Abba, Father. The Spirit itself beareth witness with our spirit, that we are the children of God: and if children, then heirs, heirs of God, and joint heirs with Christ.
(2) ii. 16. For 'by the works of the law shall no flesh be justified (Ps. cxliii. 2).'	iii. 20. For 'by the works of the law shall no flesh be justified before him.'

In both passages the quotation is oblique: in both the clause 'by the works of the law' is inserted by way of explanation: in both 'flesh' is substituted for 'living man' (πᾶσα σὰρξ for πᾶς ζῶν of the LXX, which agrees also with the Hebrew): and in both the application of the text is the same.

GALATIANS.	ROMANS.
(3) ii. 19. For I through the law am dead to the law, that I might live to God.	vii. 4. Ye also are become dead to the law...that we should bear fruit unto God. Comp. vi. 2—5.
ii. 20. I am crucified with Christ. Comp. v. 24, vi. 14.	vi. 6. Our old man is crucified with him.
Nevertheless I live, yet not I, but Christ liveth in me.	vi. 8. Now if we be dead with Christ, we believe that we shall also live with him. vi. 11. Alive unto God through Jesus Christ.
(4) iv. 23, 28. He of the freewoman was by promise...we, brethren, as Isaac was, are the children of promise.	ix. 7, 8. 'In Isaac shall thy seed be called.' That is...the children of the promise are counted for the seed.
(5) v. 14. All the law is fulfilled in one word, namely, (ἐν τῷ), Thou shalt love thy neighbour as thyself.	xiii. 8, 9, 10. He that loveth another, hath fulfilled the law;... it is briefly comprehended in this saying, namely, (ἐν τῷ), Thou shalt love thy neighbour as thyself... love is the fulfilling of the law.
(6) v. 16. Walk in the Spirit, and ye shall not fulfil the lust of the flesh.	viii. 4. In us who walk not after the flesh, but after the Spirit.
v. 17. For the flesh lusteth	vii. 23, 25. I see another law

Parallel passages.

Galatians.	Romans.
against the spirit, and the spirit against the flesh, and these are contrary the one to the other.	in my members, warring against the law of my mind...with the mind I myself serve the law of God, but with the flesh the law of sin.
So that ye cannot do the things that ye would.	vii. 15. What I would, that I do not, but what I hate, that I do. Comp. vv. 19, 20.
v. 18. But if ye be led of the spirit, ye are not under the law.	viii. 2. The law of the spirit of life...hath made me free from the law of sin and death. Comp. vii. 6.
(7) vi. 2. Bear ye one another's burdens.	xv. 1. We that are strong ought to bear the infirmities of the weak[1].

The resemblance is manifold.

It will be unnecessary to add many words on a similarity so great as these passages exhibit. Observe only that it is manifold and various. Sometimes it is found in a train of argument more or less extended, and certainly not obvious: sometimes in close verbal coincidences where the language and thoughts are unusual, or where a quotation is freely given, and where the coincidence therefore was less to be expected: sometimes in the same application of a text, and the same comment upon it, where that application and comment have no obvious reference to the main subject of discussion. There is no parallel to this close resemblance in St Paul's Epistles, except in the case of the letters to the Colossians and Ephesians. Those letters were written about the same time and sent by the same messenger; and I cannot but think that we should be doing violence to historic probability by separating the Epistles to the Galatians and Romans from each other by an interval of more than a few months, though in this instance the similarity is not quite so great as in the other.

Galatians written about the same time with,

[1] In the above extracts I have only altered the English version where our translators have given different renderings for the same Greek word. Besides these broader coincidences, the following words and phrases are peculiar to the two Epistles: *βαστάζειν, δουλεία, ἐλευθερόω, ἴδε, κατὰ ἄνθρωπον λέγω (ἀνθρώπινον λέγω), κατάρα καταρᾶσθαι, κῶμοι, μακαρισμός, μέθη, οἱ τὰ τοιαῦτα πράσσοντες, ὀφειλέτης, παραβάτης, παρ' ὅ, τί ἔτι; τί λέγει ἡ γραφή;*

But the comparison advances us yet another stage towards the solution of our problem. There can be no reasonable doubt which of the two epistles contains the earlier expression of the thoughts common to both. The Epistle to the Galatians stands in relation to the Roman letter, as the rough model to the finished statue; or rather, if I may press the metaphor without misapprehension, it is the first study of a single figure, which is worked into a group in the latter writing. To the Galatians the Apostle flashes out in indignant remonstrance the first eager thoughts kindled by his zeal for the Gospel striking suddenly against a stubborn form of Judaism. To the Romans he writes at leisure, under no pressure of circumstances, in the face of no direct antagonism, explaining, completing, extending the teaching of the earlier letter, by giving it a double edge directed against Jew and Gentile alike. The matter, which in the one epistle is personal and fragmentary, elicited by the special needs of an individual church, is in the other generalised and arranged so as to form a comprehensive and systematic treatise. Very few critics of name have assigned a priority of date to the Roman Epistle.

but before Romans.

Thus connected by striking affinities with these two epistles, the letter to the Galatians seems naturally to claim an intermediate position, as a chronological link between them. Its claim, I think, is well illustrated, if it is not vindicated, by a comparison of the lists of sins in the three epistles, with which I shall close this attempt to trace their common features.

A connecting link between 2 Corinthians and Romans.

2 Corinthians.	Galatians.	Romans.
Strife, *emulation*, *wraths*, *factions*, *backbitings*, *whisperings*, swellings, tumults ...... *uncleanness* and *fornication* and *lasciviousness*. xii. 20, 21.	*Fornications*, *uncleanness*, *lasciviousness*, idolatry, witchcraft, hatred, *strife*, *emulations*, *wraths*, *factions*, seditions, heresies, *envies*, *murders*, *drunkennesses*, *revellings*, and such like. v. 19—21.	Unrighteousness, wickedness, covetousness, maliciousness, full of *envy*, *murder*, strife, deceit, malignity, *whisperers*, *backbiters*, etc., i. 29, 30; in *revellings* and *drunkennesses*, in chamberings and wantonnesses, in *strife* and *emulation*. xiii. 13.

But if on the other hand this sequence is altered by inter-

The continuity broken in the received order.

posing the letters to the Corinthians between those to the Galatians and Romans, the dislocation is felt at once. It then becomes difficult to explain how the same thoughts, argued out in the same way and expressed in similar language, should appear in the Galatian and reappear in the Roman Epistle, while in two letters written in the interval they have no place at all, or at least do not lie on the surface. I cannot but think that the truths which were so deeply impressed on the Apostle's mind, and on which he dwelt with such characteristic energy on two different occasions, must have forced themselves into prominence in any letter written meanwhile.

The order here adopted accords best with

4. Again, if it is found that the order here maintained accords best with the history of St Paul's personal sufferings at this period, so far as we can decipher it, as well as with the progress of his controversy with the Judaizers, such an accordance will not be without its value. I shall take these two points in order.

(i) St Paul's personal history.

(i) In the First Epistle to the Corinthians he alludes to his sufferings for the Gospel more than once. He refers to them in one passage at some length[1], to point a contrast between the humiliation of the teacher and the exaltation of the taught. He speaks of himself as suffering every privation, as treated with every kind of contempt. And he alludes once and again to these afflictions, as witnesses to the immortality of man. 'If in this life only we have hope in Christ, we are of all men most miserable[2].' 'Why stand we in jeopardy every hour? I protest I die daily. If I fought with beasts at Ephesus, what advantageth it me, if the dead rise not[3]?' But the mention of them is only occasional; it does not colour the whole epistle. In the Second Epistle the case is very different. Here it is the one topic from beginning to end. His physical sufferings have increased meanwhile: and to them have been added mental agonies far more severe. Tribulation and comfort—strength and weakness—glorying and humiliation—alternate throughout

[1] 1 Cor. iv. 9—13.
[2] 1 Cor. xv. 19.
[3] 1 Cor. xv. 30—32.

the epistle[1]. But though the whole letter is one outpouring of affliction, yet we feel that the worst is already past. The first ray of sunshine has pierced the gloom. The penitence of the Corinthian Church has made him 'exceeding joyful in all his tribulation[2].' We are not surprised therefore, when, after the lapse of a few months, we find the Apostle writing in a strain of less impassioned sorrow. In the Epistle to the Romans persecution is sometimes mentioned, but in the more tranquil tone of one recalling past experiences, when the conflict is already over and the victory won.

Reference to his sufferings in Galatians.

In the Epistle to the Galatians again he says but little of his own sufferings. He is too absorbed in the momentous question at issue to speak much of himself. Yet once or twice the subject is introduced. A sentence at the close of the letter especially shows how it occupies his thoughts, even when all mention of it is repressed. After adding in his own handwriting a few sentences of earnest remonstrance, he sums up with these words, 'From henceforth let no man trouble me; for I bear in my body the marks of the Lord Jesus.' It is his final appeal, before which all opposition and controversy must give way. Does not this seem like the language of one, who has lately passed through a fiery trial, and who, looking back upon it in the first moment of abatement, while the recollection is still fresh upon him, sees in his late struggles a new consecration to a life of self-denial, and an additional seal set upon his Apostolic authority? In other words, does it not seem to follow naturally *after* the tumult of affliction, which bursts out in the Second Epistle to the Corinthians?

Perhaps this passage too, in connexion with the events of the year preceding, may serve to throw light on one or two otherwise obscure hints in this epistle. 'If I *still* preach circumcision, why am I then persecuted[3]?' 'If I were *still* pleasing men, I should not have been a *servant of Christ*[4].'

[1] 2 Cor. i. 3—10, iv. 7—11, iv. 16—v. 4, vi. 4—10, vii. 4—7, xi. 23—28, xii. 7—10, 12.

[2] 2 Cor. vii. 4.

[3] Gal. v. 11.

[4] Gal. i. 10.

May we not connect these expressions with the words, '*Henceforth* let no man trouble me; for I bear in my body *the marks of the Lord Jesus*[1]'? These sufferings marked a crisis in his spiritual life, an epoch to date from. In the permanent injuries then inflicted upon him, he delighted to see the tokens of his service to his Lord, the signs of ownership, as it were, branded on him. Henceforth Jesus was his Master, henceforth he was the slave of Christ, in a fuller sense than he had been hitherto[2]. It is at least remarkable, that in the epistle which follows next upon this, he designates himself 'a slave of Jesus Christ[3],' a title there adopted for the first time.

(ii) The progress of the Judaic opposition.

(ii) The same result which is thus obtained from an examination of St Paul's personal history, seems to follow also from the progress of his controversy with his Judaizing opponents.

In the Epistle to the Corinthians the controversy has not yet assumed a very definite shape. He scarcely once meets his opponents on *doctrinal* ground. He is occupied in maintaining his *personal* authority against those who strove to undermine it, resting their claims, in some cases at least, on a more intimate connexion with the Lord. Doubtless doctrinal error would be the next step, and this the Apostle foresaw. But hitherto he speaks with some reserve on this point, not knowing the exact position which his antagonist would take up. The heresy combated in the Galatian Epistle is much more matured. The personal antagonism remains as before, while the doctrinal opposition has assumed a distinct and threatening form.

For how different is St Paul's language in the two cases. He tells both Churches indeed in almost the same words, that

[1] Gal. vi. 17.

[2] It is related of George Herbert that when he was inducted into the cure of Bemerton he said to a friend, 'I beseech God that my humble and charitable life may so win upon others as to bring glory to my Jesus, *whom I have this day taken to be my Master and Governor;* and I am so proud of His service, that I will always call Him *Jesus my Master*,' etc. 'And,' adds his biographer, 'he seems to rejoice in that word *Jesus*, and say that the adding these words *my Master* to it, and the often repetition of them, seemed to perfume his mind,' etc. I. Walton's *Life of Herbert*.

[3] Rom. i. 1.

'circumcision is nothing, and uncircumcision is nothing[1],' but then his practical comment in the two cases presents a striking contrast. To the Corinthians he says; 'Is any man called being circumcised? let him not be uncircumcised; Is any called in uncircumcision? let him not be circumcised[2]': to the Galatians; 'Behold, I Paul say unto you, that if ye be circumcised Christ shall profit you nothing; and again I testify, etc.[3]' In the one epistle he is dealing with a hypothetical case; he speaks as if to guard against future error. In the other he is wrestling with an actual evil present in its most virulent form. If circumcision is but one point, it at least contains all implicitly: 'Every man that is circumcised is a debtor to do the whole law.'

Corresponding progress in the statement of doctrine.

Corresponding to this advance on the part of his antagonists we find a growing fulness in St Paul's exposition of those doctrines with which the errors of the Judaizers were in direct conflict. Such is the case with his account of the temporary purpose of the law, especially in its negative effect as 'multiplying sin.' In the Corinthian Epistles the subject is dismissed with a casual sentence, pregnant with meaning indeed, but standing quite alone. 'The strength of sin is the law[4].' In the Galatian letter it is the one prominent topic. So again with its correlative, the doctrine of justification by faith. This doctrine is incidentally alluded to more than once in the letter to Corinth[5]. In one passage especially it appears prominently; 'God was in Christ reconciling the world unto Himself, not imputing their trespasses to them: for He hath made Him to be sin for us, who knew no sin, that we might be made the righteousness (δικαιοσύνη) of God[6].' Here the doctrine is stated clearly enough, but there is no approach to the fulness with which it is set forth in the Galatian Epistle. The illustration, the antithesis, the aphorism, the scriptural sanction, are missing.

[1] 1 Cor. vii. 19, Gal. v. 6, vi. 15.
[2] 1 Cor. vii. 18.
[3] Gal. v. 2.
[4] 1 Cor. xv. 56.
[5] 1 Cor. i. 30, iv. 4, vi. 11, 2 Cor. iii. 9.
[6] 2 Cor. v. 19—21.

It is not the language which St Paul would have used, had the doctrines been as virtually denied in the Corinthian as they were in the Galatian Church.

Incidental allusions.

5. Lastly, the chronology adopted explains one or two allusions in the Epistle to the Galatians which otherwise it is difficult to account for.

Treatment of offenders.

(i) The sixth chapter commences with the exhortation, 'Brethren, though a man be overtaken in a fault, ye which are spiritual restore such an one in the spirit of meekness, considering thyself lest thou also be tempted.' There is something peculiarly earnest in the abruptness with which this command is introduced. There is a marked tenderness in the appeal to their brotherhood which prefaces it. An undercurrent of deep feeling is evident here. It is as though some care weighed on the Apostle's mind. Now if we suppose the Galatian Epistle to have been written after the Second to the Corinthians, we have at once an adequate explanation of this. A grievous offence had been committed in the Christian community at Corinth. In his first Epistle to the Church there, St Paul had appealed to the brotherhood to punish the guilty person. The appeal had not only been answered, but answered with so much promptness, that it was necessary to intercede for the offender. He commended their indignation, their zeal, their revenge; they had approved themselves clear in the matter[1]; and now they must forgive and comfort their erring brother, lest he be swallowed up with overmuch sorrow[2]. It was the recollection of this circumstance that dictated the injunction in the Galatian Epistle. The Galatians were proverbially passionate and fickle. If a reaction came, it might be attended, as at Corinth, with undue severity towards the delinquents. The epistle therefore was probably written while the event at Corinth was fresh on St Paul's mind—perhaps immediately after he had despatched Titus and the Second Epistle, and was still in suspense as to the issue—perhaps after he had himself arrived at Corinth, and witnessed too evident signs of over-severity.

[1] 2 Cor. vii. 11. [2] 2 Cor. ii. 7.

(ii) A little later on another passage occurs, in which the vehemence of St Paul's language is quite unintelligible at first sight. 'Be not deceived,' he says, 'God is not mocked: for whatsoever a man soweth, that shall he reap...Let us do good unto all men[1].' The admonition is thrown into a general form, but it has evidently a special application in the Apostle's own mind.

Backwardness in almsgiving.

An allusion in the First Epistle to the Corinthians supplies the key to the difficulty. 'As I gave orders to the Churches of Galatia, even so do ye[2].' He had solicited their alms for the suffering brethren of Judæa. The messenger, who had brought him word of the spread of Judaism among the Galatians, had also, I suppose, reported unfavourably of their liberality. They had not responded heartily to his appeal. He reproves them in consequence for their backwardness: but he wishes to give them more time, and therefore refrains from prejudging the case.

Conclusion.

For the reasons given above I have been led to place the Galatian Epistle after the letters to Corinth. They certainly do not amount to a demonstration, but every historical question must be decided by striking a balance between conflicting probabilities; and it seems to me that the arguments here advanced, however imperfect, will hold their ground against those which are alleged in favour of the earlier date. In the interval then between the writing of the Second Epistle to the Corinthians and that to the Romans, the Galatian letter ought probably to be placed. Beyond this I will not venture to define the time; only suggesting that the greeting from 'all the brethren which are with me[3]' seems naturally to apply to the little band of his fellow-travellers, and to hint that the letter was not despatched from any of the great churches of Macedonia or from Corinth. It may have been written on the journey between Macedonia and Achaia. And it is not improbable that it was during St Paul's residence in Macedonia, about the time when the Second Epistle to the Corinthians was written, that

[1] Gal. vi. 7—10. [2] 1 Cor. xvi. 1. [3] Gal. i. 2.

St Paul received news of the falling away of his Galatian converts, so that they were prominent in his mind, when he numbered among his daily anxieties 'the care of all the churches[1].' If so, he would despatch his letter to the Galatians as soon after as a suitable bearer could be found[2].

[1] 2 Cor. xi. 28.

[2] This investigation of the date of the Galatian Epistle is taken from a paper which I published in the *Journal of Class. and Sacr. Philol.* vol. III. p. 289, altered in parts. The view here maintained had also been advocated by Conybeare and Howson (II. p. 165, ed. 2), and by Bleek (*Einl. in das N. T.* pp. 418, 419); but otherwise it had not found much favour. Since the appearance of my first edition it appears to have gained ground.

IV.

GENUINENESS OF THE EPISTLE.

THE Epistle to the Galatians has escaped unchallenged amid the sweeping proscriptions of recent criticism. Its every sentence so completely reflects the life and character of the Apostle of the Gentiles that its genuineness has not been seriously questioned[1]. **Genuineness undisputed.**

Any laboured discussion of this subject would therefore be out of place. Yet it will be worth while to point to a single instance, as showing the sort of testimony which may be elicited from the epistle itself.

The account of St Paul's relations with the Apostles of the Circumcision has a double edge, as an evidential weapon. On the one hand, as an exhibition of the working of the Apostle's mind, it lies far beyond the reach of a forger in an age singularly unskilled in the analysis and representation of the finer shades of character. The suppressed conflict of feeling, the intermingling of strong protest and courteous reserve, the alternation of respectful concession and uncompromising rebuke—the grammar being meanwhile dislocated and the incidents obscured in this struggle of opposing thoughts—such a combination of features reflects one mind alone, and can have proceeded but from one author. On the other hand, looking at the passage as a narrative of events, it seems wholly impossible that the conceptions of a later age should have taken this form. The incidents are too fragmentary and in- **Internal evidence.**

[1] One exception is recorded, which may serve to point a moral.

direct, they are almost smothered in the expression of the writer's feelings, there is altogether a want of system in the narrative wholly unlike the story of a romancer. Nor indeed would it serve any conceivable purpose which a forger might be supposed to entertain. The Gnostic, who wished to advance his antipathy to Judaism under cover of St Paul's name, would have avoided any expression of deference to the Apostles of the Circumcision. The Ebionite would have shrunk with loathing from any seeming depreciation of the cherished customs or the acknowledged leaders of his race, as the tone of the author of the Clementines shows[1]. The Catholic writer, forging with a view to 'conciliation,' would be more unlikely than either to invent such a narrative, anxious as he would be to avoid any appearance of conflict between the two great teachers of the Church. The very unevenness of the incidents is the surest token of their authenticity.

External evidence. On the other hand, the external evidence, though not very considerable, is perhaps as great as might be expected from the paucity of early Christian literature, and the nature of the few writings still extant.

Apostolic Fathers. 1. The *Apostolic Fathers* in whose ears the echoes of the Apostle's voice still lingered, while blending his thoughts almost insensibly with their own, were less likely to quote directly from his written remains. Allusions and indirect citations are not wanting.

CLEMENT's words (§ 2) 'His sufferings were before your eyes' with the implied rebuke may perhaps be a faint reflection of Gal. iii. 1.

In the second so-called Epistle ascribed to Clement (§ 2), which though not genuine is a very early work, Is. liv. 1 is quoted and applied as in Gal. iv. 27.

The seven genuine Epistles of IGNATIUS contain several coincidences with this epistle.

Polyc. § 1, 'Bear all men, as the Lord beareth thee...Bear the ailments of all men,' resembles Gal. vi. 2. (See however Matth. viii. 17, Rom. xv. 1.)

Romans § 7, 'My passion is crucified,' recalls Gal. v. 24, vi. 14.

[1] See p. 61.

Philad. § 1, of the commission of the bishop, 'not of himself or through men but in the love of the Lord Jesus Christ' is an obvious reflexion of Gal. i. 1.

Romans § 2, 'I would not have you to be men-pleasers, but to please God,' resembles Gal. i. 10.

Ephes. § 18, 'The Cross a stumblingblock' may be a reminiscence of Gal. ii. 21.

In *Ephes.* § 16 the expression 'shall not inherit the kingdom of God' is probably derived from Gal. v. 21.

Compare also

Trall. § 10 with Gal. ii. 21.
Magnes. § 5 with Gal. v. 6.
Magnes. § 8 with Gal. v. 4.
Smyrn. § 10 with Gal. iv. 14.

POLYCARP more than once adopts the language of this epistle;

c. 3 'Builded up unto the faith given you, "which is the mother of us all,"' from Gal. iv. 26.

c. 5 'Knowing then that[1] "God is not mocked," we ought, etc.' from Gal. vi. 7.

c. 6 'Zealous in what is good,' may be taken from Gal. iv. 18; comp. Tit. ii. 14, 1 Pet. iii. 13 (v. l.).

c. 12 'Qui credituri sunt in Dominum nostrum et Deum Jesum Christum et in ipsius patrem, qui resuscitavit eum a mortuis,' resembles Gal. i. 1; comp. Rom. iv. 24.

2. The *Miscellaneous Writings of the Subapostolic Age* present one or two vague resemblances on which no stress can be laid. Other writings of subapostolic age.

BARNABAS. A passage in the epistle bearing his name, c. 19, 'Thou shalt communicate in all things with thy neighbour,' reflects Gal. vi. 6.

HERMAS (c. 140 A.D.?) *Sim.* ix. 13 has 'They that have believed in God through His Son and put on these spirits.' Comp. Gal. iii. 26, 27.

3. The Epistle to the Galatians is found in all the known *Canons of Scripture* proceeding from the Catholic Church in the Canons of Scripture.

[1] The expression 'knowing that' (εἰδότες ὅτι) in Polycarp seems to be a form of citation. In c. 1 it introduces a passage from Ephes. ii. 8, in c. 4 one from 1 Tim. vi. 7. It occurs once again in c. 6, 'knowing that we all are debtors of sin.' Though these words are not found either in the Canonical scriptures or in any other extant writing, they seem in force and point so far above the level of Polycarp's own manner, that I can scarcely doubt that he is quoting the language of one greater than himself. They ring almost like a sentence of St Paul.

second century. It is contained in the SYRIAC and OLD LATIN versions, completed, it would appear, some time before the close of the century. It is distinctly recognised also in the Canon of the MURATORIAN FRAGMENT (probably not later than 170 A.D.).

Apologists.

4. The *Apologists*, writing for unbelievers, naturally avoided direct quotations from the sacred writers, which would carry no weight of authority with those they addressed. Their testimony therefore is indirect.

THE EPISTLE TO DIOGNETUS, c. 4, has the expression, 'The observance (παρατήρησιν) of months and of days,' derived apparently from Gal. iv. 10, 'Ye observe (παρατηρεῖσθε) days and months etc.' In another passage, cc. 8, 9, the writer reproduces many of the thoughts of the Epistles to the Galatians and Romans.

JUSTIN MARTYR seems certainly to have known this epistle[1]. In the *Dial. c. Tryph.* cc. 95, 96, he quotes consecutively the two passages, 'Cursed is every one that continueth not, etc.' (Deut. xxvii. 26), and 'Cursed is every one that hangeth on a tree' (Deut. xxi. 23), and applies them as they are applied in Gal. iii. 10, 13. Moreover, he introduces the first in language closely resembling that of St Paul, 'Every race of men will be found under a curse (ὑπὸ κατάραν) according to the law of Moses'; and cites both passages exactly as St Paul cites them, though they differ both from the Hebrew and the LXX[2]. Again in the *Apol.* I. 53, Justin applies Isaiah liv. 1, 'Rejoice, thou barren, etc.' exactly as St Paul applies it in Gal. iv. 27. See the notes on iii. 10, 13, 28, iv. 27.

MELITO in a passage in the 'Oration to Antoninus,' lately discovered in a Syriac translation[3], uses language closely resembling Gal. iv. 8, 9.

[1] In c. 5 of the *Orat. ad Graecos*, often ascribed to Justin and generally assigned to the second century, there are two indirect quotations from this epistle, iv. 12 and v. 20, 21. A recension of this treatise however, discovered of late years in a Syriac translation (Cureton's *Spicil. Syr.* p. 61), bears the name of Ambrose, by whom probably is meant the friend and pupil of Origen.

[2] In Deut. xxvii. 26, ὃς οὐκ ἐμμ. ἐν πᾶσιν τοῖς γεγραμμένοις ἐν τῷ βιβλίῳ τοῦ νόμου τοῦ π. αὐτά, for the LXX (which is nearer to the Hebrew) πᾶς ὁ ἄνθρωπος ὅστις οὐκ ἐμμ. ἐν πᾶσιν τοῖς λόγοις τοῦ ν. τούτου τοῦ π. αὐτούς: in Deut. xxi. 23, Ἐπικατάρατος πᾶς, where the LXX, following the Hebrew, has Κεκατηραμένος ὑπὸ Θεοῦ πᾶς.

[3] Cureton's *Spicil. Syr.* p. 49, *Spicil. Solesm.* II. p. 1. The authorship however is doubted; see Otto *Apol. Christ.* IX. p. 460. A close parallel to Gal. iv. 8 appears also in 'the doctrine of Addæus' (Cureton's *Anc. Syr. Doc.*

ATHENAGORAS, *Suppl.* c. 16, speaks of sinking down 'to the weak and beggarly elements,' quoting from Gal. iv. 9.

5. The evidence of *Heretical writers*, while it is more direct, is also more important, as showing how widely the epistle was received. Most of the references quoted below seem to belong to the first half of the century.

Heretical writers.

THE OPHITES appear to have made great use of this epistle. Several direct quotations from it were found in their writings; e.g. Gal. iv. 26, see Hippol. *Haeres.* v. 7, p. 106; Gal. iv. 27, see Hippol. v. 8, p. 114; Gal. iii. 28, vi. 15, see Hippol. v. 7, p. 99.

JUSTIN, the Gnostic, alludes to Gal. v. 17: Hippol. v. 26, p. 155.

THE VALENTINIANS made use of it, Iren. i. 3. 5. A comment on Gal. vi. 14 is given by Irenæus from their writings, apparently from the works of Ptolemæus[1].

MARCION included it in his Canon and attached great importance to it. See p. 36, note 1. Comp. also the note on iii. 19.

TATIAN recognised it, quoting vi. 8 in support of his ascetic views: Hieron. *Comm. ad Gal.* ad loc.[2]

6. Neither is the testimony of *Adversaries* of the second century wanting to the authenticity of this epistle.

Adversaries of St Paul.

CELSUS, writing against the Christians, says contemptuously, 'Men who differ so widely among themselves and inveigh against each other most shamefully in their quarrels, may all be heard using the words (λεγόντων τό) "The world is crucified unto me and I unto the world."' (Gal. vi. 14.) 'This is the only sentence,' adds Origen, 'that Celsus seems to have recollected from Paul' (Orig. *c. Cels.* v. 64).

THE EBIONITE AUTHOR OF THE CLEMENTINE HOMILIES, writing in a spirit of bitter hostility to St Paul, who is covertly attacked in the person of Simon Magus, represents St Peter addressing Simon thus, 'Thou hast confronted and withstood me (ἐναντίος ἀνθέστηκάς μοι). If thou hadst not been an adversary, thou wouldest not have calumniated and reviled my preaching...If thou callest me condemned (κατεγνωσμένον), thou accusest God

p. 9); but this may be accidental, as there is no other recognition of St Paul in the work. In another document of the same collection (p. 56) there is seemingly a reference to Gal. vi. 17. See also *Clem. Hom.* IX. 1.

[1] See the Latin of Iren. i. 8. 5 ad fin., and comp. Westcott *Canon*, p. 304 (ed. 4).

[2] To this list should be added Theodotus, *Exc. ap. Clem. Alex.* c. 53, p. 982 (Potter), where Gal. iii. 19, 20 is quoted: but the date and authorship of these excerpts are uncertain.

who revealed Christ to me': *Hom.* xvii. 19. See Gal. ii. 11, to which the allusion is obvious, and from which even the expressions are taken. Again, where Simon is accused of 'allegorizing the words of the law to suit his own purpose' (ii. 22), we can hardly mistake the reference to Gal. iv. 21 sq. In a third passage also St Peter maintaining the observance (παρατήρησιν) complains that 'One who had learnt from the tradition of Moses, blaming the people for their sins, contemptuously called them sons of new-moons and sabbaths' (xix. 22): comp. Gal. iv. 10. Other resemblances, noted in Lagarde's edition (p. 31), are less striking: viii. 4 to Gal. i. 6; xviii. 21 to Gal. i. 8; viii. 18 (δι' ἀγγέλου νόμος ὡρίσθη) to Gal. iii. 19; ix. 1 to Gal. iv. 8. See more on this subject in the dissertation on 'St Paul and the Three' at the end of this volume.

Apocryphal Acts.

7. Of *Apocryphal Acts* relating to St Paul one extant work at least seems to date from the second century:

Acts of Paul and Thecla § 40 (apparently the work referred to by Tertullian, *de Baptism.* § 17). The sentence, 'For he that wrought with thee unto the Gospel wrought with me also unto baptism,' is moulded on Gal. ii. 8.

Irenæus, Clement, and Tertullian.

8. Owing to the nature of the earliest Christian writings, the testimony hitherto brought forward has been for the most part indirect. As soon as a strictly *Theological* literature springs up in the Church, we find the epistle at once quoted distinctly and by name. This is the case with the writers of the close of the second century, Irenæus, Clement of Alexandria and Tertullian. From their position as representatives of widely separate branches of the Church, and their manner of quotation, which shows that the writings thus cited were recognised and authoritative, the importance of their testimony is much greater than might be inferred from their comparatively late date[1].

[1] In compiling this account of the external evidence in favour of the epistle I have made use of Lardner's *Credibility*, of Kirchhofer's *Quellensammlung*, and especially of Westcott's *History of the Canon*. I have however gone over the ground independently, and added to the references.

V.

CHARACTER AND CONTENTS OF THE EPISTLE.

IN discussing the relation of this epistle to the contemporaneous letters, I have dwelt on those features which it shares in common with them. It remains to point out some characteristics which are peculiarly its own.

Unity of purpose.

I. The Epistle to the Galatians is especially distinguished among St Paul's letters by its unity of purpose[1]. The Galatian apostasy in its double aspect, as a denial of his own authority and a repudiation of the doctrine of grace, is never lost sight of from beginning to end. The opening salutation broaches this twofold subject. The name 'Paul' has no sooner passed from his lips, than he at once launches into it. The long historical explanation which succeeds is instinct with this motive in all its details. The body of the letter, the doctrinal argument, is wholly occupied with it. The practical exhortations which follow all or nearly all flow from it, either as cautions against a rebound to the opposite extreme, or as suggesting the true rule of life of which the Galatians were following the counterfeit. Lastly, in the postscript he again brings it prominently forward. The two closing sentences reflect the twofold aspect of the one purpose, which has run through the letter. 'Henceforth let no man trouble me. The grace of the Lord Jesus Christ be with your spirit.' Thus his last

[1] Ewald *Paulus*, p. 55, 'Kein anderes sendschreiben ist so sehr wie dieses aus einem gedanken entsprungen, und keines ergiesst sich wie dieses in einem mächtig stürmischen aber unaufhaltsamen und ununterbrochenen strome.'

words echo his first: 'Paul an Apostle not from men'; 'God who called you in the grace of Christ.'

Contrast to the allied epistles.

In this respect it contrasts strongly with the two letters to Corinth with which it possesses so many features in common. Like the First Epistle to the Corinthians, it was written with an immediate purpose to correct actual errors. But the difference is striking. The factions at Corinth were manifold, the irregularities were irregularities of detail not founded on any one broad principle of error, and the epistle necessarily reflects this varied character. Like the Second Epistle to the Corinthians again, it is a complete reflection of the Apostle's inner life. Yet the contrast is not less marked than before. In the one epistle he pours out his feelings without restraint, recurring to his own experiences, his own sorrows, freely and without any definite purpose. In the other the mention of himself is always subordinated to the purpose of the letter; however tumultuous may be the workings of his soul, they are all forced into this one channel. He never speaks of himself but to enforce the authority of his office or the liberty of the Gospel.

Its sustained severity.

2. The sustained severity of this epistle is an equally characteristic feature with its unity of purpose. The Galatians are not addressed as the 'saints in Christ,' 'the faithful brethren.' The Apostle has no congratulations, no word of praise, for this apostate Church. Even on the Corinthians, in spite of all their shortcomings, he could lavish expressions of commendation and love. But the case is different here. The charity which 'hopeth against hope' seems to be strained to the utmost. For this once only the pervading type of his epistles is abandoned in the omission of the opening thanksgiving. The argument is interrupted every now and then by an outburst of indignant remonstrance. He is dealing with a thoughtless half-barbarous people. They have erred like children, and must be chastised like children. Rebuke may prevail where reason will be powerless.

The body of the letter seems to have been written by an amanuensis, but the final sentences were in the Apostle's own handwriting. It was his wont to add a few words at the close of his epistles, either to vouch for their authorship, or to impress some truth more strongly on his readers. Here the urgency of the case leads him to do more. In a few eager rugged sentences he gives an epitome of the contents of the epistle[1]. These sentences are condensed beyond the ordinary compression of the Apostle's style. The language almost bursts with the surcharge of feeling. The very forms of the letters too bear witness to his intense earnestness. He writes in large bold characters to arrest the eye and rivet the mind. He has been accused of vacillation. There has been no want of firmness in the tone of the letter, and there shall be none in the handwriting. No man can henceforth question or misapprehend the Apostle's meaning. **Postscript in St Paul's own hand.**

A rough analysis of the epistle separates it into three sections of two chapters each, the first couplet (i, ii) containing the personal or narrative portion, the second (iii, iv) the argumentative or doctrinal, and the third (v, vi) the hortatory or practical. It will be borne in mind however, that in a writer like St Paul any systematic arrangement must be more or less artificial, especially where, as in the present instance, he is stirred by deep feelings and writes under the pressure of an urgent necessity. The main breaks however, occurring at the end of the second and fourth chapters, suggest this threefold division; and though narrative, argument, and exhortation, are to some extent blended together, each portion retains for the most part its own characteristic form. **Threefold division.**

The following is a more exact analysis of the contents of the epistle.

I. PERSONAL, chiefly in the form of a narrative. **Analysis of the epistle.**

1. The salutation and ascription of praise so worded as to introduce the main subject of the letter (i. 1—5).

2. The Apostle rebukes the Galatians for their apostasy, denounces the false teachers, and declares the eternal truth of the Gospel which he preached (i. 6—10).

[1] Gal. vi. 11—18. See the notes on πηλίκοις γράμμασιν ἔγραψα.

Analysis of the epistle.

3. This Gospel came directly from God.

(i) He received it by special revelation (i. 11, 12).

(ii) His previous education indeed could not have led up to it, for he was brought up in principles directly opposed to the liberty of the Gospel (i. 13, 14).

(iii) Nor could he have learnt it from the Apostles of the Circumcision, for he kept aloof from them for some time after his conversion (i. 15—17).

(iv) And when at last he visited Jerusalem, his intercourse with them was neither close nor protracted, and he returned without being known even by sight to the mass of the believers (i. 18—24).

(v) He visited Jerusalem again, it is true, after a lapse of years, but he carefully maintained his independence. He associated with the Apostles on terms of friendly equality. He owed nothing to them (ii. 1—10).

(vi) Nay more: at Antioch he rebuked Peter for his inconsistency. By yielding to pressure from the ritualists, Peter was substituting law for grace, and so denying the fundamental principle of the Gospel (ii. 11—21).

[This incident at Antioch forms the link of connexion between the first and second portions of the epistle. The error of the Galatians was the same with that of the formalists whom St Peter had countenanced. Thus St Paul passes insensibly from the narrative to the doctrinal statement.]

II. Doctrinal, mostly argumentative.

1. The Galatians are stultifying themselves. They are substituting the flesh for the Spirit, the works of the law for the obedience of faith, forgetting the experience of the past and violating the order of progress (iii. 1—5).

2. Yet Abraham was justified by faith, and so must it be with the true children of Abraham (iii. 6—9).

3. The law, on the contrary, so far from justifying, did but condemn, and from this condemnation Christ rescued us (iii. 10—14).

4. Thus He fulfilled the promise given to Abraham, which being prior to the law could not be annulled by it (iii. 15—18).

5. If so, what was the purpose of the law? (iii. 19).

(i) It was an inferior dispensation, given as a witness against sin, a badge of a state of bondage, not as contrary to, but as preparing for, the Gospel (iii. 19—23).

(ii) And so through the law we are educated for the freedom of the Gospel (iii. 24—29).

(iii) Thus under the law we were in our nonage, but now we are our own masters (iv. 1—7). Analysis of the epistle.

(iv) Yet to this state of tutelage the Galatians are bent on returning (iv. 8—11).

At this point the argument is broken off, while the Apostle reverts to his personal relations with his converts, and reprobates the conduct of the false teachers (iv. 12—20).

6. The law indeed bears witness against itself. The relation of the two covenants of law and of grace, with the triumph of the latter, are typified by the history of Hagar and Sarah. The son of the bondwoman must give place to the son of the free (iv. 21—31).

'We are the children of the free.' This word 'free' is the link of connexion with the third part of the epistle.

III. Hortatory. Practical applications.

1. Hold fast by this *freedom*, which your false teachers are endangering (v. 1—12).
2. But do not let it degenerate into license. Love is the fulfilment of the law. Walk in the Spirit, and the Spirit will save you from licentiousness, as it saves you from formalism, both being carnal. Your course is plain. The works of the Spirit are easily distinguished from the works of the flesh (v. 13—26).
3. Let me add two special injunctions:
   (i) Show forbearance and brotherly sympathy (vi. 1—5).
   (ii) Give liberally (vi. 6—10).

Conclusion in the Apostle's own handwriting (vi. 11).

4. Once more: beware of the Judaizers, for they are insincere. I declare to you the true principles of the Gospel. Peace be to those who so walk (vi. 12—16).
5. Let no man deny my authority, for I bear the brand of Jesus my Master (vi. 17).
6. Farewell in Christ (vi. 18).

The armoury of this epistle has furnished their keenest weapons to the combatants in the two greatest controversies which in modern times have agitated the Christian Church; the one a struggle for liberty within the camp, the other a war of defence against assailants from without; the one vitally affecting the doctrine, the other the evidences of the Gospel. Its place in modern controversy.

The reformation.

When Luther commenced his attack on the corruptions of the mediæval Church, he chose this epistle as his most efficient engine in overthrowing the mass of error which time had piled on the simple foundations of the Gospel. His commentary on the Galatians was written and rewritten. It cost him more labour, and was more highly esteemed by him, than any of his works[1]. If age has diminished its value as an aid to the study of St Paul, it still remains and ever will remain a speaking monument of the mind of the reformer and the principles of the reformation.

Rationalism.

Once again, in the present day, this epistle has been thrust into prominence by those who deny the divine origin of the Gospel. In this latter controversy however it is no longer to its doctrinal features, but to its historical notices, that attention is chiefly directed. 'The earliest form of Christianity,' it is argued, 'was a modified Judaism. The distinctive features of the system current under this name were added by St Paul. There was an irreconcilable opposition between the Apostle of the Gentiles and the Apostles of the Jews, a personal feud between the teachers themselves and a direct antagonism between their doctrines. After a long struggle St Paul prevailed, and Christianity—our Christianity—was the result.' The Epistle to the Galatians affords at once the ground for, and the refutation of, this view. It affords the ground, for it discovers the mutual jealousy and suspicions of the Jew and Gentile converts. It affords the refutation, for it shows the true relations existing between St Paul and the Twelve. It presents not indeed a colourless uniformity of feeling and opinion, but a far higher and more instructive harmony, the general agreement amidst some lesser differences and some human failings, of men animated by the same divine Spirit and working together for the same hallowed purpose, fit inmates of that Father's house in which are many mansions.

[1] 'The Epistle to the Galatians,' said Luther, 'is my epistle; I have betrothed myself to it: it is my wife.' See Seckendorf *de Lutheran.* L. I. § lxxxv. p. 139.

ΠΡΟΣ ΓΑΛΑΤΑΣ.

WHY SEEK YE THE LIVING AMONG THE DEAD?

The old order changeth, yielding place to new,
And God fulfils Himself in many ways.

ΠΡΟΣ ΓΑΛΑΤΑΣ.

ΠΑΥΛΟΣ ἀπόστολος οὐκ ἀπ' ἀνθρώπων οὐδὲ δι' ἀνθρώπου, ἀλλὰ διὰ Ἰησοῦ Χριστοῦ καὶ Θεοῦ πατρὸς

1—5. The two threads which run through this epistle—the defence of the Apostle's own authority, and the maintenance of the doctrine of grace —are knotted together in the opening salutation. By expanding his official title into a statement of his direct commission from God (ver. 1), St Paul meets the *personal* attack of his opponents; by dwelling on the work of redemption in connexion with the name of Christ (ver. 4), he protests against their *doctrinal* errors. See the introduction, p. 63.

'PAUL AN APOSTLE, whose authority does not flow from any human source, and whose office was not conferred through any human mediation, but through Jesus Christ, yea through God the Father Himself who raised Him from the dead—together with all the brethren in my company—to the CHURCHES OF GALATIA. Grace the fountain of all good things, and peace the crown of all blessings, be unto you from God the Father and our Lord Jesus Christ, who gave Himself for our sins that He might rescue us from the tyranny of this present age with all its sins and miseries, according to the will of our God and Father, whose is the glory throughout all the ages. Amen.'

1. οὐκ ἀπ' ἀνθρώπων οὐδὲ δι' ἀνθρώπου] '*not of men, nor yet by man.*' The first preposition denotes the fountain-head whence the Apostle's authority springs, the second the channel through which it is conveyed. Thus in the first clause he distinguishes himself from the false apostles, who did not derive their commission from God at all; in the second he ranks himself with the Twelve, who were commissioned directly from God. The prepositions therefore retain their proper sense. Διά, as distinguished from ἀπό, is used consistently in the New Testament to denote the *means* or *instrument*, especially as describing either (1) the operations of our Lord, as the Word of God, *e.g.* 1 Cor. viii. 6 εἷς Κύριος Ἰησοῦς Χριστὸς δι' οὗ τὰ πάντα, or (2) the human agency employed in carrying out the divine purpose, *e.g.* 1 Cor. iii. 5 διάκονοι δι' ὧν ἐπιστεύσατε. The change of preposition ('of,' 'by') in this passage carries with it the change of number also ('men,' 'man'). Titles and offices which emanate from a body of men will be conferred by their single representative. The acts of the Senate took effect through the prince, those of the Sanhedrin through the high-priest. The transition to the singular moreover, independently of its own fitness, would suggest itself in anticipation of the clause διὰ Ἰησοῦ Χριστοῦ, which was to follow.

ἀλλὰ διὰ Ἰησοῦ Χριστοῦ] To what event does the Apostle here refer? When did he receive his commission from Christ Himself? In 1 Cor. ix. 1, he speaks of his having 'seen the Lord Jesus,' as a token of his apostleship; and this seems naturally to refer to the appearance on the way to Damascus, Acts ix. 3 sq. From this point of time therefore his commission dated.

τοῦ ἐγείραντος αὐτὸν ἐκ νεκρῶν, [2]καὶ οἱ σὺν ἐμοὶ πάντες ἀδελφοί, ταῖς ἐκκλησίαις τῆς Γαλατίας. [3]χάρις ὑμῖν καὶ εἰρήνη ἀπὸ Θεοῦ πατρὸς καὶ Κυρίου ἡμῶν Ἰησοῦ

It was essentially this revelation of our Lord which set him apart for his high office, though the outward investiture may have taken place through human agency at a later date: see Acts ix. 15—17, xiii. 2, 3. The intervention of the prophets and Church of Antioch may perhaps have given a colouring to the false representation that he was an 'Apostle of men.' See p. 98.

καὶ Θεοῦ πατρός] It might be expected that the first preposition (ἀπὸ) would have been resumed here, as more appropriate. It is incorrect however to say that διὰ is loosely used; for if there be any laxity of expression, it is rather in the connexion of the sentences than in the use of the prepositions. At the same time the Apostle's language, as it stands, is more forcible. By including both clauses under the same preposition, he expresses with greater emphasis the *directness* of his divine commission. The channel of his authority (διὰ) coincides with its source (ἀπό). The point of the sentence would have been blunted by inserting ἀπό. Nor indeed is the extension of διὰ to the second clause a violation of its strict meaning, which is observed perhaps with greater precision in the New Testament than elsewhere, owing to its recognised function, as describing the *mediatorial* office of the Son. Ἀπό, though by far the most common, is not the only preposition which may be used in speaking of the Father. He is the beginning, middle, and end of all His works (ἐξ αὐτοῦ καὶ δι' αὐτοῦ καὶ εἰς αὐτόν, Rom. xi. 36), and may therefore be regarded as the instrument, no less than the source, in the fulfilment of His own purposes. This mode of expression will be adopted especially, where the writer is speaking of God's manifestation of Himself in some special act, as here in the raising of Jesus from the dead. Comp. iv. 7, 1 Cor. i. 9, and see Winer, *Gramm.* § xlvii. p. 473 sq. Marcion (Hieron. *ad l.*) cut the knot by omitting καὶ Θεοῦ πατρός, and apparently reading ἑαυτὸν for αὐτόν.

Here the Apostle's words are '*By* Jesus Christ *and* God the Father': immediately after he writes '*From* God the Father, *and* our Lord Jesus Christ.' The one expression supplements the other: 'Thou, Father, in Me, and I in Thee' (John xvii. 21).

τοῦ ἐγείραντος αὐτὸν ἐκ νεκρῶν] '*who raised Him from the dead.*' This expression occurs elsewhere with a more general reference to Christian faith or Christian life: Rom. iv. 24, viii. 11; comp. 1 Cor. xv. 15. Here it has a special bearing on St Paul's apostleship, as the context shows. 'I was commissioned by the risen and glorified Lord: I am in all respects an Apostle, a qualified witness of His resurrection, and a signal instance of His power.'

2. οἱ σὺν ἐμοὶ πάντες ἀδελφοί] '*all the brethren who are with me.*' Probably the small band of his fellow-travellers is meant. See Phil. iv. 21, where he distinguishes 'the brethren who are with him' from 'all the saints,' *i.e.* from the resident members of the Church of Rome from which he is writing. For the bearing of this phrase on the date of the epistle, see p. 55. This company perhaps included Timothy (2 Cor. i. 1) and Erastus (Acts xix. 22). He may also at this time have been rejoined by Titus with the two brethren from Corinth (2 Cor. viii. 16—24), and may have had with him besides some of those who accompanied him afterwards on his return to Asia, as Tychicus and Trophimus

Χριστοῦ, [4]τοῦ δόντος ἑαυτὸν περὶ τῶν ἁμαρτιῶν ἡμῶν, ὅπως ἐξέληται ἡμᾶς ἐκ τοῦ αἰῶνος τοῦ ἐνεστῶτος πονη-

4. ὑπὲρ τῶν ἁμαρτιῶν.

for instance (Acts xx. 4, 5), if indeed they are not to be identified with the two brethren already mentioned.

The patristic writers, followed by several modern commentators, see in this expression a desire on the part of the Apostle to fortify his teaching by the sanction of others: 'Faciens eis pudorem, quod contra omnes sentiunt,' says Victorinus. Such a motive seems alien to the whole spirit of this epistle, in which all human authority is set aside. The Apostle in fact dismisses the mention of his companions as rapidly as possible in one general expression. He then returns to the singular, '*I* marvel,' which he retains throughout the epistle. Paul's authority has been challenged, and Paul alone answers the challenge.

ταῖς ἐκκλησίαις τῆς Γαλατίας] '*to the Churches of Galatia.*' On this mode of address, as marking the earlier epistles, see 1 Thess. i. 1. The abruptness of the language here is remarkable. Elsewhere the Apostle adds some words of commendation. The Church of the Thessalonians, for instance, is 'in God the Father and the Lord Jesus Christ' (1 Thess. i. 1, 2 Thess. i. 1): that of the Corinthians is composed of those 'sanctified in Christ Jesus, called to be saints' (1 Cor. i. 2, comp. 2 Cor. i. 1). The omission of any expression of praise in addressing the Galatians shows the extent of their apostasy; see p. 64.

3. χάρις ὑμῖν καὶ εἰρήνη, κ.τ.λ.] On this form of salutation see the notes 1 Thess. i. 1.

4. τοῦ δόντος ἑαυτόν, κ.τ.λ.] '*who gave Himself for our sins.*' A declaration of the true ground of acceptance with God. The Galatians had practically ignored the atoning death of Christ: comp. ii. 21, v. 4.

περὶ τῶν ἁμαρτιῶν] The MSS here, as in several other passages, are divided between περὶ and ὑπέρ, though here the balance of authority is perhaps in favour of περί. Generally it may be said that περὶ is used of *things*, ὑπὲρ of *persons*, as 1 Pet. iii. 18 ὅτι καὶ Χριστὸς ἅπαξ περὶ ἁμαρτιῶν ἀπέθανεν δίκαιος ὑπὲρ ἀδίκων, but exceptions are very numerous, and in Heb. v. 3 we have περὶ ἑαυτοῦ προσφέρειν περὶ ἁμαρτιῶν (not ὑπὲρ ἁμαρτιῶν, as some read), though just before (ver. 1) the expression used is προσφέρῃ ὑπὲρ ἁμαρτιῶν. Where περὶ is used of persons, it is frequently explained by some clause added, *e.g.* Matt. xxvi. 28 τὸ περὶ πολλῶν ἐκχυννόμενον εἰς ἄφεσιν ἁμαρτιῶν. With this compare the parallel passages Luke xxii. 19, 20 (ὑπὲρ ὑμῶν), Mark xiv. 24 (ὑπὲρ πολλῶν, the correct reading), where there is no explanatory clause. All this follows from the meaning of the prepositions, ὑπὲρ having a sense of 'interest in,' which is wanting to περί. The distinction is marked in Athenag. *Resurr.* 1, λόγων διττῶν τῶν μὲν ὑπὲρ τῆς ἀληθείας των δὲ περὶ τῆς ἀληθείας κ.τ.λ. (comp. § 11). Neither conveys the idea of a *vicarious* act (ἀντί), though such will frequently appear in the context. On ὑπὲρ and περὶ see Winer § xlvii. p. 479, and especially Wieseler's note here.

ἐξέληται] '*deliver*' strikes the keynote of the epistle. The Gospel is a rescue, an emancipation from a state of bondage. See esp. iv. 9, 31, v. 1, 13.

τοῦ αἰῶνος τοῦ ἐνεστῶτος πονηροῦ] the correct reading, in which the detached position of πονηροῦ is emphatic: 'with all its evils.' Comp. Arist. *Eth. Nic.* i. 13 καὶ γὰρ τἀγαθὸν ἀνθρώπινον ἐζητοῦμεν καὶ τὴν εὐδαιμονίαν ἀνθρωπίνην, *Polit.* ii. 9 τῶν γ' ἀδικημάτων ἑκουσίων τὰ πλεῖστα συμβαίνει κ.τ.λ. The reading of the received text, τοῦ

ρου κατὰ τὸ θέλημα τοῦ Θεοῦ καὶ πατρὸς ἡμῶν [5]ᾧ ἡ δόξα εἰς τοὺς αἰῶνας τῶν αἰώνων· ἀμήν.

ἐνεστῶτος αἰῶνος πονηροῦ, is grammatically simpler, but less forcible.

The author of the Clementines, who was certainly acquainted with this epistle (see p. 61), seems to have St Paul's expression in mind, *Epist. Clem.* 1, ἐπὶ τοῦ ἐνεστῶτος πονηροῦ τὸν ἐσόμενον ἀγαθὸν ὅλῳ τῷ κόσμῳ μηνύσας βασιλέα (where αἰῶνος found in some texts after πονηροῦ is evidently an interpolation). If so, he appears to have interpreted the words 'from the æon, the dominion, of the present evil one': comp. 1 John v. 19 ὁ κόσμος ὅλος ἐν τῷ πονηρῷ κεῖται, Barnab. § 2. At all events a possible interpretation is thus suggested. Comp. Polyb. xviii. 38. 5 τὸν ἐνεστῶτα βασιλέα.

τοῦ αἰῶνος τοῦ ἐνεστῶτος] The present transitory world, elsewhere ὁ νῦν αἰών, *e.g.* 1 Tim. vi. 17, ὁ αἰὼν τοῦ κόσμου τούτου Ephes. ii. 2, and most frequently ὁ αἰὼν οὗτος, *e.g.* Rom. xii. 2, as opposed to the other world, the world of eternity, ὁ αἰὼν ἐκεῖνος Luke xx. 35, ὁ αἰὼν ὁ ἐρχόμενος Luke viii. 20, αἰὼν μέλλων Hebr. vi. 5, and often in the plural, οἱ αἰῶνες οἱ ἐπερχόμενοι Ephes. ii. 7, οἱ αἰῶνες τῶν αἰώνων, and οἱ αἰῶνες simply. This age, this world, is under a 'god' (2 Cor. iv. 4) or 'rulers' (1 Cor. ii. 6) of its own, who are opposed to the Eternal God, the King of the ages, ὁ βασιλεὺς τῶν αἰώνων, 1 Tim. i. 17. See especially Ephes. ii. 2—7, and comp. [Clem. Rom.] ii. § 6 ἔστιν δὲ οὗτος ὁ αἰὼν καὶ ὁ μέλλων δύο ἐχθροί. The Apostles speak of themselves and their generation as living on the frontier of two æons, the Gospel transferring them as it were across the border. The distinction of time between the two, which is the primary distinction, becomes lost in the moral and spiritual conception.

It has been proposed to take ἐνεστὼς here in the sense of 'impending,' as referring to the final apostasy. In other passages however ἐνεστῶτα is plainly 'present' as opposed to μέλλοντα 'future,' Rom. viii. 38, 1 Cor. iii. 22 (comp. Heb. ix. 9), in accordance with the sense it bears in the language of grammar, where ὁ χρόνος ὁ ἐνεστὼς is 'the present tense.' Comp. Philo *de Plant. Noe* ii. § 27, p. 346 M τριμεροῦς χρόνου, ὃς εἰς τὸν παρεληλυθότα καὶ ἐνεστῶτα καὶ μέλλοντα τέμνεσθαι πέφυκεν. Even in passages where it seems at first sight to have the sense 'impending, *soon* to come,' as in 1 Cor. vii. 26 διὰ τὴν ἐνεστῶσαν ἀνάγκην, 2 Thess. ii. 2 ἐνέστηκεν ἡ ἡμέρα, its proper meaning is more appropriate.

κατὰ τὸ θέλημα] '*by the will of God*' and not by our own merits. St Paul is still insisting on the dispensation of grace impugned by the false teachers. Compare τοῦ καλέσαντος, ver. 6.

τοῦ Θεοῦ καὶ πατρὸς ἡμῶν] Comp. Phil. iv. 20. Does ἡμῶν refer to Θεοῦ as well as πατρός, 'Our God and Father'? On the whole this seems probable; for the article, not being necessary before Θεοῦ, seems to be added to bind the two clauses together and connect both with ἡμῶν. The same construction is justified in the case of the similar expression, ὁ Θεὸς καὶ πατὴρ Ἰησοῦ Χριστοῦ (2 Cor. i. 3, Ephes. i. 3), by John xx. 17, 'I ascend to my Father and your Father, and to my God and your God.' See Fritzsche on Rom. III. p. 233. In ver. 1 the word 'Father' refers especially though not solely to Christ, in ver. 4 to mankind, while in ver. 3 it seems to be used absolutely.

5. Speaking of the mercy of God, as shown in man's redemption through the death of Christ, the Apostle bursts out in an ascription of praise. 'Infinitis beneficiis infinita gloria debetur,' says Pelagius. For similar outbursts of thanksgiving see Rom. vii. 25, ix. 5, xi. 36, 2 Cor. ix. 15, Ephes. iii. 20.

[6]Θαυμάζω ὅτι οὕτως ταχέως μετατίθεσθε ἀπὸ τοῦ καλέσαντος ὑμᾶς ἐν χάριτι Χριστοῦ εἰς ἕτερον εὐαγ-

ἡ δόξα] '*the glory*, which is pre-eminently such, the glory which belongs to him': comp. Joh. xvii. 5. The article is almost universally found with δόξα in these doxologies. Contrast with this the absence of the article in Rom. ii. 10, 1 Cor. xi. 15. It is probable therefore that we should supply ἐστὶν in such cases rather than ἔστω. It is an affirmation rather than a wish. Glory is the essential attribute of God. See 1 Pet. iv. 11 ᾧ ἐστὶν ἡ δόξα καὶ τὸ κράτος, and the doxology added to the Lord's prayer, Matt. vi. 13.

εἰς τοὺς αἰῶνας τῶν αἰώνων] '*for endless ages*,' opposed to the present finite and transitory age (ver. 4). Compare Ephes. ii. 2, 7, where this opposition is brought out more strongly.

6—9. An indignant expression of surprise takes the place of the usual thanksgiving for the faith of his converts. This is the sole instance where St Paul omits to express his thankfulness in addressing any church. See the introduction, p. 64.

'I marvel that ye are so ready to revolt from God who called you, so reckless in abandoning the dispensation of grace for a different gospel. A different gospel, did I say? Nay, it is not another. There cannot be two gospels. Only certain men are shaking your allegiance, attempting to pervert the Gospel of Christ. A vain attempt, for the Gospel perverted is no Gospel at all. Yea, though we ourselves or an angel from heaven (were it possible) should preach to you any other gospel than that which we have preached hitherto, let him be accursed. I have said this before, and I repeat it now. If any man preaches to you any other gospel than that which ye were taught by us, let him be accursed.'

6. οὕτως ταχέως] '*so quickly*.' If by 'so quickly' we understand 'so soon,' it must mean 'so soon after your conversion,' as the words following show. For the bearing of this expression on the date of the epistle see p. 41. It is possible however that ταχέως here may signify 'readily,' 'rashly,' *i.e.* quickly after the opportunity is offered, a sense which the present tense (μετατίθεσθε) would facilitate. See 1 Tim. v. 22 χεῖρας ταχέως μηδενὶ ἐπιτίθει, 2 Thess. ii. 2 εἰς τὸ μὴ ταχέως σαλευθῆναι. In this case there will be no reference to any independent point of time.

μετατίθεσθε] '*are turning renegades*'; the middle voice, as may be seen from the passages quoted below. Μετατίθεσθαι is used (1) of desertion or revolt, *i.e.* of military or political defection, as in Polyb. xxvi. 2. 6 ταχέως καὶ τοὺς πολιτευομένους μετατίθεσθαι πρὸς τὴν Ῥωμαίων αἵρεσιν, and frequently (2) of a change in religion, philosophy, or morals, 1 Kings xxi. 25 ὡς μετέθηκεν αὐτὸν Ἰεζάβελ ἡ γυνὴ αὐτοῦ, Iambl. *Protrept.* c. 17 μετατίθεσθαι ἀπὸ τοῦ ἀπλήστως καὶ ἀκολάστως ἔχοντος βίου ἐπὶ τὸν κοσμίως. Dionysius of Heraclea, who from being a Stoic became an Epicurean, was called μεταθέμενος, 'turncoat' (ἄντικρυς ἀποδὺς τὸν τῆς ἀρετῆς χιτῶνα ἀνθινὰ μετημφιάσατο Athen. vii. p. 281 D). The word is frequently used however of 'conversion' in a good sense, as in Justin *Apol.* II. pp. 83 B, 91 D, etc.

τοῦ καλέσαντος ὑμᾶς ἐν χάριτι] '*Him who called you in grace*.' St Paul here states the distinctive features of the true Gospel which the Galatians had set aside: *first*, as regards its *source*, that conversion comes of God ('Him that called you') and not of themselves; and *secondly*, as regards the *instrument*, that it is a covenant of grace, not of works. For the omission of Θεοῦ, see the note on i. 15.

γέλιον, 7 ὃ οὐκ ἔστιν ἄλλο, εἰ μή τινές εἰσιν οἱ ταράσσοντες ὑμᾶς καὶ θέλοντες μεταστρέψαι τὸ εὐαγγέλιον

Χριστοῦ] is generally omitted in the Latin authorities, while some others read Ἰησοῦ Χριστοῦ, Χριστοῦ Ἰησοῦ, and even Θεοῦ. All these may possibly have been glosses to explain τοῦ καλέσαντος. Certainly the passage seems to gain in force by the omission. The implied antithesis between the true gospel of grace and the false gospel of works thus stands out in bolder relief: comp. Ephes. ii. 8 τῇ χάριτί ἐστε σεσωσμένοι. It is found however in the best MSS, and is supported by such passages as Acts xv. 11, διὰ τῆς χάριτος τοῦ Κυρίου Ἰησοῦ πιστεύομεν σωθῆναι. If retained, it must be taken after χάριτι, and not with τοῦ καλέσαντος as in the Peshito, for ὁ καλέσας in St Paul's language is always the Father.

6, 7. εἰς ἕτερον εὐαγγ., κ.τ.λ.] '*to a second, a different gospel, which is not another.*' This is not an admission in favour of the false teachers, as though they taught the one Gospel, however perverted (comp. Phil. i. 15, 18). Such a concession would be quite alien to the spirit of this passage. 'It is not another gospel,' the Apostle says, 'for there cannot be two gospels, and as it is not the same, it is no gospel at all.' The relative ὃ cannot without harshness be referred to anything else but ἕτερον εὐαγγέλιον.

ἕτερον] implies a difference of kind, which is not involved in ἄλλο. The primary distinction between the words appears to be, that ἄλλος is another as 'one besides,' ἕτερος another as 'one of two.' The fundamental sense of ἕτερος is most clearly marked in its compounds, as ἑτερόφθαλμος, 'one-eyed.' Thus ἄλλος adds, while ἕτερος distinguishes. Now when our attention is confined to two objects, we naturally compare and contrast them; hence ἕτερος gets to signify 'unlike, opposite,' as Xen. *Cyrop.* viii. 3. 8 ἥν μου κατηγορήσῃς......εἰσαῦθις ὅταν διακονῶ, ἑτέρῳ μοι χρήσῃ διακόνῳ, *i.e.* 'changed,' where ἄλλῳ could not stand. In Exod. i. 8 ἀνέστη δὲ βασιλεὺς ἕτερος ἐπ' Αἴγυπτον, it is a translation of חדש 'novus'; and the idea of *difference* is frequently prominent in the word as used in the LXX. Thus while ἄλλος is generally confined to a negation of identity, ἕτερος sometimes implies the negation of resemblance. See 2 Cor. xi. 4, where the two words are used appropriately, as they are here. In many cases however they will be interchangeable: comp. Matt. xi. 3 with Luke vii. 20. Hesychius explains ἕτερον· ἄλλον· ἢ ἀλλοῖον· ἢ ἐν τοῖν δυοῖν· ἢ ἀριστερόν, νέον, δεύτερον.

7. εἰ μή τινές, κ.τ.λ.] 'Only in this sense is it another gospel, in that it is an attempt to pervert the one true Gospel.' Εἰ μὴ seems always to retain, at least in this stage of the language, its proper *exceptive* sense, and is not simply *oppositive*, though it frequently approaches nearly to ἀλλά; see the note on i. 19. Here the following θέλοντες, which is slightly emphatic ('attempting to, though without success'), justifies the exception taken by εἰ μή.

τινές εἰσιν οἱ ταράσσοντες] a somewhat unusual construction for οἱ ταράσσουσιν. It occurs however even in classical writers; *e.g.* Soph. *Œd. Col.* 1023 ἄλλοι γὰρ οἱ σπεύδοντες, Lysias *pro Arist. bon.* § 57 εἰσὶ δέ τινες οἱ προαναλίσκοντες (the latter passage is quoted with others by Winer, § xviii. p. 136), and more commonly in the New Testament, *e.g.* Col. ii. 8 βλέπετε μή τις ἔσται ὁ συλαγωγῶν, Luke xviii. 9. See the note on iii. 21. For τινὲς applied by St Paul to his adversaries, see ii. 12, 1 Cor. iv. 18, 2 Cor. iii. 1, x. 2. Other interpretations of this clause have been proposed, all of which seem to do violence either to the sense or the grammar.

τοῦ Χριστοῦ. 8ἀλλὰ καὶ ἐὰν ἡμεῖς ἢ ἄγγελος ἐξ οὐρανοῦ εὐαγγελίζηται [ὑμῖν] παρ' ὃ εὐηγγελισάμεθα
ὑμῖν, ἀνάθεμα ἔστω. 9ὡς προειρήκαμεν καὶ ἄρτι πάλιν

ταράσσοντες] not 'troubling your minds,' but 'raising seditions among you, shaking your allegiance,' a continuation of the metaphor of μετατίθεσθε. The phrase ταράττειν τὴν πόλιν is commonly used of factions, *e.g.* Aristoph. *Eq.* 863. See the note on v. 10.

μεταστρέψαι] properly, 'to reverse, to change to the opposite,' and so stronger than διαστρέψαι, which is simply 'to distort,' 'wrench': comp. Arist. *Rhet.* i. 15 καὶ τὸ τοῦ Ξενοφάνους μεταστρέψαντα φατέον κ.τ.λ. What was the idea prominent in the Apostle's mind when he called this heresy a 'reversal' of the Gospel may be gathered from iii. 3.

τοῦ Χριστοῦ] On the genitive see the notes on 1 Thess. ii. 2.

8, 9. The difference of moods in these two verses is to be noticed. In the former, a pure hypothesis is put forward, in itself highly improbable (εὐαγγελίζηται): in the latter, a fact which had actually occurred, and was occurring (εὐαγγελίζεται).

καὶ ἐάν] preserves its proper sense of 'etiamsi,' as distinguished from ἐὰν καὶ 'etsi.' See Hermann *Viger* p. 832, Jelf *Gramm.* § 861. In other words, it introduces a highly improbable supposition. With this passage contrast the meaning of ἐὰν καὶ as it occurs in vi. 1, ἐὰν καὶ προλημφθῇ.

ἡμεῖς] '*we.*' St Paul seems never to use the plural when speaking of himself alone. Here it would include those who had been his colleagues in preaching to the Galatians, such as Silas and Timothy. The latter especially would be referred to, as he seems to have been with the Apostle on both visits to Galatia, and was probably in his company when this letter was written. See the note on i. 2.

ὑμῖν] is doubtful, being found both before and after εὐαγγελίζηται in different texts, and in some omitted entirely.

παρ' ὃ] On the interpretation of these words a controversy on 'tradition' has been made to hinge, Protestant writers advocating the sense of 'besides' for παρά, Roman Catholics that of 'contrary to.' The context is the best guide to the meaning of the preposition. St Paul is here asserting the oneness, the integrity of his Gospel. It will not brook any rival. It will not suffer any foreign admixture. The idea of 'contrariety' therefore is alien to the general bearing of the passage, though independently of the context the preposition might well have this meaning.

ἀνάθεμα] is the common (Hellenistic), ἀνάθημα the classical (Attic) form. See Lobeck *Phryn.* pp. 249, 445, *Paralip.* p. 417. But though originally the same, the two forms gradually diverged in meaning; ἀνάθημα getting to signify 'devoted' in a good, and ἀνάθεμα in a bad sense. See Trench. *N. T. Synon.* § v. p. 14; Fritzsche on Rom. ix. 3. This is a common phenomenon in all languages, *e.g.* in English 'cant,' 'chant,' 'human,' 'humane,' with other examples given in Trench *Study of Words*, p. 156; see also Max Müller's *Science of Language*, 2nd ser. p. 262 sq. Such divergences of meaning are generally to be traced to the different sources from which the varying forms are derived. In the present instance the distinction seems to have arisen from the fact that the sense 'an accursed thing' would be derived chiefly through the Hellenist writers of the LXX, the sense 'an offering' mostly

λέγω, εἴ τις ὑμᾶς εὐαγγελίζεται παρ' ὃ παρελάβετε, ἀνάθεμα ἔστω. [10]ἄρτι γὰρ ἀνθρώπους πείθω ἢ τὸν

through classical authors. The distinction of meaning however is only general, not universal. Pseudo-Justin, *Quaest. et resp.* 121 (p. 190, Otto), assigns both meanings to ἀνάθεμα, as Theodoret (on Rom. ix. 3) does to ἀνάθημα. 'Ανάθημα occurs only once in the New Testament, Luke xxi. 5, and there in the sense of 'an offering,' in accordance with the distinction given above.

It is doubted whether ἀνάθεμα here means 'excommunicated' or 'accursed'; *i.e.* whether it refers to ecclesiastical censure or spiritual condition. The latter alone seems tenable; for (1) it is the LXX. translation of the Hebrew חרם, *e.g.* Josh. vii. 1, 12. This word is used in the Old Testament of a person or thing set apart and devoted to destruction, because hateful to God. Hence in a spiritual application it denotes the state of one who is alienated from God by sin. But on the other hand it seems never to signify 'excommunicated,' a sense which is not found till much later than the Christian era. (2) In no passage is the sense of ecclesiastical censure very appropriate to ἀνάθεμα, ἀναθεματίζειν, where they occur in the New Testament, and in some, as Rom. ix. 3, 1 Cor. xiii. 3, it is obviously excluded. Here, for instance, it is inconsistent with the ἄγγελος ἐξ οὐρανοῦ. In course of time ἀνάθεμα, like the corresponding חרם, underwent a change of meaning, getting to signify 'excommunicated,' and this is the common patristic sense of the word. It was not unnatural therefore, that the fathers should attempt to force upon St Paul the ecclesiastical sense with which they were most familiar, as Theodoret does for instance, on 1 Cor. xvi. 22, explaining ἀνάθεμα ἔστω by ἀλλότριος ἔστω τοῦ κοινοῦ σώματος τῆς ἐκκλησίας.

9. ὡς προειρήκαμεν] '*as we have told you before*,' probably on the occasion of his second visit, when he already discerned unhealthy symptoms in the Galatian Church. See p. 25. The distinction between the singular (λέγω) where St Paul is writing in his own person, and the plural (προειρήκαμεν) where he is speaking of the joint labours of himself and his colleagues, is to be observed. See the note on ἡμεῖς ver. 8.

καὶ ἄρτι πάλιν] '*so now again*.' ἄρτι here denotes strictly present, as opposed to past time—a late use of the word. See Lobeck *Phryn.* p. 18 sq.

πάλιν] '*again*' is not to be referred, as it is taken by some, to the preceding verse, in the sense 'I repeat what I have just said.' Against this interpretation two objections lie: (1) St Paul in that case would have used the singular προείρηκα (which indeed is found in some texts), as throughout the epistle he writes in his own person alone; and (2) The words καὶ ἄρτι mark some greater distinction of time than this interpretation would allow.

ὑμᾶς εὐαγγελίζεται] In classical writers this verb takes only a dative of the person, in later Greek it has indifferently a dative or an accusative. See Lobeck *Phryn.* p. 266 sq. and Ellicott on 1 Thess. iii. 6.

10. 'Let him be accursed, I say. What, does my boldness startle you? Is *this*, I ask, the language of a timeserver? Will any say *now* that, careless of winning the favour of God, I seek to conciliate men, to ingratiate myself with men? If I had been content thus to compromise, I should have been spared all the sufferings, as I should have been denied all the privileges, of a servant of Christ.'

ἄρτι γάρ] What is the opposition implied in this *now*? It can scarcely be referred, as some refer it, to the

Θεόν; ἢ ζητῶ ἀνθρώποις ἀρέσκειν; εἰ ἔτι ἀνθρώποις ἤρεσκον, Χριστοῦ δοῦλος οὐκ ἂν ἤμην.

11 Γνωρίζω δὲ ὑμῖν, ἀδελφοί, τὸ εὐαγγέλιον τὸ εὐ-

11. γνωρίζω γάρ.

time before his conversion. 'Conciliation' is no fit term to apply to the fierce bigotry of Saul, the persecutor of the Church of Christ. The errors of his early career are the offspring of blind zeal, and not of worldly policy (1 Tim. i. 13). The explanation is doubtless to be found in the charges of inconsistency brought against him by the Judaizers. They had misrepresented certain acts of his past life, and branded him as a temporiser. There shall be no doubt about his language *now*. He had formerly, they said, preached the Mosaic law, because forsooth he had become as a Jew to the Jews. Let them judge *now* whether he would make concessions to conciliate those who had a leaning towards Judaism. This ἄρτι has therefore no connexion with the ἄρτι of ver. 9. The suppressed allusion to the Judaizers also explains the particle γάρ: 'I speak thus strongly, *for* my language shall not be misconstrued, shall wear no semblance of compromise.'

ἀνθρώπους πείθω ἢ τὸν Θεόν] '*do I conciliate, make friends of men or of God?*' Though the idea of persuasion is not strictly applicable in the case of God (comp. 2 Cor. v. 11, ἀνθρώπους πείθομεν, Θεῷ δὲ πεφανερώμεθα), yet πείθω is fitly extended to the second clause in reference to the language of his enemies. 'You charge me with a policy of conciliation. Yes; I conciliate God.' 'De humano usu sumptum est,' says Jerome. On the article Bengel pointedly remarks: 'ἀνθρώπους, *homines;* hoc sine articulo: at mox τὸν Θεόν, *Deum* cum articulo. Dei solius habenda est ratio.' See also the note on iv. 31.

ἀνθρώποις ἀρέσκειν] So 1 Thess. ii. 4: comp. ἀνθρωπάρεσκοι, Ephes. vi. 6, Col. iii. 22 (with the note).

ἔτι] '*still.*' After what? 'After all that has befallen me: after all the experiences I have had.' Compare the ἔτι of v. 11. Both passages find an explanation in vi. 17; '*Henceforth* let no man trouble me.' See the introduction, p. 51. The ἔτι does not imply that St Paul ever had been a time-server. It is equivalent to, 'at this stage,' 'at this late date.' The insertion of γὰρ after εἰ in the received text is one of the many attempts of transcribers to smooth down the ruggedness of St Paul's style.

Χριστοῦ δοῦλος οὐκ ἂν ἤμην] '*I should not have been a servant of Christ,*' perhaps with an indirect reference to the marks of persecution which he bore on his body (τὰ στίγματα τοῦ Ἰησοῦ, vi. 17); 'I should not have been branded as His slave, I should not have suffered for Him.' Comp. v. 11, 'If I yet preach circumcision, why am I yet persecuted?'

11, 12. 'I assure you, brethren, the Gospel you were taught by me is not of human devising. I did not myself receive it from man, but from Jesus Christ. I did not learn it, as one learns a lesson, by painful study. It flashed upon me, as a revelation from Jesus Christ.'

11. Γνωρίζω ὑμῖν] '*I declare to you*' introduces some statement on which the Apostle lays special emphasis, 1 Cor. xii. 3, xv. 1, 2 Cor. viii. 1. (Compare the similar phrase, 'I would not have you ignorant.') Both this phrase and the following, κατὰ ἄνθρωπον, are confined to the epistles of this chronological group.

The best authorities are nearly equally divided between δὲ and γάρ.

αγγελισθὲν ὑπ' ἐμοῦ, ὅτι οὐκ ἔστιν κατὰ ἄνθρωπον.
12 οὐδὲ γὰρ ἐγὼ παρὰ ἀνθρώπου παρέλαβον αὐτὸ οὔτε
ἐδιδάχθην, ἀλλὰ δι' ἀποκαλύψεως Ἰησοῦ Χριστοῦ.
13 ἠκούσατε γὰρ τὴν ἐμὴν ἀναστροφήν ποτε ἐν τῷ Ἰου-

12. οὐδὲ ἐδιδάχθην.

The former, resuming the subject which has been interrupted by his defence of himself, is more after the Apostle's manner, while the latter would seem the obvious connecting particle to transcribers. On the other hand δὲ may possibly have been substituted for γὰρ here, because it is found with γνωρίζω (-ζομεν) in 1 Cor. xv. 1, 2 Cor. viii. 1.

ἔστιν] is here only the copula. The present tense is used instead of the imperfect to show the permanence and unchangeableness of his Gospel. See ii. 2.

κατὰ ἄνθρωπον] 'after any human fashion or standard.' See on iii. 15.

12. οὐδὲ γὰρ ἐγώ] 'For to go a step farther back, *neither* did *I myself* receive it from man.' The force of the particle οὐδὲ is best sought for in the context. Οὐδὲ ἐγὼ παρέλαβον answers to τὸ εὐαγγελισθὲν ὑπ' ἐμοῦ οὐκ ἔστιν, as παρὰ ἀνθρώπου answers to κατὰ ἄνθρωπον. Others explain it '*I* as little as the Twelve,' '*I* in whom perhaps it might have been expected': but such interpretations are not reflected in the context.

παρὰ ἀνθρώπου παρέλαβον] The idea in the preposition is sufficiently wide to include both the ἀπὸ and διὰ of ver. 1. I do not think the distinction given by Winer § xlvii. p. 463, and others, between λαμβάνειν παρὰ Κυρίου and λαμβάνειν ἀπὸ Κυρίου (1 Cor. xi. 23), as denoting respectively direct and indirect communication, can be insisted upon. It is true, that while ἀπὸ contemplates only the giver, παρὰ in a manner connects the giver with the receiver, denoting the *passage* from the one to the other, but the links of the chain between the two may be numerous, and in all cases where the idea of transmission is prominent παρὰ will be used in preference to ἀπό, be the communication direct or indirect; so Phil. iv. 18 δεξάμενος παρὰ Ἐπαφροδίτου τὰ παρ' ὑμῶν: comp. Plat. *Symp.* 202 E. The verb παραλαμβάνειν may be used either of the ultimate receiver or of any intermediate agent, provided that the idea of transmission be retained; *i.e.* it may be either (1) to receive as transmitted to oneself, 2 Thess. iii. 6, or (2) to receive so as to transmit to others. In this latter sense it is used of the Apostles, who receiving the Gospel directly from the Lord passed it to others. See 1 Cor. xi. 23, xv. 1, 3, and compare παραγγελία.

οὔτε ἐδιδάχθην] The authorities being nearly equally divided between οὔτε and οὐδέ, I have with some hesitation retained the former in the text, as being the less regular collocation (οὐδὲ...οὔτε), and therefore more likely to be altered. In this case another οὔτε is to be understood before παρέλαβον, the δὲ of οὐδὲ having reference to the former sentence. See Winer § lv. 6, p. 617, and esp. A. Buttmann p. 315.

ἐδιδάχθην is added to explain and enforce παρὰ ἀνθρώπου παρέλαβον, and thus to bring out the contrast with δι' ἀποκαλύψεως: 'I received it not by *instruction* from man but by *revelation* from Christ.' For a somewhat similar contrast see Cic. *pro Mil.* c. 4, 'Est enim haec, judices, non scripta sed nata lex; quam non didicimus, accepimus, legimus, verum ex natura ipsa arripuimus, hausimus, expressimus.'

13, 14. 'My early education is a

δαϊσμῷ, ὅτι καθ' ὑπερβολὴν ἐδίωκον τὴν ἐκκλησίαν τοῦ
Θεοῦ καὶ ἐπόρθουν αὐτήν, [14]καὶ προέκοπτον ἐν τῷ Ἰου-
δαϊσμῷ ὑπὲρ πολλοὺς συνηλικιώτας ἐν τῷ γένει μου,
περισσοτέρως ζηλωτὴς ὑπάρχων τῶν πατρικῶν μου

proof that I did not receive the Gospel from man. I was brought up in a rigid school of ritualism, directly opposed to the liberty of the Gospel. I was from age and temper a staunch adherent of the principles of that school. Acting upon them, I relentlessly persecuted the Christian brotherhood. No human agency therefore could have brought about the change. It required a direct interposition from God.'

13. ἠκούσατε] '*ye heard*,' 'I told you, when I was with you.' The history of his past career as a persecutor formed part of his preaching: see Acts xxii. 2—21, xxvi. 4—23, 1 Cor. xv. 8—10: comp. Phil. iii. 6, 1 Tim. i. 13. The A.V., 'ye *have* heard,' gives a wrong meaning.

ἀναστροφήν ποτε] for the more usual ποτε ἀναστροφήν, as ver. 23 ὁ διώκων ἡμᾶς ποτέ. Similar displacements of words, which would ordinarily come between the article and substantive, are frequent in the New Testament. See on 1 Thess. i. 1; and Winer § xx. p. 169 sq.

Ἰουδαϊσμῷ] '*observance of Jewish rites*.' The word does not in itself imply any disparagement. Comp. 2 Macc. ii. 21 τοῖς ὑπὲρ τοῦ Ἰουδαϊσμοῦ φιλοτίμως ἀνδραγαθήσασιν, xiv. 38 σῶμα καὶ ψυχὴν ὑπὲρ τοῦ Ἰουδαϊσμοῦ παραβεβλημένος, and Ἰουδαΐζειν Gal. ii. 14. Though perhaps originally coined by the heathen and, as used by them, conveying some shadow of contempt, it would, when neutralised among the Jews themselves, lose this idea and even become a title of honour. The case of Χριστιανός, likewise a term of reproach in the first instance, is a parallel.

ἐπόρθουν κ.τ.λ.] '*I devastated the Church*,' as Acts ix. 21 οὐχ οὗτός ἐστιν ὁ πορθήσας ἐν Ἱερουσαλὴμ τοὺς ἐπικαλουμένους κ.τ.λ. Compare ἐλυμαίνετο τὴν ἐκκλησίαν, Acts viii. 3.

14. συνηλικιώτας] '*of my own age*,' who embraced the religion of their fathers with all the ardour of youthful patriotism. The Attics use the simple form ἡλικιώτης, while the compound belongs to the later dialect. Compare the similar instances of πολίτης (συμπολίτης, Ephes. ii. 19), φυλέτης (συμφυλέτης, 1 Thess. ii. 14), etc. In this class of words the later language aims at greater definiteness. The rule however is not absolute, but only expresses a general tendency. See Lobeck *Phryn.* pp. 172, 471.

ἐν τῷ γένει μου] '*in my race*,' i.e. among the Jews, an incidental proof that St Paul is addressing Gentile converts. See p. 26, note 3. In the same way, Rom. xvi. 7, 21, he mentions certain Jews as his 'kinsmen' (συγγενεῖς). Comp. also Rom. ix. 3 ὑπὲρ τῶν ἀδελφῶν μου τῶν συγγενῶν μου κατὰ σάρκα.

περισσοτέρως ζηλωτὴς ὑπάρχων] The adverb περισσοτέρως, which is frequent in St Paul, seems always to retain its comparative force. Here it is explained by ὑπὲρ πολλούς. For ζηλωτὴς ὑπάρχων comp. Acts xxi. 20 πάντες ζηλωταὶ τοῦ νόμου ὑπάρχουσιν. St Paul seems to have belonged to the extreme party of the Pharisees (Acts xxii. 3, xxiii. 7, xxvi. 5, Phil. iii. 5, 6), whose pride it was to call themselves 'zealots of the law, zealots of God.' To this party also had belonged Simon, one of the Twelve, thence surnamed the zealot, ζηλωτὴς or καναναῖος, i.e. קנאן. A portion of

παραδόσεων. [15]ὅτε δὲ εὐδόκησεν ὁ ἀφορίσας με ἐκ κοιλίας μητρός μου καὶ καλέσας διὰ τῆς χάριτος αὐτοῦ [16]ἀποκαλύψαι τὸν υἱὸν αὐτοῦ ἐν ἐμοὶ ἵνα εὐαγγελί-

those extreme partizans, forming into a separate sect under Judas of Galilee, took the name of 'zealots' *par excellence*, and distinguished themselves by their furious opposition to the Romans: Joseph. *Antiq.* xviii. 1. 1, 6. See Ewald *Gesch. des Volkes Isr.* v. p. 25 sq, p. 322, vi. p. 340.

τῶν πατρικῶν μου παραδόσεων] '*of the traditions handed down from my fathers.*' It is doubtful whether the law of Moses is included in this expression. In Josephus τὰ ἐκ παραδόσεως τῶν πατέρων (*Antiq.* xiii. 10. 6), ἡ πατρῴα παράδοσις (*ib.* 16. 2), are the Pharisaic traditions, as distinguished from the written law. See also Matth. xv. 2, 3, 6, Mark vii. 3, 5, 8, 9, 13. These passages seem to show that the word παράδοσις, which might in itself include equally well the written law, signified in the mouth of a Jew the traditional interpretations and additions (afterwards embodied in the Mishna), as distinguished from the text on which they were founded and which they professed to supplement.

15—17. 'Then came my conversion. It was the work of God's grace. It was foreordained, before I had any separate existence. It was not therefore due to any merits of my own, it did not spring from any principles of my own. The revelation of His Son in me, the call to preach to the Gentiles, were acts of His good pleasure. Thus converted, I took no counsel of human advisers. I did not betake myself to the elder Apostles, as I might naturally have done. I secluded myself in Arabia, and, when I emerged from my retirement, instead of going to Jerusalem, I returned to Damascus.'

15. ὁ ἀφορίσας] '*who set me apart*, devoted me to a special purpose': Rom. i. 1 ἀφωρισμένος εἰς εὐαγγέλιον Θεοῦ. See also Acts xiii. 2 ἀφορίσατε δή μοι κ.τ.λ. The words ὁ Θεὸς of the received text are to be struck out as a gloss, though a correct one. Similar omissions are frequent in St Paul; see i. 6, ii. 8, iii. 5, v. 8, Rom. viii. 11, Phil. i. 6, 1 Thess. v. 24.

Observe how words are accumulated to tell upon the one point on which he is insisting—the sole agency of God as distinct from his own efforts: εὐδόκησεν, ἀφορίσας, ἐκ κοιλίας μητρός μου, καλέσας, χάριτος αὐτοῦ.

ἐκ κοιλίας μητρός μου] '*from before my birth*, before I had any impulses, any principles of my own.' For the expression see Judges xvi. 17 ἅγιος Θεοῦ ἐγώ εἰμι ἀπὸ κοιλίας μητρός μου, Is. xliv. 2, 24, xlix. 1, 5 ὁ πλάσας με ἐκ κοιλίας δοῦλον ἑαυτῷ, Psalm lxx. 6 ἐκ κοιλίας μητρός μου σύ μου εἶ σκεπαστής, and frequently in the LXX. The preposition seems to be merely temporal. The A. V., 'who separated me from my mother's womb,' obscures, if it does not misinterpret, the sense.

καλέσας διὰ τῆς χάριτος αὐτοῦ] See the note on i. 6.

16. Three separate stages in the history of the Apostle's consecration to his ministry seem to be mentioned here. *First*, the predestination to his high office, which dated from before his birth (ὁ ἀφορίσας με κ.τ.λ.); *Secondly*, the conversion and call to the Apostleship, which took place on the way to Damascus, Acts ix. 3 sq (καλέσας διὰ τῆς χάριτος αὐτοῦ); and *Thirdly*, the entering upon his ministry in fulfilment of this call, Acts ix. 20 sq, xiii. 2, 3 (ἀποκαλύψαι ἐν ἐμοὶ ἵνα εὐαγγελίζωμαι).

The distinction of these three stages seems well marked; and if so, this de-

ζωμαι αὐτὸν ἐν τοῖς ἔθνεσιν, εὐθέως οὐ προσανεθέμην
σαρκὶ καὶ αἵματι, 17 οὐδὲ ἀνῆλθον εἰς Ἱεροσόλυμα
πρὸς τοὺς πρὸ ἐμοῦ ἀποστόλους, ἀλλὰ ἀπῆλθον εἰς
Ἀραβίαν, καὶ πάλιν ὑπέστρεψα εἰς Δαμασκόν· 18 ἔπ-

17. οὐδὲ ἀπῆλθον εἰς Ἱερ.

termines the meaning of *ἐν ἐμοί.* It does not speak of a revelation made *inwardly to himself*, but of a revelation made *through him to others.* The preposition *ἐν* is used in preference to *διά*, because St Paul was not only the instrument in preaching the Gospel, but also in his own person bore the strongest testimony to its power. He constantly places his conversion in this light; see ver. 24 *ἐδόξαζον ἐν ἐμοὶ τὸν Θεόν*, 1 Tim. i. 16 *διὰ τοῦτο ἠλεήθην ἵνα ἐν ἐμοὶ πρώτῳ ἐνδείξηται Χριστὸς Ἰησοῦς τὴν ἅπασαν μακροθυμίαν πρὸς ὑποτύπωσιν τῶν μελλόντων πιστεύειν κ.τ.λ.*, 2 Cor. xiii. 3 *τοῦ ἐν ἐμοὶ λαλοῦντος Χριστοῦ*, Phil. i. 30. The rendering of *ἐν ἐμοὶ* 'within me,' i.e. 'in my heart,' seems neither to suit the context so well, nor to be so natural in itself.

εὐθέως οὐ προσανεθέμην κ.τ.λ.] '*forthwith, instead of conferring with flesh and blood, etc., I departed to Arabia.*' On *ἀνατίθεσθαι* see the note ii. 2. In the double compound *προσανατίθεσθαι* the idea of *communication* or *consultation* is stronger. The use of the word in heathen writers indirectly illustrates its sense here. It is employed especially of consulting soothsayers, and the like, as in Chrysippus (in Suidas, s.v. *νεοττός*) *προσαναθέσθαι ὀνειροκρίτῃ*, Diod. Sic. xvii. 116 *τοῖς μάντεσι προσαναθέμενος περὶ τοῦ σημείου.* Comp. Lucian *Jup. Trag.* § 1 (II. p. 642) *ἐμοὶ προσανάθου, λάβε με σύμβουλον πόνων.* See the note ii. 6.

For *σαρκὶ καὶ αἵματι* compare our Lord's words to St Peter, Matt. xvi. 17 'Flesh and blood did not reveal it unto thee.'

17. *ἀνῆλθον*] '*I came up.*' This verb and *ἀναβαίνειν* are used especially of visiting Jerusalem, situated in the high lands of Palestine, as *κατέρχεσθαι, καταβαίνειν*, are of leaving it. See Luke x. 30, Acts xi. 27, xii. 19, xv. 1, 2, xxi. 15, xxv. 1, 6, 7, and especially Acts xviii. 22, xxiv. 1. In the two last passages *ἀναβαίνειν* and *καταβαίνειν* are used absolutely without any mention of Jerusalem, this being implied in the expressions 'going up,' 'going down.' Here the various reading *ἀπῆλθον* has great claims to a place in the text. Both words occur in the context and it is difficult to say in favour of which reading the possible confusion of transcribers may more justly be urged. Perhaps however it is improbable that St Paul should have written *ἀπῆλθον* twice consecutively, as the repetition makes the sentence run awkwardly; though in Rom. viii. 15, 1 Cor. ii. 13, Heb. xii. 18, 22, something of the kind occurs.

τοὺς πρὸ ἐμοῦ ἀποστόλους] '*those who were Apostles before me,*' possibly including others besides the Twelve, especially James. See below, p. 95, note 4. For the expression compare Rom. xvi. 7, *οἵτινές εἰσιν ἐπίσημοι ἐν τοῖς ἀποστόλοις οἳ καὶ πρὸ ἐμοῦ γέγοναν ἐν Χριστῷ*, where however the construction is doubtful.

εἰς Δαμασκόν] A danger which threatened St Paul's life on this occasion seems to have left a deep impression on his mind, and is mentioned by him in another epistle, nearly contemporaneous with this, 2 Cor. xi. 32.

18—24. 'Not till three years were past did I go up to Jerusalem. My object in doing so was to confer with Cephas. But I did not remain with

ειτα μετὰ ἔτη τρία ἀνῆλθον εἰς Ἱεροσόλυμα ἱστορῆσαι Κηφᾶν, καὶ ἐπέμεινα πρὸς αὐτὸν ἡμέρας δεκαπέντε· [19]ἕτερον δὲ τῶν ἀποστόλων οὐκ εἶδον, εἰ μὴ

18. μετὰ τρία ἔτη.

him more than a fortnight; and of all the other Apostles I saw only James the Lord's brother. As in the sight of God, I declare to you that every word I write is true. Then I went to the distant regions of Syria and Cilicia. Thus I was personally unknown to the Christian brotherhood in Judæa. They had only heard that their former persecutor was now preaching the very faith which before he had attempted to destroy: and they glorified God for my conversion.'

18. ἔπειτα μετὰ ἔτη τρία] From what point of time are these three years reckoned? Probably from the great epoch of his life, from his conversion. The 'straightway' of ver. 16 leads to this conclusion; '*At first* I conferred not with flesh and blood, it was only *after the lapse of three years* that I went to Jerusalem.'

Ἱεροσόλυμα] is generally a neuter plural. In Matt. ii. 3 however we have πᾶσα Ἱεροσόλυμα. See A. Buttmann *Gramm.* p. 16. On the forms Ἱεροσόλυμα and Ἱερουσαλήμ see the note iv. 26.

ἱστορῆσαι Κηφᾶν] '*to visit Cephas.*' ἱστορῆσαι is somewhat emphatic: 'A word used,' says Chrysostom, 'by those who go to see great and famous cities.' It is generally said of things and places; less commonly, as here, of persons: comp. Joseph. *Bell. Jud.* vi. 1. 8 ἀνὴρ ὢν ἐγὼ κατ' ἐκεῖνον ἱστόρησα τὸν πόλεμον, and *Clem. Hom.* viii. 1, etc. St Peter is mentioned by St Paul only in this epistle and 1 Corinthians. Κηφᾶν is the right reading here, though there is respectable authority for Πέτρον. If the existing authorities are to be trusted, St Paul seems to have used the Aramaic and Greek names indifferently. Allowance ought to be made however for the tendency to substitute the more usual Πέτρος for the less common Κηφᾶς, e.g. here and ii. 9, 11, 14. In the Peshito Version Cephas, as the Aramaic name, is not unnaturally adopted throughout this epistle.

δεκαπέντε] A later form for the more classical πεντεκαίδεκα. This and the analogous forms of numerals occur frequently in the MSS of Greek authors of the post-classical age, but in many cases are doubtless due to the transcribers writing out the words at length, where they had only the numeral letters before them. The frequent occurrence of these forms however in the *Tabulae Heracleenses* is a decisive testimony to their use, at least in some dialects, much before the Christian era. They are found often in the LXX.

St Paul's visit on this occasion was abruptly terminated. He left on account of a plot against his life (Acts ix. 29) and in pursuance of a vision (Acts xxii. 17—21).

19. εἰ μὴ Ἰάκωβον] Is James here styled an Apostle or not? Are we to translate, 'I saw no other Apostle save James,' or 'I saw no other Apostle but only James'? It will be seen that the question is not whether εἰ μὴ retains its *exceptive* force or not, for this it seems always to do (see note on i. 7), but whether the exception refers to the whole clause or to the verb alone. That the latter is quite a possible construction will appear from Matth. xii. 4, Luke iv. 26, 27, Gal. ii. 16, Rev. xxi. 27; see Fritzsche on Rom. III. p. 195. But on the other hand the sense of ἕτερον naturally links it with

Ἰάκωβον τὸν ἀδελφὸν τοῦ Κυρίου. [20] ἃ δὲ γράφω ὑμῖν, ἰδοὺ ἐνώπιον τοῦ Θεοῦ ὅτι οὐ ψεύδομαι. [21] ἔπειτα ἦλθον εἰς τὰ κλίματα τῆς Συρίας καὶ τῆς Κιλικίας. [22] ἤμην δὲ

εἰ μή, from which it cannot be separated without harshness, and ἕτερον carries τῶν ἀποστόλων with it. It seems then that St James is here called an Apostle, though it does not therefore follow that he was one of the Twelve (see the detached note, p. 95). The plural in the corresponding account Acts ix. 27, 'He brought (Paul) to the Apostles,' is also in favour of this sense, but this argument must not be pressed.

20. ἰδοὺ ἐνώπιον τοῦ Θεοῦ] A form of asseveration equivalent to 'I call you to witness,' and so followed by ὅτι. See 2 Tim. ii. 14, iv. 1 διαμαρτύρεσθαι ἐνώπιον τοῦ Θεοῦ. For ἰδοὺ elsewhere in the New Testament is an interjection or adverb, never a verb, so that there is an objection to making it govern ὅτι here. Perhaps however the occurrence of ἴδε ὅτι in the LXX, Ps. cxix. 159, Lam. i. 20, may justify such a construction here. The strength of St Paul's language is to be explained by the unscrupulous calumnies cast upon him by his enemies. See the note 1 Thess. v. 27.

21. In the corresponding narrative of St Luke it is related that the brethren at Jerusalem, discovering the plot against St Paul's life, 'took him down to Cæsarea and despatched him to Tarsus' (Acts ix. 30); and later on, that Barnabas went to Tarsus and sought out Saul, and having found him brought him to Antioch, where they taught for a whole year before returning to Jerusalem (xi. 25—30). The Cæsarea mentioned there is doubtless *Stratonis*, and not *Philippi*, as some maintain. Not only was this the more probable route for him to take, but St Luke's language requires it; for (1) The words κατήγαγον, ἐξαπέστειλαν, imply a seaport and an embarkation: and (2) Cæsarea, without any addition to distinguish it, is always the principal city of the name. It appears therefore that St Luke represents St Paul as sailing from Cæsarea on his way to Tarsus; and comparing this account with the notice here, we must suppose either (1) That St Paul did not go direct to Tarsus but visited Syria on the way; or (2) That he visited Syria from Tarsus, and after preaching there returned again to Tarsus where he was found by Barnabas; St Luke having, on either of these hypotheses, omitted to record this visit to Syria; or (3) That St Paul's words here 'Syria and Cilicia' are not intended to describe the *order* in which he visited the two countries. This last is the most probable supposition. Cilicia has geographically a greater affinity with Syria than with Asia Minor. See Conybeare and Howson, I. p. 130. The less important country is here named after the more important. 'Cilicia,' says Ewald, 'was constantly little better than an appendage of Syria,' *Gesch. des V. Isr.* VI. p. 406. At this time however it was under a separate administration. The words τὰ κλίματα seem to show that 'Syria and Cilicia' are here mentioned under one general expression, and not as two distinct districts.

τὰ κλίματα] Rom. xv. 23, 2 Cor. xi. 10. A comparatively late word, see Lobeck *Paral.* p. 418. It is found in Pseudo-Aristot. *de Mundo* c. x, and several times in Polybius.

22. ἤμην ἀγνοούμενος κ.τ.λ.] '*I remained personally unknown.*' A strong form of the imperfect, as ἀκούοντες ἦσαν 'they kept hearing' (ver. 23): see Winer, § xlv. 5, p. 437 sq.

ἀγνοούμενος τῷ προσώπῳ ταῖς ἐκκλησίαις τῆς Ἰουδαίας ταῖς ἐν Χριστῷ, [23]μόνον δὲ ἀκούοντες ἦσαν ὅτι Ὁ διώκων ἡμᾶς ποτὲ νῦν εὐαγγελίζεται τὴν πίστιν ἥν ποτε ἐπόρθει, [24]καὶ ἐδόξαζον ἐν ἐμοὶ τὸν Θεόν.

ταῖς ἐκκλησίαις κ.τ.λ.] '*unknown to the Churches of Judæa*' generally, as distinguished from that of Jerusalem; comp. John iii. 22. To the latter he could not have failed to be known, as might be inferred from the account here, even without the narrative of his energetic preaching in the Acts. From Jerusalem he was hurried off to Cæsarea, and there embarking he left the shores of Palestine. The other churches of Judæa therefore had no opportunity of knowing him. Judæa is here distinguished from Jerusalem, as Italy is frequently distinguished from Rome, e.g. probably Hebr. xiii. 24. The addition ταῖς ἐν Χριστῷ was necessary when speaking of the Christian brotherhoods of Judæa; for the unconverted Jewish communities might still be called 'the Churches of Judæa.' See the note on 1 Thess. ii. 14, τῶν ἐκκλησιῶν τοῦ Θεοῦ τῶν οὐσῶν ἐν τῇ Ἰουδαίᾳ ἐν Χριστῷ Ἰησοῦ.

23. ὅτι] introduces an abrupt change from the oblique to the direct mode of speaking, e.g. Acts xiv. 22, xxiii. 22. So it is used frequently in introducing a quotation, e.g. Gal. iii. 10.

Ὁ διώκων ἡμᾶς ποτέ] '*Our persecutor of former times*'; ὁ διώκων being used as a substantive, i.e. without reference to time, as Matt. xxvii. 40 ὁ καταλύων τὸν ναόν: see Winer, § xlv. 7, p. 444. On the position of ποτέ, see the note on ver. 13.

τὴν πίστιν] It is a striking proof of the large space occupied by 'faith' in the mind of the infant Church, that it should so soon have passed into a synonym for the Gospel. See Acts vi. 7. Here its meaning seems to hover between the Gospel and the Church. For the various senses of πίστις, see the notes on iii. 23, vi. 10, and the detached note on the term 'faith.'

24. ἐν ἐμοί] See the note ver. 16, and comp. Is. xlix. 3 δοῦλός μου εἶ σὺ Ἰσραὴλ καὶ ἐν σοὶ ἐνδοξασθήσομαι. 'He does not say,' adds Chrysostom, 'they marvelled at me, they praised me, they were struck with admiration of me, but he attributes all to grace. They glorified God, he says, in me.'

St Paul's sojourn in Arabia.

Obscurity of the incident.

A veil of thick darkness hangs over St Paul's visit to Arabia. Of the scenes among which he moved, of the thoughts and occupations which engaged him while there, of all the circumstances of a crisis which must have shaped the whole tenour of his after life, absolutely nothing is known. 'Immediately,' says St Paul, 'I went away into Arabia.' The historian passes over the incident without a mention. It is a mysterious pause, a moment of suspense in the Apostle's history, a breathless calm which ushers in the tumultuous storm of his active missionary life.

Yet it may be useful to review the speculations to which this incident has given rise, even though we cannot hope to arrive at any definite result; for, if such a review bears no other fruit, it will at least bring out more clearly the significance of the incident itself.

Conjectures as to the place.

Of the place of the Apostle's sojourn various opinions have been held. Arabia is a vague term, and affords scope for much conjecture.

(1) El Belka.

1. The Arabic translator[1], whose language gives him a fictitious claim to a hearing on such a point, renders the passage 'Immediately I went to El Belka.' In like manner in Gal. iv. 25 he translates, 'This Hagar is Mount Sinai in El Belka, and is contiguous to Jerusalem.' Now the only district, so far as I can discover, which bears or has borne the name of El Belka, is the region lying to the east and north-east of the Dead Sea[2]. If so, how are we to account for this translation of Ἀραβία by El Belka? That the same rendering of the word in both passages arose from the translator's connecting them together in some way, can scarcely be doubted. Was his starting-point then a misapprehension of the meaning of συνστοιχεῖ in the second passage, which he renders 'is contiguous to[3],' and arguing from this, did he suppose that part of Arabia to be meant in both passages, which was nearest to Jerusalem? Or on the other hand, did he start from some tradition of St Paul's preaching in 'El Belka,' and having thus defined from the first passage the meaning of 'Arabia,' did he apply it to the second passage also? But in any case how could he talk of Mount Sinai in 'El Belka'? Was this ignorance of geography? or must we resort to the improbable supposition that some wandering Arab tribe, which gave its name to the country in the neighbourhood of the Dead Sea, at one time occupied the region about Sinai? At all events the tradition here preserved about St Paul, if it be a tradition, is of little worth, as the translator seems to have lived at a comparatively late date[4].

[1] The Arabic version of the Polyglotts, which was made directly from the Greek. The translator not unfrequently gives geographical comments. See Hug *Einleit.* § cix, I. p. 431. The other Arabic version, the Erpenian, translated from the Syriac, retains 'Arabia.'

[2] See Burckhardt *Trav. in Syria* App. III, Ritter *Erdkunde* XII. p. 426 sq, Stanley's *Sinai and Palestine* pp. 95, 319.

[3] For this rendering however he might plead the authority of several ancient commentators. See the notes on iv. 25.

[4] Hug l. c. states that the translator has unexpectedly revealed his country by his rendering of Acts ii. 10,

(2) The country near Damascus.

2. Arabia, in the widest use of the term, might extend to the gates of Damascus, and even include that city itself. 'You cannot any of you deny,' says Justin, arguing against his Jew as to the interpretation of a passage in one of the prophets, 'that Damascus belongs and did belong to Arabia, though now it has been assigned to Syrophœnicia[1].' Thus no very distant journey would be necessary to reach Arabia. A retirement in the immediate neighbourhood of Damascus would suffice, and such a visit, especially if it were brief, might well be passed over by the historian as a merely temporary interruption of the Apostle's long residence in that city, which was unknown to him, or which knowing, he did not care to record. Into these wild regions then, beyond the sway of Roman dominion, beyond the reach of civilization, far away from all his old haunts and associations, it is thought that the Apostle plunged himself in the first tumult of his newly-acquired experiences[2].

This explanation however is open to objection. It gives to 'Arabia' an extension, which at all events seems not to have been common, and which even the passage of Justin shows to have required some sort of justification. It separates the Arabia of the first chapter from the Arabia of the fourth. And lastly, it deprives this visit of a significance which, on a more probable hypothesis, it possesses in relation to this crisis of St Paul's life.

(3) Mount Sinai.

3. For if we suppose that the Apostle at this critical moment betook himself to the Sinaitic peninsula, the scene of the giving of the law, then his visit to Arabia becomes full of meaning. He was attracted thither by a spirit akin to that which formerly had driven Elijah to the same region[3]. Standing on the threshold of the new covenant, he was anxious to look upon the birthplace of the old: that dwelling for a while in seclusion in the presence of 'the mount that burned with fire,' he might ponder over the transient glories of the 'ministration of death,' and apprehend its real purpose in relation to the more glorious covenant which

τὰ μέρη τῆς Λιβύης τῆς κατὰ Κυρήνην, 'and the territories of Africa which is *our country*.' There can scarcely be a doubt however that here كورتنا 'our country' is a corrupt reading of كورينا 'Cyrene,' the change involving only a slight alteration in one letter. See Lagarde *de N. T. ad vers. Orient. fidem edendo*, Berl. 1857, p. 3, referred to in Bleek's *Einl.* p. 737. Such geographical notices as that of El Belka point to a more eastern origin.

[1] *Dial. c. Tryph.* p. 305 A. See also other authorities in Conybeare and Howson, I. p. 117, 118. Tertullian (*adv. Jud.* c. 9 and *adv. Marc.* iii. 13) obviously copies Justin and must not be considered an independent authority. The words of Justin *εἰ καὶ νῦν προσνενέμηται τῇ Συροφοινίκῃ λεγομένῃ* seem to refer to the arrangement of these provinces by Hadrian. See Becker and Marquardt *Röm. Alterth.* III. 1, p. 195 sqq and comp. [Bardesanes] *de Fato*, in Cureton's *Spicil. Syr.* p. 30. On the limits of Arabia see also Ephr. Syr. *Op. Syr.* I. p. 464 sq.

[2] See the instructive passage in Ewald, *Gesch. des Volkes Isr.* VI. p. 398. Ewald however, though he takes St Paul into this region, guards against the objections which I have alleged in the text, by supposing him to travel as far as Sinai also (p. 400).

[3] 1 Kings xix. 8—18. It is worth noticing that this region is connected with Damascus in the history of Elijah as well as of St Paul; 'Go return on thy way to the wilderness of Damascus.'

was now to supplant it. Here, surrounded by the children of the desert, the descendants of Hagar the bondwoman, he read the true meaning and power of the law[1]. In the rugged and barren region, whence it issued, he saw a fit type of that bleak desolation which it created and was intended to create in the soul of man. In the midst of such scenes and associations, his spirit was attuned to harmony with his divine mission, and fitted to receive fresh 'visions and revelations of the Lord.' Thus in the wilderness of Sinai, as on the Mount of the transfiguration, the three dispensations met in one. Here Moses had received the tables of the law amid fire and tempest and thick darkness. Here again Elijah, the typical prophet, listened to the voice of God, and sped forth refreshed on his mission of righteousness. And here lastly, in the fulness of time, St Paul, the greatest preacher of Him of whom both the law and the prophets spoke, was strengthened and sanctified for his great work, was taught the breadth as well as the depth of the riches of God's wisdom, and transformed from the champion of a bigoted and narrow tradition into the large-hearted Apostle of the Gentiles[2].

Significance of this sojourn.

What was the length of this sojourn we can only conjecture. The interval between his conversion and his first visit to Jerusalem, St Paul here states to have been three years. The notices of time in St Luke are vague, but not contradictory to this statement[3]. From Damascus St Paul tells us he went away into Arabia, whence he returned to Damascus. St Luke represents him as preaching actively in this city after his conversion, not mentioning and apparently not aware of any interruption, though his narrative is not inconsistent with such. It seems probable then that St Paul's visit to Arabia took place early in this period before he

Its duration.

[1] A stronger argument for St Paul's visit to Sinai might be drawn from his reference to Hagar, the supposed Arabic name of Sinai (Gal. iv. 25), which he was not likely to have heard anywhere but on the spot: comp. Stanley *Sinai and Palestine* p. 50. But the reading and the interpretation alike are highly doubtful. See the notes there.

[2] The significance of Sinai, as the holy place of inspiration, will be felt by readers of *Tancred*.

[3] The notices of time in the narrative of the Acts are these: He remained with the disciples in Damascus *some days* (ἡμέρας τινὰς) and *straightway* (εὐθέως) he began to preach (ἐκήρυσσεν)... and Saul was the more strengthened... and when *many days* (ἡμέραι ἱκαναὶ) were accomplishing (ἐπληροῦντο) the Jews took counsel to slay him, in consequence of which he left and went to Jerusalem (ix. 20—26). Ἡμέραι ἱκαναὶ is an indefinite period in St Luke, which may vary according to circumstances; Acts ix. 43, xviii. 18, xxvii. 7. Certainly the idea connected with ἱκανὸς in his language is that of largeness rather than smallness; comp. Luke vii. 12, Acts xx. 37 (ἱκανὸς κλαυθμός). In the LXX it is frequently employed to translate שדי 'mighty,' e.g. Ruth i. 20, 21. Again the wide use of the Hebrew ימים, which St Luke is copying, allows of almost any extension of time. Hence πολλαὶ ἡμέραι in the LXX denotes any indefinite period however long; Gen. xxxvii. 34, 2 Sam. xiv. 2, 1 Kings iii. 11 ('a long life'). Even Demosthenes, *de Cor.* p. 258, can speak of the interval between the battles of Haliartus and Corinth as οὐ πολλαὶ ἡμέραι, though they were fought in different years and many important occurrences happened in the mean time. The difference between the vague 'many days' of the Acts and the definite 'three years' of the Epistle is such as might be expected from the circumstances of the two writers.

commenced his active labours[1]. '*Immediately*,' he says, 'instead of conferring with flesh and blood, I went into Arabia.' The silence of the historian is best accounted for on the supposition that the sojourn there was short; but as St Luke's companionship with the Apostle commenced at a much later date, no great stress must be laid on the omission. Yet on the other hand there is no reason for supposing it of long duration. It was probably brief—brief enough not to occupy any considerable space in the Apostle's history, and yet not too brief to serve the purpose it was intended to serve.

Its purpose.

For can we doubt that by this journey he sought seclusion from the outer world, that his desire was to commune with God and his own soul amid these hallowed scenes, and thus to gather strength in solitude for his active labours? His own language implies this; 'I conferred *not with flesh and blood*, but departed into Arabia.' The fathers for the most part take a different view of this incident. They imagine the Apostle hurrying forth into the wilds of Arabia, burning to impart to others the glad tidings which had so suddenly burst upon himself. 'See how fervent was his soul,' exclaims Chrysostom, 'he was eager to occupy lands yet untilled; he forthwith attacked a barbarous and savage people, choosing a life of conflict and much toil[2].' This comment strikes a false note. Far different at such a crisis must have been the spirit of him, whose life henceforth was at least as conspicuous for patient wisdom and large sympathies, as for intense self-devotion. He retired for a while, we may suppose, that

'Separate from the world, his breast
Might duly take and strongly keep
The print of Heaven[3].'

And what place more fit for this retirement than that holy ground,

'Where all around, on mountain, sand, and sky,
God's chariot wheels have left distinctest trace[4]'?

[1] It must in this case be placed before the notice of his active preaching, ix. 20 καὶ εὐθέως, κ.τ.λ. Some have put it later and seen an indirect allusion to it in the expression μᾶλλον ἐνεδυναμοῦτο, ver. 22; but there is no trace of a chronological notice in these words, and such an allusion is scarcely natural.

[2] Similarly also Victorinus, Hilary, Theodore Mops., Theodoret, Primasius, and the Œcumenian commentator. Some of the Latin fathers might have been helped to this view by a curious blunder arising out of the Latin translation 'non acquievi carni et sanguini,' 'I did not *rest in* flesh and blood,' which Victorinus explains, 'Omnino laboravi carnaliter,' adding 'Caro enim et sanguis homo exterior totus est.' Tertullian however, *de Resurr. Carn.* c. 50, quotes the passage, 'Statim non retulerit ad carnem et sanguinem,' explaining it, 'id est ad circumcisionem, id est ad Judaismum.' Jerome supposes that St Paul preached in Arabia, but that his preaching was unsuccessful. His comment is curious. Why, he asks, is this visit to Arabia, of which we know nothing, which seems to have ended in nothing, recorded at all? It is an allegory from which we must extract a deep meaning. Arabia is the Old Testament. In the law and the prophets St Paul sought Christ, and having found Him there, he returned to Damascus, 'hoc est ad sanguinem et passionem Christi.' So fortified, he went to Jerusalem, 'locum visionis et pacis.' This interpretation is doubtless borrowed from Origen.

[3] *Christian Year, 13th Sunday after Trinity*, said of Moses.

[4] *Christian Year, 9th Sunday after Trinity*, said of Elijah.

St Paul's first visit to Jerusalem.

The visit to Jerusalem mentioned at the close of the first chapter of this epistle is doubtless the same with that recorded in the ninth chapter of the Acts[1]. Whatever difficulties seem to stand in the way of our identifying them, the fact that in each narrative this is stated to have been St Paul's first appearance in Jerusalem since his conversion and to have followed after a sojourn in Damascus, must be considered conclusive. Nor indeed is there any inconsistency in the two narratives. Though they contain but few incidents in common, they for the most part run parallel with each other; and even in particulars in which there is no coincidence, there is at least no direct contradiction. On the other hand the *aspect* of events presented in the two accounts is confessedly different. And this will almost always be the case in two independent narratives. In the case of St Paul and St Luke this divergence is due to two causes:

The same event narrated by St Paul and St Luke

but under different aspects owing to

First. The different *position* of the two writers, the one deriving his information at second-hand, the other an eyewitness and an actor in the scenes which he describes. In such cases the one narrator will present rather the external view of events, while the other dwells on their inner history, on those relations especially which have influenced his own character and subsequent actions: the former will frequently give broad and general statements of facts, where the latter is precise and definite.

(1) Their respective positions.

Secondly. The different *objects* of the two writers. The one sets himself to give a continuous historical account; the other introduces incidents by way of allusion rather than of narrative, singling out those especially which bear on the subject in hand. In the particular instance before us, it is important to observe this divergence of purpose. St Luke dwells on the change which had come over Saul, transforming the persecutor of the Gospel into the champion of the Gospel. St Paul asserts his own independence, maintaining that his intercourse with the leaders and the Church of the Circumcision had been slight. The standing-point of the historian is determined by the progress of events, that of the Apostle by the features of the controversy. Thus occupying different positions, they naturally lay stress each on a different class of facts, for the most part opposite to, though not inconsistent with, each other.

(2) Their difference of aim.

The narratives may best be compared by considering the incidents under two heads;

1. *St Paul's intercourse with the Apostles.* The narrative of the Acts relates that when St Paul visited Jerusalem he was regarded with suspicion by the disciples; that Barnabas introduced him to 'the Apostles,' relating the circumstances of his conversion and his zeal for the Gospel when converted; and that after this he moved about freely in their company. These are just the incidents which would strike the external observer as important. On the other hand St Paul says nothing of Barnabas. His relations with Barnabas had no bearing on the subject in hand, his obligations to

St Paul's relations (1) with the Twelve,

[1] ix. 26—30. Compare St Paul's later reference to this residence at Jerusalem, Acts xxii. 17—21.

the Apostles of the Circumcision. In all that relates to that subject he is precise and definite, where the author of the Acts is vague and general. He states the exact time of his sojourn, fifteen days. He mentions by name the members of the apostolate whom alone he saw—Peter in whose house he resided, and James to whom as head of the Church of Jerusalem he would naturally pay a visit. This is sufficient to explain the account of his 'going in and out' with the Apostles in the Acts, though the language of the historian is not what would have been used by one so accurately informed as the Apostle himself. It is probable that the other Apostles were absent on some mission, similar to that of Peter to Lydda and Joppa which is recorded just after (ix. 32—43); for there were at this time numberless churches scattered throughout 'Judæa and Galilee and Samaria' (ix. 31), which needed supervision.

(2) with the Jewish Christians.

2. *St Paul's intercourse with the Jewish Church at large.* At first sight there appears to be a wide difference between the two accounts. St Luke tells of his attempting to 'join himself to the disciples,' of his 'going in and out,' of his 'speaking boldly in the name of the Lord Jesus and disputing,' while St Paul himself states that 'he was unknown by face unto the churches of Judæa.' Yet on examining the narratives more closely this discrepancy is reduced to very narrow limits. St Luke confines his sojourn especially to Jerusalem, and his preaching to a small section of unbelievers, not the genuine Jews but the Hellenists[1]. He relates moreover that St Paul's visit terminated abruptly[2], owing to a plot against his life, and that he was hurried off to Cæsarea, whence he forthwith embarked. To a majority therefore of the Christians at Jerusalem he *might*, and to the Churches of Judæa at large he *must*, have been personally unknown. But though the two accounts are not contradictory, the impression left by St Luke's narrative needs correcting by the more precise and authentic statement of St Paul.

The name and office of an Apostle.

Meaning of the term in classical writers.

The word ἀπόστολος in the first instance is an adjective signifying 'despatched' or 'sent forth.' Applied to a person, it denotes more than ἄγγελος. The 'Apostle' is not only the messenger, but the delegate of the person who sends him. He is entrusted with a mission, has powers conferred upon him[3]. Beyond this, the classical usage of the term gives no

[1] ix. 28. The restrictions ἐν [or εἰς] Ἱερουσαλὴμ and πρὸς τοὺς Ἑλληνιστὰς are the more noticeable, in that they interfere with the leading feature of St Luke's narrative, the publicity of Saul's conversion.

[2] ix. 29. Compare Acts xxii. 18, 'Make haste and get thee quickly out of Jerusalem.'

[3] It occurs of a person in Herod. i. 21, v. 38. With this exception, no instances are given in the Lexicons of its use by classical authors even of a late date with any other but the Attic meaning; nor have I succeeded in finding any myself, though Hesychius explains ἀπόστολος· στρατηγὸς κατὰ πλοῦν πεμπόμενος. This is probably an instance where

aid towards understanding the meaning of the Christian apostolate. Its special sense denoting 'a naval expedition, a fleet despatched on foreign service,' seems to have entirely superseded every other meaning in the Attic dialect; and in the classical Greek of a later period also, except in this sense, the word appears to be of very rare occurrence.

Its use among the Jews.

A little more light, and yet not much more, is thrown on the subject by the use of the term among the Jews. It occurs but once in the LXX, in 1 Kings xiv. 6, as a translation of שָׁלוּחַ, where it has the general sense of a messenger, though with reference to a commission from God[1]. With the later Jews however, and it would appear also with the Jews of the Christian era, the word was in common use. It was the title borne by those who were despatched from the mother city by the rulers of the race on any foreign mission[2], especially such as were charged with collecting the tribute paid to the temple service[3]. After the destruction of Jerusalem the 'Apostles' formed a sort of council about the Jewish patriarch, assisting him in his deliberations at home, and executing his orders abroad[4]. Thus in

the Attic usage has ruled the literary language, the word having meanwhile preserved in the common dialect the sense which it has in Herodotus and which reappears in the LXX and New Testament and in the official language of the Jews. See the notes on κατηχεῖν, vi. 6; πτύρεσθαι, Phil. i. 28; γογγυσμός, Phil. ii. 14.

[1] It was also used by Symmachus to translate צִיר in Is. xviii. 2: see below. The word ἀποστολή occurs in a few passages in the LXX, and ἀποστέλλω is the common translation of שָׁלַח. Justin therefore (*Dial. c. Tryph.* c. 75, p. 300 D) is so far justified in saying that the prophets are called apostles, καὶ ἄγγελοι καὶ ἀπόστολοι τοῦ Θεοῦ λέγονται οἱ ἀγγέλλειν τὰ παρ' αὐτοῦ ἀποστελλόμενοι προφῆται...λέγει γὰρ ἐκεῖ ὁ Ἡσαΐας ἀπόστειλόν με. The Syriac renders ἀπόστολος by the word corresponding to the Hebrew.

[2] Such for instance as the bearers of the instructions contemplated in Acts xxviii. 21, οὔτε γράμματα περὶ σοῦ ἐδεξάμεθα ἀπὸ τῆς Ἰουδαίας οὔτε παραγενόμενός τις τῶν ἀδελφῶν ἀπήγγειλεν. Eusebius (*Montf. Coll. Nov.* II. 425), evidently thinking o this passage, says: ἀποστόλους δὲ εἰσέτι νῦν ἔθος ἐστὶν Ἰουδαίοις ὀνομάζειν τοὺς ἐγκύκλια γράμματα παρὰ τῶν ἀρχόντων αὐτῶν ἐπικομιζομένους. The passage in Isaiah xviii. 1, 2, which is read in the LXX, Οὐαὶ...ὁ ἀποστέλλων ἐν θαλάσσῃ ὅμηρα καὶ ἐπιστολὰς βιβλίνας ἐπάνω τοῦ ὕδατος, and in which for ὅμηρα Symmachus had ἀποστόλους, was interpreted to refer to these 'apostles' of the Jews who instigated the people against the Christians; and some even thought that in the words following, πορεύσονται γὰρ ἄγγελοι κοῦφοι πρὸς ἔθνος κ.τ.λ., the true Apostles were referred to in contrast with the false. See Procopius *in Esaiam*, l.c. and Eusebius, l.c. The LXX version is entirely wrong and the comment worthless in itself, but it affords a valuable illustration of St Paul's references to the 'false apostles,' and especially to the commendatory letters, 2 Cor. iii. 1. See also Jerome, *Comm. ad Gal.* i. 1, 'Usque hodie a patriarchis Judæorum apostolos mitti etc.'

[3] See Cod. Theodos. XVI. Tit. viii. 14, 'Superstitionis indignae est, ut archisynagogi sive presbyteri Judaeorum vel quos ipsi *apostolos* vocant, qui ad exigendum aurum atque argentum a patriarcha certo tempore diriguntur etc.,' with the learned comment of J. Gothofred. The collection of this tribute was called ἀποστολή, Julian *Epist.* 25 τὴν λεγομένην παρ' ὑμῖν ἀποστολὴν κωλυθῆναι.

[4] See the important passage in Epiphanius, *Haer.* XXX. p. 128, τῶν παρ' αὐτοῖς ἀξιωματικῶν ἀνδρῶν ἐναρίθμιος ἦν. εἰσὶ δὲ οὗτοι μετὰ τὸν πατριάρχην ἀπό-

designating His immediate and most favoured disciples 'Apostles,' our Lord was not introducing a new term[1] but adopting one which from its current usage would suggest to His hearers the idea of a highly responsible mission[2].

Mistake of restricting the title to the Twelve.

At the first institution of the office the Apostles were twelve in number. According to the prevailing view this limit was strictly observed, an exception however being made in the case of St Paul. Nay so far has the idea of this restriction of number been carried by some, that they hold the election of Matthias to have been a hasty and ill-advised act, and to have been subsequently reversed by an interposition of God, St Paul being substituted in his place[3]. It is needless to say that the narrative of St Luke does not betray the faintest trace of such a reversal. And with regard to the general question, it will I think appear, that neither the Canonical Scriptures nor the early Christian writings afford sufficient ground for any such limitation of the apostolate.

Its use in the Gospels does not favour this.

In the Gospels the word 'Apostle' is of comparatively rare occurrence. Those, whom it is customary with us to designate especially 'the Apostles,' are most often entitled either generally 'the disciples' or more definitely 'the Twelve.' Where the word does occur, it is not so used as to lend any countenance to the idea that it is in any way restricted to the Twelve. In St Matthew it is found once only, and there it is carefully defined, 'the *twelve* Apostles' (x. 2). In St Mark again it occurs in one passage alone, where it has a special reference to the act of *sending them forth* (vi. 30, οἱ ἀπόστολοι, compare ἀποστέλλειν, ver. 7). In St John likewise it appears once only, and there in its general sense of a messenger, a delegate, without any direct reference to the Twelve (xiii. 16). St Luke uses the word more frequently, and indeed states explicitly that our Lord gave this name to the Twelve[4], and in his Gospel it is a common designation for them. But, if we are disposed to infer from this that the title was in any way restricted to them, we are checked by remembering that the same evangelist elsewhere extends it to others—not to Paul only, but to Barnabas also[5].

στολοι καλούμενοι, προσεδρεύουσι δὲ τῷ πατριάρχῃ, κ.τ.λ.; and p. 134, συμβέβηκε...γέρας τῷ Ἰωσήππῳ τῆς ἀποστολῆς δοῦναι τὴν ἐπικαρπίαν· καὶ μετ' ἐπιστολῶν οὗτος ἀποστέλλεται εἰς τὴν Κιλικῶν γῆν, κ.τ.λ.

[1] There is no direct evidence indeed that the term was in use among the Jews before the destruction of Jerusalem: but it is highly improbable that they should have adopted it from the Christians, if it had not been current among them before; and moreover Christian writers speak of this Jewish apostolate, as an old institution which still lingered on.

[2] Our Lord Himself is so styled Hebr. iii. 1, 'The apostle and high priest of our profession'; the best comment on which expression is Joh. xvii. 18; 'As thou hast sent (ἀπέστειλας) me into the world, even so have I also sent (ἀπέστειλα) them into the world.' Comp. Justin *Apol.* I. c. 63, pp. 95 D, 96 C.

[3] See Schaff *History of the Apostolic Church*, II. p. 194.

[4] Luke vi. 13 ἐκλεξάμενος ἀπ' αὐτῶν δώδεκα οὓς καὶ ἀποστόλους ὠνόμασεν.

[5] Acts xiv. 4, 14. The word ἀπόστολος occurs 79 times in the New Testament, and of these 68 instances are in St Luke and St Paul. ἀποστολὴ occurs four times only, thrice in St Paul and once in St Luke.

In the account of the foundation of the apostolate then, and in the language used in the Gospels of the Twelve, there is no hint that the number was intended to be so limited. It is true that twelve is a typical number, but so is seven also. And if the first creation of the diaconate was not intended to be final as regards numbers, neither is there any reason to assume this of the first creation of the apostolate. The qualification for and the nature of the office in the latter case necessarily imposed a severer limit than in the former, but otherwise they stand on the same footing with respect to an increase in their numbers. The Twelve were primarily the Apostles of the Circumcision, the representatives of the twelve tribes[1]. The extension of the Church to the Gentiles might be accompanied by an extension of the apostolate. How far this extension was carried, it may be a question to consider; but the case of St Paul clearly shows that the original number was broken in upon. In the figurative language of the Apocalypse indeed the typical number twelve still remains[2]. But this is only in accordance with the whole imagery of the book, which is essentially Jewish. The Church there bears the name of Jerusalem. The elect are sealed from the twelve tribes, twelve thousand from each. It would be as unreasonable to interpret the restriction literally in the one case, as in the other. The 'twelve Apostles of the Lamb' in the figurative language of St John represent the apostolate, perhaps the general body of Christian pastors, as the elect of the twelve tribes represent the elect of Christendom.

Twelve a typical number.

And as a matter of fact we do not find the term Apostle restricted to the Twelve with only the exception of St Paul[3]. St Paul himself seems in one passage to distinguish between 'the Twelve' and 'all the Apostles,' as if the latter were the more comprehensive term (1 Cor. xv. 5, 7). It appears both there and in other places[4] that James the Lord's brother

Other Apostles beside the Twelve.

[1] Matth. xix. 28, Luke xxii. 30: comp. Barnab. § 8 *οὖσιν δεκαδύο εἰς μαρτύριον τῶν φυλῶν ὅτι δεκαδύο αἱ φυλαὶ τοῦ Ἰσραήλ*. See Justin *Dial. c. Tryph.* 42, p. 260 c. An Ophite writing represented the Twelve as actually taken from the twelve tribes: Hippol. *Haer.* v. 8, p. 109.

[2] Rev. xxi. 14 'And the walls of the city had twelve foundations, and in them the names of the twelve apostles of the Lamb.'

[3] Those instances are here disregarded, where the term is used in the sense of an apostle or delegate of a church, e.g. the brethren (2 Cor. viii. 23 *ἀπόστολοι ἐκκλησιῶν*) and Epaphroditus (Phil. ii. 25 *ὑμῶν δὲ ἀπόστολος*). Such persons are not spoken of as apostles of Christ. Yet this free use of the term seems to show that it had not such a rigid and precise application as is generally supposed.

[4] In 1 Cor. xv. 7, 'After that he was seen of James, then of all the apostles,' St Paul certainly appears to include James among the Apostles. See also the note on Gal. i. 19, where he is apparently so entitled. In 1 Cor. ix. 5, *ὡς καὶ οἱ λοιποὶ ἀπόστολοι καὶ οἱ ἀδελφοὶ τοῦ Κυρίου καὶ Κηφᾶς*, it seems probable that St Paul is singling out certain Apostles in 'the brethren of the Lord' as well as in 'Cephas,' whether we suppose *λοιποὶ* to be used in distinction to the persons thus specified, or to Paul and Barnabas who are mentioned just after. Still it is a question which of the 'brethren of the Lord' are meant. Jude is said to have been married (Euseb. *H. E.* iii. 20), but he seems to disclaim for himself the title of an Apostle (Jude 17, 18). Whether Hegesippus (Euseb. *H. E.* ii. 23) considered

is styled an Apostle. On the most natural interpretation of a passage in the Epistle to the Romans, Andronicus and Junias, two Christians otherwise unknown to us, are called distinguished members of the apostolate, language which indirectly implies a very considerable extension of the term[1]. In 1 Thess. ii. 6 again, where in reference to his visit to Thessalonica he speaks of the disinterested labours of himself and his colleagues, adding 'though *we* might have been burthensome to you, being *Apostles* of Christ,' it is probable that under this term he includes Silvanus, who had laboured with him in Thessalonica and whose name appears in the superscription of the letter[2].

Barnabas. But, if some uncertainty hangs over all the instances hitherto given, the apostleship of Barnabas is beyond question. St Luke records his consecration to the office as taking place at the same time with and in the same manner as St Paul's (Acts xiii. 2, 3). In his account of their missionary labours again, he names them together as 'Apostles,' even mentioning Barnabas first (Acts xiv. 4, 14). St Paul himself also in two different

James as an Apostle or not, may be questioned: his words are, Διαδέχεται δὲ τὴν ἐκκλησίαν μετὰ τῶν ἀποστόλων ὁ ἀδελφὸς τοῦ Κυρίου Ἰάκωβος (comp. Acts v. 29). The Clementines seem certainly to exclude him, as do also the *Apost. Const.* viii. 46. See below note 5, p. 100.

[1] Rom. xvi. 7 Ἀσπάσασθε Ἀνδρόνικον καὶ Ἰουνίαν τοὺς συγγενεῖς μου καὶ συναιχμαλώτους μου, οἵτινές εἰσιν ἐπίσημοι ἐν τοῖς ἀποστόλοις, οἳ καὶ πρὸ ἐμοῦ γέγοναν ἐν Χριστῷ. Except to escape the difficulty involved in such an extension of the apostolate, I do not think the words οἵτινές εἰσιν ἐπίσημοι ἐν τοῖς ἀποστόλοις would have been generally rendered, 'who are highly esteemed by the Apostles.' The Greek fathers took the more natural interpretation. Origen says, 'Possibile est et illud intellegi quod fortassis ex illis septuaginta duobus qui et ipsi apostoli nominati sunt, fuerint:' Chrysostom still more decisively, τὸ ἀποστόλους εἶναι μέγα· τὸ δὲ ἐν τούτοις ἐπισήμους εἶναι, ἐννόησον ἡλίκον ἐγκώμιον, and similarly Theodoret. In this case Ἰουνίαν (or Ἰουνιᾶν) is probably a man's name, Junias contracted from Junianus, as it is taken by Origen (*on Rom.* xvi. 21, T. IV. p. 582 D, and especially on xvi. 39, *ib.* p. 686 E) and by several modern critics. Chrysostom however, in spite of his interpretation, considers that it is a woman's name: βαβαί, πόση τῆς γυναικὸς ταύτης ἡ φιλοσοφία, ὡς καὶ τῆς τῶν ἀποστόλων ἀξιωθῆναι προσηγορίας.

[2] Not Timothy, though Timothy also had been with him at Thessalonica, and his name, like that of Silvanus, is joined to the Apostle's own in the opening salutation. But Timothy is distinctly excluded from the apostolate in 2 Cor. i. 1, Col. i. 1, 'Paul an Apostle and Timothy the brother'; and elsewhere, when St Paul links Timothy's name with his own, he drops the title of Apostle, e.g. Phil. i. 1 'Paul and Timotheus, *servants* of Jesus Christ.'

In 1 Cor. iv. 9, 'I think that God hath set forth us the Apostles last etc.,' he might seem to include Apollos, who is mentioned just before, ver. 6. But Apollos is distinctly excluded from the apostolate by one who was a contemporary and probably knew him. Clement of Rome, § 47, speaking of the dissensions of the Corinthians in St Paul's time, says, προσεκλίθητε ἀποστόλοις μεμαρτυρημένοις (i.e. St Peter and St Paul) καὶ ἀνδρὶ δεδοκιμασμένῳ παρ' αὐτοῖς (Apollos). If therefore there is a reference in 1 Cor. iv. 9 to any individual person besides St Paul (which seems doubtful), I suppose it to be again to Silvanus, who had assisted him in laying the foundation of the Corinthian Church (2 Cor. i. 19). For the circumstance which disqualified Apollos and Timotheus from being Apostles, see below, p. 98.

epistles holds similar language. In the Galatian letter he speaks of Barnabas as associated with himself in the Apostleship of the Gentiles (ii. 9); in the First to the Corinthians he claims for his fellow-labourer all the privileges of an Apostle, as one who like himself holds the office of an Apostle and is doing the work of an Apostle (ix. 5, 6). If therefore St Paul has held a larger place than Barnabas in the gratitude and veneration of the Church of all ages, this is due not to any superiority of rank or office, but to the ascendancy of his personal gifts, a more intense energy and self-devotion, wider and deeper sympathies, a firmer intellectual grasp, a larger measure of the Spirit of Christ[1].

It may be added also, that only by such an extension of the office could any footing be found for the pretensions of the false apostles (2 Cor. xi. 13, Rev. ii. 2). Had the number been definitely restricted, the claims of these interlopers would have been self-condemned.

But if the term is so extended, can we determine the limit to its extension? This will depend on the answer given to such questions as these: What was the nature of the call? What were the necessary qualifications for the office? What position did it confer? What were the duties attached to it?

The facts gathered from the New Testament are insufficient to supply a decisive answer to these questions; but they enable us to draw roughly the line, by which the apostolate was bounded.

Rank of an Apostle.

(i) The Apostles comprised the *first order* in the Church (1 Cor. xii. 28, 29, Ephes. iv. 11). They are sometimes mentioned in connexion with the prophets of the Old dispensation[2], sometimes with the prophets of the New[3]. It is in the latter sense, that the Church is said to be built 'on the foundation of the Apostles and prophets.' The two orders seem to have been closely allied to each other in the nature of their spiritual gifts, though the Apostle was superior in rank and had administrative functions which were wanting to the prophet.

Tests of Apostleship.

(ii) In an important passage (1 Cor. ix. 1, 2) where St Paul is maintaining his authority against gainsayers and advancing proofs of his Apostleship, he asks 'Have I not seen the Lord Jesus Christ? Are not ye our work in the Lord?' It would appear then;

(1) Quali-

First, that the having seen Christ was a necessary condition of the

[1] In the printed texts of *Clem. Rec.* i. 60 Barnabas is identified with Matthias, and thus made an Apostle, without extending the number beyond twelve; 'Post quem Barnabas qui et Matthias qui in locum Judae subrogatus est apostolus.' But the correct reading is doubtless 'Barsabas,' which is found in the MS in Trinity College Library at Cambridge, as well as in several mentioned by Cotelier. Thus the account is a confused version of the incident in the Acts. The Syriac translation strangely enough has 'Barabbas' in two places.

[2] Luke xi. 49, 2 Pet. iii. 2, and so perh. Rev. xviii. 20: comp. Polyc. § 6.

[3] Ephes. ii. 20, iii. 5. That the 'prophets' in these passages are to be so understood, appears (1) from the order, the Apostles being named before the prophets; (2) from the expression in Ephes. iii. 5, *ὡς νῦν ἀπεκαλύφθη τοῖς ἁγίοις ἀποστόλοις αὐτοῦ καὶ προφήταις.* It is in this same epistle also (iv. 11) that the prophets are directly mentioned as the next order to the Apostles in the Christian Church.

fication for the office. apostolic office. It may be urged indeed that St Paul is here taking the ground of his Judaizing opponents, who affected to lay great stress on personal intercourse with the Lord, and argues that even on their own showing he is not wanting in the qualifications for the Apostleship. This is true. But independently of St Paul's language here, there is every reason for assuming that this was an indispensable condition (Luke xxiv. 48, Acts i. 8). An Apostle must necessarily have been an eye-witness of the resurrection. He must be able to testify from direct knowledge to this fundamental fact of the faith. The two candidates for the vacant place of Judas were selected because they possessed this qualification of personal intercourse with the Saviour, and it is directly stated that the appointment is made in order to furnish 'a witness of His resurrection' (Acts i. 21—23). This knowledge, which was before lacking to St Paul, was supplied by a miraculous interposition, so as to qualify him for the office. All the others, who are called or seem to be called Apostles in the New Testament, may well have satisfied this condition. Andronicus and Junias were certainly among the earliest disciples (Rom. xvi. 7), and may have seen the Lord, if not while His earthly ministry lasted, at all events during the forty days after the resurrection. Barnabas was a well-known and zealous believer in the first days of the Christian Church (Acts iv. 36), and is reported to have been one of the Seventy. James and the other brethren of the Lord were at least so far qualified. Silas also, who was a leading man in the Church of Jerusalem (Acts xv. 22), might well have enjoyed this privilege.

To be a witness of the resurrection.

Apollos and Timothy not qualified.

On the other hand, it is not probable that this qualification was possessed either by Apollos or by Timothy, who were both comparatively late converts, and lived far away from the scenes of our Lord's ministry, the one at Alexandria (Acts xviii. 24), the other at Lystra (Acts xvi. 1, 2). And to these, as has been pointed out, the name of an Apostle is indirectly denied, though from their prominent position in the Church and the energy and success of their missionary labours, they of all men, after St Paul and the Twelve, might seem to lay claim to this honourable title.

The outward commission how given.

But though it was necessary that an Apostle should have been an eye-witness of the Lord's resurrection, it does not follow that the actual *call to the Apostleship* should come from an outward personal communication with our Lord, in the manner in which the Twelve were called. With Matthias it certainly was not so. The commission in his case was received through the medium of the Church. Even St Paul himself seems to have been invested with this highest office of the Church in the same way. His conversion indeed may be said in some sense to have been his call to the Apostleship. But the actual investiture, the completion of his call, as may be gathered from St Luke's narrative, took place some years later at Antioch (Acts xiii. 2). It was then at length that he, together with Barnabas, was set apart by the Spirit acting through the Church, for the work to which God had destined him, and for which he had been qualified by the appearance on the way to Damascus. Hitherto both alike are styled only 'prophets.' From this point onward both alike are 'Apostles.'

But *secondly*, in the passage already referred to, St Paul lays much more stress on his possessing the powers of an Apostle, as a token of the truthfulness of his claims. 'If I be not an Apostle to others,' he says to the Corinthians, 'at least I am to you.' Their conversion was the seal of his Apostleship (1 Cor. ix. 2). In another passage he speaks in like manner of his having wrought the *signs* of an Apostle among them (2 Cor. xii. 12). The signs, which he contemplates in these passages, our modern conceptions would lead us to separate into two classes. The one of these includes moral and spiritual gifts—patience, self-denial, effective preaching; the other comprises such powers as we call supernatural, 'signs, wonders, and mighty deeds.' St Paul himself however does not so distinguish them, but with more of reverence regards them rather as different manifestations of 'one and the self-same Spirit.' (2) Signs of an Apostle.

But essential as was the possession of these gifts of the Spirit to establish the claims of an Apostle, they seem to have been possessed at least in some degree by all the higher ministers of the Church, and therefore do not afford any distinctive test, by which we are enabled to fix the limits of the Apostleship.

Such then is the evidence yielded by the notices in the New Testament —evidence which, if somewhat vague in itself, is sufficient to discountenance the limitation of the Apostolate in the manner generally conceived.

And such for the most part is the tendency of the notices found in the Christian writers of the ages immediately following. They use the term indeed vaguely and inconsistently, sometimes in a narrower, sometimes in a wider sense, than the New Testament writings would seem to warrant; but on the whole the impression is left from their language, that no very rigid limitation of the office was present to their minds. Wide use of the term

The allusions in the writings of the Apostolic fathers are for the most part too general to build any inference upon. They all look upon themselves as distinct from the Apostles[1]. Several of them include St Paul by name in the Apostolate. Clement moreover speaks of the Apostles as having been sent forth by Christ himself (§ 42), and in another passage he obviously excludes Apollos from the number[2]. More important however, as showing the elasticity of the term, is a passage in Hermas, where he represents the 'Apostles and teachers' under one head as forty in number[3], selecting this doubtless as a typical number in accordance with the figurative character of his work. in the Apostolic fathers,

Writers of the subsequent ages are more obviously lax in their use of the title. At a very early date we find it applied to the Seventy, without however placing them on the same level with the Twelve. This application and succeeding writers,

[1] Clem. § 42, Ignat. *Rom.* § 4, Polyc. § 6, Barnab. §§ 5, 8, *Ep. ad Diogn.* § 11.

[2] § 47. See above, note 2, p. 96. Eusebius, iii. 39, infers that Papias distinguished Aristion and John the Presbyter, who had been personal disciples of the Lord, from the Apostles. This may be so; but from his language as quoted it can only be safely gathered that he distinguished them from the Twelve.

[3] Hermas *Sim.* ix. 15, 16: comp. *Vis.* iii. 5, *Sim.* ix. 25. The data with regard to the age of Hermas are (1) that he was a contemporary of Clement (*Vis.* ii. 4); and (2) that his work was written while his brother Pius was bishop of Rome (circ. 140), *Fragm. Murat.* in Routh *Rel. Sacr.* I. p. 396. He cannot therefore have been the Hermas mentioned by St Paul (Rom. xvi. 14), as several ancient writers suppose.

occurs even in Irenæus and Tertullian[1], the earliest extant writers who dwell on this or kindred subjects. About the same time Clement of Alexandria not only calls Barnabas an Apostle, but confers the title on Clement of Rome also[2]. Philip the Evangelist is so styled occasionally; but in some instances at least he has been confused with Philip, one of the Twelve[3]. Origen discusses the term as capable of a very wide application[4]; and Eusebius, accounting for St Paul's expression (1 Cor. xv. 7), speaks of 'numberless apostles' besides the Twelve[5].

still recognising Twelve as typical.

Nor will it weigh as an argument on the other side, that many writers speak of the Twelve as the founders of the Church, or argue on the typical significance of this number in the Apostolate[6]: for some of those, who hold this language most strongly, elsewhere use the term Apostle in a very extended application; and the rest either distinctly acknowledge the Apostolic office of St Paul, or indirectly recognise his authority by quoting from his writings or endorsing his teaching.

[1] Iren. ii. 21. 1; Tertull. *adv. Marc.* iv. 24, 'Adlegit et alios septuaginta apostolos super duodecim,' referring for an illustration of the numbers to Exod. xv. 27, 'And they came to Elim, where were twelve wells of water, and threescore and ten palm-trees.' See also Origen quoted above, p. 96. In the Gospel the Seventy are not indeed called 'Apostles,' but the verb *ἀποστέλλειν* is applied to them, and they are spoken of as 'seventy *others*' (Luke x. 1), in reference to the mission of the Twelve. In the *Ancient Syriac Documents*, edited by Cureton, this extension is distinctly and repeatedly given to the term; e.g. p. 3, 'Thaddæus the Apostle one of the Seventy'; p. 34, 'Addæus the Apostle one of the seventy-two Apostles.'

[2] For Barnabas see *Strom.* ii. p. 445, 447 (ed. Potter); for Clement of Rome, *Strom.* iv. p. 609. Elsewhere Clement calls Barnabas *ἀποστολικός*, adding that he was one of the Seventy, *Strom.* ii. p. 489.

[3] See *Colossians*, p. 45 sq. In the *Apost. Const.* (vi. 7) he is called *Φίλιππος ὁ συναπόστολος ἡμῶν*.

[4] Origen *in Joann.* Tom. IV. p. 430, ed. Delarue.

[5] *H. E.* i. 12 *εἶθ' ὡς παρὰ τούτους, κατὰ μίμησιν τῶν δώδεκα πλείστων ὅσων ὑπαρξάντων ἀποστόλων, οἷος καὶ αὐτὸς ὁ Παῦλος ἦν, προστίθησι λέγων· Ἔπειτα ὤφθη τοῖς ἀποστόλοις πᾶσι.* Comp. Theodoret on 1 Cor. xii. 28. There is however no authority for the statement of the latter, 1 Tim. iii. 1, that the order afterwards called bishops were formerly called apostles. See *Philippians*, p. 193 sq.

Certain early commentators on Isaiah xvii. 6 saw a reference to fourteen Apostles, making up the number by including Paul and Barnabas, or Paul and James the Lord's brother: see Euseb. *in Is.* xvii. 6, and Hieron. *in Is.* IV. pp. 194, 280, ed. Vallarsi. The *Apost. Const.* (viii. 46) recognise thirteen, including St Paul and excluding St James. Of really early writings the Clementine Homilies and Recognitions alone seem to restrict the number to twelve. This restriction served the purpose of the writers, enabling them to exclude St Paul. At the same time the exclusion of St James is compensated by assigning to him the title of 'bishop of bishops.'

[6] Barnab. § 8, referred to above, p. 95, note 1: Justin, *Dial.* p. 260 C: comp. *Apol.* I. p. 78 A, *ἀπὸ γὰρ Ἱερουσαλὴμ ἄνδρες δεκαδύο τὸν ἀριθμὸν ἐξῆλθον εἰς τὸν κόσμον*: Iren. iv. 21. 3, 'dodecastylum firmamentum Ecclesiae,' ib. *Fragm.* p. 843 (Stieren): Tertull. *adv. Marc.* iv. 13 asks 'Cur autem duodecim apostolos elegit et non alium quemlibet numerum?', and refers in answer to the twelve springs at Elim, the twelve jewels on Aaron's breastplate, etc. Comp. Theodot. in *Clem. Alex.* p. 975 (Potter). In *Clem. Hom.* ii. 23 the Apostles are compared to the twelve months of the year: comp. *Clem. Recogn.* iv. 35, 36.

The passages referred to are, I think, sufficient to show that ancient writers for the most part allowed themselves very considerable latitude in the use of the title. Lower down than this it is unnecessary to follow the stream of authority. The traditions of later ages are too distant to reflect any light on the usage of Apostolic times.

II. [1]Ἔπειτα διὰ δεκατεσσάρων ἐτῶν πάλιν ἀνέβην εἰς Ἱεροσόλυμα μετὰ Βαρνάβα, συνπαραλαβὼν καὶ Τίτον· [2]ἀνέβην δὲ κατὰ ἀποκάλυψιν, καὶ ἀνεθέμην αὐτοῖς

II. 1, 2. 'An interval of fourteen years elapsed. During the whole of this time I had no intercourse with the Apostles of the Circumcision. Then I paid another visit to Jerusalem. My companion was Barnabas, who has laboured so zealously among the Gentiles, whose name is so closely identified with the cause of the Gentiles. With him I took Titus also, himself a Gentile. And here again I acted not in obedience to any human adviser. A direct revelation from God prompted me to this journey.'

διὰ δεκατεσσάρων ἐτῶν] Are the fourteen years to be counted from St Paul's conversion, or from the visit to Jerusalem just recorded? The following considerations seem to decide in favour of the latter view: (1) The stress of the argument lies on the length of the interval during which he had held no communication with the Judaic Apostles; and (2) Individual expressions in the passage tend the same way: the use of διὰ δ. ἐτῶν, in preference to μετὰ δ. ἔτη, implies that the whole interval was a blank so far as regards the matter in hand, the intercourse of St Paul with the Twelve; and the words πάλιν ἀνέβην, '*again* I went up,' refer us back to the former visit, as the date from which the time is reckoned. As the latter visit (supposing it to be the same with that of Acts xv.) is calculated independently to have taken place about A.D. 51, the date of the first visit will according to this view be thrown back to about A.D. 38, and that of the conversion to about A.D. 36, the Jewish mode of reckoning being adopted. For διά, 'after the lapse of,' see Acts xxiv. 17, and Winer, § xlvii. p. 475.

καὶ Τίτον] Titus is included in the 'certain others' of Acts xv. 2, and is specially named here on account of the dispute to which he gave rise (ver. 3). He was sent from Antioch with others whose names are not mentioned, probably as a representative of the Gentile Christians; just as on the return of the mission the Apostles of the Circumcision sent back Judas and Silas to represent the Jewish believers, Acts xv. 27. The incident would present itself all the more vividly to St Paul's mind, inasmuch as Titus was much in his thoughts, if not actually in his company, at the time when this epistle was written. See 2 Cor. ii. 13, vii. 6, 13—15, viii. 16, 23, xii. 18.

κατὰ ἀποκάλυψιν] '*by revelation.*' In St Luke's narrative (Acts xv. 2) he is said to have been sent by the Church at Antioch. The revelation either prompted or confirmed the decision of the Church. See the detached note, p. 125.

2. 'Arrived at Jerusalem, I set forth the principles of the Gospel, as I had preached it and still preach it to the Gentiles—the doctrine of grace, the freedom from the ceremonial law. This explanation I gave in a private conference with the leading Apostles of the Circumcision. In all this I had one object in view; that the Gospel might have free course among the Gentiles, that my past and present labours might not be thwarted by opposition or misunderstanding.'

ἀνεθέμην] The middle ἀνατίθεσθαι has the sense 'to relate with a view to consulting,' 'to refer,' as 2 Macc. iii. 9; see also Acts xxv. 14, τῷ βασιλεῖ ἀνέθετο τὰ κατὰ τὸν Παῦλον, where the idea of *consultation* is brought out very clearly in the context, vv. 20, 26. 'Inter conferentes,' says Jerome here, 'aequalitas est; inter docentem et discentem minor est ille, qui discit.' See the notes on προσανατίθεσθαι, i. 16, ii. 6.

τὸ εὐαγγέλιον ὃ κηρύσσω ἐν τοῖς ἔθνεσιν, κατ' ἰδίαν δὲ τοῖς δοκοῦσιν, μή πως εἰς κενὸν τρέχω ἢ ἔδραμον.

ὃ κηρύσσω] '*I preach*,' not ἐκήρυσσον, 'I preached,' for his Gospel had not changed. See the note on οὐκ ἔστιν, i. 11.

κατ' ἰδίαν δὲ τοῖς δοκοῦσιν] '*but in private to those of repute*.' The foregoing αὐτοῖς is best referred to the Christians of Jerusalem generally, as implied from Ἱεροσόλυμα (ver. 1). If so, this clause, which follows, is inserted not to exclude a public conference, but to emphasize his private consultations. These private communications probably preceded the general congress, which occupies the prominent place in St Luke's narrative (Acts xv. 6 sqq) and seems to be alluded to in the Acts, though not very distinctly, in the words (xv. 4), 'They declared what things God had done with them.' The private consultation was a wise precaution to avoid misunderstanding: the public conference was a matter of necessity to obtain a recognition of the freedom of the Gentile Churches.

τοῖς δοκοῦσιν] '*the men of repute, of position*.' See Eur. *Hec.* 294 λόγος γὰρ ἔκ τ' ἀδοξούντων ἰὼν κἀκ τῶν δοκούντων, with Pflugk's note; *Heracl.* 897 εὐτυχίαν ἰδέσθαι τῶν πάρος οὐ δοκούντων, Herodian vi. 1 τῆς συγκλήτου βουλῆς τοὺς δοκοῦντας καὶ ἡλικίᾳ σεμνοτάτους κ.τ.λ. The expression itself therefore is a term of honour, and conveys no shadow of depreciation. So far as it is coloured with any tinge of disparagement here, this is due (1) to the repetition of the word δοκοῦντες, (2) to the addition of στῦλοι εἶναι, εἶναί τι, the latter especially, and (3) to the contrast implied in the whole passage, between the estimation in which they were held and the actual services they rendered to him. On the other hand, it will be seen (1) That this disparagement is relative, not absolute; a negation of the exclusive claims urged for them by the Judaizing party, not a negation of their Apostolic rank and worth; (2) That the passage itself contains direct evidence of mutual respect and recognition between St Paul and the Twelve (vv. 8, 9, 10).

On the tense of τοῖς δοκοῦσιν see the note on ver. 6.

μή πως εἰς κενὸν τρέχω κ.τ.λ.] '*lest I might be running, or had run, to no purpose*.' The kindred passage 1 Thess. iii. 5, μήπως ἐπείρασεν ὑμᾶς ὁ πειράζων καὶ εἰς κενὸν γένηται ὁ κόπος ἡμῶν, seems to show that τρέχω is here the subjunctive rather than the indicative, this being moreover the more likely mood in itself. See the note there. The use of the subjunctive (τρέχω) here, rather than the optative (τρέχοιμι), is in accordance with the spirit of the later Greek, which prefers the more direct mode of speech in all such cases. In the New Testament the optative seems *never* to occur with particles of design etc.; see Winer § xli. p. 360. In the second clause the change of mood from the subjunctive (τρέχω) to the indicative (ἔδραμον) is rendered necessary by the change of tense, since the consequences of the past were no longer contingent but inevitable: comp. iv. 11.

τρέχω] is a reference to St Paul's favourite metaphor of the stadium; see v. 7 and the note there. For the expression εἰς κενὸν τρέχειν comp. Phil. ii. 16, where, as here, it refers to his missionary career.

But what is the drift of the passage? Is it a natural expression of misgiving on the part of St Paul, who was not altogether satisfied with the soundness of his teaching, until he had consulted with the Apostles of the Circumcision? So Tertullian takes it, *adv. Marc.* i. 20, v. 3, and esp. iv. 2. This is perhaps the *prima facie* sense of the passage, slightly favoured by οὐδὲν προσανέθεντο, ver. 6. But on the other hand such an admission would be so entirely

3 ἀλλ' οὐδὲ Τίτος ὁ σὺν ἐμοὶ Ἕλλην ὢν ἠναγκάσθη

alien to the spirit of the passage, so destructive of St Paul's whole argument, and so unlikely under the circumstances, that this interpretation must be abandoned. The words therefore must be taken to express his fear lest the Judaic Christians, by insisting on the Mosaic ritual, might thwart his past and present endeavours to establish a Church on a liberal basis. By conferring with them, and more especially with the Apostles of the Circumcision, he might not only quiet such lurking anxiety (μήπως) as he felt, but also, if there were any lack of unanimity, win them over to his views.

3. St Paul is here distracted between the fear of saying too much and the fear of saying too little. He must maintain his own independence, and yet he must not compromise the position of the Twelve. How can he justify himself without seeming to condemn them? There is need of plain speaking and there is need of reserve. In this conflict of opposing aims and feelings the sense of the passage is well-nigh lost. The meaning of individual expressions is obscure. The thread of the sentence is broken, picked up, and again broken. From this shipwreck of grammar it is even difficult to extricate the main incident, on which the whole controversy hinges. Was Titus circumcised or was he not? This is not only a reasonable question, but a question which thoughtful writers have answered in different ways. On the whole, the following reasons seem to decide for the negative. (1) The incident is apparently brought forward to show that St Paul had throughout contended for the liberty of the Gentiles; that he had not, as his enemies insinuated, at one time conceded the question of circumcision. It is introduced by way of evidence, not of apology. (2) It is difficult to reconcile the view that Titus was circumcised with individual expressions in the passage. St Paul could scarcely say 'we yielded no not for an hour' in the same breath in which he confessed to this most important of all concessions: he could hardly claim for such an act the merit of preserving 'the truth of the Gospel,' i.e. the liberty of the Gentile Christians, which it was most calculated to compromise. In order to maintain that view, it is necessary to lay undue stress on the words ἠναγκάσθη, and τῇ ὑποταγῇ, which from their position seem quite unemphatic: as if the former signified that the circumcision of Titus was an act of grace, not of compulsion; and the latter, that the Apostle in yielding was not doing homage to superior authority. (3) Taking into account the narrative in the Acts, both the occasion and the person were most inopportune for such a concession. There was an agitation among the Judaizers to force the rite of circumcision on the Gentile converts. Paul and Barnabas had gone up from Antioch in order to protect them from this imposition. They were accompanied by certain representatives of the Gentile Church, of whom Titus was one. No act could be conceived more fatal to the interests of St Paul's clients at such a moment, or less likely to have been permitted by him. Accordingly the vast majority of early writers take the view that Titus was not circumcised, even though in many instances they adopted a reading (the omission of οἷς οὐδὲ in ver. 5) most unfavourable to this conclusion. See p. 122.

St Paul is here indirectly meeting a charge brought against him. Shortly before he visited Galatia the first time, he had caused Timothy to be circumcised (Acts xvi. 3). This fact, which can scarcely have been unknown to the Galatians, for Timothy accompanied him on his visit, may have afforded a handle to the calumnies of his enemies. There was a time, they said,

περιτμηθῆναι· [4]διὰ δὲ τοὺς παρεισάκτους ψευδαδέλ-

when he himself insisted on circumcision. Comp. v. 11 and the note on i. 10. By stating how he acted in the case of Titus, who was truly a Gentile, he rebuffs this assertion.

3—5. 'But while I held conferences with the Apostles of the Circumcision, I did not yield to the clamours of the disciples of the Circumcision. An incident which occurred will show this. Titus, as a Gentile who was intimately acquainted with me, was singled out as a mark for their bigotry. An attempt was made to have him circumcised. Concession was even urged upon me in high quarters, as a measure of prudence to disarm opposition. The agitators, who headed the movement, were no true brethren, no loyal soldiers of Christ. They were spies who had made their way into the camp of the Gospel under false colours and were striving to undermine our liberty in Christ, to reduce us again to a state of bondage. I did not for a moment yield to this pressure. I would not so compromise the integrity of the Gospel, the freedom of the Gentile Churches.'

3. οὐδὲ Τίτος] '*not even Titus.*' Why 'not even'? Is it (1) 'not even Titus, who as my fellow-labourer would be brought constantly in contact with the Jews, and therefore might well have adopted a conciliatory attitude towards them'? Compare the case of Timothy, Acts xvi. 3, 'Him would Paul have *go forth with him*, and took and circumcised him on account of the Jews, etc.' In this case ὁ σὺν ἐμοὶ is emphatic. Or is it (2) 'not even Titus, though the pressure exerted in his case was so great'? A more exact knowledge of the circumstances than we possess would alone enable us to answer this question. Perhaps both ideas may be combined here.

Ἕλλην ὤν] '*being a Greek,*' perhaps giving the reason why the point was not conceded. There seems to be a tacit allusion to the case of Timothy. 'You maintain,' St Paul seems to argue, 'that I allowed the validity of the Mosaic law in circumcising Timothy (Acts xvi. 1, 3). But Timothy was half of Jewish parentage. How did I act in the case of Titus, a true Gentile? I did not yield for a moment.'

In Ἕλλην all idea of nationality is lost: comp. Mark vii. 26 Ἑλληνὶς Συροφοινίκισσα (or Σύρα Φοινίκισσα) τῷ γένει. Thus the Peshito sacrificing the letter to the spirit frequently translates Ἕλλην 'an Aramæan,' e.g. here and iii. 28. See *Colossians*, p. 390.

ἠναγκάσθη] '*was compelled*,' though the pressure was extreme. This pressure doubtless came from the more bigoted Judaizers, the converted Pharisees mentioned in Acts xv. 5.

4. What part was taken in the dispute by the Apostles of the Circumcision? This question, which forces itself upon us at this stage of St Paul's narrative, is not easily answered. On the whole it seems probable that they recommended St Paul to yield the point, as a charitable concession to the prejudices of the Jewish converts: but convinced at length by his representations, that such a concession at such a time would be fatal, they withdrew their counsel and gave him their support. Such an account of the transaction seems to accord alike with the known facts and with the probabilities of the case. It is consistent with the timid conduct of Peter at Antioch shortly after (Gal. ii. 11), and with the politic advice of James at a later date (Acts xxi. 20). It was the natural consequence of their position, which led them to regard tenderly the scruples of the Jewish converts. It supplies probable antecedents to the events of the Apostolic congress. And lastly, it best explains St Paul's language here. The sensible undercurrent of

φους, οἵτινες παρεισῆλθον κατασκοπῆσαι τὴν ἐλευθερίαν ἡμῶν, ἣν ἔχομεν ἐν Χριστῷ Ἰησοῦ, ἵνα ἡμᾶς καταδουλώσουσιν, [5] οἷς οὐδὲ πρὸς ὥραν εἴξαμεν τῇ ὑποταγῇ, ἵνα

feeling, the broken grammar of the sentence, the obvious tenour of particular phrases, all convey the impression, that though the final victory was complete, it was not attained without a struggle, in which St Paul maintained at one time almost single-handed the cause of Gentile freedom.

διὰ δὲ τοὺς παρεισάκτους κ.τ.λ.] '*But* to satisfy, to disarm, the false brethren, the traitorous spies of the Gospel'—At this point the connexion of the sentence is snapped, and we are left to conjecture as to the conclusion. It seems as if St Paul intended to add, 'the leading Apostles urged me to yield.' But instead of this a long parenthesis interposes, in the course of which the main proposition of the sentence is lost sight of. It is again resumed in a different form, 'from those then who were held in repute,' ver. 6. Then again it disappears in another parenthesis. Once more it is taken up and completed, transformed by this time into a general statement, 'well, they of reputation added nothing to me in conference.' The counsels of the Apostles of the Circumcision are the hidden rock on which the grammar of the sentence is wrecked. For διὰ τοὺς παρ. ψευδ. compare Acts xvi. 3 περιέτεμεν αὐτὸν διὰ τοὺς Ἰουδαίους.

Of other possible explanations two deserve to be considered; (1) That there is an ellipsis of οὐκ ἠναγκάσθη περιτμηθῆναι or οὐ περιετμήθη after διὰ τοὺς παρεισ. ψευδαδ. So Fritzsche, *Opusc.* p. 181. (2) That the parenthesis flows back into the main proposition, so that the regular construction would have been διὰ τοὺς παρεισ. ψευδαδ. οὐδὲ πρὸς ὥραν εἴξαμεν, the οἷς being redundant. See the note, ver. 6. So Winer, § lxiii. p. 711 sq. But as Titus would not have been circumcised under any circumstances, the refusal to yield could scarcely be attributed to the pressure from the false brethren. If either of these explanations were adopted, St Paul's meaning must be: 'To the scruples of the *weaker* brethren I would have conceded the point, but the teaching of the *false* brethren made concession impossible.' So in fact Augustine takes it, *de Mendac.* § 8 (VI. p. 424, ed. Ben.).

παρεισάκτους, παρεισῆλθον] The metaphor is that of spies or traitors introducing themselves by stealth into the enemy's camp, as in Jude 4 παρεισέδυσαν γάρ τινες ἄνθρωποι. See Plut. *Popl.* 17 ἐπιβουλεύων δὲ τὸν Πορσίναν ἀνελεῖν παρεισῆλθεν εἰς τὸ στρατόπεδον, Polyb. i. 7. 3, ii. 55. 3. For παρεισάγειν see 2 Pet. ii. 1. The adjective occurs in Strabo, xvii. p. 794 παρείσακτος ἐπικληθεὶς Πτολεμαῖος. The camp thus stealthily entered is the Christian Church. Pharisees at heart, these traitors assume the name and garb of believers.

κατασκοπῆσαι] '*to act as spies on.*' κατασκοπεῖν generally signifies 'to examine carefully,' the form κατασκοπεύειν being most frequently used where the notion of treachery is prominent. For instances of the sense in the text however see 2 Sam. x. 3, 1 Chron. xix. 3.

καταδουλώσουσιν] '*reduce to abject slavery.*' The reading of the received text, καταδουλώσωνται, is a correction of some classicist, introduced for two reasons: (1) To substitute the middle voice, which is more common in classical writers; the transcriber not seeing that the sense here requires the active; 'enslave not to themselves, but to an external power, the law of

ἡ ἀλήθεια τοῦ εὐαγγελίου διαμείνῃ πρὸς ὑμᾶς. 6 ἀπὸ δὲ τῶν δοκούντων εἶναί τι· ὁποῖοί ποτε ἦσαν, οὐδέν

Moses.' (2) To restore the usual classical government of ἵνα with the conjunctive. Ἵνα however is found several times in the New Testament with the indicative future, and sometimes even with the indicative present, as in iv. 17: see Winer, § xli. p. 360 sq. This, though not a classical usage, is justified by similar constructions of ὅπως, ὄφρα, in classical writers.

5. οἷς οὐδὲ κ.τ.λ.] '*to whom we*,' Paul and Barnabas, who were sent to Jerusalem to plead the cause of the Gentile Christians, '*yielded no not for an hour.*' For the omission of οἷς οὐδὲ in some texts see the detached note, p. 122.

τῇ ὑποταγῇ] '*by the submission* which was required of us,' or possibly 'the submission with which we are taunted,' as in 2 Cor. i. 17 μήτι ἄρα τῇ ἐλαφρίᾳ ἐχρησάμην;

ἡ ἀλήθεια τοῦ εὐαγγελίου] '*the truth of the Gospel*,' i.e. the Gospel in its integrity. This expression in St Paul's language denotes the doctrine of grace, the maintenance of Christian liberty, as opposed to the false teaching of the Judaizers. See ii. 14, and comp. Col. i. 5, 6, where the same idea seems to be indirectly involved.

διαμείνῃ πρὸς ὑμᾶς] '*may abide with you*,' the Gentile Churches. See the introduction, p. 26. The idea of *firm possession* is enforced by the compound verb, by the past tense, and by the preposition.

6—9. 'The elder Apostles, I say, who are so highly esteemed, whose authority you so exclusively uphold—for myself, I care not that they once knew Christ in the flesh: God does not so judge men; He measures them not by the outward advantages they have had, not by the rank they hold, but by what they are, by what they think and do—well, these highly esteemed leaders taught me nothing new; they had no fault to find with me. On the contrary, they received me as their equal, they recognised my mission. They saw that God had entrusted to me the duty of preaching to the Uncircumcision, as He had entrusted to Peter that of preaching to the Circumcision. This was manifest from the results. My Apostleship had been sealed by my work. God had wrought by me among the Gentiles, not less than He had wrought by Peter among the Jews. This token of His grace bestowed upon me was fully recognised by James and Cephas and John, who are held in such high esteem, as pillars of the Church. They welcomed myself and Barnabas as fellow-labourers, and exchanged pledges of friendship with us. It was agreed that we should go to the Gentiles and they to the Jews.'

Much force is lost in the A. V. by translating οἱ δοκοῦντες throughout this passage as a past tense instead of a present. St Paul is speaking not of the esteem in which the leading Apostles of the Circumcision were held by the Christians of Jerusalem at the time of the conferences, but of the esteem in which they are held, while he is writing, by his Galatian converts. The mistake seems to have arisen from following the Vulgate 'qui videbantur.' The Old Latin apparently had the present in most recensions, though not consistently in all four places. Of the older English Versions, Tyndale's alone translates by a present in this verse, and the Genevan in verse 9.

τῶν δοκούντων εἶναί τι] '*those who are looked up to as authorities.*' The expression is sometimes used in a depreciatory way, as in Plat. *Apol.* 41 E ἐὰν δοκῶσί τι εἶναι μηδὲν ὄντες, *Euthyd.* 303 C τῶν πολλῶν ἀνθρώπων καὶ τῶν

μοι διαφέρει, πρόσωπον Θεὸς ἀνθρώπου οὐ λαμβάνει· ἐμοὶ γὰρ οἱ δοκοῦντες οὐδὲν προσανέθεντο, [7]ἀλλὰ τοὐναντίον ἰδόντες ὅτι πεπίστευμαι τὸ εὐαγγέλιον τῆς ἀκροβυστίας καθὼς Πέτρος τῆς περιτομῆς, [8]ὁ γὰρ

σεμνῶν δὴ καὶ δοκούντων τι εἶναι οὐδὲν ὑμῖν μέλει, *Gorg.* 472 A ἐνίοτε γὰρ ἂν καὶ καταψευδομαρτυρηθείη τις ὑπὸ πολλῶν καὶ δοκούντων εἶναί τι, and passages from later writers quoted in Wetstein: comp. Gal. vi. 3 εἰ γὰρ δοκεῖ τις εἶναί τι μηδὲν ὤν, and Ignat. *Polyc.* 3. The exact shade of meaning which it bears must always be determined by the context. Here it is depreciatory, not indeed of the Twelve themselves, but of the extravagant and exclusive claims set up for them by the Judaizers. Thus it is nearly an equivalent to οἱ ὑπερλίαν ἀπόστολοι of 2 Cor. xi. 5, xii. 11.

ὁποῖοί ποτε ἦσαν] Does ὁποῖοί ποτε here mean 'qualescunque,' or has ποτὲ its proper temporal sense 'in times past'? In a classical writer we should decide for the former: in St Paul the latter seems more probable, as ποτὲ never occurs with the meaning 'cunque' in the New Testament, and accordingly it is rendered in the Latin versions 'aliquando.' This decides the import of the whole phrase. It does not mean 'what reputation they enjoyed,' but 'what was their position, what were their advantages *in former times*,' referring to their personal intercourse with the Lord. The 'knowing Christ after the flesh' (2 Cor. v. 16) is in itself valueless in the sight of God. The same reproach is conveyed by the words here, as in 2 Cor. x. 7 τὰ κατὰ πρόσωπον βλέπετε.

πρόσωπον λαμβάνει] A translation of the Hebrew נשא פנים which signifies properly 'to accept the face' (Gesenius *Thes.* p. 916, s. v. נשא), or perhaps better, 'to raise the face' of another (opposed to הפיל פנים 'to make the countenance fall,' e.g. Job xxix. 24; comp. Gen. iv. 5), and hence 'to receive kindly,' 'to look favourably upon one.' In the Old Testament accordingly it is a neutral expression involving no subsidiary idea of *partiality*, and is much oftener found in a good than in a bad sense. When it becomes an independent Greek phrase however, the bad sense attaches to it, owing to the secondary meaning of πρόσωπον as 'a mask,' so that πρόσωπον λαμβάνειν signifies 'to regard the external circumstances of a man,' his rank, wealth, etc., as opposed to his real intrinsic character. Thus in the New Testament it has always a bad sense. Hence a new set of words, προσωπολήμπτης, προσωποληµπτεῖν, etc. which appear to occur there for the first time.

Θεὸς ἀνθρώπου] The natural order is altered for two reasons; (1) To give Θεὸς an emphatic position, and (2) To keep the contrasted words Θεὸς ἀνθρώπου together.

ἐμοὶ γὰρ κ.τ.λ.] The sentence, which was begun in ἀπὸ δὲ τῶν δοκούντων εἶναί τι and then broken off by the parenthesis, is here resumed, but in a different form, 'well, to me those of reputation communicated nothing.' See the note on ver. 4. Otherwise the γὰρ may be attached to ὁποῖοί ποτε ἦσαν οὐδέν μοι διαφέρει, the parenthesis running back into the main proposition of the sentence, 'whatever position they once held makes no matter to me: *for to me* they communicated nothing': Winer § lxiii. p. 711 sq. But the interposition of the words πρόσ. Θ. ἀνθρ. οὐ λαμβ. is an objection to this construction.

προσανέθεντο] '*communicated*,' see the note on i. 16. Προσανατίθεσθαι is 'to communicate, to impart,' whether for the purpose of giving or of obtain-

ἐνεργήσας Πέτρῳ εἰς ἀποστολὴν τῆς περιτομῆς ἐνήργη-
σεν καὶ ἐμοὶ εἰς τὰ ἔθνη, 9καὶ γνόντες τὴν χάριν τὴν
δοθεῖσάν μοι, Ἰάκωβος καὶ Κηφᾶς καὶ Ἰωάννης, οἱ
δοκοῦντες στύλοι εἶναι, δεξιὰς ἔδωκαν ἐμοὶ καὶ Βαρνάβᾳ

ing instruction. In this passage the former meaning prevails, in i. 16 the latter. The context here decides its sense: 'they imparted no fresh knowledge to me, they saw nothing defective or incorrect in my teaching; but *on the contrary*, they heartily recognised my mission.'

7. πεπίστευμαι τὸ εὐαγγ.] '*I have been entrusted with the Gospel*,' a common construction in St Paul: see the note on 1 Thess. ii. 4. The perfect here, implying a permanent commission, contrasts with the aorist in Rom. iii. 2 ἐπιστεύθησαν τὰ λόγια τοῦ Θεοῦ.

τὸ εὐαγγ. τῆς ἀκροβυστίας] denotes a distinction of sphere and not a difference of type: see Tertul. *Praescr. Haer.* 23 'Inter se distributionem officii ordinaverunt, non separationem evangelii, nec ut *aliud* alter sed ut *aliis* alter praedicarent.'

8. ὁ ἐνεργήσας Πέτρῳ] '*He that worked for Peter*.' For the omission of ὁ Θεὸς comp. i. 6, 15; for ἐνεργεῖν see the note on 1 Thess. ii. 13. The dative Πέτρῳ ought probably to be translated 'for Peter,' not 'in Peter'; comp. Prov. xxxi. 12 ἐνεργεῖ γὰρ τῷ ἀνδρὶ (γυνὴ ἀνδρεία) εἰς ἀγαθὰ πάντα τὸν βίον. As ἐνεργεῖν is an inseparable compound, it is doubtful whether the preposition could govern Πέτρῳ, and accordingly the construction elsewhere is ἐνεργεῖν ἔν τινι. Comp. *Acta Paul. et Thecl.* § 40 ὁ γὰρ σοὶ συνεργήσας εἰς τὸ εὐαγγέλιον κἀμοὶ συνήργησεν εἰς τὸ λούσασθαι.

9. Of the two words ἰδόντες and γνόντες, the former describes the *apprehension* of the outward tokens of his commission, as evinced by his successful labours; the latter the *conviction* arrived at in consequence that the grace of God was with him: see iv. 8, 9.

Ἰάκωβος καὶ Κηφᾶς καὶ Ἰωάννης] The best supported and doubtless the right reading. The variation Πέτρος καὶ Ἰάκωβος καὶ Ἰωάννης arose from the desire of maintaining the precedence of St Peter. On the other hand the correct text presents two coincidences with the narrative of the Acts, which deserve notice. *First.* In i. 19 James is styled the Lord's brother, while here and in ver. 12 this designation is dropped. St Luke's narrative explains this omission. In the interval between St Paul's two visits James the son of Zebedee had been put to death. No term of distinction therefore was now needed, as there was no likelihood of confusion, James the son of Alphaeus though an Apostle not holding any very prominent rank. *Secondly.* The relative positions here assigned to Peter and James accord exactly with the account in the Acts. When St Paul is speaking of the missionary office of the Church at large, St Peter holds the foremost place (ver. 7, 8); when he refers to a special act of the Church of Jerusalem, St James is mentioned first (ver. 9). See Acts xii. 17, xv. 13, xxi. 18.

στύλοι] '*pillars*.' A natural metaphor occurring now and then in classical writers (e.g. Eur. *Iph. T.* 57 στῦλοι γὰρ οἴκων εἰσὶ παῖδες ἄρσενες, and Æsch. *Agam.* 897), but commonly used by the Jews in speaking of the great teachers of the law. See the examples given in Schöttgen: comp. *Clem. Hom.* xviii. 14 ἑπτὰ στύλους ὑπάρξαντας κόσμῳ, said of the patriarchs. So in Clem. Rom. § 5 the Apostles Peter and Paul are called οἱ μέγιστοι καὶ δικαιότατοι στύλοι; comp. Iren. iv. 21. 3. In this metaphor the

κοινωνίας, ἵνα ἡμεῖς εἰς τὰ ἔθνη, αὐτοὶ δὲ εἰς τὴν περιτομήν· [10] μόνον τῶν πτωχῶν ἵνα μνημονεύωμεν, ὃ καὶ ἐσπούδασα αὐτὸ τοῦτο ποιῆσαι.

Church is regarded as the house or temple of God; as Rev. iii. 12 ποιήσω αὐτὸν στύλον ἐν τῷ ναῷ τοῦ Θεοῦ μου: comp. 1 Tim. iii. 15. The accent of στύλος is doubtful. On the one hand the υ is universally long in poetry even of a late date (see Rost u. Palm, *Griech. Wörterb.* s. v., and comp. *Orac. Sib.* iii. 250, 251). On the other, the authority of the oldest accents in the MSS, and the quantity of the Latin 'stylus,' are in favour of στῦλος. The latter not improbably represents the common pronunciation of the Apostolic age. See Lipsius *Gramm. Unters.* p. 43.

δεξιὰς ἔδωκαν] '*gave pledges.*' The outward gesture is lost sight of in this expression, as appears from the fact that the plural δεξιὰς δοῦναι, δεξιὰς λαμβάνειν, is often used of a single person; 1 Macc. xi. 50, 62, xiii. 50. As a symbol of contract or friendship this does not appear prominently in the Old Testament (Ezr. x. 19, and perhaps 2 Kings x. 15; see below on κοινωνίας); nor is it especially Jewish. In the patriarchal times the outward gesture which confirmed an oath was different, Gen. xxiv. 2. The giving the right hand however was a recognised pledge of fidelity with other Eastern nations, with the Persians especially (Corn. Nep. *Dat.* c. 10 'fidemque de ea re more Persarum dextra dedisset,' Diod. xvi. 43 ἔστι δὲ ἡ πίστις αὕτη βεβαιοτάτη παρὰ τοῖς Πέρσαις, comp. Justin xi. 15. 13); and from Persian influence the symbol and the phrase may have become more common among the Jews. Even Josephus (*Ant.* xviii. 9. 3) speaks of this not as a Jewish practice, but as μέγιστον παρὰ πᾶσι τοῖς ἐκείνῃ βαρβάροις παράδειγμα τοῦ θαρσεῖν τοῖς ὁμιλοῦσιν, in reference to Artabanus the Parthian king. Where personal communication was inconvenient, it was customary to send images of right hands clasped, as a token of friendship: Xen. *Anab.* ii. 4. 1 δεξιὰς παρὰ βασιλέως φέροντες, *Ages.* 3. 4; comp. Tacit. *Hist.* i. 54, ii. 8.

κοινωνίας] '*of fellowship*,' not a superfluous addition, for 'to give the hand' (נתן יד) in the language of the Old Testament, like the Latin 'do manus,' generally signifies 'to surrender,' e.g. Lament. v. 6, 2 Chron. xxx. 8: see Gesen. *Thes.* p. 566.

ἵνα ἡμεῖς] The ellipsis of the verb occurs in St Paul under various conditions. A foregoing ἵνα is one of these; see 1 Cor. i. 31, 2 Cor. viii. 13, Rom. iv. 16: comp. 2 Cor. viii. 11.

10. 'Henceforth our spheres of labour were to be separate. One reservation however was made. They asked me to continue, as I had done hitherto, to provide for the wants of the poor brethren of Judæa. Independently of their request, it was my own earnest desire.'

μόνον] '*only* they asked us': comp. Ignat. *Rom.* 5 μόνον ἵνα Ἰησοῦ Χριστοῦ ἐπιτύχω. For similar instances of an ellipsis after μόνον, see vi. 12, 2 Thess. ii. 7 μόνον ὁ κατέχων ἄρτι ἕως ἐκ μέσου γένηται. The latter passage presents an exact parallel also in the derangement of the order for the sake of emphasis.

Two occasions are recorded, on which St Paul was the bearer of alms from the Gentile converts to the poor of Jerusalem; (1) on his second journey to Jerusalem, Acts xi. 29, 30, some years before the interview of which he is speaking; and (2) on his fifth and last journey, Rom. xv. 26, 27, 1 Cor. xvi. 3, 2 Cor. ix. 1 sq, Acts xxiv. 17, shortly after this letter was written. These facts throw light on the incident

11 Ὅτε δὲ ἦλθεν Κηφᾶς εἰς Ἀντιόχειαν, κατὰ πρόσωπον αὐτῷ ἀντέστην, ὅτι κατεγνωσμένος ἦν. 12 πρὸ

in the text. His past care for their poor prompted this request of the elder Apostles. His subsequent zeal in the same cause was the answer to their appeal.

ὃ καὶ ἐσπούδασα κ.τ.λ.] '*this was my own heartfelt desire.*' 'I needed no prompting to do this.' The Galatians had personal experience of this zeal, for their own alms had been solicited by St Paul for this very purpose shortly before, 1 Cor. xvi. 1—3. See the introduction, pp. 25, 55.

The transition from the plural (μνημονεύωμεν) to the singular (ἐσπούδασα) is significant. Before St Paul had any opportunity of fulfilling this request, he had parted from Barnabas; Acts xv. 39.

αὐτὸ τοῦτο] is best taken in apposition with ὅ, see Winer § xxiii. p. 184 sq; a construction not without example in classical Greek, but more frequent in the LXX and New Testament, inasmuch as it reproduces the common Hebrew idiom: comp. Mark vii. 25, Acts xv. 17, 1 Pet. ii. 24.

11—14. 'At Jerusalem, I owed nothing to the Apostles of the Circumcision. I maintained my independence and my equality. At Antioch I was more than an equal. I openly rebuked the leading Apostle of the Circumcision, for his conduct condemned itself. He had been accustomed to mix freely with the Gentiles, eating at the same table with them. But certain persons arrived from James, and he timidly withdrew himself. He had not courage to face the displeasure of the Jewish converts. The rest were carried away by his example. Even Barnabas, my colleague, and fellow-apostle of the Gentiles, went astray.'

11. Ὅτε δέ] This occurred probably during the sojourn of Paul and Barnabas at Antioch, immediately after the Apostolic congress (Acts xv. 30—40). The inconsistency which St Peter thus appears to have shown so soon after his championship of Gentile liberty at the congress, is rather in favour of than against this view; for the point of St Paul's rebuke is his inconsistency. But in fact there is scarcely an alternative. An earlier residence at Antioch (Acts xiii. 1—3) is out of the question, for St Paul is plainly narrating events in chronological order. Neither again is it probable that a later occasion (Acts xviii. 23) can be intended; for after the separation of Paul and Barnabas, there is no notice of their meeting again.

To this passage is probably to be attributed the ecclesiastical tradition that St Peter founded the Church of Antioch (Euseb. *Chron.* A.D. 44). Jerome (ad loc.) states still more definitely that he was bishop of this see first, whence he was translated to Rome. See also Euseb. *H. E.* iii. 22, 36, Chrysost. *Op.* III. p. 70, ed. Ben.

κατεγνωσμένος] not 'reprehensible,' but 'condemned.' His conduct carried its own condemnation with it, as St Paul shows vv. 15 sq: comp. Rom. xiv. 23 ὁ διακρινόμενος, ἐὰν φάγῃ, κατακέκριται, Joh. iii. 18 ὁ μὴ πιστεύων ἤδη κέκριται, Barnab. 10 κεκριμένοι ἤδη τῷ θανάτῳ, Joseph. *B. J.* ii. 8. 6 ἤδη γὰρ κατεγνῶσθαί φασι κ.τ.λ. The condemnation is not the verdict of the bystanders, but the verdict of the act itself.

This passage was made the ground of an attack on St Paul in an Ebionite fiction of the second century, where St Peter says to Simon Magus (whose name is used as a mask for St Paul), 'Thou hast withstood me to the face ...If thou callest me condemned, thou accusest God who revealed Christ to me.' See the whole passage *Clem. Hom.* xvii. 19: comp. p. 61, and the notes on ii. 13, iv. 16, 24.

τοῦ γὰρ ἐλθεῖν τινὰς ἀπὸ Ἰακώβου μετὰ τῶν ἐθνῶν συνήσθιεν· ὅτε δὲ ἦλθον, ὑπέστελλεν καὶ ἀφώριζεν ἑαυτόν, φοβούμενος τοὺς ἐκ περιτομῆς, 13 καὶ συνυπεκρίθησαν αὐτῷ [καὶ] οἱ λοιποὶ Ἰουδαῖοι, ὥστε καὶ

12. ὅτε δὲ ἦλθεν.

12. ἐλθεῖν τινὰς ἀπὸ Ἰακώβου] '*certain came from James.*' Of these nothing more can safely be inferred than that they belonged to the Church of Jerusalem. It is not improbable however, that they came invested with some powers from James which they abused. Compare the expression in the Apostolic letter (which seems to have been drawn up by him) Acts xv. 24, τινὲς ἐξ ἡμῶν ἐξελθόντες ἐτάραξαν ὑμᾶς...οἷς οὐ διεστειλάμεθα, and xv. 1 τινὲς κατελθόντες ἀπὸ τῆς Ἰουδαίας. The terms on which St James stood with believers of this stamp may be gathered from the language in Acts xxi. 20 sq.

συνήσθιεν] The Judaizers who troubled the Church at this time are described, Acts xv. 5, as converts belonging to the sect of the Pharisees. The prohibition against eating meat with the impure was one of the leading principles of this sect, Luke xv. 2. As the agape was the recognised bond of brotherhood in the infant Church, this separation struck at the very root of Christian life. St Peter's vision (see especially Acts x. 27, xi. 3) had taught him the worthlessness of these narrow traditions. He had no scruples about living ἐθνικῶς. And when in this instance he separated himself from the Gentiles, he practically dissembled his convictions.

ὅτε δὲ ἦλθον] '*but when they came.*' The reading ἦλθεν yields no good sense, whether we refer it to St James with Origen (*c. Cels.* ii. 1 ἐλθόντος Ἰακώβου) or to St Peter with other writers. I have given it a place nevertheless, as an alternative reading, on account of the weight of authority in its favour: for though it can scarcely have been the word intended by St Paul, it may possibly be due to an error of the original amanuensis. For a similar instance of a manifestly false reading highly supported and perhaps to be explained in this way, see Phil. ii. 1 εἴ τις σπλάγχνα καὶ οἰκτιρμοί. Such readings are a valuable testimony to the scrupulous exactness of the older transcribers, who thus reproduced the text as they found it, even when clearly incorrect. In this passage the occurrence of the same words ὅτε δὲ ἦλθεν, ver. 11, is the probable cause of the mistake.

ὑπέστελλεν καὶ ἀφώριζεν] '*gradually withdrew and separated himself.*' Both verbs govern ἑαυτόν: compare Polyb. vii. 17. 1 ὑπέστειλαν ἑαυτοὺς ὑπό τινα προπεπτωκυῖαν ὀφρύν. The words describe forcibly the cautious withdrawal of a timid person who shrinks from observation, ὑπέστελλεν denoting the partial, ἀφώριζεν the complete and final separation. The word ὑποστέλλειν is frequently used, as in the passage quoted, in describing strategical operations; and so far as it is metaphorical here, the metaphor seems to be derived from military rather than from nautical matters. Comp. στέλλεσθαι, 2 Thess. iii. 6.

τοὺς ἐκ περιτομῆς] not 'Jews' but 'converts *from* Judaism,' for this seems to be the force of the preposition: Acts x. 45, xi. 2, Col. iv. 11, Tit. i. 10.

13. οἱ λοιποὶ Ἰουδαῖοι] i.e. the rest of the Jewish converts resident at Antioch, who, like St Peter, had mixed freely with the Gentiles until

Βαρνάβας συναπήχθη αὐτῶν τῇ ὑποκρίσει. [14]ἀλλ' ὅτε εἶδον ὅτι οὐκ ὀρθοποδοῦσιν πρὸς τὴν ἀλήθειαν τοῦ εὐαγγελίου, εἶπον τῷ Κηφᾷ ἔμπροσθεν πάντων Εἰ σὺ

the arrival of their brethren from Jerusalem. The observance of Pharisaic practices with the latter was a genuine expression of bigotry, but with the Jews of Antioch and with St Peter it was ὑπόκρισις, the assumption of a part which masked their genuine feelings and made them appear otherwise than they were. The idea at the root of ὑπόκρισις is not a false motive entertained, but a false impression produced. The writer of the epistle prefixed to the Clementines, doubtless alluding to this passage, speaks of some who misrepresented Peter, as though he believed that the law was abolished, 'but did not preach it openly'; *Ep. Petr.* § 2. See on ver. 11.

καὶ Βαρνάβας] '*even Barnabas* my own friend and colleague, who so lately had gone up to protect the interests of the Gentiles against the pressure of the Pharisaic brethren.' It is not impossible that this incident, by producing a temporary feeling of distrust, may have prepared the way for the dissension between Paul and Barnabas which shortly afterwards led to their separation: Acts xv. 39.

From this time forward they never again appear associated together. But on the other hand, whenever St Paul mentions Barnabas, his words imply sympathy and respect. This feeling underlies the language of his complaint here, '*even* Barnabas.' In 1 Cor. ix. 6 also he connects Barnabas with himself, as one who had laboured in the same disinterested spirit and had the same claims upon the Gentile converts. Lastly in Col. iv. 10 he commends Mark to the Colossian Church, as being the cousin of Barnabas.

συναπήχθη αὐτῶν τῇ ὑποκρίσει] '*was carried away with their dissimulation*,' as the A. V. rightly. Their dissimulation was as a flood which swept every thing away with it. Comp. 2 Pet. iii. 17 ἵνα μὴ τῇ τῶν ἀθέσμων πλάνῃ συναπαχθέντες ἐκπέσητε κ.τ.λ., Zosimus *Hist.* v. 6 καὶ αὐτὴ δὲ ἡ Σπάρτη συναπήγετο τῇ κοινῇ τῆς Ἑλλάδος ἁλώσει. In all these passages the dative seems to be governed by the preposition, and cannot without harshness be taken as the instrumental case.

14, 15. 'Seeing that they had left the straight path and abandoned the true principles of the Gospel, I remonstrated with Cephas publicly. Thou thyself, though born and bred a Jew, dost nevertheless lay aside Jewish customs and livest as the Gentiles. On what plea then dost thou constrain the Gentiles to adopt the institutions of the Jews?'

14. οὐκ ὀρθοποδοῦσιν πρὸς κ.τ.λ.] i.e. 'they diverge from the straight path of the Gospel truth.' The word ὀρθοποδεῖν appears not to occur elsewhere, except in later ecclesiastical writers, where its use may be traced to this passage of St Paul. Its classical equivalent is εὐθυπορεῖν. The preposition πρὸς here denotes not the goal to be attained, but the line of direction to be observed: see Winer § xlix. p. 505. For ἡ ἀλήθεια τοῦ εὐαγγελίου see the note on ii. 5.

εἶπον] Were all the concluding verses of the chapter actually spoken by St Paul at the time, or is he adding a comment while narrating the incident afterwards to the Galatians; and if so, where does the text cease and the comment begin? To this question it seems impossible to give a definite answer. St Paul's narrative in fact loses itself in the reflexions suggested by it. Text and comment are so

Ἰουδαῖος ὑπάρχων ἐθνικῶς καὶ οὐχ Ἰουδαϊκῶς ζῇς, πῶς τὰ ἔθνη ἀναγκάζεις Ἰουδαΐζειν; [15]ἡμεῖς φύσει Ἰουδαῖοι καὶ οὐκ ἐξ ἐθνῶν ἁμαρτωλοί, [16]εἰδότες δὲ ὅτι οὐ δικαιοῦται ἄνθρωπος ἐξ ἔργων νόμου, ἐὰν μὴ διὰ πίστεως

blended together that they cannot be separated without violence. The use of the word ἁμαρτωλοί, vv. 15, 17, marks the language of one speaking as a Jew to Jews, and therefore may be regarded as part of the original remonstrance; and yet, though there is no break in the continuity from that point onward, we find at the end of the chapter that St Paul's thoughts and language have drifted away from Peter at Antioch to the Judaizers in Galatia. For similar instances where the direct language of the speaker is intermingled with the after comment of the narrator, see John i. 15—18, where the testimony of the Baptist loses itself in the thoughts of the Evangelist, and Acts i. 16—21, where St Peter's allusion to the death of Judas is interwoven with the after explanations of St Luke.

Ἰουδαῖος ὑπάρχων] almost equivalent to φύσει Ἰουδαῖοι below; see i. 14. In such cases ὑπάρχων implies a contrast between the original and the after state, e.g. in Phil. ii. 6. Here it is very emphatic; 'If you, *born and bred* a Jew, discard Jewish customs, how unreasonable to impose them on Gentiles.'

ἐθνικῶς ζῇς] i.e. mix freely with the Gentiles and thus of necessity disregard the Jewish law of meats. The present tense describes St Peter's general principles, as acted upon long before at Cæsarea (Acts x. 28), and just lately at Antioch (ver. 12), though at the exact moment when St Paul was speaking, he was living Ἰουδαϊκῶς and not ἐθνικῶς.

οὐχ Ἰουδαϊκῶς] The best MSS agree in reading the aspirated form οὐχ. For other examples of anomalous aspirates in the Greek Testament see Winer § v. p. 48, and comp. the note on Phil. ii. 23 ἀφίδω. In this particular instance the aspirate may perhaps be accounted for by the *yh* with which the Hebrew word (יהודים) represented by Ἰουδαῖοι commences.

ἀναγκάζεις] i.e. practically oblige them, though such was not his intention. The force of his example, concealing his true principles, became a species of compulsion.

Ἰουδαΐζειν] '*to adopt Jewish customs*,' opposed to ἐθνικῶς ζῇς which in connexion with Ἰουδαῖος ὑπάρχων is equivalent to ἑλληνίζεις; comp. Esth. viii. 17 καὶ πολλοὶ τῶν ἐθνῶν περιετέμοντο καὶ Ἰουδάϊζον διὰ τὸν φόβον τῶν Ἰουδαίων, Plut. *Vit. Cic.* 7 ἔνοχος τῷ Ἰουδαΐζειν. See the note on Ἰουδαϊσμός, i. 13.

15, 16. 'Only consider our own case. We were born to all the privileges of the Israelite race: we were not *sinners*, as we proudly call the Gentiles. What then? We saw that the observance of law would not justify any man, that faith in Jesus Christ was the only means of justification. Therefore we turned to a belief in Christ. Thus our Christian profession is itself an acknowledgment that such observances are worthless and void, because, as the Scripture declares, no flesh can be justified by works of law.'

Of many constructions proposed, the simplest and best is to understand the substantive verb in ver. 15, 'We (are) Jews by birth etc.' The δὲ of ver. 16, which is omitted in the received text, is certainly genuine.

15. φύσει Ἰουδαῖοι] '*Jews by birth*, not only not Gentiles, but not even proselytes. We inherited the Jewish religion. Everything was done for us, which race could do.' See especially Phil. iii. 4, 5.

Ἰησοῦ Χριστοῦ, καὶ ἡμεῖς εἰς Χριστὸν Ἰησοῦν ἐπιστεύσαμεν, ἵνα δικαιωθῶμεν ἐκ πίστεως Χριστοῦ καὶ οὐκ ἐξ ἔργων νόμου, ὅτι ἐξ ἔργων νόμου ΟΥ ΔΙΚΑΙΩΘΗΣΕΤΑΙ

16. διὰ πίστεως Χριστοῦ Ἰησοῦ.

ἐξ ἐθνῶν] Not 'of Gentile descent,' but 'taken from, belonging to the Gentiles'; comp. Acts xv. 23.

ἁμαρτωλοί] '*sinners*.' The word was almost a synonyme for ἔθνη in the religious phraseology of the Jews. See 1 Macc. ii. 44, *Clem. Hom.* xi. 16 οὕτως ὡς οὐχὶ Ἰουδαῖος, ἁμαρτωλὸς κ.τ.λ.; and compare Luke vi. 32, 33 with Matt. v. 47, and especially Matt. xxvi. 45 with Luke xviii. 32. Here ἁμαρτωλοὶ is used in preference to ἔθνη, not without a shade of irony, as better enforcing St Paul's argument. See the note on ver. 17.

16. ἐὰν μή] retains its proper meaning, but refers only to οὐ δικαιοῦται, 'He is not justified from works of law, he is not justified *except* through faith.' See the note on i. 19.

καὶ ἡμεῖς] '*we ourselves*,' notwithstanding our privileges of race. Compare καὶ αὐτοί, ver. 17.

ἐπιστεύσαμεν] '*became believers*.' See the note on 2 Thess. i. 10. The phrase πιστεύειν εἰς or ἐπί τινα is peculiarly Christian; see Winer § xxxi. p. 267. The constructions of the LXX are πιστεύειν τινί, rarely πιστεύειν ἐπί τινι or ἔν τινι, and once only ἐπί τινα, Wisd. xii. 2 πιστεύειν ἐπὶ Θεόν. The phrase, which occurs in the revised Nicene and other creeds, πιστεύειν εἰς ἐκκλησίαν, though an intelligible, is yet a lax expression, the propriety of which was rightly disputed by many of the fathers, who maintained that πιστεύειν εἰς should be reserved for belief in God or in Christ. See the passages in Suicer *Thesaur.* s. v. πιστεύειν, and Pearson *On the Creed* Art. IX.

ἐκ πίστεως Χριστοῦ] It seems almost impossible to trace the subtle process which has led to the change of prepositions here. In Rom. iii. 30, on the other hand, an explanation is challenged by the direct opposition of ἐκ πίστεως and διὰ τῆς πίστεως. Both prepositions are used elsewhere by St Paul with δικαιοῦν, δικαιοσύνη, indifferently; though where very great precision is aimed at, he seems for an obvious reason to prefer διά, as in Ephes. ii. 8, 9, Phil. iii. 9 μὴ ἔχων ἐμὴν δικαιοσύνην τὴν ἐκ νόμου ἀλλὰ τὴν διὰ πίστεως Χριστοῦ κ.τ.λ., which words present an exact parallel to the former part of this verse, οὐκ ἐξ ἔργων νόμου, ἐὰν μὴ διὰ πίστεως Ἰησοῦ Χριστοῦ. Faith is strictly speaking only the *means*, not the *source* of justification. The one preposition (διὰ) excludes this latter notion, while the other (ἐκ) might imply it. Besides these we meet also with ἐπὶ πίστει (Phil. iii. 9), but never διὰ πίστιν, 'propter fidem,' which would involve a doctrinal error. Compare the careful language in the Latin of our Article xi, '*per* fidem, non *propter* opera.'

ὅτι] is the best supported, and doubtless the correct reading. The reading of the received text διότι has probably been imported from the parallel passage, Rom. iii. 20.

ὅτι ἐξ ἔργων κ.τ.λ.] A quotation from the Old Testament, as appears from the Hebraism οὐ πᾶσα, and from the introductory ὅτι. This sentence indeed would be an unmeaning repetition of what has gone before, unless the Apostle were enforcing his own statements by some authoritative declaration. The words are therefore to be regarded as a free citation of Psalm cxliii. 2 οὐ δικαιωθήσεται ἐνώπιόν σου πᾶς ζῶν. For πᾶς ζῶν, a

πᾶϲα ϲάρξ. [17]εἰ δὲ ζητοῦντες δικαιωθῆναι ἐν Χριστῷ εὑρέθημεν καὶ αὐτοὶ ἁμαρτωλοί, ἆρα Χριστὸς ἁμαρτίας

very common Hebrew synonyme, πᾶσα σάρξ (כל־בשר) is substituted by St Paul. In Rom. iii. 20 the passage is quoted in the same form as here. In both instances St Paul adds ἐξ ἔργων νόμου as a comment of his own, to describe the condition of the people whom the Psalmist addressed. In the context of the passage in the Romans (iii. 19) this comment is justified by his explanation, that 'whatever is stated in the law applies to those under the law.'

For οὐ πᾶσα see Winer § xxvi. p. 214 sq.

17, 18, 19. 'Thus to be justified in Christ, it was necessary to sink to the level of Gentiles, to become '*sinners*' in fact. But are we not thus making Christ a minister of sin? Away with the profane thought. No! the guilt is not in abandoning the law, but in seeking it again when abandoned. Thus, and thus alone, we convict ourselves of transgression. On the other hand, in abandoning the law we did but follow the promptings of the law itself. Only by dying to the law could we live unto God.'

17. Among a vast number of interpretations which have been given of this verse, the following alone deserve consideration.

First; We may regard Χριστὸς ἁμαρτίας διάκονος as a conclusion logically inferred from the premisses, supposing them to be granted; 'If in order to be justified in Christ it was necessary to abandon the law, and if the abandonment of the law is sinful, then Christ is made a minister of sin.' In this case ἄρα is preferable to ἆρα.

If the passage is so taken, it is an attack on the premisses through the conclusion which is obviously monstrous and untenable. Now the assumptions in the premisses are twofold: (1) 'To be justified in Christ it is necessary to abandon the law,' and (2) 'To abandon the law is to become sinners'; and as we suppose one or other of these attacked, we shall get two distinct meanings for the passage, as follows: (1) It is an attempt of the Judaizing objector to show that the abandonment of the law was wrong, inasmuch as it led to so false an inference: 'To abandon the law is to commit sin; it must therefore be wrong to abandon the law in order to be justified in Christ, for this is to make Christ a minister of sin': or (2) It is an argument on the part of St Paul to show that to abandon the law is not to commit sin; 'It cannot be sinful to abandon the law, because it is necessary to abandon the law in order to be justified in Christ, and thus Christ would be made a minister of sin.'

Of these two interpretations, the latter is adopted by many of the fathers. Yet, if our choice were restricted to one or other, the former would seem preferable, for it retains the sense of ἁμαρτωλοί ('sinners' from a Jewish point of view), which it had in ver. 15, and is more consistent with the indicative εὑρέθημεν, this proposition being assumed as absolutely true by the Jewish objector. But on the other hand, it forms an awkward introduction to the verse which follows.

It is probable therefore that both should be abandoned in favour of another explanation: For

Secondly; We may regard Χριστὸς ἁμαρτίας διάκονος as an illogical conclusion deduced from premisses in themselves correct; 'Seeing that in order to be justified in Christ it was necessary to abandon our old ground of legal righteousness and to become sinners (i.e. to put ourselves in the position of the heathen), may it not be argued that Christ is thus made a

διάκονος; μὴ γένοιτο· [18]εἰ γὰρ ἃ κατέλυσα ταῦτα πάλιν οἰκοδομῶ, παραβάτην ἐμαυτὸν συνιστάνω· [19]ἐγὼ

minister of sin?' This interpretation best developes the subtle irony of ἁμαρτωλοί; 'We Jews look down upon the Gentiles as sinners: yet we have no help for it but to become sinners like them.' It agrees with the indicative εὑρέθημεν, and with St Paul's usage of μὴ γένοιτο which elsewhere in argumentative passages always negatives a false but plausible inference from premisses taken as granted. And lastly, it paves the way for the words διὰ νόμου νόμῳ ἀπέθανον which follow. In this case ἆρα is to be preferred to ἄρα, because it at once introduces the inference as a questionable one. It may be added also in favour of ἆρα, that elsewhere μὴ γένοιτο follows an interrogation. Ἆρα expresses bewilderment as to a possible conclusion. Any attempt further to define its meaning seems not to be justified either by the context here, or by its usage elsewhere. Ἆρα hesitates, while ἄρα concludes.

εὑρέθημεν] involves more or less prominently the idea of a *surprise:* comp. Rom. vii. 10, 2 Cor. xi. 12, xii. 20. Its frequent use however must be traced to the influence of the Aramaic dialect: see Cureton *Corp. Ign.* p. 271.

ἁμαρτίας διάκονος] while yet He is δικαιοσύνης διάκονος, thus making a direct contradiction in terms.

μὴ γένοιτο] 'Nay, verily,' 'Away with the thought.' This is one out of several LXX renderings of the Hebrew חלילה ('ad profana' and so 'absit,' see Gesenius *Thes.* p. 478). Another rendering of the same is ἵλεως (sc. ὁ Θεὸς) which occurs Matt. xvi. 22 ἵλεώς σοι Κύριε, 'far be it from thee, Lord': see Glass. *Phil. Sacr.* p. 538. Μὴ γένοιτο is not however confined to Jewish and Christian writings, but is frequent for instance in Arrian; see Raphel *Annot.* Rom. iii. 4.

18. 'If, after destroying the old law of ordinances, I attempt to build it up again, I condemn myself, I testify to my guilt in the work of destruction.' The pulling down and building up have reference doubtless to the Mosaic law, though expressed as a general maxim (ταῦτα). The difficulty however is to trace the connexion in γάρ.

With the interpretation of ver. 17 adopted above, it seems simplest to attach γὰρ to μὴ γένοιτο, 'Nay verily, *for*, so far from Christ being a minister of sin, there is no sin at all in abandoning the law: it is only converted into a sin by returning to the law again.' For this use of γὰρ after μὴ γένοιτο comp. Rom. ix. 14, 15, xi. 1.

παραβάτην ἐμαυτὸν συνιστάνω] '*I make myself out, establish myself, a transgressor.*' It will have been seen that much of the force of the passage depends on the sense which the Jews attached to ἁμαρτωλός. Having passed on from this to ἁμαρτία, St Paul at length throws off the studied ambiguity of ἁμαρτωλός ('a non-observer of the law,' and 'a sinner') by substituting the plain term παραβάτης.

ἐμαυτὸν συνιστάνω is opposed to Χριστὸς ἁμαρτίας διάκονος, though from its position ἐμαυτὸν cannot be very emphatic.

συνιστάνω] '*I prove*,' like συμβιβάζω, as Rom. iii. 5, v. 8; comp. 2 Cor. iii. 1.

19. Establishing the statement of the foregoing verse: '*For* in abandoning the law, I did but follow the leading of the law itself.'

ἐγώ] Not 'I Paul' as distinguished from others, for instance from the Gentile converts, but 'I Paul, the natural man, the slave of the old covenant.' The emphasis on ἐγὼ is explained by the following verse, ζῶ δὲ οὐκέτι ἐγώ κ.τ.λ.

γὰρ διὰ νόμου νόμῳ ἀπέθανον, ἵνα Θεῷ ζήσω· 20 Χριστῷ συνεσταύρωμαι· ζῶ δὲ οὐκέτι ἐγώ, ζῇ δὲ ἐν ἐμοὶ Χρισ-

διὰ νόμου νόμῳ ἀπέθανον] In what sense can one be said *through law* to have died to law? Of all the answers that have been given to this question, two alone seem to deserve consideration. The law may be said in two different ways to be παιδαγωγὸς εἰς Χριστόν. We may regard

i. *Its economical purpose.* 'The law bore on its face the marks of its transitory character. Its prophecies foretold Christ. Its sacrifices and other typical rites foreshadowed Christ. It was therefore an act of obedience to the law, when Christ came, to take Him as my master in place of the law.' This interpretation however, though quite in character with St Paul's teaching elsewhere, does not suit the present passage; For (1) The written law—the Old Testament—is always ὁ νόμος. At least it seems never to be quoted otherwise. Νόμος without the article is 'law' considered as a principle, exemplified no doubt chiefly and signally in the Mosaic law, but very much wider than this in its application. In explaining this passage therefore, we must seek for some element in the Mosaic law which it had in common with law generally, instead of dwelling on its special characteristics, as a prophetic and typical dispensation. Moreover, (2) the interpretation thus elicited makes the words διὰ νόμου νόμῳ ἀπέθανον an appeal rather to the reason and intellect, than to the heart and conscience; but the phrases 'living unto God,' 'being crucified with Christ,' and indeed the whole tenour of the passage, point rather to the moral and spiritual change wrought in the believer. Thus we are led to seek the explanation of this expression rather in

ii. *Its moral effects.* The law reveals sin; it also provokes sin; nay, in a certain sense, it may be said to create sin, for 'sin is not reckoned where there is no law' (Rom. v. 13). Thus the law is the strength of sin (1 Cor. xv. 56). At the same time it provides no remedy for the sinner. On the contrary it condemns him hopelessly, for no one can fulfil all the requirements of the law. The law then exercises a double power over those subject to it; it makes them sinners, and it punishes them for being so. What can they do to escape? They have no choice but to throw off the bondage of the law, for the law itself has driven them to this. They find the deliverance, which they seek, in Christ. See Rom. vii. 24, 25, and indeed the whole passage, Rom. v. 20—viii. 11. Thus then they pass through three stages, (1) Prior to the law—sinful, but ignorant of sin; (2) Under the law—sinful, and conscious of sin, yearning after better things; (3) Free from the law—free and justified in Christ. This sequence is clearly stated Rom. v. 20. The second stage (διὰ νόμου) is a necessary preparation for the third (νόμῳ ἀπέθανον). 'Proinde,' says Luther on iii. 19 (the edition of 1519), 'ut remissio propter salutem, ita praevaricatio propter remissionem, ita lex propter transgressionem.'

What the Mosaic ordinances were to the Jews, other codes of precepts and systems of restraints were in an inferior degree and less efficaciously to other nations. They too, like the Jews, had felt the bondage of law in some form or other. See iv. 9, v. 1, and the note on iv. 11.

νόμῳ ἀπέθανον] '*I died to law.*' For the dative comp. Rom. vi. 2, 11 (τῇ ἁμαρτίᾳ), and for the idea of 'dying to the law' Rom. vii. 1—6, esp. ver. 4 καὶ ὑμεῖς ἐθανατώθητε τῷ νόμῳ, and ver. 6 κατηργήθημεν ἀπὸ τοῦ νόμου ἀποθα-

τός· ὃ δὲ νῦν ζῶ ἐν σαρκί, ἐν πίστει ζῶ τῇ τοῦ υἱοῦ τοῦ Θεοῦ τοῦ ἀγαπήσαντός με καὶ παραδόντος ἑαυτὸν

20. τῇ τοῦ Θεοῦ καὶ Χριστοῦ τοῦ ἀγαπήσαντος.

νόντες ἐν ᾧ κατειχόμεθα (literally, 'we were nullified, i.e. discharged, by death from the law in which we were held').

20, 21. 'With Christ I have been crucified at once to the law and to sin. Henceforth I live a new life—yet not I, but Christ liveth it in me. This new life is not a rule of carnal ordinances; it is spiritual, and its motive principle is faith in the Son of God who manifested His love for me by dying for my sake. I cannot then despise God's grace. I cannot stultify Christ's death by clinging still to a justification based upon law.'

20. An expansion of the idea in the last verse.

Χριστῷ συνεσταύρωμαι] '*I have been crucified with Christ.*' A new turn is thus given to the metaphor of death. In the last verse it was the release from past obligations; here it is the annihilation of old sins. The two however are not unconnected. Sin and law loose their hold at the same time. The sense of feebleness, of prostration, to which a man is reduced by the working of the law, *the process of dying* in fact, is the moral link which unites the two applications of the image: see Rom. vii. 5, 9—11. Thus his death becomes life. Being crucified with Christ, he rises with Christ, and lives to God.

The parallel passage in the Romans best illustrates the different senses given to death. See also, for a similar and characteristic instance of working out a metaphor, the different applications of ἡμέρα in 1 Thess. v. 2—8.

For the idea of dying with Christ etc., see Rom. vi. 6 ὁ παλαιὸς ἡμῶν ἄνθρωπος συνεσταυρώθη: comp. Gal. v. 24, vi. 14, Rom. vi. 8, Col. ii. 20, ἀποθανεῖν σὺν Χριστῷ, and Rom. vi. 4, Col. ii. 12, συνταφῆναι. Comp. Ignat. *Rom.* § 7 ὁ ἐμὸς ἔρως ἐσταύρωται. The correlative idea of rising and reigning with Christ is equally common in St Paul.

ζῶ δὲ οὐκέτι ἐγώ] The order is significant; 'When I speak of living, I do not mean myself, my natural being. I have no longer a separate existence. I am merged in Christ.' See on ἐγὼ ver. 19.

ὃ δὲ νῦν ζῶ] Not exactly ἣν νῦν ζῶ ζωήν, but ὃ limits and qualifies the idea of life: '*So far as* I now live in the flesh, it is a life of faith': comp. Rom. vi. 10 ὃ γὰρ ἀπέθανεν, τῇ ἁμαρτίᾳ ἀπέθανεν ἐφάπαξ, ὃ δὲ ζῇ, ζῇ τῷ Θεῷ, Plut. *Mor.* p. 100 F ὃ καθεύδουσι, τοῦ σώματος ὕπνος ἐστὶ καὶ ἀνάπαυσις.

νῦν] '*now*': his new life in Christ, as opposed to his old life before his conversion; not his present life on earth, as opposed to his future life in heaven; for such a contrast is quite foreign to this passage.

ἐν πίστει] '*in faith*,' the atmosphere as it were which he breathes in this his new spiritual life.

The variation of reading here is perplexing. For τοῦ υἱοῦ τοῦ Θεοῦ may be pleaded the great preponderance of the older authorities: for τοῦ Θεοῦ καὶ Χριστοῦ, the testimony of a few ancient copies, and the difficulty of conceiving its substitution for the other simpler reading.

με...ἐμοῦ] 'loved *me*, gave Himself for *me*.' He appropriates to himself, as Chrysostom observes, the love which belongs equally to the whole world. For Christ is indeed the personal friend of each man individually; and is as much to him, as if He had died for him alone.

21. οὐκ ἀθετῶ κ.τ.λ.] '*I do not set at nought the grace of God.* Setting

ὑπὲρ ἐμοῦ. [21] οὐκ ἀθετῶ τὴν χάριν τοῦ Θεοῦ· εἰ γὰρ διὰ νόμου δικαιοσύνη, ἄρα Χριστὸς δωρεὰν ἀπέθανεν.

at nought I call it: *for*, if righteousness might be obtained through law, then Christ's death were superfluous.' For ἀθετῶ 'to nullify' see Luke vii. 30, 1 Cor. i. 19: its exact sense here is fixed by δωρεὰν ἀπέθανεν. 'The grace of God' is manifested in Christ's death. The connexion of γὰρ is with the idea of ἀθετῶ, and may be explained by a supplied clause, as above.

δωρεάν] not 'in vain,' but 'uselessly, without sufficient cause,' or, as we might say, 'gratuitously,' John xv. 25 ἐμίσησάν με δωρεάν (Ps. xxxiv. 19); comp. LXX of Ps. xxxiv. 7 δωρεὰν ἔκρυψάν μοι διαφθοράν, Hebr. חנם, where Symmachus had ἀναιτίως; Ecclus. xx. 23.

Various Readings in ii. 5.

The reading which is given in the text, οἷς οὐδὲ πρὸς ὥραν, is doubtless correct. Two variations however occur, which deserve notice.

1. The omission of οὐδέ. (1) The negative. Found in most texts.

The negative is found in all the Greek uncial MSS (i. e. in ℵABCEF GKLP) except D, in which however it is inserted by a later hand, and apparently in all or nearly all the Greek cursive MSS. It is expressly mentioned by the Ambrosian Hilary[1] and by Jerome[2], as the reading of the Greek copies. It is found also in the Gothic, Memphitic, Thebaic, both Syriac and other versions, and was unquestionably the original reading of the Vulgate, as it appears in all the best manuscripts of this version. It was read moreover by Marcion[3], Ephraem Syrus, Epiphanius[4], Chrysostom, Theodore of Mopsuestia, Theodoret, the Pseudo-Ignatius[5], and perhaps also by Origen[6], among the Greeks; and by Ambrose[7], Augustine[8], Jerome, Pelagius (in his text, though he comments on the other reading), and Primasius, among the Latins.

On the other hand, it is omitted in D (both Greek and Latin), and in the Latin of E; and the text is read without it by the translator of Irenæus[9], by Tertullian[10], Victorinus, the Ambrosian Hilary, Pelagius (in his commentary), and apparently Sulpicius Severus[11]. We have it moreover on the authority of Jerome[12], of Primasius[13], and of Sedulius[14], that the negative was not found in the Latin copies, and the same is implied by the language of the Ambrosian Hilary.

Omitted in some few.

In the face of this testimony, the statement of Victorinus, that it was omitted 'in plurimis codicibus et Latinis et *Graecis*,' is not worthy of credit. He may indeed have found the omission in some Greek MS or other, but even this is doubtful. No stress can be laid on the casual statement of a writer so loose and so ignorant of Greek.

Omission traced to the Old Latin.

It appears from these facts that the omission is due to some Western MS or MSS alone. The author of the Old Latin version used one of these. And to the Old Latin version all or nearly all the existing authorities for the omission may be traced. Its absence in the Greek text of D is an exception, unless the charge of Latinising sometimes brought against this

[1] *ad loc.* 'Graeci e contra dicunt: Nec ad horam cessimus, et hoc aiunt convenire causae etc.'

[2] *ad loc.* 'juxta Graecos codices est legendum: Quibus neque, etc.'

[3] Tertull. *adv. Marc.* v. 3.

[4] *Haer.* p. 112 and p. 814.

[5] *Ep. ad Tars.* § 2.

[6] Orig. *c. Cels.* vii. 21 (I. p. 709, Delarue) οὐδέποτε ἐν χώρᾳ ὑποτεταγμένος ἀνθρώποις ὡς κρείττων γενόμενος, where the conjecture οὐδὲ πρὸς ὥραν is possibly correct.

[7] *Epist.* 37.

[8] *ad loc.* and *Epist.* lxxxii. (II. p. 194, ed. Bened.).

[9] Iren. iii. 13. 3.

[10] *adv. Marc.* v. 3.

[11] *Dial.* iii. 13, p. 219 B (Migne).

[12] *ad loc.* 'hoc esse quod in codicibus legitur Latinis: Quibus ad horam etc.'

[13] *ad loc.* 'Latinus habet, Quibus ad horam cessimus.' Primasius does not himself omit it, as represented in Tisch.

[14] *Magn. Bibl. Vet. Patr.* v. 498, 'Male in Latinis codicibus legitur, Quibus ad horam cessimus.'

MS can be substantiated. Irenæus is also to be accounted for, but in this case the omission may perhaps be ascribed not to the author himself, but to his translator.

A correction however would appear to have been made in that recension which was circulated in North Italy, for the negative is found both in Ambrose and in Augustine, the former of whom used the 'Itala' as a matter of course, and the latter by choice[1].

Tertullian's charge against Marcion.

Tertullian indeed accuses Marcion of interpolating the negative; but no weight attaches to his assertion. The African father, not finding it in his own Latin copy and finding it in Marcion's recension, caught at what appeared the simplest way of accounting for the variation. He would not stop to consider whether his own copy was correct. It was enough for him that the text with the negative was more favourable to Marcion's peculiar views than without it. Tertullian makes no appeal to MSS or external authority of any kind. He argues solely on grounds of internal evidence.

The omission in the first instance is not easily accounted for. It may have been an oversight. Or possibly the Latin translator, or the transcriber of the MSS which he used, intentionally left it out, thinking, as some later critics thought, that the sense of the passage or the veracity of the Apostle required the omission. At all events the expedient of dropping the negative, as a means of simplifying the sense, is characteristic of the Latin copies. For other instances in St Paul see Gal. v. 8, Rom. v. 14, 1 Cor. v. 6, [Col. ii. 18]; comp. Joh. vi. 64, ix. 27[2].

Omission how accounted for.

The omission once made, arguments were not wanting to support it. Tertullian found that the negative vitiated the sense of the passage. He objected to it moreover as at variance with history, which showed that St Paul did yield on occasions, in circumcising Timothy for instance, and in paying the expenses of those who had taken Nazarite vows. The same arguments are brought forward by Victorinus and the Ambrosian Hilary[3]. With much greater justice Jerome maintains that it is required for the sense. But feeble as were his reasons, doubtless the authority of Tertullian, and the prejudice thus raised against this as the reading of Marcion, were fatal to its reception with many who otherwise would have conformed to the Greek text.

It is not uninteresting to observe how little influence this important various reading has had on the interpretation of the passage. The omission or insertion of οὐδέ might have been expected to decide for or against the circumcision of Titus. This however is not the case. The Latin Fathers, who left out the negative, generally maintained that he was not circumcised[4]. Several modern critics, who retain it, hold that he was.

2. The omission of οἷς.

[1] *De Doctr. Christ.* c. 15.

[2] For these references I am indebted to Reiche *Comm. Crit.* II. p. 13.

[3] 'Litterae enim hoc indicant quia cessit, et historia factum exclamat.' The passage is based on Tertullian.

[4] So Victorinus and the Ambrosian Hilary. This is also the opinion of Tertullian (*adv. Marc.* v. 3), if I understand him rightly: though Baur, *Paulus* p. 122, interprets him differently. The only exception that I have remarked is Pelagius, who however has not the same reading in the text as in the notes.

The relative is omitted in some few texts which retain οὐδέ, and retained in some few which want οὐδέ; but for the most part the two are omitted or retained together. Here again the Greek texts are as unanimous as in the former case. The obvious motive of this omission is the improvement of the grammar by the removal of a redundant word. (2) The relative.

This assumed necessity of altering the text somehow, in order to correct the grammar, may have been the first step towards the more important omission of the negative.

The later visit of St Paul to Jerusalem.

The later of the two visits to Jerusalem mentioned in the Epistle has from the earliest times been identified with the visit recorded in Acts xv. This view is taken by Irenæus [1], the first writer who alludes to the subject; and though it has not escaped unchallenged either in ancient [2] or modern days, the arguments in its favour are sufficiently strong to resist the pressure of objections to which it is fairly exposed [3]. The same with the visit of Acts xv.

I. In support of this view may be urged the positive argument from the striking coincidence of circumstances, and the negative argument from the difficulty of finding any equally probable solution, or indeed any probable solution at all besides. Arguments in favour of this view.

(i) The later visit of the Galatian Epistle coincides with the third visit of the Acts, when the so-called Apostolic Council was held, in all the most important features. The *geography* is the same. In both narratives the communications take place between Jerusalem and Antioch: in both the head-quarters of the false brethren are at the former place, their machinations are carried on in the latter: in both the Gentile Apostles go up to Jerusalem apparently from Antioch, and return thence to Antioch again. The *time* is the same, or at least not inconsistent. St Paul places the event 15 or 16 years after his conversion: St Luke's narrative implies that they (i) *Positive.* Coincidence of circumstances.

[1] Iren. iii. 13. 3 'Si quis igitur diligenter ex Actibus Apostolorum scrutetur tempus de quo scriptum est, *Ascendi Hierosolymam*, propter praedictam quaestionem, inveniet eos, qui praedicti sunt a Paulo, annos concurrentes etc.' So also apparently Tertullian, *adv. Marc.* v. 2, 3.

[2] This visit is placed *after* the third in the Acts by Chrysostom, but not further defined. It is identified with the *fifth* by Epiphanius *Haer.* xxviii. 4, p. 112. The *Chron. Pasch.* (I. p. 435 sq. ed. Dind.) places it after the incidents of Acts xiii. 1—3, and before those of Acts xv, thus apparently interpolating it between the second and third visits of the Acts.

[3] The view adopted is that of most recent critics. It is well maintained by Schott, De Wette, Conybeare and Howson, Jowett, and others. The arguments in favour of the *second* visit of the Acts are best stated by Fritzsche *Opusc.* p. 223 sq. The *fourth* visit of the Acts finds its ablest champion in Wieseler, *Galat.* p. 553 sq. The *fifth* visit has been abandoned by modern critics, as the epistle was clearly written before that time. Some few, e.g. Paley *Horae Paulinae* ch. v. no. 10, suppose this to be a journey to Jerusalem *omitted* in the Acts.

took place about the year 51[1]. The *persons* are the same: Paul and Barnabas appear as the representatives of the Gentile Churches, Cephas and James as the leaders of the Circumcision. The agitators are similarly described in the two accounts: in the Acts, as converted Pharisees who had imported their dogmas into the Christian Church; in the Epistle, as false brethren who attempt to impose the bondage of the law on the Gentile converts. The two Apostles of the Gentiles are represented in both accounts as attended: 'certain other Gentiles' (ἐξ αὐτῶν) are mentioned by St Luke; Titus, a Gentile, is named by St Paul. The *subject of dispute* is the same; the circumcision of the Gentile converts. The *character of the conference* is in general the same; a prolonged and hard-fought contest[2]. The *result* is the same; the exemption of the Gentiles from the enactments of the law, and the recognition of the Apostolic commission of Paul and Barnabas by the leaders of the Jewish Church.

A combination of circumstances so striking is not likely to have occurred twice within a few years.

(ii) *Negative.* Difficulty of other solutions.

(ii) Nor indeed can this visit be identified with any other recorded in St Luke. It has been taken by some for instance for the *second* visit of the Acts. To this supposition the date alone is fatal. The second visit of the Acts synchronizes, or nearly so[3], with the persecution and death of Herod, which latter event happened in the year 44. But at least 12 or 13, probably 15 or 16 years, had elapsed since St Paul's conversion, before he paid the visit in question. And no system of chronology at all probable will admit of so early a date for his conversion as would thus be required. But again, according to the narrative of the Acts St Paul's Apostolic mission commenced *after* the second visit[4], whereas the account in the Epistle

[1] This is calculated by a back reckoning of the time spent from the Apostolic Council to the appointment of Festus, the date of which is fixed independently at A.D. 60; see Wieseler *Chronol.* p. 66 sq.

[2] St Luke's notices are, xv. 2 γενομένης στάσεως καὶ ζητήσεως οὐκ ὀλίγης τῷ Παύλῳ καὶ τῷ Βαρνάβᾳ πρὸς αὐτούς, at Antioch; xv. 5 ἐξανέστησαν δέ τινες, at Jerusalem before the congress; xv. 7 πολλῆς δὲ ζητήσεως γενομένης, at Jerusalem at the congress.

[3] The order of events in St Luke's narrative is as follows; (1) the notice of St Paul's setting out from Antioch for Jerusalem, xi. 30; (2) the persecution of Herod, the death of James, and the imprisonment and escape of Peter, xii. 1—19; (3) the death of Herod, and the spread of the wòrd, xii. 20—24; (4) St Paul's business at Jerusalem and his departure thence, xii. 25. The narrative itself suggests the motive of this order, which is not directly chronological. Having mentioned in (1) St Paul's mission to Jerusalem, the writer is led in (2) to describe the condition of the Church there, κατ' ἐκεῖνον τὸν καιρόν. This obliges him to pass on to (3) in order to show that God defeated the purposes of man, the persecutor dying ignominiously, and the persecuted Church continuing to flourish. He then resumes the subject of (1) in (4). Thus it may be assumed, I think, that the Church was suffering from Herod's persecutions when St Paul arrived, but not that Herod was already dead. In other words, the chronological order was probably (2), (1), (4), (3).

[4] His career as an Apostle commences with Acts xiii. He had before this held a subordinate place, and his preaching had been confined to Damascus (ix. 22), Jerusalem (ix. 28), and the neighbourhood of Tarsus and Antioch (ix. 30, xi. 25 sq.; comp. also Gal. i. 21).

clearly implies that his Apostolic office and labours were well known and recognised before this conference.

Still more serious objections lie against identifying it with any later visit in the Acts—the *fourth* for instance. It is perhaps a sufficient answer to such a solution, that St Paul's connexion with Barnabas seems to have ceased before. A more fatal difficulty still would be his silence respecting the third visit, so marked with incidents, and so pregnant with consequences bearing directly on the subject of which he is treating.

II. On the other hand the identification adopted involves various difficulties, which however, when weighed, do not seem sufficient to turn the scale. These difficulties are of two classes: Objections answered.

(i) *Discrepancies* appearing to exist between the two narratives. (i) Discrepancies.

On the whole however the circumstances of the writers and the different purposes of the narrators seem sufficient to explain the divergences, real or apparent, in the two accounts: and the remarks made in comparing the two records of the former visit apply with even more force to this (see p. 91). The alleged discrepancies are these:

(*a*) In the Acts St Paul is represented as sent to Jerusalem by the Christians of Antioch to settle some disputes which had arisen there: in the Epistle he states that he went up by revelation. Here however there is no contradiction. The historian naturally records the external impulse, which led to the mission: the Apostle himself states his inward motive. 'What I did,' he says, 'I did not owing to circumstances, not as yielding to pressure, not in deference to others, but because the Spirit of God told me it was right.' The very stress which he lays on this revelation seems to show that other influences were at work. (*a*) Motive of the journey.

The following parallel cases suggest how the one motive might supplement the other.

> (*α*) In Acts ix. 29, 30, it is said, 'They went about to slay him, which when the brethren knew, they brought him down to Cæsarea, and sent him forth to Tarsus.' St Paul's own account of this incident, Acts xxii. 17 sq., is as follows: 'While I prayed in the temple I was in a trance, and saw him saying unto me, Make haste and get thee quickly out of Jerusalem, for they will not receive thy testimony concerning me, etc.'
>
> (*β*) In Acts xiii. 2—4 the mission of Paul and Barnabas is attributed both to the Holy Spirit and to the Church of Antioch: 'The Holy Ghost said, Separate me Barnabas and Saul for the work whereunto I have called them; and when they had fasted and prayed, and laid their hands on them, *they sent them away* (ἀπέλυσαν). So they being *sent forth by the Holy Ghost* (ἐκπεμφθέντες ὑπὸ τοῦ ἁγίου πνεύματος) etc.'
>
> (*γ*) Acts xv. 28, 'It seemed good to the Holy Ghost and to us.'

(*b*) St Paul speaks of his communications as made to the Apostles in private: St Luke's narrative describes a general congress of the Church. (*b*) Character of the conferences.

The divergence is due to the different aims of the two writers. St Paul is dwelling on what he owed or did not owe to the Twelve. St Luke describes the results as affecting the interests of the Church at large. St Paul mentions or rather alludes to the private history which led to the public transactions, the secret springs, as it were, which set the machinery in motion. This history can have been but partially known to St Luke, nor did it lie within his province to record it.

But in fact, while each narrative thus presents a different aspect of this chapter of history, each also contains indications that the other aspect was recognised, though not dwelt upon, by the writer. The very form of St Paul's expression, *ἀνεθέμην αὐτοῖς, κατ' ἰδίαν δὲ τοῖς δοκοῦσιν*, implies something besides the private conference; the transactions themselves—the dispute about Titus for instance—involved more or less of publicity: the purpose sought to be attained could scarcely be effected in any other way: and the fragmentary character of the Apostle's account leaves ample space for the insertion of other incidents besides those given. On the other hand St Luke alludes in a general way to conferences and discussions preceding the congress (xv. 4, 5, 6): and the speeches there delivered, the measures there proposed, are plainly the result of much wise forethought and patient deliberation on the part of the Apostles.

(*c*) Relations of St Paul with the Twelve.

(*c*) Again, it is said, the account of St Luke leaves the impression of perfect and unbroken harmony between St Paul and the Twelve; while St Paul's narrative betrays, or seems to betray, signs of dissatisfaction with their counsels. In the Acts the leading Apostles of the Circumcision stand forth as the champions of Gentile liberty: the writer of the Epistle on the other hand implies or appears to imply, that they owed to himself and Barnabas alone their emancipation from the bondage sought to be imposed upon them.

But here again the difficulty diminishes, when we try to picture to ourselves what was likely to have been the course of events. The articles of the so-called Apostolic Council were 'Articles of Peace.' To infringe no principle and yet to quiet opposition, to concede as much as would satisfy the one party and not enough to press heavily on the other—this was the object to be attained. Thus the result was a compromise. Long discussions, many misgivings, some differences of opinion, must have arisen on a question so delicate and yet so momentous; and though the unanimity of the final decision was indeed the prompting of the Holy Ghost, it would be not less contrary to all analogies of the Apostolic history, than to all human experience, to suppose that no error or weakness or prejudice had revealed itself in the process. It would seem moreover, that by the time the congress met, St Paul's work was already done. His large experience gained in contact with the Gentile Churches had told upon the Twelve. If they hesitated at first, as they may have done, they hesitated now no longer. Opinions in favour of liberal measures towards the Gentiles would come with more force from the leading Apostles of the Circumcision. His own voice raised in their cause might only inflame the passions of the bigoted and prejudice the result. So we find that when the council meets, Paul and Barnabas confine themselves to narrating the success of their labours among the Gentiles. As regards the matter under dispute they are entirely passive.

(ii) Omissions.

(ii) More startling at first sight than these apparent discrepancies are the direct omissions of St Paul, on the supposition that he is speaking of the visit of Acts xv.

(*a*) 2nd visit to Jerusalem.

(*a*) Above all, how comes it, that while enumerating his visits to Jerusalem, St Paul should mention the first and third, and pass over the second recorded in the Acts?

The answer is to be sought in the circumstances under which that visit was paid. The storm of persecution had broken over the Church of Jerusalem. One leading Apostle had been put to death; another rescued by a miracle had fled for his life. At this season of terror and confusion Paul and Barnabas arrived. It is probable that every Christian of rank had retired from the city. No mention is made of the Twelve; the salutations of the Gentile Apostles are received by 'The Elders.' They arrived charged with alms for the relief of the poor brethren of Judæa. Having deposited these in trustworthy hands, they would depart with all convenient speed. Any lengthened stay might endanger their lives. Nor indeed was there any motive for remaining. Even had St Paul purposed holding conferences with the Apostles or the Church of the Circumcision, at this moment of dire distress it would have been impossible[1]. Of this visit then, so brief and so hurried, he makes no mention here. His object is not to enumerate his journeys to Jerusalem, but to define his relations with the Twelve; and on these relations it had no bearing.

(*b*) The Apostolic decree.

(*b*) The omission of all mention of the Apostolic decree is a less considerable difficulty. The purport of the decree itself, and the form of opposition which St Paul encountered in Galatia, sufficiently explain his silence[2].

(1) The provisions of this decree seem to have been, as I have already mentioned, 'Articles of Peace.' The Apostolic letter was only addressed to the Gentile brethren 'in Antioch and Syria and Cilicia' (xv. 23), that is, to the churches more directly in communication with Palestine, and therefore materially affected by the state of feeling and practice among the Jewish Christians. There is no reason for supposing that the decree was intended to be permanent and universal. It was drawn up to meet a special emergency, and its enactments accordingly are special. The Gentile Apostles seem to have delivered it scrupulously in those churches which had been already founded and which had felt the pressure of Jewish

[1] St Luke dismisses this visit in a very few words; xi. 30 *ἀποστείλαντες πρὸς τοὺς πρεσβυτέρους διὰ χειρὸς Βαρνάβα καὶ Σαύλου*, xii. 25 *Βαρνάβας δὲ καὶ Σαῦλος ὑπέστρεψαν ἐξ Ἱερουσαλήμ, πληρώσαντες τὴν διακονίαν, συμπαραλαβόντες Ἰωάννην τὸν ἐπικληθέντα Μάρκον*. It seems probable then that all the Apostles, perhaps even James, were away. Of Peter this is all but directly stated, xii. 17. This inference accords with an ancient tradition, that twelve years was the limit of time prescribed by our Lord for the Apostles to remain at Jerusalem. It is mentioned by Apollonius (circ. A.D. 200, ap. Euseb. *H. E.* v. 18, *ὡς ἐκ παραδόσεως*), and by Clem. Alex. *Strom.* vi, p. 762, ed. Potter. The latter gives, as his authority, the *Praedicatio Petri*, and quotes the words *μετὰ δώδεκα ἔτη ἐξέλθετε εἰς τὸν κόσμον*. This carries the tradition back to an early date. On the sequence of events in this portion of the Acts, see above, p. 124, note 3.

[2] Paley has some good remarks on this decree, *Hor. Paul.* ch. v. § 11.

prejudice (Acts xvi. 4). But in the brotherhoods afterwards formed and lying beyond the reach of such influences, no notice was taken of it. St Paul's instructions for instance to the Corinthians and to the Romans[1] entirely ignore one of its provisions, the prohibition against eating meats offered to idols. He speaks of this as a matter of indifference in itself, only important as it affected each man's conscience.

(2) The object of the decree was to *relieve* the Gentile Christians from the burden of Jewish observances. It said, 'Concede so much and we will protect you from any further exactions.' The Galatians sought no such protection. They were willing recipients of Judaic rites; and St Paul's object was to show them, not that they need not submit to these burdens against their will, but that they were wrong and sinful in submitting to them.

(3) The power of the Apostles of the Circumcision, and the precedence of the mother Church, had been unduly and exclusively exalted by the Judaizers in Galatia at the expense of St Paul's authority. The Epistle to the Galatians is from beginning to end a protest against these exaggerated claims. He refuses to acknowledge any human interference, he takes his stand throughout upon his direct commission from the Lord. By appealing to a decree of a Council held at Jerusalem for sanction on a point on which his own decision as an Apostle was final, he would have made the very concession which his enemies insisted upon[2].

Patristic accounts of the collision at Antioch.

The incident is explained by St Peter's character.

The conduct of St Peter at Antioch has been a great stumblingblock both in ancient and modern times. It has been thought strange that the very Apostle, to whom was specially vouchsafed the revelation that there is nothing common or unclean, and who only a short time before this meeting at Antioch had declared himself plainly in favour of Gentile liberty, should have acted in a manner so inconsistent with all that had gone before. Accordingly some have sought to wrest St Paul's language here, and others have denied the accuracy of the narrative in the Acts. But in fact St Peter's character, as it is drawn in the Gospels, explains every difficulty.

[1] 1 Cor. x. 27 sq., Rom. xiv. 2 sq. This question will be considered more at length in the dissertation on 'St Paul and the Three.'

[2] The accounts of this crisis in the Apostolic history given by Neander *Pflanz.* I. p. 205 sq., and de Pressensé *Trois Premiers Siècles*, 1re série, I. p. 457 sq., seem to me on the whole among the most truthful, preserving a just mean between exaggerations on either side. Other references to important recent works will be given in the notes to the dissertation on 'St Paul and the Three.' Since the 1st edition of this volume was published I have read the articles of Reuss, *La Conférence de Jérusalem*, in the *Nouvelle Revue de Théologie*, XII. p. 324, XIII. p. 62. Though they contain many things with which I cannot agree, I gladly recognise the spirit of fairness in which they are written.

It is at least no surprise, that he who at one moment declared himself ready to lay down his life for his Lord's sake and even drew his sword in defence of his Master, and the next betrayed Him with a thrice repeated denial, should have acted in this case, as we infer he acted from the combined accounts of St Luke and St Paul. There is the same impulsive courage followed by the same shrinking timidity. And though St Paul's narrative stops short of the last scene in this drama, it would not be rash to conclude that it ended as the other had ended, that the revulsion of feeling was as sudden and complete, and that again he went out and wept bitterly, having denied his Lord in the person of these Gentile converts.

Becomes a controversial weapon.

The history of the patristic interpretations of this passage is painfully instructive. The orthodox fathers of the early Church were sore pressed both by heretics and unbelievers. On the one hand Ebionite writers, like the author of the Clementines, made it a ground for a personal attack on St Paul[1]. On the other, extreme Gnostics such as Marcion used it to prove the direct antagonism of Christianity to Judaism as represented by the opposition of the Gentile to the Jewish Apostle[2]. And lastly, Porphyry and other writers availed themselves of the incident as an engine of assault on Christianity itself, impugning the characters of both Apostles in language which the fathers describe as coarse and blasphemous[3]. How were these diverse attacks to be met? Tertullian, arguing against the Marcionites, resisted all temptations to wrest the plain meaning of the passage[4]. Cyprian and Ambrose moreover took it in its obvious sense[5]. The same is done also by the commentators Victorinus and Hilary. But the majority of early writers fell into the snare. Two disingenuous explanations were put forward to meet the attacks of heretics and unbelievers; each originating, it would appear, in one of the great fathers of Alexandria, and dividing between them the allegiance of subsequent writers.

Solutions proposed by

(i) Clement.

1. Clement of Alexandria maintained that the Cephas here mentioned was not the Apostle Peter, but one of the seventy disciples bearing the same name. Though the passage itself absolutely excludes such a view, it nevertheless found several adherents, and is mentioned by Eusebius[6] with-

[1] See above, p. 61, and the notes ii. 11, 13.

[2] Tertull. *adv. Marc.* i. 20, v. 3, *de Praescr.* c. 23: comp. Iren. iii. 12. 15.

[3] See esp. Hieron. *in Ep. ad Gal. praef.* (VII. p. 371, ed. Vallarsi) 'Volens et illi maculam erroris inurere et huic procacitatis, et in commune ficti dogmatis accusare mendacium, dum inter se ecclesiarum principes discrepent,' and p. 410.

[4] See the passages of Tertullian referred to, note 2.

[5] Augustin. *ap. Hieron. Op.* I. *Epist.* cxvi. The passage in Cyprian, to which Augustine appears to refer, is in *Epist.* lxxi. At the Council of Carthage too (held under Cyprian), 'Zosimus a Tharassa dixit: Revelatione facta veritatis cedat error veritati, quia et Petrus, qui prius circumcidebat, cessit Paulo veritatem praedicanti'; *Concil. Carthag.* lvi, Cypriani *Op.* p. 239, ed. Fell.

[6] Euseb. *H.E.* i. 12, referring to the 5th book of Clement's *Hypotyposeis*. The amount of support that this view obtained may be gathered from Hieron. *Op.* VII. p. 408 '*Sunt qui* Cepham...non putent Apostolum Petrum etc.,' Chrysost. *Op.* III. p. 374 πῶς οὖν τινὲς τὴν ζήτησιν ταύτην ἔλυσαν, Gregor. Magn. *in Ezech.* Lib. II. H. 6 'Sunt vero *nonnulli* qui etc.' Jerome, Chrysostom,

out condemnation. Even in modern times it has been revived[1], but has not been received with any favour.

(ii) Origen. 2. Origen started the theory[2] that the dispute between Peter and Paul was simulated; in other words, being of one mind in the matter, they got up this scene that St Paul might the more effectually condemn the Judaizers through the chief of the Apostles, who, acknowledging the justice of the rebuke, set them an example of submission. Thus he in fact substituted the much graver charge of dishonesty against both Apostles, in order to exculpate the one from the comparatively venial offence of moral cowardice and inconsistency. Nevertheless this view commended itself to a large number of subsequent writers, and for some time may be said to have reigned supreme[3]. It was enforced with much perverse ingenuity and

and Gregory all show from St Paul's context how untenable this view is. Claudius Altiss. (ad loc.) simply copies the words of Gregory, and his language must not be taken as evidence of the prevalence of the opinion in his time. Œcumenius however, or a commentator in the Œcumenian Catena, favours this view, which he incorrectly attributes to Eusebius. On the authority of Clement it became customary to insert the name Cephas in the lists of the seventy disciples, e.g. those ascribed to Hippolytus (ed. Fabricius, I app. p. 42) and to Dorotheus Tyrius (printed in Dindorf's *Chron. Pasch.* II. p. 120), and that of the *Chron. Pasch.* (I. p. 400, ed. Dind.).

Other attempts also were made in the same direction. In the Armenian Calendar Cephas is called a disciple of St Paul: Sept. 25, 'Apollo et Cephae discipulorum Pauli,' Assemann. *Bibl. Orient.* III. p. 648. In the Apostolic Constitutions of the Egyptian Church he is represented as one of the Twelve, but distinguished from Peter (ed. Tattam, p. 2).

[1] By the Jesuit Harduin. See Harduini *Op. Sel.* (Amst. 1709) p. 920. The treatise is entitled 'Cepham a Paulo reprehensum Petrum non esse,' a strange specimen of criticism. It provoked replies from Boileau, *Disquisit. Theolog. in Galat.* ii. 10, Paris, 1713; Calmet, *Dissert.* III. p. 519, Paris, 1720; Deyling, *Obs. Sacr.* II. p. 520, Lips. 1737. The first of these I have not seen: the last two might be called satisfactory, if there were any case on the opposite side.

[2] Hieron. *Epist.* cxii (I. p. 740) 'Hanc explanationem quam primus Origenes in decimo Stromateon libro ubi epistolam Pauli ad Galatas interpretatur, et caeteri deinceps interpretes sunt secuti, etc.' In an extant work however (*c. Cels.* ii. 1), where Origen alludes to the incident, there is no trace of this interpretation.

[3] See Hieron. l. c. In this letter, addressed to Augustine, he defends himself by appealing to the authority of previous writers. He also quotes the passage in his preface to the Galatians, where he mentions that in writing his commentary he has made use, besides Origen, of Didymus of Alexandria, of the Laodicene (i.e. Apollinaris), of one Alexander, 'an ancient heretic' (see Cave, *Hist. Lit.* I. p. 101), of Eusebius of Emesa, and of Theodore of Heraclea. Augustine in reply (Hieron. Op. *Epist.* cxvi, p. 775) understands him to say that the view of Origen was held by all these writers, whom he confesses himself never to have read. In the case of Jerome's master Didymus however this seems questionable; for in two passages in his extant works he speaks of St Peter's conduct as an instance of human infirmity, *de Trin.* ii. 13, p. 168, iii. 19, p. 387. Another of Jerome's masters also, Gregory Nazianzen, had taken the honest view, attributing St Peter's error however not to cowardice but to mistaken policy, *Carm.* II. p. 522, ed. Caillau, *ὡς συντράπεζος οὐ καλῶς ἦν ἔθνεσιν, εἰ καὶ τόδ' ᾤετ' ὠφελήσειν τὸν λόγον.* Unless his text is here mutilated, Gregory's memory has failed

misapplied eloquence by Chrysostom in his exposition of this epistle, and in a separate homily devoted specially to the subject[1]. And about the same time that these discourses were delivered, it found another independent and equally able advocate in Jerome, who maintained it in his commentary on the Galatians with characteristic vigour. The advocacy of Jerome gave rise to a controversy between the two great Latin fathers, which became famous in the history of the Church[2]. Augustine wrote to remonstrate with Jerome. To admit that the two leading Apostles conspired to act a lie, he represented, was in fact to undermine the whole authority of Scripture. He therefore entreated Jerome, like Stesichorus of old, to sing a palinode, adding that the truth of Christendom is incomparably more beautiful than the Helen of Greece, for offending whom the heathen poet had been struck blind[3]. Jerome replied by another classical allusion. Let Augustine beware of provoking a contest, so he hinted, in which the crushing blows of aged Entellus, if once provoked, might prove more than a match for the youth and nimbleness of Dares[4]. In the correspondence which ensued Augustine had much the best of his adversary both in argument and in temper. It closes with a letter from Augustine in which he exposes Jerome's subterfuges and demolishes his appeal to authority[5]. The glory of Augustine's victory however is somewhat tarnished by a feeble attack made at the same time on those noble labours in Biblical criticism which have earned for Jerome the gratitude of after ages.

Chrysostom.

Controversy of Jerome and Augustine.

To this letter of Augustine Jerome seems to have made no reply. His pride had been deeply wounded by the successful assaults of a younger rival, as he regarded Augustine: and a direct confession of wrong could only be expected from a nature more frank and chivalrous than Jerome's. But at a later date he tacitly adopted Augustine's view, and whether from accident or design, in the same writing, though on a different topic, made honourable mention of his former opponent[6]. With this sequel the whole

him as to the particular act which called forth St Paul's rebuke.

Still there was doubtless a vast array of authorities on Jerome's side. He challenges Augustine to produce a single writer in his favour. Augustine in reply can only name Cyprian and Ambrose.

[1] The Latin title of this homily is 'In illud, in faciem Petro restiti' (III. p. 362, ed. Ben.). The opinion of Chrysostom is alluded to by Jerome, *Epist.* cxii, and by Augustine in reply, Hieron. Op. *Epist.* cxvi.

[2] An account of this controversy is given in Möhler, *Gesammelte Schriften*, p. 1 sq. For a summary of the points of dispute, see the commentary of Thomas Aquinas on this epistle. The correspondence itself may be found in any edition of the works either of Jerome or of Augustine. The references here given are to Vallarsi's edition of Jerome. Owing to the extraordinary delay and consequent complication in the correspondence, it is not easy to determine the order of the letters, and in this respect none of the editions which I have consulted seem altogether satisfactory. Augustine discusses the passage again more briefly, *de Mendacio*, § 8, VI. p. 424.

[3] Hieron. Op. I, *Ep.* lxvii.

[4] Ib. *Ep.* cii. See Augustine's reply, *Ep.* cx.

[5] Ib. *Ep.* cxvi.

[6] Hieron. *c. Pelag.* i. 22 (II. p. 718). This treatise (iii. 19, *ib.* p. 804) ends with an honourable mention of Augustine, who had written against the same heresy which Jerome is combating. It is just possible that Jerome, while

controversy, as well in the nature of the dispute itself, as in the courageous rebuke of the younger father and the humble penitence of the elder, has seemed to some to reflect the original dispute of the Apostles at Antioch, and thus to be a striking illustration of and comment on the text out of which it arose[1].

Later writers.

The great name of Augustine seems to have swayed later writers towards the reasonable view of the incident, and from this time forward the forced explanation of Origen finds but little support[2]. Theodore of Mopsuestia indeed, a contemporary of the two Latin fathers, does not pretend to arbitrate between their opinions, and perhaps not more than this was to be expected from the friend of Chrysostom. And by Greek commentators even of a later date the false interpretation is once and again revived[3]. But in the West the influence of Augustine was more powerful; and it is much to the credit of writers of the Latin Church, that even when directly interested in maintaining the supremacy of St Peter, they for the most part reject this perverted account of the passage, content to draw from it the higher lesson of the paramount claims of truth over respect for rank and office, and to dwell on St Peter's conduct as a noble example of humility in submitting to rebuke from an inferior in age and standing[4].

writing this, had in mind the tribute of respect paid to St Paul in 2 Pet. iii. 15. Other passages in which Jerome has been thought tacitly to surrender his former view are, *adv. Jovin.* i. 15 (II. p. 264), *c. Rufin.* iii. 2 (II. p. 532), *Comm. in Philem.* (VII. p. 755); but the inference is scarcely borne out by the passages themselves. Jerome's change of opinion did not escape Augustine, who alludes to it in a letter to Oceanus, August. *Epist.* clxxx (I. p. 634, ed. Ben.).

[1] e.g. Möhler *Gesamm. Schr.* p. 18.

[2] Primasius (circ. 550), commenting on this epistle, omits to notice the opinion of Origen and Jerome. Strangely enough the commentary of Theodoret (circ. 450) on those verses is wanting in the MSS. What view he took cannot with safety be gathered from the extant context. It might be inferred however from another passage of Theodoret, *in Ezech.* xlviii. 35 (II. p. 1046, ed. Schulze), that he gave a straightforward explanation of the incident. In the *Dial. de S. Trin.* i. 24, falsely ascribed to Athanasius (Athan. *Op.* II. p. 421, ed. Ben.), this is plainly the case, but the ground for attributing this work to Theodoret is very slender indeed; the probable author being Maximus monachus (circ. 650).

[3] It is maintained by one of the commentators in the Œcumenian Catena and by Theophylact. Both these writers would derive their opinions from Chrysostom rather than from Jerome.

[4] See especially Gregor. Magn. *in Ezech.* Lib. II. Hom. 6 'quatenus qui primus erat in apostolatus culmine, esset primus et in humilitate,' and Pope Agapetus, Baron. *Ann.* sub ann. 535: comp. Facundus x. 2 (Gallandi II. p. 772).

III. [1]Ὦ ἀνόητοι Γαλάται, τίς ὑμᾶς ἐβάσκανεν, οἷς κατ' ὀφθαλμοὺς Ἰησοῦς Χριστὸς προεγράφη ἐσταυρω-

III. 1. In the last paragraph of the foregoing chapter St Paul began by speaking of the incident at Antioch, but his thoughts have been working round gradually to the false teachers in Galatia, and have moulded his language accordingly. He is thus led to dwell on the direct antagonism to the Gospel involved in the conduct of the Judaizers, which tacitly assumes that a man may be justified by his own works. It is a practical denial of the efficacy of Christ's death. This thought is intolerable to him, and he bursts out into the indignant remonstrance with which this chapter opens.

'Christ's death in vain? O ye senseless Gauls, what bewitchment is this? I placarded Christ crucified before your eyes. You suffered them to wander from this gracious proclamation of your King. They rested on the withering eye of the sorcerer. They yielded to the fascination and were riveted there. And the life of your souls has been drained out of you by that envious gaze.'

ἐβάσκανεν] '*fascinated you.*' St Paul's metaphor is derived from the popular belief in the power of the evil eye. Comp. Ignat. *Rom.* § 3 οὐδέποτε ἐβασκάνατε οὐδένα (or οὐδενί), Wisd. iv. 12 βασκανία γὰρ φαυλότητος ἀμαυροῖ τὰ καλά, and see especially the discussion in Plutarch, *Symp.* v. 7, p. 680 C περὶ τῶν καταβασκαίνειν λεγομένων καὶ βάσκανον ἔχειν ὀφθαλμὸν ἐμπεσόντος λόγου κ.τ.λ. If the derivation of βασκαίνειν now generally adopted (see Benfey *Wurzel.* II. p. 104), from βάζω, βάσκω (φάσκω), be correct, the word originally referred to witchery by spells or incantations ('mala fascinare lingua'); but as it occurs in actual use, it denotes the blighting influence of the evil eye, of which meaning indeed the popular but now exploded derivation (διὰ φαέων, καίνουσαν Tzetz.) is an evidence. See Bacon's *Essays* ix. This belief is not confined to the East or to ancient times, but is common in some countries of Europe even now. In parts of Italy the power of the 'occhio cattivo' or 'jettatura' is said to be a deeply rooted popular superstition. On its wide prevalence see the references in Winer's *Realwörterb.* s. v. *Zauberei*, and in an article by O. Jahn, *über den Aberglauben des bösen Blicks etc.* in the *Verhandl. der Sächs. Gesellsch.* 1855, p. 31. The word βασκαίνειν then in this passage involves two ideas; (1) The baleful influence on the recipient, and (2) The envious spirit of the agent. This latter idea is very prominent in the Hebrew רע עין ('envious' or 'covetous,' e.g. Prov. xxiii. 6, Tobit iv. 16, Ecclus. xiv. 10, and compare the ὀφθαλμὸς πονηρὸς of the Gospels); and in the Latin *invideo* it has swallowed up every other meaning. The false teachers envy the Galatians this liberty in Christ, have an interest in subjecting them again to bondage: see iv. 17, vi. 12, and 2 Cor. xi. 20. This idea however is subordinate to the other, for where βασκαίνειν signifies directly 'to envy,' it generally takes a dative like the Latin 'invideo': see Lobeck *Phryn.* p. 463. Jerome besides sees in the metaphor here an allusion to the spiritual 'infancy' of the Galatians. It is true indeed that children were regarded as most susceptible of βασκανία (διότι πολλὴν ἔχουσιν εὐπάθειαν καὶ τρόπον τῆς φύσεως, Alex. Aphrod. *Probl. Phys.* ii. 53: see also the passages in Jahn, p. 39), and such an allusion would be very significant here; but the metaphor must not be overcharged.

ἐβάσκανεν (for which some copies read ἐβάσκηνεν) is probably the first aorist with ᾱ; see Ignat. l. c. On

μένος; ²τοῦτο μόνον θέλω μαθεῖν ἀφ' ὑμῶν, ἐξ ἔργων νόμου τὸ πνεῦμα ἐλάβετε ἢ ἐξ ἀκοῆς πίστεως;

forms in η and α, see Buttmann *Ausf. Sprachl.* § 101. 4, A. Buttmann p. 35, and Lobeck *Phryn.* p. 25, *Paral.* p. 22.

The words τῇ ἀληθείᾳ μὴ πείθεσθαι of the received text have no place here, but are added from v. 7.

οἷς κατ' ὀφθαλμούς] '*before whose eyes*': comp. Arist. *Ran.* 626 ἵνα σοὶ κατ' ὀφθαλμοὺς λέγῃ. This expression is slightly stronger than πρὸ ὀφθαλμῶν, as bringing out the idea of a *confronting*.

As the blighting influence passed from the eye of the bewitcher, so also was the eye of the recipient the most direct channel of communication: see esp. Alexand. Aphrod. *Probl. Phys.* ii. 53 ὥσπερ ἰώδη τινὰ καὶ φθοροποιὸν ἀκτῖνα ἐξιοῦσιν ἀπὸ τῆς κόρης αὐτῶν καὶ αὕτη εἰσιοῦσα διὰ τῶν ὀφθαλμῶν τοῦ φθονουμένου τρέψει τὴν ψυχὴν καὶ τὴν φύσιν κ.τ.λ., Heliod. *Æth.* iii. 7 διὰ τῶν ὀφθαλμῶν τὰ πάθη ταῖς ψυχαῖς εἰστοξεύονται (these references I owe to Jahn, p. 33); and comp. Ecclus. xviii. 18 δόσις βασκάνου ἐκτήκει ὀφθαλμούς, xiv. 8, *Test. xii Patr.* Is. 4. To let the eye rest on the sorcerer therefore was to yield to the fascination. This the Galatians had done; 'So deeply had they drunken in That look, those shrunken serpent eyes, That all their features were resigned To this sole image in their mind.'

προεγράφη] '*was posted up, placarded.*' The verb προγράφειν is capable of two meanings; (1) 'To write beforehand,' as Rom. xv. 4 ὅσα γὰρ προεγράφη εἰς τὴν ἡμετέραν διδασκαλίαν ἐγράφη. This sense however is excluded here, as the words κατ' ὀφθαλμοὺς forbid the supposition that the Apostle is here speaking of the *predictions* of the Old Testament, even if such a sense were otherwise likely. (2) 'To write up in public, to placard.' It is the common word to describe all public notices or proclamations, e.g. Arist. *Av.* 450 ὅ τι ἂν προγράφωμεν ἐν τοῖς πινακίοις: comp. Justin *Apol.* ii. p. 52 B ἐὰν δὲ ὑμεῖς τοῦτο προγράψητε, ἡμεῖς τοῖς πᾶσι φανερὸν ποιήσομεν. These would sometimes be notices of a trial or condemnation; comp. Jude 4 οἱ πάλαι προγεγραμμένοι εἰς τοῦτο τὸ κρίμα, with Demosth. p. 1151 τοὺς πρυτάνεις προγράφειν αὐτῷ τὴν κρίσιν ἐπὶ δύο ἡμέρας, Plut. *Camill.* 9 τῆς δίκης προγεγραμμένης: and this meaning is assigned to the word here by several ancient commentators. The context however seems to require rather the sense 'placarded, publicly announced as a magisterial edict or proclamation.' This placard ought to have kept their eyes from wandering, and so to have acted as a charm (βασκάνιον or προβασκάνιον, *Epist. Jer.* 69) against all Judaic sorceries. The compound verb προγράφειν seems never to be used of *painting*, as some take it here.

ἐν ὑμῖν is omitted after προεγράφη in deference to the best authorities. It is difficult however to account for its insertion in some early copies, unless it crept in from ver. 5. If retained, it ought probably to be regarded as a redundant expression enforcing the idea of οἷς κατ' ὀφθαλμούς, and to be taken with προεγράφη.

2, 3, 4. 'I have only one question to ask you. The gifts of the Spirit which ye have received, to what do ye owe them? To works performed in bondage to law, or to the willing hearing that comes of faith? What monstrous folly is this then! Will you so violate the divine order of progress? After taking your earliest lessons in the *Spirit*, do you look to attaining perfection through the *flesh?* To what purpose then did ye suffer persecution from these carnal teachers of the law? Will ye now

[3]οὕτως ἀνόητοί ἐστε; ἐναρξάμενοι πνεύματι νῦν σαρκὶ ἐπιτελεῖσθε; [4]τοσαῦτα ἐπάθετε εἰκῇ; εἴ γε

stultify your past sufferings? I cannot believe that ye will.'

2. ἀκοῆς] in itself may mean either 'a hearing' or 'a report.' For the latter sense see Rom. x. 16, quoted from the LXX of Is. liii. 1. The former meaning however is more probable here, as presenting a better contrast to ἔργων, which requires some word expressing the part taken by the Galatians themselves: comp. 1 Thess. ii. 13.

πίστεως] '*which comes of faith*,' the subjective genitive. The parallelism of Rom. x. 17, ἄρα ἡ πίστις ἐξ ἀκοῆς, ἡ δὲ ἀκοὴ διὰ ῥήματος, is only apparent. A true parallel is the phrase ὑπακοὴ πίστεως, Rom. i. 5, xvi. 26. At all events πίστεως cannot be considered equivalent to τῆς πίστεως (see on i. 23), taken as an objective genitive, with the sense 'listening to the doctrines of *the* faith.'

3. οὕτως] refers to what follows: 'How senseless to reverse the natural order of things!'

ἐναρξάμενοι ἐπιτελεῖσθε] These words occur together 2 Cor. viii. 6, Phil. i. 6. Both of them, the former especially, are employed of religious ceremonials, and it is possible that the idea of a sacrifice may underlie their use here. For ἐνάρχεσθαι of the initiatory rites see Pollux viii. 83, and comp. e.g. Eur. *Iph. Aul.* 1471; for ἐπιτελεῖν Herod. ii. 63 (θυσίας, εὐχωλάς), iv. 186 (νηστείας καὶ ὁρτάς).

ἐπιτελεῖσθε is perhaps the middle voice rather than the passive, as in Clem. Rom. § 55 πολλαὶ γυναῖκες ἐνδυναμωθεῖσαι...ἐπετελέσαντο πολλὰ ἀνδρεῖα, and frequently in classical writers, e.g. Plat. *Phil.* 27 C κάλλιον ἂν καὶ τὴν κρίσιν ἐπιτελεσαίμεθα. A comparison of the parallel passages 2 Cor. viii. 6, Phil. i. 6, seems to point to a transitive verb. On the other hand the middle voice is not found elsewhere in the LXX or New Testament.

4. τοσαῦτα ἐπάθετε εἰκῇ;] '*did ye suffer so much in vain?*', referring to the persecutions endured by them. For similar appeals to sufferings undergone see Gal. v. 11, 1 Cor. xv. 32, and comp. 1 Thess. ii. 14. The history indeed says nothing of persecutions in Galatia, but then it is equally silent on all that relates to the condition of the Galatian Churches: and while the converts to the faith in Pisidia and Lycaonia on the one side (Acts xiv. 2, 5, 19, 22), and in proconsular Asia on the other (2 Cor. i. 8, Acts xix. 23 sq.), were exposed to suffering, it is improbable that the Galatians alone should have escaped. If we suppose, as is most likely, that the Jews were the chief instigators in these persecutions, St Paul's appeal becomes doubly significant.

On the other hand, ἐπάθετε has been interpreted in a good sense, as if referring to the spiritual blessings of the Galatians: but πάσχειν seems never to be so used in the New Testament; and indeed such a rendering would be harsh anywhere, unless the sense were clearly defined by the context, as it is for instance in Jos. *Ant.* iii. 15. 1 τὸν θεὸν ὑπομνῆσαι μὲν ὅσα παθόντες ἐξ αὐτοῦ καὶ πηλίκων εὐεργεσιῶν μεταλαβόντες κ.τ.λ.

εἰκῇ] '*in vain.*' 'You despise that liberty in Christ for which you then suffered; you listen to those teachers, whom you then resisted even to persecution.'

εἴ γε καὶ εἰκῇ] '*if it be really in vain.*' It is hard to believe this; the Apostle hopes better things of his converts. Εἴ γε leaves a loophole for doubt, and καὶ widens this, implying an unwillingness to believe on the part of the speaker. Hermann's distinction (*ad Viger.* p. 834) that εἴγε assumes the truth of a proposition while εἴπερ leaves it doubtful, requires modifying

καὶ εἰκῇ. 5ὁ οὖν ἐπιχορηγῶν ὑμῖν τὸ πνεῦμα καὶ ἐνεργῶν δυνάμεις ἐν ὑμῖν, ἐξ ἔργων νόμου ἢ ἐξ ἀκοῆς
πίστεως; 6καθὼς Ἀβραὰμ ἐπίστευσεν τῷ Θεῷ καὶ
ἐλογίσθη αὐτῷ εἰς δικαιοσύνην. 7γινώσκετε ἄρα

before it is applied to the New Testament, where εἴπερ is, if anything, more directly affirmative than εἴγε. The alternative rendering, 'If it is only in vain and not worse than in vain,' seems harsh and improbable.

5. The question asked in ver. 2 involved the contrast of faith and works. This contrast suggests two other thoughts; (1) The violation of the law of progress committed by the Galatians (ver. 3); (2) Their folly in stultifying their former sufferings (ver. 4). The question has meanwhile been lost sight of. It is now resumed and the particle οὖν marks its resumption; 'Well then, as I said, etc.'

ὁ ἐπιχορηγῶν] '*He that supplieth bountifully*'; comp. Phil. i. 19 ἐπιχορηγίας τοῦ πνεύματος Ἰησοῦ Χριστοῦ. Even the simple word implies more or less of *liberality*, and the compound ἐπιχορηγεῖν expresses this idea more strongly. See 2 Pet. i. 5 ἐπιχορηγήσατε ἐν τῇ πίστει ὑμῶν τὴν ἀρετήν, and compare the use of the substantive ἐπιχορήγημα in Athen. iv. p. 140 c ἐπάϊκλα μὲν λέγεται ταῦτα, ὄντα οἷον ἐπιχορηγήματα τοῦ συντεταγμένου τοῖς φειδίταις ἀΐκλου, i.e. the luxuries, the superfluities of the meal.

ἐνεργῶν δυνάμεις ἐν ὑμῖν] Comp. 1 Cor. xii. 10 ἐνεργήματα δυνάμεων (with vv. 28, 29), Matt. xiv. 2 αἱ δυνάμεις ἐνεργοῦσιν ἐν αὐτῷ (comp. Mark vi. 14). These passages favour the sense 'worketh miraculous power *in* you,' rather than 'worketh miracles *among* you'; and this meaning also accords better with the context: comp. 1 Cor. xii. 6 καὶ ὁ αὐτὸς Θεὸς ὁ ἐνεργῶν τὰ πάντα ἐν πᾶσιν. What was the exact nature of these 'powers,' whether they were exerted over the physical or the moral world, it is impossible to determine. The limitations implied in 1 Cor. xii. 10, and the general use of δυνάμεις, point rather to the former. It is important to notice how here, as in the Epistle to the Corinthians, St Paul assumes the possession of these extraordinary powers by his converts as an acknowledged fact.

The verb which disappears in the ellipsis is to be supplied from the foregoing participles; 'does He do so from works etc.,' as in 2 Cor. iii. 11, Rom. xii. 7 sq.

6. The following passage vv. 6—9 was omitted in Marcion's recension of the epistle, as repugnant to his leading principle of the antagonism between the Old and New Testaments: see Tertull. *adv. Marc.* v. 3 'ostenditur quid supra haeretica industria eraserit, mentionem scilicet Abrahae,' and Hieron. *ad loc.*

καθώς] The answer to the question asked in the former verse is assumed, 'Surely of faith: and so it was with Abraham.' Καθώς, though not a good Attic word, is common in later Greek; see Lobeck *Phryn.* p. 425.

Ἀβραὰμ ἐπίστευσεν κ.τ.λ.] from the LXX of Gen. xv. 6. The Hebrew has in the second clause ויחשבה לו צדקה 'and (He) imputed it to him (for) righteousness.' It is quoted as in the LXX also in Rom. iv. 3, James ii. 23, Clem. Rom. § 10, Justin *Dial. c. Tryph.* § 119. The passage is cited also in Barnab. § 13, but too loosely and with too obvious an infusion of St Paul's language to allow of any inference as to the text used by the writer.

On the use made of this passage by Jewish writers and on the faith of Abraham see p. 158 sq.

ὅτι οἱ ἐκ πίστεως, οὗτοι υἱοί εἰσιν Ἀβραάμ. 8προϊ-
δοῦσα δὲ ἡ γραφὴ ὅτι ἐκ πίστεως δικαιοῖ τὰ ἔθνη ὁ
Θεός, προευηγγελίσατο τῷ Ἀβραὰμ ὅτι ἐνευλογηθήσονται ἐν σοὶ πάντα τὰ ἔθνη. 9ὥστε οἱ ἐκ
πίστεως εὐλογοῦνται σὺν τῷ πιστῷ Ἀβραάμ. 10ὅσοι

7. οὗτοί εἰσιν υἱοὶ Ἀβραάμ

7. The promise to Abraham, which in the passage of Genesis introduces the words just quoted, is the link of connexion with what follows.

7, 8, 9. 'An offspring, countless as the stars, was promised to Abraham. Abraham believed, and his faith was accepted as righteousness. Who then are these promised sons of Abraham? Those surely who inherit Abraham's faith. Hence the declaration of the scripture that all the *Gentiles* should be blessed in him. These are the words of foresight discerning that God justifies the Gentiles by *faith;* for so only could they be blessed in Abraham. We conclude therefore that the faithful and the faithful alone share the blessing with him.'

γινώσκετε] '*ye perceive*,' the indicative rather than the imperative. The former mood is perhaps more suited to the argumentative character of the sentence generally, as well as to the special argumentative particle ἄρα, and possibly also to the meaning of the verb γινώσκειν ('to perceive' rather than 'to know'; see the note iv. 8, 9); comp. 1 John ii. 29 ἐὰν εἰδῆτε ὅτι δίκαιός ἐστιν, γινώσκετε ὅτι πᾶς ὁ ποιῶν τὴν δικαιοσύνην ἐξ αὐτοῦ γεγέννηται. On the other hand, for the imperative see Heb. xiii. 23.

οἱ ἐκ πίστεως] 'they whose starting-point, whose fundamental principle is faith.' Comp. Rom. ii. 8 οἱ ἐξ ἐριθείας, Rom. iv. 14 οἱ ἐκ νόμου.

8. ἡ γραφή] '*the scripture*' personified. This instance stands by itself in the New Testament, the personification elsewhere not going beyond λέγει or εἶπεν, or such expressions as συνέκλεισεν, ver. 22. The attributing 'sight' to the sacred writings is however found in a not uncommon Jewish formula of reference מה ראה, 'Quid vidit?' see Schöttgen here. On the meaning of γραφή, 'a passage of Scripture,' see the note iii. 22.

δικαιοῖ] The tense denotes the certainty of God's dealings, the sure accomplishment of His purpose, as if it were actually present: see on 1 Thess. v. 2, and Winer § xi. 2, p. 280.

προευηγγελίσατο] The promise to Abraham was an *anticipation of the Gospel*, not only as announcing the Messiah, but also as involving the doctrine of righteousness by faith.

ἐνευλογηθήσονται κ.τ.λ.] A fusion of the two passages, Gen. xii. 3 καὶ [ἐν]ευλογηθήσονται ἐν σοὶ πᾶσαι αἱ φυλαὶ τῆς γῆς, and Gen. xviii. 18 καὶ ἐνευλογηθήσονται ἐν αὐτῷ (Ἀβραὰμ) πάντα τὰ ἔθνη τῆς γῆς, in both of which the LXX agrees with the Hebrew. Comp. Clem. Rom. § 10.

ἐν σοί] '*in thee*,' as their spiritual progenitor.

10, 11, 12. Having shewn by *positive* proof that justification is of faith, he strengthens his position by the *negative* argument derived from the impossibility of maintaining its opposite, justification by law. This negative argument is twofold: *First*, It is impossible to fulfil the requirements of the law, and the non-fulfilment lays us under a curse (ver. 10): *Secondly*, Supposing the fulfilment possible, still the spirit of the law is antagonistic to faith, which is else-

γὰρ ἐξ ἔργων νόμου εἰσίν, ὑπὸ κατάραν εἰσίν. γέγραπται γὰρ ὅτι ἐπικατάρατος πᾶς, ὃς οὐκ ἐμμένει πᾶσιν τοῖς γεγραμμένοις ἐν τῷ βιβλίῳ τοῦ νόμου, τοῦ ποιῆσαι αὐτά. 11 ὅτι δὲ ἐν νόμῳ οὐδεὶς δικαιοῦται παρὰ τῷ Θεῷ δῆλον, ὅτι ὁ δίκαιος

where spoken of as the source of life (vv. 11, 12).

10, 11. 'On the other hand all who depend on works of law are under a curse. This the Scripture itself declares. It utters an anathema against all who fail to fulfil every single ordinance contained in the book of the law. Again the same truth, that the law does not justify in the sight of God, appears from another Scripture which declares that the just shall live by faith.'

10. ὅσοι ἐξ ἔργων νόμου εἰσίν] '*those who are of works of law*,' whose character is founded on works of law.

ἐπικατάρατος κ.τ.λ.] A quotation from Deut. xxvii. 26. The passage is the closing sentence of the curses pronounced on Mount Ebal, and as it were the summary of the whole. The words run in the LXX, ἐπικατάρατος πᾶς ἄνθρωπος ὃς οὐκ ἐμμένει ἐν πᾶσιν τοῖς λόγοις τοῦ νόμου τούτου τοῦ ποιῆσαι αὐτούς. For τοῖς λόγοις τοῦ νόμου τούτου a slight modification is introduced by St Paul, that the sentence may explain itself. The words πᾶς, πᾶσιν, are absent in the Hebrew, though the former is found in the Peshito, and the latter in the Samar. Pentat. Jerome in this passage, referring to the Samaritan reading, attributes the omission to a wilful corruption of the text on the part of the Jews, 'ne viderentur esse sub maledicto.' The charge is of course unfounded, but it is an interesting notice of the state of the text in his day. Justin, *Dial.* § 95, p. 322 c, quotes the passage exactly in the words of St Paul, though differing from Hebrew, Greek, Syriac, and Samaritan texts, and applies it in the same way: see above, p. 60, and the note on ver. 13.

11. The same proposition proved in another way; δέ, 'Then again.'

ὁ δίκαιος κ.τ.λ.] From Habak. ii. 4, quoted also Rom. i. 17, Heb. x. 38. In the Hebrew the words run, 'Behold, his soul is uplifted (proud, stubborn), it is not right (calm, even); but the just man shall live by his steadfastness (fidelity), צדיק באמונתו יחיה.' What is the correct rendering of the first clause, whether it refers to the Chaldean invader or to the heedless Jew, may be questioned; but the second clause without doubt describes the attitude of the faithful Israelite in the season of danger. The LXX have ἐὰν ὑποστείληται, οὐκ εὐδοκεῖ ἡ ψυχή μου ἐν αὐτῷ, ὁ δὲ δίκαιός μου ἐκ πίστεως (or ἐκ πίστεώς μου) ζήσεται: see below, p. 156. The author of the Epistle to the Hebrews, who gives both clauses of the verse, though reversing the order, quotes from the LXX (see Bleek, *Heb.* l. c.).

It will thus be seen that in the first clause of the verse, the LXX, though it makes excellent sense, differs widely from the Hebrew. In the second clause again the Hebrew word אמונה is not directly 'faith,' meaning 'trust, belief,' but 'steadfastness, faithfulness.' The context however justifies πίστις, even in the sense 'trust,' as a paraphrastic rendering, and it was so translated by Symmachus, Aquila, and Theodotion, and in the other Greek versions. See p. 156, note 4. Targum Jon. has קושטהון, 'their truth.' In its original context the passage has reference to the temporal calamities inflicted by the Chaldean invasion. Here

ἐκ πίστεως ζήσεται· [12]ὁ δὲ νόμος οὐκ ἔστιν ἐκ πίστεως, ἀλλ' ὁ ποιήσας αὐτὰ ζήσεται ἐν αὐτοῖς. [13]Χριστὸς ἡμᾶς ἐξηγόρασεν ἐκ τῆς κατάρας τοῦ νόμου, γενόμενος ὑπὲρ ἡμῶν κατάρα, ὅτι γέγραπται ἐπι-

a spiritual meaning and general application are given to words referring primarily to special external incidents. Another portion of this same prophecy of Habakkuk (i. 5, comp. ii. 5) relating to the Chaldeans is similarly applied in a speech of St Paul, Acts xiii. 41, in which context (ver. 39, ἐν τούτῳ πᾶς ὁ πιστεύων δικαιοῦται) there is perhaps a tacit allusion to the words ὁ δίκαιος κ.τ.λ. quoted here.

12. 'Faith is not the starting-point of the law. The law does not take faith as its fundamental principle. On the other hand, it rigidly enforces the performance of all its enactments.'

ὁ ποιήσας κ.τ.λ.] Quoted from Lev. xviii. 5, substantially the same as in Heb., Syr., Samar. Pent., and LXX. The Targums define the meaning of 'living' by 'life eternal.' The αὐτὰ is explained by the words which in the original text precede the passage quoted, πάντα τὰ προστάγματά μου καὶ πάντα τὰ κρίματά μου, and with which St Paul assumes a familiarity in his readers.

13. 'Christ ransomed us from this curse pronounced by the law, Himself taking our place and becoming a curse for our sakes: for so says the Scripture, Cursed is every one that hangeth on the gibbet.'

ἡμᾶς] The Apostle is here thinking of the deliverance of himself and the Jewish race: see τὰ ἔθνη, ver. 14.

ἐξηγόρασεν] This verb has two meanings. (1) 'To redeem, ransom,' especially from slavery: this is its general signification: see the references in Dindorf's *Steph. Thes.* (2) 'To buy up,' as Polyb. iii. 42. 2, a somewhat exceptional sense. The former meaning is required here and iv. 5: the latter seems best suited to Ephes. v. 16, Col. iv. 5, τὸν καιρὸν ἐξαγοραζόμενοι.

κατάρα] as 2 Cor. v. 21 τὸν μὴ γνόντα ἁμαρτίαν ὑπὲρ ἡμῶν ἁμαρτίαν ἐποίησεν: comp. *Protev. Jac.* § 3, where Anna, complaining of her barrenness says, κατάρα ἐγενήθην ἐγὼ ἐνώπιον τῶν υἱῶν Ἰσραήλ. The expression is to be explained partly by the Hebrew idiom, the paucity of adjectives frequently occasioning the use of a substantive instead, but still more by the religious conception which it involves. The victim is regarded as bearing the sins of those for whom atonement is made. The curse is transferred from them to it. It becomes in a certain sense the impersonation of the sin and of the curse. This idea is very prominent in the scape-goat, Lev. xvi. 5 sq.: see especially the language of the Epistle of Barnabas, § 7, where the writer explains the scape-goat as a type of Christ. Compare also Lev. iv. 25 ἀπὸ τοῦ αἵματος τοῦ τῆς ἁμαρτίας, and iv. 29 ἐπιθήσει τὴν χεῖρα αὐτοῦ ἐπὶ τὴν κεφαλὴν τοῦ ἁμαρτήματος αὐτοῦ. In Hebrew חטאת is both a 'sin' and a 'sin-offering.' Counterparts to these types of the Great Sacrifice are found also among heathen nations, e.g. the Athenians, Arist. *Ran.* 733, Lysias *Andoc.* p. 108 φάρμακον ἀποπέμπειν καὶ ἀλιτηρίου ἀπαλλάττεσθαι, and especially the Egyptians, Herod. ii. 39 κεφαλῇ δὲ κείνῃ (i.e. of the victim) πολλὰ καταρησάμενοι φέρουσι...καταρέονται δὲ τάδε λέγοντες τῇσι κεφαλῇσι, εἴ τι μέλλοι ἢ σφίσι τοῖς θύουσι ἢ Αἰγύπτῳ τῇ συναπάσῃ κακὸν γενέσθαι, εἰς κεφαλὴν ταύτην τραπέσθαι.

γέγραπται] in Deut. xxi. 23, where the LXX runs κεκατηραμένος ὑπὸ Θεοῦ πᾶς κρεμάμενος ἐπὶ ξύλου. The passage

ΚΑΤΑΡΑΤΟΣ ΠΑΣ Ο ΚΡΕΜΑΜΕΝΟΣ ΕΠΙ ΞΥΛΟΥ, [14]ἵνα εἰς τὰ ἔθνη ἡ εὐλογία τοῦ Ἀβραὰμ γένηται ἐν Χριστῷ

14. ἐν Ἰησοῦ Χριστῷ.

is quoted by Justin, *Dial.* p. 323 c, exactly as by St Paul; see p. 60, and the note on ver. 10. Our Lord had died the death of the worst malefactors: He had undergone that punishment, which under the law betokened the curse of God. So far He had become *κατάρα*. But He was in no literal sense *κατάρατος ὑπὸ Θεοῦ*, and St Paul instinctively omits those words which do not strictly apply, and which, if added, would have required some qualification.

14. 'Thus the law, the great barrier which excluded the Gentiles, is done away in Christ. By its removal the Gentiles are put on a level with us Jews; and, so united, we and they alike receive the promise in the gift of the Spirit through our faith.' The sequence of thought here is exactly the same as in Ephes. ii. 14—18: see also Gal. iv. 5.

As regards the construction, either (1) The two clauses introduced by ἵνα are coordinate, as in 2 Cor. ix. 3, expressing the *coincidence in time* of the extension of the blessing to the Gentiles and the introduction of the dispensation of the Spirit; or (2) The second clause with ἵνα is attached to the first, expressing the *moral dependence* of the one on the other. The passage from the Ephesians already referred to favours the latter.

τὴν ἐπαγγελίαν κ.τ.λ.] '*we*, i.e. all the faithful, whether Jews or Gentiles, *may receive the promise*.' The divine promise in the New Testament is always ἐπαγγελία not ὑπόσχεσις, 'pollicitum' not 'promissum,' a gift graciously bestowed and not a pledge obtained by negotiation. Indeed the substantive ἐπαγγελία is scarcely ever used (Acts xxiii. 21 is an exception) of anything else but the divine promise. The phrase λαμβάνειν τὴν ἐπαγγελίαν is employed not of those to whom the promise is given, but of those to whom it is fulfilled; as Acts ii. 33, Heb. ix. 15. So also ἐπιτυγχάνειν τῆς ἐπαγγελίας Heb. vi. 15, περιμένειν τὴν ἐπαγγελίαν, Acts i. 4. With this use of ἐπαγγελία, compare that of ἐλπίς, πίστις, etc., for the object of faith, of hope, etc.

15—18. 'Brethren, let me draw an illustration from the common dealings of men. Even a human covenant duly confirmed is held sacred and inviolable. It cannot be set aside, it cannot be clogged with new conditions. Much more then a divine covenant. Now the promise of God was not given to Abraham alone, but to his seed. What is meant by 'his seed'? The form of expression denotes unity. It must have its fulfilment in some *one* person. This person is Christ. Thus it was unfulfilled when the law came. Between the giving of the promise then and the fulfilment of it the law intervened. And coming many hundred years after, it was plainly distinct from the promise, it did not interpret the terms of the promise. Thus the law cannot set aside the promise. Yet this would be done in effect, if the inheritance could only be obtained by obedience to the law; since the promise itself imposed no such condition.'

15. Ἀδελφοί] '*Brethren*.' There is a touch of tenderness in the appeal here, as if to make amends for the severity of the foregoing rebuke, iii. 1 sq.: comp. iv. 31, vi. 1.

κατὰ ἄνθρωπον λέγω] '*I speak after the manner of men*, I argue from the practice of men'; see Rom. iii. 5, 1 Cor. ix. 8, and Rom. vi. 19 ἀνθρώπινον λέγω. Comp. also 1 Cor. iii. 3

Ἰησοῦ, ἵνα τὴν ἐπαγγελίαν τοῦ πνεύματος λάβωμεν διὰ τῆς πίστεως.

15 Ἀδελφοί, κατὰ ἄνθρωπον λέγω. ὅμως ἀνθρώπου κεκυρωμένην διαθήκην οὐδεὶς ἀθετεῖ ἢ ἐπιδιατάσσεται.

κατὰ ἄνθρωπον περιπατεῖτε, Gal. i. 11, 1 Cor. xv. 32 εἰ κατὰ ἄνθρωπον ἐθηριομάχησα κ.τ.λ., 'If from nothing more than worldly motives I fought with beasts etc.,' where the false interpretation of κατὰ ἄνθρωπον, 'metaphorically,' has been supported by the mistaken analogy of the passage in our text. For the usage of κατὰ ἄνθρωπον in profane authors see the quotations in Wetstein on Rom. iii. 5.

ὅμως ἀνθρώπου] The force is well given in the A. V., 'though it be but a man's covenant,' i.e. καίπερ ἀνθρώπου οὖσαν, ὅμως κ.τ.λ.; comp. 1 Cor. xiv. 7 ὅμως τὰ ἄψυχα φωνὴν δίδοντα, Pausan. i. 28. 1 Κύλωνα...ἀνέθεσαν τυραννίδα ὅμως βουλεύσαντα. In classical writers this displacement of ὅμως, so as to connect it with the word or clause to which it applies, appears to occur chiefly, if not solely, with participles, and not as here and 1 Cor. xiv. 7.

The argument is here an *a fortiori* argument, as those of our Lord drawn from the affection of a human father (Luke xi. 11 sq) and from the compliance of a human judge (Luke xviii. 1 sq). See esp. Heb. vi. 16. The *a fortiori* character of the reasoning however is dismissed in the single word ὅμως, except so far as it is picked up again in τοῦ Θεοῦ (ver. 17), and does not reappear, as some have thought, in ὅς ἐστιν Χριστός.

διαθήκην] '*a covenant*.' This word (frequently in the plural διαθῆκαι) in classical writers almost always signifies 'a will, a testament.' There are some few exceptions, however, e.g. Arist. *Av.* 439 ἢν μὴ διάθωνταί γ' οἵδε διαθήκην ἐμοί. On the other hand in the LXX it is as universally used of a covenant (most frequently as a translation of בְּרִית), whether as a stipulation between two parties (συνθήκη, 'a covenant' in the strict sense) or as an engagement on the part of one. Nor in the New Testament is it ever found in any other sense, with one exception. Even in this exceptional case, Heb. ix. 15—17, the sacred writer starts from the sense of a 'covenant,' and glides into that of a 'testament,' to which he is led by two points of analogy, (1) the *inheritance* conferred by the covenant, and (2) the *death* of the person making it. 'The disposition in this case,' he says in effect, 'was a testamentary disposition, a will.' In the passage before us, on the other hand, the mere mention of the inheritance (ver. 18) is not sufficient to establish the sense 'a testament,' which is ill suited to the context: comp. Justin, *Dial. c. Tryph.* § 11, p. 228 B. Owing partly to the passage in the Epistle to the Hebrews and partly to the influence of the Latin version, which ordinarily rendered the word by 'testamentum' (as here), the idea of a *testament* connected itself inseparably with διαθήκη. As a name for the sacred books, 'testamentum' had not firmly established itself at the close of the second century, and Tertullian frequently uses 'instrumentum' instead; see esp. *adv. Marc.* iv. 1, and comp. Kaye's *Tertullian* p. 299. The LXX translators and the New Testament writers probably preferred διαθήκη to συνθήκη when speaking of the divine dispensation, because the former term, like ἐπαγγελία, better expresses the *free grace* of God. The later Greek translators frequently substituted συνθήκη, where the LXX has διαθήκη, sometimes perhaps not without a polemical aim.

16 τῷ δὲ Ἀβραὰμ ἐρρέθησαν αἱ ἐπαγγελίαι, καὶ τῷ σπέρματι αὐτοῦ. οὐ λέγει καὶ τοῖς σπέρμασιν ὡς

ἀθετεῖ] Comp. Philo *Fragm.* II. p. 675 M ἀλλὰ ὅτι ἡ διαθήκη ἀθετεῖται.

ἐπιδιατάσσεται] '*adds fresh clauses.*' Virtually the doctrine of the Judaizers was the annulling of the promise (ἀθέτησις); apparently it was but the imposing new conditions (ἐπιδιάταξις). On either shewing it was a violation of the covenant. The meaning of ἐπιδιατάσσεσθαι is partially illustrated by ἐπιδιαθήκη, which signifies 'a second will,' Joseph. *B. J.* ii. 2. 3 ἀξιῶν τῆς ἐπιδιαθήκης τὴν διαθήκην εἶναι κυριωτέραν, and § 6, *Ant.* xvii. 9. 4.

16. ἐρρέθησαν] For the form see Lobeck *Phryn.* p. 447, Buttmann *Ausf. Sprachl.* II. p. 165.

ἐπαγγελίαι] The plural, for the promise was several times repeated to Abraham: comp. Rom. ix. 4, and esp. Clem. Rom. § 10. A question has been raised as to the particular passage to which St Paul refers. In answering this question it should be observed, (1) That the words must be spoken to Abraham himself, and not to one of the later patriarchs; (2) That καὶ must be part of the quotation. These considerations restrict the reference to Gen. xiii. 15, xvii. 8, either of which passages satisfies these conditions. It is true that in both alike the inheritance spoken of refers primarily to the possession of the land of Canaan, but the spiritual application here is only in accordance with the general analogy of New Testament interpretation. See above on ver. 11.

οὐ λέγει] seems to be used impersonally, like the Attic φησὶ in quoting legal documents, the nominative being lost sight of. If so, we need not enquire whether ὁ Θεὸς or ἡ γραφὴ is to be understood. Comp. λέγει, Rom. xv. 10, Ephes. iv. 8, v. 14; and φησίν, 1 Cor. vi. 16, 2 Cor. x. 10 (v. l.).

καὶ τοῖς σπέρμασιν κ.τ.λ.] This comment of St Paul has given rise to much discussion. It has been urged that the stress of the argument rests on a grammatical error; that as the plural of זרע (the word here rendered σπέρμα) is only used to signify 'grain' or 'crops,' e.g. 1 Sam. viii. 15, the sacred writer could not under any circumstances have said 'seeds as of many.' Nor is it a complete answer to this objection that the same word in Chaldee is several times used in the plural in the sense which it has here; Gen. x. 18, Josh. vii. 14, Jer. xxxiii. 34. But the very expression in St Paul, which starts the objection, supplies the answer also. It is quite as unnatural to use the Greek σπέρματα with this meaning, as to use the Hebrew זרעים. No doubt by a forced and exceptional usage σπέρματα might be so employed, as in Plato *Legg.* ix. 853 C ἄνθρωποί τε καὶ ἀνθρώπων σπέρμασι νομοθετοῦμεν, 4 Macc. § 17 ὦ τῶν Ἀβραμιαίων σπερμάτων ἀπόγονοι παῖδες Ἰσραηλῖται, but so might the corresponding word in almost any language. This fact points to St Paul's meaning. He is not laying stress on the particular word used, but on the fact that a singular noun of some kind, a collective term, is employed, where τὰ τέκνα or οἱ ἀπόγονοι for instance might have been substituted. Avoiding the technical terms of grammar, he could not express his meaning more simply than by the opposition, 'not to thy *seeds*, but to thy *seed*.' A plural substantive would be inconsistent with the interpretation given; the singular collective noun, if it admits of plurality (as it is interpreted by St Paul himself, Rom. iv. 18, ix. 7), at the same time involves the idea of unity.

The question therefore is no longer one of grammatical accuracy, but of theological interpretation. Is this a

ἐπὶ πολλῶν, ἀλλ' ὡς ἐφ' ἑνὸς ΚΑΙ ΤΩ͂Ι CΠΕΡΜΑΤΙ COY, ὅς ἐστιν Χριστός. [17]τοῦτο δὲ λέγω· διαθήκην προκεκυρωμένην ὑπὸ τοῦ Θεοῦ ὁ μετὰ τετρακόσια καὶ

legitimate sense to assign to the seed of Abraham? Doubtless by the seed of Abraham was meant in the first instance the Jewish people, as by the inheritance was meant the land of Canaan; but in accordance with the analogy of Old Testament types and symbols, the term involves two secondary meanings. *First;* With a true spiritual instinct, though the conception embodied itself at times in strangely grotesque and artificial forms, even the rabbinical writers saw that 'the Christ' was the true seed of Abraham. In Him the race was summed up, as it were. In Him it fulfilled its purpose and became a blessing to the whole earth. Without Him its separate existence as a peculiar people had no meaning. Thus He was not only the representative, but the embodiment of the race. In this way the people of Israel is the type of Christ; and in the New Testament parallels are sought in the career of the one to the life of the other. (See especially the application of Hosea xi. 1 to our Lord in Matt. ii. 15.) In this sense St Paul used the 'seed of Abraham' here. But *Secondly;* According to the analogy of interpretation of the Old Testament in the New, the spiritual takes the place of the natural; the Israel after the flesh becomes the Israel after the spirit; the Jewish nation denotes the Christian Church. So St Paul interprets the seed of Abraham, Rom. iv. 18, ix. 7, and above, ver. 7.

These two interpretations are not opposed to each other; they are not independent of each other. Without Christ the Christian people have no existence. He is the source of their spiritual life. They are one in Him. By this link St Paul at the close of the chapter (vv. 28, 29) connects together the two senses of the 'seed of Abraham,' dwelling once more on the unity of the seed: 'Ye are all *one man* in Christ; and if ye *are part of Christ,* then ye are *Abraham's seed* and heirs according to promise.' See especially the remarks of Tholuck, *Das Alte Test. im Neuen Test.* p. 44 sq.

ἐπὶ πολλῶν] See Winer § xlvii. p. 393.

ὅς ἐστιν Χριστός] For the attraction see Winer § xxiv. p. 206 sq.

17. τοῦτο δὲ λέγω] 'Now what I mean, what I wish to say, is this.' The inference has been hitherto only hinted at indirectly; it is now stated plainly. Comp. 1 Cor. i. 12 λέγω δὲ τοῦτο, ὅτι ἕκαστος κ.τ.λ. In both passages the A.V. gives a wrong turn to the expression, translating it, 'this I say.' See also [Clem. Rom.] ii. §§ 2, 8, 12.

προκεκυρωμένην] The confirmation spoken of is not an act separate in time and subsequent to the covenant itself. The idea present to St Paul's mind is explained by Heb. vi. 17, 18.

εἰς Χριστὸν found in the received text after τοῦ Θεοῦ must be struck out as a gloss. The balance of authority is decidedly against it.

τετρακόσια κ.τ.λ.] In the prophetic passage, Gen. xv. 13, the length of the sojourn in Egypt is given in round numbers as 400 years: in the historical statement, Exod. xii. 40 sq., it is defined more exactly as 430 years. The Hebrew text in both passages implies that the residence in Egypt occupied the whole time. In the latter however the LXX inserts words so as to include the sojourn of the patriarchs in Canaan before the migration, thus reducing the actual term of residence in Egypt to about half this period. In the Vat. MS the passage runs, ἡ δὲ κατ-

τριάκοντα ἔτη γεγονὼς νόμος οὐκ ἀκυροῖ εἰς τὸ καταργῆσαι τὴν ἐπαγγελίαν. [18]εἰ γὰρ ἐκ νόμου ἡ κληρονομία, οὐκέτι ἐξ ἐπαγγελίας· τῷ δὲ Ἀβραὰμ

οἴκησις τῶν υἱῶν Ἰσραὴλ ἣν κατῴκησαν ἐν γῇ Αἰγύπτῳ καὶ ἐν γῇ Χαναὰν ἔτη τετρακόσια τριάκοντα πέντε (the last word however being erased). The Alex. MS reads παροίκησις, παρῴκησαν, adds after Χαναὰν the words αὐτοὶ καὶ οἱ πατέρες αὐτῶν, so as to bring out the revised chronology more clearly, and omits πέντε. The Samar. Pent. takes the same view, agreeing in its reading with the Alex. MS. This seems in fact to have been the received chronology. It is adopted not only by St Paul here, but by Josephus *Ant.* ii. 15. 2, by the Targum of Pseudo-Jonathan, and substantially by the Book of Jubilees (Ewald *Jahrb.* III. p. 77). On the other hand in St Stephen's speech (Acts vii. 6), and in Philo (*Quis rer. div. her.* § 54, p. 511 M), Gen. xv. 13 is referred to, which extends the sojourn in Egypt over 400 years; and this is the chronology adopted in other passages of Josephus (*Ant.* ii. 9. 1, *B. J.* v. 9. 4), who is thus inconsistent with himself. The LXX translators may have inserted the explanatory clause on grounds of internal criticism, or in deference to chronological records to which they had access in Egypt. The difficulties which attend both systems of chronology need not be considered here, as they do not affect St Paul's argument and cannot have entered into his thoughts.

18. εἰ γὰρ κ.τ.λ.] 'To abrogate and annul the promise I say, *for* this is the effect of making the inheritance dependent on law.' The γὰρ justifies the expressions 'abrogate,' 'annul,' of the previous verses. Νόμος and ἐπαγγελία are used without the article, as describing two opposing principles.

οὐκέτι] is here logical, 'this being once granted, it is not etc.,' as Rom. vii. 17, xi. 6. Ἔτι is so used frequently.

κεχάρισται] '*hath bestowed it* (the inheritance) as a free gift.' The perfect tense marks the permanence of the effects.

19, 20. 'Had the law then no purpose? Yes: but its very purpose, its whole character and history, betray its inferiority to the dispensation of grace. In four points this inferiority is seen. *First;* Instead of justifying it condemns, instead of giving life it kills: it was added to reveal and multiply transgressions. *Secondly;* It was but temporary; when the seed came to whom the promise was given, it was annulled. *Thirdly;* It did not come direct from God to man. There was a double interposition, a twofold mediation, between the giver and the recipient. There were the angels, who administered it as God's instruments; there was Moses (or the high-priest) who delivered it to man. *Fourthly;* As follows from the idea of mediation, it was of the nature of a contract, depending for its fulfilment on the observance of its conditions by the two contracting parties. Not so the promise, which, proceeding from the sole fiat of God, is unconditional and unchangeable.'

19. τί οὖν ὁ νόμος;] '*what then is the law?*', as 1 Cor. iii. 5 τί οὖν ἐστὶν Ἀπολλώς; τί δέ ἐστιν Παῦλος; the correct reading. Comp. also Rom. iii. 1.

τῶν παραβάσεων χάριν] How is this to be interpreted? Is it (1) 'To check transgressions'? comp. *Clem. Hom.* xi. 16 παραπτωμάτων χάριν ἡ τιμωρία ἕπεται; or is it rather (2) 'To create transgressions'? for 'where there is no law there is no transgression' (Rom. iv. 15). Thus law reveals (Rom. iii. 20), provokes (Rom. vii. 7, 13), multiplies (Rom. v. 20) sin or transgression. The use of χάριν (comp. 1 Joh. iii. 12) is suffi-

δι' ἐπαγγελίας κεχάρισται ὁ Θεός. 19 Τί οὖν ὁ νόμος;
τῶν παραβάσεων χάριν προσετέθη, ἄχρις οὗ ἔλθῃ
τὸ σπέρμα ᾧ ἐπήγγελται, διαταγεὶς δι' ἀγγέλων ἐν

ciently wide to admit either meaning. But the latter is to be preferred here; for (1) The language of the Epistle to the Romans shows this to be St Paul's leading conception of the purposes and functions of the law; and (2) This sense seems to be required by the expressions in the context, 'able to give life' (ver. 21), 'included all under sin' (ver. 22). Comp. ii. 19.

προσετέθη] This reading, which is much better supported than ἐτέθη, expresses more strongly the *adventitious* character of the law; comp. ἐπιδιατάσσεται ver. 15, and Rom. v. 20 νόμος δὲ παρεισῆλθεν ἵνα πλεονάσῃ τὸ παράπτωμα.

ἔλθῃ] For the omission of ἂν see A. Buttmann § 33, p. 198; for the conjunctive, the note on τρέχω ii. 2.

τὸ σπέρμα κ.τ.λ.] '*the seed to whom the promise has been given*,' i.e. Christ. ἐπήγγελται is probably a passive, as 2 Macc. iv. 27.

διαταγεὶς δι' ἀγγέλων] '*ordered*, or *administered by the medium of angels*.' The first mention of angels in connexion with the giving of the law is in the benediction of Moses, Deut. xxxiii. 2 ואתה מרבבת קדש, literally, 'and He came from (amidst) myriads of holiness,' i.e. countless angels who attend Him. Some modern commentators (see Knobel *in loc.*) obliterate the mention of angels by translating, 'He came from the heights of Kadesh,' pointing the word קדש with the LXX; but though the parallelism gains by this, the sense thus assigned to רבבת is unsupported: and Ewald, *Gesch. des V. Isr.* II. 257, still further changes רבבות into מריבת. The LXX render the words σὺν μυριάσι Κάδης, but introduce the angels in the following clause ἐκ δεξιῶν αὐτοῦ ἄγγελοι μετ' αὐτοῦ, where they must have had a different reading from our present Hebrew text (see Gesen. *Thes.* p. 358). Aquila, Symmachus, the Targums, and Jewish expositors generally, agree in the common rendering of רבבת קדש. Other allusions in the New Testament to the angels as administering the law are Acts vii. 53 ἐλάβετε τὸν νόμον εἰς διαταγὰς ἀγγέλων (comp. vv. 35, 38), Heb. ii. 2. See also Joseph. *Ant.* xv. 5. 3 ἡμῶν δὲ τὰ κάλλιστα τῶν δογμάτων καὶ τὰ ὁσιώτατα τῶν ἐν τοῖς νόμοις δι' ἀγγέλων παρὰ τοῦ Θεοῦ μαθόντων, Philo *de Somn.* p. 642 M, and the Book of Jubilees c. 1 (Ewald's *Jahrb.* II. p. 233, III. p. 74). The angels who assisted in the giving of the law hold a very important place in the later rabbinical speculations. See the interpretation of Deut. xxxiii. 2 in the Jerusalem Targum, and the passages cited by Gfrörer *Jahrh. des Heils* I. p. 226, p. 357 sq, and by Wetstein here. The theology of the schools having thus enlarged upon the casual notices in the Old Testament, a prominence was given to the mediation of angels, which would render St Paul's allusion the more significant.

In St Stephen's speech (Acts vii. 53), as in the passage of Josephus, the angels are mentioned to glorify the law, being opposed to mere human ministers. Here the motive is different. The interposition of created beings is contrasted with the direct agency of God himself. So also in Heb. ii. 2, where an *a fortiori* argument is drawn from the superiority of the salvation spoken by the Lord over the word spoken by angels (δι' ἀγγέλων). St Paul's contrast here between the directness of the one ministration and the indirectness of the other has a parallel in 2 Cor. iii. 12 sq.

χειρὶ μεσίτου· 20 ὁ δὲ μεσίτης ἑνὸς οὐκ ἔστιν, ὁ δὲ Θεὸς εἷς ἐστίν. 21 ὁ οὖν νόμος κατὰ τῶν ἐπαγγε-

ἐν χειρί] A Hebraism or Aramaism, nearly equivalent to διά: comp. Acts vii. 35. It is a frequent LXX translation of ביד, occurring especially in the expression ἐν χειρὶ Μωϋσῆ, e.g. Num. iv. 37, 41, 45, etc. In Syriac we meet with such phrases as ܒܝܕ ܪܘܚܐ (i.e. ἐν χειρὶ πνεύματος, Acts iv. 25, Pesh.), ܒܝܕ ܗܝܡܢܘܬܐ (i.e. ἐν χειρὶ πίστεως, Hab. ii. 4, Hexapl.).

μεσίτου] The mediator is Moses. This is his common title in Jewish writers. In the apocryphal ἀνάβασις or ἀνάληψις Moses says to Joshua προεθεάσατό με ὁ Θεὸς πρὸ καταβολῆς κόσμου εἶναί με τῆς διαθήκης αὐτοῦ μεσίτην, Fabric. *Cod. Pseud. V.T.* I. p. 845. See the rabbinical passages in Wetstein, and Philo *Vit. Moys.* iii. 19, p. 160 M οἷα μεσίτης καὶ διαλλακτής. There would appear to be an allusion to this recognised title of Moses also in Heb. viii. 6 (comp. ix. 15, xii. 24), where our Lord is styled 'a mediator of a better covenant.' Though the word itself does not occur in the Mosaic narrative, the mediatorial functions of Moses appear clearly, e.g. Exod. xx. 19, and Deut. v. 2, 5, Κύριος ὁ Θεὸς ὑμῶν διέθετο πρὸς ὑμᾶς διαθήκην...κἀγὼ εἱστήκειν ἀνὰ μέσον Κυρίου καὶ ὑμῶν κ.τ.λ. The reference in St Paul seems to be to the first giving of the law: if extended to its after administration, the μεσίτης would then be the high priest; see Philo *Mon.* ii. 12, p. 230 M μεθόριον ἀμφοῖν ἵνα διά μέσου τινὸς ἄνθρωποι ἱλάσκωνται Θεόν: but this extension does not seem to be contemplated here.

On the other hand Origen (IV. p. 692, ed. Delarue), misled by 1 Tim. ii. 5, understood the mediator of Christ, and, as usual, carried a vast number of later commentators with him. Thus it is taken by Victorinus, Hilary, Jerome, Augustine, and Chrysostom. So also Concil. Antioch. (Routh *Rel. Sacr.* III. p. 295), Euseb. *Eccl. Th.* i. 20. 11, Athan. *c. Apoll.* i. 12. Much earlier than Origen, Marcion would seem to have entertained this view, Hippol. *Haer.* vii. 31, p. 254. Basil however clearly showed that Moses was meant, referring to Exod. xx. 19, *de Spir. Sanct.* xiv. 33 (III. p. 27, Garnier), and it was perhaps owing to his influence that the correct interpretation was reinstated. So Theodore Mops., Theodoret, Gennadius; and comp. Didym. *in Ps.* pp. 1571, 1665 (Migne). Pelagius gives the alternative.

It will be seen that St Paul's argument here rests in effect on our Lord's divinity as its foundation. Otherwise He would have been a mediator in the same sense in which Moses was a mediator. In another and a higher sense St Paul himself so speaks of our Lord (1 Tim. ii. 5).

20. The number of interpretations of this passage is said to mount up to 250 or 300. Many of these arise out of an error as to the mediator, many more disregard the context, and not a few are quite arbitrary. Without attempting to discuss others which are not open to any of these objections, I shall give that which appears to me the most probable. The meaning of the first clause seems tolerably clear, and the range of possibility with regard to the second is not very great.

ὁ δὲ μεσίτης ἑνὸς οὐκ ἔστιν] '*no mediator can be a mediator of one.*' The very idea of mediation supposes two persons at least, between whom the mediation is carried on. The law then is of the nature of a contract between two parties, God on the one hand, and the Jewish people on the other. It is only valid so long as both parties fulfil the terms of the contract. It is therefore contingent

λιῶν [τοῦ Θεοῦ]; μὴ γένοιτο. εἰ γὰρ ἐδόθη νόμος ὁ δυνάμενος ζωοποιῆσαι, ὄντως ἐκ νόμου [ἂν] ἦν ἡ δικαιοσύνη· 22 ἀλλὰ συνέκλεισεν ἡ γραφὴ τὰ πάντα

and not absolute. The definite article with μεσίτης expresses the idea, the specific type, as 2 Cor. xii. 12 τὰ σημεῖα τοῦ ἀποστόλου, Joh. x. 11 ὁ ποιμὴν ὁ καλός: see Winer § xviii. p. 132.

ὁ δὲ Θεὸς εἷς ἐστίν] '*but God* (the giver of the promise) *is one*.' Unlike the law, the promise is absolute and unconditional. It depends on the sole decree of God. There are not two contracting parties. There is nothing of the nature of a *stipulation*. The giver is everything, the recipient nothing. Thus the primary sense of 'one' here is numerical. The further idea of unchangeableness may perhaps be suggested; but if so, it is rather accidental than inherent. On the other hand this proposition is quite unconnected with the fundamental statement of the Mosaic law, 'The Lord thy God is one God,' though resembling it in form.

21. 'Thus the law differs widely from the promise. But does this difference imply antagonism? Did the law interfere with the promise? Far otherwise. Indeed we might imagine such a law, that it would take the place of the promise, would justify and give life. This was not the effect of the law of Moses.'

τῶν ἐπαγγελιῶν] The plural. See the note on ver. 16.

νόμος ὁ δυνάμενος] '*a law, such as could*.' For the position of the article see note i. 7, and comp. Acts iv. 12.

ζωοποιῆσαι] including alike the spiritual life in the present and the glorified life in the future, for in the Apostle's conception the two are blended together and inseparable. The 'inheritance' applies to both. Compare the scriptural use of 'salvation,' 'the kingdom of heaven,' etc.

22, 23. In this metaphor, which describes the position of the Jews before Christ, two ideas are involved. *First*, that of *constraint* or *oppression*. They were brought under the dominion of sin, were locked up in its prison-house, and so were made to feel its power. *Secondly*, that of *watchful care*. They were fenced about as a peculiar people, that in due time they might become the depository of the Gospel and the centre of its diffusion. The first idea is prominent in ver. 22, the second appears in ver. 23.

22. 'On the contrary, as the passage of Scripture testifies, the law condemned all alike, yet not finally and irrevocably, but only as leading the way for the dispensation of faith, the fulfilment of the promise.'

συνέκλεισεν ἡ γραφή] The Scripture is here represented as doing that which it declares to be done.

The passage which St Paul has in mind is probably either Ps. cxliii. 2, quoted above ii. 16, or Deut. xxvii. 26, quoted iii. 10. In Rom. iii. 10—18 indeed the Apostle gathers together several passages to this same purport, and it might therefore be supposed that he is alluding here rather to the general tenour of Scripture than to any special text. But the following facts seem to show that the singular γραφὴ in the N.T. always means a *particular passage* of Scripture; (1) where the reference is clearly to the sacred writings as a whole, as in the expressions, 'searching the scriptures,' 'learned in the scriptures,' etc., the plural γραφαί is universally found, e.g. Acts xvii. 11, xviii. 24, 28. (2) We meet with such expressions as 'another scripture' (Joh. xix. 37), 'this scripture' (Luke iv. 21), 'every scripture' (2 Tim. iii. 16). (3) 'Η

ὑπὸ ἁμαρτίαν, ἵνα ἡ ἐπαγγελία ἐκ πίστεως Ἰησοῦ Χριστοῦ δοθῇ τοῖς πιστεύουσιν. 23 πρὸ τοῦ δὲ ἐλθεῖν τὴν πίστιν, ὑπὸ νόμον ἐφρουρούμεθα συνκλειόμενοι εἰς τὴν μέλλουσαν πίστιν ἀποκαλυφθῆναι. 24 ὥστε ὁ νόμος παιδαγωγὸς ἡμῶν γέγονεν εἰς Χριστόν, ἵνα ἐκ

γραφή is most frequently used in introducing a particular quotation, and in the very few instances where the quotation is not actually given, it is for the most part easy to fix the passage referred to. These instances are Joh. ii. 22 (Ps. xvi. 10; see Acts ii. 27), Joh. xvii. 12 (Ps. xli. 10; see Joh. xiii. 18), Joh. xix. 28 (Ps. lxix. 22), Joh. xx. 9 (Ps. xvi. 10). The biblical usage is followed also by the earliest fathers. The transition from the 'Scriptures' to the 'Scripture' is analogous to the transition from τὰ βιβλία to the 'Bible.'

συνέκλεισεν ὑπὸ ἁμαρτίαν] i.e. subjected to the dominion of sin without means of escape, a pregnant expression: comp. Rom. xi. 32 συνέκλεισεν γὰρ ὁ Θεὸς τοὺς πάντας εἰς ἀπείθειαν ἵνα τοὺς πάντας ἐλεήσῃ. The word συγκλείειν seems never to mean simply 'to include.' The A.V. has the more correct but somewhat ambiguous rendering 'conclude' here. Συγκλείειν εἰς is a common construction; see Fritzsche *Rom.* II. p. 545.

τὰ πάντα] The neuter is naturally used where the most comprehensive term is wanted: comp. 1 Cor. i. 27, Col. i. 20, Ephes. i. 10.

ἵνα] The consciousness of sin is a necessary step towards justification. See note ii. 19, and comp. Rom. l.c.

ἐκ πίστεως κ.τ.λ.] Not a mere tautology after τοῖς πιστεύουσιν. St Paul's opponents agreed with him that only a believer could obtain the promise. They differed in holding that he obtained it not by his faith but by his works.

23—25. 'Before the dispensation of faith came, we were carefully guarded, that we might be ready for it, when at length it was revealed. Thus we see that the law was our tutor, who watched over us as children till we should attain our manhood in Christ and be justified by faith. But, when this new dispensation came, we were liberated from the restraints of the law.'

23. ἐφρουρούμεθα συνκλειόμενοι] '*were shut up and kept in ward*': comp. Wisd. xvii. 15 ἐφρουρεῖτο εἰς τὴν ἀσίδηρον εἱρκτὴν κατακλεισθείς, Plut. *de Def. Orac.* p. 426 B οὐδὲ φρουρεῖν συγκλείσαντας τῇ ὕλῃ.

The use of πίστις in these verses (vv. 22, 23, 25) links together its extreme senses, passing from the one to the other, (1) Faith, the subjective state of the Christian, (2) *The* faith, the Gospel, the objective teaching, the system of which 'faith' is the leading feature. See the note i. 23, and p. 157.

24. παιδαγωγός] Comp. 1 Cor. iv. 15. The pædagogus or tutor, frequently a superior slave, was entrusted with the moral supervision of the child. Thus his office was quite distinct from that of the διδάσκαλος, so that the English rendering, 'schoolmaster,' conveys a wrong idea. The following passage of Plato (*Lysis* p. 208 c) is a very complete illustration of the use which St Paul makes of the metaphor; Σὲ αὐτὸν ἐῶσιν ἄρχειν σεαυτοῦ, ἢ οὐδὲ τοῦτο ἐπιτρέπουσί σοι; Πῶς γάρ, ἔφη, ἐπιτρέπουσιν; Ἀλλ' ἄρχει τίς σου; Ὅδε παιδαγωγός, ἔφη. Μῶν δοῦλος ὤν; Ἀλλὰ τί μήν; ἡμέτερός γε, ἔφη. Ἦ δεινόν, ἦν δ' ἐγώ, ἐλεύθερον ὄντα ὑπὸ δούλου ἄρχεσθαι· τί δὲ ποιῶν αὖ οὗτος ὁ παιδαγωγός σου ἄρχει; Ἄγων δήπου, ἔφη, εἰς διδασκάλου. Μῶν μὴ καὶ οὗτοί σου ἄρχουσιν,

πίστεως δικαιωθῶμεν· 25 ἐλθούσης δὲ τῆς πίστεως οὐκέτι ὑπὸ παιδαγωγόν ἐσμεν. 26 πάντες γὰρ υἱοὶ Θεοῦ ἐστὲ διὰ τῆς πίστεως ἐν Χριστῷ Ἰησοῦ· 27 ὅσοι γὰρ εἰς Χριστὸν ἐβαπτίσθητε, Χριστὸν ἐνεδύσασθε.

οἱ διδάσκαλοι; Πάντως δήπου. Παμπόλλους ἄρα σοι δεσπότας καὶ ἄρχοντας ἑκὼν ὁ πατὴρ ἐφίστησιν. On the 'pædagogus' see Becker and Marquardt *Röm. Alt.* v. 1, p. 114, and Smith's *Dict. of Antiq.* s. v. As well in his inferior rank, as in his recognised duty of enforcing discipline, this person was a fit emblem of the Mosaic law. The rabbinical writers naturalised the word παιδαγωγός, פדגוג (see Schöttgen here), and in the Jerusalem Targum it is used to translate אמן (A.V. 'a nursing father') Numb. xi. 12.

The tempting explanation of παιδαγωγὸς εἰς Χριστόν, 'one to conduct us to the school of Christ,' ought probably to be abandoned. Even if this sense did not require πρὸς Χριστὸν or εἰς Χριστοῦ, the context is unfavourable to it. There is no reference here to our Lord as a *teacher*. 'Christ' represents the freedom of mature age, for which the constraints of childhood are a preparation; compare Ephes. iv. 13 εἰς ἄνδρα τέλειον ('full grown'), εἰς μέτρον ἡλικίας τοῦ πληρώματος τοῦ Χριστοῦ. The metaphor of the pædagogus seems to have grown out of ἐφρουρούμεθα and thus the main idea is that of strict supervision. The παιδαγωγὸς had the whole moral direction of the child, so that παιδαγωγία became equivalent to 'moral training,' and the idea conveyed by the term need not be restricted to any one function. Compare Plut. *Num.* 15 ἐκ δὲ τοιαύτης παιδαγωγίας πρὸς τὸ θεῖον οὕτως ἡ πόλις ἐγεγόνει χειροήθης κ.τ.λ., and Liban. IV. 437 ed. Reiske (quoted in Wetstein) πρῶτον μὲν νόμῳ παιδαγωγήσομεν αὐτῶν τὴν προαίρεσιν, ὡς ἂν τὴν ἀπὸ τοῦ νόμου ζημίαν ἀναδυόμεναι σωφρονεῖν ἀναγκάζωνται.

25, 26. ἐσμέν, ἐστέ] See a similar instance of the interchange of the first and second persons in 1 Thess. v. 5 πάντες γὰρ ὑμεῖς υἱοὶ φωτός ἐστε καὶ υἱοὶ ἡμέρας· οὐκ ἐσμὲν νυκτὸς οὐδὲ σκότους.

26. πάντες γὰρ κ.τ.λ.] '*for ye all are sons of God by your faith*, sons of God *in Christ Jesus*.' The stress of the sentence lies on πάντες and υἱοί; '*all*,' Jews and Gentiles alike, those under the law and those without the law; '*sons*' (υἱοί), claiming therefore the privileges, the liberty of sons, so that the rigorous supervision of the tutor (παιδαγωγός) ceases when you cease to be children (παῖδες).

υἱοὶ Θεοῦ] In St Paul the expressions, 'sons of God,' 'children of God,' mostly convey the idea of *liberty*, as iv. 6, 7, Rom. viii. 14 sq (see however Phil. ii. 15), in St John of *guilelessness* and *love*, e.g. 1 Joh. iii. 1, 2, 10. In accordance with this distinction St Paul uses υἱοὶ as well as τέκνα, St John τέκνα only.

ἐν Χριστῷ Ἰησοῦ] The context shows that these words must be separated from διὰ τῆς πίστεως. They are thrown to the end of the sentence so as to form in a manner a distinct proposition, on which the Apostle enlarges in the following verses: 'You are sons by your union with, your existence in Christ Jesus.'

27. 'In Christ Jesus, I say, *for all ye, who were baptized into Christ, did put on Christ*': γὰρ introduces the explanation of the foregoing ἐν Χριστῷ Ἰησοῦ.

ἐνεδύσασθε] The metaphor has been supposed to be taken from the white garments in which the newly baptized were clothed; see Bingham *Christ. Antiq.* xi. 11, § 1. It is scarcely probable however that the ceremonial of

28 οὐκ ἔνι Ἰουδαῖος οὐδὲ Ἕλλην, οὐκ ἔνι δοῦλος οὐδὲ ἐλεύθερος, οὐκ ἔνι ἄρσεν καὶ θῆλυ· πάντες γὰρ ὑμεῖς εἷς ἐστὲ ἐν Χριστῷ Ἰησοῦ. 29 εἰ δὲ ὑμεῖς Χριστοῦ,

28. ἅπαντες γὰρ ὑμεῖς.

baptism had become so definitely fixed at this early date, that such an allusion would speak for itself. The metaphor in fact is very common in the LXX, e.g. Job viii. 22 (αἰσχύνην), xxix. 14 (δικαιοσύνην), xxxix. 19 (φόβον), Ps. xxxiv. 26 (αἰσχύνην καὶ ἐντροπήν), xcii. 1 (εὐπρέπειαν, δύναμιν), ciii. 1, etc.; comp. ἐγκομβοῦσθαι 1 Pet. v. 5. See also Schöttgen on Rom. xiii. 14. On the other hand in the context of the passage of Justin quoted below (ver. 28) there is apparently an allusion to the baptismal robes.

28, 29. 'In Christ ye are all sons, all free. Every barrier is swept away. No special claims, no special disabilities exist in Him, none *can* exist. The conventional distinctions of religious caste or of social rank, even the natural distinction of sex, are banished hence. One heart beats in all: one mind guides all: one life is lived by all. Ye are all *one man*, for ye are members of Christ. And as members of Christ ye are Abraham's seed, ye claim the inheritance by virtue of a promise, which no law can set aside.'

οὐκ ἔνι] '*there is no room for, no place for*,' negativing not the fact only, but the possibility, as James i. 17 παρ' ᾧ οὐκ ἔνι παραλλαγή. The right account of ἔνι seems to be given by Winer § xiv. p. 96. It is not a contraction of ἔνεστι, but the preposition ἐν, ἐνί, strengthened by a more vigorous accent, like ἔπι, πάρα, and used with an ellipsis of the substantive verb.

Ἕλλην] See the note ii. 3.

ἄρσεν καὶ θῆλυ] The connecting particle is perhaps changed in the third clause, because the distinction now mentioned is different in kind, no longer social but physical. There may be an allusion to Gen. i. 27 ἄρσεν καὶ θῆλυ ἐποίησεν αὐτούς, and if so, this clause will form a climax: 'even the primeval distinction of sex has ceased.' Comp. Col. iii. 11.

Either on this passage, or on some unrecorded saying of our Lord similar in import (comp. Luke xx. 35), may have been founded the mystical language attributed to our Lord in the apocryphal Gospel of the Egyptians (Clem. Alex. *Strom.* iii. p. 553, ed. Potter). Being asked by Salome when His kingdom should come, He is reported to have answered, 'When the two shall be one, and the male with the female, neither male nor female.' These obscure words were much discussed in early times and diversely interpreted, e.g. by the Ophites (Hippol. *Haer.* v. 7), by the Pseudo-Clement of Rome (Epist. 2, § 12), by Cassianus (Clem. Alex. l.c.), and by Theodotus (Clem. Alex. p. 985). Comp. also the remarks of Clement of Alexandria himself, pp. 532, 539 sq, besides the passage first cited. See the note on Clem. Rom. l.c. For another coincidence of St Paul's language with a saying attributed to our Lord, but not found in the Gospels, see 1 Thess. v. 21.

εἷς ἐστέ] '*are one man.*' Comp. Ephes. ii. 15 τοὺς δύο κτίσῃ ἐν αὐτῷ εἰς ἕνα καινὸν ἄνθρωπον, and Justin *Dial.* § 116, p. 344 B οὕτως ἡμεῖς οἱ διὰ τοῦ Ἰησοῦ ὀνόματος ὡς εἷς ἄνθρωπος πιστεύσαντες...τὰ ῥυπαρὰ ἱμάτια ἀπημφιεσμένοι κ.τ.λ., which seems to be a reminiscence of this passage of St Paul. The neuter ἕν, found in some texts, destroys the point of the expression, the oneness as *a conscious agent.*

29. Χριστοῦ] '*are part of Christ*, are members of Christ,' not merely

ἄρα τοῦ Ἀβραὰμ σπέρμα ἐστέ, κατ' ἐπαγγελίαν κληρονόμοι.

'are the property of Christ, are servants of Christ.' The argument turns on the entire *identity* of the Christian brotherhood with Christ.

ἄρα τοῦ Ἀβραάμ] '*then* being one with Christ, *ye are Abraham's seed*'; for He is that seed of Abraham, to whom the promise was given. See the note on ver. 16.

κατ' ἐπαγγελίαν] emphatic; 'heirs indeed, but heirs *by promise*, not by law.' See ver. 18.

The interpretation of Deut. xxi. 23.

This passage occupied an important place in the early controversies between the Christians and the Jews. Partly owing to this circumstance, and partly from the ambiguity of the Hebrew, it was variously interpreted and applied.

Ambiguity of the Hebrew.

The words of the original are כי קללת אלהים תלוי, 'for (the) curse of God (is) he that is hanged.' The ambiguity arises out of the construction of אלהים, since the case attached to קללת may denote either the person who pronounces the curse, as Judges ix. 57 (קללת יותם) and 2 Sam. xvi. 12 (קללתו in the Q'ri), or the person against whom the curse is pronounced, as Gen. xxvii. 13 (קללתך); in other words, it represents either a subjective or an objective genitive. As we assign one or other sense therefore to the dependent case, we get two distinct interpretations.

Two renderings.

(i) LXX and St Paul.

1. 'He that is hanged is accursed in the sight of God.' This is the rendering of the LXX, *κεκατηραμένος ὑπὸ τοῦ Θεοῦ*, adopted in substance, it would appear, by St Paul; and seems to have obtained the suffrages of most recent commentators whatever their opinions. It is certainly supported by a more exact parallel (Judges ix. 57) than the alternative rendering, and seems to suit the context better, for the sense will then be, 'Do not let the body hang after sunset; for the hanging body (of a malefactor) defiles the land, since the curse of God rests upon it.'

(ii) Judaic writers.

2. The other rendering is, 'He that hangeth is a contempt of, a reproach or insult to God.' This seems to have been the popular Jewish interpretation (shared therefore by Jewish Christians) at all events from the second century of the Christian era. The passage was so taken by the Jewish or Ebionite translators, Aquila, Theodotion, and Symmachus[1]. It is explained in this way in the ancient Jewish commentary on Deuteronomy, *Siphri*[2], and in the so-called Targum of Jonathan[3]. This rendering appeared also in the Ebionite Gospel[4]. And in one of the earliest Christian apologies, a Jewish interlocutor brought forward this text, quoting it in the form, 'He that hangeth is a reviling of God[5].' It is found more-

[1] Aquila and Theodotion rendered it *κατάρα Θεοῦ κρεμάμενος*; see Field's *Hexapla* I. p. 304. The rendering of Symmachus, as given in Latin by Jerome, was, 'quia propter blasphemiam Dei suspensus est.'

[2] 'Qua de causa iste suspenditur? Quia maledixit nomini (Dei)': see Ugolin. *Thes.* xv. p. 766.

[3] קילותא קדם אלהא למצלוב גבר, 'it is contempt before God to hang a man.'

[4] At least so I understand the language of Jerome, l.c., 'Haec verba Ebion ille haeresiarches semichristianus et semijudaeus ita interpretatus est, *ὅτι ὕβρις Θεοῦ ὁ κρεμάμενος*, id est, quia injuria Dei est suspensus.'

[5] Hieron. l.c., 'Memini me in altercatione Iasonis et Papisci quae Graeco sermone conscripta est ita reperisse, *λοιδορία Θεοῦ ὁ κρεμάμενος*, id est, 'maledictio Dei qui appensus est.' See below, p. 153, note 5.

over in the Peshito Syriac[1]. The same also would seem to be the interpretation adopted in the older Targum[2], where the passage runs, 'Since for what he sinned before God he was hanged,' but the paraphrastic freedom of this rendering leaves room for some doubt. Though these writers differ widely from each other as to the meaning to be put upon the words, they agree in their rendering so far as to take אלהים as the object, not the subject, of קללת.

It may be conjectured that this rendering obtained currency at first owing to the untoward circumstances of the times. Jewish patriots were impaled or crucified as rebels by their masters whether Syrians or Romans. The thought was intolerable that the curse of God should attach to these. The spirit of the passage indeed implies nothing of this kind, but the letter was all powerful in the schools of the day: and a rendering, which not only warded off the reproach but even, if dexterously used, turned it against the persecutor, would be gladly welcomed[3]. An interpretation started in this way would at length become traditional[4].

The text used by the Jews against Christians,

But it was especially in controversies with the Christians, as I have mentioned, that the Jews availed themselves of this passage. In whatever way interpreted, it would seem to them equally available for their purpose. The 'offence of the cross' took its stand upon the letter of the lawgiver's language, and counted its position impregnable. Again and again doubtless, as he argued in the synagogues, St Paul must have had these words cast in his teeth, 'accursed of God,' or 'an insult to God,' or 'a blasphemer of God, is he that is hanged on the tree.' More than once the early Christian apologists meet and refute this inference, when writing against the Jews. This is the case with Ariston of Pella[5], with Justin Martyr[6], with Tertullian[7]. In Jerome's time the same argument was brought by the Jews against the leading fact on which the faith of a Christian rests[8]; and later literature shows that Christ crucified did not cease to be 'to the Jews a stumblingblock.'

[1] 'Because whosoever blasphemeth God shall be hanged.'

[2] So it may be inferred from a comparison with the translations of Symmachus, of the Peshito, and of the Ebionite Gospel. Otherwise the same meaning might be got from the other rendering, 'accursed of God,' and so 'a sinner in the sight of God.'

[3] Thus the Targum of Pseudo-Jonathan, after rendering the passage as given above, p. 152, note 3, adds 'unless his sins have occasioned it to him.' It is possible however that this is aimed at Christianity. At all events it presents a curious contrast to the interpretation of the older Targum.

[4] See the passages quoted in Schöttgen here. The following is the interpretation of a learned rabbi of our own time: 'L'impiccato è (produce) imprecazione contro Dio (cioè: il lasciare il cadavere esposto lungo tempo alla pubblica vista non può che irritare gli animi, e indurli ad esecrare i giudici e le leggi): e (oltracciò) non devi rendere impura la tua terra etc.,' Luzzatto *Il Pentateuco*, Trieste 1858.

[5] In the 'Dispute of Jason and Papiscus'; see above, p. 152, note 5, and Routh *Rel. Sacr.* I. p. 95.

[6] *Dial. c. Tryph.* c. 96, p. 323 C.

[7] *Adv. Judaeos* § 10.

[8] Hieron. l.c. So too in the work of Evagrius (c. 430 A.D., see Gennad. *Vir. Ill.* 50) entitled *Altercatio inter Theophilum Christianum et Simonem Judaeum*, Migne's *Patr. Lat.* XX. p. 1174 B.

and applied to death by crucifixion.

The passage in Deuteronomy, it is true, does not refer directly to crucifixion as a means of execution, but to impaling bodies after death. It has been said indeed that Philo[1] speaks of the impalement there mentioned as a mode of putting to death, but this seems to be a mistake. Philo says, that Moses would have put such malefactors to death ten thousand times over if it were possible, but not being able to kill them more than once, he *adds another penalty*, ordering murderers to be gibbeted (τιμωρίαν ἄλλην προσδιατάττεται κελεύων τοὺς ἀνελόντας ἀνασκολοπίζεσθαι). Nor, so far as I am aware, is there any evidence to show that the Jews at the time of the Christian era interpreted the passage of death by crucifixion. Crucifixion was not a Jewish punishment. The evangelist (Joh. xviii. 32) sees a providence in the delivering over of our Lord to the Romans to be put to death, so that He might die in the manner He himself had foretold. It had been employed occasionally in seasons of tumult by their own princes[2], but was regarded as an act of great atrocity. Even the Roman looked upon crucifixion with abhorrence[3]. To the Jew it was especially hateful, owing in part no doubt to the curse attaching to this ignominious exposure of the body in the passage of Deuteronomy. For though this passage did not contemplate death by crucifixion, the application was quite legitimate. It was the hanging, not the death, that brought ignominy on the sufferer and defilement on the land. Hence the Chaldee paraphrase of Deuteronomy employs the same word (צלב) which is used in several places in the Peshito Syriac to describe the crucifixion of our Lord (e.g. Gal. iii. 1). Hence also later Jews, speaking of Jesus, called Him by the same name of reproach (תלוי, 'the gibbeted one'), which they found in the original text of the lawgiver[4]. It was not that they mistook the meaning of the word, but that they considered the two punishments essentially the same. No Jew would have questioned the propriety of St Paul's application of the text to our Lord. The curse pronounced in the law was interpreted and strengthened by the national sentiment.

The words denoting 'Faith.'

Active and passive meanings of Faith

The Hebrew אמונה, the Greek πίστις, the Latin 'fides,' and the English 'faith,' hover between two meanings; *trustfulness*, the frame of mind which relies on another; and *trustworthiness*, the frame of mind which can be relied upon. Not only are the two connected together grammati-

[1] *de Spec. Leg.* § 28, II. p. 324 M.

[2] Joseph. *Ant.* xiii. 14. 2, referred to in Winer *Realw.* s. v. *Kreuzigung*. On this question see Carpzov *Appar. Crit.* p. 591. I have not seen the treatise of Bornitius mentioned by Winer, *Diss. de cruce num Ebraeor. suppl. fuerit*, Wittenb. 1644. Those who maintain that crucifixion was a Jewish punishment rely mainly on this passage of Galatians: see Lange *Obs. Sacr.* p. 163 sq.

[3] Cic. *Verr.* v. 64 'crudelissimum teterrimumque supplicium.'

[4] Eisenmenger's *Entd. Judenth.* I. pp. 88 sq, 287, 496. On the Greek terms σταυροῦν, σκολοπίζειν, etc., see Lipsius *de Cruce* i. 4 sq (*Op.* II. p. 769).

cally, as active and passive[1] senses of the same word, or logically, as subject and object of the same act; but there is a close moral affinity between them. Fidelity, constancy, firmness, confidence, reliance, trust, belief—these are the links which connect the two extremes, the passive with the active meaning of 'faith.' Owing to these combined causes, the two senses will at times be so blended together that they can only be separated by some arbitrary distinction. When the members of the Christian brotherhood, for instance, are called 'the faithful,' *οἱ πιστοί*, what is meant by this? Does it imply their constancy, their trustworthiness, or their faith, their belief? In all such cases it is better to accept the latitude, and even the vagueness, of a word or phrase, than to attempt a rigid definition, which after all can be only artificial. And indeed the loss in grammatical precision is often more than compensated by the gain in theological depth. In the case of 'the faithful' for instance, does not the one quality of heart carry the other with it, so that they who are trustful are trusty also[2]; they who have faith in God are stedfast and immovable in the path of duty? sometimes combined.

The history of the terms for 'faith' in the three sacred languages of Christian theology is instructive from more points of view than one.

1. The Hebrew word signifying 'to believe, to trust,' is the *Hiphil* האמין. The *Kal* אמן would mean 'to strengthen, support, hold up,' but is only found in the active participle, used as a substantive with the special sense, 'one who supports, nurses, trains a child' (*παιδαγωγός*, see note, Gal. iii. 24), and in the passive participle 'firm, trustworthy.' The *Niphal* accordingly means, 'to be firm, lasting, constant, trusty'; while the *Hiphil* האמין, with which we are more directly concerned, is, 'to hold trustworthy, to rely upon, believe' (taking either a simple accusative or one of the prepositions, ב or ל), and is rendered *πιστεύω* in the LXX, e.g. Gen. xv. 6. But there is in biblical Hebrew no corresponding substantive for 'faith,' the active principle. Its nearest representative is אמונה, 'firmness, constancy, trustworthiness.' This word is rendered in the LXX most frequently by *ἀλήθεια, ἀληθινός* (twenty-four times), or by *πίστις, πιστός, ἀξιόπιστος* (twenty times); once it is translated *ἐστηριγμένος* (Exod. xvii. 12), once *πλοῦτος* (Ps. xxxvi. 3, where Symm. had *διηνεκῶς*, Aq. *πίστιν*). It will thus be seen that אמונה properly represents the passive sense of *πίστις*, as indeed the form of the word shows. But it will at times approach near to the active sense; for constancy under temptation or danger with an Israelite could only spring from reliance on Jehovah. And something of this transitional or double sense it has in the passage of Habakkuk ii. 4[3]. The latitude of the LXX translation, *πίστις*, in that passage has helped out this meaning; and in St Paul's application it is brought still more prominently forward. i. Hebrew. אֱמוּנָה

Thus in its biblical usage the word אמונה can scarcely be said ever to have the sense 'belief, trust,' though sometimes approaching towards it.

[1] Throughout this note I have used the terms 'active' and 'passive' in reference to the act of *believing*. If referred to the act of *persuading* they would of course change places.

[2] 'Qui fortis est, idem est fidens,' says Cicero, *Tusc.* iii. 7.

[3] See the note on Gal. iii. 11.

The influence of the Greek rendering however doubtless reacted upon the original, and in the rabbinical Hebrew it seems decidedly to have adopted

Aramaic. this meaning (see Buxtorf *Lex. Rabbin.* s. v.). The Aramaic dialects did something towards fixing this sense by an active form, derived from the same root אמן, but from the conjugation *Aphel* (corresponding to the Hebrew *Hiphil*). Thus in the Chaldee of the Targum of Jonathan, the word denoting the faith of Abraham, Gen. xv. 6, is הימנותא, and the Syriac renders πίστις in the New Testament by the same word ܗܝܡܢܘܬܐ.

ii. Greek. πίστις. Classical writers.

2. Unlike the Hebrew, the Greek word seems to have started from the active meaning. In its earliest use it is opposed to 'distrust'; Hesiod *Op.* 342 πίστεις δ' ἄρ τοι ὁμῶς καὶ ἀπιστίαι ὤλεσαν ἄνδρας (comp. Theogn. 831 πίστει χρήματ' ἀπώλεσ' ἀπιστίῃ δ' ἐσάωσα); and this is perhaps the sense most favoured by analogy[1]. But even if it had not originally the passive sense of faith side by side with the active, it soon acquired this meaning also, e.g. Æsch. *Fragm.* 276 οὐκ ἀνδρὸς ὅρκοι πίστις ἀλλ' ὅρκων ἀνήρ: and πίστις became a common technical term for a 'proof.' The transition was aided by the indefiniteness of the grammatical form, and such phrases as πίστιν ἔχειν τινός formed a link of connexion between the two. The English word 'persuasion' will show how easily the one sense may pass into the other. In the same manner πιστὸς has both meanings, 'trusty,' as Hom. *Il.* xvi. 147 πιστότατος δέ οἱ ἔσκε, and 'trustful,' as Æsch. *Prom.* 917 τοῖς πεδαρσίοις κτύποις πιστός. So also ἄπιστος means both 'incredulous' (Hom. *Od.* xiv. 150), and 'incredible' (Æsch. *Prom.* 832).

Old Testament.

With this latitude of use these words passed into the language of theology. In the Old Testament, there being no Hebrew equivalent to the active meaning[2], πίστις has always the passive sense, 'fidelity,' 'constancy[3],' unless the passage in Habakkuk be regarded as an exception[4]. So again there is no clear instance of πιστὸς with any but the passive sense.

[1] Compare λῆστις, μνῆστις, Buttm. *Ausf. Sprachl.* § 119. 24.

[2] As illustrating this fact, it is worth noticing that the word 'faith' occurs only twice in the Authorised Version of the Old Testament, Deut. xxxii. 20 ('children in whom is no faith,' אֵמֻן, where it is plainly passive), and Hab. ii. 4; see note 4.

[3] Besides אמונה, it occurs as a rendering of אמון, אמנה, אמת, and once as a paraphrase of לענות, Prov. xv. 28. In all these words the passive sense is evident.

[4] ii. 4. The original reading of the LXX is not clear. In the Vat. and Sin. MSS it is ὁ δὲ δίκαιος ἐκ πίστεώς μου, in the Alex. and others ὁ δὲ δίκαιός μου ἐκ πίστεως. In Hebr. x. 38 too (though not without various readings) μου follows δίκαιος. Comp. also Clem. Alex. *Strom.* ii. p. 432, Potter. With these data it is difficult to decide between two solutions; either (1) It may be inferred from the varying position of μου that the word had no place in the original text of the LXX; in this case St Paul (Gal. iii. 11, Rom. i. 17) may have quoted directly from the LXX; or (2) Ἐκ πίστεώς μου was the original reading, afterwards altered into μου ἐκ πίστεως to remove any ambiguity as to the sense. In this latter case the LXX translators must have read באמונתי 'my faith' (for באמונתו 'his faith,' the present Hebrew text), and perhaps intended their rendering ἐκ πίστεώς μου to be understood, 'by faith in me' (see however Rom. iii. 3 τὴν πίστιν τοῦ Θεοῦ). That the Hebrew text was the same in the first and second centuries as at present, may be inferred not only from St Paul's

The usage of the Apocrypha is chiefly valuable as showing how difficult it is to discriminate the two meanings, where there is no Hebrew original to act as a check, and how easily the one runs into the other; e.g. Ecclus. xlvi. 15 ἐν πίστει αὐτοῦ ἠκριβάσθη προφήτης καὶ ἐγνώσθη ἐν πίστει αὐτοῦ πιστὸς ὁράσεως, 1 Macc. ii. 52 Ἀβραὰμ οὐχὶ ἐν πειρασμῷ εὑρέθη πιστὸς καὶ ἐλογίσθη αὐτῷ εἰς δικαιοσύνην; Ecclus. xlix. 10 ἐλυτρώσατο αὐτοὺς ἐν πίστει ἐλπίδος. In these passages the active sense seems to be forcing itself into notice; and the writings of Philo, to which I shall have to refer presently, show that at the time of the Christian era πίστις, 'faith,' 'belief,' had a recognised value as a theological term. Apocrypha.

In the New Testament πίστις is found in both its passive and its active sense. On the one hand it is used for constancy, trustworthiness, whether of the immutable purpose of God, Rom. iii. 3 τὴν πίστιν τοῦ Θεοῦ καταργήσει, or of good faith, honesty, uprightness in men, Matt. xxiii. 23 ἀφήκατε τὰ βαρύτερα τοῦ νόμου, τὴν κρίσιν καὶ τὸ ἔλεος καὶ τὴν πίστιν (see the note on Gal. v. 22). On the other hand, as 'faith,' 'belief,' it assumes in the teaching of our Lord, enforced and explained by St Paul, the foremost place in the phraseology of Christian doctrine. From this latter sense are derived all those shades of meaning by which it passes from the abstract to the concrete; from faith, the subjective state, to *the* faith, the object of faith, the Gospel, and sometimes, it would appear, the embodiment of faith, the Church (see Gal. i. 23, iii. 22—26, vi. 10). New Testament.

All other senses however are exceptional, and πίστις, as a Christian virtue, certainly has the active meaning, 'trust,' 'belief.' But the use of the adjective οἱ πιστοὶ for the Christian brotherhood cannot be assigned rigidly either to the one meaning or the other. Sometimes the context requires the active, as Joh. xx. 27 μὴ γίνου ἄπιστος ἀλλὰ πιστός (comp. Gal. iii. 9), sometimes the passive, as Apoc. ii. 10 γίνου πιστὸς ἄχρι θανάτου. But when there is no context to serve as a guide, who shall say in which of the two senses the word is used? For the one it may be urged that the passive sense of πιστὸς is in other connexions by far the most common, even in the New Testament; for the other, that its opposite ἄπιστος certainly means an 'unbeliever.' Is not a rigid definition of the sense in such a case groundless and arbitrary? For why should the sacred writers have used with this meaning only or with that a term whose very comprehensiveness was in itself a valuable lesson[1]? πιστός.

application of the passage (supposing him to quote from the Hebrew), but also from the fact that *all* the Greek Versions collected by Origen so read it. See Jerome on Gal. iii. 11, and on Hab. ii. 4, *Op.* VI. p. 608 sq (ed. Vall.).

[1] The difficulty of exact definition in similar cases is pointed out in a suggestive essay in Jowett's *Epistles of St Paul* II. p. 101 (2nd ed.). With Prof. Jowett's applications of his principles I am far from agreeing in many cases, and I consider his general theory of the looseness of St Paul's language an entire mistake; but as a protest against the tendency of recent criticism to subtle restrictions of meaning, unsupported either by the context or by confirmed usage, this essay seems to me to be highly valuable. The use of οἱ πιστοὶ is an illustration of this difficulty. The expression τὸ εὐαγγέλιον τοῦ Χριστοῦ is another. What is meant by 'the Gospel of Christ'? Is it the Gospel which speaks of Christ, or the Gospel which was delivered by Christ,

iii. Latin. *fides.*

3. It has been seen that the meaning of the Greek πίστις was reflected on its Hebrew original. No less was this meaning infused into its Latin rendering. The verb πιστεύω was naturally translated by 'credo,' but this root supplied no substantive corresponding to πίστις, no adjective (for 'credulus' was stamped with a bad meaning) corresponding to πιστός. Words were therefore borrowed from another source, 'fides,' 'fidelis.' Now 'fides,' as it appears in classical writers up to the time when it is adopted into Christian literature, is not so much 'belief, trust,' as 'fidelity, trustworthiness, credit.' Its connexion in some expressions however led the way toward this active meaning, at the very threshold of which it had already arrived[1]. In the absence therefore of any exact Latin equivalent to the active sense of πίστις[2], the coincidence of 'fides' with some meanings of the Greek word, and the tendency already manifested to pass into the required sense 'belief, trust,' suggested it as the best rendering. Its introduction into Christian literature at length stamped it with a new image and superscription. In the case of the adjective 'fideles' again, the passive sense was still more marked, but here too there was no alternative, and the original πιστοὶ was, as we have seen, sufficiently wide to admit it as at all events a partial rendering.

English.

The English terms 'faith, faithful,' derived from the Latin, have inherited the latitude of meaning which marked their ancestry; and it is perhaps a gain that we are able to render πίστις, πιστοί, by comprehensive words which, uniting in themselves the ideas of 'trustfulness' and 'trustworthiness,' of 'Glauben' and 'Treue,' do not arbitrarily restrict the power of the original.

The faith of Abraham.

Results of the fore-

From the investigation just concluded it appears that the term 'Faith' can scarcely be said to occur at all in the Hebrew Scriptures of the Old

or the Gospel which belongs to Christ? or rather, does it not combine all these meanings in itself?

[1] Instances of such expressions are, 'facere fidem alicui,' 'habere fidem alicui'; comp. Ter. *Heaut.* iii. 3. 10 'Mihi fides apud hunc est me nihil facturum.' The trustworthiness, demonstrability, proof of the object, transferred to the subject, becomes 'assurance, conviction,' and so Cicero *Parad.* 9, in reference to arguments in public speaking says, 'fides est firma opinio.' See the whole passage. This sense of 'conviction' is, I believe, the nearest approach to the Christian use of the term. It never, so far as I am aware, signifies trustfulness, confidence, as a quality inherent or abiding in a person. To assert a negative however is always dangerous, and possibly wider knowledge or research would prove this position untenable. At all events the ordinary sense of 'fides' in classical writers is 'trustworthiness, credit, fidelity to engagements.'

[2] The Latin language indeed offered two words of a directly active meaning, 'fidentia' and 'fiducia'; but the former of these seems never to have obtained a firm footing in the language (see Cic. *de Inv.* ii. 163, 165, *Tusc.* iv. 80), and the signification of both alike was too pronounced for the sense required. 'Fidentia' does not occur at all in the Latin translations (if the Concordance to the Vulgate is sufficient evidence); 'fiducia' is not uncommon, frequently as a rendering of παρρησία, less often of πεποίθησις, θάρσος, but never of πίστις. Fides, fiducia, occur together in Senec. *Ep.* 94.

Testament. It is indeed a characteristic token of the difference between the two covenants, that under the Law the '*fear* of the Lord' holds very much the same place as '*faith* in God,' '*faith* in Christ,' under the Gospel. *Awe* is the prominent idea in the earlier dispensation, *trust* in the later. At the same time, though the word itself is not found in the Old Testament, the idea is not absent; for indeed a trust in the Infinite and Unseen, subordinating thereto all interests that are finite and transitory, is the very essence of the higher spiritual life. going investigation.

In Abraham, the father of the chosen race, this attitude of trustfulness was most marked. By faith he left home and kindred, and settled in a strange land: by faith he acted upon God's promise of a race and an inheritance, though it seemed at variance with all human experience: by faith he offered up his only son, in whom alone that promise could be fulfilled[1]. Thus this one word 'faith' sums up the lesson of his whole life. And when, during the long silence of prophecy which separated the close of the Jewish from the birth of the Christian Scriptures, the Hebrews were led to reflect and comment on the records of their race, this feature of their great forefather's character did not escape notice. The two languages, which having supplanted the Hebrew, had now become the vehicles of theological teaching, both supplied words to express their meaning. In the Greek πίστις, in the Aramaic הימנותא, the hitherto missing term was first found. Lesson of Abraham's faith

As early as the First Book of Maccabees attention is directed to this lesson: 'Was not Abraham found faithful in temptation, and it was imputed unto him for righteousness[2]?' Here however it is touched upon very lightly. But there is, I think, sufficient evidence to show that at the time of the Christian era the passage in Genesis relating to Abraham's faith had become a standard text in the Jewish schools, variously discussed and commented upon, and that the interest thus concentrated on it prepared the way for the fuller and more spiritual teaching of the Apostles of Christ. becomes a thesis of the schools.

This appears to have been the case in both the great schools of Jewish theology, in the Alexandrian or Græco-Judaic, and the Rabbinical or Jewish proper, under which term we may include the teaching of the Babylonian dispersion as well as of Palestine, for there does not seem to have been any marked difference between the two.

Of the Alexandrian School indeed Philo is almost the sole surviving representative, but he represents it so fully as to leave little to be desired. In Philo's writings the life and character of Abraham are again and again commented upon[3]. The passage of Genesis (xv. 6), doubly familiar to us from the applications in the New Testament, is quoted or referred to at (i) Alexandrian Judaism.

[1] Acts vii. 2—5, Rom. iv. 16—22, Heb. xi. 8—12, 17—19.

[2] 1 Macc. ii. 52. Other less distinct references in the Apocrypha to the faith of Abraham are 2 Macc. i. 2, Ecclus. xliv. 19—21. In both passages πιστὸς occurs, but not πίστις.

[3] The history of Abraham is made the direct subject of comment in the works of Philo entitled *De Migrat. Abrah.* I. p. 436 (Mangey), *De Abrah.* II. p. 1, *Quaest. in Gen.* p. 167 (Aucher), besides being discussed in scattered passages, especially in *Quis Rer. Div. Her.* I. p. 473, *De Mutat. Nom.* I. p. 578.

Philo's comments on Gen. xv. 6.

least ten times[1]. Once or twice Philo, like St Paul, comments on the second clause of the verse, the imputation of righteousness to Abraham, but for the most part the coincidence is confined to the remarks on Abraham's faith. Sometimes indeed faith is deposed from its sovereign throne by being co-ordinated with piety[2], or by being regarded as the reward[3] rather than the source of a godly life. But far more generally it reigns supreme in his theology. It is 'the most perfect of virtues[4],' 'the queen of virtues[5].' It is 'the only sure and infallible good, the solace of life, the fulfilment of worthy hopes, barren of evil and fertile in good, the repudiation of the powers of evil, the confession of piety, the inheritance of happiness, the entire amelioration of the soul, which leans for support on Him who is the cause of all things, who is able to do all things, and willeth to do those which are most excellent[6].' They that 'preserve it sacred and inviolate' have 'dedicated to God their soul, their senses, their reason[7].' Such was the faith of Abraham, a 'most stedfast and unwavering faith,' in the possession of which he was 'thrice blessed indeed[8].'

The story of Abraham an allegory.

But in order to appreciate the points of divergence from, as well as of coincidence with, the Apostolic teaching in Philo's language and thoughts, it is necessary to remember the general bearing of the history of Abraham in his system. To him it was not a history, but an allegory; or, if a history as well, it was as such of infinitely little importance. The three patriarchs represent the human soul united to God by three different means, Abraham by instruction, Isaac by nature, Jacob by ascetic discipline[9]. Abraham therefore is the type of *διδασκαλικὴ ἀρετή*, he is the man who arrives at the knowledge of the true God by teaching (xii. 6)[10]. And

His migrations.

this is the meaning of his successive migrations, from Chaldæa to Charran, from Charran to the promised land[11]. For Chaldæa, the abode of astrology, represents his uninstructed state, when he worships the stars of heaven and sets the material universe in the place of the great First Cause. By the divine monition he departs thence to Charran. What then is Charran?

[1] *Leg. Alleg.* I. p. 132, *Quod Deus Imm.* I. p. 273, *de Migr. Abr.* I. p. 443, *Quis Rer. Div. Her.* I. pp. 485, 486, *de Mut. Nom.* I. pp. 605, 606, 611, *de Abr.* II. p. 39, *de Praem. et Poen.* II. p. 413, *de Nob.* II. p. 442.

[2] *de Migr. Abr.* I. p. 456 *τίς οὖν ἡ κόλλα* (i.e. which unites him to God); *τίς; εὐσέβεια δήπου καὶ πίστις.*

[3] *de Praem. et Poen.* II. p. 412 *ἐκ τύφου μεθορμισάμενος πρὸς ἀλήθειαν, διδακτικῇ χρησάμενος ἀρετῇ πρὸς τελείωσιν ἆθλον αἱρεῖται τὴν πρὸς τὸν Θεὸν πίστιν.*

[4] *Quis Rer. Div. Her.* I. p. 485 *τὴν τελειοτάτην ἀρετῶν πίστιν.*

[5] *de Abr.* II. p. 39 *τὴν βασιλίδα τῶν ἀρετῶν.*

[6] *de Abr.* l.c. I am not sure that I have caught the meaning of the words, *κακοδαιμονίας ἀπόγνωσις, εὐσεβείας γνῶσις, εὐδαιμονίας κλῆρος*, nor is it easy to find an adequate English rendering for them.

[7] *Quis Rer. Div. Her.* I. p. 487.

[8] *de Praem. et Poen.* II. p. 413 *ἀκλινοῦς καὶ βεβαιοτάτης πίστεως κ.τ.λ.*, comp. *de Nob.* II. p. 442.

[9] *Διδασκαλία, φύσις, ἄσκησις*, *de Mut. Nom.* I. p. 580, *de Abr.* I. p. 9, *de Praem. et Poen.* I. p. 412.

[10] The change of name from Abram to Abraham betokens this progress, *de Cherub.* I. p. 139, *de Mut. Nom.* I. p. 588, *de Abr.* II. p. 13, *Quaest. in Gen.* p. 213 (Aucher).

[11] On the meaning of Chaldæa and Charran see *de Migr. Abr.* I. p. 463 sq, *de Somn.* I. p. 626 sq, *de Abr.* II. p. 11 sq, *de Nob.* II. p. 441, *Quaest. in Gen.* p. 167 (Aucher).

The name itself, signifying 'a cave,' supplies the answer: the *senses* are denoted thereby[1]. He must submit to be instructed by these, and thus to learn by observation the true relations and bearings of the material world. This however is only a half-way house on his journey towards his destined goal. From Charran he must go forward to the land of promise; from the observation on the senses he must advance to the knowledge of the one true invisible God. And the rest of the story must be similarly explained. For what is meant by his leaving home and kindred? Surely nothing else but his detaching himself from the influence of the senses, from the domination of external things[2]. What again by the inheritance and the seed promised to him? The great nation, the numerous progeny, are the countless virtues which this frame of mind engenders[3]: the inheritance is the rich possession of wisdom, the lordship of the spirit over the domain of the senses[4]. And are not its very boundaries significant? The region comprises all that lies between the river of Egypt on the one hand, the symbol of material, and the river Euphrates on the other, the symbol of spiritual blessings[5].

His race and inheritance.

If as full a record had been preserved of the Rabbinical Schools of Palestine and Babylonia during the Apostolic age, we should probably have found that an equally prominent place was assigned to the faith of Abraham in their teaching also. The interpretation put upon the passage, and the lessons deduced from it, would indeed be widely different; but the importance of the text itself must have been felt even more strongly where the national feeling was more intense. The promise to Abraham, the charter of their existence as a people, was all important to them, and its conditions would be minutely and carefully scanned.

(ii) Rabbinical Judaism.

In the fourth Book of Esdras, one of the very few Jewish writings which can be attributed with any confidence to the Apostolic age, great stress is laid on faith. In the last days, it is said, 'the land of faith shall be barren' (or 'the land shall be barren of faith,' iii. 2). The seal of eternal life is set on those who 'have treasured up faith' (iv. 13). The wicked are described as 'not having had faith in God's statutes and having neglected His works' (v. 24). Immunity from punishment is promised to the man 'who can escape by his works and by his faith whereby he has believed' (ix. 8). God watches over those 'who have good works and faith in the Most High' (xiii. 31)[6].

4 Esdras.

There is however other evidence besides. For though the extant works of Rabbinical Judaism are, as written documents and in their present form, for the most part the productions of a later age, there can be little doubt that they embody more ancient traditions, and therefore reflect fairly, though with some exceptions, the Jewish teaching at the Christian era. Thus the importance then attached to faith, and the significance assigned

[1] *de Migr. Abr.* l.c. p. 465 τρώγλη τὸ τῆς αἰσθήσεως χωρίον, comp. *de Somn.* l. c.

[2] *de Migr. Abr.* I. p. 437.

[3] *ib.* p. 444, comp. *Quaest. in Gen.* pp. 211, 229 (Aucher).

[4] *Quis Rer. Div. Her.* I. p. 487, *Quaest. in Gen.* p. 216 (Aucher).

[5] *Quaest. in Gen.* p. 188 (Aucher).

[6] The references are taken from the text as printed in Gfrörer's *Prophet. Vet. Pseudepigr.*

to Abraham's example, may be inferred from the following passage in the Mechilta. *Mechilta* on Exodus xiv. 31[1]: 'Great is faith, whereby Israel believed on Him that spake and the world was. For as a reward for Israel's having believed in the Lord, the Holy Spirit dwelt on them...In like manner thou findest that Abraham our father inherited this world and the world to come solely by the merit of faith whereby he believed in the Lord; for it is said, *and he believed in the Lord, and He counted it to him for righteousness*...Rabbi Nehemiah says: He that taketh unto himself one precept in firm faith, on him the Holy Spirit dwelleth; for so we find in the case of our fathers, that, as a reward for their believing on the Lord, they were deemed worthy that the Holy Spirit should dwell on them...So Abraham solely for the merit of faith, whereby he believed in the Lord, inherited this world and the other...Only as a reward for their faith were the Israelites redeemed out of Egypt, for it is said, *And the people believed*...What is the cause of David's joy (in Ps. xci. 1)? It is the reward of faith, whereby our fathers believed...So Jeremiah (v. 3), *O Lord, thine eyes look upon faith*, and Habakkuk (ii. 4), *The righteous liveth of his faith*...Great is faith'; with more to the same effect. This passage should be taken in Siphri. connexion with the comment in *Siphri* on Deut. xi. 13[2]. 'The sacred text means to show that practice depends on doctrine and not doctrine on practice. And so we find too that (God) punishes more severely for doctrine than for practice, as it is said (in Hosea iv. 1), *Hear the word of the Lord etc.*' Gfrörer, to whom I am indebted for these passages, illustrates their bearing by reference to the opinions of later Jewish doctors who maintain that 'as soon as a man has mastered the thirteen heads of the faith, firmly believing therein, he is to be loved and forgiven and treated in all respects as a brother, and though he may have sinned in every possible way, he is indeed an erring Israelite, and is punished accordingly, but still he inherits eternal life[3].'

Coincidences and divergences. It were unwise to overlook the coincidences of language and thought which the contemporaneous teaching of the Jews occasionally presents to the Apostolic writings. The glory of the scriptural revelation does not pale because we find in the best thoughts of men 'broken lights' of its own fuller splendour. Yet on the other hand the resemblance must not be exaggerated. It is possible to repeat the same words and yet to attach to them an entirely different meaning: it is possible even to maintain the same precept, and yet by placing it in another connexion to lead it to an opposite practical issue. In the case before us the divergences are quite as striking as the coincidences.

[1] Ugolin. *Thes.* XIV. p. 202.

In marked contrast to these earlier comments is the treatment of the text, Gen. xv. 6, by some later Jewish writers. Anxious, it would appear, to cut the ground from under St Paul's inference of 'righteousness by faith,' they interpreted the latter clause, 'And Abraham counted on God's righteousness,' i.e. on His strict fulfilment of His promise. See the references in Beer's *Leben Abrahams* p. 147; comp. p. 33. Such a rendering is as harsh in itself, as it is devoid of traditional support.

[2] Ugolin. *Thes.* XV. p. 554.

[3] Abarbanel *Rosh Amanah* p. 5 *a*, Maimonides on *Mishna Sanhedr.* p. 121 *a*, referred to in Gfrörer *Jahrh. des Heils* II. p. 162.

St Paul and Philo.

If we look only to the individual man, faith with Philo is substantially the same as faith with St Paul. The lessons drawn from the history of Abraham by the Alexandrian Jew and the Christian Apostle differ very slightly. Faith is the postponement of all present aims and desires, the sacrifice of all material interests, to the Infinite and Unseen. But the philosopher of Alexandria saw no *historical* bearing in the career of Abraham. As he was severed from the heart of the nation, so the pulses of the national life had ceased to beat in him. The idea of a chosen people retained scarcely the faintest hold on his thoughts. Hence the only lesson which he drew from the patriarch's life had reference to himself. Abraham was but a type, a symbol of the individual man. The promises made to him, the rich inheritance, the numerous progeny, had no fulfilment except in the growth of his own character. The Alexandrian Jew, like the heathen philosopher, was exclusive, isolated, selfish. With him the theocracy of the Old Testament was emptied of all its meaning: the covenant was a matter between God and his own spirit. The idea of a *Church* did not enter into his reckoning. He appreciated the significance of Abraham's *faith*, but Abraham's *seed* was almost meaningless to him.

St Paul and Judaism proper.

On the other hand Judaism proper was strong where Alexandrian Judaism was weak, and weak where it was strong. The oppressive rule of Syrians and Romans had served only to develope and strengthen the national feeling. 'We are Abraham's sons, we have Abraham to our father': such was their religious war-cry, full of meaning to every true Israelite. It was a protest against selfish isolation. It spoke of a corporate life, of national hopes and interests, of an outward community, a common brotherhood, ruled by the same laws and animated by the same feelings. In other words, it kept alive the idea of a *Church*. This was the point of contact between St Paul's teaching and Rabbinical Judaism. But their agreement does not go much beyond this. With them indeed he upheld the faith of Abraham as an example to Abraham's descendants. But, while they interpreted it as a rigorous observance of outward ordinances, he understood by it a spiritual state, a steadfast reliance on the unseen God. With them too he clung to the fulfilment of the promise, he cherished fondly the privileges of a son of Abraham. But to him the link of brotherhood was no longer the same blood, but the same spirit: they only were Abraham's sons who inherited Abraham's faith.

Summary.

Thus the coincidences and contrasts of St Paul's doctrine of faith and of his application of Abraham's history with the teaching of the Jewish doctors are equally instructive. With the Alexandrian school it looked to the growth of the individual man, with the Rabbinical it recognised the claims of the society: with the one it was spiritual, with the other it was historical. On the other hand, it was a protest alike against the selfish, esoteric, individualising spirit of the one, and the narrow, slavish formalism of the other.

Other elements in St Paul's teaching.

This sketch is very far from doing justice to St Paul's doctrine of faith. In order fully to understand its force, or indeed to appreciate its leading conception, it would be necessary to take into account the atoning death and resurrection of Christ as the central object on which that faith is fixed. This however lies apart from the present question, for it has no direct bearing on the lesson drawn from Abraham's example. In a certain sense indeed the Messiah may be said to have been the object of Abraham's faith; for He, as the fulfilment of the promise, must have been dimly discerned by Abraham, as by one 'looking through a glass darkly.' And to this vague presentiment of a future Triumph or Redemption we may perhaps refer our Lord's words (John viii. 56), 'Your father Abraham rejoiced to see My day: and he saw it and was glad.' But however this may be, St Paul makes no such application of Abraham's example. He does not once allude to the Christ, as the object of the patriarch's faith.

Comparison of St Paul and St James,

To return once again to the passages from Jewish writers already cited: they are important in their bearing on the interpretation of the Apostolic writings in yet another point of view. The example of Abraham is quoted both by St Paul and St James; while the deductions which the two Apostles draw from it are at first sight diametrically opposed in terms. 'We conclude that a man is justified by faith apart from (χωρὶς) works of law,' says St Paul (Rom. iii. 28). 'A man is justified of works and not of faith only,' are the words of St James (ii. 24). Now, so long as our range of view is confined to the Apostolic writings, it seems scarcely possible to resist the impression that St James is attacking the teaching, if not of St Paul himself, at least of those who exaggerated and perverted it. But when we realise the fact that the passage in Genesis was a common thesis in the schools of the day, that the meaning of *faith* was variously explained by the disputants, that diverse lessons were drawn from it—then the case is altered. The Gentile Apostle and the Pharisaic Rabbi might both maintain the supremacy of faith as the means of salvation: but faith with St Paul was a very different thing from faith with Maimonides for instance. With the one its prominent idea is a *spiritual life*, with the other an *orthodox creed*: with the one the guiding principle is the individual conscience, with the other an external rule of ordinances: with the one faith is allied to liberty, with the other to bondage. Thus it becomes a question, whether St James's protest against reliance on faith alone has any reference, direct or indirect, to St Paul's language and teaching; whether in fact it is not aimed against an entirely different type of religious feeling, against the Pharisaic spirit which rested satisfied with a barren orthodoxy fruitless in works of charity. Whether this is the true bearing of the Epistle of St James or not, must be determined by a close examination of its contents. But inasmuch as the circles of labour of the two Apostles were not likely to intersect, we have at least a *prima facie* reason for seeking the objects of St James's rebuke elsewhere than in the disciples of St Paul, and the facts collected above destroy the force of any argument founded on the mere coincidence of the examples chosen[1].

illustrated by the facts collected.

[1] This view of the Epistle of St James is taken by Michaelis (VI. p. 302, Marsh's 2nd ed.). It is also adopted by Neander: see especially his *Pflanzung* p. 567 (4te aufl.). He there refers, in illustration of this Jewish mode of thinking against which he supposes the epistle to be directed, to Justin *Dial. c. Tryph.* p. 370 D οὐχ ὡς ὑμεῖς ἀπατᾶτε ἑαυτοὺς καὶ ἄλλοι τινὲς ὑμῖν ὅμοιοι (i.e. Judaizing Christians) κατὰ τοῦτο, οἳ λέγουσιν ὅτι, κἂν ἁμαρτωλοὶ ὦσι θεὸν δὲ γινώσκουσιν, οὐ μὴ λογίσηται αὐτοῖς Κύριος ἁμαρτίαν: and to the *Clem. Hom.* iii. 6. Several later writers have maintained the same view. For more on this subject see the Dissertation on 'St Paul and the Three.'

IV. ¹Λέγω δέ, ἐφ' ὅσον χρόνον ὁ κληρονόμος νήπιός

IV. 1—7. In the former paragraph St Paul starting from the figure of the pædagogus had been led to speak of the sonship of the faithful in Christ. The opening verses of this chapter are an expansion of the same image. The heir in his nonage represents the state of the world before the Gospel. In drawing out the comparison, St Paul seems to include Gentiles as well as Jews under this 'tutelage,' all having more or less been subject to a system of positive ordinances, and so far gone through a disciplinary training. In the image itself however there are two points to be cleared up.

First. Is the father of the heir represented as dead or living? On the one hand individual expressions point to the decease of the father; a very unnatural meaning must otherwise be forced upon the words, 'heir,' 'guardian,' 'lord of all.' On the other hand the metaphor in its application refers to a living Father. The latter consideration must yield to the former. The point of the comparison lies not in the circumstances of the father, but of the son. All metaphors must cease to apply at some point, and the death of the father is the limit here imposed by the nature of the case. Our Father never dies; the inheritance never passes away from Him: yet nevertheless we succeed to the full possession of it.

Secondly. It has been questioned whether St Paul borrows the imagery here from Roman or from Jewish law, or even, as some maintain, from a special code in force in Galatia. In the absence of very ample information, we may say that, so far as he alludes to any definite form of the law of guardianship, he would naturally refer to the Roman; but, as the terms are not technically exact (e.g. νήπιος, προθεσμία), he seems to put forward rather the general conception of the office of a guardian, than any definite statute regulating it. His language indeed agrees much better with our simpler modern practice, than with Roman law, which in this respect was artificial and elaborate.

'I described the law as our tutor. I spoke of our release from its restraints. Let me explain my meaning more fully. An heir during his minority is treated as a servant. Notwithstanding his expectations as the future lord of the property, he is subject to the control of guardians and stewards, until the time of release named in his father's will arrives. In like manner mankind itself was a minor before Christ's coming. It was subject, like a child, to the discipline of external ordinances. At length when the time was fully arrived, God sent His own Son into the world, born of a woman as we are, subject to law as we are, that He might redeem and liberate those who are so subject, and that we all might receive our destined adoption as sons. Of this sonship God has given us a token. He sent forth into our hearts the Spirit of His Son, which witnesses in us and cries to Him as to a Father. Plainly then, thou art no more a servant, but a son; and, as a son, thou art also an heir, through the goodness of God.'

1. Λέγω δέ] 'But what I would say is this,' introducing an expansion or explanation of what has gone before: see v. 16, Rom. xv. 8, and for the more definite τοῦτο δὲ λέγω, Gal. iii. 17 (with the note), 1 Cor. i. 12.

νήπιος] '*an infant.*' As this does not appear to have been a technical term in Greek, or at least in Attic law (where the distinction is between παῖς and ἀνήρ), it probably represents the Latin 'infans.' If so, its use here, though sufficiently exact for the purposes of the comparison, is not technically precise. The 'infantia' of a

ἐστιν, οὐδὲν διαφέρει δούλου κύριος πάντων ὤν, ²ἀλλὰ ὑπὸ ἐπιτρόπους ἐστὶν καὶ οἰκονόμους ἄχρι τῆς προθεσ-

Roman child ended with his seventh year, after which he was competent to perform certain legal acts, but he was not entirely emancipated from a state of tutelage till he entered on his twenty-fifth year, having passed through several intermediate stages. See Savigny *Röm. Recht.* III. p. 25 sq. Νήπιος seems to be here 'a minor' in any stage of his minority. The word is opposed to ἀνήρ, 1 Cor. xiii. 11, Ephes. iv. 13, 14: comp. Dion. Hal. iv. 9, Gruter *Inscr.* p. 682. 9. See Philo *Leg. ad Cai.* 4, II. p. 549 νήπιον ἔτι ὄντα κομιδῇ καὶ χρῄζοντα ἐπιτρόπων καὶ διδασκάλων καὶ παιδαγωγῶν.

οὐδὲν διαφέρει δούλου] The minor was legally in much the same position as the slave. He could not perform any act, except through his legal representative. This responsible person, the guardian in the case of the minor, the master in the case of the slave, who represented him to the state, and whose sanction was necessary for the validity of any contract undertaken on his behalf, was termed in Attic law κύριος, Meier *Att. Proc.* p. 450. Prospectively however, though not actually, the minor was κύριος πάντων, which the slave was not.

2. ἐπιτρόπους καὶ οἰκονόμους] '*controllers of his person and property.*' The language is intended, as the plurals show, to be as comprehensive as possible. It is therefore vain to search for the exact technical term in Roman law corresponding to each word. The Latin fathers translate them variously; 'curatores et actores' *Vict.*, *Hil.*, *Interp. Orig.*; 'tutores et actores' *Pelag.*, *Hier.*; 'procuratores et actores' *Aug.*; 'tutores et dispensatores' *Interp. Theod. Mops.* The distinction given in the above translation seems the most probable. The ἐπίτροποι are the boy's legal representatives, his guardians (whether 'curatores' or 'tutores' in Roman law); the οἰκονόμοι, stewards or bailiffs appointed to manage his household or property. The word ἐπίτροπος elsewhere in the New Testament, Matt. xx. 8, Luke viii. 3, is 'a steward.' Adopted into the Rabbinical language (אפיטרופוס) it has a comprehensive meaning, signifying sometimes a guardian, sometimes a steward: see Schöttgen here and on Luke viii. 3.

τῆς προθεσμίας] sc. ἡμέρας, '*the day appointed beforehand,*' generally as a limit to the performance or non-performance of an action; in this case as the time at which the office of guardian ceases. A difficulty however presents itself in πατρός. In Roman law the term was fixed by statute, so that the father did not generally exercise any control over it. It has been supposed indeed, that St Paul refers to some exceptional legislation by which greater power was given to the Galatians in this respect: but this view seems to rest on a mistaken interpretation of a passage in Gaius (i. § 55). It would appear however, that by Roman law some discretion was left to the father, at all events in certain cases; see Gaius § 186 'Si cui testamento tutor *sub condicione aut ex die certo* datus sit': comp. Justinian's *Instit.* I. xiv. 3; and probably more exact information would show that the law was not so rigorous as is often assumed. Considering then (1) That though the term of guardianship was not generally settled by the will of the testator, the choice of persons was, and (2) That in appointments made for special purposes this power was given to the testator; the expression in question will perhaps not appear out of place, even if St Paul's illustration be supposed to be drawn directly from Roman law.

3. ἡμεῖς] '*we,*' Jews and Gentiles

μίας τοῦ πατρός. ³οὕτως καὶ ἡμεῖς, ὅτε ἦμεν νήπιοι, ὑπὸ τὰ στοιχεῖα τοῦ κόσμου ἦμεν δεδουλωμένοι· ⁴ὅτε

alike, as appears from the whole context. See the note on ver. 11.

τα στοιχεῖα] '*the elements*,' originally 'the letters of the alphabet,' as being set in rows. From this primary sense the word gets two divergent meanings among others, both of which have been assigned to it in this passage; (1) 'The physical elements' (2 Pet. iii. 10, 12, Wisd. vii. 17), as earth, fire, etc. (Hermas *Vis.* iii. 13), and especially the heavenly bodies: comp. *Clem. Hom.* x. 9, 25, Justin *Apol.* ii. p. 44 A τὰ οὐράνια στοιχεῖα, *Dial.* p. 285 C. They were probably so called chronologically, as the elements of time (Theoph. *ad Aut.* i. 4 ἥλιος καὶ σελήνη καὶ ἀστέρες στοιχεῖα αὐτοῦ εἰσίν, εἰς σημεῖα καὶ εἰς καιροὺς καὶ εἰς ἡμέρας καὶ εἰς ἐνιαυτοὺς γεγονότα): (2) 'The alphabet of learning, rudimentary instruction'; as Heb. v. 12.

The former sense is commonly adopted by the fathers, who for the most part explain it of the observance of days and seasons, regulated by the heavenly bodies. So Hilar., Pelag., Chrysost., Theod. Mops., Theodoret; comp. *Ep. ad Diog.* § 4. Victorinus strangely interprets it of the influence of the stars on the heathen not yet emancipated by Christ; and Augustine supposes that St Paul is referring to the Gentile worship of the physical elements. The two latter interpretations are at all events excluded by ἡμεῖς, which must include Jews. The agreement in favour of this sense of στοιχεῖα may, I think, be attributed to the influence of a passage in the *Praedicatio Petri*, quoted in Clem. Alex. *Strom.* vi. (p. 760, Potter), Orig. *in Ioann.* iv. 22 (IV. p. 226, Delarue), in which the worship of the Jews is classed with that of the heathen; inasmuch as, professing to know God, they were in fact by this observance of days and seasons λατρεύοντες ἀγγέλοις καὶ ἀρχαγγέλοις, μηνὶ καὶ σελήνῃ. At all events I can scarcely doubt that this interpretation of στοιχεῖα became current through Origen's influence. It seems to be much more in accordance with the prevailing tone of Alexandrian theology, than with the language and teaching of St Paul. Comp. Philo *de Migr. Abr.* p. 464 M.

On the other hand a few of the fathers (Jerome, Gennadius, Primasius) adopt the other sense, 'elementary teaching.' This is probably the correct interpretation, both as simpler in itself and as suiting the context better. St Paul seems to be dwelling still on the rudimentary character of the law, as fitted for an earlier stage in the world's history. The expression occurs again in reference to formal ordinances, Col. ii. 8 κατὰ τὴν παράδοσιν τῶν ἀνθρώπων κατὰ τὰ στοιχεῖα τοῦ κόσμου, and ii. 20 εἰ ἀπεθάνετε σὺν Χριστῷ ἀπὸ τῶν στοιχείων τοῦ κόσμου, τί ὡς ζῶντες ἐν κόσμῳ δογματίζεσθε; In these passages the words of the context which are emphasized seem to show that *a mode of instruction* is signified by τὰ στοιχεῖα τοῦ κόσμου.

τοῦ κόσμου] '*of the world*,' i.e. having reference to material and not to spiritual things, formal and sensuous. The force of τοῦ κόσμου is best explained by the parallel passages already cited, Col. ii. 8, 20. See below, vi. 14.

4. τὸ πλήρωμα τοῦ χρόνου] The ideas involved in this expression may be gathered from the context. It was 'the fulness of time.' *First;* In reference to the *Giver*. The moment had arrived which God had ordained from the beginning and foretold by His prophets for Messiah's coming. This is implied in the comparison ἡ προθεσμία τοῦ πατρός. *Secondly;* In reference to the *recipient*. The Gospel was withheld until the world had arrived at mature age: law had worked out its educational purpose and now was su-

δὲ ἦλθεν τὸ πλήρωμα τοῦ χρόνου, ἐξαπέστειλεν ὁ Θεὸς τὸν υἱὸν αὐτοῦ, γενόμενον ἐκ γυναικός, γενόμενον ὑπὸ νόμον, 5 ἵνα τοὺς ὑπὸ νόμον ἐξαγοράσῃ, ἵνα τὴν υἱοθε-

perseded. This educational work had been twofold: (1) *Negative*: It was the purpose of all law, but especially of the Mosaic law, to deepen the conviction of sin and thus to show the inability of all existing systems to bring men near to God. This idea, which is so prominent in the Epistle to the Romans, appears in the context here, vv. 19, 21. (2) *Positive*. The comparison of the child implies more than a negative effect. A moral and spiritual expansion, which rendered the world more capable of apprehending the Gospel than it would have been at an earlier age, must be assumed, corresponding to the growth of the individual; since otherwise the metaphor would be robbed of more than half its meaning.

The primary reference in all this is plainly to the Mosaic law: but the whole context shows that the Gentile converts of Galatia are also included, and that they too are regarded as having undergone an elementary discipline, up to a certain point analogous to that of the Jews. See the remarks on ver. 11.

πλήρωμα] '*the complement*.' On this word see *Colossians*, p. 257 sq.

ἐξαπέστειλεν] '*He sent forth from Himself*, as His representative': '*ex* caelo *a* sese,' says Bengel. This word assumes the pre-existence of the Son, but must not be pressed to imply also the unity with the Father, for it is commonly used in later Greek in speaking of any mission.

γενόμενον ἐκ γυναικός] i.e. taking upon Himself our human nature; comp. Job xiv. 1, Matt. xi. 11. These passages show that the expression must not be taken as referring to the miraculous incarnation. See Basil *de Spir. Sanct.* v. 12.

γενόμενον ὑπὸ νόμον] not τὸν νόμον; for though Christ was born under the Mosaic law, the application of the principle is much wider. See the note on the next verse.

5. The two clauses correspond to those of the foregoing verse in an inverted order by the grammatical figure called chiasm; 'The Son of God was born a man, that in Him all men might become sons of God; He was born subject to law, that those subject to law might be rescued from bondage.' At the same time the figure is not arbitrarily employed here, but the inversion arises out of the necessary sequence. The abolition of the law, the rescue from bondage, was a prior condition of the universal sonship of the faithful. See the note on iii. 14.

τοὺς ὑπὸ νόμον] again not τὸν νόμον. St Paul refers primarily to the Mosaic law, as at once the highest and most rigorous form of law, but extends the application to all those subject to any system of positive ordinances. We seem to have the same extension, starting from the law of Moses, in 1 Cor. ix. 20, ἐγενόμην τοῖς Ἰουδαίοις ὡς Ἰουδαῖος... τοῖς ὑπὸ νόμον ὡς ὑπὸ νόμον.

ἐξαγοράσῃ] See the note on iii. 13.

ἵνα, ἵνα] For the repetition of ἵνα, and for the general connexion of thought, see the note iii. 14. In this passage it is perhaps best to take the two as independent of each other, inasmuch as the two clauses to which they respectively refer are likewise independent. Comp. Ephes. v. 26, 27.

τὴν υἱοθεσίαν] not 'the sonship,' but 'the adoption as sons.' Υἱοθεσία seems never to have the former sense; see Fritzsche on Rom. viii. 15. Potentially indeed men were sons before Christ's coming (ver. 1), but actually they were only slaves (ver. 3). His coming conferred upon them the privileges of sons: 'Adoptionem propterea dicit,'

σίαν ἀπολάβωμεν. [6]ὅτι δέ ἐστε υἱοί, ἐξαπέστειλεν ὁ Θεὸς τὸ πνεῦμα τοῦ υἱοῦ αὐτοῦ εἰς τὰς καρδίας ἡμῶν, κρᾶζον Ἀββᾶ ὁ πατήρ. [7]ὥστε οὐκέτι εἶ δοῦλος, ἀλλὰ

says Augustine with true appreciation, 'ut distincte intelligamus unicum Dei filium.' We are sons by grace; He is so by nature.

ἀπολάβωμεν] The exact sense of the preposition will depend on the meaning assigned to υἱοθεσίαν. If υἱοθεσία be taken as adoption, ἀπολάβωμεν must signify 'receive *as destined for*, *as promised to* us,' or, as Augustine says, 'nec dixit *accipiamus*, sed *recipiamus*, ut significaret hoc nos amisisse in Adam, ex quo mortales sumus.' At all events it cannot be equivalent to λάβωμεν. The change to the first person plural marks the universality of the sonship: '*we*, those under law and those free from law, alike.'

6. ὅτι ἐστὲ υἱοί] '*because ye are sons*.' The presence of the Spirit is thus a witness of their sonship. The force of this clause is best explained by the parallel passage, Rom. viii. 15, 16. St Paul seems here to be dwelling on the same idea as in iii. 2. Their reconciliation with God was complete without works of law, the gift of the Spirit being a proof of this. See also Acts x. 44, xi. 15—18, xv. 8.

κρᾶζον] The word denotes earnest and importunate prayer, as in Is. xix. 20: comp. James v. 4.

Ἀββᾶ ὁ πατήρ] Abba is the Aramaic equivalent to the Greek πατήρ. The combination of the two words seems to have been a liturgical formula. It occurs in Mark xiv. 36 in the mouth of our Lord, and also in Rom. viii. 15, in a passage closely resembling this. The origin of this formula may be explained in two ways. *First*, It originated with the Hellenistic Jews who would naturally adhere with fondness to the original word consecrated in their prayers by long usage, and add to it the equivalent in the Greek language which they ordinarily spoke. In this case, in the passage of St Mark the words ὁ πατήρ may perhaps be an addition of the Evangelist himself, explaining the Aramaic word after his wont. *Secondly*, It may have taken its rise among the Jews of Palestine after they had become acquainted with the Greek language. In this case it is simply an expression of importunate entreaty, illustrating the natural mode of emphasizing by repetition of the same idea in different forms. This latter explanation seems simpler, and best explains the expression as coming from our Lord's lips. It is moreover supported by similar instances given in Schöttgen, II. p. 252: e.g. a woman entreating a judge addresses him מרי כירי, the second word being κύριε, the Greek equivalent to the Aramaic מרי 'my Lord.' For other examples see Rev. ix. 11 (Ἀπολλύων, Ἀβαδδών), xii. 9, xx. 2 (Σατανᾶς, Διάβολος). Whichever explanation be adopted, this phrase is a speaking testimony to that fusion of Jew and Greek which prepared the way for the preaching of the Gospel to the heathen. Accordingly St Paul in both passages seems to dwell on it with peculiar emphasis, as a type of the union of Jew and Gentile in Christ: comp. iii. 28.

Ἀββᾶ] In Chaldee אַבָּא, in Syriac ܐܒܐ. In the latter dialect it is said to have been pronounced with a double *b* when applied to a spiritual father, with a single *b* when used in its first sense: see Bernstein's *Lex.* s. v. and comp. Hoffmann, *Gramm. Syr.* I. 1, § 17. With the double letter at all events it has passed into the European languages, as an ecclesiastical term, 'abbas,' 'abbot.' The Peshito in rendering Ἀββᾶ ὁ πατήρ can only repeat the word, '*Father our Father*,' in all

υἱός· εἰ δὲ υἱός, καὶ κληρονόμος διὰ Θεοῦ. 8ἀλλὰ τότε μὲν οὐκ εἰδότες Θεὸν ἐδουλεύσατε τοῖς φύσει μὴ οὖσιν θεοῖς· 9νῦν δὲ γνόντες Θεόν, μᾶλλον δὲ γνωσθέντες

three passages where the expression occurs.

ὁ πατήρ] The nominative with the article is here used for an emphatic vocative, as e.g. Luke viii. 54 ἡ παῖς, ἔγειρε. See Winer, § xxix. p. 227. This is a Hebraism; comp. Gesen. *Heb. Gramm.* § 107.

7. ὥστε] '*therefore*,' in reference to all that has gone before; 'Seeing (1) that this naturally follows when your minority has come to an end; and (2) that you have direct proof of it in the gift of the Spirit, the token of sonship.'

οὐκέτι εἶ] '*thou art no longer*,' now that Christ has come. The appeal is driven home by the successive changes in the mode of address; *first*, 'we, all Christians, far and wide, Jews and Gentiles alike' (ἀπολάβωμεν, ver. 5); *next*, 'you, my Galatian converts' (ἐστέ, ver. 6); *lastly*, 'each individual man who hears my words' (εἶ, ver. 7).

εἰ δὲ υἱός, καὶ κληρονόμος] Comp. Rom. viii. 17 εἰ δὲ τέκνα, καὶ κληρονόμοι. It has been made a question whether St Paul is here drawing his illustrations from Jewish or from Roman law. In answer to this it is perhaps sufficient to say, that so far as he has in view any special form of law, he would naturally refer to the Roman, as most familiar to his readers. And indeed the Roman law of inheritance supplied a much truer illustration of the privileges of the Christian, than the Jewish. By Roman law all the children, whether sons or daughters, inherited alike (comp. iii. 28 οὐκ ἔνι ἄρσεν καὶ θῆλυ); by Jewish, the sons inherited unequally, and except in default of male heirs the daughters were excluded; Michaelis *Laws of Moses* III. 3, § 1. See a paper of C. F. A. Fritzsche in Fritzsch. *Opusc.* I. p. 143.

διὰ Θεοῦ] '*heir* not by virtue of birth, or through merits of your own, but *through God* who adopted you.' For διὰ see the note on i. 1. This is doubtless the right reading, having the preponderance of authority in its favour. All other variations, including that of the received text, κληρονόμος Θεοῦ διὰ Χριστοῦ, are apparently substitutions of a common expression for one which is unusual and startling.

8—11. 'Nevertheless, in an unfilial spirit, ye have subjected yourselves again to bondage, ye would fain submit anew to a weak and beggarly discipline of restraint. And how much less pardonable is this now! For then ye were idolaters from ignorance of God, but now ye have known God, or rather have been known of Him. Ye are scrupulous in your observance of months and seasons and years. Ye terrify me, lest all the toil which I have expended on you should be found vain.'

ἀλλά] '*yet still*, in spite of your sonship,' referring not to ἐδουλεύσατε with which it stands in close proximity, but to the more remote ἐπιστρέφετε (ver. 9); comp. Rom. vi. 17 χάρις δὲ τῷ Θεῷ, ὅτι ἦτε δοῦλοι, ὑπηκούσατε δὲ ἐκ καρδίας κ.τ.λ. The intervening words (ver. 8) are inserted to prepare the way for πάλιν.

τότε μὲν οὐκ εἰδότες] 'Then it was through ignorance of God that ye were subject etc.'; a partial excuse for their former bondage. For the expression εἰδέναι Θεὸν see 1 Thess. iv. 5, 2 Thess. i. 8.

τοῖς φύσει μὴ οὖσιν θεοῖς] '*to those who by nature were not gods*,' i.e. μὴ οὖσιν θεοῖς ἀλλὰ δαιμονίοις; comp. 1 Cor. x. 20 ἃ θύουσιν [τὰ ἔθνη], δαιμονίοις καὶ οὐ Θεῷ θύουσιν. This is the correct order. On the other hand in the reading of the received text, τοῖς μὴ φύσει οὖσιν θεοῖς, the negative affects φύσει; i.e. μὴ φύσει ἀλλὰ λόγῳ, 'not by na-

ὑπὸ Θεοῦ, πῶς ἐπιστρέφετε πάλιν ἐπὶ τὰ ἀσθενῆ καὶ πτωχὰ στοιχεῖα, οἷς πάλιν ἄνωθεν δουλεύειν θέλετε; 10 ἡμέρας παρατηρεῖσθε καὶ μῆνας καὶ καιροὺς

ture, but by repute'; comp. 1 Cor. viii. 5 εἰσὶν λεγόμενοι θεοί.

9. γνόντες] '*having discerned, recognised*,' to be distinguished from the preceding εἰδότες. See 1 Joh. ii. 29 ἐὰν εἰδῆτε ὅτι δίκαιός ἐστιν, γινώσκετε ὅτι καὶ πᾶς κ.τ.λ., John xxi. 17, Ephes. v. 5, 1 Cor. ii. 11: comp. Gal. ii. 7, 9. While οἶδα 'I know' refers to the knowledge of facts absolutely, γινώσκω 'I recognise,' being relative, gives prominence either to the *attainment* or the *manifestation* of the knowledge. Thus γινώσκειν will be used in preference to εἰδέναι; (1) where there is reference to some earlier state of ignorance, or to some prior facts on which the knowledge is based; (2) where the ideas of 'thoroughness, familiarity,' or of 'approbation,' are involved: these ideas arising out of the stress which γινώσκειν lays on the *process* of reception. Both words occur very frequently in the First Epistle of St John, and a comparison of the passages where they are used brings out this distinction of meaning clearly.

γνωσθέντες ὑπὸ Θεοῦ] added to obviate any false inference, as though the reconciliation with God were attributable to a man's own effort. See 1 Cor. viii. 2 εἴ τις δοκεῖ ἐγνωκέναι τι, οὔπω ἔγνω καθὼς δεῖ γνῶναι· εἰ δέ τις ἀγαπᾷ τὸν Θεόν, οὗτος ἔγνωσται ὑπ' αὐτοῦ: comp. 1 Cor. xiii. 12. God knows man, but man knows not God or knows Him but imperfectly. See also 1 Joh. iv. 10 οὐχ ὅτι ἡμεῖς ἠγαπήκαμεν τὸν Θεόν, ἀλλ' ὅτι αὐτὸς ἠγάπησεν ἡμᾶς.

πῶς ἐπιστρέφετε] The Apostle's eagerness to remonstrate leads him to interrupt by an interrogation the natural flow of the sentence as marked out by the foregoing words. A present tense is used, for the change was still going on; comp. i. 6 μετατίθεσθε.

ἀσθενῆ καὶ πτωχά] '*weak*,' for they have no power to rescue man from condemnation; '*beggarly*,' for they bring no rich endowment of spiritual treasures. For ἀσθενῆ see Rom. viii. 3 τὸ ἀδύνατον τοῦ νόμου (comp. Gal. iii. 21), Heb. vii. 18 τὸ ἀσθενὲς καὶ ἀνωφελές.

πάλιν ἄνωθεν] a strong expression to describe the completeness of their *relapse*.

10. ἡμέρας κ.τ.λ.] Comp. Col. ii. 16 ἐν μέρει ἑορτῆς ἢ νεομηνίας ἢ σαββάτων, which passage explains the expressions here, stopping short however of ἐνιαυτοί. The ἡμέραι are the days recurring weekly, the sabbaths: μῆνες, the monthly celebrations, the new moons: καιροί, the annual festivals, as the passover, pentecost, etc.; ἐνιαυτοί, the sacred years, as the sabbatical year and the year of jubilee. Comp. Judith viii. 6 χωρὶς προσαββάτων καὶ σαββάτων καὶ προνουμηνιῶν καὶ νουμηνιῶν καὶ ἑορτῶν καὶ χαρμοσυνῶν οἴκου Ἰσραήλ, Philo *de Sept.* p. 286 M. ἵνα τὴν ἑβδομάδα τιμήσῃ κατὰ πάντας χρόνους ἡμερῶν καὶ μηνῶν καὶ ἐνιαυτῶν κ.τ.λ. For μῆνες in the sense it has here comp. Is. lxvi. 23 καὶ ἔσται μὴν ἐκ μηνὸς καὶ σάββατον ἐκ σαββάτου. On this use of καιρὸς for an *annually* recurring season see Mœris p. 214 (Bekker), Ὥρα ἔτους, Ἀττικοί· καιρὸς ἔτους, Ἕλληνες: and Hesychius, Ὥρα ἔτους· καιρὸς ἔτους· τὸ ἔαρ καὶ τὸ θέρος.

ἐνιαυτούς] It has been calculated (Wieseler, *Chron. Synops.* p. 204 sq and here) that the year from autumn 54 to autumn 55 was a sabbatical year; and an inference has been drawn from this as to the date of the epistle. The enumeration however seems to be intended as general and exhaustive, and no special reference can be assumed.

On the Christian observance of days in reference to this prohibition of St

καὶ ἐνιαυτούς; 11 φοβοῦμαι ὑμᾶς, μή πως εἰκῇ κεκοπίακα εἰς ὑμᾶς.

Paul see the excellent remarks of Origen, *c. Cels.* viii. 21—23.

παρατηρεῖσθε] *'ye minutely, scrupulously observe,'* literally 'ye go along with and observe': comp. Ps. cxxix. 3 ἐὰν ἀνομίας παρατηρήσῃς, Joseph. *Ant.* iii. 5. 5 παρατηρεῖν τὰς ἑβδομάδας, *Clem. Hom.* xix. 22 ἀμελήσαντες τὴν παρατήρησιν. In this last passage, which enjoins the observance of days (ἐπιτηρήσιμοι ἡμέραι), there is apparently an attack on St Paul; see above, p. 61. There seems to be no authority for assigning to παρατηρεῖν the sense 'wrongly observe,' nor is the analogy of such words as παρακούειν sufficiently close to bear it out. Here the middle voice still further enforces the idea of interested, assiduous observance; comp. Luke xiv. 1.

11. κεκοπίακα] the indicative mood, because the speaker suspects that what he fears has actually happened. Herm. on Soph. *Aj.* 272 says, 'μή ἐστι verentis quidem est sed indicantis simul putare se ita esse ut veretur.' See Winer § lvi. p. 631 sq.

In the above passage St Paul expressively describes the Mosaic law, as a rudimentary teaching, the alphabet, as it were, of moral and spiritual instruction. The child must be taught by definite rules, learnt by rote. The chosen race, like the individual man, has had its period of childhood. During this period, the mode of instruction was tempered to its undeveloped capacities. It was subject to a discipline of absolute precepts, of external ordinances.

It is clear however from the context, that the Apostle is not speaking of the Jewish race alone, but of the heathen world also before Christ—not of the Mosaic law only, but of all forms of law which might be subservient to the same purpose. This appears from his including his Galatian hearers under the same tutelage. Nor is this fact to be explained by supposing them to have passed through a stage of Jewish proselytism on their way to Christianity. St Paul distinctly refers to their previous idolatrous worship (ver. 8), and no less distinctly and emphatically does he describe their adoption of Jewish ritualism, as a *return* to the weak and beggarly discipline of childhood, from which they had been emancipated when they abandoned that worship.

But how, we may ask, could St Paul class in the same category that divinely ordained law which he elsewhere describes as 'holy and just and good' (Rom. vii. 12), and those degraded heathen systems which he elsewhere reprobates as 'fellowship with devils' (1 Cor. x. 20)?

The answer seems to be that the Apostle here regards the higher element in heathen religion as corresponding, however imperfectly, to the lower element in the Mosaic law. For we may consider both the one and the other as made up of two component parts, the *spiritual* and the *ritualistic*.

Now viewed in their *spiritual* aspect there is no comparison between the one and the other. In this respect the heathen religions, so far as they added anything of their own to that sense of dependence on God which is innate in man and which they could not entirely crush (Acts xiv. 17, xvii. 23, 27, 28, Rom. i. 19, 20), were wholly bad; they were profligate and soul-destroying, were the prompting of devils. On the contrary in the Mosaic law the spiritual element was most truly divine. But this does not enter into our reckoning here. For Christianity has appropriated all that was spiritual in its predecessor. The Mosaic dispensation was a foreshadowing, a germ of the Gospel: and thus, when

[12]Γίνεσθε ὡς ἐγώ, ὅτι κἀγὼ ὡς ὑμεῖς, ἀδελφοί, δέομαι ὑμῶν· οὐδέν με ἠδικήσατε· [13]οἴδατε δὲ ὅτι δι'

Christ came, its spiritual element was of necessity extinguished or rather absorbed by its successor. Deprived of this, it was a mere mass of lifeless ordinances, differing only in degree, not in kind, from any other ritualistic system.

Thus the *ritualistic* element alone remains to be considered, and here is the meeting point of Judaism and Heathenism. In Judaism this was as much lower than its spiritual element, as in Heathenism it was higher. Hence the two systems approach within such a distance of each other that they can under certain limitations be classed together. They have at least so much in common that a lapse into Judaism can be regarded as a relapse to the position of unconverted Heathenism. Judaism was a system of bondage like Heathenism. Heathenism had been a disciplinary training like Judaism.

It is a fair inference, I think, from St Paul's language here, that he does place Heathenism in the same category with Judaism in this last respect. Both alike are στοιχεῖα, 'elementary systems of training.' They had at least this in common, that as ritual systems they were made up of precepts and ordinances, and thus were representatives of 'law' as opposed to 'grace,' 'promise,' that is, as opposed to the Gospel. Doubtless in this respect even the highest form of heathen religion was much lower and less efficient than the Mosaic ritual. But still in an imperfect way they might do the same work: they might act as a restraint, which multiplying transgressions and thus begetting and cherishing a conviction of sin prepared the way for the liberty of manhood in Christ.

Thus comparing the two together from the point of view in which St Paul seems to consider them, we get as the component parts of each: JUDAISM; (1) The *spiritual*—absolutely good, absorbed in the Gospel; (2) The *ritualistic*—relatively good, στοιχεῖα: HEATHENISM; (1) The *ritualistic*—relatively good, στοιχεῖα; (2) The *spiritual*—absolutely bad, antagonistic to the Gospel.

If this explanation of St Paul's meaning be correct, it will appear on the one hand that his teaching has nothing in common with Goethe's classification, when he placed Judaism at the head of Ethnic religions. On the other hand it will explain the intense hatred with which the Judaizers, wholly unable to rise above the level of their sectarian prejudices and take a comprehensive view of God's providence, regarded the name and teaching of St Paul.

12—16. 'By our common sympathies, as brethren I appeal to you. I laid aside the privileges, the prejudices of my race: I became a Gentile, even as ye were Gentiles. And now I ask you to make me some return. I ask you to throw off this Judaic bondage, and to be free, as I am free. Do not mistake me; I have no personal complaint; ye did me no wrong. Nay, ye remember, when detained by sickness I preached the Gospel to you, what a hearty welcome ye gave me. My infirmity might well have tempted you to reject my message. It was far otherwise. Ye did not spurn me, did not loathe me; but received me as an angel of God, as Christ Jesus Himself. And what has now become of your felicitations? Are they scattered to the winds? Yet ye *did* felicitate yourselves then. Yea, I bear you witness, such was your gratitude, ye would have plucked out your very eyes and have given them to me. What then? Have I made you my enemies by telling the truth?'

12. Γίνεσθε ὡς ἐγώ κ.τ.λ.] Of the

ἀσθένειαν τῆς σαρκὸς εὐηγγελισάμην ὑμῖν τὸ πρότερον· [14]καὶ τὸν πειρασμὸν ὑμῶν ἐν τῇ σαρκί μου οὐκ ἐξου-

meaning of the first clause there can be but little doubt; 'Free yourself from the bondage of ordinances, as I am free.' Of the second two interpretations deserve to be considered; (1) 'For I was once in bondage as ye are now,' i.e. κἀγὼ ἤμην Ἰουδαῖος ὡς ὑμεῖς νῦν Ἰουδαΐζετε. So Eusebius (of Emesa?), Chrysostom, Jerome, and apparently Pseudo-Justin *Orat. ad Graec.* § 5; see p. 60 note 1: (2) 'For I abandoned my legal ground of righteousness, I became a Gentile like you,' i.e. κἀγὼ ἐγενόμην Ἕλλην ὡς ὑμεῖς ἦτε Ἕλληνες; comp. ii. 17, 1 Cor. ix. 21. This latter sense is simpler grammatically, as it understands the same verb which occurs in the former clause, ἐγενόμην, not ἤμην. It is also more in character with the intense personal feeling which pervades the passage. The words so taken involve an appeal to the affection and gratitude of the Galatians; 'I gave up all those time-honoured customs, all those dear associations of race, to become like you. I have lived as a Gentile that I might preach to you Gentiles. Will you then abandon me when I have abandoned all for you?' This sense is well adapted both to the tender appeal 'brethren, I beseech you,' and to the eager explanation which follows 'ye did me no wrong.' For the expression comp. Ter. *Eun.* i. 2. 116 'meus fac sis postremo animus, quando ego sum tuus.'

οὐδέν με ἠδικήσατε] To these words two different meanings have been assigned; (1) 'Ye never disobeyed me before; do not disobey me now': (2) 'I have no personal ground of complaint.' The latter seems better adapted to the context. Possibly however the real explanation is hidden under some unknown circumstances to which St Paul alludes; see below on δι' ἀσθένειαν.

13. οἴδατε δέ] '*on the contrary ye know.*'

δι' ἀσθένειαν τῆς σαρκός] '*on account of an infirmity in my flesh.*' St Paul seems to have been detained in Galatia by illness, so that his infirmity was the cause of his preaching there; see pp. 23, 24. The fact that his preaching among them was thus in a manner compulsory made the enthusiastic welcome of the Galatians the more commendable. If this interpretation seems somewhat forced, it is only because we are ignorant of the circumstances to which St Paul refers: nor is it more harsh than any possible explanation which can be given of the preceding οὐδέν με ἠδικήσατε. For the expression compare Thucyd. vi. 102 αὐτὸν δὲ τὸν κύκλον [αἱρεῖν] Νικίας διεκώλυσεν· ἔτυχε γὰρ ἐν αὐτῷ δι' ἀσθένειαν ὑπολελειμμένος. Alluding to this afterwards in an impassioned appeal, Nicias might well have said, δι' ἀσθένειαν ἔσωσα τὸν κύκλον. At all events this is the only rendering of the words which the grammar admits. No instance has been produced, until a much later date, which would at all justify our explaining δι' ἀσθένειαν, as if it were δι' ἀσθενείας or ἐν ἀσθενείᾳ, as is frequently done. The ambiguity of the Latin 'per infirmitatem' gave the Latin fathers a license of interpretation which the original does not allow: Jerome however recognises the proper meaning of the preposition, though wrongly explaining it 'propter infirmitatem carnis *vestrae*.' Of the Greek fathers, Chrysost., Theodoret, and Theod. Mops. slur over the preposition, interpreting the passage however in a way more consonant with the sense ἐν ἀσθενείᾳ. Photius (? *ap. Oecum.*) is the first, so far as I have noticed, who boldly gives the ungrammatical rendering μετὰ ἀσθενείας.

τὸ πρότερον] '*on the former of my*

θενήσατε οὐδὲ ἐξεπτύσατε, ἀλλὰ ὡς ἄγγελον Θεοῦ ἐδέξασθέ με, ὡς Χριστὸν Ἰησοῦν. [15]ποῦ οὖν ὁ μακαρισ-

15. τίς οὖν ὁ μακαρισμός.

two visits.' Τὸ πρότερον, which derives a certain emphasis from the article, cannot be simply equivalent to πάλαι, 'some time ago.' It may mean either (1) 'formerly,' with a direct and emphatic reference to some later point of time; comp. Joh. vi. 62, ix. 8, 1 Tim. i. 13, or (2) 'on the former of two occasions.' In the present passage it is difficult to explain the emphasis, if we assign the first of these two meanings to it, so that we have to fall back upon the second as the probable interpretation. The expression therefore seems to justify the assumption of *two* visits to Galatia before this letter was written; see pp. 25, 41.

14. τὸν πειρασμὸν ὑμῶν κ.τ.λ.] '*your temptation which was in my flesh,*' i.e. St Paul's bodily ailment, which was a trial to the Galatians and which might have led them to reject his preaching. Πειρασμός, like the corresponding English word 'temptation,' is employed here by a laxity of usage common in all languages for 'the thing which tempts or tries.' On this concrete sense of substantives in -μός, see Buttm. *Ausf. Sprachl.* § 119. 23. *anm.* 11. The apparent harshness of the expression here, 'your temptation ye did not despise nor loathe,' is explained and in some degree relieved by the position of τὸν πειρασμὸν ὑμῶν at the beginning of the sentence. These words are used without a distinct anticipation of what is to follow, the particular sense of the verb to be employed being yet undecided and only suggested afterwards, as the sentence runs on, by the concrete sense which the intervening words ἐν τῇ σαρκί μου have given to πειρασμόν.

For ὑμῶν some texts have μου τόν, the received reading, others simply τόν. Considering however that the weight of authority is strongly in favour of ὑμῶν (see below, p. 186, note 1) and that the transcribers were under every temptation to soften a harsh and at first sight unintelligible phrase by altering or omitting the pronoun, this reading ought certainly to be retained. On the other hand, supposing μου to be the original reading, some have accounted for the variation ὑμῶν (Reiche, *Comm. Crit.* II. p. 54) by supposing that it was substituted by some scribe who was jealous for the honour of St Paul: but an emendation, which introduced so much confusion in the sense, was not likely to be made. As for τόν, it seems to be merely the insertion of a classicist.

οὐκ ἐξουθενήσατε οὐδὲ ἐξεπτύσατε] 'ye did not treat with contemptuous indifference or with active loathing.' As ἀποπτύειν is more usual than ἐκπτύειν in this metaphorical sense, the latter seems to be preferred here for the sake of the alliteration.

15. ποῦ οὖν ὁ μακαρισμὸς ὑμῶν;] The reading of the received text differs from this in two points: (1) It inserts ἦν after οὖν. This is certainly to be omitted, as very deficient in authority and perhaps also as giving a wrong sense to the passage. (2) It reads τίς for ποῦ. On this point there is more difficulty. The weight of direct evidence is certainly in favour of ποῦ, but on the other hand it is more probable that ποῦ should have been substituted for τίς than conversely; especially as several Greek commentators (Theod. Mops., Theodoret, Severianus) who read τίς explain it by ποῦ.

If the reading τίς be adopted, the choice seems to lie between two out of many interpretations which have been proposed: (1) 'How hollow, how meaningless was your rejoicing' (understanding ἦν); (2) 'What has be-

μός ὑμῶν; μαρτυρῶ γὰρ ὑμῖν ὅτι, εἰ δυνατόν, τοὺς ὀφθαλμοὺς ὑμῶν ἐξορύξαντες ἐδώκατέ μοι. [16]ὥστε ἐχθρὸς ὑμῶν γέγονα ἀληθεύων ὑμῖν; [17]Ζηλοῦσιν ὑμᾶς οὐ

come of your rejoicing? where has it vanished?' (understanding ἐστίν). In the latter sense it would coincide in meaning with ποῦ οὖν ὁ μακαρισμός, which can only be taken in one way. This interpretation seems more natural than the former.

ὁ μακαρισμὸς ὑμῶν] '*your felicitation of yourselves*,' 'your happiness in my teaching,' as the sense seems to require. ὑμῶν is probably the subjective genitive, though the Galatians were at the same time also the object of the μακαρισμός. Others understand by these words either their felicitation of St Paul, or his felicitation of them, but neither of these meanings is so appropriate to the context; not the former, because the word μακαρισμὸς would ill express their *welcoming* of him; not the latter, for St Paul is dwelling on the change of feeling which *they themselves* had undergone. For μακαρισμός, 'beatitudo,' see Rom. iv. 6, 9, and Clem. Rom. § 50.

μαρτυρῶ] '*I bear witness*,' see the note on 1 Thess. ii. 12.

εἰ δυνατὸν κ.τ.λ.] '*if it had been possible*, if you could have benefited me thereby, you would have plucked out your very eyes, would have given me that which is most precious to you.' For καὶ τοὺς ὀφθαλμοὺς compare the Old Testament phrase to 'keep as the apple of one's eye' (e.g. Ps. xvii. 8), and the references in Wetstein. See below, p. 191, note.

ἐδώκατε] '*ye had given*.' The suppression of the condition expresses more vividly their readiness; see Winer § xlii. p. 321. The insertion of ἂν in the received text enfeebles the sense.

16. ὥστε] '*therefore*' ought naturally to be followed by a direct assertion; but shunning this conclusion and hoping against hope, the Apostle substitutes an interrogative; 'Can it be that I have become your enemy?'

ἐχθρὸς ὑμῶν] '*your enemy*.' It was a term by which the Judaizers of a later age, and perhaps even at this time, designated St Paul; *Clem. Hom. Ep. Petr.* § 2 τοῦ ἐχθροῦ ἀνθρώπου ἄνομόν τινα καὶ φλυαρώδη προσηκάμενοι διδασκαλίαν, *Clem. Recogn.* i. 70: see p. 61. This quotation suggests that ἄνομος was another of these hostile names which he is parrying in 1 Cor. ix. 21 μὴ ὢν ἄνομος Θεοῦ.

ἀληθεύων] probably referring to some warnings given during his second visit. See the introduction p. 25. Compare the proverb, Ter. *Andr.* i. 1. 41, 'obsequium amicos, *veritas odium* parit.'

17. From speaking of the former interchange of affection between himself and his Galatian converts, he goes on to contrast their relations with the false teachers: 'I once held the first place in your hearts. Now you look upon me as an enemy. Others have supplanted me. Only enquire into their aims. True, they pay court to you: but how hollow, how insincere is their interest in you! Their desire is to shut you out from Christ. Thus you will be driven to pay court to them.'

Ζηλοῦσιν] '*they pay court to*.' As ζηλοῦν would seem to have one and the same sense throughout this passage, its more ordinary meanings with the accusative, as 'to admire, emulate, envy,' must be discarded. It signifies rather 'to busy oneself about, take interest in,' a sense which lies close to the original meaning of ζῆλος, if correctly derived from ζέω. See 2 Cor. xi. 2, ζηλῶ γὰρ ὑμᾶς Θεοῦ ζήλῳ: so also Plut. *Mor.* p. 448 E ὑπὸ χρείας τὸ πρῶτον ἕπονται καὶ ζηλοῦσιν, ὕστερον δὲ

καλῶς, ἀλλὰ ἐκκλεῖσαι ὑμᾶς θέλουσιν, ἵνα αὐτοὺς ζηλοῦτε. [18]καλὸν δὲ ζηλοῦσθαι ἐν καλῷ πάντοτε, καὶ
μὴ μόνον ἐν τῷ παρεῖναί με πρὸς ὑμᾶς, [19]τεκνία μου, οὓς

19. τέκνα μου.

καὶ φιλοῦσιν: 1 Cor. xii. 31, xiv. 1, 39, Ezek. xxxix. 25.

ἀλλά] is connected not with ζηλοῦσιν, but with οὐ καλῶς: comp. Æsch. *Eum.* 458 ἔφθιθ' οὗτος οὐ καλῶς, μολὼν ἐς οἶκον, ἀλλά νιν κελαινόφρων ἐμὴ μήτηρ κατέκτα.

ἐκκλεῖσαι ὑμᾶς] '*to exclude, to debar you.*' If it is asked 'from what?', the reply is to be sought in the tendency of the false teaching. By insisting on ceremonial observances, they were in fact shutting out the Galatians from Christ. The idea is the same as in v. 4 κατηργήθητε ἀπὸ τοῦ Χριστοῦ, τῆς χάριτος ἐξεπέσατε. The reading ἡμᾶς, though it gives a good sense, is almost destitute of authority.

ἵνα αὐτοὺς ζηλοῦτε] '*that*, having no refuge elsewhere, *you may pay court to them.*' For the present indicative after ἵνα comp. 1 Cor. iv. 6 ἵνα μὴ φυσιοῦσθε: a usage quite unclassical, but often found in later writers; see Winer § xli. p. 362. The future indicative with ἵνα is comparatively common, as e.g. ii. 4. The attempt to give ἵνα with the indicative a *local* sense (quo in statu), as opposed to a *final* (e.g. Fritzsche on Matth. p. 836 sq), may mislead, as seeming to assume that there is an essential difference between the *local* and the *final* ἵνα. The *final* sense is derived from the *local*, the relation of cause and effect in all languages being expressed by words originally denoting relations in space. Thus the difference of meaning between ἵνα ποιεῖτε and ἵνα ποιῆτε is not in the adverb, which is of constant value, but in the moods.

ζηλοῦτε δὲ τὰ κρείττω χαρίσματα is interpolated here in many copies from 1 Cor. xii. 31; comp. iii. 1, note.

18. καλὸν δὲ ζηλοῦσθαι κ.τ.λ.] The number of possible explanations is limited by two considerations: (1) That ζηλοῦν must have the same sense as in the preceding verse, a paronomasia, though frequent in St Paul, being out of place here: (2) That ζηλοῦσθαι must be passive and not middle; a transitive sense of ζηλοῦσθαι, even if it were supported by usage elsewhere, being inexplicable here in the immediate neighbourhood of the active ζηλοῦν.

With these limitations only two interpretations present themselves, which deserve to be considered. *First;* 'I do not grudge the court which is paid to you. I do not desire a monopoly of serving you. It is well that in my absence your interests should be looked after by others. Only let them do it in an honourable cause.' *Secondly;* 'I do not complain that they desire your attentions, or you theirs. These things are good in themselves. I myself am not insensible to such attachments. I remember how warm were your feelings towards me, when I was with you. I would they had not grown cold in my absence.' The difference between the two consists mainly in the turn given to μὴ μόνον ἐν τῷ παρεῖναί με. The objection to the latter sense is, that it *supplies too much.* But this abrupt and fragmentary mode of expression is characteristic of St Paul when he is deeply moved: and this interpretation suits the general context so much better—especially the tender appeal which immediately follows, 'my little children'—that it is to be preferred to the other.

The reading ζηλοῦσθε, found in the two best MSS, is in itself but another

πάλιν ὠδίνω μέχρις οὗ μορφωθῇ Χριστὸς ἐν ὑμῖν. 20 ἤθελον δὲ παρεῖναι πρὸς ὑμᾶς ἄρτι καὶ ἀλλάξαι τὴν φωνήν μου, ὅτι ἀποροῦμαι ἐν ὑμῖν.

way of writing the infinitive ζηλοῦσθαι, the sounds ε and αι being the same. It was however liable to be mistaken for an imperative, and is so translated in the Vulgate.

19. This verse should be taken with the preceding and the punctuation regulated accordingly. It is difficult to explain δέ, ver. 20, if τεκνία μου be made the beginning of a new sentence. The connexion of thought seems to be as follows: 'I have a right to ask for constancy in your affections. I have a greater claim on you than these new teachers. They speak but as strangers to strangers; I as a mother to her children with whom she has travailed.' Comp. 1 Cor. iv. 14, 'Though ye have ten thousand tutors in Christ, yet have ye not many fathers.'

τεκνία μου] '*my little children*,' a mode of address common in St John, but not found elsewhere in St Paul. This however is no argument for the reading τέκνα in preference to τεκνία, for St Paul does not elsewhere use the vocatives τέκνα, τέκνον, except in Ephes. vi. 1, Col. iii. 20, where he could not possibly have had τεκνία, and in 1 Tim. i. 18, 2 Tim. ii. 1, where τεκνίον would have been inappropriate. Here the diminutive, expressing both the tenderness of the Apostle and the feebleness of his converts, is more forcible. It is a term at once of affection and rebuke. The reading τέκνα however is very highly supported and may perhaps be correct.

πάλιν ὠδίνω] 'I travailed with you once in bringing you to Christ. By your relapse you have renewed a mother's pangs in me.' There is no allusion here, as some have thought, to the new birth in the Spirit (παλιγγενεσία) as opposed to the old birth in the flesh.

μορφωθῇ ἐν ὑμῖν] i.e. 'until you have taken the form of Christ,' as the embryo developes into the child. Compare the similar expression of 'growing up into the full stature of Christ,' Ephes. iv. 13. The words μορφωθῇ ἐν ὑμῖν have been otherwise explained as a different application of the former metaphor, the Apostle's converts being put no longer in the place of the child, but of the mother. Such inversions of a metaphor are characteristic of St Paul (see the notes 1 Thess. ii. 7, v. 4), but here the explanation is improbable. St Paul would have shrunk instinctively from describing the relation of Christ to the believer by that of the unborn child to its mother, thereby suggesting, however indirectly, the idea of subordination.

For an elaborate application of the metaphor in the text see the Epistle of the Churches of Vienne and Lyons, Euseb. v. 1 §§ 40, 41, especially the words οἱ πλείους ἀνεμητροῦντο καὶ ἀνεκυΐσκοντο κ.τ.λ.

20. ἤθελον δὲ κ.τ.λ.] '*but*, speaking of my presence, *I would I had been present with you now*.' The δὲ catches up the passing thought of παρεῖναι (v. 18), before it escapes; comp. 1 Cor. i. 16 ἐβάπτισα δὲ καὶ τὸν Στεφανᾶ οἶκον. The connexion of this clause with the previous παρεῖναι requires that the sentence should be continuous, and that there should be no full stop after πρὸς ὑμᾶς (ver. 18); see the note on ver. 19. All other explanations seem harsh. Δὲ has been connected for instance with the vocative, but there is here no abrupt transition from one person to another, which alone would justify such an expression as τεκνία μου, ἤθελον δέ.

ἤθελον as ηὐχόμην Rom. ix. 3, ἐβουλόμην Acts xxv. 22. The thing is

[21]Λέγετέ μοι, οἱ ὑπὸ νόμον θέλοντες εἶναι, τὸν νόμον οὐκ ἀκούετε; [22]γέγραπται γὰρ ὅτι Ἀβραὰμ δύο
υἱοὺς ἔσχεν, ἕνα ἐκ τῆς παιδίσκης καὶ ἕνα ἐκ τῆς ἐλευ-

spoken of in itself, prior to and independently of any conditions which might affect its possibility; see Winer § xli. p. 352, and the note Philem. 13.

ἄρτι] See the note i. 9.

ἀλλάξαι τὴν φωνήν μου] not 'to modify my language from time to time as occasion demands,' for this is more than the phrase will bear, but 'to change my present tone.' The change meant is surely from severity to gentleness, and not from less to greater severity, as it has often been taken. His anxiety to mitigate the effects of his written rebuke has an exact parallel in his dealings with the Corinthian offender; see esp. 2 Cor. ii. 5 sq.

ἀποροῦμαι ἐν ὑμῖν] '*I am perplexed about you*, I am at a loss how to deal with you'; comp. 2 Cor. vii. 16 *θαρρῶ ἐν ὑμῖν*. The idea of inward questioning is expressed more strongly by *ἀπορεῖσθαι* than by *ἀπορεῖν*. It is probably a middle rather than a passive; though *ἀπορεῖν* is found as a transitive verb in *Clem. Hom.* i. 11 *ἀπορεῖν αὐτὸν πειρώμενοι ὡς βάρβαρόν τινα δαιμονῶντα*, if the text be not corrupt.

21—27. 'Ye who vaunt your submission to law, listen while I read you a lesson out of the law. The Scripture says that Abraham had two sons, the one the child of the bondwoman, the other the child of the free. The child of the bondwoman, we are there told, came into the world in the common course of nature: the child of the free was born in fulfilment of a promise. These things may be treated as an allegory. The two mothers represent two covenants. The one, Hagar, is the covenant given from Mount Sinai, whose children are born into slavery (for Sinai is in Arabia, the land of Hagar and the Hagarenes), and this covenant corresponds to the earthly Jerusalem, which is in bondage with her children. The other answers to the heavenly Jerusalem, which is free—I mean the Church of Christ, our common mother. In her progeny is fulfilled the prophetic saying, which bids the barren and forsaken wife rejoice, because her offspring shall be far more numerous than her rival's, who claims the husband for herself.'

21. *οἱ ὑπὸ νόμον κ.τ.λ.*] '*ye, who would be subject to law*, who must needs submit to bondage in some way or other.' Observe here again the distinction between *νόμος* and *ὁ νόμος*, and see the notes on ii. 19, iv. 4, 5.

τὸν νόμον] '*the law*,' when referring to the written word, either comprises the whole of the Old Testament writings (e.g. Rom. iii. 19), or is restricted to the Pentateuch (e.g. Rom. iii. 21, Luke xxiv. 44).

οὐκ ἀκούετε] '*will ye not listen to?*' Matt. x. 14, xiii. 13, Luke xvi. 29. The other interpretation, 'Is not the law constantly read to you?' (comp. Acts xv. 21, 2 Cor. iii. 14), is less probable, because less simple. The various reading *ἀναγινώσκετε*, which has respectable authority, is evidently a gloss on this latter sense assigned to the word.

22. *γέγραπται*] '*it is stated in the scriptures*,' introducing a general reference, and not a direct quotation; as in 1 Cor. xv. 45. See Genesis xvi, xxi.

τῆς παιδίσκης] '*the bondmaid*'; comp. Gen. xvi. 1 *ἦν δὲ αὐτῇ παιδίσκη Αἰγυπτία, ᾗ ὄνομα Ἄγαρ*. The word seems to have exclusively the sense of a *servant* in the New Testament and later Greek; not so in classical writers. See Lobeck *Phryn.* p. 239 *παιδίσκη· τοῦτο ἐπὶ τῆς θεραπαίνης οἱ νῦν τιθέασιν, οἱ δ' ἀρχαῖοι ἐπὶ τῆς νεάνιδος.*

θέρας. [23]ἀλλ' ὁ [μὲν] ἐκ τῆς παιδίσκης κατὰ σάρκα γεγέννηται, ὁ δὲ ἐκ τῆς ἐλευθέρας διὰ τῆς ἐπαγγελίας. [24]ἅτινά ἐστιν ἀλληγορούμενα. αὗται γάρ εἰσιν δύο

23. ἀλλ'] '*but*,' i.e. although sons of the same father. The opposition implied in ἀλλὰ is illustrated by Rom. ix. 7 οὐδ' ὅτι εἰσὶν σπέρμα Ἀβραάμ, πάντες τέκνα, and ix. 10 ἐξ ἑνὸς κοίτην ἔχουσα.

κατὰ σάρκα] i.e. 'in the common course of nature.' In some sense Ishmael was also a child of promise (Gen. xvi. 10), but in his case the course of nature was not suspended, as the promise was made after his conception. It must be remembered however that in his choice of words here St Paul regards not only the original history, but the typical application, the Jews being the children of Abraham after the flesh, the Christians his children by the promise.

γεγέννηται] the perfect, 'is recorded as born,' 'is born, as we read': comp. 1 Tim. ii. 14 ἡ δὲ γυνὴ ἐξαπατηθεῖσα ἐν παραβάσει γέγονεν.

24. ἅτινα] '*now all these things*'; not simply ἃ 'which *particular* things,' but ἅτινα 'which *class* of things': comp. Col. ii. 23 ἅτινά ἐστιν λόγον μὲν ἔχοντα σοφίας, i.e. precepts of this sort (with the note).

ἀλληγορούμενα] The word has two senses: (1) 'To speak in an allegory,' e.g. Joseph. *Ant.* procem. 4 τὰ μὲν αἰνιττομένου τοῦ νομοθέτου δεξιῶς τὰ δὲ ἀλληγοροῦντος κ.τ.λ.; (2) 'To treat or interpret as an allegory,' e.g. Philo *de Vit. Cont.* § 3, II. p. 475 M ἐντυγχάνοντες γὰρ τοῖς ἱεροῖς γράμμασι φιλοσοφοῦσι τὴν πάτριον φιλοσοφίαν ἀλληγοροῦντες, ἐπειδὴ σύμβολα τὰ τῆς ῥητῆς ἑρμηνείας νομίζουσι φύσεως ἀποκεκρυμμένης ἐν ὑπονοίαις δηλουμένης, *Clem. Hom.* vi. 18, 20, and frequently: comp. Plut. *Op. Mor.* p. 363 D ὥσπερ Ἕλληνες Κρόνον ἀλληγοροῦσι τὸν Χρόνον κ.τ.λ. It is possible that St Paul uses the word in this latter sense, referring to some recognised mode of interpretation. Comp. the note on συνστοιχεῖ ver. 25, and see the remarks p. 198.

St Paul uses ἀλληγορία here much in the same sense as he uses τύπος 1 Cor. x. 11 ταῦτα δὲ τυπικῶς συνέβαινεν, not denying the historical truth of the narrative, but superposing a secondary meaning. By a stricter definition ἀλληγορία and τύπος were distinguished as denoting the former a fictitious, the latter a true narrative. See the definition of ἀλληγορία, Heracl. *Alleg. Hom.* 5 ὁ ἄλλα μὲν ἀγορεύων τρόπος ἕτερα δὲ ὧν λέγει σημαίνων. Hence the jealousy of the Antiochene fathers (Chrysostom, Severianus, Theod. Mops.) in explaining that St Paul uses the word καταχρηστικῶς here and does not deny the historical truth of the narrative.

The author of the *Clem. Hom.* (ii. 22) indirectly attacks this allegory: see the introduction, p. 61.

αὗται γάρ κ.τ.λ.] '*for these women are* (represent) *two covenants*.' Εἰσιν 'are' not actually, but mystically or typically; Matt. xiii. 39, xxvi. 26—28, 1 Cor. x. 4. The article before δύο must be omitted.

μία μέν] '*one of them*, which was given *from Mount Sinai, bearing children unto bondage*.' The true antithesis would have been ἑτέρα δέ, but it melts away in the general fusion of the sentence, vv. 25, 26. For γεννῶσα used of a *mother*, see Luke i. 13: it occurs so in Xen. *de Rep. Lac.* i. 3, and occasionally elsewhere, especially in later writers.

ἥτις] '*inasmuch as she*.' ἡ would simply declare the fact, ἥτις places it in dependence on the context.

25. τὸ γὰρ Σινᾶ κ.τ.λ.] '*for Sinai is a mountain in Arabia*,' i.e. in the land of bondsmen, themselves de-

διαθῆκαι, μία μὲν ἀπὸ ὄρους Σινᾶ, εἰς δουλείαν γεννῶσα,
ἥτις ἐστὶν Ἄγαρ· 25 τὸ γὰρ Σινᾶ ὄρος ἐστὶν ἐν τῇ Ἀ-
ραβίᾳ· συνστοιχεῖ δὲ τῇ νῦν Ἰερουσαλήμ, δουλεύει γὰρ

scended from Hagar. The stress lies on ἐν τῇ Ἀραβίᾳ, not on ὄρος, which is unemphatic; or perhaps we should render the words, 'Mount Sinai is in Arabia' (comp. Athan. *de Decr.* 7, I. p. 168, for τὸ Σινᾶ ὄρος), as this gives a better sense. The Arabians are called 'sons of Hagar,' Baruch iii. 23: see Ewald *Gesch. des V. Isr.* I. p. 418. St Paul's language here is further illustrated by the prominence given to Hagar in the national legends of the Arabs, where she is represented as the lawful wife of Abraham: see d'Herbelot *Bibl. Or.* s. v. Hagiar. The word is preserved also in the name of several Arab tribes, e.g. the Hagarenes or Hagarites of the Old Testament (Ps. lxxxiii. 6, הַגְרִים, Ἀγαρηνοί; and 1 Chron. v. 19, הַגְרִיאִים, Ἀγαραῖοι, comp. ver. 10), and the Ἀγραῖοι of heathen writers (Eratosth. in Strabo xvi. p. 767), if these be not the same. A place on the Persian gulf is still so called. It is to the Sinaitic peninsula apparently that Hagar flees (Gen. xvi. 7, 14), and possibly some portion of it may have borne her name in St Paul's time; see below, p. 197.

The clause τὸ γὰρ Σινᾶ κ.τ.λ. is parenthetical, and the nominative to συνστοιχεῖ is μία διαθήκη.

For the various readings in this passage and for different interpretations of the word 'Hagar,' see the detached notes p. 192 sq.

συνστοιχεῖ] '*answers to*'; literally, 'belongs to the same row or column with.' In military language συστοιχία denotes a *file*, as συζυγία does a *rank* of soldiers; comp. Polyb. x. 21. 7. The use of this word here is best illustrated by the Pythagorean συστοιχίαι of opposing principles (Arist. *Eth. N.* i. 6, *Metaph.* i. 5), which stood thus;

Good,	Bad,
Finite,	Infinite,
One,	Many,
Permanent,	Changing,
etc.	etc.

Similar also were the συστοιχίαι of grammarians, who so arranged the letters of the alphabet according to the organs of speech (comp. Athen. xi. p. 501 B), or the words derived from the same root according to the ending (Arist. *Rhet.* i. 7, *Top.* ii. 9). The allegory in the text then may be represented by συστοιχίαι thus;

Hagar, the bond-woman.	Sarah, the free-woman.
Ishmael, the child after the flesh.	Isaac, the child of promise.
The old covenant.	The new covenant.
The earthly Jerusalem.	The heavenly Jerusalem.
etc.	etc.

The old covenant is thus σύστοιχος with the earthly Jerusalem, but ἀντίστοιχος to the heavenly. It is not improbable that St Paul is alluding to some mode of representation common with Jewish teachers to exhibit this and similar allegories. Strangely enough the fathers with but few exceptions translate συνστοιχεῖ 'borders upon,' 'is contiguous to,' which is scarcely true even in the most forced sense of contiguity.

τῇ νῦν Ἰερουσαλήμ] The metropolis of the Jews is taken to represent the whole race.

δουλεύει γάρ κ.τ.λ.] '*is in* spiritual *bondage with her children*,' just as Hagar was in social bondage with her child Ishmael. For τῶν τέκνων αὐτῆς see Matt. xxiii. 37.

26. ἡ ἄνω Ἰερουσαλήμ] St Paul here uses an expression familiar to rabbinical teachers, but detaches it from

μετὰ τῶν τέκνων αὐτῆς· [26] ἡ δὲ ἄνω Ἰερουσαλὴμ ἐλευθέρα ἐστίν, ἥτις ἐστὶν μήτηρ ἡμῶν. [27] γέγραπται γάρ, ΕΥ̓ΦΡΆΝΘΗΤΙ ΣΤΕῖΡΑ Ἡ ΟΥ̓ ΤΊΚΤΟΥΣΑ, ῬΗ͂ΞΟΝ ΚΑῚ ΒΌΗΣΟΝ

those sensuous and material conceptions with which they invested it. See the treatise *de Hieros. Coelest.* in Schöttgen's *Hor. Hebr.* I. p. 1205. With them it is an actual city, the exact counterpart of the earthly Jerusalem in its topography and its furniture: with him it is a symbol or image, representing that spiritual city of which the Christian is even now a denizen (Phil. iii. 20). See Heb. xii. 22 Ἰερουσαλὴμ ἐπουράνιος, Rev. iii. 12 καινὴ Ἰερουσαλήμ, xxi. 2 ἁγία Ἰερουσαλήμ: comp. *Test. xii. Patr.* Dan 5, *Clem. Rec.* i. 51. The contrast between the two scenes, as they appeared to the eye, would enhance, if it did not suggest, the imagery of St Paul here. On the one hand, Mount Sion, of old the joy of the whole earth, now more beautiful than ever in the fresh glories of the Herodian renaissance, glittering in gold and marble (Joseph. *B. J.* v. 5. 6); on the other, Sinai with its rugged peaks and barren sides, bleak and desolate, the oppressive power of which the Apostle himself had felt during his sojourn there (see p. 89)—these scenes fitly represented the contrast between the glorious hopes of the new covenant and the blank despair of the old. Comp. Heb. xii. 18—22.

The Apostle instinctively prefers the Hebrew form Ἰερουσαλὴμ here for the typical city, as elsewhere in this epistle (i. 17, 18, ii. 1) he employs the Graecised form Ἱεροσόλυμα for the actual city. "Ἰερουσαλὴμ est appellatio Hebraica, originaria et sanctior: Ἱεροσόλυμα, deinceps obvia, Graeca, magis politica,' says Bengel on Rev. xxi. 2, accounting for the usage of St John ('in evangelio Ἱεροσόλυμα, in apocalypsi Ἰερουσαλήμ'), and referring to this passage in illustration. In his other epistles St Paul has always Ἰερουσαλήμ; Rom. xv. 19, 25, 26, 31, 1 Cor. xvi. 3.

μήτηρ ἡμῶν] '*the mother of us* Christians.' St Paul's expression was borrowed and adapted by Polycarp § 3 τὴν δοθεῖσαν ὑμῖν πίστιν ἥτις ἐστὶ μήτηρ πάντων ἡμῶν. From a confusion of this loose quotation with the original text, the word πάντων was early interpolated in St Paul; e.g. in Iren. (interp.) v. 35. 2. This at all events is not an improbable account of the origin of the received reading πάντων ἡμῶν; or perhaps πάντων crept in from Rom. iv. 16 ὅς ἐστιν πατὴρ πάντων ἡμῶν.

27. St Paul here illustrates the allegory by reference to a passage in Isaiah liv. 1. This passage in its context is a song of triumph anticipating the deliverance of God's afflicted people Israel from a foreign yoke. Sion has been deserted by her Lord (xlix. 14), and is mourning in her widowhood: she will be restored to favour and become the mother of a large and prosperous people. The image of conjugal union, as representing the relation of Jehovah to His people, is drawn out at some length in the context, see esp. liv. 5, 6. In order moreover fully to understand St Paul's application here, it must be remembered that in another part of the same prophecy (li. 2) God's dealings with Abraham and Sarah are pointed to as a type of His dealings with their descendants. Accordingly Jewish writers connected li. 2 with liv. 1; 'Sterilitas Abrahae et Sarae figura fuit sterilitatis Sion,' *Ir Gibborim* fol. 49. 2, quoted in Schöttgen. Here then Sarah = the chosen people = the Church of Christ.

γέγραπται γάρ] from the LXX where some few texts add καὶ τέρπου after βόησον with the Hebrew. It is quoted as St Paul quotes it in Pseudo-Clem.

Ἡ οὐκ ὠδίνουσα, ὅτι πολλὰ τὰ τέκνα τῆς ἐρήμου μᾶλλον ἢ τῆς ἐχούσης τὸν ἄνδρα. [28]ὑμεῖς δέ, ἀδελφοί, κατὰ Ἰσαὰκ ἐπαγγελίας τέκνα ἐστέ. [29]ἀλλ'

28. ἡμεῖς δέ—τέκνα ἐσμέν.

Epist. ii. § 2, and Justin, *Apol.* i. c. 53, p. 88 c, and similarly applied. On the coincidence of Justin's quotations with St Paul's see p. 60, and the notes iii. 10, 13; comp. Semisch *Just. Mart.* I. p. 258 sq (Eng. Tr.). The Hebrew differs somewhat, as do the other Greek versions (see Jerome and Procopius *in Is.* l. c.). Γὰρ links the quotation with μήτηρ ἡμῶν.

στεῖρα] The barren one is not Gentile Christendom as opposed to Jewish, but the new dispensation as opposed to the old. At the same time the image of barrenness derives its force from the introduction of the Gentile element into the Christian Church. Compare the metaphor of the ἀγριέλαιος, Rom. xi. 17.

πολλὰ τὰ τέκνα μᾶλλον ἢ] for the usual Greek πλείονα ἢ, the Hebrew idiom (רבים מן), which has no comparative, being followed.

τῆς ἐχούσης τὸν ἄνδρα] in St Paul's application, Hagar, who for a time possessed the affection of Abraham and conceived by him. She thus represents the Jewish people at one time enjoying the special favour of Jehovah.

28—V. 1. 'So, brethren, you as Christians are children of a promise, like Isaac. Nor does the allegory end here. Just as Ishmael the child born after the flesh insulted Isaac the child born after the Spirit, so is it now. But the end shall be the same now, as then. In the language of the Scripture, the bondwoman and her offspring shall be cast out of the father's house. The child of the slave cannot share the inheritance with the child of the free. Remember therefore, brethren, that you are not children of any slave, but of the free and wedded wife. I speak of that freedom, whereunto we all are emancipated in Christ. Remember this, and act upon it. Firmly resist all pressure, and do not again bow your necks under the yoke of slavery.'

28. ὑμεῖς δέ] resuming the main subject, ver. 27 being in a manner parenthetical.

κατὰ Ἰσαάκ] See Rom. ix. 7—9. The Gentiles were sprung from one 'as good as dead': they had no claims of race or descent. Thus they were sons not κατὰ σάρκα, but, like Isaac, ἐξ ἐπαγγελίας.

The reading ἡμεῖς...ἐσμέν, for ὑμεῖς ...ἐστέ, is very highly supported, but perhaps was a transcriber's correction to conform to ver. 26, 31. The direct appeal of ὑμεῖς is more forcible, and the change of persons is characteristic of St Paul; see the note ver. 7.

29. ἐδίωκεν τὸν κ.τ.λ.] The Hebrew text, Gen. xxi. 9, has simply 'laughing' (מצחק). This single word the LXX expands into παίζοντα μετὰ Ἰσαὰκ τοῦ υἱοῦ αὐτῆς. From this it may be conjectured that the verse originally ended מצחק [בבנה ביצחק] (comp. Gen. xxxix. 14, 17), the words in brackets having dropped out owing to the homœoteleuton. At all events the word seems to mean 'mocking, jeering'; 'Lusio illa illusio erat,' says Augustine pertinently (*Serm.* 3). The anger of Sarah, taken in connexion with the occasion, a festival in honour of the weaning of Isaac, seems to require it. Such also would appear to be the force of the rendering in the older Targum, מחיך. On the other hand the Book of Jubilees paraphrases the passage, 'When Sarah saw that Ishmael was merry and danced and that Abraham also rejoiced greatly thereat, she was jealous etc.' (Ewald's

ὥσπερ τότε ὁ κατὰ σάρκα γεννηθεὶς ἐδίωκεν τὸν κατὰ πνεῦμα, οὕτως καὶ νῦν. 30 ἀλλὰ τί λέγει ἡ γραφή; ἜΚΒΑΛΕ ΤῊΝ ΠΑΙΔΊΣΚΗΝ ΚΑῚ ΤῸΝ ΥἹῸΝ ΑΥ̓ΤΗ͂Σ· ΟΥ̓ ΓᾺΡ ΜῊ ΚΛΗΡΟΝΟΜΉΣΕΙ Ὁ ΥἹῸΣ ΤΗ͂Σ ΠΑΙΔΊΣΚΗΣ ΜΕΤᾺ ΤΟΥ͂

Jahrb. III. p. 13). But beyond the text itself two circumstances must be taken into account as affecting St Paul's application of it. (1) This incident which is so lightly sketched in the original narrative had been drawn out in detail in later traditions, and thus a prominence was given to it, which would add force to the Apostle's allusion, without his endorsing these traditions himself. For the rabbinical accounts of Ishmael's insolence to his brother see Beer *Leben Abraham's*, pp. 49, 170. (2) The relations between the two brothers were reproduced in their descendants. The aggressions of the Arab tribes (of the *Hagarenes* especially, see Ps. lxxxiii. 6, 1 Chron. v. 10, 19) on the Israelites were the antitype to Ishmael's mockery of Isaac. Thus in Ishmael the Apostle may have indirectly contemplated Ishmael's progeny; and he would therefore be appealing to the national history of the Jews in saying 'he that was born after the flesh persecuted him that was born after the Spirit.' For the conflicts with the Arabs in the time of Herod see esp. Joseph. *Ant.* xv. 5. 1.

οὕτως καὶ νῦν] 'So now the Church of God is persecuted by the children after the flesh.' St Paul's persecutors were at first Jews, afterwards Judaizers; but both alike were 'born after the flesh,' for both alike claimed to inherit the covenant by the performance of certain material carnal ordinances.

30. ἡ γραφή] Gen. xxi. 10, taken from the LXX which again is a close translation of the Hebrew. At the end of the quotation however St Paul has substituted τῆς παιδίσκης μετὰ τοῦ υἱοῦ τῆς ἐλευθέρας for the LXX τῆς παιδίσκης ταύτης μετὰ τοῦ υἱοῦ μου Ἰσαάκ, in order to adapt it to his own context and to save explanation. For instances of adapted quotations, which are frequent, see iii. 10 and Acts vii. 43.

The words are spoken by Sarah to Abraham, but her demand is confirmed by the express command of God, Gen. xxi. 12, 'Hearken unto her voice,' to which the later Targum adds, 'for she is a prophetess.'

οὐ μὴ κληρονομήσει] '*shall in no wise inherit*'; comp. Joh. viii. 35 ὁ δοῦλος οὐ μένει ἐν τῇ οἰκίᾳ εἰς τὸν αἰῶνα κ.τ.λ. The Law and the Gospel cannot co-exist; the Law must disappear before the Gospel. It is scarcely possible to estimate the strength of conviction and depth of prophetic insight which this declaration implies. The Apostle thus confidently sounds the death-knell of Judaism at a time when one-half of Christendom clung to the Mosaic law with a jealous affection little short of frenzy, and while the Judaic party seemed to be growing in influence and was strong enough, even in the Gentile churches of his own founding, to undermine his influence and endanger his life. The truth which to us appears a truism must then have been regarded as a paradox.

κληρονομήσει should probably be read, not κληρονομήσῃ, as being better supported here and in the LXX; comp. Winer § lvi. p. 635, and A. Buttmann p. 183.

31. διό] '*wherefore*,' as the inference from this allegorical lesson. The particle is chosen rather with a view to the obligation involved in the statement, than to the statement itself; '*wherefore* let us remember that we are not sons of a bondwoman, let us not act as bondslaves.' There are many variations of reading, but διὸ is probably correct. Some copies have

υἱοῦ τῆς ἐλευθέρας. [31]διό, ἀδελφοί, οὐκ ἐσμὲν παιδίσκης τέκνα, ἀλλὰ τῆς ἐλευθέρας [V] [1]τῇ ἐλευθερίᾳ ᾗ ἡμᾶς Χριστὸς ἠλευθέρωσεν. στήκετε οὖν καὶ μὴ πάλιν ζυγῷ δουλείας ἐνέχεσθε.

iv. 31, v. 1. τῆς ἐλευθέρας. τῇ ἐλευθερίᾳ ἡμᾶς κ.τ.λ.

ἡμεῖς δέ, others ἡμεῖς οὖν, others ἄρα or ἄρα οὖν, and one at least entirely omits the connecting particle. The difficulty in διὸ was evidently felt, but sufficient allowance was not made for St Paul's freedom in the employment of connecting particles.

οὐ παιδίσκης ἀλλά κ.τ.λ.] Observe the omission of the article before παιδίσκης; 'not of *any* bondwoman' whether Judaism or some form of heathenism, for there are *many* (see the note iv. 11), 'but of *the* freewoman, the lawful spouse, the Church of Christ, which is *one*.' See on i. 10 ἀνθρώπους πείθω ἢ τὸν Θεόν;

V. 1. τῇ ἐλευθερίᾳ ᾗ κ.τ.λ.] If this reading be adopted (see the detached note, p. 200), the words are best taken with the preceding sentence. They may then be connected either (1) with τέκνα ἐσμὲν τῆς ἐλευθέρας, 'we are sons of the free by virtue of the freedom which Christ has given us'; or (2) with τῆς ἐλευθέρας alone, 'of her who is free with that freedom which Christ etc.' The latter is perhaps the simpler construction. In either case τῇ ἐλευθερίᾳ κ.τ.λ. serves the purpose of an explanatory note.

If on the other hand we read τῇ ἐλευθερίᾳ ἡμᾶς Χριστὸς ἠλευθέρωσεν, the force of this detached sentence will be, 'Did Christ liberate us that we might be slaves? no, but that we might be free.' Compare v. 13 ἐπ' ἐλευθερίᾳ ἐκλήθητε, and especially John viii. 36 ἐὰν οὖν ὁ υἱὸς ὑμᾶς ἐλευθερώσῃ, ὄντως ἐλεύθεροι ἔσεσθε. The abruptness of the sentence, introduced without a connecting particle, has a fair parallel in Ephes. ii. 5 χάριτί ἐστε σεσωσμένοι: but the dative, '*with*' or '*in*' or '*for* freedom,' is awkward, in whatever way it is taken; see A. Buttmann p. 155.

στήκετε] '*stand firm, stand upright*, do not bow your necks to the yoke of slavery'; comp. 2 Thess. ii. 15 ἄρα οὖν, ἀδελφοί, στήκετε κ.τ.λ. The form στήκω appears not to occur earlier than the New Testament, where with two exceptions (Mark iii. 31, xi. 25) it is found only in St Paul.

πάλιν] '*again*.' Having escaped from the slavery of Heathenism, they would fain bow to the slavery of Judaism. Compare the similar expressions iv. 9 πῶς ἐπιστρέφετε πάλιν, πάλιν ἄνωθεν δουλεύειν θέλετε. For the force of these expressions see the introduction, p. 30, and the note on iv. 11.

St Paul's infirmity in the flesh.

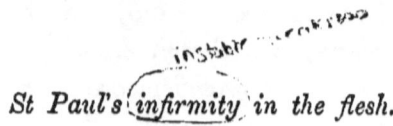

References to his infirmity.

In the Second Epistle to the Corinthians (xii. 7) St Paul, after speaking of the abundant revelations vouchsafed to him, adds that 'a thorn' or rather 'a stake' was 'given him in his flesh, a messenger of Satan sent to buffet him,' and thus to check the growth of spiritual pride. In the Epistle to the Galatians again (iv. 13, 14) he reminds his converts how he had 'preached to them through infirmity of the flesh,' commending them at the same time because they 'did not despise nor loathe their temptation in his flesh, but received him as an angel of God, as Christ Jesus.'

In the latter passage there is a variation of reading, which has some bearing on the interpretation. For '*my* temptation,' which stands in the received text, the correct reading seems certainly to be '*your* temptation,' as I have quoted it[1].

These passages so closely resemble each other that it is not unnatural to suppose the allusion to be the same in both. If so, the subject seems to have been especially present to St Paul's thoughts at the season when these two epistles were written; for they were written about the same time.

What then was this 'stake in the flesh,' this 'infirmity of the flesh,' which made so deep an impression on his mind?

Different accounts.

Diverse answers have been given to this question[2], shaped in many instances by the circumstances of the interpreters themselves, who saw in the Apostle's temptation a more or less perfect reflexion of the trials which beset their own lives. How far such subjective feelings have influenced the progress of interpretation, will appear from the following list of conjectures, which I have thrown into a rough chronological order.

i. A bodily complaint (tradition).

1. It was some bodily ailment. This, which is the natural account of the incident, is also the first in point of time. A very early tradition defined the complaint; 'per dolorem, ut aiunt, auriculae vel capitis,' says Tertullian *de Pudic.* § 13. And this statement is copied or confirmed by Jerome (Gal. l. c.), 'Tradunt eum gravissimum capitis dolorem saepe perpessum.' The headache is mentioned also by Pelagius and Primasius (both

[1] Of the three readings, τὸν πειρασμόν μου τὸν ἐν, τὸν πειρασμὸν τὸν ἐν (omitting μου), and τὸν πειρασμὸν ὑμῶν ἐν (omitting τόν), I have no hesitation in preferring the last; for (1) it is the most difficult of the three; (2) it accounts for the remaining two (see the note on the passage); and (3) it has far higher support than the others in the ancient copies. The Thebaic Version reads τὸν πειρασμόν μου, as I have ascertained (see Scrivener's *Introduction*, p. 351, ed. 2). Eusebius of Emesa here (Cramer's *Catena*, p. 65) and Origen on Ephes. iii. 14 (Cramer's *Catena*, p. 158) have a mixed reading τὸν πειρασμὸν ὑμῶν τὸν ἐν κ.τ.λ. Eusebius is overlooked by Tischendorf.

[2] A long list of references to writers who have discussed this question is given in Wolf *Cur. Philol.* on 2 Cor. xii. 7. I have to acknowledge my obligations chiefly to Calov. *Bibl. Illustr.* on 2 Cor. l. c., and Stanley's *Corinthians*, p. 563 sq (2nd ed.). I have had no opportunity of using Bertholdt *Opusc.* 134 sq, to which I find frequent references in recent commentaries.

on 2 Cor. l. c.). Others seem to have followed a different tradition as to the complaint in question[1]; but in some form or other *illness* was the solution which suggested itself to the earliest writers. This appears to be the idea of Irenæus, the first writer who alludes to the subject, and of Victorinus, the first extant commentator on the Epistle to the Galatians[2].

ii. Persecution (Greek fathers).

2. 'Nay, not so,' argued Chrysostom (2 Cor., Gal.), as others probably had argued before him; 'it cannot have been a headache, it cannot have been any physical malady. God would not have delivered over the body of His chosen servant to the power of the devil to be tortured in this way. The Apostle is surely speaking of opposition encountered, of suffering endured from his enemies.' And so for a time, and with a certain class of expositors, the thorn in the flesh assumed the form of persecution, whether from the direct opponents of the Gospel or from the Judaizers within the pale of the Church. This interpretation again was perhaps not uninfluenced by the circumstances of the times. At all events it would find a ready welcome, when the memory of the Diocletian persecution was fresh and when the Church was torn asunder by internal feuds. It appears at least as early as the middle of the fourth century in Eusebius of Emesa (Cramer's *Catena*, Gal. l. c.) among the Greek, and the Ambrosian Hilary (2 Cor., Gal.) among the Latin fathers. It is adopted also by Augustine (Gal.), by Theodore of Mopsuestia (Gal.), by Theodoret (2 Cor., Gal.), by Photius (? *ap. Œcum.*, 2 Cor., Gal.), and by Theophylact (2 Cor., Gal.)[3]. Thus it is especially the interpretation of the Greek commentators, though not confined to them.

But in spite of such strong advocacy, this account of St Paul's thorn in the flesh at all events cannot be correct. The passages, which allude to it, point clearly to something inseparable from the Apostle, to some affliction which he himself looked upon and which was looked upon by others as part of himself. Any calamity overtaking him from without fails to explain the intense personal feeling with which his language is charged.

Jerome.

The state of opinion on this subject at the close of the fourth century

[1] An ancient writer (Cotel. *Mon. Eccles.* I. p. 252) says *τριχῶν ἐποιησάμεθα τὴν ἀφαίρεσιν· συναφέλωμεν αὐταῖς καὶ τοὺς ἐν τῇ κεφαλῇ σκόλοπας· κομάσαντες γὰρ οὗτοι ἐπιπλέον ἡμᾶς ὀδυνῶσι· τὸ μὲν γὰρ τρίχωμα ἡμῶν ἦν ὁ κατὰ τὸν βίον κόσμος, τιμαί, δόξαι, χρημάτων κτήσεις, κ.τ.λ.*, on which the editor (p. 756) absurdly enough remarks, 'ex toto contextu suspicari datur a nostro per *σκόλοπα animalcula* quae caput pungunt intellecta esse.' The context, if I mistake not, fails to bear out this remark, but Cotelier's conjectural interpretation is treated as a fact by recent writers, and so this is added to the list of traditional accounts of St Paul's complaint. The list is still further swelled by understanding of St Paul the maladies which Nicetas (see below, note 3) attributes to Gregory Nazianzen. Aquinas mentions the opinion, 'quod fuit vehementer afflictus dolore iliaco' (colic), but I have not noticed it in any earlier writer. On the whole the tradition of the headache (*κεφαλαλγία*) is fairly constant.

[2] Iren. v. 3. 1, but his language is obscure. Victorinus says, 'infirmus carne,' but this again is not free from ambiguity.

[3] It was so taken apparently also by Greg. Naz. *Orat.* xx. (*de laud. Basil.*) ad fin. (see the note of Nicetas), and by Basil, *Reg. Fus. Tract.* ad fin. (II. p. 400, Garnier).

may be inferred from the alternative explanations which Jerome offers in his commentary on the Galatians, derived in part from tradition, but partly without doubt conjectural. These are four in number: (1) St Paul's carnal preaching of the Gospel, as addressed to babes; (2) His mean personal appearance; (3) Some bodily malady, traditionally reported as headache; (4) Persecutions endured by him[1].

iii. Carnal thoughts (Ascetics).

3. 'No,' thought the monks and ascetics of a somewhat later date, 'not persecution. It was surely something which we can realise, something which we have experienced in ourselves. Must he not have felt those same carnal longings, by which we have been dogged in our solitude, and which rise up hydra-like with seven-fold force as we smite them down? From these Paul thrice entreated the Lord to be delivered, as we have entreated Him; and was only answered, as we have been answered, by the indirect assurance, *My grace is sufficient for thee.*' This interpretation does not appear in a very tangible form before the sixth century, but earlier writers had used language which prepared the way for it[2]. Throughout the middle ages it seems to have been very generally received; and Roman Catholic writers have for the most part adopted it. So it is taken by Aquinas, Bellarmine (*de Monach.* c. 30), Corn. a Lapide[3], and Estius. Luther is probably correct when he attributes the prevalence of this interpretation to the influence of the Latin version, which renders σκόλοψ τῇ σαρκὶ by 'stimulus carnis.'

This account again of St Paul's thorn in the flesh may confidently be set aside. In such a temptation he could not have 'gloried'; nor would this struggle, hidden as it must have been in his own heart, have exposed him to the contempt of others. But indeed from painful trials of this kind we have his own assurance that he was free: 'I would,' he says, 'that all men were even as myself' (1 Cor. vii. 7). 'Ah no,' said Luther, 'he was too hard pressed by the devil to think of such things.'

iv. Spiri-

4. And in turn Luther propounded his own view of the thorn in the

[1] Ephraem Syrus (on Gal. iv. 18), a little earlier than Jerome, says 'Either disease of his limbs or temptation from his enemies.'

[2] Jerome *Epist.* xxii (ad Eustoch.) § 5, says: 'Si apostolus vas electionis et separatus in evangelium Christi ob carnis aculeos et incentiva vitiorum reprimit corpus suum, etc.,' quoting Rom. vii. 24, but he makes no reference to either of the passages in St Paul which relate to his 'thorn in the flesh,' and in § 31 of the same letter he says, 'Si aliquis te afflixerit dolor, legito, *datus est mihi stimulus carnis meae*,' evidently explaining it of some *bodily pain*. The passage in Augustine, Ps. lviii. Serm. ii. (IV. pp. 572, 3), is vague, and need not necessarily refer to this kind of temptation. Pelagius gives, as one interpretation, 'naturalem infirmitatem'; Primasius more definitely, though still only as an alternative explanation, 'alii dicunt titillatione carnis stimulatum.' Gregory the Great, *Mor.* viii. c. 29, writes, 'Sic Paulus ad tertium caelum raptus ducitur, paradisi penetrans secreta considerat, et tamen ad semetipsum rediens contra carnis bellum laborat, legem aliam in membris sustinet.' Comp. also x. 10. And thus, as time went on, this opinion gained strength, till at length it assumed the coarsest and most revolting form.

[3] Corn. a Lapide on 2 Cor. xii. 7 almost exalts this interpretation into an article of faith: 'Videtur communis fidelium sensus, qui hinc libidinis tentationem stimulum carnis vocant: vox autem populi est vox dei.'

flesh. He complained that the older churchmen were unable from their position to appreciate St Paul's meaning, and thus he consciously threw into the interpretation of the passage his own personal experiences. It was certainly not carnal longing, he thought; it was not any bodily malady. It might mean external persecution, as others had maintained, but he inclined more and more to the view that *spiritual trials* were intended, faint-heartedness in his ministerial duties, temptations to despair or to doubt, blasphemous suggestions of the devil[1]. This view naturally commends itself to the leaders of a new form of religious belief, owing to the difficulties of their position; and spiritual temptation was the account of St Paul's trial in which the reformers generally acquiesced. From them it found its way into Protestant writers of a later date, subject however to some modifications which adapted it to the more equable temper and the more settled opinions of their own day. tual trials (Reformers).

Lastly, having thus travelled round the entire circle of possible interpretation, criticism has returned to the point from which it started. *Bodily ailment* of some kind has been felt by most recent writers to be the only solution which meets all the conditions of the question. Recent critics.

These conditions are as follows: (1) The Apostle speaks of physical pain of a very acute kind; for nothing less can be implied by his metaphor of a stake driven through his flesh[2]. (2) The malady, whatever its nature, was very humiliating to himself, for he speaks of it as a set-off against his spiritual privileges and a check to his spiritual pride. (3) He seems to regard it, as he could not but regard such suffering, as a great trial to his constancy and resolution, a grievous hindrance to the Gospel in itself, a powerful testimony to the Gospel when overcome as he was enabled to overcome it. (4) His suffering was such that he could not conceal it from others. It seems to have attacked him in the course of his public ministrations, so that he feared it might expose him to the contempt and even loathing of his hearers. (5) In the meanness of his personal presence, of which he was Conditions of the problem.

[1] In his shorter and earlier commentary on the Galatians (1519) Luther explains it of 'persecution'; in his later and fuller work (1535) he combines spiritual temptations with persecution; and lastly in the Table-talk he drops persecution and speaks of spiritual trials only, xxiv. § 7 (vol. XXII. p. 1092 of the Halle edition). This last passage forms a striking contrast to the language of a Lapide quoted in the last note. 'Those were high spiritual temptations,' says Luther, 'which no papist has understood,' with more in the same strain. Thus each of these writers makes his own interpretation in a manner a test of orthodoxy. Other references in Luther's works to the 'thorn in the flesh' are, vol. VIII. p. 959, XI. p. 1437, XII. p. 561.

[2] This seems to be the meaning of σκόλοψ: see the notes of Meyer and Stanley on 2 Cor. xii. 7. Robertson, *Lectures on the Corinthians* lix, lx, speaks of the thorn as peculiarly suggestive of some 'secret sorrow'; for 'a thorn is a small invisible cause of suffering.' The Greek word however suggests no such idea; nor is it consistent with the fear of contempt or loathing expressed in the Galatian Epistle. This slight blemish, occurring where it does, may well be overlooked in the latest utterance of one who spoke from deep personal experience, having himself maintained a hard struggle against 'fightings without' and 'fears within,' and 'borne about in the body the dying of the Lord Jesus.' The lesson of St Paul's sufferings is nowhere more powerfully brought out than in this exposition of the thorn in the flesh.

so acutely sensible (2 Cor. x. 10), we may perhaps trace the permanent effects of his painful malady. (6) His disease was recurring. We first read of it in connexion with his visions and revelations fourteen years before the Second Epistle to the Corinthians was written. If the two were nearly coincident, as his language seems to imply, he must have had an attack about the year 44, and this, as it would appear, for the first time. Again we hear of it about the year 51 or 52, when he first preached in Galatia. On this occasion at least it would seem to have hung about him for some time. For from Greece he writes to the Thessalonians, that he had desired to visit them more than once, but 'Satan had hindered him' (1 Thess. ii. 18), an expression which may perhaps be connected with the 'messenger of Satan, the thorn in the flesh' in one of the passages under consideration; and writing afterwards to the Corinthians of this same period of his life, he reminds them that he came among them 'in infirmity and in fear and in much trembling' (1 Cor. ii. 3). Lastly, from the twin references to his malady, in the Second Epistle to the Corinthians and in the Epistle to the Galatians, it may be inferred that he had a fresh attack about the years 57, 58, when these letters were written, and to this he may allude in part when he speaks in the former of these epistles of having 'despaired even of life,' of having 'had the sentence of death in himself' (2 Cor. i. 8, 9).

Parallel of King Alfred.

The life of the greatest and best of English kings presents so close a parallel to the Apostle's thorn in the flesh, that I cannot forbear quoting the passage at length, though the illustration is not my own[1].

"It was in the midst of these rejoicings (on the occasion of his marriage) that Alfred was *suddenly attacked* by an illness, the sight of which struck dumb the loud joy of the guests, and for which neither they nor all the physicians of the day could account...Others thought it was the unexpected return of a painful malady to which he had been subject at an early age.

"We are informed what the malady really was in an account which is not quite clear...On passing from childhood to youth...he begged for some protection against his passions, for some corporal suffering which might arm him against temptation, so that his spirit might be enabled to raise him above the weakness of the flesh. On this, we are told, heaven sent him his illness, which Asser describes as a kind of eruption. For many years it caused him the most horrible torture, which was so intense that *he himself began to despair of his life.* One day...the royal youth...prostrated himself in silent devotion and prayed to God for pity. For fear of being rendered by his bodily infirmities, or perhaps by leprosy *or blindness,* incapable of exercising the royal power or *despicable in the sight of the world,* had long obtained possession of his soul and induced him to *pray for his deliverance* from such a plague. Every other lighter trial he was willing to undergo, provided it only spared him for what he was accustomed to look on as his destined office. Not long after...in consequence of his fervent prayers, we are informed that all signs of his malady disappeared.

"And now in the very moment that he had taken to himself a wife,

[1] The passage is quoted in Jowett, I. p. 368 (2nd ed.). The value of the illustration is diminished by the suspicion attaching to the so-called Asser.

in the very moment that the marriage-guests were drinking and carousing noisily in the festive halls, the evil against which (? warum) he had prayed overtook him. He was *suddenly seized with fear and trembling;* and to the very hour that Asser wrote, to a good old age, *he was never sure of not being attacked by it.* There were instants when this visitation seemed *to render him incapable of any exertion*, either intellectual or bodily: but the repose of a day, a night, or even an hour, would always raise his courage again. Under the weight of this bodily infirmity, which was probably of an epileptic nature, he learned, by the force of his unyielding will, to overcome the heaviest cares that ever weighed upon any ruler engaged in a contest with a most terrible foe, and under the weight of corporeal weakness and the cares of the outer world, to prosecute unceasingly his great purpose." Pauli's *Life of Alfred*, pp. 122—125 (Eng. Transl.).

In the mystery which hangs over the whole subject, in its physical symptoms, and in its influence on his own character and feelings, Alfred's malady is a most striking counterpart to the infirmity of St Paul; and the coincidence is the less open to suspicion, since neither Asser, who is the original authority for the fact, nor Pauli, whose account I have quoted, seems to have been struck by the parallel.

Unless then we accept the earliest tradition of this infirmity, and assume that the Apostle suffered from acute pain in the head (an account which considering his nervous sensibility is perhaps sufficient to explain the feeling of humiliation and the fear of contempt which his malady inspired), we should be tempted by the closeness of the parallel to conjecture that it was of the nature of epilepsy. Recent criticism has offered other conjectures in abundance. Of these, the view that it was a complaint in the eyes deserves especially to be mentioned, as having been supported by the most ingenious advocacy and found the largest number of adherents: but it does not, I think, sufficiently recognise the conditions of the problem, as stated above; while the direct arguments, on which it is founded, seem to melt away under the light of careful examination[1]. Conclusion.

[1] It is put forward in a lively and interesting paper in Dr J. Brown's *Horae Subsecivae.* But the foundation on which this opinion is built seems to me scarcely strong enough to bear it; for (1) The stress of the argument rests on what I cannot but think a mistaken interpretation of Gal. iv. 15, 'If it had been possible, ye would have plucked out your eyes and have given them to me.' Here the English version has 'your *own* eyes,' which lends some countenance to the idea that St Paul intended to say they would have replaced his eyes with their own, if it could have been done: but the Greek is τοὺς ὀφθαλμοὺς ὑμῶν, where ὑμῶν is as unemphatic as possible, so that the meaning is not '*your* eyes,' but 'your *eyes*.' (2) The expression πηλίκα γράμματα (vi. 11) is thought to be illustrated by this view of St Paul's complaint, as though his defective eyesight explained the allusion to the *size of the letters*, or *the length of the epistle*, whichever way we take it. It seems to me that a much better account can be given of that expression: see the note there. (3) It is supposed that this defective eyesight was a permanent effect of the temporary blindness which seized the Apostle on the way to Damascus; and that thus his thorn in the flesh was eminently fitted to be a check on spiritual pride produced by his 'visions and revelations.' But the narrative of the Acts implies, if it does not state, that this blindness was *completely* healed;

The various readings in iv. 25.

Variations.

The following are the variations of text, which the opening clause of this verse presents.

(i) τὸ γὰρ Σινᾶ ὄρος ἐστίν. So it is read in ℵCFG, 17; in the Old Latin (f.g.), Vulgate, Æthiopic, and Armenian Versions; in Origen[1], Epiphanius[2], Cyril[3], and Damascene; in Victorinus, the Ambrosian Hilary ('Sina *autem* mons,' in his text), Augustine, Jerome, Pelagius, Primasius, and probably *all* the Latin fathers. This is also the reading of the Gothic Version, except that it omits γάρ. The Thebaic Version reads similarly, 'quae vero mons Sina est.' The MS ℵ after ἐστὶν adds ὄν, in which respect it stands alone (except apparently the Memphitic Version); and Epiphanius transposes Σινᾶ and ὄρος.

(ii) τὸ Ἄγαρ Σινᾶ ὄρος ἐστίν. So the Memphitic Version as read by Boetticher; but Wilkins inserts a δέ.

(iii) τὸ δὲ Ἄγαρ Σινᾶ ὄρος ἐστίν. Such is the reading of ABDE, 37, 73, 80, lectionary 40.

(iv) τὸ γὰρ Ἄγαρ Σινᾶ ὄρος ἐστίν. So KLP with the vast majority of cursive manuscripts, with both Syriac Versions, and with the Greek commentators generally, Chrysostom, Theodore of Mopsuestia, Theodoret, Theophylact, and the Œcumenian Catena. This also is apparently the reading of Ephraem Syrus.

(v) τὸ γὰρ Ἄγαρ ὄρος ἐστὶν found only in the Latin of D and E[4].

Reading adopted.

It will thus be seen that the strongest, because the most varied, testimony is in favour of the first of these readings. And there is also this weighty argument on the same side, that supposing it to have been the

and the passage in 2 Corinthians refers to incidents which occurred only fourteen years before the letter was written, and therefore much later than the Apostle's conversion. (4) To the arguments already considered, some have added the expression ἀτενίζειν, 'to look steadfastly,' twice used of St Paul (Acts xiii. 9, xxiii. 1), as indicating a defective vision; but, not to mention that the word occurs frequently in the Acts of others besides St Paul, this 'steadfast gaze' would seem, if anything, to imply a *powerful* eye. Thus it may be connected with the tradition or fiction, dating at least from the second century, that St Paul was σύνοφρυς (Acta Paul. et Thecl. § 3). The overhanging brows and piercing glance made up at least a consistent and characteristic portrait of the Apostle, if not a true likeness. On the other hand it is *possible* that he suffered from weak eyes, and this may account for the incident of Acts xxiii. 5; but it is not implied in Gal. iv. 15, and does not explain the strong expressions used of his 'stake in the flesh,' though perhaps it might be one of the consequences of that infirmity. St Paul's language implies some more *striking* complaint.

[1] *In Cant.* ii. (III. p. 52, ed. Delarue), extant only in a Latin translation.

[2] *Haeres.* p. 695.

[3] *Glaphyr.* I. p. 75 (ed. Auberti). Cyril is said in other passages to read τὸ δὲ Ἄγαρ and τὸ γὰρ Ἄγαρ, but I am unable to verify the statement.

[4] The Ambrosian Hilary (in his commentary) is also quoted in favour of this reading, but his words do not bear out the inference.

original reading we have on the whole a more probable explanation of the variations in the text, than on any other hypothesis. By the negligence or confusion of a scribe τὸ Ἄγαρ might easily be substituted for τὸ γάρ, the word Ἄγαρ occurring in the immediate context[1]. As a next step a connecting particle must be supplied; and δὲ or γὰρ was inserted according to the caprice or judgment of the transcriber, thus producing the second and third readings. Lastly, the word Σινᾶ, now rendered superfluous, was expelled to relieve the passage, and hence arose the fourth variation, which indeed is too feebly supported to deserve consideration. The reading which I am here advocating is adopted by the two great masters of textual criticism, Bentley[2] and Lachmann. Westcott and Hort however relegate it to their margin.

Such seems to be the most probable account of the passage. Otherwise the earlier conjecture of Bentley, that we have here a gloss transferred from margin to text, has much to recommend it. Bentley himself indeed read it τὸ δὲ Ἄγαρ συστοιχεῖ τῇ νῦν Ἰερουσαλήμ, but it seems simpler, if any such solution be adopted, to erase the whole clause τὸ γὰρ...... ἐν τῇ Ἀραβίᾳ. This hypothesis derives some colour from the fact that there is a slight variation of reading in the connecting particles of the following clauses, as if the connexion had been disturbed by the insertion of the gloss.

The meaning of Hagar in iv. 25.

If the word Hagar be omitted, the passage is capable of a very easy and natural interpretation; 'Sinai,' St Paul argues, 'is situated in Arabia, the country of Hagar's descendants, the land of bondslaves.' And such too seems to be the most probable account of his meaning, even if with the received text we retain Hagar; 'This Hagar is Mount Sinai in Arabia,' i.e. it represents Mount Sinai, because Mount Sinai is in Arabia, the land of Hagar and her descendants. It is not ἡ Ἄγαρ, the woman Hagar, but τὸ Ἄγαρ, the thing Hagar, the Hagar of the allegory, the Hagar which is under discussion[3].

Probable interpretation of 'Hagar.'

[1] The commentary of Theodore Mops. on this passage shows how easily Ἄγαρ might be foisted in. The Greek text of this writer (in Cramer's *Catena*) has ἀλλ' Ἄγαρ ἥ τε ἔρημος πᾶσα κ.τ.λ., which makes no sense. The Latin translation runs '*sed et* solitudo omnis,' which doubtless represents the original reading, ἀλλὰ καὶ ἥ τε ἔρημος πᾶσα. Windischmann's conjecture to account for the insertion of Ἄγαρ in the text of St Paul is more ingenious than probable. He supposes a critical note, ἀ. γάρ (i. e. ἄλλοι· γάρ), marking a various reading in the connecting particle, to have been transferred from the margin to the text.

[2] In his text of the epistle as given in *Bentleii Crit. Sacr.* p. 108. This text is much later than his 'Epistola ad Millium' (Ib. p. 45), in which he starts the hypothesis of a gloss. This hypothesis was adopted by Mill and others.

[3] τὸ denotes that 'Hagar' is regarded not as a person, but as an object of thought or of speech. For this use of the neuter article see Winer § xviii. p. 135, A. Buttmann p. 84. It need not necessarily mean 'the *word* Hagar'; compare for instance Ephes. iv. 9 τὸ δὲ

Such substantially was the interpretation put upon the passage by some of the ablest among the Greek commentators. 'The law was given in the very place,' says Theodore of Mopsuestia (the sense is somewhat distorted through the medium of a bad Latin translation), 'which belongs to that race whence Hagar also was.' 'About that mountain,' says Theodoret, 'are the tents of the descendants of Hagar (τὸ τῆς Ἄγαρ ἐσκήνωται γένος).' 'The Saracens,' remarks a third writer, perhaps Severianus[1], 'the descendants of Ishmael, dwell in the desert which reaches as far as Mount Sinai.' Similarly Ephraem Syrus: 'For this Hagar is Mount Sinai which is in the land of the Arabs, and it is a type of (a likeness to) Jerusalem, for it is in subjection and bondage with its sons under the Romans.'

This however is not the interpretation generally adopted by those who retain the received reading. They suppose the Apostle to be calling attention not to the locality of Sinai but to the meaning of the word Hagar: 'The word Hagar in the language of the Arabians denotes Mount Sinai.' This interpretation, which prevails widely, is put in its most attractive form by Dean Stanley. 'There is another traveller through Arabia,' he writes, 'at this time, on whose visit to Mount Sinai we should look with still greater interest. *I went into Arabia*, says St Paul, in describing his conversion to the Galatians. It is useless to speculate; yet when in a later chapter of the same epistle the words fall upon our ears, *This Hagar is Mount Sinai in Arabia*, it is difficult to resist the thought, that he too may have stood upon the rocks of Sinai, and heard from Arab lips the often repeated "Hagar," "rock," suggesting the double meaning to which that text alludes[2].' 'Hagar[3]' in Arabic means 'a rock,' or rather 'a stone'; and it is maintained that this Arabic word 'Hagar' was a common local name for Sinai, or at all events was appropriated to it in some special way.

Hagar taken for a name of Sinai.

Objections to this.

Independently of any questions that may rise on the interpretation, I have endeavoured to show that 'Hagar' ought to be expelled from the text on the ground of external authority alone. Yet, if it be a fact that Hagar is really another name for Sinai, this fact will go some little way towards reinstating Ἄγαρ; and on this account, as well as in deference to the advocacy it has found, it will be worth while to consider the difficulties which beset this interpretation.

ἀνέβη τί ἐστιν; where τὸ is the *statement*, for the preceding *word* was not ἀνέβη, but ἀναβάς. The Ambrosian Hilary (after the middle of the fourth century) explains it 'causam Agar': a very early example of the sense which this word bears in the Romance languages, 'cosa,' 'chose.'

[1] In Cramer's *Catena*. It is anonymous (ἄλλος πάλιν φησίν), but in the immediate neighbourhood there is a note assigned to Severianus.

[2] *Sinai and Palestine* p. 50; see above, p. 89.

[3] حاجر pronounced '*Chagar*' (or rather '*Chajar*'). The Arabic alphabet has two letters, ح and خ, a softer and a harsher sound, corresponding to the one Hebrew guttural ח (*Ch*eth). The initial letter of 'Hagar,' 'a stone,' is the former of these, a soft guttural *Ch*, and not a simple aspirate. The second letter of the word is ج, corresponding to the Hebrew ג, our G, but generally pronounced by the Arabs softly like the English J, as we pronounce it in *gem*. I shall in this note represent ح by *Ch*, ج by *G*, both in Italics.

1. The evidence on which the assumed fact rests is both deficient in amount and suspicious in character. Not more than two independent witnesses, if they be independent, have, so far as I know, been produced.

(1) Inconclusive evidence.

(i) Chrysostom at the close of the fourth century in his exposition of this epistle writes somewhat obscurely; 'Hagar was the name of the bondmaid; and Mount Sinai is so interpreted in their native tongue (τὸ δὲ Σινᾶ ὄρος οὕτω μεθερμηνεύεται τῇ ἐπιχωρίῳ αὐτῶν γλώττῃ);' and afterwards he speaks of the mountain as 'bearing the same name with the bondmaid (ὁμώνυμον τῇ δούλῃ).' To the same effect writes Theophylact, who is often a mere echo of Chrysostom, as do one or two anonymous commentators in the Œcumenian Catena, without doubt deriving their information from the same source[1].

Chrysostom.

(ii) The Bohemian traveller Harant, who visited Sinai in the year 1598, says: 'The Arabian and Mauritanian heathen call Mount Sinai *Agar* or *Tur*[2].' Though, for anything that is found in the context, this might have been written without a thought of the passage of St Paul, yet I think it hardly probable. Luther, following Erasmus, had maintained this interpretation; and from the enormous popularity of his commentaries on the Galatians, it is likely that they were known to Harant, who himself ultimately became a protestant. If so, he did not necessarily derive his information from the Arabs on the spot, but may have accepted without question the popular statement, as more recent travellers have done.

Harant.

Their statements accounted for.

In later works of travel I have not found any direct personal testimony to this assumed fact. If there be any, it will from the nature of the case require careful sifting. The word 'Hagar' (*Chagar*) meaning 'a rock,' or 'a stone,' must be heard again and again from native lips in this wild region[3]; and a traveller, once possessed of the idea, might easily elicit the word from his Arab guide by a leading question, and on the strength of an

[1] Chrysostom's interpretation of the passage in St Paul may perhaps underlie the account of the word 'Hagar' given in Bar Bahlul's Syriac Lexicon, p. 417: ܗܓܪ ܒܣܘܪܝܐ ܗܘ ܛܘܪܐ جبل : ܘܐܣܛܪܐ هاجر. This extract, which is taken from the MS in the Cambridge University Library, I owe to the kindness of R. L. Bensly, Esq., of Caius College.

[2] Harant's authority is generally quoted at secondhand through Büsching's *Erdbeschr.* I. I. p. 603 (Hamb. 1792). In Harant's work itself, *Der Christliche Ulysses* (Nürnb. 1678), the passage runs: 'Den Berg Synai nennen die Arabische und Mauritanische Heyden *Agar* oder *Tur:* Weissenberg, wie auch *Tucla*, wie *Odoardo Barbosa nel' summ. del' Ind. Orient.* bezeuget.' The work was written in Bohemian, but translated into German by his brother and published by his nephew (see Balbinus *Bohem. Doct.* II. p. 104). [A friend, who has consulted the Bohemian original, informs me that *Weissenberg* is a miswriting of the name of a traveller whom Harant quotes, and that *Tucla* is there written *Turla*.] I give the passage of Barbosa to which Harant refers, as it stands in the copies which I have consulted. The title is *Primo volume delle Navigationi e Viaggi* (Venet. 1550 and 1554); *Libro di Odoardo Barbessa* or *Barbosa*, p. 313 (323), 'passato il detto monte Sinai, il quale i Mori dimandano Turla.'

[3] The index to Ritter's *Erdkunde*, Sinai etc. II. p. 1331, s.v. 'Hadschar,' 'Hadjar,' etc., names several 'stones' on and about Sinai; 'Hadschar Elma,' 'Hadsjar rükkâbe,' 'Hadj Musa,' etc.

answer thus obtained unsuspiciously confirm the statement that it was a local name for the mountain.

Thus the independent testimony to this supposed fact is confined to Chrysostom and Harant, or, if my supposition with regard to Harant be correct, to Chrysostom alone. To Chrysostom then, if I mistake not, or to some earlier writer whom he copied, this statement is due. Nor should we be doing any injustice to one who makes St Paul speak of Sinai as 'contiguous to Jerusalem,' were we to suppose that having heard of some place bearing the name 'Hagar' whether in Arabia Petræa or in some district bordering upon the Sinaitic mountains, (for the name seems to have been not uncommon[1],) he compressed the geography of the whole region and assigned this name to Mount Sinai itself, imagining that he had thus found the key to St Paul's meaning[2]. It is at least worthy of notice that no mention whatever of this assumed fact, or the interpretation based on it, is made either by his friend Theodore of Mopsuestia, or by Theodoret the pupil of Theodore, both natives of Antioch, and both acquainted with his work. Probably they were better informed on the subject, and for this reason tacitly abandoned Chrysostom's explanation.

2. But supposing it were proved that Sinai were so called by the Arabs, this word '*Ch*agar' is not written or pronounced in the same way as the proper name 'Hagar,' and etymologically the two are entirely distinct. The proper name 'Hagar,' with the simple aspirate (הגר, in Arabic هاجر), signifies 'a wanderer or fugitive,' being connected with the Arabic 'Hegira'

[1] Older critics, as Bochart and others (le Moyne *Var. Sacr.* p. 834, Pfeiffer *Op.* I. p. 504), assert that Petra itself bears the name Hagar (*Ch*agar) in Arabic writers, just as in Greek it is called Πέτρα, and in Hebrew סלע, words having the same meaning 'rock.' This statement however is founded on a twofold error; (1) The vocalisation of the proper name referred to is not '*Ch*agar,' but *Chigr*'; and (2) The place which bears this name 'El *Chigr*' in Arabic writers is not Petra itself, but a station several days south of Petra on the pilgrims' route between Damascus and Mecca. See Ewald *Paulus* p. 493 sq, Robinson's *Palestine etc.* II. p. 522. There is no evidence that Petra itself was so called.

There is a place חַגְרָא, '*Ch*agra,' mentioned four times in the Targum of Onkelos, Gen. xvi. 7, 14, xx. 1, Exod. xv. 22. In the second passage it is substituted for 'Bered,' in the remaining three for 'Shur,' of the original text. It must therefore have lain somewhere at the south of Palestine in the desert on the way to Egypt. In Gen. xvi. 7 it occurs in connexion with the flight of Hagar.

I venture to conjecture that there was also a place 'Hagar' (whether حاجر or هاجر) in Belka, and that the appearance of 'Belka' in the Arabic version of Gal. i. 17 and iv. 25 (see above, p. 87) is to be explained by this fact.

[2] Wieseler explains Chrysostom's meaning in a different way, insisting on the strict sense of *μεθερμηνεύεται*. According to Fürst *Concord.* and *Hebr. Handb.* s. v., סיני signifies 'rocky,' so that *interpreted* in Arabic it would be حاجر, and to this identity of meaning in 'Sinai' and 'Hagar' he supposes Chrysostom to allude. But even if the account which Fürst gives of the word סיני were altogether satisfactory, it would still remain in the highest degree improbable that Chrysostom should be acquainted with an etymology so abstruse.

the familiar term for the flight of Mahomet (compare also the Hebrew גור and יגר). Thus it has nothing in common with '*Chagar*,' 'a stone' (حاجر), which if it occurred in Hebrew would be written חגר. It is true that the gutturals are closely allied, and were sometimes confounded[1]; and this circumstance would deserve to be considered, if the supposed name for Sinai were supported by sufficient testimony: but where this is wanting, the false etymology throws an additional obstacle, to say the least, in the way of our accepting the explanation in question. Nor will it appear very probable that St Paul should have set aside the true derivation, when it is given and allegorized by his contemporary Philo[2].

It seems much more probable indeed, if St Paul is alluding to any local name of Sinai, that he should have regarded the true etymology, and that the name in question was not חגר 'rock,' but הגר 'wanderer.' This latter name was at least not uncommon among the Arab tribes; and it is far from unlikely, though direct evidence is wanting, that a settlement of these 'wanderers,' these children of 'Hagar,' occupied the country about Sinai in St Paul's day and gave it their name for the time.

3. But lastly, is it probable, supposing this to have been St Paul's meaning, that he would have expressed himself as he has done? If in writing to a half-Greek, half-Celtic people he ventured to argue from an Arabic word at all, he would at all events be careful to make his drift intelligible. But how could his readers be expected to put the right interpretation on the words 'this Hagar is Mount Sinai in Arabia'? How could they

(3) St Paul's language.

[1] The close alliance between the gutturals is shown, (1) By their interchange in the same language in different words connected or identical in meaning and obviously derived from the same root, e.g. מהר and מחר, צהר and צחר; (2) By their interchange in different languages of the Semitic family, e.g. Heb. בזה and Syr. ܒܙܚ (Hoffmann, *Gramm. Syr.* p. 123), or in different dialects of the same language, e.g. in the Aramaic dialects the Syriac ܚܢܢ compared with the Chaldee נחן (see Gesen. *Thes.* p. 359, Fürst *Aram. Idiome* § 45); (3) By the confusion of sound in the same language or dialect, e.g. a Judæan in the story professes himself unable to distinguish between אִמַּר, 'a lamb,' עֲמַר, 'wool,' חֲמַר, 'wine,' and חֲמוֹר, 'an ass,' as pronounced by a Galilean, when the latter wants to make a purchase; see Fürst, *ib.* § 15. There was the same confusion also in the Samaritan pronunciation of the gutturals; Gesen. *Lehrgeb.* § 32. 1. On the relation of the gutturals to each other, see Ewald, *Ausf. Lehrb. d. Heb. Spr.* § 39 sq.

Assemani indeed (*Bibl. Or.* III. 2, p. 753) gives an instance of the interchange of the gutturals *He* and *Cheth* in this very word Hagar: 'Hagar ܗܓܪ, Arabibus حاجر Hagiar, hoc est, Petra; Ptolemaeo Agra, unde Agraei populi Arabiae juxta sinum Persicum, etc.' But is there not a misprint or an error here? Was this place ever written in Arabic otherwise than with a simple aspirate as in Syriac? At all events Winer (*Realw.* s.v. *Hagariter*) is wrong in understanding Assemani's remark of the station between Damascus and Mecca (see p. 196, note 1), and has been blindly followed by others.

[2] παροίκησις, *Leg. Alleg.* I. p. 135 M, *Sacr. Ab. et Ca.* I. p. 170 (παροικεῖ σοφίᾳ, οὐ κατοικεῖ). Another derivation of Hagar, or rather a play upon the word, was הא אגרך, 'here is thy wages'; see Beer *Leben Abraham's* p. 148.

possibly understand, knowing nothing of Arabic, that he meant to say, 'this word Hagar in the Arabic tongue stands for Mount Sinai'? Even if it be granted that his readers were acquainted with the fact which was the key to his meaning, is *ἐν τῇ Ἀραβίᾳ* at all a likely expression to be used by any writer for *ἐν τῇ Ἀραβικῇ γλώσσῃ* or *Ἀραβιστί*, unless it were made intelligible by the context? Yet this is the meaning generally assigned to *ἐν τῇ Ἀραβίᾳ* by those commentators, ancient or modern, who adopt the interpretation in question, and indeed seems to be required to justify that interpretation.

In the face of these difficulties, it seems at least improbable that the point of the passage is the identity of 'Hagar' and 'Sinai' as different names of the same mountain, and the reading which retains 'Hagar' in the text loses any support which it may seem to draw from this identity, assumed as a fact.

Philo's allegory of Hagar and Sarah[1].

In giving an allegorical meaning to this passage of the Old Testament narrative St Paul did not stand alone. It might be inferred indeed from his own language that such applications of the history of Hagar and Sarah were not uncommon in the schools of his day[2]. But, however this may be, it is more than once so applied in the extant works of Philo. I have already pointed out the contrast presented by his treatment of the history of Abraham in general to the lessons which it suggests to the Apostle of the Gentiles. This contrast extends to the application of the allegorical method to this portion of the sacred narrative. Philo's allegory is as follows.

hilo's llegory, Abraham—the human soul progressing towards the knowledge of God—unites himself first with Sarah and then with Hagar. These two alliances stand in direct opposition the one to the other[3]. Sarah, the princess—for such is the interpretation of the word[4]—is divine wisdom. To her therefore Abraham is bidden to listen in all that she says. On the other hand Hagar, whose name signifies 'sojourning' (*παροίκησις*), and points therefore to something transient and unsatisfying, is a preparatory or intermediate

[1] For Philo's allegory of Hagar and Sarah, see esp. *de Congr. Quaer. Erud. Gr.* I. p. 519 sq, esp. pp. 521, 522, 530, 592, and *Quaest. in Gen.* p. 189 sq, 233 sq (Aucher). Compare also *Leg. Alleg.* I. p. 135, *de Cherub.* I. p. 139 sq, *de Prof.* I. p. 546, *de Abr.* II. p. 52, *de Somn.* I. p. 656.

[2] See the notes on *συνστοιχεῖ* and *ἀλληγορούμενα*.

[3] *de Abr.* II. p. 15 *ἐναντιώτατοι δὲ ἀλλήλοις εἰσὶν οἱ λεχθέντες γάμοι.*

[4] In some passages Philo still further refines on the change in her name (Gen. xvii. 15): e.g. *de Mut. Nom.* I. p. 590, *Quaest. in Gen.* p. 229 (Aucher), *de Cherub.* I. p. 139. Her first name Σάρα (שׂרי) is ἀρχή μου, her after-name Σάρρα (שׂרה) is ἄρχουσα (see Hieron. *Quaest. in Gen.*, III. p. 331). Thus they are related to each other as the special to the general, as the finite and perishable to the infinite and imperishable.

training—the instruction of the schools—secular learning, as it might be termed in modern phrase[1]. Hence she is fitly described as an Egyptian, as Sarah's handmaid. Abraham's alliance with Sarah is at first premature. He is not sufficiently advanced in his moral and spiritual development to profit thereby. As yet he begets no son by her. She therefore directs him to go in to her handmaid, to apply himself to the learning of the schools. This inferior alliance proves fruitful at once. At a later date and after this preliminary training he again unites himself to Sarah; and this time his union with divine wisdom is fertile. Not only does Sarah bear him a son, but she is pointed out as the mother of a countless offspring[2]. Thus is realised the strange paradox that 'the barren woman is most fruitful.' Thus in the progress of the human soul are verified the words of the prophet, spoken in an allegory, that 'the desolate hath many children[3].'

But the allegory does not end here. The contrast between the mothers is reproduced in the contrast between the sons. Isaac represents the wisdom of the wise man, Ishmael the sophistry of the sophist[4]. Sophistry must in the end give place to wisdom. The son of the bondwoman must be cast out and flee before the son of the princess[5].

compared with St Paul's.

Such is the ingenious application of Philo—most like and yet most unlike that of St Paul. They both allegorize, and in so doing they touch upon the same points in the narrative, they use the same text by way of illustration. Yet in their whole tone and method they stand in direct contrast, and their results have nothing in common. Philo is, as usual, wholly unhistorical. With St Paul on the other hand Hagar's career is an allegory, because it is a history. The symbol and the thing symbolized are the same in kind. The simple passage of patriarchal life represents in miniature the workings of God's providence hereafter to be exhibited in grander proportions in the history of the Christian Church. The Christian

[1] *ἡ μέση καὶ ἐγκύκλιος παιδεία* is Philo's favourite phrase, e.g. *de Cherub.* I. p. 139.

[2] *de Congr. Quaer. Erud. Gr.* I. p. 519 *ταύτην Μωϋσῆς, τὸ παραδοξότατον, καὶ στεῖραν ἀποφαίνει καὶ πολυγονωτάτην*: comp. *de Mut. Nom.* I. pp. 599, 600, where he adds *κατὰ τὸ ᾀδόμενον ᾆσμα ὑπὸ τῆς χάριτος Ἄννης ἥ φησιν, Στεῖρα ἔτεκεν ἑπτὰ ἡ δὲ πολλὴ ἐν τέκνοις ἠσθένησε* (1 Sam. ii. 5).

[3] *de Execr.* II. p. 434 *ἡ γὰρ ἔρημος, ᾗ φησὶν ὁ προφήτης, εὔτεκνός τε καὶ πολύπαις, ὅπερ λόγιον καὶ ἐπὶ ψυχῆς ἀλληγορεῖται* (Is. liv. 1). The coincidence with St Paul is the more striking inasmuch as Philo very rarely goes beyond the Pentateuch in seeking subjects for allegorical interpretation. There is indeed no mention of Sarah and Hagar here, but it appears, both from the context and from parallel passages, that they are present to his mind.

[4] *de Sobr.* I. p. 394 *σοφίαν μὲν Ἰσαάκ, σοφιστείαν δὲ Ἰσμαὴλ κεκλήρωται*: comp. *de Cherub.* I. p. 140, and other passages referred to in p. 198, note 1. The names give Philo some trouble. Isaac of course signifies 'laughter,' betokening the joy which comes of divine wisdom; see, besides the passages just referred to, *Leg. Alleg.* I. p. 131, *Quod Det. Pot.* I. pp. 203, 215. Ishmael he contrasts with Israel, the one signifying the *hearing* God, the other the *seeing* God (איש ראה אל, 'vir videns deum'; comp. Hieron. *in Gen.* III. p. 357). Thus they are opposed to each other, as *ἀκοὴ* to *ὅρασις*, as the fallacious to the infallible, as the *σοφιστὴς* to the *σοφός*, *de Prof.* I. p. 577, *de Mut. Nom.* I. p. 609.

[5] *de Cherub.* I. p. 140.

Apostle and the philosophic Jew move in parallel lines, as it were, keeping side by side and yet never once crossing each other's path.

And there is still another point in which the contrast between the two is great. With Philo the allegory is the whole substance of his teaching; with St Paul it is but an accessory. He uses it rather as an illustration than an argument, as a means of representing in a lively form the lessons before enforced on other grounds. It is, to use Luther's comparison, the painting which decorates the house already built.

Bearing on Inspiration.

At the same time we need not fear to allow that St Paul's mode of teaching here is coloured by his early education in the rabbinical schools. It were as unreasonable to stake the Apostle's inspiration on the turn of a metaphor or the character of an illustration or the form of an argument, as on purity of diction. No one now thinks of maintaining that the language of the inspired writers reaches the classical standard of correctness and elegance, though at one time it was held almost a heresy to deny this. 'A treasure contained in earthen vessels,' 'strength made perfect in weakness,' 'rudeness in speech, yet not in knowledge,' such is the far nobler conception of inspired teaching, which we may gather from the Apostle's own language. And this language we should do well to bear in mind. But on the other hand it were mere dogmatism to set up the intellectual standard of our own age or country as an infallible rule. The power of allegory has been differently felt in different ages, as it is differently felt at any one time by diverse nations. Analogy, allegory, metaphor—by what boundaries are these separated the one from the other? What is true or false, correct or incorrect, as an analogy or an allegory? What argumentative force most be assigned to either? We should at least be prepared with an answer to these questions, before we venture to sit in judgment on any individual case.

The various readings in v. I.

The variations of reading in this verse are the more perplexing, in that they seriously affect the punctuation, and thereby the whole texture of the passage. The main variations are threefold.

(1) Position of οὖν.

I. The position of οὖν.

(i) It stands after στήκετε in ℵABCFGP and a few of the better cursive MSS; in f, g, the Vulgate, Gothic, Memphitic, Thebaic[1], Æthiopic, Armenian, and perhaps the Peshito Syriac[2] versions; in Origen[3], Basil[4], and Cyril[5]; in Victorinus, Augustine, and others. The Memphitic version also inserts γὰρ with τῇ ἐλευθερίᾳ.

[1] I have ascertained this from the MS belonging to Lord Crawford and Balcarres.

[2] This is doubtful, the order of the words being altered in this version.

[3] *in Exod.* H. 3 (II. p. 139), *in Jud.* H. 9 (II. p. 477), both extant only in Latin.

[4] *Mor.* 14 (II. p. 247, Garnier), according to some of the best MSS. In the printed editions however it stands after ἐλευθερίᾳ. In the *de Bapt.* (II. p. 641, Garnier), a treatise ascribed to Basil but of doubtful authorship, its place is after στήκετε.

[5] *Glaphyr.* I. p. 75.

(ii) Its position is after ἐλευθερίᾳ in C (by a third hand) KL and very many cursive MSS, in Marcus Monachus[1], Damascene, Theophylact, and Œcumenius.

(iii) It is omitted in DE (both Greek and Latin); in the Vulgate and later Syriac; in Ephraem Syrus, in Theodore of Mopsuestia and Theodoret, in Jerome, Pelagius, the Ambrosian Hilary, and others. It is wanting also in Chrysostom, who however supplies a connecting particle, reading τῇ γὰρ ἐλευθερίᾳ κ.τ.λ.

In Asterius[2] οὖν is absent after ἐλευθερίᾳ, but, as the context is wanting, it is impossible to say whether it occurred after στήκετε or not.

Thus it will be seen that the balance of authority is decidedly in favour of placing οὖν after στήκετε; and this is probably the correct reading. The displacement (ii) and the omission (iii) were, it would seem, different expedients to relieve the awkwardness in the position of the connecting particle, on the supposition that the sentence began with τῇ ἐλευθερίᾳ.

(2) Position of ἡμᾶς.

2. The position of ἡμᾶς. It is found,

(i) Before Χριστὸς in ℵABDEFGP and some cursive MSS, in Origen (Latin translation), Theodore of Mopsuestia (Latin translation), and Cyril[3].

(ii) After Χριστὸς in CKL and many cursive MSS, and in Chrysostom, Theodoret, Asterius, Marcus Monachus, and Damascene.

(iii) After ἠλευθέρωσεν in Theophylact.

The versions and the Latin fathers vary, the majority placing it after Χριστός; but this is plainly a case where no great stress can be laid on such evidence. The transposition would be made unintentionally in the course of translation (Χριστὸς ἡμᾶς being perhaps the more natural order), so that one authority in favour of ἡμᾶς Χριστὸς is of more weight than a number against it. The order ἡμᾶς Χριστὸς may therefore be retained with confidence.

(3) The relative.

3. Besides these, there still remains a third and more important variation.

(i) Τῇ ἐλευθερίᾳ ᾗ is read in D (by the correction of later hands[4]) EKL and the great majority of cursives, in both Syriac versions, in Basil, Chrysostom, Theodore of Mopsuestia (Latin), Theodoret (twice), Cyril, Asterius, Marcus Monachus, Theophylact, and Œcumenius. The Æthiopic has 'quia Christus nos liberavit; et state igitur.'

(ii) τῇ ἐλευθερίᾳ alone is found in ℵABCDP and a few cursive MSS, in the Thebaic and Memphitic versions, and in Damascene and others.

(iii) ᾗ ἐλευθερίᾳ in FG, in the old Latin, Vulgate, and Gothic versions, in Marcion (or rather Tertullian[5]), Origen (Latin translation[6]), in Victorinus, Augustine, Jerome, and others.

[1] Gallandi VIII. p. 47.

[2] *In Ps.* v. Hom. 5, Cotel. *Mon. Eccl.* II. p. 46.

[3] The Latin of D has 'qua libertate nostra.' It has been suggested to me that *tra* was originally a direction to transpose 'nos.'

[4] 'D** et D*** praeposuerunt η, praetereaque D** addidit signa quibus η χς ante ημας ponendum esse significaret, sed videntur ea signa rursus deleta esse.' Tischendorf *Cod. Clarom.*

[5] *adv. Marc.* v. 4.

[6] *in Gen.* H. 7 (II. p. 78), *in Cant.* i. 6 (III. p. 52).

Thus our choice seems to lie between (i) and (ii), and on the whole the first seems more probable than the second. For, though the balance of direct evidence is against it, the following considerations may be urged in its favour.

First. The reading τῇ ἐλευθερίᾳ without ᾗ is so difficult as to be almost unintelligible. At a certain point Bengel's rule, 'proclivi scriptioni praestat ardua,' attains its maximum value; beyond this point it ceases to apply. And in the present instance it is difficult to give an interpretation to the words which is not either meaningless or ungrammatical.

Secondly. Supposing τῇ ἐλευθερίᾳ ᾗ to have been the original reading, the omission of ᾗ in some texts admits of a very simple explanation. Standing immediately before ἡμᾶς (which in its proper position, as we have seen, precedes Χριστός) it would easily drop out through the carelessness of transcribers. In this case too the transposition Χριστὸς ἡμᾶς for ἡμᾶς Χριστὸς was probably made for the sake of euphony to avoid the juxtaposition of ᾗ ἡμᾶς which came together in the original text.

At the same time the testimony in favour of τῇ ἐλευθερίᾳ alone is so strong, that I have hesitated to set it aside altogether and have therefore retained it at the foot as an alternative reading.

The third reading, ᾗ ἐλευθερίᾳ, found chiefly in the Latin copies, is not very easily accounted for, but was perhaps substituted for τῇ ἐλευθερίᾳ ᾗ as a more elegant expression or as a retranslation from the loose Latin rendering 'qua libertate.'

The words being thus determined, the punctuation is best decided by the position of the connecting particle, and the sentence will run, τῆς ἐλευθέρας τῇ ἐλευθερίᾳ ᾗ ἡμᾶς Χριστὸς ἠλευθέρωσεν. Στήκετε οὖν κ.τ.λ.

[2]Ἴδε ἐγὼ Παῦλος λέγω ὑμῖν, ὅτι, ἐὰν περιτέμνησθε, Χριστὸς ὑμᾶς οὐδὲν ὠφελήσει· [3]μαρτύρομαι δὲ πάλιν παντὶ ἀνθρώπῳ περιτεμνομένῳ, ὅτι ὀφειλέτης ἐστὶν

2—6. 'Let there be no misunderstanding. I Paul myself declare to you that if you submit to circumcision, you forfeit all advantage from Christ. I have said it once, and I repeat it again with a solemn protest. Every man, who is circumcised, by that very act places himself under the law; he binds himself to fulfil every single requirement of the law. You have no part in Christ, you are outcasts from the covenant of grace, you who seek justification in obedience to law. There is a great gulf between you and us. We, the true disciples of Christ, hope to be justified of faith, not of works, in the Spirit, not in the flesh.'

2. At this point St Paul assumes a severer tone in condemning the observance of the law. It is not only a useless imposition, a slavish burden; it is pernicious and fatal in itself.

Ἴδε] so to be accented rather than ἰδέ. According to the ancient grammarians, the pronunciation of common dialect was ἴδε, λάβε, of the Attic ἰδέ, λαβέ. See Winer § vi. p. 55 sq.

ἐγὼ Παῦλος] What is the exact force of this? Is it (1) *An assertion of authority?* 'I Paul, who received a direct commission from Christ, who have done and suffered so much for the Gospel and for you, who have so strong a claim on your hearing'? Or is it rather (2) *An indirect refutation of calumnies?* 'I Paul, who have myself preached circumcision forsooth, who say smooth things to please men, who season my doctrine to the tastes of my hearers'? For the latter sense, see 2 Cor. x. 1, where the words αὐτὸς δὲ ἐγὼ Παῦλος are used in combating the contemptuous criticism of his enemies; and compare his tone in i. 10 of this epistle; 'do I *now* persuade men?' See also the notes on ii. 3, v. 11, and the introduction, p. 28. For the former sense compare perhaps Ephes. iii. 1. The two ideas are not incompatible: they are equally prominent elsewhere in this epistle, and may both have been present to St Paul's mind, when he thus asserts *himself* so strongly.

περιτέμνησθε] '*suffer yourselves to be circumcised*'; see the note on περιτεμνομένῳ ver. 3.

3. The argument is this; 'Circumcision is the seal of the law. He who willingly and deliberately undergoes circumcision, enters upon a compact to fulfil the law. To fulfil it therefore he is bound, and he cannot plead the grace of Christ; for he has entered on another mode of justification.'

μαρτύρομαι δὲ πάλιν] 'Christ benefit you? *nay, I protest again.*' The adversative sense of δὲ is to be explained by the idea of ὠφελήσει. Πάλιν refers to the preceding λέγω; 'I have said it, and I repeat it with protestation.'

μαρτύρομαι] '*I protest,*' i.e. I assert as in the presence of witnesses. The word signifies properly 'to call to witness'; and is never, except perhaps in very late Greek, equivalent to μαρτυρῶ, 'I bear witness.' See the notes on 1 Thess. ii. 12. For the dative ἀνθρώπῳ compare Acts xx. 26. This use of the dative is a remnant of the fuller construction μαρτύρεσθαί τινί τι (Judith vii. 28 μαρτυρόμεθα ὑμῖν τὸν οὐρανὸν καὶ τὴν γῆν), the accusative being suppressed and the verb used absolutely without reference to the person of the witness.

περιτεμνομένῳ] '*who undergoes circumcision,*' as περιτέμνησθε ver. 2, and οἱ περιτεμνόμενοι vi. 13 (the better reading). In all these cases the present tense is more appropriate than

ὅλον τὸν νόμον ποιῆσαι. [4]κατηργήθητε ἀπὸ Χριστοῦ, οἵτινες ἐν νόμῳ δικαιοῦσθε, τῆς χάριτος ἐξεπέσατε. [5]ἡμεῖς γὰρ πνεύματι ἐκ πίστεως ἐλπίδα δικαιοσύνης ἀπεκδεχόμεθα· [6]ἐν γὰρ Χριστῷ ['Ιησοῦ] οὔτε περιτομή

the past. It is not the fact of their *having been circumcised* which St Paul condemns (for this is indifferent in itself), but the fact of their *allowing themselves to be circumcised*, being free agents.

4. κατηργήθητε, ἐξεπέσατε] The aorists represent the consequences as instantaneous; 'Ye are *then and there* shut out from Christ.' For similar instances see Joh. xv. 6 ἐὰν μή τις μείνῃ ἐν ἐμοί, ἐβλήθη ἔξω ὡς τὸ κλῆμα, Rev. x. 7: comp. Winer § xl. p. 345.

κατηργήθητε ἀπὸ Χριστοῦ] a pregnant expression for κατηργήθητε καὶ ἐχωρίσθητε ἀπὸ Χριστοῦ, 'Ye are nothing as regards Christ, ye are entirely separate from Him'; as Rom. vii. 2, 6; comp. 2 Cor. xi. 3 φθαρῇ τὰ νοήματα ὑμῶν ἀπὸ τῆς ἁπλότητος, Col. ii. 20.

οἵτινες δικαιοῦσθε] '*all ye who seek your justification.*' See on περιτεμνομένῳ, ver. 3.

ἐξεπέσατε] '*are driven forth, are banished* with Hagar your mother': see iv. 30 ἔκβαλε τὴν παιδίσκην. The words ἐκπίπτειν and ἐκβάλλειν are correlatives in this sense; e.g. Thucyd. vi. 4 ὑπὸ Σαμίων καὶ ἄλλων Ἰώνων ἐκπίπτουσιν...τοὺς δὲ Σαμίους Ἀναξίλας Ῥηγίνων τύραννος οὐ πολλῷ ὕστερον ἐκβαλὼν κ.τ.λ. For the form ἐξεπέσατε see Lobeck *Phryn.* p. 724, Winer § xiii. p. 86.

5. ἡμεῖς γάρ] '*for we*, who are in union with Christ, *we* who cling to the covenant of grace.' γὰρ introduces an argument from the opposite, as in iii. 10.

πνεύματι] '*spiritually*,' or '*by the Spirit*.' It is almost always difficult and sometimes, as here, impossible to say when πνεῦμα refers directly to the Holy Spirit and when not. From the nature of the case the one sense will run into the other, the spiritual in man, when rightly directed, being a manifestation, an indwelling of the Divine Spirit.

ἐλπίδα] here used in a concrete sense, 'the thing hoped for'; comp. Col. i. 5 τὴν ἐλπίδα τὴν ἀποκειμένην ὑμῖν, Tit. ii. 13 προσδεχόμενοι τὴν μακαρίαν ἐλπίδα, Heb. vi. 18; and see the note on ἐπαγγελία, iii. 14.

ἀπεκδεχόμεθα] '*wait eagerly*,' or perhaps '*patiently*'; used especially in speaking of the future redemption; comp. Rom. viii. 19, 23, 25, 1 Cor. i. 7, Phil. iii. 20. Compare the ἀπὸ in ἀποκαραδοκία, and see a paper by C. F. A. Fritzsche in *Fritzsch. Opusc.* p. 156.

6. γάρ] explaining the emphatic πνεύματι ἐκ πίστεως which has gone before: '*By the Spirit*, for the dispositions of the flesh, such as circumcision or uncircumcision, are indifferent: *from faith*, for faith working by love is all powerful in Christ Jesus.'

St Paul had before pronounced a direct and positive condemnation of circumcision. He here indirectly qualifies this condemnation. Circumcision is neither better nor worse than uncircumcision in itself (see especially 1 Cor. vii. 18—20, Gal. vi. 15). The false sentiment which attends it, the glorying in the flesh, makes the difference, and calls down the rebuke.

πίστις κ.τ.λ.] 'In his stat totus Christianismus,' says Bengel.

ἐνεργουμένη] '*working*'; the middle voice according to the general usage of St Paul. The Spirit of God or the Spirit of Evil ἐνεργεῖ; the human agent or the human mind ἐνεργεῖται: see the note on 1 Thess. ii. 13. On the other hand ἐνεργεῖσθαι is never passive in St Paul (as it seems to be taken here by Tertullian *adv. Marc.* v. 4, 'di-

τι ἰσχύει οὔτε ἀκροβυστία, ἀλλὰ πίστις δι' ἀγάπης
ἐνεργουμένη.
7 Ἐτρέχετε καλῶς· τίς ὑμᾶς ἐνέκοψεν ἀληθείᾳ μὴ
πείθεσθαι; 8 ἡ πεισμονὴ οὐκ ἐκ τοῦ καλοῦντος ὑμᾶς.

cendo per dilectionem perfici'), and therefore this passage does not express the doctrine of 'fides caritate formata.'

These words δι' ἀγάπης ἐνεργουμένη bridge over the gulf which seems to separate the language of St Paul and St James. Both assert a principle of practical energy, as opposed to a barren, inactive theory.

Observe in these verses the connexion between the triad of Christian graces. The same sequence—faith, love, hope—underlies St Paul's language here, which appears on the surface in 1 Thess. i. 3, Col. i. 4, 5. See the note on the former of these two passages.

7—11. 'Ye were running a gallant race. Who has checked you in your mid career? Whence this disloyalty to the truth? Be assured, this change of opinion comes not of God by whom ye are called. The deserters are only few in number? Yes, but the contagion will spread: for what says the proverb? *A little leaven leaveneth the whole lump.* Do not mistake me: I do not confound *you* with *them:* I confidently hope in Christ that *you* will be true to your principles. But the ringleader of this sedition—I care not who he is or what rank he holds—shall bear a heavy chastisement. What, brethren? A new charge is brought against me? I preach circumcision forsooth? If so, why do they still persecute me? It is some mistake surely! Nay, we shall work together henceforth! there is no difference between us now! I have ceased to preach the Cross of Christ! The stumblingblock in the way of the Gospel is removed!'

7. Ἐτρέχετε καλῶς] '*Ye were running bravely,*' again a reference to St Paul's favourite metaphor of the stadium. See ii. 2, 1 Cor. ix. 24—27, Phil. iii. 14, 2 Tim. iv. 7.

ἐνέκοψεν] a metaphor derived from military operations. The word signifies 'to break up a road' (by destroying bridges etc.) so as to render it impassable, and is therefore the opposite of προκόπτειν, 'to clear a way,' 'to act as pioneer'; comp. Greg. Naz. *Or.* xiv. 31 (I. p. 279 ed. Ben.) ἡ κακίας ἐγκοπτομένης δυσπαθείᾳ τῶν πονηρῶν ἢ ἀρετῆς ὁδοποιουμένης εὐπαθείᾳ τῶν βελτιόνων. Hence it originally took a *dative* of the person, e.g. Polyb. xxiv. 1. 12, but the metaphor being subsequently lost sight of, the dative was replaced by an accusative, as always in the New Testament, e.g. Acts xxiv. 4, 1 Thess. ii. 18. Compare the passive, Rom. xv. 22, 1 Pet. iii. 7. See the note on φθονοῦντες, ver. 26.

The testimony in favour of ἐνέκοψεν is overwhelming. Otherwise the received reading ἀνέκοψεν suits the metaphor of the stadium better; for ἀνακόπτειν 'to beat back' would apply to the ῥαβδοῦχοι (Thuc. v. 50) who kept the course: comp. Lucian *Nigr.* § 35 (I. p. 77) ἐξέπιπτόν τε καὶ ἀνεκοπτόμην, Polyc. § 5 ἀνακόπτεσθαι ἀπὸ τῶν ἐπιθυμιῶν. The word ἐγκόπτειν seems to have given offence to transcribers: in 1 Thess. ii. 18, as here, ἀνακόπτειν stands as a various reading; in Acts xxiv. 4, 1 Pet. iii. 7, ἐκκόπτειν.

8. πεισμονή] with a faint reference to the preceding πείθεσθαι; 'You have refused to *obey* the truth, you have rendered another *obedience* which is not of God.' πεισμονή (Ignat. *Rom.* 3, Justin *Apol.* I. c. 53, p. 17 E; comp. πλησμονή, Col. ii. 23), like the English 'persuasion,' may be either active or

9 μικρὰ ζύμη ὅλον τὸ φύραμα ζυμοῖ. 10 ἐγὼ πέποιθα εἰς ὑμᾶς ἐν Κυρίῳ, ὅτι οὐδὲν ἄλλο φρονήσετε· ὁ δὲ ταράσσων ὑμᾶς βαστάσει τὸ κρίμα, ὅστις ἐὰν ᾖ. 11 ἐγὼ

passive; 'the act of persuading,' referring to the false teachers; or 'the state of one persuaded,' referring to the Galatians themselves. The latter is perhaps simpler.

τοῦ καλοῦντος] i.e. God, as always in St Paul; see Usteri *Paul. Lehrbegr.* p. 269, and comp. i. 6, 15. The present is preferred here to the aorist, because the stress is laid on the *person* rather than the *act;* see the note on 1 Thess. v. 24, and comp. Winer § xlv. p. 444.

9. This proverb is quoted also in 1 Cor. v. 6. Comp. Hosea vii. 4.

Does it apply here (1) To the *doctrine?* 'If you begin by observing the law in a few points, you will end by selling yourselves wholly to it' (comp. v. 3); or (2) To the *persons?* 'Though the Judaizers may be but few now, the infection will spread to the whole body.' The latter is far more probable: for the prominent idea in the context is that of a small and compact body disturbing the peace of the Church; and the metaphor is thus applied also in 1 Cor. v. 7, where again it refers to the contagious example of a few evil-doers.

The leaven of Scripture is always a symbol of evil, with the single exception of the parable (Matt. xiii. 33, Luke xiii. 20, 21), as it is for the most part also in rabbinical writers: see Lightfoot on Matt. xvi. 6 and Schöttgen on 1 Cor. v. 6. Heathen nations also regarded leaven as unholy. Plutarch, *Quaest. Rom.* 109 (p. 289 E), in answer to the question why the Flamen Dialis was not allowed to touch leaven, explains it, ἡ ζύμη καὶ γέγονεν ἐκ φθορᾶς αὐτὴ καὶ φθείρει τὸ φύραμα μιγνυμένη. See Trench *On the Parables*, p. 111.

For the expression ζυμοῦν τὸ φύραμα see Exod. xii. 34.

10. ἐγώ] emphatic, '*I*, who know you so well, who remember your former zeal': iv. 14, 15.

πέποιθα] still dwelling on the same word, πείθεσθαι πεισμονή; see Winer § lxviii. p. 793 sq.

εἰς ὑμᾶς] '*in regard to you*'*;* see Winer § xlix. p. 496: comp. 2 Cor. viii. 22 πεποιθήσει πολλῇ τῇ εἰς ὑμᾶς, 2 Cor. ii. 3 πεποιθὼς ἐπὶ πάντας ὑμᾶς ὅτι κ.τ.λ., 2 Thess. iii. 4 πεποίθαμεν ἐν Κυρίῳ ἐφ' ὑμᾶς ὅτι κ.τ.λ. As in the passage last cited, ἐν Κυρίῳ here denotes not the object of the writer's confidence, but the sphere in which it is exercised.

οὐδὲν ἄλλο φρονήσετε] '*none otherwise minded,*' either (1) 'than I bid you,' for though no direct command immediately precedes these words, there is one implied; or, as seems more probable, (2) 'than ye were before this disorder broke out'; see ἐτρέχετε καλῶς, ver. 7.

ταράσσων] '*raises seditions*, excites tumults among you,' the metaphor being continued in ἀναστατοῦντες ver. 12. See the note on i. 7.

βαστάσει] '*shall bear* as a burden; it shall press grievously on him': see vi. 2, 5.

κρίμα] On the accent of this word, which is κρῖμα in classical writers, see Lobeck *Paral.* p. 418, Fritzsche *Rom.* I. p. 96, Lipsius *Gram. Unters.* p. 40. Compare the note on στύλοι, ii. 9.

ὅστις ἐὰν ᾖ] i.e. 'whatever may be his position in the Church, however he may vaunt his personal intercourse with the Lord.' See 2 Cor. x. 7.

11. At this point the malicious charge of his enemies rises up before the Apostle; 'Why you do the same thing yourself; you caused Timothy to be circumcised.' To this he replies: 'What do *I*, who have incurred the deadly hatred of the Judaizers, who

δέ, ἀδελφοί, εἰ περιτομὴν ἔτι κηρύσσω, τί ἔτι διώκομαι; ἄρα κατήργηται τὸ σκάνδαλον τοῦ σταυροῦ· 12 ὄφελον καὶ ἀποκόψονται οἱ ἀναστατοῦντες ὑμᾶς.

am exposed to continual persecution from them, do *I* preach circumcision?'

ἔτι κηρύσσω] For an explanation of this ἔτι, see the note i. 10. Perhaps however it should be explained rather by the form which the slander of his enemies would take; 'You *still* preach circumcision, though you have become a Christian: why should not we *continue* to do the same?'

τί ἔτι] The second ἔτι is probably argumentative, 'this being the case,' as in Rom. iii. 7, ix. 19.

ἄρα] 'so it appears!' ἄρα introduces a false statement or inference also in 1 Cor. v. 10, xv. 14, 15, 18, 2 Cor. i. 17. It is here ironical; 'So I have adopted their mode of justification; I am silent about the Cross of Christ! no one takes offence at my preaching now; all goes on pleasantly enough!' The σταυρὸς here stands for the atoning death of Christ. The crucifixion of the Messiah was in itself a stumbling-block to the Jews, but preached as the means of atonement, it became doubly so: comp. 1 Cor. i. 23.

σκάνδαλον] almost confined, it would appear, to biblical and ecclesiastical Greek. σκανδάληθρον however is a classical word, e.g. Arist. *Ach.* 687.

12. After this abrupt digression St Paul returns again to the false brethren: 'Why do they stop at circumcision?' he asks indignantly, 'why do they not mutilate themselves, like your priests of Cybele?' The severity of the irony may be compared with 2 Cor. xi. 19, 'Ye suffer fools gladly, seeing ye yourselves are wise.'

Circumcision under the law and to the Jews was the token of a covenant. To the Galatians under the Gospel dispensation it had no such significance. It was merely a bodily mutilation, as such differing rather in degree than in kind from the terrible practices of the heathen priests. Compare Phil. iii. 2, 3 βλέπετε τὴν κατατομήν· ἡμεῖς γάρ ἐσμεν ἡ περιτομή, where the same idea appears, clothed in similar language.

ὄφελον] Comp. 1 Cor. iv. 8, 2 Cor. xi. 1, in both of which passages the irony is plain. In this construction with the indicative, which appears only in later writers, the original meaning of ὄφελον is lost sight of, and it is treated as a mere particle; see Winer § xli. p. 377, A. Buttmann § 139, 10, p. 185.

ἀποκόψονται] will not admit the rendering of the A. V., 'I would they were even cut off.' On the other hand the meaning given above is assigned to ἀποκόψονται by all the Greek commentators, I believe, without exception (the Latin fathers, who read 'abscindantur' in their text, had more latitude), and seems alone tenable. See for instance ἀποκεκομμένος, Deut. xxiii. 1, and indeed ἀποκόπτεσθαι was the common term for this mutilation. If it seems strange that St Paul should have alluded to such a practice at all, it must be remembered that as this was a recognised form of heathen self-devotion, it could not possibly be shunned in conversation, and must at times have been mentioned by a Christian preacher. For the juxtaposition of περιτέμνειν and ἀποκόπτειν see Dion Cassius lxxix. 11 (quoted by Bentley *Crit. Sacr.* p. 48), and compare Diod. Sic. iii. 31. The remonstrance is doubly significant as addressed to Galatians, for Pessinus one of their chief towns was the home of the worship of Cybele in honour of whom these mutilations were practised: comp. Justin *Apol.* i. p. 70 E ἀποκόπτονταί τινες καὶ εἰς μητέρα θεῶν τὰ μυστήρια ἀναφέρουσι. See also [Bardesanes] *de Fato* § 20, in Cureton's *Spic. Syr.* p. 32. Thus by 'glorying in the flesh' the Galatians were returning in a very marked way

13 Ὑμεῖς γὰρ ἐπ' ἐλευθερίᾳ ἐκλήθητε, ἀδελφοί· μόνον μὴ τὴν ἐλευθερίαν εἰς ἀφορμὴν τῇ σαρκί, ἀλλὰ διὰ τῆς ἀγάπης δουλεύετε ἀλλήλοις. 14 ὁ γὰρ πᾶς νόμος ἐν ἑνὶ λόγῳ πεπλήρωται, ἐν τῷ ἀγαπήσεις τὸν

to the bondage of their former heathenism. See iv. 9, v. 1.

ἀναστατοῦντες] stronger than ταράσσοντες; 'They not only incite you to sedition, but they overthrow the whole framework of your heavenly polity.' For ἀναστατοῦν, a word unknown to classical writers, who would use ἀναστάτους ποιεῖν instead, see Acts xvii. 6, xxi. 38. 'Well does he say ἀναστατοῦντες,' remarks Chrysostom, 'for abandoning their country and their freedom and their kindred in heaven, they compelled them to seek a foreign and a strange land; banishing them from the heavenly Jerusalem and the free, and forcing them to wander about as captives and aliens.'

13. This is the justification of the indignant scorn poured on their offence: 'They are defeating the very purpose of your calling: ye were called not for bondage, but for liberty.'

ἐπ' ἐλευθερίᾳ] For καλεῖν ἐπὶ see 1 Thess. iv. 7: comp. Ephes. ii. 10, and Winer § xlviii. p. 492.

μόνον μή] Here he suddenly checks himself, to avoid misunderstanding; 'Liberty and not licence.' It may be that here, as in the Corinthian Church, a party opposed to the Judaizers had shown a tendency to Antinomian excess. At all events, such an outburst was ever to be dreaded in a body of converted heathens, whether as a protest against or a rebound from the strict formalism which the Judaic party sought to impose on the Church; and in this case the passionate temperament of a Celtic people would increase the Apostle's uneasiness. Comp. Rom. vi. 1 sq, Phil. iii. 13 sq (notes).

μόνον μή κ.τ.λ.] '*only turn not your liberty.*' Some MSS supply δῶτε, which is perhaps a retranslation from 'detis' of the Latin versions. For similar instances of ellipsis see the notes ii. 9, 10. The omission of the verb after the prohibitive μή is common in animated passages in classical writers: e.g. Arist. *Ach.* 345 ἀλλὰ μή μοι πρόφασιν. See the instances in Jelf's *Gramm.* § 897. Comp. Matt. xxvi. 5 μὴ ἐν τῇ ἑορτῇ.

ἀφορμήν] The word is peculiar to St Paul among the New Testament writers, occurring Rom. vii. 8, 11, 2 Cor. v. 12, xi. 12 (twice), 1 Tim. v. 14.

διὰ τῆς ἀγάπης δουλεύετε] Both ἀγάπης and δουλεύετε are emphatic. St Paul's meaning may be expressed by a paraphrase thus; 'Your desire to be in bondage: I too recommend to you a *bondage*, the subservience of mutual *love*. Temper your liberty with this bondage, and it will not degenerate into licence.' A similar contrast between true and false servitude appears in 1 Pet. ii. 16 ὡς ἐλεύθεροι καὶ μὴ ὡς ἐπικάλυμμα ἔχοντες τῆς κακίας τὴν ἐλευθερίαν, ἀλλ' ὡς Θεοῦ δοῦλοι.

14. 'Ye profess yourselves anxious to fulfil the law; I show you a simple and comprehensive way of fulfilling it.' See vi. 2. The idea of completeness is brought out by an accumulation of separate expressions, 'the entire law,' 'a single precept,' 'is fulfilled already.'

ὁ πᾶς νόμος] '*the entire law.*' The idea of *totality* is expressed more strongly by the exceptional position of the article instead of the more usual order πᾶς ὁ νόμος; comp. 1 Tim. i. 16 τὴν ἅπασαν μακροθυμίαν, Plat. *Gorg.* p. 470 E ἐν τούτῳ ἡ πᾶσα εὐδαιμονία ἐστίν, Ignat. *Magn.* 1 τὴν πᾶσαν ἐπήρειαν.

πεπλήρωται] '*is summarily fulfilled.*' For the force of the perfect see Winer § xl. p. 341, A. Buttmann p. 172. Tertullian (*adv. Marc.* p. 4)

ΠΛΗΣΙΟΝ ΣΟΥ ὩΣ ΣΕΑΥΤΌΝ. [15]εἰ δὲ ἀλλήλους δάκνετε καὶ κατεσθίετε, βλέπετε μὴ ὑπ' ἀλλήλων ἀναλωθῆτε.

[16]Λέγω δέ, πνεύματι περιπατεῖτε, καὶ ἐπιθυμίαν σαρκὸς οὐ μὴ τελέσητε. [17]ἡ γὰρ σὰρξ ἐπιθυμεῖ κατὰ

hints that Marcion perverted the meaning of the tense to suit his purpose, 'si sic vult intelligi *adimpleta est*, quasi jam non adimplenda.' The present πληροῦται in the received text enfeebles the sense. The meaning of πληροῦν here is not to 'sum up, comprehend,' but 'to perform, complete,' as appears from the parallel passage, Rom. xiii. 8 ὁ ἀγαπῶν τὸν ἕτερον, νόμον πεπλήρωκεν; so that ἐν ἑνὶ λόγῳ, 'in one maxim or precept,' means 'in the observance of one maxim or precept.'

ἐν τῷ] probably neuter, in apposition to the sentence; comp. Rom. xiii. 9, 10. See above on iv. 25.

τὸν πλησίον] In the original text (Lev. xix. 18) the word 'neighbour' is apparently restricted to the Jewish people: 'Thou shalt not bear any grudge against the *children of thy people*, but thou shalt love *thy neighbour* as thyself.' From the question of the lawyer (Luke x. 29) it may be inferred that the meaning of this term was a common theme for discussion. Our Lord extends and spiritualises its meaning; and in this comprehensive sense, as applying to the universal brotherhood of men, St Paul here uses it. See Tholuck *Bergpredigt*, v. 43.

σεαυτόν] The received text has ἑαυτόν, which some would retain against the authority of the best MSS on the ground that it was altered by scribes ignorant of this usage of ἑαυτοῦ for the first and second persons. The case however with respect to the New Testament seems to stand thus; that whereas (1) in the plural we always find ἑαυτῶν etc., never ἡμῶν αὐτῶν, ὑμῶν αὐτῶν etc., as mere reflexives, yet (2) in the singular there is not one decisive instance of ἑαυτοῦ in the first or second person; the authority of the best MSS being mostly against it. See A. Buttmann p. 99; and for the testimony of the MSS in this text (Lev. xix. 18) as quoted in the N. T., Tischendorf on Rom. xiii. 9.

15. βλέπετε κ.τ.λ.] A sort of parenthetic warning; 'The contest will not end in a victory to either party, such as you crave. It will lead to the common extinction of both.' St Paul returns to his main subject again in ver. 16. See the introduction, p. 33, note 3.

16—18. 'This is my command. Walk by the rule of the Spirit. If you do so, you will not, you cannot, gratify the lusts of the flesh. Between the *Spirit* and the *flesh* there is not only no alliance; there is an interminable, deadly feud. (You feel these antagonistic forces working in you: you would fain follow the guidance of your conscience, and you are dragged back by an opposing power.) And if you adopt the rule of the *Spirit*, you thereby renounce your allegiance to the *law*.'

In this passage the Spirit is doubly contrasted, first, with the *flesh*, and secondly, with the *law*. The flesh and the law are closely allied: they both move in the same element, in the sphere of outward and material things. The law is not only no safeguard against the flesh, but rather provokes it; and he who would renounce the flesh, must renounce the law also. We have here germs of the ideas more fully developed in the Epistle to the Romans.

16. πνεύματι] the dative of the rule or direction: see the notes v. 25, vi. 16.

οὐ μὴ τελέσητε] '*ye shall in no wise fulfil*.' A strong form of the future especially frequent in later Greek; see Lobeck *Phryn*. p. 724.

τοῦ πνεύματος, τὸ δὲ πνεῦμα κατὰ τῆς σαρκός· ταῦτα γὰρ ἀλλήλοις ἀντίκειται, ἵνα μή, ἃ ἐὰν θέλητε, ταῦτα ποιῆτε. [18]εἰ δὲ πνεύματι ἄγεσθε, οὐκ ἐστὲ ὑπὸ νόμον.

17. τὸ δὲ πνεῦμα] '*but the Spirit* strives, fights *against the flesh.*' As ἐπιθυμεῖν cannot apply to the Spirit, some other verb must be supplied in the second clause. Throughout this passage the πνεῦμα is evidently the Divine Spirit; for the human spirit in itself and unaided does not stand in direct antagonism to the flesh. See Müller's *Doctrine of Sin* I. p. 354 sq.

ταῦτα γὰρ κ.τ.λ.] A parenthetical clause, suggested by what has gone before, but not bearing on the main argument. It is an appeal to their own consciousness; 'Have you not evidence of these two opposing principles in your own hearts? How otherwise do you not always obey the dictates of your conscience?'

ἵνα] here seems to denote simply the *result*, whereas in classical writers it always expresses the *purpose*. For this late use of the word see the note on 1 Thess. v. 4.

ἃ ἐὰν θέλητε] The parallel passage, Rom. vii. 15, 16, determines the meaning of θέλειν here. It denotes the promptings of the conscience; 'video meliora proboque.'

18. πνεύματι ἄγεσθε] Comp. Rom. viii. 14 ὅσοι γὰρ πνεύματι Θεοῦ ἄγονται.

οὐκ ἐστὲ ὑπὸ νόμον] 'You have escaped from the dominion of law.' See on ver. 23. An anonymous writer in Cramer's *Catena* p. 81 (where the words are wrongly assigned to Chrysostom) says, οὐ νόμῳ τῷ ἀπειλοῦντι δούλοις, πνεύματι δὲ τῷ ἄγοντι τέκνα Θεοῦ. For νόμος without the article, see iii. 18, iv. 4, 5.

19. 'Would you ascertain whether you are walking by the Spirit? Then apply the plain practical test.'

ἅτινα] '*such as are*,' not ἅ, 'which are'; the list not being exhaustive, but giving instances only. See on iv. 24.

Though no systematic classification is to be looked for in the catalogue which follows, yet a partial and unconscious arrangement may perhaps be discerned. The sins here mentioned seem to fall into four classes: (1) *Sensual passions*, 'fornication, uncleanness, licentiousness'; (2) *Unlawful dealings in things spiritual*, 'idolatry, witchcraft'; (3) *Violations of brotherly love*, 'enmities...murders'; (4) *Intemperate excesses*, 'drunkenness, revellings.' From early habit and constant association a Gentile Church would be peculiarly exposed to sins of the first two classes. The third would be a probable consequence of their religious dissensions, inflaming the excitable temperament of a Celtic people. The fourth seems to be thrown in to give a sort of completeness to the list, though not unfitly addressed to a nation whose Gallic descent perhaps disposed them too easily to these excesses; see the introduction p. 13.

πορνεία κ.τ.λ.] The same three words occur together in a different order 2 Cor. xii. 21. The order here is perhaps the more natural; πορνεία a special form of impurity, ἀκαθαρσία uncleanness in whatever guise, ἀσέλγεια an open and reckless contempt of propriety.

ἀκαθαρσία] Comp. Rom. i. 24. There is no sufficient ground for assigning to this word the sense 'covetousness'; see the note on 1 Thess. ii. 3.

ἀσέλγεια] '*wantonness*.' A man may be ἀκάθαρτος and hide his sin; he does not become ἀσελγής until he shocks public decency. In classical Greek the word ἀσέλγεια generally signifies insolence or violence towards another, as it is defined in Bekker's *Anecd.* p. 451, ἡ μετ' ἐπηρεασμοῦ καὶ θρασύτητος βία. In the later language, in the New Testament for instance, the prominent

19φανερὰ δέ ἐστιν τὰ ἔργα τῆς σαρκός, ἅτινά ἐστιν
πορνεία, ἀκαθαρσία, ἀσέλγεια, 20εἰδωλολατρεία, φαρμακεία, ἔχθραι, ἔρις, ζῆλος, θυμοί, ἐριθεῖαι, διχοστασίαι,

20. ἔχθραι, ἔρεις.

idea is sensuality, according to the loose definition in Etym. Magn. ἑτοιμότης πρὸς πᾶσαν ἡδονήν: comp. Polyb. xxxvii. 2 πολλή δέ τις ἀσέλγεια καὶ περὶ τὰς σωματικὰς ἐπιθυμίας αὐτῷ συνεξηκολούθει. Thus it has much the same range of meaning as ὕβρις.

20. In spiritual things two sins are named; εἰδωλολατρεία the open recognition of false gods, and φαρμακεία the secret tampering with the powers of evil.

φαρμακεία] not 'poisoning' here, but '*sorcery, witchcraft*,' as its association with 'idolatry' shows: comp. Rev. xxi. 8 φαρμακοῖς καὶ εἰδωλολάτραις. On the different kinds of φαρμακεία see especially Plato *Legg.* xi. pp. 932, 933: comp. Philo *de Migr. Abr.* p. 449 M ἢ οὐχ ὁρᾷς τοὺς ἐπαοιδοὺς καὶ φαρμακευτὰς ἀντισοφιστεύοντας τῷ θείῳ λόγῳ, *Quod Det. Pot.* p. 198 M τοὺς ἐν Αἰγύπτῳ τῷ σώματι σοφιστὰς οὓς φαρμακέας ὀνομάζει, Plato *Symp.* p. 203 D δεινὸς γόης καὶ φαρμακεὺς καὶ σοφιστής. This is a common sense of φαρμακεύς, φαρμακεία, in the LXX. It is a striking coincidence, if nothing more, that φαρμακεῖαι were condemned by a very stringent canon of the council held at Ancyra the capital of Galatia (about A.D. 314); see Hefele *Concilieng.* I. p. 209. For the prevalence of γοητεία in Asia Minor see Greg. Naz. *Orat.* iv. 31 (I. p. 91); comp. 2 Tim. iii. 13.

20, 21. ἔχθραι κ.τ.λ.] A principle of order may be observed in the enumeration which follows; (1) ἔχθραι, a general expression opposed to ἀγάπη, breaches of charity in feeling or in act: from this point onward the terms are in an ascending scale: (2), (3) ἔρις 'strife,' not necessarily implying self-interest; ζῆλος 'rivalry,' in which the idea of self-assertion is prominent: (4), (5) θυμοὶ 'wraths,' a more passionate form of ἔρις; ἐριθεῖαι 'factious cabals,' a stronger development of ζῆλος: (6), (7) hostility has reached the point where the contending parties separate; such separation is either temporary (διχοστασίαι 'divisions'), or permanent (αἱρέσεις 'sects, heresies'): (8) φθόνοι, a grosser breach of charity than any hitherto mentioned, the wish to deprive another of what he has; (9) φόνοι, the extreme form which hatred can take, the deprivation of life.

The first four words ἔρις ζῆλος θυμοὶ ἐριθεῖαι occur in the same order 2 Cor. xii. 20: comp. Rom. xiii. 13.

ζῆλος] '*emulation, rivalry*,' not necessarily, like φθόνος, in a bad sense, and in fact with classical writers it is generally used otherwise. But as it is the tendency of Christian teaching to exalt the gentler qualities and to depress their opposites, ζῆλος falls in the scale of Christian ethics (see Clem. Rom. §§ 4—6), while ταπεινότης for instance rises.

θυμοί] '*outbursts of wrath*.' On θυμὸς in its relation to ὀργή, as the outward manifestation to the inward feeling, see Trench, *N. T. Syn.* § xxxvii. p. 123. The plural is frequent even in classical writers: see Lobeck on Soph. *Aj.* 716.

ἐριθεῖαι] '*caballings*.' Derived from ἔριθος, the word signifies properly 'working for hire'; hence it gets to mean 'the canvassing of hired partizans' (Suidas, ἐριθεύεσθαι ὅμοιόν ἐστι τῷ δεκάζεσθαι, καὶ γὰρ ἡ ἐριθεία εἴρηται ἀπὸ τῆς τοῦ μισθοῦ δόσεως) and hence more generally 'factiousness'; comp. Arist. *Polit.* v. [viii.] 3, μεταβάλλουσι δ' αἱ πολιτεῖαι καὶ ἄνευ στάσεως διά τε τὰς ἐριθείας ὥσπερ ἐν Ἡραίᾳ· ἐξ αἱρετῶν γὰρ διὰ τοῦτο ἐποίησαν κληρωτάς, ὅτι

αἱρέσεις, [21]φθόνοι, [φόνοι], μέθαι, κῶμοι, καὶ τὰ ὅμοια τούτοις· ἃ προλέγω ὑμῖν καθὼς [καὶ] προεῖπον, ὅτι οἱ τὰ τοιαῦτα πράσσοντες βασιλείαν Θεοῦ οὐ κληρονομήσουσιν. [22]ὁ δὲ καρπὸς τοῦ πνεύματός ἐστιν ἀγάπη,

ἠροῦντο τοὺς ἐριθευομένους. Thus it has no connexion with ἔρις, unless indeed both are to be referred ultimately to the same root ἔρω ἔρδω, as is maintained by Lobeck *Pathol.* p. 365. Comp. Fritzsche *Rom.* I. p. 143. For ἐριθεία following upon ζῆλος see James iii. 14, εἰ δὲ ζῆλον πικρὸν ἔχετε καὶ ἐριθείαν, and ib. ver. 16.

αἱρέσεις] A more aggravated form of διχοστασίαι, when the divisions have developed into distinct and organized parties: comp. 1 Cor. xi. 18 ἀκούω σχίσματα ἐν ὑμῖν ὑπάρχειν καὶ μέρος τι πιστεύω, δεῖ γὰρ καὶ αἱρέσεις ἐν ὑμῖν εἶναι, and the remarks of Tertullian *de Praescr. Haer.* § 5, thereon.

21. φθόνοι] On the distinction of ζῆλος the desire to be as well off as another, and φθόνος the desire to deprive another of what he has, see Aristotle *Rhet.* ii. 9, 10, 11, who says, διὸ καὶ ἐπιεικές ἐστιν ὁ ζῆλος καὶ ἐπιεικῶν, τὸ δὲ φθονεῖν φαῦλον καὶ φαύλων. Compare Trench *N. T. Syn.* § xxvi. p. 82, and to the references there given add Æsch. *Agam.* 939 ὁ δ' ἀφθόνητός γ' οὐκ ἐπίζηλος πέλει, and Thucyd. ii. 64.

φόνοι] is omitted by some editors with a few of the most ancient texts, as an interpolation from Rom. i. 29, where φθόνου φόνου occur together. The fact however of the same alliteration occurring in another epistle written about the same time is rather in its favour, and the omission in some texts may be due to the carelessness of a copyist transcribing words so closely resembling each other. The reading must therefore remain doubtful. Comp. Eur. *Troad.* 763 φθόνου φόνου τε. For the paronomasia see Winer § lxviii. p. 658.

μέθαι, κῶμοι] as Rom. xiii. 13; comp. Dion Cass. lxv. 3 μέθαι τε καὶ κῶμοι.

ἃ προλέγω κ.τ.λ.] For the construction comp. Joh. viii. 54 ὃν ὑμεῖς λέγετε ὅτι Θεὸς ὑμῶν ἐστίν.

προεῖπον] probably on the occasion of his second visit. See i. 9, iv. 13, 16, and the introduction p. 25.

βασιλείαν κ.τ.λ.] Comp. 1 Cor. vi. 9, 10, xv. 50.

22. ὁ δὲ καρπός] The Apostle had before mentioned the *works* of the flesh; he here speaks of the *fruit* of the Spirit. This change of terms is significant. The flesh is a rank weed which produces no fruit properly so called (comp. Eph. v. 9, 11, Rom. vi. 21); and St Paul's language here recals the contrast of the fig and vine with the thorn and the thistle in the parable, Matt. vii. 16 sq.

22, 23. The difficulty of classification in the list which follows is still greater than in the case of the works of the flesh. Nevertheless some sort of order may be observed. The catalogue falls into three groups of three each. The first of these comprises Christian habits of mind in their more general aspect, 'love, joy, peace'; the second gives special qualities affecting a man's intercourse with his neighbour, 'long-suffering, kindness, beneficence'; while the third, again general in character like the first, exhibits the principles which guide a Christian's conduct, 'honesty, gentleness, temperance.'

ἀγάπη κ.τ.λ.] The fabric is built up, story upon story. Love is the foundation, joy the superstructure, peace the crown of all.

μακροθυμία κ.τ.λ.] This triad is again arranged in an ascending scale; μακροθυμία is *passive*, 'patient endurance under injuries inflicted by others';

χαρά, εἰρήνη, μακροθυμία, χρηστότης, ἀγαθωσύνη, πίστις, [23]πραΰτης, ἐγκράτεια. κατὰ τῶν τοιούτων οὐκ ἔστιν νόμος. [24]οἱ δὲ τοῦ Χριστοῦ Ἰησοῦ τὴν σάρκα ἐσταύρωσαν σὺν τοῖς παθήμασιν καὶ ταῖς ἐπιθυμίαις.

χρηστότης, *neutral*, 'a kindly disposition towards one's neighbours' not necessarily taking a practical form; ἀγαθωσύνη, *active*, 'goodness, beneficence' as an energetic principle. For the first two words compare 1 Cor. xiii. 4 ἡ ἀγάπη μακροθυμεῖ χρηστεύεται. The second is distinguished from the third as the ἦθος from the ἐνέργεια; χρηστότης is potential ἀγαθωσύνη, ἀγαθωσύνη is energizing χρηστότης. They might be translated by 'benignitas' and 'bonitas' respectively, as Jerome renders them here, or by 'benevolentia' and 'beneficentia.' Other distinctions which have been given of these words are discussed in Trench's *N. T. Syn.* § lxiii. p. 218 sq.

πίστις] seems not to be used here in its theological sense 'belief in God.' Its position points rather to the passive meaning of faith, 'trustworthiness, fidelity, honesty,' as in Matt. xxiii. 23, Tit. ii. 10; comp. Rom. iii. 3. See above, p. 157. Possibly however it may here signify 'trustfulness, reliance,' in one's dealings with others; comp. 1 Cor. xiii. 7 ἡ ἀγάπη...πάντα πιστεύει.

23. πραΰτης] '*meekness*' is joined with πίστις (used apparently in the same sense as here) in Ecclus. xlv. 4 ἐν πίστει καὶ πραΰτητι αὐτοῦ ἡγίασεν (sc. Μωϋσῆν). On the meaning of πραΰτης see Trench *N. T. Syn.* §§ xlii, xliii. p. 140 sq; and on the varying forms πρᾶος (-ότης), πραΰς (-ΰτης), Lobeck *Phryn.* p. 403, Lipsius *Gram. Unters.* p. 7. The forms in υ are the best supported in the New Testament: see A. Buttmann pp. 23, 24.

κατὰ τῶν τοιούτων κ.τ.λ.] '*against such things.*' Law exists for the purpose of restraint, but in the works of the Spirit there is nothing to restrain; comp. 1 Tim. i. 9 εἰδὼς τοῦτο, ὅτι δικαίῳ νόμος οὐ κεῖται, ἀνόμοις δὲ καὶ ἀνυποτάκτοις κ.τ.λ. Thus then the Apostle substantiates the proposition stated in ver. 18, 'If ye are led by the Spirit, ye are not under law.'

24. οἱ δὲ τοῦ Χριστοῦ Ἰησοῦ] '*now they that are of Christ Jesus.*' Several of the Greek fathers strangely connected τοῦ Χριστοῦ with τὴν σάρκα, 'these persons have crucified the flesh of Christ,' explaining it in various ways; see e.g. Clem. Alex. *Fragm.* 1015 (Potter). Origen however, who so took it, seems not to have had δὲ in his text, and therefore made οἱ a relative agreeing with τῶν τοιούτων, which he took as masculine. See Jerome's note here.

Ἰησοῦ] which is struck out in the received text, ought probably to be retained. It is found in several of the oldest texts, and the omission in others is easily accounted for by the unusual order ὁ Χριστὸς Ἰησοῦς. This order occurs also in Ephes. iii. 1, 11, Col. ii. 6, but in both passages with some variation of reading.

ἐσταύρωσαν] '*crucified.*' The aorist is to be explained either (1) By reference to the time of their becoming members of Christ in baptism, as Rom. vi. 6 ὁ παλαιὸς ἡμῶν ἄνθρωπος συνεσταυρώθη; or (2) As denoting that the change is complete and decisive, without reference to any distinct point of time; see the note on ver. 4, κατηργήθητε.

τοῖς παθήμασιν κ.τ.λ.] '*the affections and the lusts*'; comp. Col. iii. 5, 1 Thess. iv. 5, and see Trench *N. T. Syn.* § lxxxvii. p. 305. The two words are chiefly distinguished as presenting vice on its passive and its active side respectively. Comp. Joseph. [?] *Macc.* § 3. At the same time παθήματα perhaps retains something of the meaning which

25 εἰ ζῶμεν πνεύματι, πνεύματι καὶ στοιχῶμεν. 26 μὴ γινώμεθα κενόδοξοι, ἀλλήλους προκαλούμενοι, ἀλλήλους φθονοῦντες.

26. ἀλλήλοις φθονοῦντες.

it has in Greek philosophy; and, if so, it is more comprehensive than ἐπιθυμίαι; see for instance Arist. *Eth. Nic.* ii. 4 λέγω δὲ πάθη μὲν ἐπιθυμίαν ὀργὴν φόβον θράσος κ.τ.λ.

25. 'You have crucified your old selves: you are dead to the flesh and you live to the Spirit. Therefore conform your conduct to your new life.' See Gal. ii. 19, 20, and especially Rom. vi. 2—14, where the same thoughts are expanded.

The 'life to the Spirit,' of which the Apostle here speaks, is an ideal rather than an actual life; it denotes a state which the Galatians were put in the way of attaining rather than one which they had already attained. Otherwise the injunction 'walk also by the Spirit' were superfluous. Comp. Col. iii. 1, Ephes. iv. 30. This is always St Paul's way of speaking. Members of the Christian brotherhood are in his language the 'saints,' the 'elect,' by virtue of their admission into the Church. It remains for them to make their profession a reality.

εἰ ζῶμεν πνεύματι] '*if we live to the Spirit.*' The dative here is safest interpreted by the corresponding datives in the parallel passage, Rom. vi. 2, 10, τῇ ἁμαρτίᾳ ἀποθανεῖν, ver. 11 νεκροὺς μὲν τῇ ἁμαρτίᾳ ζῶντας δὲ τῷ Θεῷ: comp. also Rom. xiv. 8, Κυρίῳ ζῶμεν, Κυρίῳ ἀποθνήσκομεν, 2 Cor. v. 15.

πνεύματι καὶ στοιχῶμεν] '*let us also walk by the Spirit.*' The dative with στοιχεῖν, περιπατεῖν, etc., marks the *line* or *direction;* as Polyb. xxviii. 5, 6 βουλόμενοι στοιχεῖν τῇ τῆς συγκλήτου προθέσει. Comp. Fritzsche *Rom.* III. p. 142, and A. Buttmann p. 160. See above v. 16 (with the note), vi. 16.

26. St Paul works round again to the subject of ver. 15, and repeats his warning. It is clear that something had occurred which alarmed him on this point. See the introduction, p. 14.

There is a gradation in the phrases used here. Vainglory provokes contention; contention produces envy.

γινώμεθα] not ὦμεν. This vainglorying was a *departure* from their spiritual standard.

κενόδοξοι] '*vainglorious.*' So κενοδοξία, Phil. ii. 3, and occasionally in Polybius and later writers. In Wisd. xiv. 14 κενοδοξία seems to mean rather 'vain opinion,' 'folly.'

προκαλούμενοι] '*provoking, challenging to combat.*' Both this word and φθονεῖν are ἅπαξ λεγόμενα in the New Testament. In the LXX φθονεῖν occurs once only, Tob. iv. 16; προκαλεῖσθαι never.

ἀλλήλους φθονοῦντες] I have ventured to place the accusative in the text rather than the dative, in deference to a few excellent authorities, though I am not aware of any other example of φθονεῖν with an accusative of the person. It seems to be one out of many instances of the tendency of later Greek to produce uniformity by substituting the more usual case of the object for the less usual; see the note on ἐγκόπτειν ver. 7. Comp. also Heb. viii. 8 μεμφόμενος αὐτούς (the correct reading). So too πολεμεῖν takes an accusative, e.g. Ignat. *Trall.* 4.

VI. 1—5. 'As brethren, I appeal to you. Act in a brotherly spirit. I have just charged you to shun vainglory, to shun provocation and envy. I ask you now to do more than this. I ask you to be gentle even to those whose guilt is flagrant. Do any of you profess to be spiritually-minded? Then correct the offender in a spirit of tenderness. Correct and reinstate him. Remember your own weakness; reflect that you too may be tempted

VI. Ἀδελφοί, ἐὰν καὶ προλημφθῇ ἄνθρωπος ἔν τινι παραπτώματι, ὑμεῖς οἱ πνευματικοὶ καταρτίζετε τὸν τοιοῦτον ἐν πνεύματι πραΰτητος, σκοπῶν σεαυτὸν μὴ

some day, and may stand in need of like forgiveness. Have sympathy one with another. Lend a ready hand in bearing your neighbours' burdens. So doing you will fulfil the most perfect of all laws—the law of Christ. But if any one asserts his superiority, if any one exalts himself above others, he is nothing worth, he is a vain self-deceiver. Nay rather let each man test *his own work*. If this stands the test, then his boast will be his own, it will not depend on comparison with others. Each of us has his own duties, his own responsibilities. Each of us must carry his own load.'

1. ἀδελφοί] '*Brothers.*' 'A whole argument lies hidden under this one word,' says Bengel. See iii. 15, iv. 12 and especially vi. 18.

The fervour and pathos of this appeal are perhaps to be explained by certain circumstances which engaged St Paul's attention at this time. A grave offence had been committed in the Church of Corinth. St Paul had called upon the Corinthian brethren to punish the offender; and his appeal had been promptly and zealously responded to. He had even to protest against undue severity, to interpose for the pardon of the guilty one. The remembrance of this incident still fresh on his mind may be supposed to have dictated the injunction in the text. The striking resemblance in his tone here to 2 Cor. ii. 6—8, where he is speaking of the Corinthian offender, bears out this conjecture. See the introduction, p. 54.

ἐὰν καί] See the note on i. 8.

προλημφθῇ] '*be surprised, detected* in the act of committing any sin,' so that his guilt is placed beyond a doubt. For this sense of προλαμβάνειν, 'to take by surprise, to overpower before one can escape,' see Wisd. xvii. 16 προλημφθεὶς τὴν δυσάλυκτον ἔμενεν ἀνάγκην: comp. κατείληπται, Joh. viii. 4. The word cannot here mean 'be betrayed into sin,' for neither will the preposition ἐν admit this meaning, nor is it well suited to the context.

ὑμεῖς οἱ πνευματικοί] St Paul had once and again urged them to walk by the Spirit (v. 16, 25). This explains the form of address here; 'Ye who have taken my lesson to heart, ye who would indeed be guided by the Spirit.' Their readiness to forgive would be a test of their spirituality of mind. It might indeed be supposed that the Apostle was here addressing himself especially to the party of more liberal views, who had taken his side against the Judaizers, and in their opposition to ritualism were in danger of paying too little regard to the weaker brethren; comp. Rom. xv. 1 ἡμεῖς οἱ δυνατοί. In this case there would be a slight shade of irony in πνευματικοί. The epistle however betrays no very distinct traces of the existence of such a party in the Galatian Churches (see v. 13), and indeed the context here is far too general to apply to them alone. For οἱ πνευματικοί, see 1 Cor. ii. 13, 15, iii. 1.

καταρτίζετε] '*correct, restore.*' The idea of punishment is quite subordinate to that of amendment in καταρτίζετε, which on this account is preferred here to κολάζετε or even νουθετεῖτε, though the latter occurs in a similar passage, 2 Thess. iii. 15 μὴ ὡς ἐχθρὸν ἡγεῖσθε ἀλλὰ νουθετεῖτε ὡς ἀδελφόν. On καταρτίζειν see the note 1 Thess. iii. 10. It is used especially as a surgical term, of setting a bone or joint; see the passages in Wetstein on Matt. iv. 21.

ἐν πνεύματι πραΰτητος] Comp. 1 Cor. iv. 21 ἐν ἀγάπῃ πνεύματί τε πραΰτητος.

καὶ σὺ πειρασθῇς. [2]ἀλλήλων τὰ βάρη βαστάζετε, καὶ οὕτως ἀναπληρώσετε τὸν νόμον τοῦ Χριστοῦ. [3]εἰ γὰρ δοκεῖ τις εἶναί τι μηδὲν ὤν, φρεναπατᾷ ἑαυτόν· [4]τὸ δὲ

2. οὕτως ἀναπληρώσατε.

Gentleness is a characteristic of true spirituality. By their conduct towards wrong-doers their claim to the title of *πνευματικοὶ* would be tested.

σκοπῶν] The transition from the plural to the singular gives the charge a direct personal application; 'each one of you individually.' Compare the *καὶ σύ*, and see the note on iv. 7.

2. 'If you must needs impose *burdens* on yourselves, let them be the burdens of mutual sympathy. If you must needs observe a *law*, let it be the law of Christ.' The Apostle seems to have used both *βάρη* and *νόμον* (the latter certainly), with a reference to the ritualistic tendencies of the Galatians; see above vv. 13, 14. For the idea of the *burden* of the Mosaic law compare especially Luke xi. 46 *φορτίζετε τοὺς ἀνθρώπους φορτία δυσβάστακτα*, Acts xv. 10 *ἐπιθεῖναι ζυγὸν ὃν οὔτε οἱ πατέρες ἡμῶν οὔτε ἡμεῖς ἰσχύσαμεν βαστάσαι*, ver. 28 *μηδὲν πλέον ἐπιτίθεσθαι ὑμῖν βάρος*. For the 'law of Christ,' always in contrast to the law of Moses, see 1 Cor. ix. 21 *ἔννομος Χριστοῦ*, Rom. iii. 27 *διὰ ποίου νόμου; τῶν ἔργων; οὐχί, ἀλλὰ διὰ νόμου πίστεως*, viii. 2 *ὁ νόμος τοῦ πνεύματος τῆς ζωῆς κ.τ.λ.*; comp. James i. 25, ii. 12.

ἀλλήλων τὰ βάρη κ.τ.λ.] Comp. Matt. viii. 17, Rom. xv. 1 *τὰ ἀσθενήματα τῶν ἀδυνάτων βαστάζειν*, Ignat. *Polyc.* 1. *πάντας βάσταζε ὡς καί σε ὁ Κύριος*, and again *πάντων τὰς νόσους βάσταζε*, *Epist. ad Diogn.* § 10 *ὅστις τὸ τοῦ πλησίον ἀναδέχεται βάρος*. Here the position of *ἀλλήλων* is emphatic: 'These are the burdens I would have you bear —not the vexatious ritual of the law, but your neighbour's errors and weaknesses, his sorrows and sufferings.'

ἀναπληρώσετε] '*ye will rigorously fulfil*,' the idea of completeness being contained in the preposition. It is difficult to decide here between the readings *ἀναπληρώσετε* and *ἀναπληρώσατε*, the external authority for either being nearly balanced. On the whole the preference may perhaps be given to *ἀναπληρώσετε* as having the versions for the most part in its favour, such testimony being in a case like the present less open to suspicion than any other. On the other hand *ἀναπληρώσατε* makes excellent sense; the past tense, so far from being an objection, is its strongest recommendation; for this tense marks the completeness of the act, and thus adds to the force of the preposition, 'fulfil the law *then and there*.' See the passages in Winer § xliii. p. 393.

τοῦ Χριστοῦ] is added in a manner *παρὰ προσδοκίαν*; 'the law not of Moses but of Christ.'

3. These words are connected with the first verse of the chapter, the second being an amplification of and inference from the first.

εἰ γὰρ δοκεῖ τις κ.τ.λ.] Comp. Plat. *Apol.* p. 41 E *ἐὰν δοκῶσί τι εἶναι μηδὲν ὄντες*, Arrian *Epict.* ii. 24 *δοκῶν μέν τις εἶναι ὢν δ' οὐδείς*: and for *οὐδὲν εἶναι*, see 1 Cor. xiii. 2, 2 Cor. xii. 11.

μηδὲν ὤν] '*being nothing*,' i.e. 'seeing that he is nothing,' not 'if he is nothing,' for the very fact of his thinking highly of himself condemns him. 'His estimate,' says Chrysostom, 'is a leading proof of his vileness.' In Christian morality self-esteem is vanity and vanity is nothingness. With the Christian it is 'not I but the grace of God which is with me': see 1 Cor. iii. 7, xv. 9, 10, 2 Cor. iii. 5.

φρεναπατᾷ] '*deceives by his fancies*,' comp. Tit. i. 10 *ματαιολόγοι καὶ φρεναπάται*. More is implied by this word

ἔργον ἑαυτοῦ δοκιμαζέτω ἕκαστος, καὶ τότε εἰς ἑαυτὸν μόνον τὸ καύχημα ἕξει, καὶ οὐκ εἰς τὸν ἕτερον· 5 ἕκαστος γὰρ τὸ ἴδιον φορτίον βαστάσει.

than by ἀπατᾶν, for it brings out the idea of *subjective fancies* and thus enforces the previous δοκεῖ. It was possibly coined by St Paul, for it seems not to be found in any earlier writer, and at a later date occurs chiefly, if not solely, in ecclesiastical authors.

4. τὸ δὲ ἔργον ἑαυτοῦ] '*his own work*'; ἔργον, emphatic by its position, stands in contrast to δοκεῖ and φρεναπατᾷ; and this contrast is enhanced by the addition of ἑαυτοῦ.

δοκιμαζέτω] '*let him test, examine*'; see the notes on 1 Thess. ii. 4, v. 21.

εἰς ἑαυτὸν κ.τ.λ.] '*in himself and not by comparison with others.*' 'Probitas in re, non in collatione,' says Castalio. For the preposition compare Ephes. iii. 16 κραταιωθῆναι εἰς τὸν ἔσω ἄνθρωπον, Rom. iv. 20, xv. 2, xvi. 6, etc.: Winer § xlix. p. 496.

τὸ καύχημα] '*his ground for boasting*'; καύχημα is the matter of καύχησις; compare Rom. iii. 27 with iv. 2, and 2 Cor. i. 12 ἡ γὰρ καύχησις ἡμῶν αὕτη ἐστὶν κ.τ.λ. with i. 14 ὅτι καύχημα ὑμῶν ἐσμέν.

τὸν ἕτερον] '*his neighbour.*' For the article compare Rom. ii. 1, xiii. 8, 1 Cor. vi. 1, x. 24, 29.

5. Having started from the precept 'bear one another's loads,' the Apostle has worked round to an apparently contradictory statement 'each man must bear his own burden.' This expression of complementary truths under antagonistic forms is characteristic of St Paul. For instances of similar paradoxes of expression see Phil. ii. 12, 13 'work out *your own* salvation, for it is *God* that worketh in you,' or 2 Cor. xii. 10 'when I am weak, then I am strong.' Compare also his language in speaking of the law, Romans vi, vii.

τὸ ἴδιον φορτίον] It is difficult to establish any precise distinction between φορτίον here and βάρη, ver. 2. This much difference however there seems to be, that the latter suggests the idea of an adventitious and oppressive burden, which is not necessarily implied in the former; so that βάρη points to a load of which a man may fairly rid himself when occasion serves, φορτίον to a load which he is expected to bear. Thus φορτίον is a common term for a man's pack, e.g. Xen. *Mem.* iii. 13. 6. Here it is perhaps an application of the common metaphor of Christian warfare in which each soldier bears his own kit (φορτίον), as each is supplied with his own provisions (ἐφόδια, Clem. Rom. 2), and each receives his proper pay (ὀψώνια 1 Cor. ix. 7, Ignat. *Pol.* 6). The soldier of Christ sets out on his march, 'Non secus ac patriis acer Romanus in armis Injusto sub fasce viam cum carpit.' If so, βαστάζειν τὸ ἴδιον φορτίον refers rather to the discharge of the obligations themselves than to the punishment undergone for their neglect.

βαστάσει] 'is appointed to bear, must bear.' Each man has certain responsibilities imposed on him individually, which he cannot throw off. For the future tense see ii. 16, Winer § xl. p. 296.

6. 'I spoke of bearing one another's burdens. There is one special application I would make of this rule. Provide for the temporal wants of your teachers in Christ.' Δὲ arrests a former topic before it passes out of sight; see the note iv. 20. Otherwise it might be taken as qualifying the clause which immediately precedes: 'Each man must bear his own burden; but this law does not exempt you from supporting your spiritual teachers.' Such a turn of the sentence however, inas-

[6]Κοινωνείτω δὲ ὁ κατηχούμενος τὸν λόγον τῷ κατηχοῦντι ἐν πᾶσιν ἀγαθοῖς. [7]μὴ πλανᾶσθε, Θεὸς οὐ μυκτηρίζεται· ὃ γὰρ ἐὰν σπείρῃ ἄνθρωπος, τοῦτο καὶ θερίσει·

much as it is not obvious, might be expected to be marked in some more decided way than by the very faint opposition implied by δέ.

6. κοινωνείτω] '*let him impart to*'; literally 'let him go shares with.' The word is properly intransitive and equivalent to κοινωνὸς εἶναι 'to be a partner with.' It may be construed with all three cases: (1) The genitive of the thing which is participated in: once only in the New Testament, Heb. ii. 14 κεκοινώνηκεν αἵματος καὶ σαρκός; comp. Prov. i. 11, 2 Macc. xiv. 25. In this case the verb may denote either the person who gives or the person who receives. (2) The accusative of the thing imparted, as Æsch. *c. Ctes.* p. 63 οἱ ἀποδόμενοι καὶ κατακοινωνήσαντες τὰ τῆς πόλεως ἰσχυρά, a rare construction not found perhaps with the simple verb, and due in the passage quoted to the preposition. (3) The dative, which is explained by the idea of *partnership* implied in κοινωνός, and expresses the person or thing *with* which the other makes common cause. He who κοινωνεῖ in this case may be either the receiver, as Rom. xv. 27 τοῖς πνευματικοῖς αὐτῶν ἐκοινώνησαν τὰ ἔθνη, or the giver, as Rom. xii. 13 ταῖς χρείαις τῶν ἁγίων κοινωνοῦντες. Here the latter is intended.

κατηχούμενος] '*instructed.*' The word in this sense is not peculiar to biblical Greek. κατήχησις 'oral instruction' occurs as early as Hippocrates p. 28. 25 κατηχήσιος ἰδιωτέων, and probably κατηχεῖν 'to instruct' was in common use in the other dialects, though it would seem to have been banished from the Attic of the classical period. See the remarks on ἀπόστολος, p. 92 note 3.

ἐν πᾶσιν ἀγαθοῖς] '*in all good things.*' The obligation of the hearers of the word to support the ministers of the word is again and again insisted upon by St Paul, though he seldom asserted his own claims; see 1 Thess. ii. 6, 9, 2 Cor. xi. 7 sq, Phil. iv. 10 sq, 1 Tim. v. 17, 18, and especially 1 Cor. ix. 11. The resemblance of language in this last passage leaves no doubt that St Paul is here speaking of imparting temporal goods. The metaphor of sowing and reaping both there and in the very close parallel, 2 Cor. ix. 6, has reference to liberality in almsgiving. The more general sense which has been assigned to this passage, 'let the taught sympathize with the teacher in all good things,' is not recommended either by the context or by St Paul's language elsewhere. For ἀγαθοῖς, 'temporal blessings,' see Luke i. 53, xii. 18, 19, xvi. 25. Compare Barnabas § 19 κοινωνήσεις ἐν πᾶσι τῷ πλησίον σου.

7, 8. 'What? you hold back? Nay, do not deceive yourselves. Your niggardliness will find you out. You cannot cheat God by your fair professions. You cannot mock *Him*. According as you sow, thus will you reap. If you plant the seed of your own selfish desires, if you sow the field of the flesh, then when you gather in your harvest, you will find the ears blighted and rotten. But if you sow the good ground of the Spirit, you will of that good ground gather the golden grain of life eternal.'

7. οὐ μυκτηρίζεται] '*is not mocked.*' Μυκτηρίζειν, which is properly 'to turn up the nose at,' 'to treat with contempt,' involves as a secondary meaning the idea of contradicting one's language by one's gesture or look, and so implies an outward avowal of

8ὅτι ὁ σπείρων εἰς τὴν σάρκα ἑαυτοῦ ἐκ τῆς σαρκὸς
θερίσει φθοράν, ὁ δὲ σπείρων εἰς τὸ πνεῦμα ἐκ τοῦ
πνεύματος θερίσει ζωὴν αἰώνιον. 9τὸ δὲ καλὸν ποι-

respect neutralised by an indirect expression of contempt. In other words it conveys the idea of *irony*, whether this irony be dissembled or not. Thus μυκτὴρ is frequently connected with εἰρωνεία, as in Lucian *Prom.* c. 1; compare Pollux ii. 78 καὶ τὸν εἴρωνά τινες μυκτῆρα καλοῦσι. In writers on rhetoric μυκτηρισμὸς is ordinarily treated as a species of εἰρωνεία; see for instance four different treatises on 'tropes' in the *Rhet. Graec.* III. pp. 205, 213, 235, 254 (ed. Spengel). Similarly Quintilian, viii. 6, 59, well defines it, 'dissimulatus quidam sed non latens risus.' Such is the force of μυκτηρίζεται in this passage: 'you cannot with impunity turn your professions to contempt, you cannot with God indulge in a *postica sanna*.'

ὃ γὰρ ἐὰν κ.τ.λ.] A common proverb not only in the Bible (Job iv. 8), but elsewhere; e.g. Cic. *de Orat.* ii. 65 'ut sementem feceris, ita metes,' and Gorgias in Arist. *Rhet.* iii. 3 σὺ δὲ ταῦτα αἰσχρῶς μὲν ἔσπειρας κακῶς δὲ ἐθέρισας (see Plato *Phaedr.* 260 C, Thompson's note). It occurs in 2 Cor. ix. 6, of the contributions for the brethren of Judaea. To this object the Galatians also had been asked to contribute (1 Cor. xvi. 1). We may therefore conjecture that niggardliness was a besetting sin with them (see p. 14); that they had not heartily responded to the call; and that St Paul takes this opportunity of rebuking their backwardness, in passing from the obligation of supporting their ministers to a general censure of illiberality. See p. 55.

8. The former verse speaks of the *kind of seed* sown (ὃ ἐὰν σπείρῃ). In the present the metaphor is otherwise applied, and the harvest is made to depend on the *nature of the ground* in which it is cast (εἰς), as in the parable of the sower. In moral husbandry sowers choose different soils, as they choose different seeds. The harvest depends on both the one and the other. For St Paul's diversified application of metaphors, see the notes on ii. 20, iv. 19.

ἑαυτοῦ] which disturbs the equilibrium of the clauses, is added to bring out the idea of *selfishness*.

φθοράν] '*rottenness, corruption*.' The field of the flesh yields not full and solid ears of corn, which may be gathered up and garnered for future use, but only blighted and putrescent grains. Comp. 1 Cor. xv. 42 σπείρεται ἐν φθορᾷ, Col. ii. 22 ἅ ἐστιν πάντα εἰς φθορὰν τῇ ἀποχρήσει. The metaphor suggests that φθορὰν should be taken in its primary physical sense. At the same time in its recognised secondary meaning as a moral term, it is directly opposed to life eternal, and so forms the link of connexion between the emblem and the thing signified. In ζωὴ αἰώνιος the metaphor is finally abandoned.

9. Having passed from a particular form of beneficence (ver. 6) to beneficence in general (vv. 7, 8), the Apostle still further enlarges the compass of his advice; 'Nay, in doing what is honourable and good let us never tire.' Compare 2 Thess. iii. 13 μὴ ἐγκακήσητε καλοποιοῦντες. The word καλοποιεῖν includes ἀγαθοποιεῖν and more, for while τὰ ἀγαθὰ are beneficent actions, kind services, etc., things good in their results, τὰ καλὰ are right actions, such as are beautiful in themselves, things absolutely good. In this passage, as in 2 Thess. *l. c.*, the antithesis of καλὸν and κακὸν seems to be intended, though it can scarcely be translated into English; 'in *well* doing let us not show an *ill* heart.'

οὖντες μὴ ἐγκακῶμεν· καιρῷ γὰρ ἰδίῳ θερίσομεν μὴ ἐκλυόμενοι. 10 ἄρα οὖν ὡς καιρὸν ἔχομεν, ἐργαζώμεθα

ἐγκακῶμεν] '*turn cowards, lose heart*'; ἐγκακεῖν or ἐνκακεῖν is the correct word in the New Testament, not ἐκκακεῖν. It is read persistently in a few of the best MSS, though in all six passages where it occurs ἐκκακεῖν is found as a various reading; see the note on 2 Thess. iii. 13.

καιρῷ ἰδίῳ] '*at its proper season*,' i.e. the regular time for harvest; comp. 1 Tim. ii. 6, vi. 15, Tit. i. 3.

μὴ ἐκλυόμενοι] '*if we faint not*,' as husbandmen overcome with heat and fatigue. Comp. James v. 7. For ἐκλύεσθαι compare 1 Macc. iii. 17, Matt. xv. 32, Mark viii. 3. On the synonymes here used Bengel remarks: 'ἐκκακεῖν [rather ἐγκακεῖν] est in *velle*, ἐκλύεσθαι est in *posse*.' To this it may be added that ἐκλύεσθαι is a consequence of ἐγκακεῖν; the prostration of the powers following on the submission of the will.

10. ὡς καιρὸν ἔχομεν] '*as we find a seasonable time*, as opportunity presents.' The καιρὸς here answers to the καιρὸς of the former verse. There is a time for sowing as there is a time for harvest. Ὡς is perhaps best translated as above. There is however no objection to rendering it '*while* we have time'; comp. Joh. xii. 35 ὡς τὸ φῶς ἔχετε (as it is read in the best MSS), Ignat. *Smyrn.* 9 ὡς ἔτι καιρὸν ἔχομεν, [Clem. Rom.] ii. 8 ὡς οὖν ἐσμὲν ἐπὶ γῆς, *ib.* § 9 ὡς ἔχομεν καιρόν. The distinction is introduced by translation; the original ὡς covers both meanings.

τοὺς οἰκείους κ.τ.λ.] '*the members of the household of the faith*': compare Ephes. ii. 19 συνπολῖται τῶν ἁγίων καὶ οἰκεῖοι τοῦ Θεοῦ. Similarly the Church is elsewhere spoken of as the *house* of God, 1 Tim. iii. 15, 1 Pet. iv. 17; comp. 1 Pet. ii. 5, Heb. iii. 6. We need not therefore hesitate to assign this meaning to οἰκεῖοι here. Comp. *Clem. Rec.* p. 45, l. 31 (Syr.). In this case τῆς πίστεως will probably be nearly equivalent to τοῦ εὐαγγελίου; see above, p. 157. On the other hand, οἰκεῖός τινος is not an uncommon phrase in profane writers for 'acquainted with,' e.g. φιλοσοφίας, γεωγραφίας, ὀλιγαρχίας, τυραννίδος, τρυφῆς; see the passages in Wetstein: but this sense would be insipid here.

11. At this point the Apostle takes the pen from his amanuensis, and the concluding paragraph is written with his own hand. From the time when letters began to be forged in his name (2 Thess. ii. 2, iii. 17), it seems to have been his practice to close with a few words in his own handwriting as a precaution against such forgeries. Frequently he confined himself to adding the final benediction (2 Thess. iii. 17, 18), with perhaps a single sentence of exhortation, as 'If any one love not the Lord Jesus Christ, etc.' (1 Cor. xvi. 21—24), or 'Remember my bonds' (Col. iv. 18). In the present case he writes a whole paragraph, summing up the main lessons of the epistle in terse eager disjointed sentences. He writes it too in large bold characters, that his handwriting may reflect the energy and determination of his soul (see above, p. 65). To this feature he calls attention in the words which follow.

Ἴδετε κ.τ.λ.] '*Look you in what large letters I write with mine own hand.*' In the English version the words are translated 'How *large a letter* I have written with mine own hand.' It is true indeed that γράμματα sometimes signifies 'a letter' (Acts xxviii. 21, 1 Macc. v. 10, comp. Ignat. *Polyc.* 7, *Clem. Hom.* xii. 10), and therefore πηλίκα γράμματα might mean 'how long a letter'; but on the other hand, it seems equally clear that

τὸ ἀγαθὸν πρὸς πάντας, μάλιστα δὲ πρὸς τοὺς οἰκείους τῆς πίστεως.

11 Ἴδετε πηλίκοις ὑμῖν γράμμασιν ἔγραψα τῇ ἐμῇ

γράμμασιν γράφειν 'to write *with letters*' cannot be used for γράμματα γράφειν 'to write *a letter*.' On this account the other interpretation must be preferred. But what is the Apostle's object in calling attention to the handwriting? Does he, as Chrysostom and others have supposed, point to the rude ill-formed characters in which the letter was written, as though he gloried in his imperfect knowledge of Greek? But where is there any mention of rudeness of form? and is it at all probable that St Paul who had received a careful education at Jerusalem and at Tarsus, the great centres of Jewish and of Greek learning, should have betrayed this childlike ignorance and even gloried in it? Or again does he, as others imagine, refer to the physical difficulties under which he was labouring, the irregularity of the handwriting being explained by his defective eyesight or by his bodily suffering? But here again πηλίκοις denotes size only, not irregularity; and altogether this explanation is forced into the passage from without, nor does the sentence in this case contain the key to its own meaning. Theodore of Mopsuestia has caught the point of the expression, explaining it ἄγαν μείζοσιν ἐχρήσατο γράμμασιν ἐμφαίνων ὅτι οὔτε αὐτὸς ἐρυθριᾷ οὔτε ἀρνεῖται τὰ λεγόμενα. The boldness of the handwriting answers to the force of the Apostle's convictions. The size of the characters will arrest the attention of his readers in spite of themselves.

ὑμῖν] Its right place is after πηλίκοις, though a few MSS have transposed the words. Standing therefore in this position, it cannot well be taken with ἔγραψα, 'I write' or 'I wrote *to you*'; but is connected rather with πηλίκοις, which it emphasizes, 'how large, *mark you*'; see e.g. Plat. *Theaet.* p. 143 E ἀκοῦσαι πάνυ ἄξιον οἵῳ ὑμῖν τῶν πολιτῶν μειρακίῳ ἐντετύχηκα.

ἔγραψα] '*I write*,' the epistolary aorist, conveniently translated by a present. According to the view here adopted, it marks the point at which St Paul takes the pen into his own hand. For other instances of this epistolary ἔγραψα see Philem. 19, 21, 1 Pet. v. 12, 1 Joh. ii. 14, 21, 26, v. 13; comp. ἐπέστειλα, Heb. xiii. 22. The objection, that the aorist cannot be so used except at the close of a letter and in reference to what goes before, seems to be groundless; for (1) it fails to recognise the significance of the epistolary aorist, the explanation of the past tense being that events are referred to *the time at which the letter is received:* (2) There are clear instances of the past tense used as here, e.g. in *Mart. Polyc.* § 1 ἐγράψαμεν ὑμῖν, ἀδελφοί, τὰ κατὰ τοὺς μαρτυρήσαντας, these words occurring immediately after the opening salutation; comp. ἔπεμψα, Acts xxiii. 30, 2 Cor. ix. 3, Ephes. vi. 22, Col. iv. 8. The usage of the epistolary past (the imperfect and pluperfect) is still more marked in Latin, and is clearly explained by Madvig *Gr.* § 345. Thus ἔγραψα in no way prejudices the question whether the whole letter or the last paragraph only was written by St Paul.

12, 13. 'Certain men have an *object* in displaying their zeal for carnal ordinances. These are they, who would force circumcision upon you. They have no sincere belief in its value. Their motive is far different. They hope thereby to save themselves from persecution for professing the cross of Christ. For only look at their incon-

χειρί. [12]ὅσοι θέλουσιν εὐπροσωπῆσαι ἐν σαρκί, οὗτοι ἀναγκάζουσιν ὑμᾶς περιτέμνεσθαι, μόνον ἵνα τῷ σταυρῷ τοῦ Χριστοῦ μὴ διώκωνται. [13]οὐδὲ γὰρ οἱ περιτεμνόμενοι αὐτοὶ νόμον φυλάσσουσιν, ἀλλὰ θέλουσιν ὑμᾶς

sistency. They advocate circumcision, and yet they themselves neglect the ordinances of the law. They would make capital out of your compliance; they would fain boast of having won you over to these carnal rites.'

It was not against bigotry alone that St Paul had to contend; his opponents were selfish and worldly also; they could not face the obloquy to which their abandonment of the Mosaic ordinances would expose them; they were not bold enough to defy the prejudices of their unconverted fellow-countrymen. And so they attempted to keep on good terms with them by imposing circumcision on the Gentile converts also, and thus getting the credit of zeal for the law. Even the profession of Jesus as Messiah by the Christians was a less formidable obstacle to their intercourse with the Jews than their abandonment of the law.

12. εὐπροσωπῆσαι κ.τ.λ.] '*to show fair in the flesh*,' i.e. 'to make a pretentious display of their religion in outward ordinances.' The emphasis seems to lie as much on εὐπροσωπῆσαι as on ἐν σαρκί, so that the idea of *insincerity* is prominent in the rebuke. Thus the expression is a parallel to our Lord's comparison of the whited sepulchres, οἵτινες ἔξωθεν φαίνονται ὡραῖοι (Matt. xxiii. 27). The adjective εὐπρόσωπος is not uncommon in classical Greek, and generally has this sense, 'specious, plausible,' e.g. Demosth. p. 277 λόγους εὐπροσώπους καὶ μύθους συνθεὶς καὶ διεξελθών. The verb εὐπροσωπίζειν (?) occurs in Symmachus, Ps. cxli. 6.

ἐν σαρκί] '*in the flesh*,' i.e. in external rites. It has been taken by some as equivalent to σαρκικοὶ ὄντες, but, besides that this interpretation is harsh in itself, ἐν σαρκὶ here cannot well be separated from ἐν τῇ ὑμετέρᾳ σαρκὶ of the following verse.

μόνον ἵνα] seemingly elliptical; 'only (their object in doing so is) that they may not etc.' See the note on ii. 10.

τῷ σταυρῷ τοῦ Χριστοῦ] not as it is sometimes taken, 'with the sufferings of Christ,' but 'for professing the cross of Christ.' A comparison with ver. 14 and v. 11 seems to place this beyond a doubt. The cross of Christ and the flesh are opposed, as faith and works. They are two antagonistic principles, either of which is a denial of the other. For the dative of the *occasion* compare Rom. xi. 20, 30, 2 Cor. ii. 13.

διώκωνται] The reading διώκονται, however well supported, can only be regarded as a careless way of writing διώκωνται. In the same way in ver. 10 many texts read ἐργαζόμεθα for ἐργαζώμεθα; compare Rom. v. 1, ἔχομεν and ἔχωμεν.

13. οὐδὲ γὰρ κ.τ.λ.] '*for even the advocates of circumcision themselves do not keep the law.*' The allusion here is not to the *impossibility* of observing the law, the distance from Jerusalem for instance preventing the due sacrifices, for this would argue no moral blame; but to the *insincerity* of the men themselves, who were not enough in earnest to observe it rigorously.

οἱ περιτεμνόμενοι] '*the circumcision party*, the advocates of circumcision.' See the apt quotation from the apocryphal book *Act. Petr. et Paul.* § 63 (p. 28, ed. Tisch.), where Simon says of the two Apostles, οὗτοι οἱ περιτεμνόμενοι πανοῦργοί εἰσιν, to which St Paul replies, πρὸ τοῦ ἡμᾶς ἐπιγνῶναι

περιτέμνεσθαι, ἵνα ἐν τῇ ὑμετέρᾳ σαρκὶ καυχήσωνται.
14ἐμοὶ δὲ μὴ γένοιτο καυχᾶσθαι, εἰ μὴ ἐν τῷ σταυρῷ
τοῦ κυρίου ἡμῶν Ἰησοῦ Χριστοῦ, δι' οὗ ἐμοὶ κόσμος ἐ-
σταύρωται κἀγὼ κόσμῳ. 15οὔτε γὰρ περιτομή τι ἐστὶν

τὴν ἀλήθειαν σαρκὸς ἔσχομεν περιτομήν· ὅτε δὲ ἐφάνη ἡ ἀλήθεια, ἐν τῇ καρδίας περιτομῇ καὶ περιτεμνόμεθα καὶ περιτέμνομεν: and compare the somewhat similar classical usage in the expression οἰρέοντες Plat. *Theaet.* p. 181 A. See the note i. 23. If this interpretation be correct, the present tense leaves the question open whether the agitators were converted Jews or converted proselytes. The former is more probable; for proselytes would not be so dependent on the good opinion of the unconverted Jews. The balance of authority is perhaps in favour of reading περιτεμνόμενοι rather than περιτετμημένοι, as the versions which have a present tense may safely be urged in favour of the former, while those which have a past cannot with the same confidence be alleged to support the latter; but independently of external authority, a preference must be given to περιτεμνόμενοι, as probably the original reading, of which περιτετμημένοι is so obvious a correction.

νόμον] 'They are no rigorous observers of *law*,' regarded as a principle. On the absence of the article, see the references in the note on v. 18.

ὑμᾶς, ὑμετέρᾳ] opposed to αὐτοί; 'Indifferent *themselves*, they make capital out of *you*.'

ἐν τῇ ὑμετέρᾳ κ.τ.λ.] i.e. that they may vaunt your submission to this carnal rite and so gain credit with the Jews for proselytizing. Comp. Phil. iii. 3 καυχώμενοι ἐν Χριστῷ Ἰησοῦ καὶ οὐκ ἐν σαρκὶ πεποιθότες.

14. 'For myself—God forbid I should glory in anything save in the cross of Christ. On that cross I have been crucified to the world and the world has been crucified to me. Henceforth we are dead each to the other. In Christ Jesus old things have passed away. Circumcision is not and uncircumcision is not. All external distinctions have vanished. The new spiritual creation is all in all.'

μὴ γένοιτο] with the infinitive. This is the common construction in the LXX, Gen. xliv. 7, 17, Josh. xxii. 29, xxiv. 16, 1 Kings xxi. 3, 1 Macc. ix. 10, xiii. 5.

ἐν τῷ σταυρῷ] Again not 'in my sufferings for Christ' (2 Cor. xii. 9, 10), but 'in His sufferings for me' (Phil. iii. 3). The offence of the cross shall be my proudest boast.

δι' οὗ] probably refers to σταυρῷ; 'The cross of Christ is the instrument of my crucifixion as of His; for I am crucified with Him' (ii. 20). If the relative had referred to Χριστοῦ, we should have expected rather ἐν ᾧ or σὺν ᾧ. For the same image as here compare Col. ii. 14 αὐτὸ ἦρκεν ἐκ τοῦ μέσου προσηλώσας αὐτὸ τῷ σταυρῷ (i.e. it was nailed with Christ to the cross, and rent as His body was rent); and for the general purport of the passage, Col. ii. 20, 'If ye died with Christ from the rudiments of the world, why as if living in the world are ye subject to ordinances?' This κόσμος, the material universe, is the sphere of external ordinances.

Some texts insert the article before κόσμος and κόσμῳ—before either or both. It should be expunged in both places with the best MSS. The sentence thus gains in terseness.

15. This verse has been variously lengthened out and interpolated from the parallel passage, v. 6. Some of these interpolations have very considerable MS authority. The reading

οὔτε ἀκροβυστία, ἀλλὰ καινὴ κτίσις. 16 καὶ ὅσοι τῷ κανόνι τούτῳ στοιχήσουσιν, εἰρήνη ἐπ' αὐτοὺς καὶ ἔλεος,

adopted is the shortest form, and doubtless represents the genuine text.

οὔτε γὰρ κ.τ.λ.] In this annihilation of the world all external distinctions have ceased to be. This sentence occurs again, v. 6 and 1 Cor. vii. 19, in substantially the same words.

Nevertheless this passage is said by several ancient authors (Photius *Amphil.* Qu. 183, G. Syncellus *Chronogr.* p. 27; see also Cotel. on *Apost. Const.* vi. 16, *Cod. Bodl. Æthiop.* p. 24) to be a quotation from the 'Revelation of Moses.' A sentiment however, which is the very foundation of St Paul's teaching, was most unlikely to have been expressed in any earlier Jewish writing; and, if it really occurred in the apocryphal work in question, this work must have been either written or interpolated after St Paul's time; see Lücke *Offenb. d. Johann.* I. p. 232. Cedrenus (*Hist. Comp.* p. 4) states that the Revelation of Moses was identified by some persons (φασί τινες) with the 'Little Genesis.' This latter title is another name for the Book of Jubilees, which of late years has been discovered in an Æthiopic translation. In the Book of Jubilees however the words in question do not occur; see Ewald's *Jarhb.* III. p. 74.

καινὴ κτίσις] '*a new creature.*' Compare the parallel passage, 2 Cor. v. 17 εἴ τις ἐν Χριστῷ καινὴ κτίσις. This phrase καινὴ κτίσις, בריה חדשה, is a common expression in Jewish writers for one brought to the knowledge of the true God. See the passages in Schöttgen I. p. 704. The idea of spiritual enlightenment as a creating anew appears also in παλιγγενεσία 'regeneration'; see also Ephes. iv. 24 καινὸν ἄνθρωπον κτισθέντα; comp. Ephes. ii. 10, 15, Col. iii. 10; and 2 Cor. iv. 16, ἀνακαινοῦσθαι.

16. 'On all those who shall guide their steps by this rule may peace and mercy abide; for they are the true Israel of God.'

ὅσοι] '*as many as;* no matter whether they are of the circumcision or of the uncircumcision.'

στοιχήσουσιν] '*shall walk.*' This reading is to be preferred to στοιχοῦσιν, both as having somewhat higher support and as being slightly more difficult. It is at the same time more expressive as implying the *continuance* of this order. Compare ii. 16, Rom. iii. 30, and see Winer § xl. p. 350.

τῷ κανόνι τούτῳ] '*by this line,*' corresponding to the meaning of στοιχεῖν. Κανὼν is the carpenter's or surveyor's line by which a direction is taken. In 2 Cor. x. 13, 16, it is used metaphorically, where the image is taken from surveying and mapping out a district, so as to assign to different persons their respective parcels of ground. For the several senses through which this word has passed, and for its ecclesiastical meaning especially, see Westcott *On the Canon*, App. A, p. 541 sq. On the dative see the notes, v. 16, 25; comp. Phil. iii. 16 τῷ αὐτῷ στοιχεῖν, where κανόνι is interpolated in some texts from this passage.

καὶ ἐπὶ τὸν Ἰσραὴλ κ.τ.λ.] '*yea upon the Israel of God.*' Israel is the sacred name for the Jews, as the nation of the Theocracy, the people under God's covenant: see Trench's *N. T. Syn.* § xxxix. p. 129 sq, and compare Ephes. ii. 12 ἀπηλλοτριωμένοι τῆς πολιτείας τοῦ Ἰσραήλ, Rom. ix. 4 οἵτινές εἰσιν Ἰσραηλῖται, ὧν ἡ υἱοθεσία κ.τ.λ. (comp. 2 Cor. xi. 22, Phil. iii. 5), John i. 48 ἴδε ἀληθῶς Ἰσραηλίτης, compared with ver. 50 σὺ βασιλεὺς εἶ τοῦ Ἰσραήλ. St Paul is perhaps referring here to the benediction εἰρήνη ἐπὶ τὸν Ἰσραήλ, which closes Psalms cxxv, cxxviii, and must have been a familiar sound in the ears of all devout Israelites.

The 'Israel of God' is in implied

καὶ ἐπὶ τὸν Ἰσραὴλ τοῦ Θεοῦ. [17] τοῦ λοιποῦ κόπους μοι μηδεὶς παρεχέτω· ἐγὼ γὰρ τὰ στίγματα τοῦ Ἰησοῦ ἐν τῷ σώματί μου βαστάζω.

contrast to the 'Israel after the flesh' (1 Cor. x. 18); comp. Rom. ix. 6 οὐ γὰρ πάντες οἱ ἐξ Ἰσραὴλ οὗτοι Ἰσραήλ, Gal. iii. 29, Phil. iii. 3. It stands here not for the faithful converts from the circumcision alone, but for the spiritual Israel generally, the whole body of believers whether Jew or Gentile; and thus καὶ is *epexegetic*, i.e. it introduces the same thing under a new aspect, as in Heb. xi. 17, etc.; see Winer § liii. p. 545 sq.

17. St Paul closes the epistle, as he had begun it, with an uncompromising assertion of his office: 'Henceforth let no man question my authority: let no man thwart or annoy me. Jesus is my Master, my Protector. His brand is stamped on my body. I bear this badge of an honourable servitude.'

τοῦ λοιποῦ] '*henceforth*' differs from τὸ λοιπόν, as 'in the time to come' from 'throughout the time to come.' Compare νυκτὸς and νύκτα. In the New Testament it occurs only here and Ephes. vi. 10, where however the received reading is τὸ λοιπόν.

τὰ στίγματα] '*the brands*,' i.e. the marks of *ownership* branded on his body. These στίγματα were used; (1) In the case of *domestic slaves*. With these however branding was not usual, at least among the Greeks and Romans, except to mark such as had attempted to escape or had otherwise misconducted themselves, hence called στιγματίαι, 'literati' (see the ample collection of passages in Wetstein), and such brands were held a badge of disgrace; Pseudo-Phocyl. 212 στίγματα μὴ γράψῃς ἐπονειδίζων θεράποντα, Senec. *de Benef.* iv. 37, 38. (2) *Slaves attached to some temple* (ἱερόδουλοι) or persons devoted to the service of some deity were so branded: Herod. ii. 113 ὅτεῳ ἀνθρώπων ἐπιβάληται στίγματα ἱρά, ἑωυτὸν διδοὺς τῷ θεῷ, οὐκ ἔξεστι τούτου ἅψασθαι, Lucian *de Dea Syr.* § 59 στίζονται δὲ πάντες οἱ μὲν ἐς καρποὺς οἱ δὲ ἐς αὐχένας; Philo *de Mon.* II. p. 221 M.: comp. 3 Macc. ii. 29. The passage of Lucian is a good illustration of Rev. xiii. 16, 17. (3) *Captives* were so treated in very rare cases. (4) *Soldiers* sometimes branded the name of their commander on some part of their body; see Deyling *Obs. Sacra* III. p. 427. The metaphor here is most appropriate, if referred to the second of these classes. Such a practice at all events cannot have been unknown in a country which was the home of the worship of Cybele. A ἱερὸς δοῦλος is mentioned in a Galatian inscription, Texier *Asie Mineure* I. p. 135.

The brands of which the Apostle speaks were doubtless the permanent marks which he bore of persecution undergone in the service of Christ: comp. 2 Cor. iv. 10 τὴν νέκρωσιν τοῦ Ἰησοῦ ἐν τῷ σώματι περιφέροντες, xi. 23. See the introduction, p. 51 sq.

Whether the stigmata of St Francis of Assisi can be connected by any historical link with a mistaken interpretation of the passage, I do not know. Bonaventura in his life of this saint (§ 13. 4) apostrophizes him in the language of St Paul, 'Jam enim propter stigmata Domini Jesu quae in corpore tuo portas, nemo debet tibi esse molestus'; and the very use of the word 'stigmata' (which is retained untranslated in the Latin Versions) points to such a connexion. On the other hand, I am not aware that this interpretation of the passage was current in the age of St Francis. A little later Aquinas paraphrases the words, 'portabat insignia passionis Christi,' but explains this expression away in the next sentence.

18 Ἡ χάρις τοῦ Κυρίου ἡμῶν Ἰησοῦ Χριστοῦ μετὰ τοῦ πνεύματος ὑμῶν, ἀδελφοί. ἀμήν.

Ἰησοῦ] So it is read in the majority of the older MSS. All other variations, including the received reading τοῦ κυρίου Ἰησοῦ, are inferior, for the personal name of the owner alone is wanted.

βαστάζω] St Chrysostom has probably caught the right idea, οὐκ εἶπεν ἔχω ἀλλὰ βαστάζω, ὥσπερ τις ἐπὶ τροπαίοις μέγα φρονῶν. Compare the use of περιφέροντες in 2 Cor. iv. 10 already quoted. For βαστάζω see Acts ix. 15.

18. μετὰ τοῦ πνεύματος ὑμῶν] '*with your spirit*'; perhaps in reference to the carnal religion of the Galatians, as Chrysostom suggests. This allusion however must not be pressed, for the same form of benediction occurs in Philem. 25, 2 Tim. iv. 22.

ἀδελφοί] '*brothers*,' in an unusual and emphatic position; comp. Philem. 7. St Paul's parting word is an expression of tenderness; 'Ita mollitur,' says Bengel, 'totius epistolae severitas.' See the note on vi. 1.

THE patristic commentaries on the Galatians, extant either whole or in part, are perhaps more numerous than on any other of St Paul's Epistles. The earlier of these have for the most part an independent value; the later are mere collections or digests of the labours of preceding writers and have no claim to originality. In the list which follows an asterisk is prefixed to the name of the author in cases where fragments only remain.

In drawing up this account I have had occasion to refer frequently to Cave's *Script. Eccles. Hist. Liter.* (Oxon. 1740), to Fabricius's *Bibliotheca Græca* (ed. Harles), and to Schröckh's *Christliche Kirchengeschichte.* Special works relating to the subject, to which reference is also made, are Simon's *Histoire Critique des Principaux Commentateurs du N. T.* (1693), Rosenmüller's *Historia Interpretationis Librorum Sacrorum* (1795—1814), and a treatise by J. F. S. Augustin in Nösselt's *Opusc.* III. p. 321 sq. Books of reference.

1. EARLIER COMMENTARIES. 1. EARLIER COMMENTARIES.

(a) *Greek and Syrian Fathers.* (a) *Greek and Syrian.*

(i) *ORIGENES († 253). The recently discovered list of Origen's works drawn up by Jerome mentions fifteen books on the Epistle to the Galatians, besides seven homilies on the same (Redepenning in Niedner's *Zeitschr.* 1851, pp. 77, 78); while the same Jerome in the preface to his Commentary (VII. p. 370, ed. Vall.) says of this father, 'Scripsit ille vir in epistolam Pauli ad Galatas quinque proprie volumina et decimum Stromatum suorum librum commatico super explanatione ejus sermone complevit: tractatus quoque varios et excerpta quae vel sola possint sufficere composuit.' The two accounts are not irreconcileable. Of this vast apparatus not a single fragment remains in the original, and only two or three have been preserved in a Latin dress either in the translation of Pamphilus's *Apology* (Origen, *Op.* IV. p. 690, Delarue), or in Jerome's *Commentary* (Gal. v. 13). On the other hand there can be no doubt that all subsequent writers are directly or indirectly indebted to him to a very large extent. Jerome especially avows his obligations to this father of Biblical criticism. In my notes I have had occasion to mention Origen's name chiefly in connexion with fanciful speculations or positive errors, because his opinion has rarely been recorded by later writers, except where his authority was needed to sanction some false or questionable interpretation: but the impression thus produced is most unjust to his reputation. In spite of his very patent faults, which it costs nothing to denounce, a very considerable part of what is valuable in subsequent commentaries, whether ancient or modern, is due to him. A deep thinker, an accurate grammarian, a most laborious worker, and a most earnest Christian, he not only laid the foundation, but to a very great extent built up the fabric of Biblical interpretation. Origen.

(ii) EPHRAEM SYRUS († 378), the deacon of Edessa. An Armenian version of a commentary on the Scriptures, including St Paul's Epistles, Ephraem Syrus.

purporting to be by this author, was published at Venice in 1836[1]. If this work be genuine, it ought to be of some value for the text at all events, if not for the interpretation. On this writer see Cave I. p. 235, Fabricius VIII. p. 217, Schröckh XV. p. 527; and the article by E. Rödiger in Herzog's *Real-Encyclopaedie*, with the references there given. Lagarde (*Apost. Const.* p. vi) very decidedly maintains the genuineness of these Armenian works; and Rödiger seems also to take this view. In the few passages which I have had the opportunity of testing, both the readings and the interpretation are favourable to their genuineness[2].

School of Antioch. The five writers whose names follow all belong to the great Antiochene school of interpreters. For its grammatical precision, and for its critical spirit generally, this school was largely indebted to the example of Origen, whose principles were transmitted to it through Lucian of Antioch and Pamphilus of Cæsarea, both ardent Biblical critics and both martyrs in the Diocletian persecution; but in its method of exposition it was directly opposed to the great Alexandrian, discarding the allegorical treatment of Scripture and maintaining for the most part the simple and primary meaning. The criticisms of these commentators on Gal. iv. 21—31 exhibit the characteristic features of the school to which they belonged. Theodore of Mopsuestia is its best typical exponent, being at once the most original thinker and the most determined antagonist of the allegorists. On the Antiochene school see Neander *Church Hist.* II. p. 498, III. p. 497 sq (Eng. trans.), Reuss *Gesch. d. Heil. Schr.* § 518 (3te ausg.), Kihn *Die Bedeutung der Antioch. Schule* (1867), Th. Forster *Chrysostom u. sein Verhältniss zur Antiochenischen Schule* (1869).

Eusebius of Emisa. (iii) *EUSEBIUS EMISENUS († about 360), so called from the name of his see Emesa or Emisa (Hums), a native of Edessa. A few fragments of his work are preserved in Cramer's *Catena*, pp. 6, 8, 12, 20, 28, 32, 40, 44, 57, 62, 64, 65, 67, 91. It is described by Jerome, as 'ad Galatas libri decem' (*de Vir. Illustr.* c. 91). Eusebius enjoyed a great reputation with his contemporaries, and these scanty fragments seem to indicate an acute and careful expositor. His writings are the subject of monographs by Augusti *Eusebii Emeseni Opusc. Graec.* etc. 1829, and by Thilo *Ueber die Schriften d. Euseb. v. Alexandrien u. d. Euseb. v. Emisa* (1832). See also Fabricius VII. p. 412, Schröckh V. p. 68 sq. The publication of Cramer's *Catena* has since added materials for an account of this writer.

Chrysostom. (iv) JOANNES CHRYSOSTOMUS († 407). This father's commentary on the Galatians differs from his expositions of other parts of the New Testament, in that it is not divided into separate discourses, nor interrupted by long perorations, which in his Homilies break the continuity of the subject. This gives it compactness and adds considerably to its value. At the same time

[1] Zenker *Bibl. Orient.* also mentions as published at Venice in 1833 a book by Aucher, bearing the title *S. P. Ephraemi Syri Comment. in Epist. S. Pauli etc. ex antiquissima Armenica versione nunc primum latinitate donatum.* But it is not included in a recent catalogue of the works printed at the Armenian press at Venice, and though advertised, seems never to have appeared.

[2] Through the kindness of Dr Rieu of the British Museum I have been able in some important passages to give the readings and interpretations of Ephraem in my commentary. [On this work see further in *Essays on Supernatural Religion*, 1889, p. 287 sq.]

it would seem from its character to have been intended for oral delivery. It is an eloquent popular exposition, based on fine scholarship. The date is uncertain, except that it was written at Antioch, i.e. before A.D. 398, when St Chrysostom became Patriarch of Constantinople (see the preface of the Benedictine edition, x. p. 655). It appears not to have been known to Jerome when he wrote his own commentary. In his controversy with Augustine indeed, which arose out of that commentary, he alludes to the opinion of Chrysostom on the collision of the Apostles at Antioch, but distinctly refers to a separate homily of the great preacher devoted to this special subject ('proprie super hoc capitulo latissimum exaravit librum,' Hieron. *Epist.* cxii. See above, p. 131 sq). The exposition of the Galatians may be read in the Benedictine edition of Chrysostom's works x. p. 657; or still better in Field's edition of the Homilies (Oxon. 1852).

(v) *SEVERIANUS (about 400), bishop of Gabala in Syria, first the friend and afterwards the opponent of Chrysostom; see Schröckh x. p. 458 sq. He wrote an *Expositio in Epistolam ad Galatas* (Gennad. *de Vir. Illustr.* c. 21, Hier. *Op.* II. p. 981). Gennadius speaks of him as 'in divinis scripturis eruditus.' Several fragments of this work are preserved in Cramer's *Catena*, pp. 16, 18, 23, 29, 39, 40, 55, 58, 59, 64, 66, 70, 82, 93, and one at least in the Œcumenian commentary (Gal. i. 13). Like most writers of the Græco-Syrian School he maintained the literal meaning of Scripture against the allegorists. See Cave I. p. 375, Fabricius x. p. 507. Severianus.

(vi) THEODORUS MOPSUESTENUS († 429), a native of Tarsus, so called from the see of Mopsuestia which he held. He wrote commentaries on all St Paul's Epistles; see Ebed Jesu's Catalogue in Assemann. *Bibl. Orient.* III. p. 32. Several fragments of these in the original are preserved in the *Catena*[1], and have been collected and edited by O. F. Fritzsche *Theod. Mops. Comment. in N. T.* (1847). This editor had before written a monograph *De Theodori Mopsuesteni Vita et Scriptis* (1836). Fritzsche's monograph and collection of fragments are reprinted in the edition of Theodore's works in Migne's *Patrol. Græc.* LXVI. But though only portions survive in the Greek, the complete commentaries on the smaller epistles from Galatians to Philemon inclusive are extant in a Latin translation. These commentaries, from Philippians onwards, had been long known in the compilation of Rabanus Maurus (Migne's *Patrol. Lat.* CXII), where they are incorporated nearly entire under the name of Ambrose; and a few years since Dom Pitra, *Spicil. Solesm.* I. p. 49 sq (1852), printed the expositions of the Galatians, Ephesians, and Philemon complete, and supplied the omissions and corrected the errors in the extracts on the remaining epistles in Rabanus, ascribing the work however to Hilary of Poitiers. Theodore of Mopsuestia.

In the Corbey MS which he used, these commentaries of Theodore on the shorter epistles were attached to the exposition of the Ambrosiaster or pseudo-Ambrose (who seems to have been one Hilary: see below, p. 232) on Romans and Corinthians, and the two together were entitled *Expositio Sancti Ambrosii in Epistolas B. Pauli*. This circumstance accounts for their being assigned to St Ambrose in Rabanus, as it also suggested the

[1] The fragments assigned to Theodore in Mai *Nov. Patr. Bibl.* VII. 1. p. 408 are none of his, but belong to Theodoret.

conjecture of Dom Pitra, that the great Hilary was their author. The true authorship was ascertained by Professor Hort[1] from a comparison with the Greek fragments of Theodore, and pointed out by him in the *Journ. of Clas. and Sacr. Phil.* IV. p. 302 (Camb. 1859). Though much marred by an indifferent Latin translator[2], this commentary is inferior in importance to the works of Jerome and Chrysostom alone among the patristic expositions now extant. Theodore was a leader of religious thought in his day, and as an expositor he has frequently caught the Apostle's meaning where other commentators have failed[3]. Among his contemporaries he had a vast reputation, and was called by the Nestorian Christians 'the Interpreter' *par excellence:* see Renaudot *Lit. Orient.* II. p. 616. In the Catholic Church of a later date the imputation of heresy overshadowed and darkened his fame. On this writer see Fabricius x. p. 346 sq (esp. p. 359), Rosenmüller III. p. 250 sq, Schröckh xv. p. 197 sq.

(vii) THEODORETUS († about 458), bishop of Cyrus, a native of Antioch and a disciple of Theodore. His commentaries on St Paul are superior to his other exegetical writings and have been assigned the palm over all patristic expositions of Scripture. See Schröckh XVIII. p. 398 sq, Simon p. 314 sq, Rosenmüller IV. p. 93 sq, and the monograph of Richter *de Theodoreto Epist. Paulin. interprete* (Lips. 1822). For appreciation, terseness of expression, and good sense, they are perhaps unsurpassed, and, if the absence of faults were a just standard of merit, they would deserve the first place; but they have little claim to originality, and he who has read Chrysostom and Theodore of Mopsuestia will find scarcely anything in Theodoret which he has not seen before. It is right to add however that Theodoret himself modestly disclaims any such merit. In his preface he apologizes for attempting to interpret St Paul after two such men (μετὰ τὸν δεῖνα καὶ τὸν δεῖνα) who are 'luminaries of the world': and he professes nothing more than to gather his stores 'from the blessed fathers.' In these expressions he alludes doubtless to Chrysostom and Theodore.

lius. (viii) EUTHALIUS, afterwards bishop of Sulce (supposed to have been in Egypt, but as no such place is known to have existed there, probably Sulce in Sardinia is meant; see the *Notitia* printed in Hierocl. *Synecd.* p. 79, ed. Parthey), wrote his work while a young man in the year 458. On his date see Zacagni *Collect. Mon. Vet.* I. pp. 402, 536, Fabricius IX. p. 287. Euthalius *edited* the Epistles of St Paul, dividing them into chapters (κεφάλαια) and verses (στίχοι), writing a general preface and arguments to the several epi-

[1] Whilst the first edition of this work was going through the press, my attention was directed by Dr Hort to an article by J. L. Jacobi in the *Deutsche Zeitschr. f. Christl. Wissensch.* Aug. 1854, in which, unknown to him, his conclusions had been anticipated. A more recent writer (Reinkens *Hilarius von Poitiers*, Schaffhausen 1864) states fairly the objections to Dom Pitra's view, but is apparently ignorant that the question of authorship is no longer a matter of conjecture.

[2] Thus for instance he makes Theodore fall into the common error of interpreting συνστοιχεῖ, Gal. iv. 25, 'is contiguous to' ('affinis,' 'confinis'); but the context, as well as the Greek fragment which has ἰσοδυναμεῖ, shows that the blunder is the translator's own.

[3] The first volume of a very careful edition of these Commentaries has recently appeared, by the Rev. H. B. Swete, Cambridge, 1880.

stles, and marking and enumerating the scriptural quotations. The divisions into chapters and the headings of the chapters he borrowed from some earlier writer (Zacagni, p. 528), probably the same whose date is given as A.D. 396 (ib. 536). Mill conjectures this person to have been Theodore of Mopsuestia; *Proleg.* pp. lxxxvi, lxxxvii. Reasons however have been assigned for thinking that Euthalius in this work was largely indebted to a much earlier critic, Pamphilus the martyr († 309): see Tregelles in *Horne's Introduction*, p. 27. On the stichometry of Euthalius see Mill *Proleg.* p. xc, Scrivener's *Introduction*, pp. 49, 58, and especially Tregelles, l. c. Though not a commentary, the work is sufficiently important in its bearing on the criticism of St Paul's Epistles to deserve a place here. It was first printed entire in Zacagni's *Collect. Mon. Vet.* I. p. 402 sq, and may be found in Gallandi x. p. 197 sq.

Gennadius.

(ix) *GENNADIUS († 471), patriarch of Constantinople. A few extracts in the printed editions of the Œcumenian Catena bear the name of Gennadius, and the number might be increased by consulting the MSS. I suppose these are rightly attributed to the patriarch of Constantinople, among whose works they are included in Migne's *Patrol. Græc.* LXXXV. p. 1611, for they can scarcely be assigned to any other of the name. So far as I know, there is no record of any work on St Paul by this or any Gennadius. The fragments on the Galatians indeed are so scanty that they do not in themselves warrant us in assuming a special work on this epistle, but the numerous extracts on the Epistle to the Romans in Cramer's *Catena* must certainly have been taken from a continuous exposition.

Photius.

(x) *PHOTIUS († about 891), patriarch of Constantinople. For the fullest information on the writings of this great man, see Fabricius x. p. 670 sq. Large fragments bearing the name of Photius are preserved in the Œcumenian Catena, taken it would appear from a Commentary on St Paul's Epistles no longer extant. Cave indeed asserts (II. p. 49) that a MS exists in the Cambridge University Library, and this statement is repeated by Fabricius, XI. p. 33, and others. This is a mistake. The MS in question (Ff. I. 30), which is incorrectly labelled with the name of Photius, proves—as far at least as relates to the Epistle to the Galatians—to contain a collection of notes identical with that of the Œcumenian Catena. It is accurately described in the new Catalogue. These fragments of Photius do not contribute much that is new to the criticism of St Paul, but they are an additional testimony to the extensive learning and intellectual vigour of the writer.

(b) *Latin.*

(b) *Latin Fathers.*

Victorinus.

(i) C. MARIUS VICTORINUS (about 360), an African, surnamed the Philosopher, converted to Christianity in old age, taught rhetoric at Rome when Jerome was a boy. He wrote commentaries apparently on all St Paul's Epistles (Hieron. *de Vir. Illustr.* 101, *præf. ad Gal.*), of which the expositions of the Galatians, Philippians, and Ephesians alone are extant. They were first published by Mai *Script. Vet. Nov. Coll.* III. 2, p. 1 (1828), and may be found in Migne *Patr. Lat.* VIII. p. 1145. It is difficult to understand the reputation which Victorinus had for eloquence. His work on the Galatians is obscure, confused, and as an exposition almost worthless, but it now and then preserves a curious fact (e.g. about the Symmachians, p. 16) and is interesting as the earliest extant commentary on this epistle. There is a lacuna from v. 18 to the end of the chapter. On this writer see Mai's Preface, p. x sq, and the article in Smith's *Dict. of Biography*.

Hilary. (ii) AMBROSIASTER, so called because his commentary was wrongly ascribed to St Ambrose and is commonly printed with the works of that father: see the Benedictine Edition, II. App. p. 20 sq. It is however quoted by Augustine (*cont. Duas Epist. Pelag.* iv. 7, x. p. 472, ed. Ben.) under the name 'sanctus Hilarius,' and is generally ascribed in consequence to Hilary the Roman deacon who lived about the middle of the fourth century and attached himself to the Luciferian schism. The epithet 'sanctus' however is not likely to have been applied by St Augustine to this person, and it must remain doubtful what Hilary was intended, except that we cannot possibly ascribe these commentaries to the great Hilary of Poitiers. The author, whoever he was, wrote during the pontificate of Damasus (see his note on 1 Tim. iii. 15) who was bishop of Rome from 366 to 384. See Schröckh VI. p. 210, XIV. p. 310. This work, which includes the thirteen epistles of St Paul, is one of the best Latin commentaries. A good account of it is given in Simon p. 133 sq: see also Rosenmüller III. p. 589 sq. I have generally quoted this commentator as the Ambrosian Hilary, or as Hilary simply.

Jerome. (iii) EUSEBIUS SOPHRONIUS HIERONYMUS. His '*Commentarii in Epistolam ad Galatas*' (VII. p. 367 ed. Vallarsi) were written about the year 387 (*Hieron. Vit.* XI. p. 104). In his preface he speaks of himself as undertaking a task unattempted by any Latin writer (he afterwards excepts Victorinus, of whom he speaks contemptuously), and treated by very few even of the Greeks in a manner worthy of the dignity of the subject. It is clear from this that he had not seen the work of the Ambrosiaster, which perhaps had only been published a few years before. Of the Greeks he singles out Origen, whose labours he extols highly and whom he professes to have followed. Besides Origen, he mentions having read Didymus (of Alexandria, who died in 396 at an advanced age: see Fabricius IX. p. 269) whom in allusion to his blindness he calls 'my seer' (videntem meum), one Alexander whom he designates an ancient heretic (of whom nothing is known), 'the Laodicene who has lately left the church' (meaning Apollinarius; see Fabricius VIII. p. 589), Eusebius of Emisa, and Theodorus of Heraclea († about 355; see Fabricius IX. p. 319). Of these writers he speaks loosely as having left 'nonnullos commentariolos,' which were not without their value. All these he read and digested before commencing his own work. Though abounding in fanciful and perverse interpretations, violations of good taste and good feeling, faults of all kinds, this is nevertheless the most valuable of all the patristic commentaries on the Epistle to the Galatians: for the faults are more than redeemed by extensive learning, acute criticism, and lively and vigorous exposition.

Augustine. (iv) AURELIUS AUGUSTINUS; '*Expositio Epistolae ad Galatas*,' written about 394 and apparently without consulting previous commentators (see p. 130, note 3), of whom he shows no knowledge. The great excellences of Augustine as an 'Interpreter of Scripture' are sufficiently vindicated by

Archbishop Trench (in his introduction to the 'Exposition of the Sermon on the Mount') against the attacks of writers who had too little sympathy with his tone of mind to appreciate his merits: but spiritual insight, though a far diviner gift than the critical faculty, will not supply its place. In this faculty Augustine was wanting, and owing to this defect, as a continuous expositor he is disappointing. With great thoughts here and there, his commentary on the Galatians is inferior as a whole to several of the patristic expositions.

(v) PELAGIUS, the great heresiarch, wrote his commentaries on the thirteen epistles of St Paul in Rome, and therefore not later than 410, before the Pelagian controversy broke out. Strangely enough in the middle of the 6th century, when Cassiodorus wrote, learned men assigned them to Pope Gelasius. Stranger still they have at a later date been fathered upon Jerome, and are generally printed in the editions of his works (XI. 2, p. 135 ed. Vall.). The true authorship however is established almost beyond a doubt by the quotations and references of Augustine and Marius Mercator, the contemporaries of Pelagius. On the other hand some of the passages given by Marius Mercator are wanting in the extant copies; but history supplies the clue to this perplexity. About the middle of the sixth century Cassiodorus (*Inst. Div. Lit.* c. 8), finding this commentary tainted with Pelagian errors, expurgated the Epistle to the Romans by removing the heretical passages, and thus set an example, as he tells us, which might be followed the more easily by others in the remaining epistles[1]. In its present form then this commentary is mutilated. The notes are pointed and good, but meagre. The high estimation in which they were held, in spite of the cloud which hung over their author, and the fact of their being attributed both to Gelasius and to Jerome, are high testimonies to their merits. Good accounts of this commentary will be found in Simon p. 236 sq, Schröckh XIV. p. 338 sq, and Rosenmüller III. p. 503 sq. Pelagius.

(vi) MAGNUS AURELIUS CASSIODORUS († after 562). '*Complexiones in Epistolas Apostolorum, in Acta, et in Apocalypsin,*' first brought to light and published by Scipio Maffei in 1721. It was reprinted by Chandler (1722 and 1723), and may be found in Migne's *Patrol. Lat.* LXX. p. 1343. This work consists of a few reflexions on detached passages, utterly valueless in themselves. It has a peculiar interest however as containing traces of 1 Joh. v. 7. See Schröckh XVI. p. 153, Rosenmüller V. p. 412 sq. Cassiodorus.

2. SECONDARY COMMENTARIES, excerpts, compilations, and collections of variorum notes, mostly of a later date. 2. LATER COMMENTARIES.

(a) *Greek Writers.* (a) *Greek.*

These are compiled from the Greek fathers already mentioned, but especially from Chrysostom.

[1] Migne's *Patrol. Lat.* LXX. p. 1119 sq. The identity of the work of which Cassiodorus speaks with this commentary is inferred from his description, for he does not himself mention the true author, though protesting against assigning it to Gelasius. On the other hand Cassiodorus a little later mentions what apparently he regards as another work the description of which would suit this commentary equally well: 'Tertium vero codicem reperi epistolarum Sancti Pauli, qui a nonnullis beati Hieronymi adnotationes brevissimas dicitur continere, quem vobis pariter Christo largiente dereliqui.'

Damascene. (i) JOANNES DAMASCENUS (about 750). A commentary on St Paul's Epistles, being an epitome of Chrysostom (see Fabricius IX. p. 281, Schröckh XX. p. 207), printed in Jo. Damasc. *Op.* II. p. 1 sq (ed. Le Quien).

Cramer's Catena. (ii) ANONYMOUS CATENA (date uncertain), first published by Cramer (Oxon. 1842). The authorship of the comments is very frequently noted (though not always correctly) either in the text or in the margin, but sometimes they are anonymous. The portion on the Galatians seems to be made up entirely of extracts from four commentators. Chrysostom is by far the largest contributor; Theodore of Mopsuestia comes next; and a few fragments (enumerated above, pp. 228, 229) bear the names of Eusebius of Emisa and Severianus. Of the anonymous fragments, those which belong to Chrysostom and Theodore can be verified: and such as remain after this verification ought probably to be assigned to either Eusebius or Severianus.

Œcumenius. (iii) ŒCUMENIUS (10th century), bishop of Tricca in Thessaly. The work which bears his name is a catena on the Acts and Epistles, to which he is one of the less important contributors. See especially Simon p. 458, and comp. Fabricius VIII. p. 693, Rosenmüller IV. p. 263. Though this commentary seems to be anonymous in the MSS, it appears on the whole more probable than not, from internal evidence, that Œcumenius was also the compiler of the Catena, adding to it a few notes of his own. The affirmative is maintained by Hentenius in the preface to his edition (Paris, 1630); the negative by J. F. S. Augustin *de Cat. Patr. Græc.* p. 366. There are considerable variations in the different MSS of this work; see Fabricius l. c. p. 696, and Cramer's *Catena* p. 411. The names on the margin of the printed editions in the portion relating to the Galatians are Photius (apparently by far the largest contributor), Joannes (i.e. Chrysostom), Gennadius, Severianus, Theodoret, Cyril, and Œcumenius. The MSS in some instances supply names to extracts which in the printed editions are anonymous. The few extracts from Cyril do not appear to be taken from a commentary on this epistle.

Theophylact. (iv) THEOPHYLACTUS (latter part of the 11th century), archbishop of Acris in Bulgaria. His commentary on St Paul's Epistles is founded chiefly on Chrysostom, with the aid of some other of the Greek fathers. The manner of execution has secured it a high reputation, but it possesses no independent value. On this commentary see Simon p. 403, Augustin p. 346, comp. Fabricius VII. p. 591.

To these should be added the commentary of EUTHYMIUS ZIGABENUS (about 1110), which is said to exist in MS, but has never been printed.

(b) *Latin.* (b) *Latin Writers.*

These are derived from the four Latin commentators, Hilary (Ambrosiaster), Jerome, Augustine, and Pelagius, directly or indirectly.

Primasius. (i) PRIMASIUS (about 550), bishop of Adrumetum in Africa, wrote a commentary on all St Paul's Epistles, including the Epistle to the Hebrews and the Apocalypse. It is a brief and fairly executed compilation from the Latin fathers already noticed, the most successful of these secondary commentaries. The editio princeps is by Gagnée (Lyons, 1537). This work is printed also in the *Magn. Bibl. Vet. Patr.* VI. 2, p. 18 sq and in Migne's *Patrol. Lat.* LXVIII. p. 415. See Rosenmüller V. p. 12, Cave I. p. 525, Schröckh XVII. p. 538.

It will be seen that the majority of the commentaries which follow were written about the middle of the ninth century within a period of a few years. The interest in Biblical studies was evidently very keen at this time, especially in France, and may be traced to the influence of our own Alcuin. I have already had occasion to speak of a similar period of activity in the history of Biblical interpretation during the latter half of the fourth and beginning of the fifth centuries, having its head-quarters at Antioch. In one respect these movements present a remarkable parallel. The first followed upon the establishment of Christianity as the religion of the Roman Empire under Constantine; the second upon the consolidation and extension of Western Christendom under Charlemagne. Thus the two most prominent epochs in the history of Biblical interpretation during the early centuries were ushered in by the two political events which exerted incomparably the greatest influence on the practical working of the Church; and it seems not unreasonable to attribute them in some measure to the stimulus given by these events. In real importance however the second of these two epochs in Biblical criticism bears no comparison with the first. It was feeble in character, and wholly unoriginal, and has therefore left no permanent stamp on the interpretation of Scripture. The Commentaries on the Epistle to the Galatians belonging to this period are derived entirely from one or more of the four great Latin expositors already mentioned either directly or through the medium of Primasius, together with the Latin translation of Theodore's work (then attributed to St Ambrose) which was made use of in some cases, and here and there a passage culled from the writings of Gregory the Great. Yet among these commentators, who were thus content to compile from the labours of their predecessors, are found the names of some of the ablest and most famous churchmen of their day. Revival of Biblical learning.

(ii) SEDULIUS (Scotus? 8th or 9th century?). '*In omnes S. Pauli Epistolas Collectaneum*,' compiled from the Latin fathers, a direct reference being occasionally given. This writer, whenever he lived, is certainly to be distinguished from Sedulius the Christian poet of the 5th century, with whom he has been confused. See Cave II. p. 15, Simon p. 379. This commentary is printed in *Magn. Bibl. Vet. Patr.* V. 1, p. 438, and in Migne's *Patrol. Lat.* CIII. p. 181. Sedulius.

(iii) CLAUDIUS TAURINENSIS († about 840), less correctly called 'Altissiodorensis' or 'Autissiodorensis' (of Auxerre), a Spaniard by birth, but bishop of Turin. Of his commentaries on St Paul, the exposition of the Epistle to the Galatians alone is printed (*Magn. Bibl. Vet. Patr.* IX. p. 66, Migne's *Patrol. Lat.* CIV. p. 838), but other portions exist or did exist in MS, and references are made to them in Simon p. 353 sq, where the fullest account of this writer will be found. See also Schröckh XXIII. p. 281, Cave II. p. 16. Claudius.

(iv) FLORUS LUGDUNENSIS, surnamed 'Magister' († after 852). A commentary on St Paul's Epistles, being a catena from the works of Florus.

Augustine. The portion relating to the Galatians is not taken from Augustine's exposition of the epistle, but is culled from his works generally. This commentary is printed among the works of Bede (VI. p. 690, ed. Basil. 1563), to whom it was ascribed; but the probable authorship was pointed out by Mabillon *Vet. Anal.* pp. 18, 488 (1723). On this work see Simon p. 339, Cave II. p. 24. It is printed in Migne's *Patrol. Lat.* CXIX. p. 363.

Rabanus Maurus. (v) RABANUS MAURUS († 856), archbishop of Mentz. *Enarrationum in Epistolas B. Pauli libri triginta*, a catena from the fathers, the names being given. The commentary on the Galatians in this collection is made up of large extracts from Jerome, Augustine, and the pseudo-Ambrose (see above p. 229), with one or two passages from extraneous writers, e.g. Gregory the Great. In Migne's *Patrol. Lat.* CXI, CXII.

Glossa Ordinaria. (vi) WALAFREDUS STRABO or Strabus († 849), a disciple of Rabanus, is the reputed author of the *Glossa Ordinaria* on the Scriptures, compiled from the fathers and especially from the catena of his master. It was the standard commentary during the middle ages and had an immense reputation. See Rosenmüller V. p. 135, and especially Simon p. 377. Printed in Migne's *Patrol. Lat.* CXIV. p. 570.

Haymo. (vii) HAYMO, bishop of Halberstadt († 853), wrote a commentary on St Paul's Epistles, which has been attributed also to his contemporary REMIGIUS (of Lyons?). See Cave II. pp. 28, 42, Schröckh XXIII. p. 283, Simon p. 365. Printed in Migne's *Patrol. Lat.* CXVII. p. 669.

Atto, Lanfranc, Bruno, Herveus. Later commentaries still, differing little in character from those just enumerated and for the most part equally unoriginal, are those of ATTO VERCELLENSIS († about 960), Migne's *Patrol. Lat.* CXXXIV. p. 491; see Schröckh XXIII. p. 302: of LANFRANC († 1089), an interlinear gloss and commentary, Migne CL. p. 259; see Simon p. 385, Schröckh XXIV. p. 334; the authorship however has been questioned: of BRUNO CARTHUSIANUS († 1101), the founder of the order, Migne CLIII. p. 281; see Simon p. 387: and of HERVEUS DOLENSIS (about 1130), Migne CLXXXI. p. 1129; see Cave II. pp. 187, 213, Simon p. 386. The authorship of the last-mentioned work is doubtful; it has been wrongly assigned to Anselm of Canterbury, but there is some authority for attributing it to his namesake of Laon.

DISSERTATIONS.

I.

WERE THE GALATIANS CELTS OR TEUTONS?

II.

THE BRETHREN OF THE LORD.

III.

ST PAUL AND THE THREE.

I.

WERE THE GALATIANS CELTS OR TEUTONS?

FOLLOWING the universal tradition of ancient writers, I have hitherto assumed that the remarkable people who settled in the heart of Asia Minor were members of the great Celtic family and brothers of the Gauls occupying the region west of the Rhine. And this tradition is confirmed in a striking way by the character and temperament of the Asiatic nation. A Teutonic origin however has been claimed for them by several writers, more especially commentators on this epistle; and this claim it will be necessary now to consider.

Teutonic theory.

How or when this theory arose I do not know: but it seems, in some form or another, to have been held as early as the beginning of the sixteenth century; for Luther takes occasion by it to read his countrymen a wholesome lesson. 'Some think,' he says, 'that we Germans are descended from the Galatians. Neither is this divination perhaps untrue, for we Germans are not much unlike them in temper. And I also am constrained to wish there were in my countrymen more steadfastness and constancy: for in all things we do, at the first brunt we be very hot, but when the heat of our first affections is burnt out, anon we become more slack, and look, with what rashness we begin things, with the same we throw them aside again and neglect them[1]'; and he goes on to reproach them with their waning interest in the cause of the Reformation. Doubtless the rebuke was well deserved; but Luther did injustice to his

Luther's rebuke.

[1] Luther's later commentary on Gal. i. 6.

countrymen in representing this as a special failing of the Teutonic race. The Roman historians at all events favourably contrast the constancy of the Germans with the fickleness of the Gauls.

French and German writers.

More recently a skirmishing battle has been fought over the carcase of this extinct nation, as if it were a point of national honour to claim possession. 'For ourselves,' says a French traveller, 'we cannot remember without a sentiment of national pride, that the Gauls penetrated to the very centre of Asia Minor, established themselves there, and left in that country imperishable monuments of themselves. If the name of Franks is the general term by which Eastern nations designate the inhabitants of Europe, it is because our ancestors have influenced in a remarkable manner the destinies of the East from the earliest ages of our history[1].' Contrast with this the language held by German commentators. 'Thus,' says Wieseler, after summing up the arguments in favour of his view, 'it can scarcely be doubtful that the Galatians are indeed the first German people to whom the Word of the Cross was preached[2].' 'The Epistle to the Galatians,' writes Olshausen, 'is addressed to Germans, and it was the German Luther who in this Apostolical Epistle again recognised and brought to light the substance of the Gospel.'

The question is not so simple as at first sight it might appear. Accustomed ourselves to dwell on the distinctive features of Celts and Germans, and impressed with the striking contrasts between the two races, we can scarcely imagine any confusion possible. But with

Testimony of Greeks and Romans.

the ancients the case was different. In their eyes Gauls and Germans alike were savage and lawless tribes, living in the far North beyond the pale of civilisation, and speaking an unknown language. The contrast to Greeks and Romans, which they observed in both alike, obscured the minor differences between one barbarian and another. As time opened out new channels of communication, they became more and more alive to the distinction between the two races[3]. In

[1] Texier in the *Revue des deux Mondes*, 1841, IV. p. 575.

[2] *Galater* p. 528.

[3] The authorities will be found in Diefenbach's *Celtica* II. They are very fairly and clearly stated also in Brandes *Kelten und Germanen* (Leipz. 1857). See especially his summary, p. ix. The only really important exception among ancient authors is Dion Cassius, who

Cæsar the line of separation is roughly traced: in Tacitus it is generally sharp and well-defined. But without doubt the two were sometimes confused; and this fact alone rescues the theory of the Teutonic origin of the Galatians from the imputation of a mere idle paradox.

Still historical scepticism must have some limit; and it would require a vast mass of evidence on the other side to overcome the very strong presumption from the agreement of ancient authorities, both Greek and Roman. Classical writers uniformly regard the ruthless hordes who poured into Italy and sacked Rome, the sacrilegious invaders who attacked the temple at Delphi, and the warlike immigrants who settled in the heart of Asia Minor, as belonging to one and the same race, as Gauls sprung from that Celtic nation whose proper home was north of the Alps and west of the Rhine. On this point there is little or no wavering, I believe, from first to last. It would not be strange that an incorrect view of the affinities of some obscure tribe, springing up in the early twilight of history, when the intercourse between distant nations was slight and intermitted, should pass unchallenged. But it is less easy to understand how, when a widespread race had played so important a part in the history of the world for some centuries, when civilised nations had been brought into close contact with them in the far East and West and at different points along a line extending with some interruptions across the whole of Europe and even into Asia, when the study of their language and manners had long been within the reach of the curious, so vital an error should still have held its ground. All ethnology would become hopeless, if testimony so strong were lightly set aside. There must have been many who for purposes of commerce or from love of travel or in discharge of some official duty or

Force of this evidence.

persistently makes the Rhine the boundary-line between the *Gauls* on the left bank, and the *Celts* on the right bank. See Brandes p. 202. Thus he identifies the Celts with the Germans, and distinguishes them from the Gauls. Extreme paradoxes have been held by some recent writers. On the one hand Holtzmann, *Kelten und Germanen* (1855), maintains that the Celts and Germans of the ancients (the inhabitants of Gaul as well as of Germany) were Teutonic in the language of modern ethnography (see esp. p. 157); on the other, Mone, *Celtische Forschungen* (1857), is of opinion that Germany as well as Gaul was of old occupied by races which we should call Celtic.

through missionary zeal had visited both the mother country of the Gauls and their Asiatic settlement, and had seen in the language and physiognomy and national character of these distant peoples many striking features which betokened identity of race.

Jerome's account of the Galatians.

The testimony of one of these witnesses is especially valuable. Jerome, who writes at the close of the fourth century, had spent some time both in Gaul proper and in Galatia[1]. He had thus ample opportunities of ascertaining the facts. He was moreover eminently qualified by his critical ability and linguistic attainments for forming an opinion. In the preface to his Commentary on the Galatians[2] he expresses himself to the following effect; 'Varro and others after him have written voluminous and important works on this race: nevertheless he will not quote heathen writers; he prefers citing the testimony of the Christian Lactantius. This author states that the Galatæ were so called from the whiteness of their complexion (γάλα), described by Virgil (*Æn.* viii. 660), *Tum lactea colla auro innectuntur*, informing us also that a horde of these Gauls arrived in Asia Minor, and there settled among the Greeks, whence the country was called Gallo-Græcia and afterwards Galatia. No wonder, adds Jerome, after illustrating this incident by other migrations between the East and the West, that the Galatians are called fools and slow of understanding[3], when Hilary, the Rhone of Latin eloquence, himself a Gaul and a native of Poitiers, calls the Gauls stupid (indociles). It is true that Gaul produces orators, but then Aquitania boasts a Greek origin, and the Galatians are not descended from these but from the fiercer Gaulish tribes (de ferocioribus Gallis sint profecti).' Though betraying the weakness common to all ancient

[1] Jerome mentions his visit to Galatia (totius Galatiae iter), and his sojourn in Gaul (Rheni semibarbarae ripae) in the same letter (*Epist.* iii, I. pp. 10, 12). While in Gaul, he appears to have stayed some time 'apud Treveros' (*Epist.* v, I. p. 15). Elsewhere he tells us that he paid this visit to Gaul when a very young man (adolescentulus, *adv. Jovin.* ii. 7, II. p. 335). Lastly, in his commentary on this epistle (VII. p. 430), he mentions having seen Ancyra the capital of Galatia.

[2] II. p. 425.

[3] It is scarcely necessary to say that Jerome here misses the point of St Paul's rebuke. The Galatians were intellectually quick enough (see p. 15, note 1). The 'folly' with which they are charged arose not from obtuseness but from fickleness and levity; the very versatility of their intellect was their snare. The passage of Hilary to which Jerome refers is not extant.

writers when speculating on questions of philology, this passage taken in connexion with its context implies a very considerable knowledge of facts; and if Jerome agreed with the universal tradition in assuming the Galatians to be genuine Gauls, I can hardly doubt that they were so.

Its indirect value.

But beyond the testimony borne to Jerome's personal knowledge and conviction, this passage suggests another very important consideration. The influence of the Christian Church must have been largely instrumental in spreading information of this kind. The Roman official was under no obligation to learn the language of the people whom he governed; but the Christian missionary could not hope for success unless he were able to converse freely with his hearers. In this way the practical study of languages was promoted by the spread of the gospel far more than it had ever been by the growth of the Roman empire[1]. At the same time the feeling of brotherhood inspired by Christianity surmounted the barriers of race and language and linked together the most distant nations. There is no more striking phenomenon in the history of the early centuries than the close and sympathetic intercourse kept up between churches as far apart as those of Asia and Gaul. These communications could scarcely have failed to clear up the error as to the origin of the Galatian people, if any error existed.

The Galatians spoke the same language with the Treveri,

But great reliance has been placed by those who advocate the Teutonic descent of the Galatians on the words with which Jerome concludes the passage above quoted; 'Besides the Greek,' he says, 'which is spoken throughout the East, the Galatians use as their native tongue a language almost identical with that of the Treveri; for any corruption they may have introduced need not be taken into account[2].' The Treveri, it is affirmed, were Germans and spoke a German tongue[3].

[1] 'The science of language,' says Prof. Max Müller, 'owes more than its first impulse to Christianity. The pioneers of our science were those very apostles who were commanded to go into all the world and preach the Gospel to every creature; and their true successors, the missionaries of the whole Christian Church' (*Science of Language*, 1st series, p. 121).

[2] See above, p. 12, note 2. The correct form is *Treveri*, not *Treviri*: see Glück *Die bei Cæsar vorkommenden Keltischen Namen* (1857), p. 155.

[3] Even Niebuhr, who maintained the Celtic origin of the Galatians, con-

who were Gauls,

This question is not free from difficulty. The fact that German is now spoken and has been spoken for many centuries in the district corresponding to the ancient Treveri (Treves) is in itself a presumption in favour of this view. Nor is the testimony of ancient writers so decisive as to remove every shadow of doubt.

Yet the balance of evidence is doubtless on the side of the Celtic extraction of this tribe. Tacitus indeed in one passage says that they, like the Nervii, eagerly affected a German origin, but he expresses no opinion of his own; and by distinguishing certain races whom he mentions immediately after as 'unquestionably Germans,' he evidently throws some doubt on the validity of their claims[1]. Elsewhere he speaks of them plainly as Belgians and Gauls[2]. The testimony of Cæsar leans the same way, though here again there is some indistinctness; 'Being harassed by constant wars, owing to their proximity to Germany, they did not differ much in their warlike habits from the Germans[3]'; but he too expressly calls them Gauls or Belgians elsewhere[4].

sidered that German was the language of the Treveri, and accounted for Jerome's statement by supposing him to have heard some Germans who had recently settled in Galatia (*Vorträge über Röm. Gesch.* II. p. 181). This view is opposed by Dr Latham (*Germania of Tacitus*, p. 98, comp. p. cxlv), who upholds the testimony of Jerome. In a later work (Prichard's *Celtic Nations*, p. 106 sq) he somewhat impugns that testimony, suggesting that Jerome was mistaken, and starting the theory that the Galatians were neither Gauls nor Germans, but Slavonians.

[1] Tac. *Germ.* 28 'Treveri et Nervii circa adfectationem Germanicae originis ultro ambitiosi sunt, tamquam per hanc gloriam sanguinis a similitudine et inertia Gallorum separentur. Ipsam Rheni ripam haud dubie Germanorum populi colunt, Vangiones, Triboci, Nemetes.' Strabo (iv. p. 194) says Τρηουΐροις δὲ συνεχεῖς Νερουΐοι καὶ τοῦτο Γερμανικὸν ἔθνος. If καὶ τοῦτο here refers to Τρηουΐροις, which however is very questionable (see Ukert II. 2, p. 361, note 65), it would seem that Strabo did not care to dispute their claims.

[2] *Ann.* i. 43, 44, iii. 44, *Hist.* iv. 71, 73.

[3] *Bell. Gall.* viii. 25 'Treveros quorum civitas propter Germaniae vicinitatem quotidianis exercitata bellis cultu et feritate non multum a Germanis differebat.'

[4] *Bell. Gall.* ii. 4, 24, v. 3, 45, vi. 2, 7, 8, vii. 63. So too Mela iii. 2 calls them 'clarissimi Belgarum.' Dion Cassius in like manner, xxxix. 47, xl. 31, li. 20, separates them from his Κελτοί (i.e. Germans). See Diefenb. *Celt.* II. p. 10 sq. In some of these passages they (as well as the Nervii) are spoken of as Gauls, in others as Belgians. This latter designation cannot be regarded as conclusive, inasmuch as some writers have maintained that the Belgians were themselves a German race. The evidence however is irresistibly strong in favour of their Gallic parentage. The facts of the case seem to be as follows; (1) The names of places and, what is more important, of persons among the

And this is fully borne out by the less questionable evidence supplied by the names of places and of persons among the Treveri, which equally with other Belgian names betoken their Celtic origin.

The country of the Treveri indeed has long been occupied by a German-speaking population, but history is not silent as to the change. About the close of the third century a colony of Franks settled in the waste lands of the Nervii and Treveri[1]. This was somewhat more than half a century before Jerome visited the place. The old Celtic language cannot have died out in so short a time. Gradually it was displaced by the German of the Frankish immigrants, reinforced by fresh hordes of their fellow-countrymen; but in the cities especially, where the remnants of the old population were gathered together, it would still continue to be the vulgar tongue; and Jerome's acquaintance with the inhabitants would naturally be confined for the most part to the towns[2].

but subsequently replaced by German settlers.

Belgæ are Celtic. Thus we find proper names having well-known Celtic terminations, and occasionally even identical with the names of Gallic places and heroes: see Zeuss *Die Deutschen etc.* p. 189. This is true even of the Treveri, e.g. Cingetorix (*Bell. Gall.* v. 3) compared with Vercingetorix (*ib.* vii. 4); see Brandes, p. 84. (2) Cæsar relates that the maritime parts of Britain were peopled by the Belgæ (v. 12, comp. ii. 4), and the British on the sea-coasts were certainly Celts. These facts seem decisive. On the other hand (3) Cæsar speaks of a difference of language between the three divisions of Gaul, the Belgæ, the Aquitani, and the Celtæ ('hi omnes lingua institutis legibus inter se differunt,' i. 1), but this is most naturally explained of various dialects of the same language, as in fact Strabo represents it (who however excepts the Aquitani), ὁμογλώττους δ' οὐ πάντας, ἀλλ' ἐνίους μικρὸν παραλλάττοντας ταῖς γλώτταις, iv. p. 176. (4) Cæsar relates 'plerosque Belgas esse ortos ab Germanis' (ii. 4, comp. Tac. *Germ.* 2); but this very expression implies that the staple of the population was Celtic, and it becomes simply a question to what extent they were leavened by the infusion of a German element. The statement of this question by Brandes, p. 80 sq, seems very fair and reasonable.

Of the two great branches of the Celtic family philologers for the most part assign the ancient Belgæ to the Cymric (see Diefenbach II. p. 58 sq, Thierry I. p. 153, 4me ed., Brandes p. 85 sq), and as the tradition seems to connect the Galatians with the Belgæ, we may, in the absence of any direct evidence, look for their modern affinities rather in the Welsh than in the Irish or the Gael. A careful examination of local words and names in Galatia might even now clear up some difficulties.

[1] Eumen. *Paneg. Constantio Cæs.* c. 21, 'Tuo, Maximiane Auguste, nutu Nerviorum et Treverorum arva jacentia laetus postliminio restitutus et receptus in leges Francus excoluit,' *Paneg. Vet.* p. 207 Gruter; comp. *ib. Paneg. Constantino Aug.* cc. 5, 6, Gruter p. 181. See Brandes pp. 243, 267, Gibbon's *Decline and Fall* c. xiii; comp. *ib.* c. xix.

[2] Perrot (*De la Disparition de la Langue Gauloise en Galatie*, p. 180 sq in the *Revue Celtique*, no. 2, Août

Evidence afforded by the Galatian language.

But the evidence for the Celtic parentage of the Galatians is not confined to the testimony of ancient writers, however well informed. The Galatian language itself is a witness free from all suspicion of ignorance or perjury. And considering that a mere handful of words, chiefly proper names, has alone survived, the evidence thence derived is far fuller than might have been anticipated[1].

(1) Terminations of proper names of places

(1) Several Galatian names of places and persons exhibit Celtic terminations. These are as follows:

Of *places:*

-BRIGA. Eccobriga (*Itin. Ant.* p. 203, ed. Wess., *Tab. Peut.*); Ipetobrigen (*Itin. Hieros.* p. 574). It signifies 'a hill'; see Zeuss *Gr. Celt.* p. 101, Glück p. 126.

-IACUM. Rosologiacum (*Itin. Ant.* p. 143); Acitorihiacum (*Tab. Peut.*); Teutobodiaci (Plin. v. 42); Timoniacenses (? Plin. v. 42). On this very common Celtic termination see Zeuss *G. C.* p. 772.

and persons.

Of *persons:*

-GNATUS. Eposognatus (Polyb. xxii. 20): compare Critognatus, Boduognatus (Cæsar), and several Celtic names in inscriptions; (gnath, 'consuetus'; Zeuss *G. C.* p. 82, and compare *ib.* p. 19).

-MARUS. Combolomarus (Liv. xxxviii. 19); Chiomara (Polyb. xxii. 21); compare Virdumarus, Indutiomarus (Cæsar), and other names in Gallic inscriptions; (mar, 'magnus'; see Zeuss *G. C.* p. 19, Glück p. 77).

-ORIUS. Acichorius (Paus. x. 19. 4): Orestorius (Paus. x. 22. 2); Comontorius (Polyb. iv. 46. 3); see Zeuss *G. C.* p. 741.

-RIX. Adiatorix[2] (Cic. *Fam.* ii. 12, Strabo xii. p. 534); Albiorix,

1870) seeks to invalidate Jerome's testimony altogether, but his arguments do not seem to me to be substantial. He believes that the Celtic language had died out in Galatia itself some centuries before; and he therefore supposes that this father thoughtlessly copies a statement of some earlier writer, and applies it to his own time, regardless of the anachronism. Jerome's assertion however has every appearance of being founded on personal knowledge.

[1] The account which follows perhaps needs some apology from one who has no pretensions to Celtic scholarship and may possibly betray great ignorance. But the investigation could not well be avoided, while the facts seemed to lie very much on the surface. At all events the general results will not, I think, be invalidated by any inaccuracy or weakness that there may be in the details.

[2] The first element in this word also occurs in several Celtic names, Adiatunnus, Adiatumarus, etc., Glück p. 1.

Ateporix (Boeckh *Inscr.* 4039); a very common Celtic termination, e.g. Dumnorix, Ambiorix, Vercingetorix, etc.; ('rex,' 'princeps,' Zeuss *G. C.* p. 25, where instances are given).

-TARUS, -TORUS; Bogodiatorus (Strabo xii. p. 567); Brogitarus (Cic. *Harusp. Resp.* 28); Deiotarus (Cic. *pro Reg. Deiot.*, comp. Boeckh *Inscr.* 4072). See Zeuss *G. C.* p. 823.

(2) But it is not only in the terminations that the Celtic origin of the language is seen. It appears unmistakeably also in a large proportion of the Galatian names and words which have been preserved.

(2) Galatian names and words.

Strabo tells us (xii. p. 567) that the great council of the Galatian people met at a place called DRYNÆMETUM (Δρυναίμετον). Now nemetum ('nemed') is a good Celtic word for a temple: we meet with it for instance in Augustonemetum, 'the temple of Augustus,' at Clermont in the Auvergne; in Vernemetum, 'the great temple,' in the province of Bordeaux, of which it is said

Drynæmetum.

> Nomine Vernemetis voluit vocitare vetustas,
> Quod quasi *fanum ingens* Gallica lingua refert[1];

in another Vernemetum also in Britain (*Itin. Ant.* p. 479); and in several other names: comp. Diefenb. *Celt.* I. p. 83, II. p. 329, Zeuss *G. C.* pp. 11, 186, Glück p. 75. The first syllable of Drynæmetum again represents the Celtic (Welsh) *derw*, 'quercus,' whence Druid ('*derwydd*'), Derwent, etc.: see Zeuss *G. C.* pp. 8, 16, and Diefenb. I. p. 160. Thus 'Drynæmetum' is the 'oak-shrine' or the 'grove temple,' recalling a characteristic feature of the old Celtic worship which prevailed in Britain and Gaul.

Again the names of several of the Galatian chieftains betray their Celtic extraction. The leader of the expedition against Greece, of which the Galatian immigration was an offshoot, bears the same name with the Gaulish captain who sacked Rome; he too, like his predecessor, is a BRENNUS—no proper name but a good Celtic word signifying a 'prince' or 'chieftain' (Thierry *Hist. des Gaul.* I. p. 160, Zeuss *G. C.* p. 101). A second name assigned to this same king was

Galatian chieftains.

[1] Venant. Fortun. i. 9.

PRAUSUS, 'the terrible' (Strab. iv. p. 187; see Thierry I. p. 218, and especially Diefenb. II. p. 252). Again, another commander in this expedition is called CERETHRIUS, 'the famous, the glorious' (Pausan. x. 19. 4; *certh*, 'celebrated,' *certhrwyz*, 'glory'; Thierry I. p. 219, from Owen's *Welsh Dict.*). BOLGIUS again (Pausan. *ib.*), also written Belgius (Justin. xxiv. 5), presents the same Celtic root which appears in 'Belgæ' (comp. Diefenb. I. p. 200, II. pp. 61 sq, 267). The name of ACICHORIUS too (Pausan. l. c.) or Cichorius (Diod. xxii. fragm.), who is associated with Brennus in the command, taken as a Celtic word, describes his office (*cyçwiawr*, 'colleague,' Thierry I. p. 225).

and others.

Among later Galatian names of persons we meet with GÆZATODIASTUS (Boeckh *Inscr.* 4039), doubtless to be connected with the 'Gesatæ' of whom we read among the western Gauls, and whose name, signifying 'warriors,' is derived from the Gallic word *gesum*, 'a spear' (Cæs. *B. G.* iii. 4; comp. Serv. in Virg. *Æn.* viii. 662, Diefenb. I. p. 126); and BROGORIS (Boeckh *Inscr.* 4118), the root of which appears in Brogitarus, Allobroges, etc.; Zeuss *G. C.* p. 106; Glück p. 27. Again the name BITUITUS, Bitovitus, or Bitœtus, seems to occur both in Asiatic (Appian *Mithr.* 111) and in European Gaul (ib. *Celt.* 12, Liv. *Epit.* lxi); for the reasons given (Wernsdorff p. 164) for assigning the first of these, who slew Mithridates, to the western nation seem insufficient. Nor is this the only proper name which links the two countries together. Strabo (xiii. p. 625) mentions one ADOBOGION, a Galatian; the name Adbogius appears on an inscription relating to Rhenish Gaul (Steiner *Cod. Inscr. Rom. Rhen.* no. 440).

Galatian tribes.

Again, of the three tribes which composed the Galatian people two at least proclaim their Celtic descent in their names. The TECTOSAGÆ or Tectosages bear identically the same name with a tribe of western Gauls (Cæs. *B. G.* vi. 24) whom we find moving eastward and occupying a district which was properly German (see Diefenb. II. p. 264 sq). Similarly both the component parts of TOLISTOBOGII, the name of the second of these tribes, claim a Celtic affinity. The word is variously written, but its original Celtic form would seem to be represented by Tolosatobogii. Tolosa was a common Gallic name for places (Diefenb. II. p. 339), and has survived both in the French Toulouse and in the Spanish Tolosa. It is connected moreover with the name and history of the other Galatian tribe already discussed. 'Tolosa Tectosagum' is especially mentioned (Mela ii. 5; comp. Plin. iii. 5); and according to the ancient legend a portion of the Tectosages returning from the Delphic expedition 'to their ancient country Tolosa,' and being afflicted by a pestilence, bethought them of averting the wrath of heaven by sinking their ill-gotten gains in the neighbouring lake (Justin. xxxii. 3; comp. Strab. iv. p. 188, Dion. Cass. *Exc.* I. p. 133, ed. L. Dind.). The riddle of this legend I shall not attempt to read; I simply quote it to show the connexion of the Gallic Tolosa with the Asiatic settlement. Indeed this name occurs in Galatia itself under the form Tolosocorium (*Tab. Peut.*), and Τόλαστα χωρίον (Ptol. v. 4). The second element in the composition of Tolostobogii or Tolostoboii is no less Celtic. It is the name borne by the tribe of the Boii which plays so prominent a part in early Gallic history, and is not uncommon as a termination of other Celtic names (see instances in Zeuss *G. C.* p. 69, comp. p. 58, and compare the proper name Adobogius already referred to). Even in the third and remaining tribe the TROCMI Celtic affinities have been pointed out (Diefenb. I. p. 256, Zeuss *G. C.* p. 28), but these are obscure and far from convincing[1].

Other Galatian words.

Of Galatian words besides proper names very few indeed have been recorded. The explanations given of these may be found in Diefenbach (see his references II. p. 251). Among others which are less patent, one is certainly a good Celtic word μάρκα, mentioned

[1] Diefenbach, *Celt.* II. p. 248, quotes Solinus (c. 42) as mentioning a Galatian tribe 'Ambiani,' this being the ancient Gaulish name for the modern 'Amiens.' But there seems to be an accidental error here. In the most recent and most critical edition of Solinus (c. 41, ed. Mommsen, 1864) the word is 'Ambitoti'; and in the corresponding passage of Pliny (v. 42), from which Solinus borrowed, Sillig reads 'Ambitouti.' Though the MSS in both authors present some variations, there seems to be no authority for Ambiani.

I notice also that the names of several Galatian places begin with Reg-, as Reganagalla, Regemnezus, Regemaurecium, Regetmocata, Regomori; see Wernsdorff pp. 232, 3. This may be the same word which appears in many Gallic names, as Rigodulum, Rigomagus, etc.; see Diefenbach I. p. 53, II. p. 331, Zeuss *G. C.* p. 25.

by Pausanias (x. 19) as the name for a horse among the Gauls of the Delphic expedition (Diefenb. I. p. 67).

Result. In gathering together the evidence in favour of the Celtic extraction of the Galatians as afforded by their language I have omitted many questionable affinities; and even of those which are given some perhaps will appear uncertain. But taken as a whole the evidence, if I mistake not, places the result beyond a doubt; and the few German etymologies real or imagined, which have been alleged on the other side, will be quite insufficient to turn the scale. Thus it is asserted that the names of the leaders of the Asiatic expedition, LUTARIUS and LEONNORIUS, are both German; and that the Galatian tribe TEUTOBODIACI and the Galatian town GERMANOPOLIS point very clearly to the same origin. On these four words the whole stress of the Teutonic theory may be said to rest.

Supposed German affinities,

And if they had stood alone, the German affinities of these names might perhaps have been accepted. But with the vast mass of evidence on the other side, it becomes a question whether some more satisfactory account cannot be given of them. Thus Lutarius (or Luturius) is said to be the same name with the Frankish *Lothaire* and the Saxon *Luther*, and therefore Teutonic (see Graff *Althochd. Sprachsch.* IV. p. 555); but among the Gallic chieftains one Lucterius is mentioned (Cæsar *B. G.* vii. etc.), and the identity of the names Lutarius and Lucterius is at least not improbable (Diefenb. II. p. 253; Zeuss, *G. C.* p. 78, derives the name Lucterius from luct, 'agmen,' 'pars': see also p. 180). Again the other Galatian commander Leonnorius has certainly a namesake in a genuine Celtic saint, a native of Britain (*Acta Sanct.* Jul. I. see Diefenb. II. p. 254), and there seems to be no reason for assigning a Teutonic parentage to this word. In the name Teutobodiaci indeed the first component seems very plainly to mean 'German': but, even granting that this is not one of those very specious but very deceptive affinities which are the snares of comparative philology, the word need not imply that the tribe itself was Teutonic. If the second component is rightly taken to denote victory ('buad,' 'buaid,' comp. Boadicea, Bodiocasses, Bodiontici, Bodicus, etc.; see Zeuss *G. C.* p. 27, Glück

how to be explained.

p. 53), then the Teutobodiaci were not necessarily Teutons any more than Thessalonica was Thessalian. The remaining word Germanopolis seems in its very form to betray its later origin, or at all events to mark some exceptional occupants other than the main population of the country.

A possible German element.

It is quite possible indeed, as Thierry supposes (I. p. 225), that swept away with the hordes of Gaulish invaders a small body of Germans also settled in Asia Minor, and this may be the true account of the names Lutarius and Teutobodiaci. We know that of all the Gauls the Belgians were most mixed up with the Germans, and it is with the Belgian members of the Celtic family especially that the Gauls of the Asiatic settlement seem to be connected. But the evidence is scarcely strong enough to bear the strain of the German theory, even when pared down to these very meagre dimensions. Beyond this we cannot go without doing violence to history.

Conclusion.

There is every reason then for believing that the Galatian settlers were genuine Celts, and of the two main subdivisions into which modern philologers have divided the Celtic race, they seem rather to have belonged to the Cymric, of which the Welsh are the living representatives. Thus in the age when St Paul preached, a native of Galatia spoke a language essentially the same with that which was current in the southern part of Britain. And if—to indulge a passing fancy—we picture to ourselves one of his Asiatic converts visiting the far West to barter the hair cloths of his native country for the useful metal which was the special product of this island, we can imagine that finding a medium of communication in a common language he may have sown the first seeds of the Gospel and laid the foundations of the earliest Church in Britain.

II.

THE BRETHREN OF THE LORD[1].

Two rival theories.

IN the early ages of the Church two conflicting opinions were held regarding the relationship of those who in the Gospels and Apostolic Epistles are termed 'the brethren of the Lord.' On the one hand it was maintained that no blood relationship existed; that

[1] The interest in this subject, which was so warmly discussed towards the close of the fourth century, has been revived in more recent times by the publication of Herder's *Briefe Zweener Brüder Jesu in unserem Kanon* (1775), in which the Helvidian hypothesis is put forward. Since then it has formed the subject of numberless monographs, dissertations, and incidental comments. The most important later works, with which I am acquainted, are those of Blom, *De τοῖς ἀδελφοῖς et ταῖς ἀδελφαῖς τοῦ Κυρίου* (Leyden, 1839); of Schaf, *Das Verhältniss des Jakobus Bruders des Herrn zu Jakobus Alphäi* (Berlin, 1842); and of Mill, *The accounts of our Lord's Brethren in the New Testament vindicated etc.* (Cambridge, 1843). The two former adopt the Helvidian view; the last is written in support of St Jerome's hypothesis. Blom gives the most satisfactory statement which I have seen of the patristic authorities, and Schaf discusses the Scriptural arguments most carefully. I am also largely indebted to the ability and learning of Mill's treatise, though he seems to me to have mistaken the general tenor of ecclesiastical tradition on this subject. Besides these monographs I have also consulted, with more or less advantage, articles on the subject in works of reference or periodicals, such as those in *Studien u. Kritiken* by Wieseler; *Die Söhne Zebedäi Vettern des Herrn* (1840, p. 648), and *Ueber die Brüder des Herrn, etc.* (1842, p. 71). In preparing for the second edition I looked over the careful investigation in Laurent's *Neutest. Studien* p. 155 sq (1866), where the Helvidian hypothesis is maintained, but saw no reason to make any change in consequence. The works of Arnaud, *Recherches sur l'Epître de Jude*, and of Goy (Mont. 1845), referred to in Bishop Ellicott's *Galatians* i. 19, I have not seen. My object in this dissertation is mainly twofold; (1) To place the Hieronymian hypothesis in its true light, as an effort of pure criticism unsupported by any traditional sanction; and (2) To say a word on behalf of the Epiphanian solution, which seems, at least of late years, to have met with the fate reserved for *τὰ μέσα* in literature and theology, as well as in politics, *ὑπ' ἀμφοτέρων ἢ ὅτι οὐ ξυνηγωνίζοντο ἢ φθόνῳ τοῦ περιεῖναι διεφθείροντο.* I suppose it was because he considered it idle to discuss a theory which had no friends, that Prof. Jowett (on Gal. i. 19), while balancing the claims of the other two solutions, does not even mention the existence of this, though in the early centuries it was the received account.

these brethren were in fact sons of Joseph by a former wife, before he espoused the Virgin; and that they are therefore called the Lord's brethren only in the same way in which Joseph is called His father, having really no claim to this title but being so designated by an exceptional use of the term adapted to the exceptional fact of the miraculous incarnation. On the other hand certain persons argued that the obvious meaning of the term was the correct meaning, and that these brethren were the Lord's brethren as truly as Mary was the Lord's mother, being her sons by her husband Joseph. The former of these views was held by the vast majority of orthodox believers and by not a few heretics; the latter was the opinion of a father of the Church here and there to whom it occurred as the natural inference from the language of Scripture, as Tertullian for instance, and of certain sects and individuals who set themselves against the incipient worship of the Virgin or the one-sided asceticism of the day, and to whom therefore it was a very serviceable weapon of controversy.

A third propounded by Jerome.

Such was the state of opinion, when towards the close of the fourth century Jerome struck out a novel hypothesis. One Helvidius, who lived in Rome, had attacked the prevailing view of the superiority of virgin over married life, and in doing so had laid great stress on the example of the Lord's mother who had borne children to her husband. In or about the year 383 Jerome, then a young man, at the instigation of 'the brethren' wrote a treatise in reply to Helvidius, in which he put forward his own view[1]. He maintained that the Lord's brethren were His cousins after the flesh, being sons of Mary the wife of Alphæus and sister of the Virgin. Thus, as he boasted, he asserted the virginity not of Mary only but of Joseph also.

Names assigned to these three.

These three accounts are all of sufficient importance either from their real merits or from their wide popularity to deserve consideration, and I shall therefore investigate their several claims. As it will be convenient to have some short mode of designation,

[1] *Adv. Helvidium de Perpetua Virginitate B. Mariæ*, II. p. 206 (ed. Vall.). Comp. *Comment. ad Gal.* i. 19.

I shall call them respectively the *Epiphanian*, the *Helvidian*, and the *Hieronymian* theories, from the names of their most zealous advocates in the controversies of the fourth century when the question was most warmly debated.

Arbitrary assumptions

But besides the solutions already mentioned not a few others have been put forward. These however have been for the most part built upon arbitrary assumptions or improbable combinations of known facts, and from their artificial character have failed to secure any wide acceptance. It is assumed for instance, that two persons of the same name, James the son of Alphæus and James the Lord's brother, were leading members of the Church of Jerusalem, though history points to one only[1]; or that James the Lord's brother mentioned in St Paul's Epistles is not the same James whose name occurs among the Lord's brethren in the Gospels, the relationship intended by the term 'brother' being different in the two cases[2]; or that 'brethren' stands for 'foster-brethren,' Joseph having undertaken the charge of his brother Clopas' children after their father's death[3]; or that the Lord's brethren had a double parentage, a legal as well as an actual father, Joseph having raised seed to his deceased brother Clopas by his widow according to the levirate law[4]; or lastly, that the cousins of Jesus were rewarded with the title of His brethren, because they were His steadfast disciples, while His own brothers opposed Him[5].

to be set aside.

All such assumptions it will be necessary to set aside. In themselves indeed they can neither be proved nor disproved. But it is safer to aim at the most probable deduction from known facts than to build up a theory on an imaginary foundation. And, where the question is so intricate in itself, there is little temptation to

[1] e.g. Wieseler *Ueber die Brüder etc.*, l.c., p. 80 sq. According to this writer the James of Gal. ii. 9 and of the Acts is the son of Alphæus, not the Lord's brother, and therefore different from the James of i. 19. See his notes on Gal. i. 19, ii. 9. An ancient writer, the pseudo-Dorotheus (see below, p. 286, note), had represented two of the name as bishops of Jerusalem, making the son of Alphæus the successor of the Lord's brother.

[2] The writers mentioned in Schaf, p. 11.

[3] Lange in *Herzog's Real-Encycl.* in the article 'Jakobus im N.T.'

[4] Theophylact; see below, p. 290.

[5] Renan *Vie de Jésus* p. 24. But in *Saint Paul* p. 285 he inclines to the Epiphanian view.

introduce fresh difficulties by giving way to the license of conjecture.

Relation of the three accounts.

To confine ourselves then to the three accounts which have the greatest claim to a hearing. It will be seen that the hypothesis which I have called the Epiphanian holds a middle place between the remaining two. With the Helvidian it assigns an intelligible sense to the term 'brethren': with the Hieronymian it preserves the perpetual virginity of the Lord's mother. Whether or not, while uniting in itself the features which have recommended each of these to acceptance, it unites also their difficulties, will be considered in the sequel.

From a critical point of view however, apart from their bearing on Christian doctrine and feeling, the Helvidian and Epiphanian theories hang very closely together, while the Hieronymian stands apart. As well on account of this isolation, as also from the fact which I have hitherto assumed but which I shall endeavour to prove hereafter, that it was the latest born of the three, it will be convenient to consider the last-mentioned theory first.

Jerome's statement.

St Jerome then states his view in the treatise against Helvidius somewhat as follows:

The son of Alphæus is the Lord's brother;

The list of the Twelve Apostles contains two of the name of James, the son of Zebedee and the son of Alphæus. But elsewhere we read of a James the Lord's brother. What account are we to give of this last James? Either he was an Apostle or he was not. If an Apostle, he must be identified with the son of Alphæus, for the son of Zebedee was no longer living: if not an Apostle, then there were three persons bearing this name. But in this case how can a certain James be called 'the less,' a term which implies only one besides? And how moreover can we account for St Paul's language 'Other of the Apostles saw I none, save James the Lord's brother' (Gal. i. 19)? Clearly therefore James the son of Alphæus and James the Lord's brother are the same person.

the Virgin's sister being his mother.

And the Gospel narrative explains this identity. Among the Lord's brethren occur the names of James and Joseph. Now it is stated elsewhere that Mary the mother of James the less and of

Joseph (or Joses) was present at the crucifixion (Matt. xxvii. 56, Mark xv. 40). This Mary therefore must have been the wife of Alphæus, for Alphæus was the father of James. But again in St John's narrative (xix. 25) the Virgin's sister 'Mary of Cleophas (Clopas)' is represented as standing by the cross. This carries us a step in advance. The last-mentioned Mary is to be identified with the wife of Alphæus and mother of James. Thus James the Lord's brother was in reality the Lord's cousin.

Meaning of the term Brethren.

But, if His cousin, how is he called His brother? The following is the explanation. The term 'brethren' is used in four different senses in Holy Scripture: it denotes either (1) actual brotherhood or (2) common nationality, or (3) kinsmanship, or (4) friendship and sympathy. These different senses St Jerome expresses by the four words 'natura, gente, cognatione, affectu.' In the case of the Lord's brethren the third of these senses is to be adopted: brotherhood here denotes mere relationship, just as Abraham calls his nephew Lot brother (Gen. xiii. 8), and as Laban uses the same term of Jacob his sister's son (Gen. xxix. 15).

Jerome's theory supplemented.

So far St Jerome, who started the theory. But, as worked out by other writers and as generally stated, it involves two particulars besides.

Alphæus the same with Clopas.

(i) *The identity of Alphæus and Clopas.* These two words, it is said, are different renderings of the same Aramaic name חלפי or ܚܠܦܝ (Chalphai), the form Clopas being peculiar to St John, the more completely grecized Alphæus taking its place in the other Evangelists. The Aramaic guttural *Cheth*, when the name was reproduced in Greek, might either be omitted as in Alphæus, or replaced by a κ (or χ) as in Clopas. Just in the same way Aloysius and Ludovicus are recognised Latin representatives of the Frankish name Clovis (Clodovicus, Hludovicus, Hlouis)[1].

This identification however, though it materially strengthens his theory, was unknown to Jerome himself. In the course of his argument he confesses plainly that he does not know why Mary is called Clopæ, (or Cleophæ, as he writes it): it may be, he suggests,

[1] This illustration is taken from Mill, p. 236.

after her father or from her family surname ('gentilitate familiae') or for some other reason[1]. In his treatise on Hebrew names too he gives an account of the word Alphæus which is scarcely consistent with this identity[2]. Neither have I found any traces of it in any of his other works, though he refers several times to the subject. In Augustine again, who adopts Jerome's hypothesis and his manner of stating it, it does not anywhere appear, so far as I know. It occurs first, I believe, in Chrysostom who incidentally speaks of James the Lord's brother as 'son of Clopas,' and after him in Theodoret who is more explicit (both on Gal. i. 19)[3]. To a Syrian Greek, who, even if he were unable to read the Peshito version, must at all events have known that Chalphai was the Aramæan rendering or rather the Aramæan original of Ἀλφαῖος, it might not unnaturally occur to graft this identification on the original theory of Jerome.

Jude the Lord's brother one of the Twelve,

(ii) *The identity of Judas the Apostle and Judas the Lord's brother.* In St Luke's catalogues of the Twelve (Luke vi. 16, Acts i. 13) the name 'Judas of James' (Ἰούδας Ἰακώβου) occurs. Now we find a Judas also among the four brethren of the Lord (Matt. xiii. 55, Mark vi. 3); and the writer of the epistle, who was doubtless the Judas last mentioned, styles himself 'the brother of James' (Jude 1). This coincidence suggests that the ellipsis in 'Judas of James' should be supplied by *brother* as in the English version, not by *son* which would be the more obvious word. Thus Judas the Lord's brother, like James, is made one of the Twelve. I do not know when the Hieronymian theory received this fresh accession, but, though the gain is considerable in apparent strength at least, it does not appear, so far as I have noticed, to have occurred to Jerome himself.

and perhaps Simon also.

And some have gone a step farther. We find not only a James and a Judas among the Lord's brethren, but also a Symeon or

[1] *adv. Helvid.* § 15, II. p. 219.

[2] '*Alphæus*, fugitivus [חלף; the Greek of Origen was doubtless *οἰχόμενος*, see p. 626], sed melius millesimus [אלף] vel doctus [אלף]'; III. p. 89: and again, '*Alphæus*, millesimus, sive super os [?עלפה] ab ore non ab osse.' ib. p. 98. Thus he deliberately rejects the derivation with a *Cheth*, which is required in order to identify 'Alphæus' with 'Clopas.' Indeed, as he incorrectly wrote Cleopas (or Cleophas) for Clopas with the Latin version, this identification was not likely to occur to him.

[3] See below, p. 289.

Simon. Now it is remarkable that these three names occur together in St Luke's list of the Twelve: James (the son) of Alphæus, Simon called Zelotes, and Judas (the brother) of James. In the lists of the other Evangelists too these three persons are kept together, though the order is different and Judas appears under another name, Lebbæus or Thaddæus. Can this have been a mere accident? Would the name of a stranger have been inserted by St Luke between two brothers? Is it not therefore highly probable that this Simon also was one of the Lord's brethren? And thus *three* out of the four are included among the Twelve[1].

Without these additions the theory is incomplete; and indeed they have been so generally regarded as part of it, that advocates and opponents alike have forgotten or overlooked the fact that Jerome himself nowhere advances them. I shall then consider the theory as involving these two points; for indeed it would never have won its way to such general acceptance, unless presented in this complete form, where its chief recommendation is that it combines a great variety of facts and brings out many striking coincidences.

Jerome himself

But before criticizing the theory itself, let me prepare the way by divesting it of all fictitious advantages and placing it in its true light. The two points to which attention may be directed, as having been generally overlooked, are these:

(i) claims no traditional sanction for his theory,

(1) *Jerome claims no traditional support for his theory.* This is a remarkable feature in his treatise against Helvidius. He argues the question solely on critical and theological grounds. His opponent had claimed the sanction of two older writers, Tertullian and Victorinus of Pettaw. Jerome in reply is obliged to concede him Tertullian, whose authority he invalidates as 'not a member of the Church,' but denies him Victorinus. Can it be doubted that if he could have produced any names on his own side he would only too gladly have done so? When for instance he is maintaining

[1] It is found in Sophronius (?), who however confuses him with Jude; 'Simon Cananaeus cognomento Judas, frater Jacobi episcopi, qui et successit illi in episcopatum etc.'; Hieron. *Op.* II. p. 958. Compare the pseudo-Hippolytus (I. App. p. 30, ed. Fabric.). Perhaps the earliest genuine writing in which it occurs is Isidor. Hispal. *de Vit. et Ob. Sanct.* c. 81. See Mill p. 248.

the virginity of the Lord's mother, a feature possessed by his theory in common with the Epiphanian, he is at no loss for authorities: Ignatius, Polycarp, Irenæus, Justin, and many other 'eloquent apostolic men' occur to him at once[1]. But in support of his own account of the relationship he cannot, or at least does not, name a single writer; he simply offers it as a critical deduction from the statements of Scripture[2]. Again in his later writings, when he refers to the subject, his tone is the same: '*Some* suppose them to have been sons of Joseph: it is *my* opinion, *I* have maintained in my book against Helvidius, that they were the children of Mary the Virgin's sister[3].' And the whole tenor of patristic evidence, as I shall hope to show, is in accordance with this tone. No decisive instance can be produced of a writer holding Jerome's view, before it was propounded by Jerome himself.

(ii) and does not hold it consistently,

(2) *Jerome does not hold his theory staunchly and consistently.* The references to the subject in his works taken in chronological order will speak for themselves. The theory is first propounded, as we saw, in the treatise against Helvidius written about 383, when he was a young man. Even here his main point is the perpetual virginity of the Lord's mother, to which his own special solution is quite subordinate: he speaks of himself as not caring to fight hard ('contentiosum funem non traho') for the identity of Mary of Cleophas with Mary the mother of James and Joses, though this is the pivot of his theory. And, as time advances, he seems to hold to his hypothesis more and more loosely. In his commentary on the Epistle to the Galatians (i. 19) written about 387 he speaks very vaguely: he remembers, he says, having when at Rome written a treatise on the subject, with which such as it is he ought to be satisfied ('qualiacunque sunt illa quae scripsimus his contenti esse debemus'); after which he goes on inconsistently

[1] See however below, p. 278, note 1.

[2] He sets aside the appeal to authority thus: 'Verum nugas terimus, et fonte veritatis omisso opinionum rivulos consectamur,' *adv. Helvid.* 17.

[3] *de Vir. Illustr.* 2 'ut *nonnulli* existimant, Joseph ex alia uxore; ut autem *mihi* videtur Mariae sororis matris Domini......filius'; *Comment. in Matth.* xii. 49 (VII. p. 86) '*Quidam* fratres Domini de alia uxore Joseph filios suspicantur...*nos* autem, sicut in libro quem contra Helvidium scripsimus continetur etc.'

but wavers in his view, enough, 'Suffice it now to say that James was called the Lord's brother on account of his high character, his incomparable faith, and extraordinary wisdom: the other Apostles also are called brothers (John xx. 17; comp. Ps. xxii. 22), but he preeminently so, to whom the Lord at His departure had committed the sons of His mother (i.e. the members of the Church of Jerusalem)'; with more to the same effect: and he concludes by showing that the term Apostle, so far from being confined to the Twelve, has a very wide use, adding that it was 'a monstrous error to identify this James with the Apostle the brother of John[1].' In his Catalogue of Illustrious Men (A.D. 392) and in his Commentary on St Matthew (A.D. 398) he adheres to his earlier opinion, referring in the passages already quoted[2] to his treatise against Helvidius, and taunting those who considered the Lord's brethren to be the sons of Joseph by a former wife with 'following the ravings of the apocryphal writings and inventing a wretched creature (mulierculam) Melcha

and seems at length to abandon it. or Escha by name[3].' Yet after all in a still later work, the Epistle to Hedibia (about 406 or 407), enumerating the Maries of the Gospels he mentions Mary of Cleophas the maternal aunt of the Lord and Mary the mother of James and Joses as distinct persons, adding 'although others contend that the mother of James and

[1] 'Quod autem exceptis duodecim quidam vocentur apostoli, illud in causa est, omnes qui Dominum viderant et eum postea praedicabant fuisse apostolos appellatos'; and then after giving instances (among others 1 Cor. xv. 7) he adds, 'Unde vehementer erravit qui arbitratus est Jacobum hunc de evangelio esse apostolum fratrem Johannis;... hic autem Jacobus episcopus Hierosolymorum primus fuit cognomento Justus etc.' (VII. p. 396). These are just the arguments which would be brought by one maintaining the Epiphanian account. Altogether Jerome's language here is that of a man who has committed himself to a theory of which he has misgivings, and yet from which he is not bold enough to break loose.

[2] See p. 259, note 3.

[3] 'Sequentes deliramenta apocryphorum et quandam Melcham vel Escham mulierculam confingentes.' *Comm. in Matth.* l. c. 'Nemo non videt,' says Blom, p. 116, 'illud nomen אשה [wife, woman] esse mere fictitium, nec minus posterius [prius] מלכה [queen].' (Comp. Julius Africanus in Routh's *Rel. Sacr.* II. p. 233, 339.) If so, the work must have been the production of some Jewish Christian. But Escha is not a very exact representation of אשה (Ishah). On the other hand, making allowance for the uncertain vocalisation of the Hebrew, the two daughters of Haran (Gen. xi. 29) bear identically the same names: 'the father of Milcah (LXX Μελχά) and the father of Iscah (יסכה) LXX Ἰεσχά).' Doubtless these names were borrowed thence.

Joses was His aunt[1].' Yet this identification, of which he here speaks with such indifference, was the keystone of his own theory. Can it be that by his long residence in Bethlehem, having the Palestinian tradition brought more prominently before him, he first relaxed his hold of and finally relinquished his own hypothesis?

If these positions are correct, the Hieronymian view has no claim to any traditional sanction—in other words, there is no reason to believe that time has obliterated any secondary evidence in its favour—and it must therefore be investigated on its own merits.

And compact and plausible as it may seem at first sight, the theory exposes, when examined, many vulnerable parts. Objections to Jerome's theory.

(1) The instances alleged notwithstanding, the sense thus assigned to 'brethren' seems to be unsupported by biblical usage. (1) Use of the word Brethren. In an affectionate and earnest appeal intended to move the sympathies of the hearer, a speaker might not unnaturally address a relation or a friend or even a fellow-countryman as his 'brother.' And even when speaking of such to a third person he might through warmth of feeling and under certain aspects so designate him. But it is scarcely conceivable that the cousins of any one should be commonly and indeed exclusively styled his 'brothers' by indifferent persons; still less, that one cousin in particular should be singled out and described in this loose way, 'James the Lord's brother.'

(2) But again: the Hieronymian theory when completed supposes two, if not three, of the Lord's brethren to be in the number of the Twelve. (2) Relation of the Lord's brethren to the Twelve, This is hardly reconcileable with the place they hold in the Evangelical narratives, where they appear sometimes as distinct from, sometimes as antagonistic to the Twelve. Only a short time before the crucifixion they are disbelievers in the Lord's divine mission (John vii. 5). Is it likely that St John would have made this unqualified statement, if it were true of one only or at most of two out of the four? Jerome sees the difficulty and meets it by saying that James was 'not one of those that disbelieved.' But what if Jude and Simon also belong to the Twelve? After the Lord's Ascension, it is true, His brethren appear in company with

[1] *Epist.* cxx, 1. p. 826. Comp. Tischendorf's *Evang. Apocr.* p. 104.

the Apostles, and apparently by this time their unbelief has been converted into faith. Yet even on this later occasion, though with the Twelve, they are distinguished from the Twelve; for the latter are described as assembling in prayer 'with the women and Mary the mother of Jesus and [with] His brethren' (Acts i. 14).

especially James and Jude.

And scarcely more consistent is this theory with what we know of James and Jude in particular. James, as the resident bishop or presiding elder of the mother Church, held a position hardly compatible with the world-wide duties which devolved on the Twelve. It was the essential feature of his office that he should be stationary; of theirs, that they should move about from place to place. If on the other hand he appears sometimes to be called an Apostle (though not one of the passages alleged is free from ambiguity), this term is by no means confined to the Twelve and might therefore be applied to him in its wider sense, as it is to Barnabas[1]. Again, Jude on his part seems to disclaim the title of an Apostle (ver. 17); and if so, he cannot have been one of the Twelve.

(3) Their connexion with Joseph and Mary.

(3) But again: the Lord's brethren are mentioned in the Gospels in connexion with Joseph His reputed father and Mary His mother, never once with Mary of Clopas (the assumed wife of Alphæus). It would surely have been otherwise, if the latter Mary were really their mother.

(4) James the less.

(4) Jerome lays great stress on the epithet *minor* applied to James, as if it implied *two only*, and even those who impugn his theory seem generally to acquiesce in his rendering. But the Greek gives not 'James the Less' but 'James the *little*' (ὁ μικρός). Is it not most natural then to explain this epithet of his height[2]? 'There were many of the name of James,' says Hegesippus, and the short stature of one of these might well serve as a distinguishing mark. This interpretation at all events must be regarded as more probable than explaining it either of his comparative youth or of inferior rank and influence. It will be remembered that there

[1] See above, p. 95.

[2] As in Xen. *Mem.* I. 4. 2 Ἀριστόδημον τὸν μικρὸν ἐπικαλούμενον, referring to stature, as appears from Plato, *Symp.* 173 B; and in Arist. *Ran.* 708 Κλειγένης ὁ μικρός.

is no Scriptural or early sanction for speaking of the son of Zebedee as 'James the Great.'

(5) The mention of Jude in the lists of the Twelve.

(5) The manner in which Jude is mentioned in the lists of the Twelve is on this hypothesis full of perplexities. In the first place it is necessary to translate Ἰακώβου not 'the son' but 'the brother of James,' though the former is the obvious rendering and is supported by two of the earliest versions, the Peshito Syriac and the Thebaic, while two others, the Old Latin and Memphitic, leave the ellipsis unsupplied and thus preserve the ambiguity of the original. But again, if Judas were the brother of James, would not the Evangelist's words have run more naturally, 'James the son of Alphæus and Jude his brother,' or 'James and Jude the sons of Alphæus,' as in the case of the other pairs of brothers? Then again, if Simon Zelotes is not a brother of James, why is he inserted by St Luke between the two? If he also is a brother, why is the designation of brotherhood (Ἰακώβου) attached to the name of Judas only?

Moreover in the different lists of the three Evangelists the Apostle in question is designated in three different ways. In St Matthew (x. 3) he is called Lebbæus (at least according to a well-supported reading); in St Mark (iii. 18) Thaddæus; and in St Luke 'Jude of James.' St John again having occasion to mention him (xiv. 22) distinguishes him by a negative, 'Judas not Iscariot[1].' Is

[1] The perplexity is increased by the Curetonian Syriac, which for Ἰούδας οὐχ ὁ Ἰσκαριώτης reads ܝܗܘܕܐ ܬܐܘܡܐ, 'Judas Thomas,' i.e. 'Judas the Twin.' It seems therefore that the translator took the person intended by St John to be not the *Judas Jacobi* in the list of the Twelve, but the *Thomas Didymus*, for Thomas was commonly called Judas in the Syrian Church; e.g. Euseb. *H. E.* i. 13 Ἰούδας ὁ καὶ Θωμᾶς, and *Acta Thomae* 1 Ἰούδᾳ Θωμᾷ τῷ καὶ Διδύμῳ (ed. Tisch. p. 190); see Assemani *Bibl. Orient.* I. pp. 100, 318, Cureton's *Syriac Gospels* p. li, *Anc. Syr. Documents* p. 33. As Thomas (Δίδυμος), 'the Twin,' is properly a surname, and this Apostle must have had some other name, there seems no reason for doubting this very early tradition that he also was a Jude. At the same time it is highly improbable that St John should have called the same Apostle elsewhere Thomas (Joh. xi. 16, xiv. 5, xx. 24 etc.) and here Judas, and we may therefore conclude that he is speaking of two different persons. The name of the other brother is supplied in *Clem. Hom.* ii. 1 προσέτι δὲ Θωμᾶς καὶ Ἐλιέζερος οἱ δίδυμοι.

The Thebaic version again for οὐχ ὁ Ἰσκαριώτης substitutes ὁ Κανανίτης. Similarly in Matth. x. 3 for Θαδδαῖος some of the most important MSS of the Old Latin have 'Judas Zelotes'; and in the Canon of Gelasius Jude the writer of the epistle is so designated. This points to some connexion or confusion with Simon Zelotes. See p. 258, note.

it possible, if he were the Lord's brother Judas, he would in all these places have escaped being so designated, when this designation would have fixed the person meant at once?

(6) Punctuation of Joh. xix. 25.

(6) Lastly; in order to maintain the Hieronymian theory it is necessary to retain the common punctuation of John xix. 25, thus making 'Mary of Clopas' the Virgin's sister. But it is at least improbable that two sisters should have borne the same name. The case of the Herodian family is scarcely parallel, for Herod was a family name, and it is unlikely that a humble Jewish household should have copied a practice which must lead to so much confusion. Here it is not unlikely that a tradition underlies the Peshito rendering which inserts a conjunction: 'His mother and his mother's sister, *and* Mary of Cleophas and Mary Magdalene[1].' The Greek at all events admits, even if it does not favour, this interpretation, for the arrangement of names in couples has a parallel in the lists of the Apostles (e.g. Matt. x. 2—4).

Jerome's hypothesis must be abandoned

I have shown then, if I mistake not, that St Jerome pleaded no traditional authority for his theory, and that therefore the evidence in its favour is to be sought in Scripture alone. I have examined the Scriptural evidence, and the conclusion seems to be, that though this hypothesis, supplemented as it has been by subsequent writers, presents several striking coincidences which attract attention, yet it involves on the other hand a combination of difficulties—many of these arising out of the very elements in the

[1] See Wieseler *Die Söhne Zebedäi etc.* p. 672. This writer identifies the sister of the Lord's mother (John xix. 25) with Salome (Mark xv. 40, xvi. 1), who again is generally identified with the mother of Zebedee's children (Matt. xxvii. 56); and thus James and John, the sons of Zebedee, are made cousins of our Lord. Compare the pseudo-Papias, p. 273, note; and see the various reading 'Ιωάννης for 'Ιωσὴφ in the list of the Lord's brethren in Matt. xiii. 55. But as we are told that there were *many other women* present also (Mark xv. 41, comp. Luke xxiv. 10),—one of whom, Joanna, is mentioned by name—both these identifications must be considered precarious. It would be strange that no hint should be given in the Gospels of the relationship of the sons of Zebedee to our Lord, if it existed.

The Jerusalem Syriac lectionary gives the passage John xix. 25 not less than three times. In two of these places (pp. 387, 541, the exception being p. 445) a stop is put after 'His mother's sister,' thus separating the words from 'Mary of Cleophas' and suggesting by punctuation the same interpretation which the Peshito fixes by inserting a conjunction.

hypothesis which produce the coincidences—which more than counterbalances these secondary arguments in its favour, and in fact must lead to its rejection, if any hypothesis less burdened with difficulties can be found.

Thus, as compared with the Hieronymian view, both the Epiphanian and the Helvidian have higher claims to acceptance. They both assign to the word brethren its natural meaning; they both recognise the main facts related of the Lord's brethren in the Gospels—their unbelief, their distinctness from the Twelve, their connexion with Joseph and Mary—and they both avoid the other difficulties which the Hieronymian theory creates.

and replaced by one of the remaining two.

And moreover they both exhibit a coincidence which deserves notice. A very short time before the Lord's death His brethren refuse to accept His mission: they are still unbelievers. Immediately after His ascension we find them gathered together with the Apostles, evidently recognising Him as their Master. Whence comes this change? Surely the crucifixion of one who professed to be the Messiah was not likely to bring it about. He had claimed to be King of Israel and He had been condemned as a malefactor: He had promised His followers a triumph and He had left them persecution. Would not all this confirm rather than dissipate their former unbelief? An incidental statement of St Paul explains all; 'Then He was seen of James.' At the time when St Paul wrote, there was but one person eminent enough in the Church to be called James simply without any distinguishing epithet—the Lord's brother, the bishop of Jerusalem. It might therefore reasonably be concluded that this James is here meant. And this view is confirmed by an extant fragment of the Gospel according to the Hebrews, the most important of all the apocryphal gospels, which seems to have preserved more than one true tradition, and which expressly relates the appearance of our Lord to His brother James[1] after His resurrection.

A coincidence common to both.

This interposition, we may suppose, was the turning-point in the religious life of the Lord's brethren; the veil was removed at

[1] See below, p. 274.

once and for ever from their hearts. In this way the antagonistic notices in the Gospels—first the disbelief of the Lord's brethren, and then their assembling together with the Apostles—are linked together; and harmony is produced out of discord.

Objections to both.

Two objections however are brought against both these theories, which the Hieronymian escapes.

(1) Repetition of names.

(1) They both, it is objected, assume the existence of two pairs of cousins bearing the same names, James and Joseph the sons of Alphæus, and James and Joseph the Lord's brothers. If moreover we accept the statement of Hegesippus[1] that James was succeeded in the bishopric of Jerusalem by Symeon son of Clopas, and also admit the identification of Clopas with Alphæus, we get a third name Symeon or Simeon common to the two families. Let us see what this objection really amounts to.

Cousinhood on either mothers

It will be seen that the cousinhood of these persons is represented as a cousinhood on the mothers' side, and that it depends on three assumptions: (1) The identification of James the son of Alphæus in the list of the Twelve with James the Little the son of Mary: (2) The identification of 'Mary of Clopas' in St John with Mary the mother of James and Joses in the other Evangelists: (3) The correctness of the received punctuation of John xix. 25, which makes 'Mary of Clopas' the Virgin's sister. If any one of these be rejected, this cousinhood falls to the ground. Yet of these three assumptions the second alone can safely be pronounced more likely than not[2] (though we are expressly told that 'many other women' were present), for it avoids the unnecessary multiplication of Maries. The first must be considered highly doubtful, seeing that James was a very common name; while the third is most improbable, for it gives two sisters both called Mary—a difficulty far surpassing that of supposing two or even three cousins bearing the same name. On the other hand, if, admitting the second identification and supplying the ellipsis in 'Mary of Clopas' by 'wife[3],' we combine

[1] See below, p. 276 sq.

[2] Eusebius however makes 'Mary of Clopas' a different person from Mary the mother of James and Joses; *Quaest. ad Marin.* ii. 5 (*Op.* IV. p. 945, Migne).

[3] As ἡ τοῦ Κλωπᾶ may mean either the *daughter* or the *wife* or the *mother*

with it the statement of Hegesippus[1] that Clopas the father of Symeon was brother of Joseph, we get three cousins, James, Joses, and Symeon, *on their fathers' side*. Yet this result again must be considered on the whole improbable. I see no reason indeed for doubting the testimony of Hegesippus, who was perhaps born during the lifetime of this Symeon, and is likely to have been well informed. But the chances are against the other hypotheses, on which it depends, being both of them correct. The identification of Clopas and Alphæus will still remain an open question[2].

or fathers' side improbable.

of Clopas, this expression has been combined with the statement of Hegesippus in various ways. See for instance the apocryphal gospels, *Pseudo-Matth. Evang.* 52 (ed. Tisch. p. 104), *Evang. Inf. Arab.* 29 (ib. p. 186), and the marginal note on the Philoxenian version, Joh. xix. 25, besides other references which will be given in the account of the patristic authorities.

[1] The statement of Hegesippus suggests a solution which would remove the difficulty. We might suppose the two Maries to have been called sisters, as having been married to two brothers; but is there any authority for ascribing to the Jews an extension of the term 'sister' which modern usage scarcely sanctions?

[2] Of the three names *Alphæus* (the father of Levi or Matthew, Mark ii. 14, and the father of James, Matt. x. 3, Mark iii. 18, Luke vi. 15, Acts i. 13), *Clopas* (the husband or father or son of Mary, Joh. xix. 25), and *Cleopas* (the disciple journeying to Emmaus, Luke xxiv. 18), it is considered that the two former are probably identical, and the two latter certainly distinct. Both positions may be disputed with some reason. In forming a judgment, the following points deserve to be considered; (1) In the Greek text there is no variation of reading worth mentioning; Clopas is certainly the reading in St John, and Cleopas in St Luke. (2) The versions however bring them together. Cleopæ (or Cleophæ) is read in the Peshito, Old Latin, Memphitic, Vulgate, and Armenian text of St John. (3) Of these the evidence of the Peshito is particularly important in a matter relating to Aramaic names. While for Ἀλφαῖος in all five places it restores what was doubtless the original Aramaic form ܚܠܦܝ, Chalphai; on the other hand, it gives the same word ܩܠܝܘܦܐ Kleōpha (i.e. Κλεόπας) in Luke xxiv. 18 and in John xix. 25, if the printed texts may be trusted. The Jerusalem Syriac too renders Κλωπᾶς by ܩܠܝܘܦܣ (Kleophas), and Ἀλφαῖος by ܚܠܦܝ (Chalphai). (4) The form Κλωπᾶς, which St John's text gives, is confirmed by Hegesippus (Euseb. *H. E.* iii. 11), and there is every reason to believe that this was a common mode of writing some proper name or other with those acquainted with Aramaic; but it is difficult to see why, if the word intended to be represented were Chalphai, they should not have reproduced it more exactly in Greek. The name Χαλφὶ in fact does occur in 1 Macc. xi. 70. (5) It is true that Κλεόπας is strictly a Greek name contracted from Κλεόπατρος, like Ἀντίπας from Ἀντίπατρος, etc. But it was a common practice with the Jews to adopt the genuine Greek name which bore the closest resemblance in sound to their own Aramaic name, either side by side with it or in place of it, as Simon for Symeon, Jason for Jesus; and thus a man, whose real Aramaic name was Clopas, might grecize the word and call himself Cleopas. On these grounds it appears to me that, viewing the question as one of names merely, it is quite as reasonable to identify Clopas with Cleopas as with

The names are common.

But, whether they were cousins or not, does the fact of two families having two or three names in common constitute any real difficulty? Is not this a frequent occurrence among ourselves? It must be remembered too that the Jewish names in ordinary use at this time were very few, and that these three, James, Joses, and Symeon, were among the most common, being consecrated in the affections of the Jews from patriarchal times. In the list of the Twelve the name of James appears twice, Symeon twice. In the New Testament no less than twelve persons bear the name of Symeon or Simon, and nearly as many that of Joseph or Joses[1].

Alphæus. But the identification of names does not carry with it the identification of persons. St Paul's Epaphras for instance is probably a different person from his Epaphroditus.

A Jewish name 'Alfius' occurs in an inscription ALFIVS . IVDA . ARCON . ARCOSINAGOGVS (Inscr. Gudii, p. cclxiii. 5), and possibly this is the Latin substitute for Chalphai or Chalphi, as 'Αλφαῖος is the Greek; Alfius being a not uncommon Latin name. One would be tempted to set down his namesake also, the 'fenerator Alfius' or 'Alphius' of Horace (*Epod.* ii. 67, see Columella I. 7. 2), for a fellow-countryman, if his talk were not so pagan.

[1] I am arguing on the supposition that Joses and Joseph are the same name, but this is at least doubtful. In St Matthew, according to the best authorities, the Lord's brother (xiii. 55) is 'Ιωσήφ, the son of Mary (xxvii. 56) 'Ιωσῆς. In St Mark on the other hand the latter word is found (the genitive being differently written 'Ιωσῆτος or 'Ιωσῆ, though probably Tregelles is right in preferring the former in all three passages), whether referring to the Lord's brother (vi. 3) or to the son of Mary (xv. 40, 47). Thus if existing authorities in the text of St Mark are to be trusted, there is no distinction between the names. Yet I am disposed to think with Wieseler (*die Söhne Zebedäi etc.* p. 678) that St Matthew's text suggests the real difference, and that the original reading in Mark vi. 3 was 'Ιωσήφ; but if so, the corruption was very ancient and very general, for 'Ιωσήφ is found in ℵ alone of the uncial manuscripts. A similar confusion of these names appears in the case of Barsabbas, Acts i. 23, and Barnabas, iv. 36; in the former case we find a various reading 'Joses' for 'Joseph,' in the latter we should almost certainly read 'Joseph' for 'Joses' of the received text. I am disposed to think the identification of the names Joses and Joseph improbable for two reasons: (1) It seems unlikely that the same name should be represented in Greek by two such divergent forms as 'Ιωσῆς, making a genitive 'Ιωσῆτος, and 'Ιωσήφ or 'Ιώσηπος, which perhaps (replaced by a genuine Greek name) became 'Ηγήσιππος. (2) The Peshito in the case of the commoner Hebrew or Aramaic names restores the original form in place of the somewhat disfigured Greek equivalent, e.g. Juchanon for 'Ιωάννης, Zabdai for Ζεβεδαῖος. Following this rule, it ought, if the names were identical, to have restored ܝܘܣܦ (Joseph) for the Greek 'Ιωσῆς, in place of which it has ܝܘܣܐ (Jōsī, Jausī, or Jūsī). In Matt. xxvii. 56, Mark xv. 40, the Memphitic Version separates Μαρία [ἡ τοῦ] 'Ιακώβου [τοῦ μικροῦ] and 'Ιωσῆ[τος] μήτηρ, making them two different persons. [On the other hand, similar instances of abbreviation, e.g. Ashe for Asher, Jochana for Jochanan, Shabba for Shabbath, are produced; see Delitzsch in Laurent *Neutest. Stud.* p. 168.]

In the index to Josephus may be counted nineteen Josephs, and twenty-five Simons[1].

And moreover is not the difficulty, if difficulty there be, diminished rather than increased on the supposition of the cousinhood of these two families? The name of a common ancestor or a common relative naturally repeats itself in households connected with each other. And from this point of view it is worthy of notice that the names in question actually occur in the genealogies of our Lord. Joseph's father is Jacob or James in St Matthew (i. 15, 16); and in St Luke's table, exclusively of our Lord's reputed father, the name Joseph or Joses occurs twice at least[2] in a list of thirty-four direct ancestors.

(2) 'Mary the mother of James.'

(2) When a certain Mary is described as 'the mother of James,' is it not highly probable that the person intended should be the most celebrated of the name—James the Just, the bishop of Jerusalem, the Lord's brother? This objection to both the Epiphanian and Helvidian theories is at first sight not without force, but it will not bear examination. Why, we may ask, if the best known of all the Jameses were intended here, should it be necessary in some passages to add the name of a brother Joses also, who was a person of no special mark in the Church (Matt. xxvii. 56, Mark xv. 40)? Why again in others should this Mary be designated 'the mother of Joses' alone (Mark xv. 47), the name of his more famous brother being suppressed? In only two passages is she called simply 'the mother of James'; in Mark xvi. 1, where it is explained by the fuller description which has gone before 'the mother of James and Joses' (xv. 40); and in Luke xxiv. 10, where no such explanation can be given. It would seem then that this Mary and this James, though not the most famous of their respective names and therefore not at once distinguishable when mentioned alone,

[1] The popularity of this name is probably due to Simon Maccabæus.

[2] And perhaps not more than twice Ἰωσήφ (vv. 24, 30). In ver. 26 Ἰωσὴχ seems to be the right reading, where the received text has Ἰωσήφ; and in ver. 29 Ἰησοῦ, where it has Ἰωσῆ. Possibly Ἰωσὴχ may be a corruption for Ἰωσὴφ through the confusion of ף and ך, which in their older forms resemble each other closely; but if so, it is a corruption not of St Luke's text, but of the Hebrew or Aramaic document from which the genealogy was derived.

were yet sufficiently well known to be discriminated from others, when their names appeared in conjunction.

The two theories compared. The objections then which may be brought against both these theories in common are not very serious; and up to this point in the investigation they present equal claims to acceptance. The next step will be to compare them together, in order to decide which of the two must yield to the other.

(1) Relation of the brethren to Joseph and Mary. 1. The Epiphanian view assumes that the Lord's brethren had really no relationship with Him; and so far the Helvidian has the advantage. But this advantage is rather seeming than real. It is very natural that those who called Joseph His father should call Joseph's sons His brethren. And it must be remembered that this designation is given to Joseph not only by strangers from whom at all events the mystery of the Incarnation was veiled, but by the Lord's mother herself who knew all (Luke ii. 48). Even the Evangelist himself, about whose belief in the miraculous conception of Christ there can be no doubt, allows himself to speak of Joseph and Mary as 'His father and mother' and 'His parents[1].' Nor again is it any argument in favour of the Helvidian account as compared with the Epiphanian, that the Lord's brethren are found in company of Mary rather than of Joseph. Joseph appears in the evangelical history for the last time when Jesus is twelve years old (Luke ii. 43); during the Lord's ministry he is never once seen, though Mary comes forward again and again. There can be little doubt therefore that he had died meanwhile.

(2) Virginity of Mary. 2. Certain expressions in the evangelical narratives are said to imply that Mary bore other children besides the Lord, and it is even asserted that no unprejudiced person could interpret them otherwise. The justice of this charge may be fairly questioned. The context in each case seems to suggest another explanation of these expressions, which does not decide anything one way or the other. St Matthew writes that Joseph 'knew not' his wife '*till* (ἕως οὗ)

[1] Luke ii. 33 ὁ πατὴρ αὐτοῦ καὶ ἡ μήτηρ, ii. 41, 43 οἱ γονεῖς αὐτοῦ, the correct reading. Later transcribers have taken offence and substituted 'Joseph and Mary,' 'Joseph and His mother,' in all three places.

she brought forth a son' (i. 25)[1]; while St Luke speaks of her bringing forth 'her *firstborn* son' (ii. 7). St Matthew's expression however, '*till* she brought forth,' as appears from the context, is intended simply to show that Jesus was not begotten in the course of nature; and thus, while it denies any previous intercourse with her husband, it neither asserts nor implies any subsequent intercourse[2]. Again, the prominent idea conveyed by the term 'firstborn' to a Jew would be not the birth of other children, but the special consecration of this one. The typical reference in fact is foremost in the mind of St Luke, as he himself explains it, '*Every male that openeth the womb* shall be called holy to the Lord' (ii. 23). Thus 'firstborn' does not necessarily suggest 'later-born,' any more than 'son' suggests 'daughter.' The two words together describe the condition under which in obedience to the law a child was consecrated to God. The 'firstborn son' is in fact the Evangelist's equivalent for the 'male that openeth the womb.'

It may indeed be fairly urged that, if the Evangelists had considered the perpetual virginity of the Lord's mother a matter of such paramount importance as it was held to be in the fourth and following centuries, they would have avoided expressions which are at least ambiguous and might be taken to imply the contrary; but these expressions are not in themselves fatal to such a belief.

Whether in itself the sentiment on which this belief was founded be true or false, is a fit subject of enquiry; nor can the present question be considered altogether without reference to it. If it be true, then the Epiphanian theory has an advantage over the Helvidian, as respecting or at least not disregarding it; if false, then it may be thought to have suggested that theory, as it certainly did the Hieronymian, and to this extent the theory itself must lie under suspicion. Into this enquiry however it will not be necessary to enter. Only let me say that it is not altogether correct to represent this belief as suggested solely by the false asceticism of the early Church which exalted virginity at the expense of married life. It

[1] τὸν πρωτότοκον ought to be rejected from St Matthew's text, having been interpolated from Luke ii. 7.

[2] For parallel instances see Mill, p. 304 sq.

appears in fact to be due quite as much to another sentiment which the fathers fantastically expressed by a comparison between the conception and the burial of our Lord. As after death His body was placed in a sepulchre 'wherein never man before was laid,' so it seemed fitting that the womb consecrated by His presence should not thenceforth have borne any offspring of man. It may be added also, that the Epiphanian view prevailed especially in Palestine where there was less disposition than elsewhere to depreciate married life, and prevailed too at a time when extreme ascetic views had not yet mastered the Church at large.

(3) Our Lord's dying words.

3. But one objection has been hurled at the Helvidian theory with great force, and as it seems to me with fatal effect, which is powerless against the Epiphanian[1]. Our Lord in His dying moments commended His mother to the keeping of St John; 'Woman, behold thy son.' The injunction was forthwith obeyed, and 'from that hour that disciple took her unto his own home' (John xix. 26, 27). Yet according to the Helvidian view she had no less than four sons besides daughters living at the time. Is it conceivable that our Lord would thus have snapped asunder the most sacred ties of natural affection? The difficulty is not met by the fact that her own sons were still unbelievers. This fact would scarcely have been allowed to override the paramount duties of filial piety. But even when so explained, what does this hypothesis require us to believe? Though within a few days a special appearance is vouchsafed to one of these brethren, who is destined to rule the mother Church of Jerusalem, and all alike are converted to the faith of Christ; yet she, their mother, living in the same city and joining with them in a common worship (Acts i. 14), is consigned to the care of a stranger of whose house she becomes henceforth the inmate.

Conclusion.

Thus it would appear that, taking the scriptural notices alone, the Hieronymian account must be abandoned; while of the remaining two the balance of the argument is against the Helvidian and in favour of the Epiphanian. To what extent the last-men-

[1] This argument is brought forward not only by Jerome, but also by Hilary of Poitiers, Ambrose, and Epiphanius, who all held the view which I have designated by the name of the last of the three.

tioned theory can plead the prestige of tradition, will be seen from the following catena of references to the fathers and other early Christian writings[1].

[1] The testimony of Papias is frequently quoted at the head of the patristic authorities, as favouring the view of Jerome. The passage in question is an extract, to which the name of this very ancient writer is prefixed, in a Bodleian MS, no. 2397, of the date 1302 or 1303. It is given in Grabe's *Spicil.* II. p. 34, Routh's *Rel. Sacr.* I. p. 16, and runs as follows: 'Maria mater Domini: Maria Cleophae, sive Alphei uxor, quae fuit mater Jacobi episcopi et apostoli et Symonis et Thadei et cujusdam Joseph: Maria Salome uxor Zebedei mater Joannis evangelistae et Jacobi: Maria Magdalene: istae quatuor in Evangelio reperiuntur. Jacobus et Judas et Joseph filii erant materterae Domini; Jacobus quoque et Joannes alterius materterae Domini fuerunt filii. Maria Jacobi minoris et Joseph mater, uxor Alphei, soror fuit Mariae matris Domini, quam Cleophae Joannes nominat vel a patre vel a gentilitatis familia vel alia causa. Maria Salome a viro vel a vico dicitur: hanc eandem Cleophae quidam dicunt quod duos viros habuerit. Maria dicitur illuminatrix sive stella maris, genuit enim lumen mundi; sermone autem Syro Domina nuncupatur, quia genuit Dominum.' Grabe's description 'ad marginem expresse adscriptum lego *Papia*' is incorrect; the name is not in the margin but over the passage as a title to it. The authenticity of this fragment is accepted by Mill, p. 238, and by Dean Alford on Matth. xiii. 55. Two writers also in Smith's *Biblical Dictionary* (s. vv. 'Brother' and 'James'), respectively impugning and maintaining the Hieronymian view, refer to it without suspicion. It is strange that able and intelligent critics should not have seen through a fabrication which is so manifestly spurious. Not to mention the difficulties in which we are involved by some of the statements, the following reasons seem conclusive: (1) The last sentence 'Maria dicitur etc.' is evidently very late, and is, as Dr Mill says, 'justly rejected by Grabe.' Grabe says, 'addidit is qui descripsit ex suo'; but the passage is continuous in the MS, and there is neither more nor less authority for assigning this to Papias than the remainder of the extract. (2) The statement about 'Maria uxor Alphei' is taken from Jerome (*adv. Helvid.*) almost word for word, as Dr Mill has seen; and it is purely arbitrary to reject this as spurious and accept the rest as genuine. (3) The writings of Papias were in Jerome's hands, and eager as he was to claim the support of authority, he could not have failed to refer to testimony which was so important and which so entirely confirms his view in the most minute points. Nor is it conceivable that a passage like this, coming from so early a writer, should not have impressed itself very strongly on the ecclesiastical tradition of the early centuries, whereas in fact we discover no traces of it.

For these reasons the extract seemed to be manifestly spurious; but I might have saved myself the trouble of examining the Bodleian MS and writing these remarks, if I had known at the time, that the passage was written by a mediæval namesake of the Bishop of Hierapolis, Papias the author of the 'Elementarium,' who lived in the 11th century. This seems to have been a standard work in its day, and was printed four times in the 15th century under the name of the Lexicon or Vocabulist. I have not had access to a printed copy, but there is a MS of the work (marked Kk. 4. 1) in the Cambridge University Library, the knowledge of which I owe to Mr Bradshaw, the librarian. The variations from the Bodleian extract are unimportant. It is strange that though Grabe actually mentions the later Papias the author of the Dictionary, and Routh copies his note, neither the one nor the other got on the right track.

Hebrew Gospel.

1. The GOSPEL ACCORDING TO THE HEBREWS, one of the earliest and most respectable of the apocryphal narratives, related that the Lord after His resurrection 'went to James and appeared to him; for James had sworn that he would not eat bread from that hour in which the Lord had drunk the cup (biberat calicem Dominus), till he saw Him risen from the dead.' Jesus therefore 'took bread and blessed it and brake it and gave it to James the Just and said to him, My brother, eat thy bread, for the Son of Man has risen from the dead' (Hieron. *de Vir. Illustr.* 2). I have adopted the reading 'Dominus,' as the Greek translation has Κύριος, and it also suits the context better; for the point of time which we should naturally expect is not the institution of the eucharist but the Lord's death[1]. Our Lord had more than once spoken of His sufferings under the image of draining the cup (Matt. xx. 22, 23, xxvi. 39, 42, Mark x. 38, 39, xiv. 36, Luke xxii. 42)[2]; and He is represented as using this metaphor here. If however we retain 'Domini,' it must be allowed that the writer represented James the Lord's brother as present at the last supper, but it does not follow that he regarded him as one of the Twelve. He may have assigned to him a sort of exceptional position such as he holds in the Clementines, apart from and in some respects superior to the Twelve, and thus his presence at this critical time would be accounted for. At all events this passage confirms the tradition that the James mentioned by St Paul (1 Cor. xv. 7) was the Lord's brother; while at the same time it is characteristic of a Judaic writer whose aim it would be to glorify the head of his Church at all hazards, that an appearance, which seems in reality to have been vouchsafed to this James to win him over from his unbelief, should be represented as a reward for his devotion.

Gospel of Peter.

2. The GOSPEL ACCORDING TO PETER was highly esteemed by the Docetæ of the second century. Towards the close of that century,

I made the discovery while the first edition of this work was passing through the press [1865].

[1] There might possibly have been an ambiguity in the Hebrew original owing to the absence of case-endings, as Blom suggests (p. 83): but it is more probable that a transcriber of Jerome carelessly wrote down the familiar phrase 'the cup of the Lord.'

[2] Comp. *Mart. Polyc.* 14 ἐν τῷ ποτηρίῳ τοῦ Χριστοῦ σου.

Serapion, bishop of Antioch, found it in circulation at Rhossus a Cilician town, and at first tolerated it: but finding on examination that, though it had much in common with the Gospels recognised by the Catholic Church, there were sentiments in it favourable to the heretical views that were secretly gaining ground there, he forbad its use. In the fragment of Serapion preserved by Eusebius (*H. E.* vi. 12)[1], from which our information is derived, he speaks of this apocryphal work as if it had been long in circulation, so that its date must be about the middle of the second century at the latest, and probably somewhat earlier. To this gospel Origen refers, as stating that the Lord's brethren were Joseph's sons by a former wife and thus maintaining the virginity of the Lord's mother[2].

3. PROTEVANGELIUM JACOBI, a purely fictitious but very early narrative, dating probably not later than the middle of the second century, represents Joseph as an old man when the Virgin was espoused to him, having sons of his own (§ 9, ed. Tisch. p. 18) but no daughters (§ 17, p. 31), and James the writer of the account apparently as grown up at the time of Herod's death (§ 25, p. 48). Following in this track, subsequent apocryphal narratives give a similar account with various modifications, in some cases naming Joseph's daughters or his wife. Such are the *Pseudo-Matthæi Evang.* (§ 32, ed. Tisch. p. 104), *Evang. de Nativ. Mar.* (§ 8, *ib.* p. 111), *Historia Joseph.* (§ 2, *ib.* p. 116), *Evang. Thomæ* (§ 16, p. 147), *Evang. Infant. Arab.* (§ 35, p. 191), besides the apocryphal Gospels mentioned by Jerome (*Comm. in Matth.* T. VII. p. 86) which were different from any now extant[3]. Doubtless these accounts, so far as they step beyond the incidents narrated in the Canonical Gospels, are pure fabrications, but the fabrications would scarcely have taken this form, if the Hieronymian view of the Lord's brethren had been received or even known when they were written. It is to these sources that Jerome refers when he taunts the holders of the Epiphanian view with following 'deliramenta apocryphorum.'

Protevangelium and other apocryphal gospels.

4. The EARLIEST VERSIONS, with the exception of the Old Latin

Older Versions.

[1] For this fragment see Routh's *Rel. Sacr.* I. p. 452, and Westcott *History of the Canon*, p. 385.

[2] See below, p. 281.

[3] As appears from the fact mentioned by Jerome; see above, p. 260, note 3.

and Memphitic which translate the Greek literally and preserve the same ambiguities, give renderings of certain passages bearing on the subject, which are opposed to the Hieronymian view. The CURETONIAN SYRIAC translates Μαρία Ἰακώβου (Luke xxiv. 10) 'Mary the *daughter* of James.' The PESHITO in John xix. 25 has, 'His mother and His mother's sister *and* Mary of Cleopha and Mary Magdalene'; and in Luke vi. 16, Acts i. 13, it renders 'Judas *son* of James.' One of the old Egyptian versions again, the THEBAIC, in John xix. 25 gives 'Mary *daughter* of Clopas,' and in Luke vi. 16, Acts i. 13 'Judas *son* of James.'

Clementine writings.

5. The CLEMENTINE HOMILIES, written, it would appear, not late in the second century to support a peculiar phase of Ebionism, speak of James as being '*called* the brother of the Lord' (ὁ λεχθεὶς ἀδελφὸς τοῦ Κυρίου, xi. 35), an expression which has been variously interpreted as favouring all three hypotheses (see Blom, p. 88: Schliemann *Clement.* pp. 8, 213), and is indecisive in itself[1]. It is more important to observe that in the Epistle of Clement prefixed to this work and belonging to the same cycle of writings James is styled not Apostle, but Bishop of Bishops, and seems to be distinguished from and in some respects exalted above the Twelve.

6. In the portion of the Clementine Recognitions, which seems to have been founded on the ASCENTS OF JAMES, another very early Ebionite writing[2], the distinction thus implied in the Homilies is explicitly stated. The Twelve Apostles after disputing severally with Caiaphas give an account of their conference to James the chief of Bishops; while James the son of Alphæus is distinctly mentioned among the Twelve as one of the disputants (i. 59).

Hegesippus.

7. HEGESIPPUS (about 160), a Hebrew Christian of Palestine, writes as follows: 'After the martyrdom of James the Just on the same charge as the Lord, his paternal uncle's child Symeon the son of Clopas is next made bishop, who was put forward by all as the second in succession, being cousin of the Lord' (μετὰ τὸ μαρτυρῆσαι Ἰάκωβον

[1] The word λεχθεὶς is most naturally taken, I think, to refer to the *reputed* brotherhood of James, as a consequence of the reputed fatherhood of Joseph, and thus to favour the Epiphanian view. See the expressions of Hegesippus, and of Eusebius, pp. 277, 278.

[2] See the next dissertation.

τὸν δίκαιον ὡς καὶ ὁ Κύριος ἐπὶ τῷ αὐτῷ λόγῳ, πάλιν ὁ ἐκ τοῦ θείου αὐτοῦ Συμεὼν ὁ τοῦ Κλωπᾶ καθίσταται ἐπίσκοπος, ὃν προέθεντο πάντες ὄντα ἀνεψιὸν τοῦ Κυρίου δεύτερον[1], Euseb. *H. E.* iv. 22). If the passage be correctly rendered thus (and this rendering alone seems intelligible[2]), Hegesippus distinguishes between the relationships of James the Lord's brother and Symeon His cousin. So again, referring apparently to this passage, he in another fragment (Euseb. *H. E.* iii. 32) speaks of 'the child of the Lord's paternal uncle, the aforesaid Symeon son of Clopas' (ὁ ἐκ θείου τοῦ Κυρίου ὁ προειρημένος Συμεὼν υἱὸς Κλωπᾶ), to which Eusebius adds, 'for Hegesippus relates that Clopas was the brother of Joseph.' Thus in Hegesippus Symeon is never once called the Lord's brother, while James is always so designated. And this argument powerful in itself is materially strengthened by the fact that, where Hegesippus has occasion to mention Jude, he too like James is styled 'the Lord's brother'; 'There still survived members of the Lord's family (οἱ ἀπὸ γένους τοῦ Κυρίου) grandsons of Judas who was called His brother according to the flesh' (τοῦ κατὰ σάρκα λεγομένου αὐτοῦ ἀδελφοῦ); Euseb. *H. E.* iii. 20. In this passage the word 'called' seems to me to point to the Epiphanian rather than the Helvidian view, the brotherhood of these brethren, like the fatherhood of Joseph, being reputed but not real. In yet another passage (Euseb. *H. E.* ii. 23) Hegesippus relates that 'the Church was committed in conjunction with the Apostles[3] to the charge of (διαδέχεται τὴν ἐκκλησίαν μετὰ τῶν ἀποστόλων) the Lord's brother James,

[1] For δεύτερον comp. Euseb. *H. E.* iii. 14.

[2] A different meaning however has been assigned to the words: πάλιν and δεύτερον being taken to signify '*another* child of his uncle, *another* cousin,' and thus the passage has been represented as favouring the Hieronymian view. So for instance Mill p. 253, Schaf p. 64. On the other hand see Credner *Einl.* p. 575, Neander *Pflanz.* p. 559 (4te aufl.). To this rendering the presence of the definite article alone seems fatal (ὁ ἐκ τοῦ θείου not ἕτερος τῶν ἐκ τοῦ θείου); but indeed the whole passage appears to be framed so as to distinguish the relationships of the two persons; whereas, had the author's object been to represent Symeon as a brother of James, no more circuitous mode could well have been devised for the purpose of stating so very simple a fact. Let me add that Eusebius (*l.c.*) and Epiphanius (*Haeres.* pp. 636, 1039, 1046, ed. Petav.) must have interpreted the words as I have done.

Whether αὐτοῦ should be referred to Ἰάκωβον or to Κύριος is doubtful. If to the former, this alone decides the meaning of the passage. This seems the more natural reference of the two, but the form of expression will admit either.

[3] Jerome (*de Vir. Ill.* § 2) renders it 'post apostolos,' as if μετὰ τοὺς ἀποστόλους; Rufinus correctly 'cum apostolis.'

who has been entitled Just by all from the Lord's time to our own day; for many bore the name of James.' From this last passage however no inference can be safely drawn; for, supposing the term 'Apostles' to be here restricted to the Twelve, the expression μετὰ τῶν ἀποστόλων may distinguish St James not *from* but *among* the Apostles; as in Acts v. 29, 'Peter and the Apostles answered.'

Thus the testimony of Hegesippus seems distinctly opposed to the Hieronymian view, while of the other two it favours the Epiphanian rather than the Helvidian. If any doubt still remains, the fact that both Eusebius and Epiphanius, who derived their information mainly from Hegesippus, gave this account of the Lord's brethren materially strengthens the position. The testimony of an early Palestinian writer who made it his business to collect such traditions is of the utmost importance.

Tertullian.

8. TERTULLIAN's authority was appealed to by Helvidius, and Jerome is content to reply that he was not a member of the Church ('de Tertulliano nihil amplius dico quam ecclesiae hominem non fuisse,' *adv. Helvid.* § 17). It is generally assumed in consequence that Tertullian held the Lord's brethren to be sons of Joseph and Mary. This assumption, though probable, is not absolutely certain. The point at issue in this passage is not the particular opinion of Helvidius respecting the Lord's brethren, but the virginity of the Lord's mother. Accordingly in reply Jerome alleges on his own side the authority of others[1], whose testimony certainly did not go beyond

[1] 'Numquid non possum tibi totam veterum scriptorum seriem commovere: Ignatium, Polycarpum, Irenaeum, Justinum Martyrem, multosque alios apostolicos et eloquentes viros?' (*adv. Helvid.* 17). I have already (p. 130, note 3) mentioned an instance of the unfair way in which Jerome piles together his authorities. In the present case we are in a position to test him. Jerome did not possess any writings of Ignatius which are not extant now; and in no place does this apostolic father maintain the perpetual virginity of St Mary. In one remarkable passage indeed (*Ephes.* 19), which is several times quoted by subsequent writers, he speaks of the virginity of Mary as a mystery, but this refers distinctly to the time before the birth of our Lord. To this passage which he elsewhere quotes (*Comment. in Matth.* T. VII. p. 12), Jerome is doubtless referring here.

In Cowper's *Syriac Miscell.* p. 61, I find an extract, 'Justin one of the authors who were in the days of Augustus and Tiberius and Gaius wrote in the third discourse: That Mary the Galilean, who was the mother of Christ who

this one point and had no reference to the relationship of the Lord's brethren. Thus too the more distinct passages in the extant writings of Tertullian relate to the virginity only (*de Carn. Christ.* c. 23 and passim, *de Monog.* c. 8). Elsewhere however, though he does not directly state it, his argument seems to imply that the Lord's brethren were His brothers in the same sense in which Mary was His mother (*adv. Marc.* iv. 19, *de Carn. Christ.* 7). It is therefore highly probable that he held the Helvidian view. Such an admission from one who was so strenuous an advocate of asceticism is worthy of notice.

Clement of Alexandria.

9. CLEMENT OF ALEXANDRIA (about A.D. 200) in a passage of the Hypotyposeis preserved in a Latin translation by Cassiodorus (the authorship has been questioned but without sufficient reason[1]) puts forward the Epiphanian solution; 'Jude, who wrote the Catholic Epistle, being one of the sons of Joseph and [the Lord's] brother, a man of deep piety, though he was aware of his relationship to the Lord, nevertheless did not say he was His brother; but what said he? *Jude the servant of Jesus Christ*, because He was his Lord, *but brother of James;* for this is true; he was his brother, being Joseph's [son]'[2] (ed. Potter, p. 1007). This statement is explicit.

Latin fragment.

was crucified in Jerusalem, had not been with a husband. And Joseph did not repudiate her, but Joseph continued in holiness without a wife, he and his five sons by a former wife: and Mary continued without a husband.' The editor assigns this passage to Justin Martyr; but not to mention the anachronism, the whole tenor of the passage and the immediate neighbourhood of similar extracts shows that it was intended for the testimony (unquestionably spurious) of some contemporary heathen writer to the facts of the Gospel.

[1] We read in Cassiodorus (*de Inst. Div. Lit.* 8), 'In epistolas autem canonicas Clemens Alexandrinus presbyter, qui et Stromateus vocatur, id est, in epistola (-am?) S. Petri prima (-am?) S. Johannis prima (-am?) et secunda (-am?) et Jacobi quaedam Attico sermone declaravit. Ubi multa quidem subtiliter sed aliqua incaute loquutus est, quae nos ita transferri fecimus in Latinum, ut exclusis quibusdam offendiculis purificata doctrina ejus securior possit hauriri.' If 'Jude' be substituted for 'James,' this description exactly applies to the Latin notes extant under the title *Adumbrationes.* This was a very easy slip of the pen, and I can scarcely doubt that these notes are the same to which Cassiodorus refers as taken from the Hypotyposeis of Clement. Dr Westcott (*Canon*, p. 401) has pointed out in confirmation of this, that while Clement elsewhere directly quotes the Epistle of St Jude, he never refers to the Epistle of St James. Bunsen has included these notes in his collection of fragments of the Hypotyposeis, *Anal. Anten.* I. p. 325. It should be added that the statement about the relationship of Jude must be Clement's own and cannot have been inserted by Cassiodorus, since Cassiodorus in common with the Latin Church would naturally hold the Hieronymian hypothesis.

[2] 'Frater erat ejus [filius] Joseph.' The insertion of 'filius' (with Bunsen) is

Quotations in Eusebius.

On the other hand, owing to an extract preserved in Eusebius, his authority is generally claimed for the Hieronymian view; 'Clement,' says Eusebius, 'in the sixth book of the Hypotyposeis gives the following account: *Peter and James and John*, he tells us, *after the resurrection of the Saviour were not ambitious of honour, though the preference shown them by the Lord might have entitled them to it, but chose James the Just Bishop of Jerusalem.* The same writer too in the seventh book of the same treatise gives this account also of him (James the Lord's brother); *The Lord after the resurrection delivered the gnosis to James the Just*[1] *and John and Peter. These delivered it to the rest of the Apostles; and the rest of the Apostles to the seventy, of whom Barnabas was one. Now there are two Jameses, one the Just who was thrown down from the pinnacle (of the temple) and beaten to death with a club by a fuller, and another who was beheaded*' (*H. E.* ii. 1). This passage however proves nothing. Clement says that there were two of the name of James, but he neither states nor implies that there were two only.

necessary for the sense, whether Cassiodorus had it or not. Perhaps the Greek words were ἀδελφὸς αὐτοῦ τῶν Ἰωσήφ, which would account for the omission.

[1] Credner, *Einl.* p. 585, condemns the words τῷ δικαίῳ as spurious. Though it might be inferred from the previous extract given by Eusebius that the son of Zebedee is meant here, I believe nevertheless that they are genuine. For (1) They seem to be required as the motive for the explanation which is given afterwards of the different persons bearing the name James. (2) It is natural that a special prominence should be given to the same three Apostles of the Circumcision who are mentioned in Gal. ii. 9 as the pillars of Jewish Christendom. (3) Eusebius introduces the quotation as relating to James the Just (περὶ αὐτοῦ), which would not be a very good description if the other James were the prominent person in the passage. (4) I find from Hippolytus that the Ophite account singled out James the Lord's brother as a possessor of the esoteric gnosis, ταῦτά ἐστιν ἀπὸ πολλῶν πάνυ λόγων τὰ κεφάλαια ἅ φησιν παραδεδωκέναι Μαριάμνῃ τὸν Ἰάκωβον τοῦ Κυρίου τὸν ἀδελφόν, *Haeres.* x. 6, p. 95. Clement seems to have derived his information from some work of a Jewish Gnostic complexion, perhaps from the Gospel of the Egyptians with which he was well acquainted (*Strom.* iii. pp. 529 sq, 553, ed. Potter); and as Hippolytus tells us that the Ophites made use of this Gospel (τὰς δὲ ἐξαλλαγὰς ταύτας τὰς ποικίλας ἐν τῷ ἐπιγραφομένῳ κατ' Αἰγυπτίους εὐαγγελίῳ κειμένας ἔχουσιν, *ib.* v. 7, p. 98), it is probable that the account of Clement coincided with that of the Ophites. The words τῷ δικαίῳ are represented in the Syriac translation of Eusebius of which the existing MS (Brit. Mus. add. 14,639) belongs to the 6th century.

I hold τῷ δικαίῳ therefore to be the genuine words of Clement, but I do not feel so sure that the closing explanation δύο δὲ γεγόνασιν Ἰάκωβοι κ.τ.λ. is not an addition of Eusebius. This I suppose to be Bunsen's opinion, for he ends his fragment with the preceding words I. p. 321.

His sole object was to distinguish the son of Zebedee from the Lord's brother; and the son of Alphæus, of whom he knew nothing and could tell nothing, did not occur to his mind when he penned this sentence. There is in this passage nothing which contradicts the Latin extract; though indeed in a writer so uncritical in his historical notices[1] such a contradiction would not be surprising[2].

10. ORIGEN († A.D. 253) declares himself very distinctly in favour of the Epiphanian view, stating that the brethren were sons of Joseph by a deceased wife[3]. Elsewhere[4] indeed he says that St Paul 'calls this James the Lord's brother, not so much on account of his kinsmanship or their companionship together, as on account of his character and language,' but this is not inconsistent with the explicit statement already referred to. In one passage he writes at some length on the subject; 'Some persons, on the ground of a tradition in the Gospel according to Peter, as it is entitled, or the Book of James (i.e. the Protevangelium), say that the brothers of Jesus were Joseph's sons by a former wife to whom he was married before Mary. Those who hold this view wish to preserve the honour of Mary in virginity throughout...And I think it reasonable that as Jesus was the first-fruit of purity and chastity among men, so Mary was among women: for it is not seemly to ascribe the first-fruit of virginity to any other woman but her' (*in Matt.* xiii. 55, III. p. 462)[5]. This passage

[1] For instance he distinguished Cephas of Gal. ii. 9 from Peter (see above, p. 129), and represented St Paul as a married man (Euseb. *H. E.* iii. 30).

[2] On the supposition that Clement held the Hieronymian theory, as he is represented even by those who themselves reject it, the silence of Origen, who seems never to have heard of this theory, is quite inexplicable. Epiphanius moreover, who appears equally ignorant of it, refers to Clement while writing on this very subject (*Haeres.* p. 119, Petav.). Indeed Clement would then stand quite alone before the age of Jerome.

[3] *In Joann.* ii. 12 (*Catena Corder.* p. 75) ἀδελφοὺς μὲν οὐκ εἶχε φύσει, οὔτε τῆς παρθένου τεκούσης ἕτερον οὐδὲ αὐτὸς ἐκ τοῦ Ἰωσὴφ τυγχάνων· νόμῳ τοιγαροῦν ἐχρημάτισαν αὐτοῦ ἀδελφοί, υἱοὶ Ἰωσὴφ ὄντες ἐκ προτεθνηκυίας γυναικός: *Hom. in Luc.* 7 (III. p. 940, ed. Delarue) 'Hi enim filii qui Joseph dicebantur non erant orti de Maria, neque est ulla scriptura quae ista commemoret.' In this latter passage either the translator has been confused by the order in the original or the words in the translation itself have been displaced accidentally, but the meaning is clear.

[4] *c. Cels.* i. 47 (I. p. 363) οὐ τοσοῦτον διὰ τὸ πρὸς αἵματος συγγενὲς ἢ τὴν κοινὴν αὐτῶν ἀναστροφὴν ὅσον διὰ τὸ ἦθος καὶ τὸν λόγον.

[5] *Op.* III. p. 462 sq. Mill, pp. 261, 273, has strangely misunderstood the purport of this passage. He speaks of

shows not only that Origen himself favoured the Epiphanian view which elsewhere he has directly maintained, but that he was wholly unaware of the Hieronymian, the only alternative which presented itself being the denial of the perpetual virginity[1].

Apostolical Constitutions.

11. The APOSTOLICAL CONSTITUTIONS, the main part of which may perhaps be regarded as a work of the third century, though they received considerable additions in later ages, distinguish James the Lord's brother from James the son of Alphæus, making him, like St Paul, a supernumerary apostle, and thus counting fourteen in all (vi. 12, 13, 14; compare ii. 55, vii. 46, viii. 4).

Victorinus of Pettaw.

12. VICTORINUS PETAVIONENSIS (about 300) was claimed by Helvidius as a witness in his own favour. Jerome denied this and put in a counter claim. It may perhaps be inferred from this circumstance that Victorinus did little more than repeat the statements of the evangelists respecting the Lord's brethren (*adv. Helvid.* 17).

Eusebius of Cæsarea.

13. EUSEBIUS OF CÆSAREA († about 340) distinguished James the Lord's brother from the Twelve, representing him as a supernumerary apostle like St Paul (*Comm. in Isai.* in Montfaucon's *Coll. Nov. Patr.* II. p. 422; *Hist. Eccl.* i. 12; comp. vii. 19). Accordingly in another

Origen here as 'teaching the opinion of his (James the Just) being the son of Joseph, both as the sentiment of a minority among right-minded Christians and as founded on apocryphal traditions'; and so considers the note on John ii. 12, already referred to, as 'standing strangely contrasted' to Origen's statement here. If Dr Mill's attention however had been directed to the last sentence, καὶ οἶμαι λόγον ἔχειν κ.τ.λ., which, though most important, he has himself omitted in quoting the passage, he could scarcely have failed to see Origen's real meaning.

[1] The authority of Hippolytus of Portus, a contemporary of Origen, has sometimes been alleged in favour of Jerome's hypothesis. In the treatise *De XII Apostolis* ascribed to this author (ed. Fabric. I. app. p. 30) it is said of James the son of Alphæus, κηρύσσων ἐν Ἱερουσαλὴμ ὑπὸ Ἰουδαίων καταλευσθεὶς ἀναιρεῖται καὶ θάπτεται ἐκεῖ παρὰ τῷ ναῷ. He is thus confused or identified with James the Lord's brother. But this blundering treatise was certainly not written by the bishop of Portus: see Le Moyne in Fabricius I. p. 84, and Bunsen's *Hippol.* I. p. 456 (ed. 2). On the other hand in the work *De LXX Apostolis* (Fabricius I. app. p. 41), also ascribed to this writer, we find among the 70 the name of Ἰάκωβος ὁ ἀδελφόθεος ἐπίσκοπος Ἱεροσολύμων, who is thus distinguished from the Twelve. This treatise also is manifestly spurious. Again Nicephorus Callistus, *H. E.* ii. 3, cites as from Hippolytus of Portus an elaborate account of our Lord's brethren following the Epiphanian view (Hippol. *Op.* I. app. 43, ed. Fabric.); but this account seems to be drawn either from Hippolytus the Theban, unless as Bunsen (*l. c.*) supposes this Theban Hippolytus be a mythical personage, or from some forged writings which bore the name of the older Hippolytus.

passage he explains that this James was called the Lord's brother, because Joseph was his reputed father (*Hist. Eccl.* ii. 1)[1].

Cyril of Jerusalem.

14. CYRIL OF JERUSALEM († 386) comments on the successive appearances of our Lord related by St Paul, first to Peter, then to the Twelve, then to the five hundred, then to James His own brother, then to Paul His enemy; and his language implies that each appearance was a step in advance of the testimony afforded by the former (*Catech.* xiv. 21, p. 216, ed. Touttée). It may be gathered thence that he distinguished this James from the Twelve. As this however is only an inference from his language, and not a direct statement of his own, too much stress must not be laid on it. In another passage also (*Catech.* iv. 28, p. 65, *καὶ τοῖς ἀποστόλοις καὶ Ἰακώβῳ τῷ ταύτης τῆς ἐκκλησίας ἐπισκόπῳ*) Cyril seems to make the same distinction, but here again the inference is doubtful.

Hilary of Poitiers.

15. HILARY OF POITIERS († 368) denounces those who 'claim authority for their opinion (against the virginity of the Lord's mother) from the fact of its being recorded that our Lord had several brothers'; and adds, 'yet if these had been sons of Mary and not rather sons of Joseph, the offspring of a former marriage, she would never at the time of the passion have been transferred to the Apostle John to be his mother' (*Comm. in Matth.* i. 1, p. 671, ed. Bened.).

[1] Ἰάκωβον τὸν τοῦ Κυρίου λεγόμενον ἀδελφόν, ὅτι δὴ καὶ οὗτος τοῦ Ἰωσὴφ ὠνόμαστο παῖς, τοῦ δὲ Χριστοῦ πατὴρ ὁ Ἰωσήφ, ᾧ μνηστευθεῖσα ἡ παρθένος κ.τ.λ. On the whole this passage seems to be best explained by referring *οὗτος* to *Κύριος*. But this is not necessary; for *ὀνομάζεσθαι* (or *καλεῖσθαι*) *παῖς τινὸς* is a good Greek phrase to denote real as well as reputed sonship: as Æsch. *Fragm.* 285 *αἵδ' ἕπτ' Ἄτλαντος παῖδες ὠνομασμέναι*, Soph. *Trach.* 1105 *ὁ τῆς ἀρίστης μητρὸς ὠνομασμένος*, Eur. *Elect.* 935: comp. Ephes. iii. 15 *τὸν πατέρα ἐξ οὗ πᾶσα πατριὰ ὀνομάζεται*. The word *ὠνόμαστο* cannot at all events, as Mill (p. 272) seems disposed to think, imply any doubt on the part of Eusebius about the parentage of James, for the whole drift of the passage is plainly against this. The other reading, *ὅτι δὴ καὶ οὗτος τοῦ Ἰωσὴφ τοῦ νομιζομένου οἱονεὶ πατρὸς τοῦ Χριστοῦ*, found in some MSS and in the Syriac version, and preferred by Blom. p. 98, and Credner *Einl.* p. 585, I cannot but regard as an obvious alteration of some early transcriber for the sake of clearness.

Compare the expressions in i. 12 *εἷς δὲ καὶ οὗτος τῶν φερομένων ἀδελφῶν ἦν*, and iii. 7 *τοῦ Κυρίου χρηματίζων ἀδελφός*. He was a *reputed* brother of the Lord, because Joseph was His *reputed* father. See also Eusebius *On the Star*, 'Joseph and Mary and Our Lord with them and the five sons of Hannah (Anna) the first wife of Joseph' (p. 17, Wright's Transl.). The account from which this passage is taken professes to be founded on a document dating A.D. 119.

Thus he not only adopts the Epiphanian solution, but shows himself entirely ignorant of the Hieronymian.

Victorinus the Philosopher.

16. VICTORINUS THE PHILOSOPHER (about 360) takes εἰ μὴ in Gal. i. 19 as expressing not *exception* but *opposition*, and distinctly states that James was not an Apostle: 'Cum autem *fratrem* dixit, *apostolum* negavit.'

Ambrosiaster.

17. The AMBROSIAN HILARY (about 75) comments on Gal. i. 19 as follows; 'The Lord is called the brother of James and the rest in the same way in which He is also designated the son of Joseph. For some in a fit of madness impiously assert and contend that these were true brothers of the Lord, being sons of Mary, allowing at the same time that Joseph, though not His true father, was so called nevertheless. For if these were His true brothers, then Joseph will be His true father; for he who called Joseph His Father also called James and the rest His brothers.' Thus his testimony entirely coincides with that of his greater namesake. He sees only the alternative of denying the perpetual virginity as Helvidius did, or accepting the solution of the Protevangelium; and he unhesitatingly adopts the latter.

Basil.

18. BASIL THE GREAT († 379), while allowing that the perpetual virginity is not a necessary article of belief, yet adheres to it himself 'since the lovers of Christ cannot endure to hear that the mother of God ever ceased to be a virgin' (*Hom. in Sanct. Christ. Gen.* II. p. 600, ed. Garn.)[1]. As immediately afterwards he refers, in support of his view, to some apocryphal work which related that Zacharias was slain by the Jews for testifying to the virginity of the mother of Jesus (a story which closely resembles the narrative of his death in the *Protevang.* §§ 23, 24), it may perhaps be inferred that he accepted that account of the Lord's brethren which ran through these apocryphal gospels.

Gregory Nyssen.

19. His brother GREGORY NYSSEN († after 394) certainly adopted the Epiphanian account. At the same time he takes up the very untenable position that the 'Mary who is designated in the other

[1] This very moderate expression of opinion is marked by the editors with a *caute legendum* in the margin; and in Garnier's edition the treatise is consigned to an appendix as of doubtful authenticity. The main argument urged against it is the passage here referred to. (See Garnier, II. præf. p. xv.)

Evangelists (besides St John) the mother of James and Joses is *the mother of God* and none else[1],' being so called because she undertook the education of these her stepsons; and he supposes also that this James is called 'the little' by St Mark to distinguish him from James *the son of Alphæus* who was 'great,' because he was in the number of the Twelve Apostles, which the Lord's brother was not (*in Christ. Resurr.* ii. *Opp.* III. pp. 412, 413, ed. Paris, 1638).

20. The ANTIDICOMARIANITES, an obscure Arabian sect in the latter half of the fourth century, maintained that the Lord's mother bore children to her husband Joseph. These opinions seem to have produced a reaction, or to have been themselves reactionary, for we read about the same time of a sect called *Collyridians*, likewise in Arabia, who going to the opposite extreme paid divine honours to the Virgin (Epiphan. *Haeres.* lxxviii, lxxix[2]). Antidicomarianites.

21. EPIPHANIUS a native of Palestine became bishop of Constantia in Cyprus in the year 367. Not very long before Jerome wrote in defence of the perpetual virginity of the Lord's mother against the Helvidians at Rome, Epiphanius came forward as the champion of the same cause against the Antidicomarianites. He denounced them in an elaborate pastoral letter, in which he explains his views at length, and which he has thought fit to incorporate in his subsequently written treatise against Heresies (pp. 1034—1057, Epiphanius.

[1] Similarly Chrysostom, see below, p. 289, note 1. This identification of the Lord's mother with the mother of James and Joses is adopted and similarly explained also in one of the apocryphal gospels: *Hist. Joseph.* 4 (Tisch. p. 117). Possibly Gregory derived it from some such source. It was also part of the Helvidian hypothesis, where it was less out of place, and gave Jerome an easy triumph over his adversary (*adv. Helvid.* 12 etc.). It is adopted moreover by Cave (Life of St James the Less, § 2), who holds that the Lord's brethren were sons of Joseph, and yet makes James the Lord's brother one of the Twelve, identifying Joseph with Alphæus. Fritzsche also identifies these two Maries (*Matth.* p. 822, *Marc.* p. 697).

[2] The names are plainly terms of ridicule invented by their enemies. Augustine supposes the 'Antidicomarianitæ' of Epiphanius (he writes the word 'Antidicomaritæ') to be the same as the Helvidians of Jerome (*adv. Haer.* 84, VIII. p. 24). They held the same tenets, it is true, but there seems to have been otherwise no connexion between the two. Considerations of time and place alike resist this identification.

Epiphanius had heard that these opinions, which he held to be derogatory to the Lord's mother, had been promulgated also by the elder Apollinaris or some of his disciples; but he doubted about this (p. 1034). The report was probably circulated by their opponents in order to bring discredit upon them.

ed. Petav.). He moreover discusses the subject incidentally in other parts of his great work (pp. 115, 119, 432, 636), and it is clear that he had devoted much time and attention to it. His account coincides with that of the apocryphal gospels. Joseph, he states, was eighty years old or more when the Virgin was espoused to him; by his former wife he had six children, four sons and two daughters, the names of the daughters were Mary and Salome, for which names by the way he alleges the authority of Scripture (p. 1041); his sons, St James especially, were called the Lord's brethren because they were brought up with Jesus; the mother of the Lord remained for ever a virgin; as the lioness is said to exhaust her fertility in the production of a single offspring (see Herod. iii. 108), so she who bore the Lion of Judah could not in the nature of things become a mother a second time (pp. 1044, 1045). These particulars with many other besides he gives, quoting as his authority 'the tradition of the Jews' (p. 1039). It is to be observed moreover that, though he thus treats of the subject several times and at great length, he never once alludes to the Hieronymian account; and yet I can scarcely doubt that one who so highly extolled celibacy would have hailed with delight a solution which, as Jerome boasted, saved the virginity not of Mary only but of Joseph also, for whose honour Epiphanius shows himself very jealous (pp. 1040, 1046, 1047).

Helvidius, Bonosus, and Jovinianus.

22. Somewhere about the year 380 HELVIDIUS, who resided in Rome, published a treatise in which he maintained that the Lord's brethren were sons of Joseph and Mary. He seems to have succeeded in convincing a considerable number of persons, for contemporary writers speak of the Helvidians as a party. These views were moreover advocated by BONOSUS, bishop of Sardica in Illyria, about the same time, and apparently also by JOVINIANUS a monk probably of Milan. The former was condemned by a synod assembled at Capua (A.D. 392), and the latter by synods held at Rome and at Milan (about A.D. 390; see Hefele *Conciliengesch.* II. pp. 47, 48)[1].

[1] The work ascribed to Dorotheus Tyrius is obviously spurious (see Cave *Hist. Lit.* I. p. 163); and I have therefore not included his testimony in this

In earlier times this account of the Lord's brethren, so far as it was the badge of a party, seems to have been held in conjunction with Ebionite views respecting the conception and person of Christ[1]. For, though not necessarily affecting the belief in the miraculous Incarnation, it was yet a natural accompaniment of the denial thereof. The motive of these latter impugners of the perpetual virginity was very different. They endeavoured to stem the current which had set strongly in the direction of celibacy; and, if their theory was faulty, they still deserve the sympathy due to men who in defiance of public opinion refused to bow their necks to an extragavant and tyrannous superstition. Motive of the Helvidians.

We have thus arrived at the point of time when Jerome's answer to Helvidius created a new epoch in the history of this controversy. And the following inferences are, if I mistake not, fairly deducible from the evidence produced. *First:* there is not the slightest indication that the Hieronymian solution ever occurred to any individual or sect or church, until it was put forward by Jerome himself. If it had been otherwise, writers like Origen, the two Hilaries, and Epiphanius, who discuss the question, could not have failed to notice it. *Secondly:* the Epiphanian account has the highest claims to the sanction of tradition, whether the value of this sanction be great or small. *Thirdly:* this solution seems especially to represent the Palestinian view. Evidence summed up.

In the year 382 (or 383) Jerome published his treatise; and the effect of it is visible at once. Jerome's treatise.

AMBROSE in the year 392 wrote a work *De Institutione Virginis*, Ambrose.

list. The writer distinguishes James the Lord's brother and James the son of Alphæus, and makes them successive bishops of Jerusalem. See Combefis in Fabricius' *Hippol.* 1, app. p. 36.

[1] [I fear the statement in the text may leave a false impression. Previous writers had spoken of the Ebionites as holding the Helvidian view, and I was betrayed into using similar language. But there is, so far as I am aware, no evidence in favour of this assumption. It would be still more difficult to substantiate the assertions in the following note of Gibbon, *Decline and Fall* c. xvi, 'This appellation ('brethren') was at first understood in the most obvious sense, and it was supposed that the brothers of Jesus were the lawful issue of Joseph and Mary. A devout respect for the virginity of the mother of God suggested to the Gnostics, and afterwards to the Orthodox Greeks, the expedient of bestowing a second wife on Joseph, etc.'] 2nd ed.

in which he especially refutes the impugners of the perpetual virginity of the Lord's mother. In a passage which is perhaps intentionally obscure he speaks to this effect: 'The term brothers has a wide application; it is used of members of the same family, the same race, the same country. Witness the Lord's own words *I will declare thy name to my brethren* (Ps. xxii. 22). St Paul too says: *I could wish to be accursed for my brethren* (Rom. ix. 3). Doubtless they might be called brothers as sons of Joseph, not of Mary. And if any one will go into the question carefully, he will find this to be the true account. For myself I do not intend to enter upon this question: it is of no importance to decide what particular relationship is implied; it is sufficient for my purpose that the term "brethren" is used in an extended sense (i.e. of others besides sons of the same mother)[1].' From this I infer that St Ambrose had heard of, though possibly not read, Jerome's tract, in which he discourses on the wide meaning of the term: that, if he had read it, he did not feel inclined to abandon the view with which he was familiar in favour of the novel hypothesis put forward by Jerome: and lastly, that seeing the importance of cooperation against a common enemy he was anxious not to raise dissensions among the champions of the perpetual virginity by the discussion of details.

Pelagius. PELAGIUS, who commented on St Paul a few years after Jerome, adopts his theory and even his language, unless his text has been tampered with here (Gal. i. 19).

Augustine. At the same time Jerome's hypothesis found a much more weighty advocate in ST AUGUSTINE. In his commentary on the Galatians indeed (i. 19), written about 394 while he was still a presbyter, he offers the alternative of the Hieronymian and Epiphanian accounts. But in his later works he consistently maintains the view put forward

[1] The passage, which I have thus paraphrased, is 'Fratres autem gentis, et generis, populi quoque consortium nuncupari docet Dominus ipse qui dicit: *Narrabo nomen tuum fratribus meis; in medio ecclesiae laudabo te.* Paulus quoque ait: *Optabam ego anathema esse pro fratribus meis.* Potuerunt autem fratres esse ex Joseph, non ex Maria. Quod quidem si quis diligentius prosequatur inveniet. Nos ea prosequenda non putavimus, quoniam fraternum nomen liquet pluribus esse commune' (II. p. 260, ed. Ben.). St Ambrose seems to accept so much of Jerome's argument as relates to the wide use of the term 'brothers' and nothing more.

by Jerome in the treatise against Helvidius (*In Joh. Evang.* x, III. 2. p. 368, *ib.* xxviii, III. 2. p. 508; *Enarr. in Ps.* cxxvii, IV. 2. p. 1443; *Contr. Faust.* xxii. 35, VIII. p. 383; comp. *Quaest. XVII in Matth.*, III. 2. p. 285).

Western Church.

Thus supported, it won its way to general acceptance in the Latin Church; and the WESTERN SERVICES recognise only one James besides the son of Zebedee, thus identifying the Lord's brother with the son of Alphæus.

Chrysostom.

In the East also it met with a certain amount of success, but this was only temporary. CHRYSOSTOM wrote both before and after Jerome's treatise had become generally known, and his expositions of the New Testament mark a period of transition. In his Homilies on the earlier books he takes the Epiphanian view: St James, he says, was at one time an unbeliever with the rest of the Lord's brethren (on Matth. i. 25, VII. p. 77; John vii. 5, VIII. p. 284; see also on 1 Cor. ix. 4, X. p. 181 E); the resurrection was the turning-point in their career; they were called the Lord's brethren, as Joseph himself was reputed the husband of Mary (on Matth. i. 25, l. c.)[1]. Hitherto he betrays no knowledge of the Hieronymian account.

[1] A comment attributed to Chrysostom in Cramer's *Catena* on 1 Cor. ix. 4—7, but not found in the Homilies, is still more explicit; 'Αδελφοὺς τοῦ Κυρίου λέγει τοὺς νομισθέντας εἶναι αὐτοῦ ἀδελφούς· ἐπειδὴ γὰρ οὗτος ὁ χρηματίζων καὶ αὐτὸς κατὰ τὴν κοινὴν δόξαν εἶπεν αὐτούς· τοὺς δὲ υἱοὺς 'Ιωσὴφ λέγει, οἱ ἀδελφοὶ τοῦ Κυρίου ἐχρημάτισαν διὰ τὴν πρὸς τὴν θεοτόκον μνηστείαν τοῦ 'Ιωσήφ. λέγει δὲ 'Ιάκωβον ἐπίσκοπον 'Ιεροσολύμων καὶ 'Ιωσὴφ ὁμώνυμον τῷ πατέρι καὶ Σίμωνα καὶ 'Ιούδα. I give the passage without attempting to correct the text. This note reappears almost word for word in the Œcumenian catena and in Theophylact. If Chrysostom be not the author, then we gain the testimony of some other ancient writer on the same side. Compare also the pseudo-Chrysostom, *Op.* II. p. 797.

The passages referred to in the text show clearly what was Chrysostom's earlier view. To these may be added the comments on 1 Cor. xv. 7 (x. 355 D), where he evidently regards James as not one of the Twelve; on Matth. x. 2 (VII. pp. 368, 9), where he makes James the son of Alphæus a tax-gatherer like Matthew, clearly taking them to be brothers; and on Matth. xxvii. 55 (VII. p. 827 A), where, like Gregory Nyssen, he identifies Μαρία 'Ιακώβου with the Lord's mother. The accounts of Chrysostom's opinion on this subject given by Blom p. 111 sq, and Mill p. 284 note, are unsatisfactory.

The Homilies on the Acts also take the same view (IX. pp. 23 B, 26 A), but though these are generally ascribed to Chrysostom, their genuineness is very questionable. In another spurious work, *Opus imp. in Matth.*, VI. p. clxxiv E, the Hieronymian view appears; 'Jacobum Alphaei lapidantes: propter quae omnia Jerusalem destructa est a Romanis.'

But in his exposition of the Epistle to the Galatians (i. 19) he not only speaks of James the Lord's brother as if he were an apostle (which proves nothing), but also calls him the son of Clopas[1]. Thus he would appear meanwhile to have accepted the hypothesis of Jerome and to have completed it by the identification of Clopas with Alphæus. And THEODORET, who for the most part closely follows Chrysostom, distinctly repudiates the older view: 'He was not, as some have supposed, a son of Joseph, the offspring of a former marriage, but was son of Clopas and cousin of the Lord; for his mother was the sister of the Lord's mother.'

Theodoret.

Cyril of Alexandria.

But with these exceptions the Epiphanian view maintained its ground in the East. It is found again in CYRIL OF ALEXANDRIA for instance (*Glaphyr. in Gen.* lib. vii. p. 221), and seems to have been held by later Greek writers almost, if not quite, universally. In THEOPHYLACT indeed (on Matth. xiii. 55, Gal. i. 19) we find an attempt to unite the two accounts. James, argues the writer, was the Lord's reputed brother as the son of Joseph and the Lord's cousin as the son of Clopas; the one was his natural, and the other his legal father; Clopas having died childless, Joseph had raised up seed to his brother by his widow according to the law of the levirate[2]. This novel suggestion however found but little favour, and the Eastern Churches continued to distinguish between James the Lord's brother and James the son of Alphæus. The GREEK, SYRIAN, and COPTIC CALENDARS assign a separate day to each.

Theophylact.

Eastern Churches.

The table on the next page gives a conspectus of the patristic and early authorities.

[1] τὸν τοῦ Κλωπᾶ, ὅπερ καὶ ὁ εὐαγγελιστὴς ἔλεγεν. He is referring, I suppose, to the lists of the Apostles which mention James the son of *Alphæus*. See above, p. 267. This portion of his exposition however is somewhat confused, and it is difficult to resist the suspicion that it has been interpolated.

[2] See the remarks of Mill, p. 228.

View	Authorities	Grouping	Authorities
A. *Sons of Joseph and Mary.*	TERTULLIAN, HELVIDIUS, BONOSUS, JOVINIANUS (?), ANTIDICOMARIANITES.	A. or B. *'Brethren' in a strict sense. James the Just not one of the Twelve.*	EARLY VERSIONS, CLEMENTINE HOMILIES (?), ASCENTS OF JAMES, HEGESIPPUS, APOST. CONSTIT., CYRIL OF JERUSALEM (?), VICTORINUS THE PHILOSOPHER.
B. *Sons of Joseph by a former wife.*	GOSPEL OF PETER, PROTEVANGELIUM etc., CLEMENT OF ALEX., ORIGEN, EUSEBIUS, HILARY OF POITIERS, AMBROSIASTER, GREGORY OF NYSSA, EPIPHANIUS, AMBROSE, [CHRYSOSTOM], CYRIL OF ALEX., EASTERN SERVICES (Greek, Syrian, and Coptic), LATER GREEK WRITERS.	B or C. *Perpetual virginity of Mary.*	BASIL, CATHOLIC WRITERS GENERALLY.
C. *Sons of the Virgin's sister.*	JEROME, PELAGIUS, AUGUSTINE, [CHRYSOSTOM], THEODORET, WESTERN SERVICES, LATER LATIN WRITERS.		

Uncertain. HEBREW GOSPEL, VICTORINUS PETAVIONENSIS.

Levirate. THEOPHYLACT.

III.

ST PAUL AND THE THREE.

Three Apostles alone besides St Paul prominent.

THREE and three only of the personal disciples and immediate followers of our Lord hold any prominent place in the Apostolic records—James, Peter, and John; the first the Lord's brother, the two latter the foremost members of the Twelve. Apart from an incidental reference to the death of James the son of Zebedee, which is dismissed in a single sentence, the rest of the Twelve are mentioned by name for the last time on the day of the Lord's Ascension. Thenceforward they disappear wholly from the canonical writings.

And this silence also extends to the traditions of succeeding ages. We read indeed of St Thomas in India, of St Andrew in Scythia; but such scanty notices, even if we accept them as trustworthy, show only the more plainly how little the Church could tell of her earliest teachers. Doubtless they laboured zealously and effectively in the spread of the Gospel; but, so far as we know, they have left no impress of their individual mind and character on the Church at large. Occupying the foreground, and indeed covering the whole canvas of early ecclesiastical history, appear four figures alone, St Paul and the three Apostles of the Circumcision.

The four meet together at a great crisis.

Once and, it would appear, not more than once, these four great teachers met together face to face. It was the one great crisis in the history of the Church, on the issue of which was staked her future progress and triumph. Was she to open her doors wide and receive all comers, to declare her legitimate boundaries coextensive with the limits of the human race? Or was she to remain for ever narrow and sectarian, a national institution at best, but most probably a suspected minority even in her own nation?

Not less important, so far as we can see, was the question at issue, when Paul and Barnabas arrived at Jerusalem to confer with the Apostles of the Circumcision on the subject of the Mosaic ritual which then distracted the youthful Church. It must therefore be an intensely interesting study to watch the attitude of the four great leaders of the Church at this crisis, merely as a historical lesson. But the importance of the subject does not rest here. Questions of much wider interest are suggested by the accounts of this conference: What degree of coincidence or antagonism between Jewish and Gentile converts may be discerned in the Church? What were the relations existing between St Paul and the Apostles of the Circumcision? How far do the later sects of Ebionites on the one hand and Marcionites on the other, as they appear in direct antagonism in the second century, represent opposing principles cherished side by side within the bosom of the Church and sheltering themselves under the names, or (as some have ventured to say) sanctioned by the authority, of the leading Apostles? What in fact is the secret history—if there be any secret history—of the origin of Catholic Christianity?

Questions suggested by this meeting.

On this battle-field the most important of recent theological controversies has been waged: and it is felt by both sides that the Epistle to the Galatians is the true key to the position. In the first place, it is one of the very few documents of the Apostolic ages, whose genuineness has not been seriously challenged by the opponents of revelation. Moreover, as the immediate utterance of one who himself took the chief part in the incidents recorded, it cannot be discredited as having passed through a coloured medium or gathered accretions by lapse of time. And lastly, the very form in which the information is conveyed—by partial and broken allusions rather than by direct and continuous statement—raises it beyond the reach of suspicion, even where suspicion is most active. Here at least both combatants can take their stand on common ground.

Importance of the Galatian Epistle.

Nor need the defenders of the Christian faith hesitate to accept the challenge of their opponents and try the question on this issue. If it be only interpreted aright, the Epistle to the Galatians ought to present us with a true, if only a partial, solution of the problem.

Apology for this essay.

Thus the attempt to decipher the relations between Jewish and Gentile Christianity in the first ages of the Church is directly suggested by this epistle; and indeed any commentary would be incomplete which refused to entertain the problem. This must be my excuse for entering upon a subject, about which so much has been written and which involves so many subsidiary questions. It will be impossible within my limits to discuss all these questions in detail. The objections, for instance, which have been urged against the genuineness of a large number of the canonical and other early Christian writings, can only be met indirectly. Reasonable men will hardly be attracted towards a theory which can only be built on an area prepared by this wide clearance of received documents. At all events there is, I think, no unfairness in stating the case thus; that, though they are supported by arguments drawn from other sources, the general starting-point of such objections is the theory itself. If then a fair and reasonable account can be given both of the origin and progress of the Church generally, and of the mutual relations of its more prominent teachers, based on these documents assumed as authentic, a general answer will be supplied to all objections of this class.

Proposed sketch of the relations of Jewish and Gentile Christians.

I purpose therefore to sketch in outline the progressive history of the relations between the Jewish and Gentile converts in the early ages of the Church, as gathered from the Apostolic writings, aided by such scanty information as can be got together from other sources. This will be a fit and indeed a necessary introduction to the subject with which the Epistle to the Galatians is more directly concerned, the positions occupied by St Paul and the three Apostles of the Circumcision respectively.

Three main divisions

This history falls into three periods which mark three distinct stages in its progress: (1) The Extension of the Church to the Gentiles; (2) The Recognition of Gentile Liberty; (3) The Emancipation of the Jewish Churches[1]. of this subject.

1. *The Extension of the Church to the Gentiles.*

It appears from the Apostolic history that the believers in the earliest days conformed strictly to Jewish customs in their religious life, retaining the fixed hours of prayer, attending the temple worship and sacrifices, observing the sacred festivals. The Church was still confined to one nation and had not yet broken loose from the national rites and usages. But these swathing bands, which were perhaps needed to support its infancy, would only cripple its later growth, and must be thrown off, if it was ever to attain to a healthy maturity. This emancipation then was the great problem which the Apostles had to work out. The Master Himself had left no express instructions. He had charged them, it is true, to preach the Gospel to all nations, but how this injunction was to be carried out, by what changes a national Church must expand into an universal Church, they had not been told. He had indeed asserted the sovereignty of the spirit over the letter; He had enunciated the great principle—as wide in its application as the law itself—that 'Man was not made for the sabbath, but the sabbath for man'; He had pointed to the fulfilment of the law in the Gospel. So far He had discredited the law, but He had not deposed or abolished it. It was left to the Apostles themselves under the guidance of the Spirit, moulded by circumstances and moulding them in turn, to work out this great change.

The early Church of Jerusalem.

Our Lord's teaching.

[1] Important works treating of the relation between the Jewish and Gentile Christians are Lechler's *Apostolisches und Nachapostolisches Zeitalter* (2te aufl. 1857), and Ritschl's *Entstehung der Altkatholischen Kirche* (2te aufl. 1857). I am indebted to both these works, but to the latter especially, which is very able and suggestive. Ritschl should be read in his second edition, in which with a noble sacrifice of consistency to truth he has abandoned many of his former positions, and placed himself in more direct antagonism to the Tübingen school in which he was educated. The historical speculations of that school are developed in Baur's *Paulus* and *Christenthum und die Christliche Kirche der drei ersten Jahrhunderte*, in Schwegler's *Nachapostolisches Zeitalter*.

Jews of the Dispersion.

And soon enough the pressure of events began to be felt. The dispersion was the link which connected the Hebrews of Palestine with the outer world. Led captive by the power of Greek philosophy at Athens and Tarsus and Alexandria, attracted by the fascinations of Oriental mysticism in Asia, swept along with the busy whirl of social life in the city and court of the Cæsars, these outlying members of the chosen race had inhaled a freer spirit and contracted wider interests than their fellow-countrymen at home. By a series of insensible gradations—proselytes of the covenant—proselytes of the gate[1]—superstitious devotees who observed the rites without accepting the faith of the Mosaic dispensation—curious lookers-on who interested themselves in the Jewish ritual as they would in the worship of Isis or of Astarte—the most stubborn zealot of the law was linked to the idolatrous heathen whom he abhorred and who despised him in turn. Thus the train was unconsciously laid, when the spark fell from heaven and fired it.

First day of Pentecost.

The very baptism of the Christian Church opened the path for its extension to the Gentile world. On the first day of Pentecost were gathered together Hellenist Jews from all the principal centres of the dispersion. With them were assembled also numbers of incorporated Israelites, proselytes of the covenant. The former of these by contact with Gentile thought and life, the latter by the force of early habits and associations[2], would accept and interpret the new revelation in a less rigorous spirit than the Hebrew zealot of Jerusalem. Each successive festival must have been followed by similar though less striking results. The stream of Hellenists and proselytes, constantly ebbing and flowing, must have swept away fragments at least of the

[1] The distinction between proselytes of the covenant or of righteousness and proselytes of the gate is found in the Gemara: the former were circumcised, and observed the whole law; the latter acknowledged the God of Israel and conformed to Jewish worship in some respects, but stood without the covenant, not having been incorporated by the initiatory rite. The former alone, it would appear, are called *προσήλυτοι* in the New Testament; the latter, who hardly form a distinct class, are *οἱ σεβόμενοι τὸν Θεόν, οἱ εὐσεβεῖς* etc. In speaking therefore of 'proselytes of the gate' I am using a convenient anachronism.

[2] 'Trust not a proselyte,' said one of the rabbis, 'till twenty-four generations; for he holds his leaven.' Yalkut (Shimoni) on Ruth i. 11, 12, § 601. See also the passages given by Danz in Meuschen *Test. Illustr.* p. 651.

new truth, purging it of some local encumbrances which would gather about it in the mother country, and carrying it thus purged to far distant shores.

Meanwhile at Jerusalem some years passed away before the barrier of Judaism was assailed. The Apostles still observed the Mosaic ritual; they still confined their preaching to Jews by birth, or Jews by adoption, the proselytes of the covenant. At length a breach was made, and the assailants as might be expected were Hellenists. The first step towards the creation of an organised ministry was also the first step towards the emancipation of the Church. The Jews of Judæa, 'Hebrews of the Hebrews,' had ever regarded their Hellenist brethren with suspicion and distrust; and this estrangement reproduced itself in the Christian Church. The interests of the Hellenist widows had been neglected in the daily distribution of alms. Hence 'arose a murmuring of the Hellenists against the Hebrews (Acts vi. 1),' which was met by the appointment of seven persons specially charged with providing for the wants of these neglected poor. If the selection was made, as St Luke's language seems to imply, not by the Hellenists themselves but by the Church at large (vi. 2), the concession when granted was carried out in a liberal spirit. All the names of the seven are Greek, pointing to a Hellenist rather than a Hebrew extraction, and one is especially described as a proselyte, being doubtless chosen to represent a hitherto small but growing section of the community.

Appointment of Hellenist officers.

By this appointment the Hellenist members obtained a status in the Church; and the effects of this measure soon became visible. Two out of the seven stand prominently forward as the champions of emancipation, Stephen the preacher and martyr of liberty, and Philip the practical worker[1].

Effects of this measure.

[1] In Nicolas, the only one of the remaining five whose name reappears in history, liberty is degraded into licence. I see no valid reason for doubting the very early tradition that the Nicolaitans (Apoc. ii. 6, 15) derived their name from him. If there was a traitor among the Twelve, there might well be a heresiarch among the Seven. Nor is it likely that an account so discreditable to one who in the New Testament is named only in connexion with his appointment to an honourable office would have been circulated unless there were some foundation in fact. At the same time the Nicolaitans may have exaggerated and perverted the teaching of Nicolas. Irenæus (i. 26, 3) and Hippolytus (*Haer.*

Stephen's testimony.

STEPHEN is the acknowledged forerunner of the Apostle of the Gentiles. He was the first to 'look steadfastly to the end of that which is abolished,' to sound the death-knell of the Mosaic ordinances and the temple worship, and to claim for the Gospel unfettered liberty and universal rights. 'This man,' said his accusers, 'ceaseth not to speak words against the holy place and the law; for we have heard him say that this Jesus of Nazareth shall destroy this place and shall change the customs which Moses delivered us (vi. 13, 14).' The charge was only false as misrepresenting the spirit which animated his teaching. The accused attempts no denial, but pleads justification. To seal this testimony the first blood of the noble army of martyrs is shed.

Indirect consequences.

The indirect consequences of his martyrdom extend far beyond the immediate effect of his dying words. A persecution 'arose about Stephen.' The disciples of the mother Church 'were scattered abroad throughout the regions of Judæa and Samaria (viii. 1).' Some of the refugees even 'travelled as far as Phenice and Cyprus and Antioch (xi. 19).' This dispersion was, as we shall see, the parent of the first Gentile congregation. The Church of the Gentiles, it may be truly said, was baptized in the blood of Stephen.

Philip converts

The doctrine, which Stephen preached and for which he died, was carried into practice by PHILIP. The sacred narrative mentions two incidents in his career, each marking an onward stride in the free development of the Church. It is therefore not without signi-

vii. 36) believe him to have been the founder of the sect; while Clement of Alexandria (*Strom.* ii. p. 411, iii. p. 522, Potter) attributes to him an ambiguous saying that 'the flesh must be abused (*δεῖν παραχρῆσθαι τῇ σαρκί*),' of which these Nicolaitans perverted the meaning; and in attempting to clear his reputation relates a highly improbable story, which, if true, would be far from creditable. In another passage of Hippolytus, a fragment preserved in Syriac (Lagarde's *Anec. Syr.* p. 87, Cowper's *Syr. Miscell.* p. 55) and taken from the 'Discourse on the Resurrection' addressed to Mammæa, this writer again represents Nicolas as the founder of the sect, speaking of him as 'stirred by a strange spirit' and teaching that the resurrection is past (2 Tim. ii. 18), but not attributing to him any directly immoral doctrines. A common interpretation, which makes Nicolaus a Greek rendering of Balaam, is not very happy; for *Νικόλαος* does not altogether correspond with any possible derivation of Balaam, least of all with בלע עם 'the destroyer of the people,' generally adopted by those who so explain *Νικόλαος*. See below, p. 309, with the notes.

ficance that years afterwards we find him styled '*the* Evangelist' (xxi. 8), as if he had earned this honourable title by some signal service rendered to the Gospel.

1. The Samaritan occupied the border land between the Jew and the Gentile. Theologically, as geographically, he was the connecting link between the one and the other. Half Hebrew by race, half Israelite in his acceptance of a portion of the sacred canon, he held an anomalous position, shunning and shunned by the Jew, yet clinging to the same promises and looking forward to the same hopes. With a bold venture of faith Philip offers the Gospel to this mongrel people. His overtures are welcomed with joy, and 'Samaria receives the word of God.' The sacred historian relates moreover, that his labours were sanctioned by the presence of the chief Apostles Peter and John, and confirmed by an outpouring of the Holy Spirit (viii. 14—17). 'He who eats the bread of a Samaritan,' said the Jewish doctor, 'is as one who eats swine's flesh[1].' 'No Samaritan shall ever be made a proselyte. They have no share in the resurrection of the dead[2].' In opening her treasures to this hated race, the Church had surmounted the first barrier of prejudice behind which the exclusiveness of the nation

(1) The Samaritans;

[1] *Mishnah Shebiith* viii. 10.

[2] *Pirke Rabbi Eliezer* 38. The passage so well illustrates the statement in the text, that I give it in full: 'What did Ezra and Zerubbabel the son of Shealtiel and Jehoshua the son of Jehozadak? (They went) and they gathered together all the congregation into the temple of the Lord, and they brought 300 priests and 300 children and 300 trumpets and 300 scrolls of the law in their hands, and they blew, and the Levites sang and played, and they banned the Cuthæans (Samaritans) by the mystery of the ineffable name and by the writing which is written on the tables and by the anathema of the upper (heavenly) court of justice and by the anathema of the nether (earthly) court of justice, that no one of Israel should eat the bread of a Cuthæan for ever. Hence they (the elders) said: Whosoever eats the bread of a Cuthæan is as if he ate swine's flesh; and no Cuthæan shall ever be made a proselyte: and they have no share in the resurrection of the dead; for it is said (Ezra iv. 3) *Ye have nothing to do with us to build an house unto our God*, (that is) neither in this world nor in the future. And that they should have neither portion nor inheritance in Jerusalem, as it is said (Neh. ii. 20), *But ye had no portion nor right nor memorial in Jerusalem.* And they communicated the anathema to Israel which is in Babylon. And they put upon them anathema upon anathema. And king Cyrus also decreed upon them an everlasting anathema as it is said (Ezra vi. 12), *And the God that has caused His name to dwell there etc.*' Several passages bearing on this subject are collected in the article 'Samaritan Pentateuch,' by Mr E. Deutsch, in Smith's *Dictionary of the Bible*.

had entrenched itself. To be a Samaritan was to have a devil in the eyes of a rigid Jew (John viii. 48, comp. iv. 9).

(2) The Ethiopian eunuch.

2. Nor was it long before Philip broke through a second and more formidable line of defence. The blood of the patriarchs, though diluted, still flowed in the veins of the Samaritans. His next convert had no such claim to respect. A descendant of the accursed race of Ham[1], shut out from the congregation by his physical defect (Deut. xxiii. 1), the Ethiopian chamberlain laboured under a twofold disability. This double line is assailed by the Hellenist preacher and taken by storm. The desire of the Ethiopian to know and to do God's will is held by Philip to be a sufficient claim. He acts boldly and without hesitation. He accosts him, instructs him, baptizes him then and there.

Conversion of Cornelius.

The venture of the subordinate minister however still wanted the sanction of the leaders of the Church. At length this sanction was given in a signal way. The Apostles of the Circumcision, even St Peter himself, had failed hitherto to comprehend the wide purpose of God. With their fellow-countrymen they still 'held it unlawful for a Jew to keep company with or to come near an alien' (x. 28). The time when the Gospel should be preached to the Gentiles seemed not yet to have arrived: the manner in which it should be preached was still hidden from them. At length a divine vision scatters the dark scruples of Peter, teaching him to call no man 'common or unclean.' He goes himself and seeks out the devout Roman centurion Cornelius, whose household he instructs in the faith. The Gentile Church, thus founded on the same 'rock' with the Jewish, receives also the same divine confirmation. As Peter began to speak, 'the Holy Ghost fell on them, as it did' on the Jewish disciples on the first day of Pentecost (xi. 15). As if the approval of God could not be too prompt or too manifest, the usual sequence is reversed and the outpouring of the Spirit precedes the rite of baptism (x. 44—48).

Significance of this event.

The case of Cornelius does not, I think, differ essentially from the case of the Ethiopian eunuch. There is no ground for assuming

[1] Amos ix. 7, 'Are ye not as the children of the Ethiopians unto me, O children of Israel?'

that the latter was a proselyte of the covenant. His mutilation excluded him from the congregation by a Mosaic ordinance, and it is an arbitrary conjecture that the definite enactment of the law was overruled by the spiritual promise of the prophet (Is. lvi. 3—5). This liberal interpretation at all events accords little with the narrow and formal spirit of the age. Both converts alike had the inward qualification of 'fearing God and working righteousness' (x. 35); both alike were disabled by external circumstances, and the disabilities of the Ethiopian eunuch were even greater than those of the Roman centurion. If so, the significance of the conversion of the latter consists in this, that now in the case of the Gentile, as before in the case of the Samaritan, the principle asserted by the Hellenist Philip is confirmed by the Apostles of the Circumcision in the person of their chief and sealed by the outpouring of the Spirit.

Preaching to Gentiles at Antioch.

Meanwhile others were asserting the universality of the Church elsewhere, if not with the same sanction of authority, at all events with a larger measure of success. With the dying words of Stephen, the martyr of Christian liberty, still ringing in their ears, the persecuted brethren had fled from Jerusalem and carried the tidings of the Gospel to distant lands. At first they 'preached the word to none but to the Jews only' (xi. 19). At length others bolder than the rest, 'when they were come to Antioch, spake unto the Gentiles[1], preaching the Lord Jesus.' Probably this was an advance even on the conversion of the Ethiopian eunuch and of Cornelius. These two converts at all events recognised the God of the old covenant. Now for the first time, it would seem, the Gospel was offered to heathen idolaters. Here, as before, the innovators were not Hebrews but Hellenists, 'men of Cyprus and Cyrene' (xi. 20). Their success was signal: crowds flocked to hear them; and at Antioch first the brethren were called by a new name—a term of ridicule and contempt then, now the pride and glory of the civilized world. Hitherto the believers had been known as 'Galileans' or 'Nazarenes'; now they were called 'Christians.' The transition from

The name Christians.

[1] xi. 20. I cannot doubt that Ἕλληνας is correct, as the preceding Ἰουδαίους requires it; but external authority preponderates in favour of Ἑλληνιστάς.

a Jewish to a heathen term marks the point of time when the Church of the Gentiles first threatens to supersede the Church of the Circumcision.

The first step gained.

Thus the first stage in the emancipation of the Church was gained. The principle was broadly asserted that the Gospel received all comers, asking no questions, allowing no impediments, insisting on no preliminary conditions, if only it were found that the petitioner 'feared God and worked righteousness.'

2. *The Recognition of Gentile Liberty.*

It is plain that the principle, which had thus been asserted, involved consequences very much wider than were hitherto clearly foreseen and acknowledged. But between asserting a principle and carrying it out to its legitimate results a long interval must necessarily elapse, for many misgivings have to be dissipated and many impediments to be overcome.

Questions yet unsettled.

So it was with the growth of Gentile Christendom. The Gentiles were no longer refused admission into the Church unless first incorporated with Israel by the initiatory rite. But many questions remained still unsettled. What was their exact position, when thus received? What submission, if any, must they yield to the Mosaic law? Should they be treated as in all respects on an equality with the true Israelite? Was it right for the Jewish Christian so far to lay aside the traditions of his race, as to associate freely with his Gentile brother? These must necessarily in time become practical questions, and press for a solution.

Saul of Tarsus

At this point in the history of the Church a new character appears on the scene. The mantle of Stephen has fallen on the persecutor of Stephen. SAUL has been called to bear the name of Christ to the Gentiles. Descended of pure Hebrew ancestry and schooled in the law by the most famous of living teachers, born and residing in a great university town second to none in its reputation for Greek wisdom and learning, inheriting the privileges and the bearing of a Roman citizen, he seemed to combine in himself all those varied qualifications which would best fit him for this work. These wide experiences, which had lain dormant before, were quickened into thought and life by the lightning flash on the way to Damascus; and stubborn zeal was melted and fused into large-hearted and comprehensive charity. From his conversion to the present time we read only of his preaching in the synagogues at Damascus (ix. 20, 22) and to the Hellenists at Jerusalem (ix. 29). But now the moment was ripe, when he must enter upon that wider sphere of action for which he had been specially designed. The Gentile Church, founded on the 'rock,' must be handed over to the 'wise master-builder' to enlarge and complete. So at the bidding of the Apostles, Barnabas seeks out Saul in his retirement at Tarsus and brings him to Antioch. Doubtless he seemed to all to be the fittest instrument for carrying out the work so auspiciously begun. goes to Antioch.

Meanwhile events at Jerusalem were clearing the way for his great work. The star of Jewish Christendom was already on the wane, while the independence of the Gentiles was gradually asserting itself. Two circumstances especially were instrumental in reversing the positions hitherto held by these two branches of the Church. Circumstances affecting the mother Church.

1. It has been seen that the martyrdom of Stephen marked an epoch in the emancipation of the Church. The martyrdom of James the son of Zebedee is scarcely less important in its influence on her progressive career. The former persecution had sown the disciples broad-cast over heathen lands; the latter seems to have been the signal for the withdrawal of the Apostles themselves from Jerusalem. The twelve years, which according to an old tradition our Lord had assigned as the limit of their fixed residence there, had drawn to a close[1]. So, consigning the direction of the mother Church to James the Lord's brother and the presbytery, they depart thence to enter upon a wider field of action. Their withdrawal must have deprived the Church of Jerusalem of half her prestige and more than half her influence. Henceforth she remained indeed the mother Church of the nation, but she was no longer the mother Church of the world. (1) Withdrawal of the Apostles.

[1] See above, p. 127, n. 1.

(2) Famine relieved by Gentile alms.

2. About the same time another incident also contributed to lessen her influence. A severe famine devastated Palestine and reduced the Christian population to extreme want. Collections were made at Antioch, and relief was sent to the brethren in Judæa. By this exercise of liberality the Gentile Churches were made to feel their own importance: while the recipients, thus practically confessing their dependence, were deposed from the level of proud isolation which many of them would gladly have maintained. This famine seems to have ranged over many years, or at all events its attacks were several times repeated. Again and again the alms of the Gentile Christians were conveyed by the hands of the Gentile Apostles, and the Churches of Judæa laid themselves under fresh obligations to the heathen converts.

New stage of the Gospel.

Events being thus ripe, Saul still residing at Antioch is set apart by the Spirit for the Apostleship of the Gentiles to which he had been called years before.

The Gospel thus enters upon a new career of triumph. The primacy of the Church passes from Peter to Paul—from the Apostle of the Circumcision to the Apostle of the Gentiles. The centre of evangelical work is transferred from Jerusalem to Antioch. Paul and Barnabas set forth on their first missionary tour.

St Paul's first missionary journey.

Though they give precedence everywhere to the Jews, their mission is emphatically to the Gentiles. In Cyprus, the first country visited, its character is signally manifested in the conversion of the Roman proconsul, Sergius Paulus. And soon it becomes evident that the younger Church must supplant the elder. At Antioch in Pisidia matters are brought to a crisis: the Jews reject the offer of the Gospel: the Gentiles entreat to hear the message. Thereupon the doom is pronounced: 'It was necessary that the word of God should first have been spoken to you; but seeing ye put it from you and judge yourselves unworthy of everlasting life, lo we turn to the Gentiles' (xiii. 46). The incidents at Pisidian Antioch foreshadow the destiny which awaits the Gospel throughout the world. Everywhere the Apostles deliver their message to the Jews first, and everywhere the offer rejected by them is welcomed by the heathen. The mission of Paul and Barnabas is successful, but its success is confined almost wholly to the Gentiles. They return to Antioch.

The question of circumcision raised.

Hitherto no attempt had been made to define the mutual relations of Jewish and Gentile converts. All such questions, it would seem, had been tacitly passed over, neither side perhaps being desirous of provoking discussion. But the inevitable crisis at length arrives. Certain converts, who had imported into the Church of Christ the rigid and exclusive spirit of Pharisaism, stir up the slumbering feud at Antioch, starting the question in its most trenchant form. They desire to impose circumcision on the Gentiles, not only as a condition of equality, but as necessary to salvation (xv. 1). The imposition of this burden is resisted by Paul and Barnabas, who go on a mission to Jerusalem to confer with the Apostles and elders.

Accounts of the conference.

I have already given what seems to me the probable account of the part taken by the leading Apostles in these controversies[1], and shall have to return to the subject later. Our difficulty in reading this page of history arises not so much from the absence of light as from the perplexity of cross lights. The narratives of St Luke and St Paul only then cease to conflict, when we take into account the different positions of the writers and the different objects they had in view.

Twofold results.

At present we are concerned only with the results of this conference. These are twofold: *First*, the settlement of the points of dispute between the Jewish and Gentile converts: *Secondly*, the recognition of the authority and commission of Paul and Barnabas by the Apostles of the Circumcision. It will be necessary, as briefly as possible, to point out the significance of these two conclusions and to examine how far they were recognised and acted upon subsequently.

The decree a compromise.

1. The arrangement of the disputed points was effected by a mutual compromise. On the one hand it was decided once and for ever that the rite of circumcision should not be imposed on the Gentiles. On the other, concessions were demanded of them in turn; they were asked to 'abstain from meats offered to idols, and from blood, and from things strangled, and from fornication.'

[1] See above, p. 126 sq, and the notes on ii. 1—10.

Emancipating clause.

The first of these decisions was a question of principle. If the initiatory rite of the old dispensation were imposed on all members of the Christian Church, this would be in effect to deny that the Gospel was a new covenant; in other words to deny its essential character[1]. It was thus the vital point on which the whole controversy turned. And the liberal decision of the council was not only the charter of Gentile freedom but the assertion of the supremacy of the Gospel.

Restrictive clauses.

On the other hand it is not so easy to understand the bearing of the restrictions imposed on the Gentile converts. Their significance in fact seems to be relative rather than absolute. There were certain practices into which, though most abhorrent to the feelings of their Jewish brethren, the Gentile Christians from early habit and constant association would easily be betrayed. These were of different kinds: some were grave moral offences, others only violations of time-honoured observances, inwrought in the conscience of the Israelite. After the large concession of principle made to the Gentiles in the matter of circumcision, it was not unreasonable that they should be required in turn to abstain from practices which gave so much offence to the Jews. Hence the prohibitions in question. It is strange indeed that offences so heterogeneous should be thrown together and brought under one prohibition; but this is perhaps sufficiently explained by supposing the decree framed to meet some definite complaint of the Jewish brethren. If, in the course of the hot dispute which preceded the speeches of the leading Apostles, attention had been specially called by the Pharisaic party to these detested practices, St James would not unnaturally take up the subject and propose to satisfy them by a direct condemnation of the offences in question[2].

The decree disregarded by some.

It would betray great gnorance of human nature to suppose that a decision thus authoritatively pronounced must have silenced all

[1] See Ritschl, p. 127.

[2] This seems to me much simpler than explaining the clauses as enforcing the conditions under which proselytes of the gate were received by the Jews. In this latter case πορνεία will perhaps refer to unlawful marriage, e.g. within the prohibited degrees of kindred (Levit. xviii. 18), as it is interpreted by Ritschl p. 129 sq, who ably maintains this view. These difficulties of interpretation are to my mind a very strong evidence of the genuineness of the decree.

opposition. If therefore we should find its provisions constantly disregarded hereafter, it is no argument against the genuineness of the decree itself. The bigoted minority was little likely to make an absolute surrender of its most stubborn prejudices to any external influence. Many even of those, who at the time were persuaded by the leading Apostles into acquiescence, would find their misgivings return, when they saw that the effect of the decree was to wrest the sceptre from their grasp and place it in the hands of the Gentile Church.

Circumcision still insisted on.

Even the question of circumcision, on which an absolute decision had been pronounced, was revived again and again. Long after, the Judaizing antagonists of St Paul in Galatia attempted to force this rite on his Gentile converts. Perhaps however they rather evaded than defied the decree. They may for instance have no longer insisted upon it as a condition of salvation, but urged it as a title to preference. But however this may be, there is nothing startling in the fact itself.

The restrictive clauses not uniformly enforced.

But while the *emancipating* clause of the decree, though express and definite, was thus parried or resisted, the *restrictive* clauses were with much greater reason interpreted with latitude. The miscellaneous character of these prohibitions showed that, taken as a whole, they had no binding force independently of the circumstances which dictated them. They were a temporary expedient framed to meet a temporary emergency. Their object was the avoidance of offence in mixed communities of Jew and Gentile converts. Beyond this recognised aim and the general understanding implied therein the limits of their application were not defined. Hence there was room for much latitude in individual cases. St James, as the head of the mother Church where the difficulties which it was framed to meet were most felt, naturally refers to the decree seven years after as still regulating the intercourse between Jewish and Gentile converts (xxi. 25). At Antioch too and in the neighbouring Churches of Syria and Cilicia, to which alone the Apostolic letter was addressed and on which alone therefore the enactments were directly binding (xv. 23), it was doubtless long observed. The close communica-

St James.

Antioch and the neighbouring churches.

tion between these churches and Jerusalem would at once justify and secure its strict observance. We read also of its being delivered to the brotherhoods of Lycaonia and Pisidia, already founded when the council was held, and near enough to Palestine to feel the pressure of Jewish feelings (xvi. 4). But as the circle widens, its influence becomes feebler. In strictly Gentile churches it seems never to have been enforced. St Paul, writing to the Corinthians, discusses two of the four practices which it prohibits without any reference to its enactments. Fornication he condemns absolutely as defiling the body which is the temple of God (1 Cor. v. 1—13, vi. 18—20). Of eating meats sacrificed to idols he speaks as a thing indifferent in itself, only to be avoided in so far as it implies participation in idol worship or is offensive to the consciences of others. His rule therefore is this: 'Do not sit down to a banquet celebrated in an idol's temple. You may say that in itself an idol is nothing, that neither the abstaining from meat nor the partaking of meat commends us to God. All this I grant is true: but such knowledge is dangerous. You are running the risk of falling into idolatry yourself, you are certainly by your example leading others astray; you are in fact committing an overt act of treason to God, you are a partaker of the tables of devils. On the other hand do not officiously inquire when you make a purchase at the shambles or when you dine in a private house: but if in such cases you are plainly told that the meat has been offered in sacrifice, then abstain at all hazards. Lay down this rule, to give no offence either to Jews or Gentiles or to the churches of God' (1 Cor. viii. 1—13, x. 14—22). This wise counsel, if it disregards the letter, preserves the spirit of the decree, which was framed for the avoidance of offence. But St Paul's language shows that the decree itself was not held binding, perhaps was unknown at Corinth: otherwise the discussion would have been foreclosed. Once again we come across the same topics in the apocalyptic message to the Churches of Pergamos and Thyatira. The same irregularities prevailed here as at Corinth: there was the temptation on the one hand to impure living, on the other to acts of conformity with heathen worship which compromised their allegiance

St Paul to the Corinthians.

St John to the Asiatic churches.

to the one true God. Our Lord in St John's vision denounces them through the symbolism of the Old Testament history. In the Church of Pergamos, were certain Nicolaitans 'holding the doctrine of Balaam who taught Balac to cast a stumblingblock before the children of Israel, to eat things sacrificed to idols and to commit fornication' (ii. 14). At Thyatira the evil had struck its roots deeper. The angel of that Church is rebuked because he 'suffers his wife Jezebel who calls herself a prophetess, and she teacheth and seduceth God's servants to commit fornication and to eat things sacrificed to idols.' I see no reason for assuming a reference here to the Apostolic decree. The two offences singled out are those to which Gentile churches would be most liable, and which at the same time are illustrated by the Old Testament parallels. If St Paul denounces them independently of the decree, St John may have done so likewise[1]. In the matter of sacrificial meats indeed the condemnation of the latter is more absolute and uncompromising. But this is owing partly to the epigrammatic terseness and symbolic reference of the passage, partly, also, we may suppose, to the more definite form which the evil itself had assumed[2]. In both cases the practice was justified by a vaunted knowledge which held itself superior to any such restrictions[3]. But at Corinth this temper

[1] Yet the expression *οὐ βάλλω ἐφ' ὑμᾶς ἄλλο βάρος* (ii. 24) looks like a reference to the decree.

[2] The coincidence of the two Apostles extends also to their language. (1) If St John denounces the offence as a following of Balaam, St Paul uses the same Old Testament illustration, 1 Cor. x. 7, 8, 'Neither be ye idolaters, as were some of them; as it is written, The people sat down to eat and drink, and rose up to play: neither let us commit fornication, as some of them committed, and fell in one day three and twenty thousand.' (2) If St John speaks of 'casting a stumblingblock (*σκάνδαλον*) before the children of Israel,' the whole purport of St Paul's warning is 'to give no offence' (*μὴ σκανδαλίζειν*, viii. 13, *ἀπρόσκοποι γίνεσθαι*, x. 32). With all these coincidences of matter and language, it is a strange phenomenon that any critic should maintain, as Baur, Zeller, and Schwegler have done, that the denunciations in the Apocalypse are directed against St Paul himself.

[3] Comp. Apoc. ii. 24 *ὅσοι οὐκ ἔχουσιν τὴν διδαχὴν ταύτην, οἵτινες οὐκ ἔγνωσαν τὰ βαθέα τοῦ Σατανᾶ, ὡς λέγουσιν*. The false teachers boasted a knowledge of the deep things of God; they possessed only a knowledge of the deep things of Satan. St John's meaning is illustrated by a passage in Hippolytus (*Haer.* v. 6, p. 94) relating to the Ophites, who offer other striking resemblances to the heretics of the Apostolic age; *ἐπεκάλεσαν ἑαυτοὺς γνωστικούς, φάσκοντες μόνοι τὰ βάθη γινώσκειν*: see also Iren. ii. 28. 9. St Paul's rebuke is very different in form, but the same in effect. He begins each time in a strain of noble irony. 'We all have knowledge'; 'I speak as to wise men': he appears to concede,

was still immature and under restraint: while in the Asiatic churches it had outgrown shame and broken out into the wildest excesses[1].

Object of the enactments not defined.

Thus then the decree was neither permanently nor universally binding. But there was also another point which admitted much latitude of interpretation. What was understood to be the design of these enactments? They were articles of peace indeed, but of what nature was this peace to be? Was it to effect an entire union between the Jewish and Gentile churches, a complete identity of interest; or only to secure a strict neutrality, a condition of mutual toleration? Were the Gentiles to be welcomed as brothers and admitted at once to all the privileges of sons of Israel: or was the Church hereafter to be composed of two separate nationalities, as it were, equal and independent; or lastly, were the heathen converts to be recognised indeed, but only as holding a subordinate position like proselytes under the old covenant? The first interpretation is alone consistent with the spirit of the Gospel: but either of the others might honestly be maintained without any direct violation of the letter of the decree. The Church of Antioch, influenced doubtless by St Paul, took the larger and truer view; Jewish and Gentile converts lived freely together as members of one brotherhood. A portion at least of the Church of Jerusalem, 'certain who came from James,' adopted a narrower interpretation and still clung to the old distinctions, regarding their Gentile brethren as unclean and refusing to eat with them. This was not the Truth of the Gospel, it was not the Spirit of Christ; but neither was it a direct breach of compact.

St Paul's authority recognised.

2. Scarcely less important than the settlement of the disputed

to defer, to sympathize, even to encourage: and then he turns round upon the laxity of this vaunted wisdom and condemns and crushes it: 'I will eat no flesh while the world standeth, lest I make my brother to offend'; 'I would not that ye should have fellowship with devils.'

[1] The subject of εἰδωλόθυτα does not disappear with the apostolic age: it turns up again for instance in the middle of the second century, in Agrippa Castor (Euseb. *H. E.* iv. 7) writing against Basilides, and in Justin (*Dial.* 35, p. 253 D) who mentions the Basilideans among other Gnostic sects as 'participating in lawless and godless rites': comp. *Orac. Sib.* ii. 96. Both these writers condemn the practice, the latter with great severity. When the persecution began, and the Christians were required to deny their faith by participating in the sacrifices, it became a matter of extreme importance to avoid any act of conformity, however slight.

points was the other result of these conferences, the recognition of St Paul's office and mission by the Apostles of the Circumcision. This recognition is recorded in similar language in the narrative of the Acts and in the epistle to the Galatians. In the Apostolic circular inserted in the former Paul and Barnabas are commended as 'men who have hazarded their lives for the name of our Lord Jesus Christ' (xv. 26). In the conferences, as related in the latter, the three Apostles, James, Peter, and John, seeing that 'the Gospel of the uncircumcision was committed unto him,' and 'perceiving the grace that was given unto him, gave to him and Barnabas the right hand of fellowship, that they should go unto the heathen' (ii. 7—10).

Continued opposition to St Paul.

This ample recognition would doubtless carry weight with a large number of Jewish converts: but no sanction of authority could overcome in others the deep repugnance felt to one who, himself a 'Hebrew of the Hebrews,' had systematically opposed the law of Moses and triumphed in his opposition. Henceforth St Paul's career was one life-long conflict with Judaizing antagonists. Setting aside the Epistles to the Thessalonians, which were written too early to be affected by this struggle, all his letters addressed to churches, with but one exception[1], refer more or less directly to such opposition. It assumed different forms in different places: in Galatia it was purely Pharisaic; in Phrygia and Asia it was strongly tinged with speculative mysticism; but everywhere and under all circumstances zeal for the law was its ruling passion. The systematic hatred of St Paul is an important fact, which we are too apt to overlook, but without which the whole history of the Apostolic ages will be misread and misunderstood.

3. *The Emancipation of the Jewish Churches.*

Zeal for the law.

We have seen hitherto no signs of waning affection for the law in the Jewish converts to Christianity as a body. On the contrary the danger which threatened it from a quarter so unexpected seems

[1] This exception, the Epistle to the Ephesians, may be explained by its character as a circular letter to the Asiatic churches, in which special references would be out of place.

to have fanned their zeal to a red heat. Even in the churches of St Paul's own founding his name and authority were not powerful enough to check the encroachments of the Judaizing party. Only here and there, in mixed communities, the softening influences of daily intercourse must have been felt, and the true spirit of the Gospel insensibly diffused, inculcating the truth that 'in Christ was neither Jew nor Greek.'

Reasons for its observance in the mother Church.

But the mother Church of Jerusalem, being composed entirely of Jewish converts, lacked these valuable lessons of daily experience. Moreover the law had claims on a Hebrew of Palestine wholly independent of his religious obligations. To him it was a national institution, as well as a divine covenant. Under the Gospel he might consider his relations to it in this latter character altered, but as embodying the decrees and usages of his country it still demanded his allegiance. To be a good Christian he was not required to be a bad citizen. On these grounds the more enlightened members of the mother church would justify their continued adhesion to the law. Nor is there any reason to suppose that St Paul himself took a different view of their obligations. The Apostles of the Circumcision meanwhile, if conscious themselves that the law was fulfilled in the Gospel they strove nevertheless by strict conformity to conciliate the zealots both within and without the Church, were only acting upon St Paul's own maxim, who 'became to the Jews a Jew that he might gain the Jews.' Meanwhile they felt that a catastrophe was impending, that a deliverance was at hand. Though they were left in uncertainty as to the time and manner of this divine event, the mysterious warnings of the Lord had placed the fact itself beyond a doubt. They might well therefore leave all perplexing questions to the solution of time, devoting themselves meanwhile to the practical work which lay at their doors.

Fall of Jerusalem.

A.D. 70.

And soon the catastrophe came which solved the difficult problem. The storm which had long been gathering burst over the devoted city. Jerusalem was razed to the ground, and the Temple-worship ceased, never again to be revived. The Christians foreseeing the calamity had fled before the tempest; and at Pella, a city of the

Decapolis, in the midst of a population chiefly Gentile the Church of the Circumcision was reconstituted. They were warned to flee, said the story, by an oracle[1]: but no special message from heaven was needed at this juncture; the signs of the times, in themselves full of warning, interpreted by the light of the Master's prophecies plainly foretold the approaching doom. Before the crisis came, they had been deprived of the counsel and guidance of the leading Apostles. Peter had fallen a martyr at Rome; John had retired to Asia Minor; James the Lord's brother was slain not long before the great catastrophe; and some thought that the horrors of the Flavian war were the just vengeance of an offended God for the murder of so holy a man[2]. He was succeeded by his cousin Symeon, the son of Clopas and nephew of Joseph.

The church at Pella.

Under these circumstances the Church was reformed at Pella. Its history in the ages following is a hopeless blank[3]; and it would be vain to attempt to fill in the picture from conjecture. We cannot doubt however that the consequences of the fall of Jerusalem, direct or indirect, were very great. In two points especially its effects

Effects

[1] Euseb. *H. E.* iii. 5 *κατά τινα χρησμὸν τοῖς αὐτόθι δοκίμοις δι' ἀποκαλύψεως ἐκδοθέντα κ.τ.λ.*

[2] Hegesippus in Euseb. *H. E.* ii. 23 *καὶ εὐθὺς Οὐεσπασιανὸς πολιορκεῖ αὐτούς*, and the pseudo-Josephus also quoted there, *ταῦτα δὲ συμβέβηκεν Ἰουδαίοις κατ' ἐκδίκησιν Ἰακώβου τοῦ δικαίου κ.τ.λ.*

[3] The Church of Pella however contributed one author at least to the ranks of early Christian literature in Ariston, the writer of an apology in the form of a dialogue between Jason a Hebrew Christian and Papiscus an Alexandrian Jew: see Routh I. p. 93. One of his works however was written after the Bar-cochba rebellion, to which it alludes (Euseb. *H. E.* iv. 6); and from the purport of the allusion we may infer that it was this very dialogue. The expulsion of the Jews by Hadrian was a powerful common-place in the treatises of the Apologists; see e.g. Justin Martyr *Apol.* i. 47. On the other hand it cannot have been written long after, for it was quoted by Celsus (Orig. *c. Cels.* iv. 52, p. 544, Delarue). The shade of doubt which rests on the authorship of this dialogue is very slight. Undue weight seems to be attributed to the fact of its being quoted anonymously; e.g. in Westcott's *Canon*, p. 93, Donaldson's *Christian Literature etc.* II. p. 58. If I am right in conjecturing that the reference to the banishment of the Jews was taken from this dialogue, Eusebius himself directly attributes it to Ariston. The name of the author however is of little consequence, for the work was clearly written by a Hebrew Christian not later than the middle of the second century. Whoever he may have been, the writer was no Ebionite, for he explained Gen. i. 1, 'In filio fecit Deus caelum et terram' (Hieron. *Quaest. Hebr. in Gen.*, III. p. 305, ed. Vall.); and the fact is important, as this is the earliest known expression of Hebrew Christian doctrine after the canonical writings, except perhaps the Testaments of the Twelve Patriarchs.

of the change. would be powerfully felt, in the change of opinion produced within the Church itself and in the altered relations between the converted and unconverted Jews.

(1) The law loses its power. (1) The loss of their great leader at this critical moment was compensated to the Church of the Circumcision by the stern teaching of facts. In the obliteration of the Temple services they were brought at length to see that all other sacrifices were transitory shadows, faint emblems of the one Paschal Lamb, slain once and for ever for the sins of the world. In the impossibility of observing the Mosaic ordinances except in part, they must have been led to question the efficacy of the whole. And besides all this, those who had hitherto maintained their allegiance to the law purely as a national institution were by the overthrow of the nation set free henceforth from any such obligation. We need not suppose that these inferences were drawn at once or drawn by all alike; but slowly and surely the fall of the city must have produced this effect.

(2) Jews and Christians in antagonism. (2) At the same time it wholly changed their relations with their unconverted countrymen. Hitherto they had maintained such close intercourse that in the eyes of the Roman the Christians were as one of the many Jewish sects. Henceforth they stood in a position of direct antagonism. The sayings ascribed to the Jewish rabbis of this period are charged with the bitterest reproaches of the Christians, who are denounced as more dangerous than the heathen, and anathemas against the hated sect were introduced into their daily prayers[1]. The probable cause of this change is not far to seek. While the catastrophe was still impending, the Christians seem to have stood forward and denounced the national sins which had brought down the chastisement of God on their country. In the traditional notices at least this feature may be discerned. Nor could they fail to connect together as cause and effect the stubborn rejection of Messiah and the coming doom which He Himself had foretold. And when at length the blow fell, by withdrawing from the

[1] See especially Graetz *Geschichte der Juden* IV. p. 112 sq. The antagonism between the Jews and Christians at this period is strongly insisted upon by this writer, whose account is the more striking as given from a Jewish point of view.

city and refusing to share the fate of their countrymen they declared by an overt act that henceforth they were strangers, that now at length their hopes and interests were separate.

These altered relations both to the Mosaic law and to the Jewish people must have worked as leaven in the minds of the Christians of the Circumcision. Questions were asked now, which from their nature could not have been asked before. Difficulties hitherto unfelt seemed to start up on all sides. The relations of the Church to the synagogue, of the Gospel to the law, must now be settled in some way or other. Thus diversities of opinion, which had hitherto been lulled in a broken and fitful slumber, suddenly woke up into dangerous activity. The Apostles, who at an earlier date had moderated extreme tendencies and to whom all would have looked instinctively for counsel and instruction, had passed away from the scene. One personal follower of the Lord however still remained, Symeon the aged bishop, who had succeeded James[1]. At length he too was removed. After a long tenure of office he was martyred at a very advanced age in the ninth year of Trajan. His death, according to Hegesippus, was the signal for a shameless outbreak of multitudinous heresies which had hitherto worked underground, the Church having as yet preserved her virgin purity undefiled[2]. Though this early historian has interwoven many fabulous details in his account, there seems no reason to doubt the truth of the broad statement, confirmed as it is from another source[3], that this epoch was the birth-time of many forms of dissent in the Church of the Circumcision.

Difficulties and dissensions.

Symeon son of Clopas. A.D. 106.

How far these dissensions and diversities of opinion had ripened meanwhile into open schism, to what extent the majority still conformed to the Mosaic ordinances (as for instance in the practice of circumcision and the observance of the sabbath), we have no data to determine. But the work begun by the fall of Jerusalem was only

[1] Hegesippus in Euseb. *H. E.* iv. 22. This writer also mentions grandsons of Jude the Lord's brother as ruling over the Churches and surviving till the time of Trajan; *H. E.* iii. 32.

[2] Euseb. *H. E.* iii. 32 *ἐπιλέγει ὡς ἄρα μέχρι τῶν τότε χρόνων παρθένος καθαρὰ καὶ ἀδιάφθορος ἔμεινεν ἡ ἐκκλησία, ἐν ἀδήλῳ που σκότει φωλευόντων εἰσέτι τότε τῶν, εἰ καί τινες ὑπῆρχον, παραφθείρειν ἐπιχειρούντων κ.τ.λ.*: comp. iv. 22.

[3] See below, p. 325, note 5.

at length completed by the advent of another crisis. By this second catastrophe the Church and the law were finally divorced; and the malcontents who had hitherto remained within the pale of the Church become declared separatists.

Rebellion of Bar-cochba. A.D. 132—135.

A revolution of the Jews broke out in all the principal centres of the dispersion. The flame thus kindled in the dependencies spread later to the mother country. In Palestine a leader started up, professing himself to be the long promised Messiah, and in reference to the prophecy of Balaam styling himself 'Bar-cochba,' 'the son of the Star.' We have the testimony of one who wrote while these scenes of bloodshed were still fresh in men's memories, that the Christians were the chief sufferers from this rebel chieftain[1]. Even without such testimony this might have been safely inferred. Their very existence was a protest against his claims: they must be denounced and extirpated, if his pretensions were to be made good. The cause of Bar-cochba was taken up as the cause of the whole Jewish nation, and thus the antagonism between Judaism and Christianity was brought to a head. After a desperate struggle the rebellion was trampled out and the severest vengeance taken on the insurgents. The practice of circumcision and the observance of the sabbath—indeed all the distinguishing marks of Judaism—were visited with the severest penalties. On the other hand the Christians, as the avowed enemies of the rebel chief, seem to have been favourably received. On the ruins of Jerusalem Hadrian had built his new city Ælia Capitolina. Though no Jew was admitted within sight of its walls, the Christians were allowed to settle there freely[2]. Now for the first time a Gentile bishop was appointed, and the Church of Jerusalem ceased to be the Church of the Circumcision[3].

Ælia Capitolina.

The church

The account of Eusebius seems to imply that long before this

[1] Justin *Apol.* i. 31, p. 72 E, *ἐν τῷ νῦν γεγενημένῳ Ἰουδαϊκῷ πολέμῳ Βαρχωχέβας ὁ τῆς Ἰουδαίων ἀποστάσεως ἀρχηγέτης Χριστιανοὺς μόνους εἰς τιμωρίας δεινάς, εἰ μὴ ἀρνοῖντο Ἰησοῦν τὸν Χριστὸν καὶ βλασφημοῖεν, ἐκέλευεν ἀπάγεσθαι.*

[2] Justin *Apol.* i. 47, p. 84 B, *Dial.* 110, p. 337 D; Ariston of Pella in Euseb. *H. E.* iv. 6; Celsus in Orig. *c. Cels.* viii. 69.

[3] Sulpicius Severus (*H. S.* ii. 31) speaking of Hadrian's decree says, 'Quod quidem Christianae fidei proficiebat, quia tum pene omnes Christum Deum sub legis observatione credebant; nimirum id Domino ordinante dispositum, ut legis servitus a libertate fidei atque ecclesiae tolleretur.'

disastrous outbreak of the Jews the main part of the Christians had left their retirement in Pella and returned to their original home. At all events he traces the succession of bishops of Jerusalem in an unbroken line from James the Lord's brother until the foundation of the new city[1]. If so, we must imagine the Church once more scattered by this second catastrophe, and once more re-formed when the terror was passed. But the Church of Ælia Capitolina was very differently constituted from the Church of Pella or the Church of Jerusalem; a large proportion of its members at least were Gentiles[2]. Of the Christians of the Circumcision not a few doubtless accepted the conqueror's terms, content to live henceforth as Gentiles, and settled down in the new city of Hadrian. But there were others who clung to the law of their forefathers with a stubborn grasp which no force of circumstances could loosen: and henceforward we read of two distinct sects of Judaizing Christians, observing the law with equal rigour but observing it on different grounds[3].

reconstituted.

Judaizing sects.

[1] *H. E.* iii. 32, 35, iv. 5. Eusebius seems to narrate all the incidents affecting the Church of the Circumcision during this period, as taking place not at Pella but at Jerusalem.

[2] Euseb. *H. E.* iv. 6 *τῆς αὐτόθι ἐκκλησίας ἐξ ἐθνῶν συγκροτηθείσης*.

[3] As early as the middle of the second century Justin Martyr distinguishes two classes of Judaizers; those who retaining the Mosaic law themselves did not wish to impose it on their Gentile brethren, and those who insisted upon conformity in all Christians alike as a condition of communion and a means of salvation (*Dial. c. Tryph.* § 47; see Schliemann *Clement.* p. 553 sq). In the next chapter Justin alludes with disapprobation to *some* Jewish converts who held that our Lord was a mere man; and it seems not unreasonable to connect this opinion with the second of the two classes before mentioned. We thus obtain a tolerably clear view of their distinctive tenets. But the first direct and definite account of both sects is given by the fathers of the fourth century especially Epiphanius and Jerome, who distinguish them by the respective names of 'Nazarenes' and 'Ebionites.' Irenæus (i. 26. 2), Tertullian (*de Praescr.* 33), and Hippolytus (*Haer.* vii. 34, p. 257), contemplate only the second, whom they call Ebionites. The Nazarenes in fact, being for the most part orthodox in their creed and holding communion with Catholic Christians, would not generally be included in the category of heretics: and moreover, being few in number and living in an obscure region, they would easily escape notice. Origen (*c. Cels.* v. 61) mentions two classes of Christians who observe the Mosaic law, the one holding with the Catholics that Jesus was born of a Virgin, the other that he was conceived like other men; and both these he calls Ebionites. In another passage he says that both classes of Ebionites (*Ἐβιωναῖοι ἀμφότεροι*) reject St Paul's Epistles (v. 65). If these two classes correspond to the 'Nazarenes' and 'Ebionites' of Jerome, Origen's information would seem to be incorrect. On the other hand it is very

Nazarenes.

1. The NAZARENES appear at the close of the fourth century as a small and insignificant sect dwelling beyond the Jordan in Pella and the neighbouring places[1]. Indications of their existence however occur in Justin two centuries and a half earlier; and both their locality and their name carry us back to the primitive ages of Jewish Christianity. Can we doubt that they were the remnant of the fugitive Church, which refused to return from their exile with the majority to the now Gentile city, some because they were too indolent or too satisfied to move, others because the abandonment of the law seemed too heavy a price to pay for Roman forbearance?

Their tenets.

The account of their tenets is at all events favourable to this inference[2]. They held themselves bound to the Mosaic ordinances, rejecting however all Pharisaic interpretations and additions. Nevertheless they did not consider the Gentile Christians under the same obligations or refuse to hold communion with them; and in the like spirit, in this distinguished from all other Judaizing sectarians, they fully recognised the work and mission of St Paul[3]. It is stated moreover that they mourned over the unbelief of their fellow-countrymen, praying for and looking forward to the time

possible that he entirely overlooks the Nazarenes and alludes to some differences of opinion among the Ebionites properly so called; but in this case it is not easy to identify his two classes with the Pharisaic and Essene Ebionites of whom I shall have to speak later. Eusebius, who also describes two classes of Ebionites (*H. E.* iii. 27), seems to have taken his account wholly from Irenæus and Origen. If, as appears probable, both names 'Nazarenes' and 'Ebionites' were originally applied to the whole body of Jewish Christians indiscriminately, the confusion of Origen and others is easily explained. In recent times, since Gieseler published his treatise *Ueber die Nazaräer und Ebioniten* (Stäudlin u. Tzschirner *Archiv für Kirchengesch.* iv. p. 279 sq, 1819), the distinction has been generally recognised. A succinct and good account of these sects of Judaizers will be found in Schliemann *Clement.* p. 449 sq, where the authorities are given; but the discovery of the work of Hippolytus has since thrown fresh light on the Essene Ebionites. The portion of Ritschl's work (p. 152 sq) relating to these sects should be consulted.

[1] Epiphan. *Haer.* xxix. 7; comp. Hieron. *de Vir. Ill.* § 3.

[2] See the account in Schliemann, p. 445 sq, with the authorities there given and compare Ritschl p. 152 sq.

[3] Hieron. *in Is.* ix. 1 (IV. p. 130), 'Nazaraei...hunc locum ita explanare conantur: Adveniente Christo et praedicatione illius coruscante prima terra Zabulon et terra Nephthali scribarum et Pharisaeorum est erroribus liberata et gravissimum traditionum Judaicarum jugum excussit de cervicibus suis. Postea autem per evangelium apostoli Pauli, qui novissimus apostolorum omnium fuit, ingravata est, id est, multiplicata praedicatio; et in terminos gentium et viam universi maris Christi evangelium splenduit.'

when they too should be brought to confess Christ. Their doctrine of the person of Christ has been variously represented; but this seems at all events clear that, if it fell short of the Catholic standard, it rose above the level of other Judaic sects. The fierce and indiscriminate verdict of Epiphanius indeed pronounces these Nazarenes 'Jews and nothing else[1]': but his contemporary Jerome, himself no lenient judge of heresy, whose opinion was founded on personal intercourse, regards them more favourably. In his eyes they seem to be separated from the creeds and usages of Catholic Christendom chiefly by their retention of the Mosaic law.

Their relation to the Twelve.

Thus they were distinguished from other Judaizing sects by a loftier conception of the person of Christ and by a frank recognition of the liberty of the Gentile Churches and the commission of the Gentile Apostle. These distinguishing features may be traced to the lingering influence of the teaching of the Apostles of the Circumcision. To the example of these same Apostles also they might have appealed in defending their rigid observance of the Mosaic law. But herein, while copying the letter, they did not copy the spirit of their model; for they took no account of altered circumstances.

Testaments of the Twelve Patriarchs.

Of this type of belief, if not of this very Nazarene sect, an early document still extant furnishes an example. The book called the 'Testaments of the twelve Patriarchs[2]' was certainly written after

[1] *Haer.* xxx. 9.

[2] It is printed in Grabe's *Spicil. SS. Patr.* I. p. 145 sq (ed. 2, 1700), and in Fabricius *Cod. Pseudepigr. Vet. Test.* I. p. 519 sq (ed. 2, 1722), and has recently been edited with an introductory essay by Sinker (Cambridge, 1869). Ritschl in his first edition had assigned this work to a writer of the Pauline school. His opinion was controverted by Kayser in the *Strassburg. Beitr. z. den Theol. Wissensch.* III. p. 107 (1851), and with characteristic honesty he withdrew it in his second edition, attributing the work to a Nazarene author (p. 172 sq). Meanwhile Ritschl's first view had been adopted in a monograph by Vorstman *Disquis. de Test. xii. Patr.* (Roterod. 1857), and defended against Kayser. The whole tone and colouring of the book however seem to show very plainly that the writer was a Jewish Christian, and the opposite view would probably never have been entertained but for the preconceived theory that a believer of the Circumcision could not have written so liberally of the Gentile Christians and so honorably of St Paul. Some writers again who have maintained the Judaic authorship (Kayser for instance, whose treatise I only know at second hand) have got over this assumed difficulty by rejecting certain passages as interpolations. On the other hand Ewald pronounces it 'mere folly to assert that *Benj.* c. II (the prophecy about St Paul) was a later

the capture of Jerusalem by Titus and probably before the rebellion of Bar-cochba, but may be later[1]. With some alien features, perhaps stamped upon it by the individual writer, it exhibits generally the characteristics of this Nazarene sect. In this respect at least it offers a remarkable parallel, that to a strong Israelite feeling it unites the fullest recognition of the Gentile Churches. Our Lord is represented as the renovator of the law[2]: the imagery and illustrations are all Hebrew: certain virtues are strongly commended and certain vices strongly denounced by a Hebrew standard: many incidents in the lives of the patriarchs are derived from some unknown legendary Hebrew source[3]. Nay more; the sympathies of the writer are not only Judaic but Levitical. The Messiah is represented as a descendant not of Judah only but of Levi also; thus he is high priest as well as king[4]; but his priestly office is higher than his kingly, as Levi is greater than Judah[5]: the dying patriarchs one

Hebrew sympathies

addition to the work' (*Gesch. d. Volks Isr.* VII. p. 329), and certainly such arbitrary assumptions would render criticism hopeless.

Whether Ritschl is right or not in supposing that the author was actually a Nazarene, it is difficult and not very important to decide. The really important feature in the work is the complexion of the opinions. I do not think however that the mere fact of its having been written in Greek proves the author to have been a Hellenist (Ewald *ib.* p. 333).

[1] The following dates have been assigned to it by recent critics; A.D. 100–135 (Dorner), 100–120 (Wieseler), 133–163 (Kayser), 100–153 (Nitzsch, Lücke), 117–193 (Gieseler), 100–200 (Hase), about 150 (Reuss), 90–110 (Ewald). These dates except the last are taken from Vorstman p. 19 sq, who himself places it soon after the fall of Jerusalem (A.D. 70). The frequent references to this event fix the earliest possible date, while the absence of any allusion to the rebellion of Bar-cochba seems to show that it was written before that time. It is directly named by Origen (*Hom. in Jos.* XV. 6), and probably was known to Tertullian (*c. Marc.* V. 1, *Scorpiace* 13), and (as I believe) even earlier to Irenæus (*Fragm.* 17, p. 836 sq Stieren).

[2] *Levi* 10 ἀνακαινοποιοῦντα τὸν νόμον ἐν δυνάμει ὑψίστου. 'The law of God, the law of the Lord,' are constant phrases with this writer; *Levi* 13, 19, *Judas* 18, 26, *Issach.* 5, *Zabul.* 10, *Dan* 6, *Gad* 3, *Aser* 2, 6, 7, *Joseph* 11, *Benj.* 10: see also *Nepht.* 8. His language in this respect is formed on the model of the Epistle of St James, as Ewald remarks (p. 329). Thus the Law of God with him 'is one with the revealed will of God, and he never therefore understands it in the narrow sense of a Jew or even of an Ebionite.'

[3] See Ewald *Gesch.* I. p. 490.

[4] *Simeon* 5, 7, *Issach.* 5, *Dan* 5, *Nepht.* 6, 8, *Gad* 8, *Joseph* 19, besides the passages referred to in the next note.

[5] *Reuben* 6 πρὸς τὸν Λευὶ ἐγγίσατε... αὐτὸς γὰρ εὐλογήσει τὸν Ἰσραὴλ καὶ τὸν Ἰούδαν, *Judas* 21 καὶ νῦν τέκνα μου ἀγαπήσατε τὸν Λευί...ἐμοὶ γὰρ ἔδωκε Κύριος τὴν βασιλείαν κἀκείνῳ τὴν ἱερατείαν καὶ ὑπέταξε τὴν βασιλείαν τῇ ἱερωσύνῃ· ἐμοὶ ἔδωκε τὰ ἐπὶ τῆς γῆς κἀκείνῳ τὰ ἐν

after another enjoin obedience to Levi: to the Testament of Levi are consigned the most important prophecies of all: the character of Levi is justified and partially cleansed of the stain which in the Old Testament narrative attaches to it[1]. Yet notwithstanding all this, the admission of the Gentiles into the privileges of the covenant is a constant theme of thanksgiving with the writer, who mourns over the falling away of the Jews but looks forward to their final restitution. And into the mouth of the dying Benjamin he puts a prophecy foretelling an illustrious descendant who is to 'arise in after days, beloved of the Lord, listening to His voice, enlightening all the Gentiles with new knowledge'; who is to be 'in the synagogues of the Gentiles until the completion of the ages, and among their rulers as a musical strain in the mouth of all'; who shall 'be written in the holy books, he and his work and his word, and shall be the elect of God for ever[2].'

united with liberal principles.

2. But besides these Nazarenes, there were other Judaizing sects, narrow and uncompromising, to whose principles or prejudices language such as I have just quoted would be most abhorrent.

Ebionites.

The EBIONITES were a much larger and more important body than the Nazarenes. They were not confined to the neighbourhood of Pella or even to Palestine and the surrounding countries, but were found in Rome and probably also in all the great centres of the dispersion[3]. Not content with observing the Mosaic ordinances themselves, they maintained that the law was binding on all Christians alike, and regarded Gentile believers as impure because they refused to conform. As a necessary consequence they rejected the authority and the writings of St Paul, branding him as an apostate and pursuing his memory with bitter reproaches. In their theology also they were far removed from the Catholic Church, holding our

Their tenets.

οὐρανοῖς, *ib.* 25 *Λευὶ πρῶτος, δεύτερος ἐγώ*, *Nepht.* 5 *Λευὶ ἐκράτησε τὸν ἥλιον καὶ Ἰούδας φθάσας ἐπίασε τὴν σελήνην.*

[1] *Levi* 6, 7.

[2] *Benj.* 11. Besides this prophecy the work presents several coincidences of language with St Paul (see Vorstman p. 115 sq), and at least one quotation, *Levi* 6 ἔφθασε δὲ ἡ ὀργὴ Κυρίου ἐπ' αὐτοὺς εἰς τέλος, from 1 Thess. ii. 16. On the whole however the language in the moral and didactic portions takes its colour from the Epistle of St James, and in the prophetic and apocalyptic from the Revelation of St John.

[3] Epiphan. *Haer.* xxx. 18.

Lord to be a mere man, the son of Joseph and Mary, who was justified, as any of themselves might be justified, by his rigorous performance of the law[1].

Relation to the Judaizers of the apostolic age.

If the Nazarenes might have claimed some affinity to the Apostles of the Circumcision, the Ebionites were the direct spiritual descendants of those false brethren, the Judaizers of the apostolic age, who first disturbed the peace of the Antiochene Church and then dogged St Paul's footsteps from city to city, everywhere thwarting his efforts and undermining his authority. If Ebionism was not primitive Christianity, neither was it a creation of the second century. As an organization, a distinct sect, it first made itself known, we may suppose, in the reign of Trajan: but as a sentiment, it had been harboured within the Church from the very earliest days. Moderated by the personal influence of the Apostles, soothed by the general practice of their church, not yet forced into declaring themselves by the turn of events, though scarcely tolerant of others these Judaizers were tolerated for a time themselves. The beginning of the second century was a winnowing season in the Church of the Circumcision.

Another type of Ebionism,

The form of Ebionism[2], which is most prominent in early writers and which I have hitherto had in view, is purely Pharisaic; but we meet also with another type, agreeing with the former up to a certain point but introducing at the same time a new element, half ascetic, half mystical.

derived from the Essenes.

This foreign element was probably due to Essene influences. The doctrines of the Christian school bear so close a resemblance to the

[1] For the opinions of these Ebionites see the references in Schliemann p. 481 sq, and add Hippol. *Haer.* vii. 3 *εἰ γὰρ καὶ ἕτερός τις πεποιήκει τὰ ἐν νόμῳ προστεταγμένα, ἦν ἂν ἐκεῖνος ὁ Χριστός· δύνασθαι δὲ καὶ ἑαυτοὺς ὁμοίως ποιήσαντας Χριστοὺς γενέσθαι· καὶ γὰρ καὶ αὐτὸν ὁμοίως ἄνθρωπον εἶναι πᾶσιν λέγουσιν.*

[2] The following opinions were shared by all Ebionites alike: (1) The recognition of Jesus as Messiah; (2) The denial of His divinity; (3) The universal obligation of the law; (4) The rejection and hatred of St Paul. Their differences consisted in (1) Their view of what constituted the law, and (2) Their conception of the Person of Christ; e.g. whether He was born of a Virgin or in the course of nature; what supernatural endowments He had and at what time they were bestowed on Him, whether at His birth or at His baptism, etc.

The Ebionites of earlier writers, as Irenæus and Hippolytus, belong to the Pharisaic type; while those of Epiphanius are strongly Essene.

characteristic features of the Jewish sect as to place their parentage almost beyond a doubt[1]: and moreover the head-quarters of these heretics—the countries bordering on the Dead Sea—coincide roughly with the head-quarters of their prototype. This view however does not exclude the working of other influences more directly Gnostic or Oriental: and as this type of Ebionism seems to have passed through different phases at different times, and indeed to have comprehended several species at the same time, such modifications ought probably to be attributed to forces external to Judaism. Having regard then to its probable origin as well as to its typical character, we can hardly do wrong in adopting the name *Essene* or *Gnostic Ebionism* to distinguish it from the common type, *Pharisaic Ebionism* or *Ebionism proper.*

If Pharisaic Ebionism was a disease inherent in the Church of the Circumcision from the first, Essene Ebionism seems to have been a later infection caught by external contact. In the Palestinian Church at all events we see no symptoms of it during the apostolic age. It is a probable conjecture, that after the destruction of Jerusalem the fugitive Christians, living in their retirement in the neighbourhood of the Essene settlements, received large accessions to their numbers from this sect, which thus inoculated the Church with its peculiar views[2]. It is at least worthy of notice, that in a religious work emanating from this school of Ebionites the 'true Gospel' is reported to have been first propagated 'after the destruction of the holy place[3].' Its later origin,

This younger form of Judaic Christianity seems soon to have eclipsed the elder. In the account of Ebionism given by Epiphanius the Pharisaic characteristics are almost entirely absorbed in the Essene.

[1] See especially the careful investigation of Ritschl p. 204 sq.

[2] Ritschl (p. 223), who adopts this view, suggests that this sect, which had stood aloof from the temple-worship and abhorred sacrifices, would be led to welcome Christ as the true prophet, when they saw the fulfilment of His predictions against the temple. In *Clem. Hom.* iii. 15 great stress is laid on the fulfilment of these prophecies: comp. also *Clem. Recogn.* i. 37 (especially in the Syriac).

[3] *Clem. Hom.* ii. 17 *μετὰ καθαίρεσιν τοῦ ἁγίου τόπου εὐαγγέλιον ἀληθὲς κρύφα διαπεμφθῆναι εἰς ἐπανόρθωσιν τῶν ἐσομένων αἱρέσεων*: comp. *Clem. Recogn.* i. 37, 64, iii. 61 (in the Syriac, as below, p. 330, note 1). See also Epiphan. *Haer.* xxx. 2.

but greater literary activity,

This prominence is probably due in some measure to their greater literary capacity, a remarkable feature doubtless derived from the speculative tendencies and studious habits of the Jewish sect[1] to which they traced their parentage. Besides the Clementine writings which we possess whole, and the book of Elchasai of which a few fragmentary notices are preserved, a vast number of works which, though no longer extant, have yet moulded the traditions of the early Church, emanated from these Christian Essenes. Hence doubtless are derived the ascetic portraits of James the Lord's brother in Hegesippus and of Matthew the Apostle in Clement of Alexandria[2], to which the account of St Peter in the extant Clementines presents a close parallel[3].

and zealous proselytism.

And with greater literary activity they seem also to have united greater missionary zeal. To this spirit of proselytism we owe much important information relating to the tenets of the sect.

Book of Elchasai.

One of their missionaries early in the third century brought to Rome a sacred book bearing the name of Elchasai or Elxai, whence also the sect were called Elchasaites. This book fell into the hands of Hippolytus the writer on heresies[4], from whom our knowledge of it is chiefly derived. It professed to have been obtained from the Seres, a Parthian tribe, and to contain a revelation which had been first made in the third year of Trajan (A.D. 100). These Seres hold the same place in the fictions of Essene Ebionism, as the Hyperboreans in Greek legend: they are a mythical race, perfectly pure and therefore perfectly happy, long-lived and free from pain, scrupulous in the performance of all ceremonial rites and thus exempt from the penalties attaching to their neglect[5]. Elchasai, an Aramaic word

[1] Joseph. *B. J.* ii. 8. 6.

[2] *Paedag.* ii. 1 (p. 174 Potter), where St Matthew is said to have lived on seeds, berries, and herbs, abstaining from animal food. See Ritschl p. 224.

[3] *Clem. Hom.* xii. 6, comp. viii. 15, xv. 7.

[4] *Haer.* ix. 13. See a valuable paper on the Elchasaites by Ritschl in Niedner's *Zeitschrift* IV. p. 573 sq (1853), the substance of which is given also in the second edition of his *Altkatholische Kirche*. Hilgenfeld has edited the fragments of the book of Elxai in his *Novum Testamentum extra Canonem Receptum*, fasc. III. p. 153 sq (1866). The use made of it by Epiphanius is investigated by Lipsius, *Quellenkritik des Epiphan.* p. 143 sq.

[5] *Clem. Recogn.* viii. 48, ix. 19. Even in classical writers the Seres or Chinese are invested with something of an ideal character: e.g. Plin. vi. 24, Strabo xv. p. 701, Mela iii. 7. But in

signifying the 'hidden power[1],' seems to be the name of the divine messenger who communicated the revelation, and probably the title of the book itself: Hippolytus understands it of the person who received the revelation, the founder of the sect. 'Elchasai,' adds this father, 'delivered it to a certain person called Sobiai.' Here again he was led astray by his ignorance of Aramaic: Sobiai is not the name of an individual but signifies 'the sworn members[2],' to whom alone the revelation was to be communicated and who perhaps, like their Essene prototypes[3], took an oath to divulge it only to the brotherhood. I need not follow this strange but instructive notice farther. Whether this was the sacred book of the whole sect or of a part only, whether the name Elchasaism is coextensive with Essene Ebionism or not, it is unimportant for my purpose to enquire. The pretended era of this revelation is of more consequence. Whether the book itself was really as early as the reign of Trajan or whether the date was part of the dramatic fiction, it is impossible to decide[4]. Even in the latter case, it will still show that according to their own tradition this epoch marked some striking development in the opinions or history of the sect; and the date given corresponds, it will be remembered, very nearly with the epoch mentioned by Hegesippus as the birthtime of a numerous brood of heresies[5].

Its pretended date.

the passage which most strikingly illustrates this fact (*Geogr. Graec. Min.* II. p. 514, ed. Müller), the name disappears when the text is correctly read ('se regentes,' and not 'Serae gentes').

[1] חיל כסי. Epiphanius correctly explains it δύναμις κεκαλυμμένη, *Haer.* xix. 2. See Ritschl l. c. p. 581, and *Altkath. Kirche* p. 245. Other explanations of the word, given in Hilgenfeld l. c. p. 156, in M. Nicolas *Evangiles Apocryphes* p. 108 (1866), and by Geiger *Zeitsch. der Deutsch. Morgenl. Gesellsch.* XVIII. p. 824 (1864), do not recommend themselves. The name is differently written in Greek, Ηλχασαι, Ελκεσαι and Ηλξαι. The first, which is most correct, is found in Hippolytus who had seen the book.

[2] From שבע. Accordingly Hippolytus (ix. 17) relates that the Elchasaite missionary Alcibiades made a mystery of his teaching, forbidding it to be divulged except to the faithful; see Ritschl l. c. p. 589. Ewald however (*Gesch.* VII. p. 159) derives Sobiai from ܨܒܥ i.e. βαπτισταί. See also Chwolson *die Ssabier* etc. I. p. 111.

[3] Joseph. *B. J.* ii. 8. 7.

[4] Hilgenfeld (p. xxi) maintains the early date very positively against Ritschl. Lipsius (l. c.) will not pronounce an opinion.

[5] See above, p. 315 sq. In the passage there quoted Hegesippus speaks of these heresies 'as living underground, burrowing (φωλευόντων)' until the reign of Trajan. This agrees with the statement in the Homilies (ii. 17) already referred to (p. 323, note 3), that the true Gospel (i.e. Essene Ebionism) was

Essene Ebionites distinguished from Pharisaic,

Without attempting to discriminate the different forms of doctrine which this Essene Ebionism comprised in itself—to point out for instance the distinctive features of the book of Elchasai, of the Homilies, and of the Recognitions respectively—it will be sufficient to observe the broad line of demarcation which separates the Essene from the Pharisaic type[1]. Laying almost equal stress with the others on the observance of the law as an essential part of Christianity, the Essene Ebionites undertook to settle by arbitrary criticism what the law was[2]. By this capricious process they eliminated from the Old Testament all elements distasteful to them—the doctrine of sacrifices especially, which was abhorrent to Essene principles—cutting down the law to their own standard and rejecting the prophets wholly. As a compensation, they introduced certain ritual observances of their own, on which they laid great stress; more especially lustral washings and abstinence from wine and from animal food. In their Christology also they differed widely from the Pharisaic Ebionites, maintaining that the Word or Wisdom of God had been incarnate more than once, and that thus there had been more Christs than one, of whom Adam was the first and Jesus the last. Christianity in fact was regarded by them merely as the restoration of the primeval religion: in other words, of pure Mosaism before it had been corrupted by foreign accretions. Thus equally with the Pharisaic Ebionites they denied the Gospel the character of a new covenant; and, as a natural consequence, equally with them they rejected the authority and reviled the name of St Paul[3].

and allied to the Colossian heretics.

If the Pharisaic Ebionites are the direct lineal descendants of the 'false brethren' who seduced St Paul's Galatian converts from their allegiance, the Essene Ebionites bear a striking family likeness

first '*secretly* propagated' after the destruction of the temple. The opinions which had thus been progressing stealthily now showed a bold front; but whether the actual organization of the sect or sects took place now or at a still later date (after the rebellion of Bar-cochba), it is impossible to say.

[1] The chief authorities for the Essene Ebionites are Epiphanius (*Haer.* xix, xxx); Hippolytus (*Haer.* ix. 13—17) and Origen (Euseb. *H. E.* vi. 38), whose accounts refer especially to the book of Elchasai; and the Clementine writings.

[2] See *Colossians* p. 372.

[3] See Epiphan. *Haer.* xxx. 16, 25, Orig. ap. Euseb. l. c. τὸν ἀπόστολον τέλεον ἀθετεῖ; besides the passages in the Clementine writings quoted in the text.

to those other Judaizers against whom he raises his voice as endangering the safety of the Church at Colossae[1].

Of the hostility of these Christian Essenes to St Paul, as of their other typical features, a striking example is extant in the fictitious writings attributed to the Roman bishop Clement. These are preserved in two forms: the *Homilies*, extant in the Greek, apparently an uniform work, which perhaps may be assigned to the middle or latter half of the second century; and the *Recognitions*, a composite production probably later than the Homilies, founded, it would appear, partly on them or some earlier work which was the common basis of both and partly on other documents, and known to us through the Latin translation of Rufinus, who avowedly altered his original with great freedom[2].

Clementine writings.

In the Homilies Simon Magus is the impersonation of manifold heresy, and as such is refuted and condemned by St Peter. Among other false teachers, who are covertly denounced in his person, we cannot fail to recognise the lineaments of St Paul[3]. Thus St Peter

Attack on St Paul in the Homilies,

[1] See *Colossians* p. 73 sq.

[2] The only complete editions of the Homilies are those of Dressel, *Clementis Romani quae feruntur Homiliae Viginti* (1853), and of Lagarde, *Clementina* (1865); the end of the 19th and the whole of the 20th homily having been published for the first time by Dressel. The Recognitions which have been printed several times may be read most conveniently in Gersdorf's edition (Lips. 1838). A Syriac version lately published by Lagarde (*Clementis Romani Recognitiones Syriace*, Lips. et Lond. 1861) is made up partly of the Recognitions (i, ii, iii, iv), and partly of the Homilies (x, xi, xii, xiii, xiv, the xth book being imperfect). The older of the two extant MSS of this version was actually written A.D. 411, the year after the death of Rufinus; but the errors of transcription, which it exhibits, show that it was taken from an earlier MS. We are thus carried back to a very remote date. The first part, containing the early books of the Recognitions, is extremely valuable, for it enables us to measure the liberties which Rufinus took with his original. An important instance of his arbitrary treatment will be given below, p. 330, note 1. Two abridgments of the Homilies are extant. These have been edited by Dressel, *Clementinorum Epitomae duae* (Lips. 1859), one of them for the first time. Of those monographs which I have read on the relations between the different Clementine writings, the treatise of Uhlhorn, *Die Homilien und Recognitionen* etc. (Göttingen, 1854), seems to me on the whole the most satisfactory. It is dangerous to express an opinion where able critics are so divided; and the remarks in the text are not hazarded without some hesitation. Baur, Schliemann, Schwegler, and Uhlhorn, give the priority to the Homilies, Hilgenfeld and Ritschl to the Recognitions, Lehmann partly to the one and partly to the other, while Reuss and others decline to pronounce a decided opinion.

[3] See on this subject Schliemann *Clement.* pp. 96 sq, 534 sq: comp. Stanley's *Corinthians*, p. 366 sq.

charges his hearers, 'Shun any apostle, or teacher, or prophet, who does not first compare his preaching with James called the brother of my Lord and entrusted with the care of the Church of the Hebrews in Jerusalem, and has not come to you with witnesses[1]; lest the wickedness, which contended with the Lord forty days and prevailed not, should afterwards fall upon the earth as lightning from heaven and send forth a preacher against you, just as he suborned Simon against us, preaching in the name of our Lord and sowing error under the pretence of truth; wherefore He that sent us said, *Many shall come to me in sheep's clothing, but within they are ravening wolves* (xi. 35).' The allusions here to St Paul's rejection of 'commendatory letters' (2 Cor. iii. 1) and to the scene on the way to Damascus (Acts ix. 3) are clear. In another passage St Peter, after explaining that Christ must be preceded by Antichrist, the true prophet by the false, and applying this law to the preaching of Simon and himself, adds: 'If he had been known (*εἰ ἐγινώσκετο*) he would not have been believed, but now being not known (*ἀγνοούμενος*) he is wrongly believed...being death, he has been desired as if he were a saviour...and being a deceiver he is heard as if he spake the truth (ii. 17, 18).' The writer seems to be playing with St Paul's own words, 'as deceivers and yet true, as unknown and yet well known, as dying and behold we live (2 Cor. vi. 8, 9).' In a third passage there is a very distinct allusion to the Apostle's account of the conflict at Antioch in the Galatian Epistle: 'If then,' says St Peter to Simon, 'our Jesus was made known to thee also and conversed with thee being seen in a vision, He was angry with thee as an adversary, and therefore He spake with thee by visions and dreams, or even by outward revelations. Can any one be made wise unto doctrine by visions? If thou sayest he can, then why did the Teacher abide and converse with us a whole year when we were awake? And how shall we ever believe thee in this, that He was seen of thee? Nay, how could He have been seen of thee, when thy thoughts are contrary to His teaching? If having been seen and instructed of

[1] *καὶ μετὰ μαρτύρων προσεληλυθότα.* It is needless to insert *μὴ* with Schliemann and Schwegler: the negative is carried on from the former clause *μὴ πρότερον ἀντιβάλλοντα.*

Him for a single hour thou wast made an Apostle, then preach His words, expound His teaching, love His Apostles, do not fight against me His companion. For thou hast withstood and opposed me (ἐναντίος ἀνθέστηκάς μοι), the firm rock, the foundation of the Church. If thou hadst not been an adversary, thou wouldest not have calumniated and reviled my preaching, that I might not be believed when I told what I had heard myself in person from the Lord, as though forsooth I were condemned (καταγνωσθέντος) and thou wert highly regarded[1]. Nay, if thou callest me condemned (κατεγνωσμένον), thou accusest God who revealed Christ to me and assailest Him that called me blessed in my revelation[2] (xvii. 19).' In this same bitter spirit the writer would rob him of all his missionary triumphs and transfer them to his supposed rival: the Apostleship of the Gentiles, according to the Homilies, belongs not to St Paul but to St Peter: Barnabas is no more the companion nor Clement the disciple of St Paul but of St Peter[3].

Again in the letter of Peter to James prefixed to the Homilies, emanating from the same school though perhaps not part of the work itself, and if so, furnishing another example of this bitterness of feeling, St Peter is made to denounce those Gentile converts who repudiate his lawful preaching, welcoming a certain lawless and foolish doctrine of the enemy (τοῦ ἐχθροῦ ἀνθρώπου ἄνομόν τινα καὶ φλυαρώδη διδασκαλίαν), complaining also that 'certain persons attempted by crafty interpretations to wrest his words to the abolishing of the law, pretending that this was his opinion, but that he did not openly preach it,' with more to the same effect (§ 2). in the Letter of Peter,

In the Recognitions, probably a later patch-work[4], the harsher features of the Essene-Ebionite doctrine, as it appears in the Homilies, are softened down, and these bitter though indirect attacks on St Paul in the Recognitions,

[1] The existing text has καὶ ἐμοῦ εὐδοκιμοῦντος, for which some have proposed to read καὶ μὴ εὐδοκιμοῦντος. It is better perhaps to substitute σοῦ or οὐδαμοῦ for ἐμοῦ, though neither is a neat emendation. Some change however is absolutely needed.

[2] τοῦ ἐπὶ ἀποκαλύψει μακαρίσαντός με. The allusion is to Matt. xvi. 17, μακάριος εἶ κ.τ.λ.

[3] See also other references to St Paul noted above, p. 61.

[4] Not much earlier than the middle of the third century; for a portion of the treatise *de Fato*, written probably by a disciple of Bardesanes, is worked up in the later books; unless indeed this is itself borrowed from the Recognitions.

omitted; whether by the original redactor or by his translator Rufinus, it is not easy to say[1]. Thus in the portions corresponding to and probably taken from the Homilies no traces of this hostility remain. But in one passage adapted from another work, probably the 'Ascents of James[2],' it can still be discerned, the allusion having either escaped notice or been spared because it was too covert to give offence. It is there related that a certain enemy (homo quidam inimicus) raised a tumult against the Apostles and with his own hands assaulted James and threw him down from the steps of the temple, ceasing then to maltreat him, only because he believed him to be dead; and that after this the Apostles received secret information from Gamaliel, that this enemy (inimicus ille homo) had been sent by Caiaphas on a mission to Damascus to persecute and slay the disciples, and more especially to take Peter who was supposed to have fled thither (i. 70, 71)[3]. The original work, from which this

and in the Ascents of James.

portion of the Recognitions seems to have been borrowed, was much more violent and unscrupulous in its attacks on St Paul; for in the 'Ascents of James' Epiphanius read the story, that he was of Gentile parentage, but coming to Jerusalem and wishing to marry the high-priest's daughter he became a proselyte and was circumcised: then, being disappointed of his hope, he turned round and furiously attacked the Mosaic ordinances (*Haer.* xxx. 16).

[1] In one instance at least the change is due to Rufinus himself. His translation of *Clem. Recogn.* iii. 61 contains a distinct recognition of St Paul's Apostleship, 'Nonum (par) omnium gentium et illius qui mittetur seminare verbum inter gentes.' (On these *συζυγίαι* of the false and the true see above, p. 328.) But the corresponding passage in the Syriac version (p. 115, l. 20, Lagarde) is wholly different, and translated back into Greek will run thus: *ἡ δὲ ἐννάτη (συζυγία) τοῦ σπέρματος τῶν ζιζανίων καὶ τοῦ εὐαγγελίου τοῦ πεμπομένου εἰς ἐπιστροφήν, ὅταν ἐκριζωθῇ τὸ ἅγιον καὶ εἰς τὴν ἐρήμωσιν αὐτοῦ θήσουσι τὸ βδέλυγμα*: see Dan. ix. 27, and compare *Clem. Hom.* ii. 17 (quoted above, p. 323, note 3). Thus the commendation of St Paul, which is wholly alien to the spirit of these Clementine writings, disappears.

[2] Uhlhorn, p. 366. Epiphanius mentions this book, *ἀναβαθμοὶ Ἰακώβου*, as being in circulation among the Ebionites (xxx. 16). It was so called doubtless as describing the *ascents* of James up the temple-stairs, whence he harangued the people. The name and the description of its contents in Epiphanius alike favour the view that it was the original of this portion of the Recognitions. But if so, the redactor of the Recognitions must have taken the same liberties with it as he has done with the Homilies.

[3] This passage is substantially the same in the Syriac.

In the earlier part of the third century these Gnostic Ebionites seem to have made some futile efforts to propagate their views. An emissary of the sect, one Alcibiades of Apamea in Syria, appeared in Rome with the pretended revelation of Elchasai, and (thinking himself the better juggler of the two, says Hippolytus) half succeeded in cajoling the pope Callistus, but was exposed and defeated by the zealous bishop of Portus who tells the story (*Haer.* ix. 13—17). Not many years after another emissary, if it was not this same Alcibiades, appears to have visited Cæsarea, where he was confronted and denounced by Origen[1].

Activity of the sect at Rome, A.D. 219—223, and Cæsarea, A.D. 247?

This display of activity might lead to an exaggerated estimate of the influence of these Judaizing sects. It is not probable that they left any wide or lasting impression west of Syria. In Palestine itself they would appear to have been confined to certain localities lying for the most part about the Jordan and the Dead Sea. After the reconstitution of the mother Church at Ælia Capitolina the Christianity of Palestine seems to have been for the most part neither Ebionite nor Nazarene. It is a significant fact, implying more than appears at first sight, that in the Paschal controversy which raged in the middle and later half of the second century the bishops of Cæsarea and Jerusalem, of Tyre and Ptolemais, ranged themselves, not with the Churches of Asia Minor which regulated their Easter festival by the Jewish passover without regard to the day of the week, but with those of Rome and Alexandria and Gaul which observed another rule; thus avoiding even the semblance of Judaism[2]. But we have more direct testimony to the main features of Palestinian doctrine about the middle of the second century in the known opinions of two writers who lived at the time—Justin as representative of the Samaritan, and Hegesippus of the Hebrew Christianity of their day. The former of these declares himself distinctly against the two characteristic tenets of Ebionism. Against their humanitarian views he expressly argues, maintaining the divinity of Christ[3]. On the

The Churches of Palestine not Ebionite.

Paschal controversy.

Justin.

[1] Euseb. *H. E.* vi. 38. This extract is taken from Origen's Homily on the 82nd Psalm, which appears to have been delivered in Cæsarea about A.D. 247. See Redepenning *Origenes* II. p. 72.

[2] Euseb. *H. E.* v. 23, 24. See below, p. 343, note 2.

[3] *Dial.* cc. 48, 127.

universal obligation of the law he declares, not only that those who maintain this opinion are wrong, but that he himself will hold no communion with them, for he doubts whether they can be saved[1]. If, as an apologist for the Gospel against Gentile and Jew, he is precluded by the nature of his writings from quoting St Paul[2], whose name would be received by the one with indifference and by the other with hatred, he still shows by his manner of citing and applying the Old Testament that he is not unfamiliar with this Apostle's writings[3]. The testimony of Hegesippus is still more important, for his extant fragments prove him to have been a thorough Hebrew in all his thoughts and feelings. This writer made a journey to Rome, calling on the way at Corinth among other places; he expresses himself entirely satisfied with the teaching of the churches which he thus visited; 'Under each successive bishop,' he says, 'and in each city it is so as the law and the prophets and the Lord preach[4].' Was the doctrine of the whole Christian world at this

Hegesippus,

[1] *Dial.* cc. 47, 48.

[2] See Westcott's argument (*Canon* p. 116 sq) drawn from the usage of other apologists, Tertullian for instance, who does not quote even the Gospels in his Apology.

[3] See the introduction, p. 60, and the notes on iii. 28, iv. 27.

[4] In Euseb. *H. E.* iv. 22. The extract ends, γενόμενος δὲ ἐν Ῥώμῃ διαδοχὴν ἐποιησάμην μέχρις Ἀνικήτου οὗ διάκονος ἦν Ἐλεύθερος· καὶ παρὰ Ἀνικήτου διαδέχεται Σωτήρ, μεθ' ὃν Ἐλεύθερος· ἐν ἑκάστῃ δὲ διαδοχῇ καὶ ἐν ἑκάστῃ πόλει οὕτως ἔχει ὡς ὁ νόμος κηρύττει καὶ οἱ προφῆται καὶ ὁ Κύριος. If the text be correct, διαδοχὴν ἐποιησάμην must mean 'I drew up a list or an account of the successive bishops' (see Pearson in *Routh* I. p. 268 sq); and in this case Hegesippus would seem to be referring to some earlier work or earlier portion of this work, which he now supplements. Possibly however the conjectural reading διατριβὴν ἐποιησάμην, 'I continued to reside,' may be correct: but the translation of Rufinus, 'permansi inibi (i.e. Romae) donec Aniceto Soter et Soteri successit Eleutherus,' is of little or no weight on this side; for he constantly uses his fluency in Latin to gloze over his imperfect knowledge of Greek, and the evasion of a real difficulty is with him the rule rather than the exception. If we retain διαδοχήν, the words of Hegesippus would still seem to imply that he left Rome during the episcopate of Anicetus. Eusebius indeed (*H. E.* iv. 11) infers, apparently from this passage, that he remained there till Eleutherus became bishop; and Jerome (*de Vir. Ill.* 22), as usual, repeats Eusebius. This inference, though intelligible, seems hardly correct; but it shows almost conclusively that Eusebius did not read διατριβήν. The early Syriac translator of Eusebius (see above, p. 280, note) certainly read διαδοχήν. The dates of the accession of the successive bishops as determined by Lipsius are, Pius 141 (at the latest), Anicetus 154—156, Soter 166 or 167, Eleutherus 174 or 175, Victor 189, Zephyrinus 198 or 199, Callistus 217, Urbanus 222; *Chron. der Röm. Bisch.* p. 263. But there is considerable variation in the authorities, the ac-

time (A.D. 150) Ebionite, or was the doctrine of Hegesippus Catholic? There is no other alternative. We happen to possess information which leaves no doubt as to the true answer. Eusebius speaks of Hegesippus as 'having recorded the unerring tradition of the apostolic preaching' (*H. E.* iv. 8); and classes him with Dionysius of Corinth, Melito, Irenæus, and others, as one of those in whose writings 'the orthodoxy of sound faith derived from the apostolic tradition had been handed down[1].' In this Eusebius could not have been mistaken, for he himself states that Hegesippus 'left the *fullest record* of his own opinions in five books of memoirs' which were in his hands (*H. E.* iv. 22). It is surely a bold effort of recent criticism in the face of these plain facts to set down Hegesippus as an Ebionite and to infer thence that a great part of Christendom was Ebionite also. True, this writer gives a traditional account of St James which represents him as a severe and rigorous ascetic[2]; but between this stern view of life and Ebionite doctrine the interval may be wide enough; and on this showing how many fathers of the Church, Jerome and Basil for instance in the fourth century, Bernard and Dominic and Francis of Assisi in later ages, must plead guilty of Ebionism. True, he used the Hebrew Gospel; but what authority he attributed to it, or whether it was otherwise than orthodox, does not appear. True also, he appeals in a passage already quoted to the authority of 'the law and the prophets and the Lord[3]'; but this is a natural equivalent for 'the Old and New Tes-

not an Ebionite.

cession of Anicetus being placed by some as early as A.D. 150; see the lists in Clinton's *Fasti Romani* II. p. 534 sq.

[1] *H. E.* iv. 21 ὧν καὶ εἰς ἡμᾶς τῆς ἀποστολικῆς παραδόσεως ἡ τῆς ὑγιοῦς πίστεως ἔγγραφος κατῆλθεν ὀρθοδοξία.

[2] Euseb. *H. E.* ii. 23. See the account of St James below.

[3] See the passage quoted above, p. 332, note 4. For the inferences of the Tübingen school see Schwegler *Nachapost. Zeitalter* I. p. 355, Baur *Christenthum* etc. p. 78. A parallel instance will serve the purpose better than much argument. In a poem by the late Prof. Selwyn (*Winfrid, afterwards called Boniface*, Camb. 1864) the hero is spoken of as 'Printing heaven's message deeper in his soul, By reading holy writ, Prophet and Law, And fourfold Gospel.' Here, as in Hegesippus, the law is mentioned and 'the Apostle' is not. Yet who would say that this passage savours of Ebionism? Comp. Irenæus *Haer.* ii. 30. 6 'Relinquentes eloquia Domini et Moysen et reliquos prophetas,' and again in *Spicil. Solesm.* I. p. 3, and the Clementine *Epistles to Virgins* i. 12 'Sicut ex lege ac prophetis et a Domino nostro Jesu Christo didicimus' (Westcott *Canon* p. 185, 4th ed.). So too *Apost. Const.* ii. 39 μετὰ τὴν ἀνάγνωσιν τοῦ νόμου καὶ τῶν

tament,' and corresponding expressions would not appear out of place even in our own age. True lastly, he condemns the use made of the text, 'Eye hath not seen nor ear heard' etc.[1], as contradicting our Lord's words, 'Blessed are your eyes for ye see, etc.'; but he is here protesting against its perverted application by the Gnostics, who employed it of the initiated few, and whom elsewhere he severely denounces; and it is a mere accident that the words are quoted also by St Paul (1 Cor. ii. 9). Many of the facts mentioned point him out as a Hebrew, but not one brands him as an Ebionite. The decisive evidence on the other side is fatal to this inference. If Hegesippus may be taken as a type of the Hebrew Church in his day, then the doctrine of that Church was Catholic.

Ebionism not prevalent in other churches.

And if the Palestinian Churches of the second century held Catholic doctrine, we shall see little or no reason to fix the charge of Ebionism on other communities farther removed from the focus

προφητῶν καὶ τοῦ εὐαγγελίου, Hippol. *Haer.* viii. 19 *πλεῖόν τι δι' αὐτῶν...μεμαθηκέναι ἢ ἐκ νόμου καὶ προφητῶν καὶ εὐαγγελίων.*

[1] The fragment to which I refer is preserved in an extract from Stephanus Gobarus given in Photius *Bibl.* 232. After quoting the words *τὰ ἡτοιμασμένα τοῖς δικαίοις ἀγαθὰ οὔτε ὀφθαλμὸς εἶδεν οὔτε οὖς ἤκουσεν οὔτε ἐπὶ καρδίαν ἀνθρώπου ἀνέβη*, Stephanus proceeds, *'Ηγήσιππος μέντοι, ἀρχαῖός τε ἀνὴρ καὶ ἀποστολικός, ἐν τῷ πέμπτῳ τῶν ὑπομνημάτων, οὐκ οἶδ' ὅ τι καὶ παθών, μάτην μὲν εἰρῆσθαι ταῦτα λέγει καὶ καταψεύδεσθαι τοὺς ταῦτα φαμένους τῶν τε θείων γραφῶν καὶ τοῦ Κυρίου λέγοντος Μακάριοι οἱ ὀφθαλμοὶ ὑμῶν κ.τ.λ.* It is not surprising that this writer, who lived when Gnosticism had passed out of memory, should be puzzled to 'know what had come to Hegesippus': but modern critics ought not to have gone astray. Hegesippus can hardly be objecting to the passage itself, which is probably a quotation from Is. lxiv. 4. His objection therefore must be to some *application* of it. But whose application? Even had there been no direct evidence, it might have been gathered from the argument which follows that he referred to the esoteric teaching of the Gnostics; but the lately discovered treatise of Hippolytus establishes the fact that it was a favourite text of these heretics, being introduced into the form of initiation: see v. 24, 26, 27 (of Justin the Gnostic), vi. 24 (of Valentinus). This is the opinion of Lechler p. 463, Ritschl p. 267, Westcott *Canon* pp. 206, 281, Bunsen *Hippolytus* I. p. 132 (2nd ed.), and Hilgenfeld *Apost. Väter* p. 102, but otherwise *Zeitschr. f. Wiss. Theol.* 1876, p. 203 sq. Yet Baur (*Christenthum* p. 77, *Paulus* p. 221), and Schwegler (I. p. 352), forcing an unnatural meaning on the words, contend that Hegesippus is directly denying St Paul's claim to a revelation and asserting that this privilege belongs only to those who have seen and heard Christ in the flesh. It is worth noticing that the same quotation, 'eye hath not seen etc.,' is found in the Epistle of Clement (c. 34); and this epistle was referred to by Hegesippus, as the notice of Eusebius seems to imply (*H. E.* iv. 22), with approval. This very mention of Clement's epistle is in itself a secondary evidence that Hegesippus recognised the authority of St Paul.

of Judaic influences. Here and there indeed Judaism seems to have made a desperate struggle, but only to sustain a signal defeat. At Antioch this conflict began earlier and probably continued longer than elsewhere; yet the names of her bishops Ignatius, Theophilus, and Serapion, vouch for the doctrine and practice of the Antiochene Church in the second century. In Asia Minor the influence first of St Paul and then of St John must have been fatal to the ascendancy of Ebionism. A disproportionate share indeed of the faint light which glimmers over the Church of the second century is concentrated on this region: and the notices, though occasional and fragmentary, are sufficient to establish this general fact. The same is true with regard to Greece: similar influences were at work and with similar results. The Churches of Gaul took their colour from Asia Minor which furnished their greatest teachers: Irenæus bears witness to the Catholicity of their faith. In Alexandria, when at length the curtain rises, Christianity is seen enthroned between Greek philosophy and Gnostic speculation, while Judaism is far in the background. The infancy of the African Church is wrapt in hopeless darkness: but when she too emerges from her obscurity, she comes forward in no uncertain attitude, with no deep scars as of a recent conflict, offering neither a mutilated canon nor a dwarfed theology. The African Bible, as it appears in the old Latin version, contains all the books which were received without dispute for two centuries after. The African theology, as represented by Tertullian, in no way falls short of the standard of Catholic doctrine maintained in other parts of Christendom.

The Church of Rome.

But the Church of the metropolis demands special attention. At Rome, if anywhere, we should expect to see very distinct traces of these successive phenomena, which are supposèd to have extended throughout or almost throughout the Christian Church—first the supremacy of Ebionism—then the conflict of the Judaic with the Pauline Gospel—lastly, towards the close of the second century, the triumph of a modified Paulinism and the consequent birth of Catholic Christianity[1]. Yet, even if this were the history of Catho-

[1] The episcopate of Victor (about A.D. 190—200) is fixed by the Tübingen critics (see Schwegler II. p. 206 sq) as the epoch of the antijudaic revolu-

licity at Rome, it would still be an unfounded assumption to extend the phenomenon to other parts of Christendom. Rome had not yet learnt to dictate to the Church at large. At this early period she appears for the most part unstable and pliant, the easy prey of designing or enthusiastic adventurers in theology, not the originator of a policy and a creed of her own. The prerogative of Christian doctrine and practice rests hitherto with the Churches of Antioch and Asia Minor.

Heretics congregate there.

But the evidence lends no countenance to the idea that the tendencies of the Roman Church during this period were towards Ebionism. Her early history indeed is wrapt in obscurity. If the veil were raised, the spectacle would probably not be very edifying, but there is no reason to imagine that Judaism was her characteristic taint. As late heathen Rome had been the sink of all Pagan superstitions, so early Christian Rome was the meeting-point of all heretical creeds and philosophies. If the presence of Simon Magus in the metropolis be not a historical fact, it is still a carrying out of the typical character with which he is invested in early tradition, as the father of heresy. Most of the great heresiarchs—among others Valentinus, Marcion, Praxeas, Theodotus, Sabellius—taught in Rome. Ebionism alone would not be idle, where all other heresies were active. But the great battle with this form of error seems to have been fought out at an early date, in the lifetime of the Apostles themselves and in the age immediately following.

Secession of Judaizers.

The last notice of the Roman Church in the apostolic writings seems to point to two separate communities, a Judaizing Church and a Pauline Church. The arrival of the Gentile Apostle in the metropolis, it would appear, was the signal for the separation of the Judaizers, who had hitherto associated with their Gentile brethren coldly and distrustfully. The presence of St Paul must have vastly strengthened the numbers and influence of the more liberal

tion in the Roman Church. This date follows necessarily from their assumption that Hegesippus was an Ebionite; for his approval of this church extends to the episcopate of Eleutherus, the immediate predecessor of Victor; see above, p. 332, note 4. They suppose however that the current had been setting in this direction some time before.

and Catholic party; while the Judaizers provoked by rivalry redoubled their efforts, that in making converts to the Gospel they might also gain proselytes to the law[1]. Thus 'in every way Christ was preached.'

St Peter in Rome.

If St Peter ever visited Rome, it must have been at a later date than these notices. Of this visit, far from improbable in itself, there is fair if not conclusive evidence; and once admitted, we may reasonably assume that important consequences flowed from it. Where all is obscurity, conjecture on one side is fairly answered by conjecture on the other. We may venture therefore to suggest this, as a not unlikely result of the presence of both Apostles in Rome. As they had done before in the world at large, so they would agree to do now in the metropolis: they would exchange the right hand of fellowship, devoting themselves the one more especially to the Jewish, the other to the Gentile converts. Christian Rome was large enough to admit two communities or two sections in one community, until the time was ripe for their more complete amalgamation. Thus either as separate bodies with separate governments, or as a confederation of distinct interests represented each by their own officers in a common presbytery, we may suppose that the Jewish and Gentile brotherhoods at Rome were organized by the combined action of the two Apostles. This fact possibly underlies the tradition that St Peter and St Paul were joint founders of the Roman Church: and it may explain the discrepancies in the lists of the early bishops, which perhaps point to a double succession. At all events, the presence of the two Apostles must have tended to tone down antipathies and to draw parties closer together. The Judaizers seeing that the Apostle of the Circumcision, whose name they had venerated at a distance but whose principles they had hitherto imperfectly understood, was associating on terms of equality with the 'hated one,' the subverter of the law, would be led to follow his example slowly and suspiciously: and advances on the one side would be met eagerly by

A twofold church.

[1] The inferences in the text are drawn from Phil. i. 15—18, compared with Col. iv. 11 'These only (i.e. of the circumcision) are my fellow-workers etc.'

united under Clement. advances on the other. Hence at the close of the first century we see no more traces of a twofold Church. The work of the Apostles, now withdrawn from the scene, has passed into the hands of no unworthy disciple. The liberal and catholic spirit of Clement eminently fitted him for the task of conciliation; and he appears as the first bishop or presiding elder of the one Roman Church. This amalgamation however could not be effected without some opposition; the extreme Judaizers must necessarily have been embittered and alienated: and, if a little later we discern traces of Ebionite sectarianism in Rome, this is not only no surprise, but the most natural consequence of a severe but short-lived struggle.

Clement's Epistle. A.D. 95? The Epistle to the Corinthians written by Clement in the name of the Roman Church cannot well be placed after the close of the first century and may possibly date some years earlier. It is not unreasonable to regard this as a typical document, reflecting the comprehensive principles and large sympathies which had been impressed upon the united Church of Rome, in great measure perhaps by the influence of the distinguished writer. There is no early Christian writing which combines more fully than this the distinctive features of all the Apostolic Epistles, now asserting the supremacy of faith with St Paul, now urging the necessity of works with St James, at one time echoing the language of St Peter, at another repeating the very words of the Epistle to the Hebrews[1]. Not without some show of truth, the authority of Clement was claimed in after generations for writings of very different tendencies. Belonging to no party, he seemed to belong to all.

Testimony of Ignatius. A.D. 107? Not many years after this Epistle was written, Ignatius now on his way to martyrdom addresses a letter to the Roman brethren. It contains no indications of any division in the Church of the metropolis or of the prevalence of Ebionite views among his readers. On the contrary, he lavishes epithets of praise on them in the opening salutation; and throughout the letter there is not the faintest shadow of blame. His only fear is that they may be too kind to him and deprive him of the honour of martyrdom by their intercessions. To

[1] See Westcott *History of the Canon* p. 24 sq.

the Ephesians, and even to Polycarp, he offers words of advice and warning; but to the Romans he utters only the language of joyful satisfaction[1].

But in a church thus formed we might expect to meet with other and narrower types of doctrine than the Epistle of Clement exhibits. Traditional principles and habits of thought would still linger on, modified indeed but not wholly transformed by the predominance of a Catholicity which comprehended all elements in due proportion. One such type is represented by an extant work which emanated from the Roman Church during the first half of the second century[2].

Shepherd of Hermas not Ebionite.

c. A.D. 145.

In its general tone the Shepherd of Hermas confessedly differs from the Epistle of Clement; but on the other hand the writer was certainly no Ebionite, as he has been sometimes represented. If he dwells almost exclusively on works, he yet states that the 'elect of God will be saved through faith[3]': if he rarely quotes the New Testament, his references to the Old Testament are still fainter and scantier: if he speaks seldom of our Lord and never mentions Him by name, he yet asserts that the 'Son of God was present with His Father in counsel at the founding of creation[4],' and holds that the world is 'sustained by Him[5].' Such expressions no Ebionite could have used. Of all the New Testament writings the Shepherd most resembles in tone the Epistle of St James, whose language it some-

[1] This is the case, even though we should accept only the parts preserved in the Syriac as genuine; but the Greek (Vossian) Epistles are still more explicit. They distinctly acquit the Romans of any participation in heresy; speaking of them as 'united in flesh and spirit with every commandment of Christ, filled with the grace of God inseparably, and strained clear of every foreign colour (ἀποδιυλισμένοις ἀπὸ παντὸς ἀλλοτρίου χρώματος).' At the same time the writer appears in other passages as a stubborn opponent of Judaism, *Magn.* 8, 10, *Philad.* 6.

[2] On the date of the Shepherd see above, p. 99, note 3.

[3] *Vis.* iii. 8: comp. *Mand.* viii.

[4] *Sim.* ix. 12. The whole passage is striking: Πρῶτον, φημί, πάντων, κύριε, τοῦτό μοι δήλωσον· ἡ πέτρα καὶ ἡ πύλη τίς ἐστιν; Ἡ πέτρα, φησίν, αὕτη καὶ ἡ πύλη ὁ υἱὸς τοῦ Θεοῦ ἐστί. Πῶς, φημί, κύριε, ἡ πέτρα παλαιά ἐστιν, ἡ δὲ πύλη καινή; Ἄκουε, φησί, καὶ σύνιε, ἀσύνετε. ὁ μὲν υἱὸς τοῦ Θεοῦ πάσης τῆς κτίσεως αὐτοῦ προγενέστερός ἐστιν, ὥστε σύμβουλον αὐτὸν γενέσθαι τῷ πατρὶ τῆς κτίσεως αὐτοῦ· διὰ τοῦτο καὶ παλαιός ἐστιν. Ἡ δὲ πύλη διὰ τί καινή, φημί, κύριε; Ὅτι, φησίν, ἐπ' ἐσχάτων τῶν ἡμερῶν τῆς συντελείας φανερὸς ἐγένετο, διὰ τοῦτο καινὴ ἐγένετο ἡ πύλη, ἵνα οἱ μέλλοντες σώζεσθαι δι' αὐτῆς εἰς τὴν βασιλείαν εἰσέλθωσι τοῦ Θεοῦ.

[5] *Sim.* ix. 14 τὸ ὄνομα τοῦ υἱοῦ τοῦ Θεοῦ μέγα ἐστὶ καὶ ἀχώρητον καὶ τὸν κόσμον ὅλον βαστάζει. On the whole subject see Dorner *Lehre* etc. I. p. 186 sq, Westcott *Canon* p. 200 sq.

times reflects: but the teaching of St James appears here in an exaggerated and perverted form. The author lays great stress on works, and so far he copies his model: but his interpretation of works is often formal and ritualistic, and in one passage he even states the doctrine of supererogation[1]. Whether the tone of this writing is to be ascribed to the traditional feelings of Judaism yet lingering in the Church, or to the influence of a Judaic section still tolerated, or to the constitution of the author's own mind, it is impossible to say. The view of Christian ethics here presented deviates considerably, it is true, from St Paul's teaching; but the deviation is the same in kind and not greater in degree than marks a vast number of mediæval writings, and may in fact be said to characterize more or less distinctly the whole mediæval Church. Thus it affords no ground for the charge of Ebionism. Hermas speaks of law indeed, as St James speaks of it; yet by law he means not the Mosaic ordinances but the rule introduced by Christ. On the other hand his very silence is eloquent. There is not a word in favour of Judaic observances properly so called, not a word of denunciation direct or indirect against either the doctrine or the person of St Paul or his disciples. In this respect the Shepherd presents a marked contrast to the truly Ebionite work, which must be taken next in order.

Roman origin of the Clementines questioned.

The Clementine writings have been assigned with great confidence by most recent critics of ability to a Roman authorship[2]. Of the truth of this view I am very far from convinced. The great argument—indeed almost the only argument—in its favour is the fact that the plot of the romance turns upon the wanderings of this illustrious bishop of Rome, who is at once the narrator and the hero of the story. But the fame of Clement reached far beyond the limits of his own jurisdiction. To him, we are specially told by a contemporary writer, was assigned the task of corresponding with

[1] *Sim.* v. 3: comp. *Mand.* iv. 4.

[2] So for instance Baur, Schliemann, Ritschl, Hilgenfeld: and this view is adopted by Dean Milman *Latin Christianity* I. p. 31, who speaks of it as 'the unanimous opinion of those who in later days have critically examined the Clementina.' Uhlhorn is almost alone among recent critics in raising his voice against this general verdict: p. 370 sq.

foreign churches[1]. His rank and position, his acknowledged wisdom and piety, would point him out as the best typical representative of the Gentile converts: and an Ebionite writer, designing by a religious fiction to impress his views on Gentile Christendom, would naturally single out Clement for his hero, and by his example enforce the duty of obedience to the Church of the Circumcision, as the prerogative Church and the true standard of orthodoxy. At all events it is to be noticed that, beyond the use made of Clement's name, these writings do not betray any familiarity with or make any reference to the Roman Church in particular[2]. On the contrary, the scenes are all laid in the East; and the supreme arbiter, the ultimate referee in all that relates to Christian doctrine and practice, is not Peter, the Clementine Apostle of the Gentiles, the reputed founder of the Roman Church, but James the Lord's brother, the bishop of bishops, the ruler of the mother Church of the Circumcision.

If the Roman origin of these works is more than doubtful, the time of writing also is open to much question. The dates assigned to the Homilies by the ablest critics range over the whole of the second century, and some place them even later. If the Roman authorship be abandoned, many reasons for a very early date will fall to the ground also. Whenever they were written, the Homilies are among the most interesting and important of early Christian writings; but they have no right to the place assigned them in the system of a modern critical school, as the missing link between the Judaism of the Christian era and the Catholicism of the close of the second century, as representing in fact the phase of Christianity taught at Rome and generally throughout the Church during the early ages.

Their importance exaggerated.

[1] Hermas *Vis.* ii. 4 πέμψει οὖν Κλήμης εἰς τὰς ἔξω πόλεις· ἐκείνῳ γὰρ ἐπιτέτραπται.

[2] The Epistle of Clement to James, prefixed to the work, is an exception; for it gives an elaborate account of the writer's appointment by St Peter as his successor. The purpose of this letter, which is to glorify the see of Rome, shows that it was no part of and probably is later than the Homilies themselves.

If the Homilies had really been written by a Roman Christian, the slight and incidental mention of St Peter's sojourn in Rome (i. 16, comp. *Recogn.* i. 74) would have thrown considerable doubt on the fact. But if they emanated from the East, from Syria for instance, no explanation of this silence is needed.

The very complexion of the writer's opinions is such, that they can hardly have been maintained by any large and important community, at least in the West. Had they presented a purer form of Judaism, founded on the Old Testament Scriptures, a more plausible case might have been made out. But the theology of the Clementines does not lie in a direct line between the Old Testament and Catholic Christianity: it deviates equally from the one and the other. In its rejection of half the Mosaic law and much more than half of the Old Testament, and in its doctrine of successive avatars of the Christ, it must have been as repugnant to the religious sentiments of a Jew trained in the school of Hillel, as it could possibly be to a disciple of St Paul in the first century or to a Catholic Christian in the third. Moreover the tone of the writer is not at all the tone of one who addresses a sympathetic audience. His attacks on St Paul are covert and indirect; he makes St Peter complain that he has been misrepresented and libelled. Altogether there is an air of deprecation and apology in the Homilies. If they were really written by a Roman Christian, they cannot represent the main body of the Church, but must have emanated from one of the many heresies with which the metropolis swarmed in the second century, when all promulgators of new doctrine gathered there, as the largest and therefore the most favourable market for their spiritual wares.

They cannot represent the doctrine of the Roman Church.

Notice in Hippolytus.

There is another reason also for thinking that this Gnostic Ebionism cannot have obtained any wide or lasting influence in the Church of Rome. During the episcopate of Callistus (A. D. 219—223) a heretical teacher appears in the metropolis, promulgating Elchasaite doctrines substantially, though not identically, the same with the creed of the Clementines, and at first seems likely to attain some measure of success, but is denounced and foiled by Hippolytus. It is clear that this learned writer on heresies regarded the Elchasaite doctrine as a novelty, against which therefore it was the more necessary to warn the faithful Christian. If the Ebionism of the Clementines had ever prevailed at Rome, it had passed into oblivion when Hippolytus wrote.

No Ebionite leanings in the Roman Church.

The few notices of the Roman Church in the second century point to other than Ebionite leanings. In their ecclesiastical ordinances the Romans seem anxious to separate themselves as widely as possible from Jewish practices. Thus they extended the Friday's fast over the Saturday, showing thereby a marked disregard of the sabbatical festival[1]. Thus again they observed Easter on a different day from the Jewish passover; and so zealous were they in favour of their own traditional usage in this respect, that in the Paschal controversy their bishop Victor resorted to the extreme measure of renouncing communion with those churches which differed from it[2]. This controversy affords a valuable testimony to the Catholicity of Christianity at Rome in another way. It is clear that the churches ranged on different sides on this question of ritual are nevertheless substantially agreed on all important points of doctrine and practice. This fact appears when Anicetus of Rome permits Polycarp of Smyrna, who had visited the metropolis in order to settle some disputed points and had failed in arranging the Paschal question, to celebrate the eucharist in his stead. It is distinctly stated by Irenæus when he remonstrates with Victor for disturbing the peace of the Church by insisting on non-essentials[3]. In its creed the Roman Church was one with the Gallic and Asiatic Churches; and that this creed was not Ebionite, the names of Polycarp and Irenæus are guarantees. Nor is it only in the Paschal controversy that the Catholicity of the Romans may be inferred from their intercourse

Evidence of the Paschal controversy.

[1] Tertull. *de Jejun.* 14; see Neander *Ch. Hist.* I. p. 410 (Bohn).

[2] On the Paschal controversy see Euseb. *H. E.* v. 23—25. Polycrates on behalf of the Asiatic Churches claimed the sanction of St John; and there seems no reason to doubt the validity of this claim. On the other hand a different rule had been observed in the Roman Church at least as far back as the episcopate of Xystus (about 120—129) and perhaps earlier. It seems probable then that the Easter festival had been established independently by the Romans and those who followed the Roman practice. Thus in the first instance the difference of usage was no index of Judaic or antijudaic leanings: but when once attention was called to its existence, and it became a matter of controversy, the observance of the Christian anniversary on the same day with the Jewish festival would afford a handle for the charge of Judaism; and where it was a matter of policy or of principle to stand clear of any sympathy with Jewish customs (as for instance in Palestine after the collision of the Jews with the Romans), the Roman usage would be adopted in preference to the Asiatic.

[3] In Euseb. *H. E.* v. 24 ἡ διαφωνία τῆς νηστείας τὴν ὁμόνοιαν τῆς πίστεως συνίστησιν, and the whole extract.

Other communications with foreign churches.

with other Christian communities. The remains of ecclesiastical literature, though sparse and fragmentary, are yet sufficient to reveal a wide network of intercommunication between the churches of the second century; and herein Rome naturally holds a central position. The visit of Hegesippus to the metropolis has been mentioned already. Not very long after we find Dionysius bishop of Corinth, whose 'orthodoxy' is praised by Eusebius, among other letters addressed to foreign churches, writing also to the Romans in terms of cordial sympathy and respect[1]. On the Catholicity of the African Church I have already remarked: and the African Church was a daughter of the Roman, from whom therefore it may be assumed she derived her doctrine[2].

Internal condition of the Roman Church.

The gleams of light which break in upon the internal history of the Roman Church at the close of the second and beginning of the third century exhibit her assailed by rival heresies, compromised by the weakness and worldliness of her rulers, altogether distracted and unsteady, but in no way Ebionite. One bishop, whose name is not given, first dallies with the fanatical spiritualism of Montanus; then suddenly turning round, surrenders himself to the patripassian speculations of Praxeas[3]. Later than this two successive bishops, Zephyrinus and Callistus, are stated, by no friendly critic indeed but yet a contemporary writer, the one from stupidity and avarice, the other from craft and ambition, to have listened favourably to the heresies of Noetus and Sabellius[4]. It was at this point in her history that the Church of Rome was surprised by the novel doctrines of the Elchasaite teacher, whom I have already mentioned more than once. But no one would maintain that at this late date Ebionism predominated either at Rome or in Christendom generally.

Ebionites indeed there were at this time and very much later.

[1] In Euseb. *H. E.* iv. 23.

[2] Tertull. *de Praescr.* 36. Cyprian *Epist.* 48 (ed. Fell) writing to Cornelius speaks of Rome as 'Ecclesiae catholicae radicem et matricem,' in reference to the African Churches.

[3] Tertull. *adv. Prax.* 1. Tertullian, now a Montanist, writes of Praxeas who had persuaded this nameless bishop of Rome to revoke his concessions to Montanism, 'Ita duo negotia diaboli Praxeas Romae procuravit, prophetiam expulit et haeresim intulit, paracletum fugavit et patrem crucifixit.' For speculations as to the name of this bishop see Wordsworth's *Hippolytus* pp. 131, 132.

[4] Hippol. *Haer.* ix. 7 sq.

Even at the close of the fourth century, they seem to have mustered in considerable numbers in the east of Palestine, and were scattered through the great cities of the empire. But their existence was not prolonged much later. About the middle of the fifth century they had almost disappeared[1]. They would gradually be absorbed either into the Catholic Church or into the Jewish synagogue: into the latter probably, for their attachment to the law seems all along to have been stronger than their attachment to Christ. Ebionism dies out.

Thus then a comprehensive survey of the Church in the second century seems to reveal a substantial unity of doctrine and a general recognition of Jewish and Gentile Apostles alike throughout the greater part of Christendom. At the same time it could hardly happen, that the influence of both should be equally felt or the authority of both estimated alike in all branches of the Church. St Paul and the Twelve had by mutual consent occupied distinct spheres of labour; and this distribution of provinces must necessarily have produced some effect on the subsequent history of the Church[2]. The communities founded by St Paul would collect and preserve the letters of their founder with special care; while the brotherhoods evangelized by the Apostles of the Circumcision would attribute a superior, if not an exclusive, value to the writings of these 'pillars' of the Church. It would therefore be no great surprise if we should find that in individual writers of the second century and in different parts of the early Church, the Epistles of St Paul on the one hand, the Apocalypse of St John or the letter of St James on the other, were seldom or never appealed to as authorities[3]. The

[1] Theodoret, *Haer. Fab.* ii. 11, mentions the Ebionites and the Elchasaites among those of whom οὐδὲ βραχὺ διέμεινε λείψανον.

[2] Gal. ii. 9; see Westcott's *History of the Canon* p. 77 sq, ed. 4.

[3] Many false inferences however, affecting the history of the Canonical writings, have been drawn from the silence of Eusebius, which has been entirely misapprehended: see *Contemporary Review*, January, 1875, p. 169 sq, *Colossians* p. 52 sq.

The phenomenon exhibited in the *Ancient Syriac Documents* (edited by Cureton, 1864) is remarkable. Though they refer more than once to the Acts of the Apostles (pp. 15, 27, 35) as the work of St Luke and as possessing canonical authority, and though they allude incidentally to St Paul's labours (pp. 35, 61, 62), there is yet no reference to the epistles of this Apostle, where the omission cannot have been accidental (p. 32), and the most important churches founded by him,

equable circulation of all the apostolic writings was necessarily the work of time.

Use of the foregoing account.

THE foregoing account of the conflict of the Church with Judaism has been necessarily imperfect, and in some points conjectural; but it will prepare the way for a more correct estimate of the relations between St Paul and the leading Apostles of the Circumcision. We shall be in a position to view these relations no longer as an isolated chapter in history, but in connexion with events before and after: and we shall be furnished also with means of estimating the value of later traditional accounts of these first preachers of the Gospel.

St Paul.

St Paul himself is so clearly reflected in his own writings, that a distorted image of his life and doctrine would seem to be due only to defective vision. Yet our first impressions require to be corrected or rather supplemented by an after consideration. Seeing him chiefly as the champion of Gentile liberty, the constant antagonist of Jew and Judaizer, we are apt to forget that his character has another side also. By birth and education he was a Hebrew of the Hebrews: and the traditions and feelings of his race held him in honourable captivity to the very last.

His portrait in the Acts.

Of this fact the narrative of the Acts affords many striking examples. It exhibits him associating with the Apostles of the Circumcision on terms of mutual respect and love, celebrating the festivals and observing the rites of his countrymen, everywhere giving the precedence to the Jew over the Gentile.

Its truth questioned,

But the character of the witness has been called in question. This narrative, it is said, is neither contemporary nor trustworthy. It was written long after the events recorded, with the definite purpose of uniting the two parties in the Church. Thus the incidents are forged or wrested to subserve the purpose of the writer. It was part of his plan to represent St Peter and St Paul as living on friendly terms, in order to reconcile the Petrine and Pauline factions.

as Ephesus, Thessalonica, Corinth, etc., are stated to have received 'the Apostles' Hand of Priesthood from John the Evangelist' (p. 34).

The Acts of the Apostles in the multiplicity and variety of its details probably affords greater means of testing its general character for truth than any other ancient narrative in existence; and in my opinion it satisfies the tests fully. But this is not the place for such an investigation. Neither shall I start from the assumption that it has any historical value. Taking common ground with those whose views I am considering, I shall draw my proofs from St Paul's Epistles alone in the first instance, nor from all of these, but from such only as are allowed even by the extreme critics of the Tübingen school to be genuine, the Epistles to the Romans, Corinthians, and Galatians[1]. It so happens that they are the most important for my purpose. If they contain the severest denunciations of the Judaizers, if they display the most uncompromising antagonism to Judaism, they also exhibit more strongly than any others St Paul's sympathies with his fellow-countrymen.

but established by his own writings.

These then are the facts for which we have St Paul's direct personal testimony in the epistles allowed by all to be genuine. (1) *The position of the Jews.* He assigns to them the prerogative over the Gentiles; a prior right to the privileges of the Gospel, involving a prior reward if they are accepted and, according to an universal rule in things spiritual, a prior retribution if they are spurned (Rom. i. 16, ii. 9, 10). In the same spirit he declares that the advantage is on the side of the Jew, and that this advantage is 'much every way' (Rom. iii. 1, 2). (2) *His affection for his countrymen.* His earnestness and depth of feeling are nowhere more striking than when he is speaking of the Jews: 'Brethren, my heart's desire and prayer to God for Israel is, that they might be saved: for I bear them record that they have a zeal of God, but not according to knowledge' (Rom. x. 1, 2). Thus in spite of their present stubborn apostasy he will not allow that they have been cast away (xi. 1),

(1) Position of the Jews.

(2) His affection for them.

[1] These four epistles alone were accepted as genuine by Baur and Schwegler. Hilgenfeld, who may now be regarded as the chief of the Tübingen school, has in this, as in many other points, deserted the extreme position of Baur whom he calls the 'great master.' He accepts as genuine 1 Thessalonians, Philippians, and Philemon: thus substituting, as he expresses it, the sacred number Seven for the heathen Tetractys of his master: see *Zeitsch. für wissensch. Theol.* v. p. 226 (1862).

but looks forward to the time when 'all Israel shall be saved' (xi. 26). So strong indeed is his language in one passage, that commentators regarding the letter rather than the spirit of the Apostle's prayer, have striven to explain it away by feeble apologies and unnatural interpretations: 'I say the truth in Christ, I lie not, my conscience also bearing me witness in the Holy Ghost, that I have great heaviness and continual sorrow in my heart: for I could wish that myself were accursed from Christ (ἀνάθεμα εἶναι αὐτὸς ἐγὼ ἀπὸ τοῦ Χριστοῦ) for my brethren, my kinsmen according to the flesh' (Rom. ix. 1—3). (3) *His practical care for his countrymen.* The collection of alms for the poor brethren of Judæa occupies much of his attention and suggests messages to various churches (Rom. xv. 25, 26; 1 Cor. xvi. 1—6; 2 Cor. viii, ix; Gal. ii. 10). It is clear not only that he is very solicitous himself on behalf of the Christians of the Circumcision, but that he is anxious also to inspire his Gentile converts with the same interest. (4) *His conformity to Jewish habits and usages.* St Paul lays down this rule, to 'become all things to all men that he may by all means save some' (1 Cor. ix. 22). This is the key to all seeming inconsistencies in different representations of his conduct. In his epistles we see him chiefly as a Gentile among Gentiles; but this powerful moral weapon has another edge. Applying this maxim, he himself tells us emphatically that 'unto the Jews he became as a Jew, that he might gain the Jews; unto them that are under the law as under the law, that he might gain them that are under the law' (1 Cor. ix. 20). The charges of his Judaizing opponents are a witness that he did carry out his maxim in this direction, as in the other. With a semblance of truth they taunt him with inconsistency, urging that in his own practice he had virtually admitted their principles, that in fact he had himself preached circumcision[1]. (5) *His reverence for the Old Testament Scriptures.* This is a strongly marked feature in the four epistles which I am considering. They teem with quotations, while there are comparatively few in his remaining letters. For metaphor, allegory, example, argument, confirmation, he draws upon this inex-

(3) His practical care for them.

(4) His conformity to their usages.

(5) His use of the Old Testament.

[1] See above, p. 28 sq, and notes on i. 10, ii. 3, v. 2, 11.

haustible store. However widely he may have differed from his rabbinical teachers in other respects, he at least did not yield to them in reverence for 'the law and the prophets and the psalms.'

These facts being borne in mind (and they are indisputable) the portrait of St Paul in the Acts ought not to present any difficulties. It records no one fact of the Apostle, it attributes no sentiment to him, which is not either covered by some comprehensive maxim or supported by some practical instance in his acknowledged letters. On the other hand the tone of the history confessedly differs somewhat from the tone of the epistles. Nor could it possibly have been otherwise. Written in the heat of the conflict, written to confute unscrupulous antagonists and to guard against dangerous errors, St Paul's language could not give a complete picture of his relations with the Apostles and the Church of the Circumcision. Arguments directed against men, who disparaged his authority by undue exaltation of the Twelve, offered the least favourable opportunity of expressing his sympathy with the Twelve. Denunciations of Judaizing teachers, who would force their national rites on the Gentile Churches, were no fit vehicle for acknowledging his respect for and conformity with those rites. The fairness of this line of argument will be seen by comparing the differences observable in his own epistles. His tone may be said to be graduated according to the temper and character of his hearers. The opposition of the Galatian letter to the Mosaic ritual is stern and uncompromising. It was written to correct a virulent form of Judaism. On the other hand the remonstrances in the Epistle to the Romans are much more moderate, guarded by constant explanations and counterpoised by expressions of deep sympathy. Here he was writing to a mixed church of Jews and Gentiles, where there had been no direct opposition to his authority, no violent outbreak of Judaism. If then we picture him in his intercourse with his own countrymen at Jerusalem, where the claims of his nation were paramount and where the cause of Gentile liberty could not be compromised, it seems most natural that he should have spoken and acted as he is represented in the Acts. Luther denouncing the pope for idolatry and Luther rebuking Carl-

Difference in tone between the Acts and Epistles.

stadt for iconoclasm writes like two different persons. He bids the timid and gentle Melancthon 'sin and sin boldly': he would have cut his right hand off sooner than pen such words to the antinomian rioters of Munster. It is not that the man or his principles were changed: but the same words addressed to persons of opposite tempers would have conveyed a directly opposite meaning.

St Paul's relations with the Three as described in this epistle.

St Paul's language then, when in this epistle he describes his relations with the Three, must be interpreted with this caution, that it necessarily exhibits those relations in a partial aspect. The purport of this language, as I understand it, is explained in the notes: and I shall content myself here with gathering up the results.

(1) There is a general recognition of the position and authority of the elder Apostles, both in the earlier visit to Jerusalem when he seeks Peter apparently for the purpose of obtaining instruction in the facts of the Gospel, staying with him a fortnight, and in the later visit which is undertaken for the purpose, if I may use the phrase, of comparing notes with the other Apostles and obtaining their sanction for the freedom of the Gentile Churches. (2) On the other hand there is an uncompromising resistance to the extravagant and exclusive claims set up on their behalf by the Judaizers. (3) In contrast to these claims, St Paul's language leaves the impression (though the inference cannot be regarded as certain), that they had not offered a prompt resistance to the Judaizers in the first instance, hoping perhaps to conciliate them, and that the brunt of the contest had been borne by himself and Barnabas. (4) At the same time they are distinctly separated from the policy and principles of the Judaizers, who are termed false brethren, spies in the Christian camp. (5) The Apostles of the Circumcision find no fault with St Paul's Gospel, and have nothing to add to it. (6) Their recognition of his office is most complete. The language is decisive in two respects: it represents this recognition *first* as thoroughly mutual, and *secondly* as admitting a perfect equality and independent position. (7) At the same time a separate sphere of labour is assigned to each: the one are to preach to the heathen, the other to the Circumcision. There is no implication, as some have represented,

that the Gospel preached to the Gentile would differ from the Gospel preached to the Jew. Such an idea is alien to the whole spirit of the passage. Lastly, (8) Notwithstanding their distinct spheres of work, St Paul is requested by the Apostles of the Circumcision to collect the alms of the Gentiles for the poor brethren of Judæa, and to this request he responds cordially.

References to them in other epistles.

With the exception of the incident at Antioch, which will be considered presently, the Epistle to the Galatians contains nothing more bearing directly on the relations between St Paul and the Apostles of the Circumcision. Other special references are found in the Epistles to the Corinthians, but none elsewhere. These notices, slight though they are, accord with the view presented by the Galatian letter. St Paul indeed says more than once that he is 'not a whit behind the very chiefest Apostles' (τῶν ὑπερλίαν ἀποστόλων, 2 Cor. xi. 5, xii. 11), and there is in the original a slight touch of irony which disappears in the translation: but the irony loses its point unless the exclusive preference of the elder Apostles is regarded as an exaggeration of substantial claims. Elsewhere St Paul speaks of Cephas and the Lord's brethren as exercising an apostolic privilege which belonged also to himself and Barnabas (1 Cor. ix. 5), of Cephas and James as witnesses of the Lord's resurrection like himself (1 Cor. xv. 5, 7). In the last passage he calls himself (with evident reference to the elder Apostles who are mentioned immediately before) 'the least of the Apostles, who is not worthy to be called an Apostle.' In rebuking the dissensions at Corinth, he treats the name of Cephas with a delicate courtesy and respect which has almost escaped notice. When he comes to argue the question, he at once drops the name of St Peter; 'While one saith, I am of Paul, and another, I am of Apollos, are ye not carnal? What then is Apollos, and what is Paul?' Apollos was so closely connected with him (1 Cor. xvi. 12), that he could use his name without fear of misapprehension. But in speaking of Cephas he had to observe more caution: certain persons persisted in regarding St Peter as the head of a rival party, and therefore he is careful to avoid any seeming depreciation of his brother Apostle.

No antagonism between St Paul and the other Apostles.

In all this there is nothing inconsistent with the character of St Paul as drawn in the Acts, nothing certainly which represents him as he was represented by extreme partisans in ancient times, by Ebionites on the one hand and Marcionites on the other, and as he has been represented of late by a certain school of critics, in a position of antagonism to the chief Apostles of the Circumcision. I shall next examine the scriptural notices and traditional representations of these three.

St Peter claimed by Ebionites

1. The author of the Clementine Homilies makes St Peter the mouth-piece of his own Ebionite views. In the prefatory letter of Peter to James which, though possibly the work of another author, represents the same sentiments, the Apostle complains that he has been misrepresented as holding that the law was abolished but fearing to preach this doctrine openly. 'Far be it,' he adds, 'for to act so is to oppose the law of God which was spoken by Moses and to which our Lord bare witness that it should abide for ever. For thus He said, *Heaven and earth shall pass away: one jot or one tittle shall in no wise pass away from the law.* And this He said that all things might be fulfilled. Yet these persons professing to give my sentiments (τὸν ἐμὸν νοῦν ἐπαγγελλόμενοι) I know not how, attempt to interpret the words that they have heard from me more cleverly (φρονιμώτερον) than myself who spoke them, telling their pupils that this is my meaning (φρόνημα), though it never once entered into my mind (ὃ ἐγὼ οὐδὲ ἐνεθυμήθην). But if they dare to tell such falsehoods of me while I am still alive, how much more will those who come after me venture to do it when I am gone (§ 2).' It has been held by some modern critics that the words thus put into the Apostle's mouth are quite in character; that St Peter did maintain the perpetuity of the law; and that therefore the traditional account which has pervaded Catholic Christendom from the writing of the Acts to the present day gives an essentially false view of the Apostle.

I think the words quoted will strike most readers as betraying a consciousness on the part of the writer that he is treading on hollow and dangerous ground. But without insisting on this, it is important to observe that the sanction of this venerated name was claimed by other sectarians of opposite opinions. Basilides (about A.D. 130), the famous Gnostic teacher, announced that he had been instructed by one Glaucias an 'interpreter' of St Peter[1]. An early apocryphal writing moreover, which should probably be assigned to the beginning of the second century and which expressed strong anti-judaic views[2], was entitled the 'Preaching of Peter.' I do not see why these assertions have not as great a claim to a hearing as the opposite statement of the Ebionite writer. They are probably earlier; and in one case at least we have more tangible evidence than the irresponsible venture of an anonymous romance writer. The probable inference however from such conflicting statements would be, that St Peter's true position was somewhere between the two extremes. and also by opposite sects.

[1] Clem. Alex. *Strom.* vii. p. 898, Potter.

[2] On this work, the *κήρυγμα Πέτρου*, see Schwegler *Nachap. Zeit.* II. p. 30 sq. Its opposition to Judaism appears in an extant fragment preserved in Clem. Alex. *Strom.* vi. p. 760, *μηδὲ κατὰ Ἰουδαίους σέβεσθε...ὥστε καὶ ὑμεῖς ὁσίως καὶ δικαίως μανθάνοντες ἃ παραδίδομεν ὑμῖν φυλάσσεσθε, καινῶς τὸν Θεὸν διὰ τοῦ Χριστοῦ σεβόμενοι· εὕρομεν γὰρ ἐν ταῖς γραφαῖς καθὼς ὁ Κύριος λέγει· Ἰδοὺ διατίθεμαι ὑμῖν καινὴν διαθήκην κ.τ.λ.* The fragments of this work are collected by Grabe, *Spicil.* I. p. 62 sq. It was made use of by Heracleon the Valentinian, and is quoted more than once, apparently as genuine, by Clement of Alexandria.

The identity of this work with the *Praedicatio Pauli* quoted in the treatise *De Baptismo Haereticorum* printed among Cyprian's works (App. p. 30, Fell) seems to me very doubtful, though maintained by several able critics. The passage there quoted is strangely misinterpreted by Baur (*Christenthum* p. 53). I give his words, lest I should have misunderstood him: 'Auch die kirchliche Sage, welche die Apostel wieder zusammenbrachte, lässt erst am Ende nach einer langen Zeit der Trennung die gegenseitige Anerkennung zu Stande kommen. Post tanta tempora, hiess es in der Prædicatio Pauli in der Stelle, welche sich in der Cyprian's Werken angehängten Schrift de rebaptismate erhalten hat (Cypr. *Opp.* ed. Baluz. s. 365 f.), Petrum et Paulum post conlationem evangelii in Jerusalem et mutuam cogitationem [?] et altercationem et rerum agendarum dispositionem postremo in urbe, quasi tunc primum, invicem sibi esse cognitos.' Baur thus treats the comment of the writer as if it were part of the quotation. In this treatise the writer denounces the *Praedicatio Pauli* as maintaining 'adulterinum, imo internecinum baptisma'; in order to invalidate its authority, he proceeds to show its thoroughly unhistorical character; and among other instances he alleges the fact that it makes St Peter and St Paul meet in Rome as if for the first time, forgetting all about the congress at Jerusalem, the collision at Antioch, and so forth. Schwegler takes the correct view of the passage, II. p. 32.

Other early apocryphal works attributed to the chief Apostle of the Circumcision are the Gospel, the Acts, and the Apocalypse of Peter; but our information respecting these is too scanty to throw much light on the present question: on the Gospel of Peter see above, p. 274.

St Paul's notice of the occurrence at Antioch.

But we are not to look for trustworthy information from such sources as these. If we wish to learn the Apostle's real attitude in the conflict between Jewish and Gentile converts, the one fragmentary notice in the Epistle to the Galatians will reveal more than all the distorted and interested accounts of later ages: 'But when Cephas came to Antioch I withstood him to the face, for he was condemned (his conduct condemned itself). For before that certain came from James, he did eat with the Gentiles, but when they came, he withdrew and separated himself, fearing those of the circumcision: and the rest of the Jews also dissembled with him, so that even Barnabas was carried away with their dissimulation (συναπήχθη αὐτῶν τῇ ὑποκρίσει). But when I saw that they walked not straight according to the truth of the Gospel, I said unto Cephas before all, If thou, being born a Jew (Ἰουδαῖος ὑπάρχων), livest after the manner of the Gentiles and not after the manner of the Jews, how compellest thou the Gentiles to live like the Jews? etc. (ii. 11—14).'

Now the point of St Paul's rebuke is plainly this: that in sanctioning the Jewish feeling which regarded eating with the Gentiles as an unclean thing, St Peter was *untrue to his principles*, was acting hypocritically and from fear. In the argument which follows he assumes that it was the normal practice of Peter to live as a Gentile (ἐθνικῶς ζῇς and not ἐθνικῶς ἔζης), in other words, to mix freely with the Gentiles, to eat with them, and therefore to disregard the distinction of things clean and unclean: and he argues on the glaring inconsistency and unfairness that Cephas should claim this liberty himself though not born to it, and yet by hypocritical compliance with the Jews should practically force the ritual law on the Gentiles and deprive them of a freedom which was their natural right[1].

[1] I do not see how this conclusion can be resisted. According to the Tübingen view of St Peter's position, his hypocrisy or dissimulation must have consisted not in withdrawing from, but in holding intercourse with the Gentiles; but this is not the view of St Paul on any natural interpretation of his words; and certainly the Ebionite writer already quoted (p. 352) did not so understand his meaning. Schwegler (I. p. 129) explains συνυπεκρίθησαν αὐτῷ 'were hypocritical enough to side with him,' thus forcing the expression itself and severing it from the context; but even then he is obliged to acquit the other Jewish Christians at Antioch of Ebionism. Hilgenfeld (*Galater* p. 61 sq) discards Schwegler's interpretation and explains ὑπόκρισις of the self-contradiction, the unconscious inconsistency of Jewish Christian or Ebionite

How St Peter came to hold these liberal principles, so entirely opposed to the narrow traditions of his age and country, is explained by an incident narrated in the Acts. He was at one time as rigid and as scrupulous as the most bigoted of his countrymen: 'nothing common or unclean had at any time entered into his mouth (x. 14, xi. 8).' Suddenly a light bursts in upon the darkness of his religious convictions. He is taught by a vision 'not to call any man common or unclean (x. 28).' His sudden change scandalizes the Jewish brethren: but he explains and for the moment at least convinces (xi. 18).

It accords with an incident related in the Acts

And if his normal principles are explained by the narrative of the Acts, his exceptional departure from them is illustrated by his character as it appears in the Gospels. The occasional timidity and weakness of St Peter will be judged most harshly by those who have never themselves felt the agony of a great moral crisis, when not their own ease and comfort only, which is a small thing, but the spiritual welfare of others seems to clamour for a surrender of their principles. His true nobleness—his fiery zeal and overflowing love and abandoned self-devotion—will be appreciated most fully by spirits which can claim some kindred however remote with his spirit.

and with his character as given in the Gospels.

Thus the fragmentary notices in the Gospels, the Acts, and the Epistles of St Paul, combine to form a harmonious portrait of a character, not consistent indeed, but—to use Aristotle's significant phrase—consistently inconsistent (ὁμαλῶς ἀνώμαλον); and this is a much safer criterion of truth. But there is yet another source of information to be considered—his own letters. If the deficiency of external evidence forbids the use of the Second Epistle in controversy, the First labours under no such disabilities; for very few of the apostolical writings are better attested.

The First Epistle of St Peter

To this epistle indeed it has been objected that it bears too manifest traces of Pauline influence to be the genuine writing of St Peter. The objection however seems to overlook two important

shows the influence of St Paul,

principles: but inconsistency is not dissimulation or hypocrisy, and this interpretation, like the former, loses sight of the context which denounces St Peter for abandoning a certain line of conduct *from timidity*.

considerations. *First.* If we consider the prominent part borne by St Paul as the chief preacher of Christianity in countries Hellenic by race or by adoption; if we remember further that his writings were probably the first which clothed the truths of the Gospel and the aspirations of the Church in the language of Greece; we shall hardly hesitate to allow that he 'had a great influence in moulding this language for Christian purposes, and that those who afterwards trod in his footsteps could hardly depart much from the idiom thus moulded[1].' *Secondly.* It is begging the whole question to assume that St Peter derived nothing from the influence of the Apostle of the Gentiles. The one was essentially a character to impress, the other to be impressed. His superior in intellectual culture, in breadth of sympathy, and in knowledge of men, his equal in love and zeal for Christ, St Paul must have made his influence felt on the frank and enthusiastic temperament of the elder Apostle. The weighty spiritual maxims thrown out during the dispute at Antioch for instance would sink deep into his heart[2]: and taking into account the many occasions when either by his writings or by personal intercourse St Paul's influence would be communicated, we can hardly doubt that the whole effect was great.

but bears the individual stamp

But after all the epistle bears the stamp of an individual mind quite independent of this foreign element. The substratum of the thoughts is the writer's own. Its individuality indeed appears more in the contemplation of the life and sufferings of Christ, in the view taken of the relations between the believer and the world around, in the realisation of the promises made to the chosen people of old, in the pervading sense of a regenerate life and the reiterated hope of a glorious advent, than in any special development of doctrine: but it would be difficult to give any reason why, prior to experience, we should have expected it to be otherwise.

[1] Schleiermacher, *Einl. ins N. T.* p. 402 sq.

[2] See 1 Pet. ii. 24 *τὰς ἁμαρτίας ἡμῶν αὐτὸς ἀνήνεγκεν ἐν τῷ σώματι αὐτοῦ ἐπὶ τὸ ξύλον, ἵνα ταῖς ἁμαρτίαις ἀπογενόμενοι τῇ δικαιοσύνῃ ζήσωμεν.* This is the most striking instance which the epistle exhibits of coincidence with St Paul's doctrinal teaching (though there are occasionally strong resemblances of language). With it compare Gal. ii. 20 *Χριστῷ συνεσταύρωμαι· ζῶ δὲ οὐκέτι ἐγώ, ζῇ δὲ ἐν ἐμοὶ Χριστὸς κ.τ.λ.*

Altogether the epistle is anything but Ebionite. Not only is the 'law' never once named, but there is no allusion to formal ordinances of any kind. The writer indeed is essentially an Israelite, but he is an Israelite after a Christian type. When he speaks of the truths of the Gospel, he speaks of them through the forms of the older dispensation: he alludes again and again to the ransom of Christ's death, but the image present to his mind is the paschal lamb without spot or blemish; he addresses himself to Gentile converts, but he transfers to them the cherished titles of the covenant race; they are the true 'dispersion (i. 1)'; they are 'a chosen generation, a royal priesthood, a holy nation, a peculiar people (ii. 9).' The believer in Christ is the Israelite; the unbeliever the Gentile (ii. 12).

of a mind Hebrew but not Ebionite.

Corresponding to the position of St Peter as he appears in the postolic history, this epistle in its language and tone occupies a place midway between the writings of St James and St Paul. With St James it dwells earnestly on the old: with St Paul it expands to the comprehension of the new. In its denunciation of luxurious wealth, in its commendation of the simple and homely virtues, in its fond reference to past examples in Jewish history for imitation or warning, it recalls the tone of the head of the Hebrew Church: in its conception of the grace of God, of the ransom of Christ's death, of the wide purpose of the Gospel, it approaches to the language of the Apostle of the Gentiles.

Its relation to St Paul and St James.

With St Paul too the writer links himself by the mention of two names, both Christians of the Circumcision, and both companions of the Gentile Apostle; Mark who, having accompanied him on his first missionary tour, after some years of alienation is found by his side once more (Col. iv. 10), and Silvanus who shared with him the labours and perils of planting the Gospel in Europe. Silvanus is the bearer or the amanuensis of St Peter's letter; Mark joins in the salutations (v. 12, 13).

Mark and Silvanus.

Thus the Churches of the next generation, which were likely to be well informed, delighted to unite the names of the two leading Apostles as the greatest teachers of the Gospel, the brightest examples of Christian life. At Rome probably, at Antioch certainly, both these

St Peter and St Paul associated in early tradition.

Apostles were personally known. We have the witness of the one church in Clement; of the other in Ignatius. The former classes them together as the two 'noble ensamples of his own generation,' 'the greatest and most righteous pillars' of the Church, who 'for hatred and envy were persecuted even unto death (§ 5).' The latter will not venture to command the Christians of Rome, 'as Peter and Paul did; they were Apostles, he a convict; they were free, he a slave to that very hour[1].' Clement wrote before the close of the first century, Ignatius at the beginning of the second. It seems probable that both these fathers had conversed with one or other of the two Apostles. Besides Antioch and Rome, the names of St Peter and St Paul appear together also in connexion with the Church of Corinth (1 Cor. iii. 22). This church again has not withheld her voice, though here the later date of her testimony detracts somewhat from its value[2]. Dionysius bishop of Corinth, writing to the Romans during the episcopate of Soter (c. 166—174), claims kindred with them on the ground that both churches alike had profited by the joint instruction of St Peter and St Paul[3].

Rome.

Antioch.

Corinth.

Misrepresentations of extreme parties.

But though the essential unity of these two Apostles is thus recognised by different branches of the Catholic Church, a disposition to sever them seems early to have manifested itself in some quarters. Even during their own lifetime the religious agitators at Corinth would have placed them in spite of themselves at the head of rival parties. And when death had removed all fear of contradiction, extreme partisans boldly claimed the sanction of the one or the other

[1] *Rom.* 4. The words *οὐχ ὡς Πέτρος καὶ Παῦλος διατάσσομαι ὑμῖν* gain force, as addressed to the Romans, if we suppose both Apostles to have preached in Rome.

[2] The language of Clement however implicitly contains the testimony of this church at an earlier date: for he assumes the acquiescence of the Corinthians when he mentions both Apostles as of equal authority (§§ 5, 47).

[3] In Euseb. *H. E.* ii. 25 *τὴν ἀπὸ Πέτρου καὶ Παύλου φυτείαν γενηθεῖσαν Ῥωμαίων τε καὶ Κορινθίων συνεκεράσατε. καὶ γὰρ ἄμφω καὶ εἰς τὴν ἡμετέραν Κόρινθον φοιτήσαντες ἡμᾶς ὁμοίως ἐδίδαξαν, ὁμοίως δὲ καὶ εἰς τὴν Ἰταλίαν ὁμόσε διδάξαντες ἐμαρτύρησαν κατὰ τὸν αὐτὸν καιρόν.* All the MSS and the Syriac version here have *φυτεύσαντες*; but *φοιτήσαντες* is read by Georgius Syncellus, and Rufinus has 'adventantes'; the sense too seems to require it. In any case it is hardly a safe inference that Dionysius erroneously supposed the Churches of Rome and Corinth to have been *founded* by both Apostles jointly.

for their own views. The precursors of the Ebionites misrepresented the Israelite sympathies of St Peter, as if he had himself striven to put a yoke upon the neck of the Gentiles which neither their fathers nor they were able to bear. The precursors of Marcionism exaggerated the antagonism of St Paul to the Mosaic ritual, as if he had indeed held the law to be sin and the commandment neither holy nor just nor good. It seems to have been a subsidiary aim of St Luke's narrative, which must have been written not many years after the martyrdom of both Apostles, to show that this growing tendency was false, and that in their life, as in their death, they were not divided. A rough parallelism between the career of the two reveals itself in the narrative when carefully examined. Recent criticism has laid much stress on this 'conciliatory' purpose of the Acts, as if it were fatal to the credit of the narrative. But denying the inference we may concede the fact, and the very concession draws its sting. Such a purpose is at least as likely to have been entertained by a writer, if the two Apostles were essentially united, as if they were not. The truth or falsehood of the account must be determined on other grounds.

Conciliatory aim of the Acts.

2. While St Peter was claimed as their leader by the Judaizers, no such liberty seems to have been taken with the name of St John[1]. Long settled in an important Gentile city, surrounded by a numerous school of disciples, still living at the dawn of the second century, he must have secured for his teaching such notoriety as protected it from gross misrepresentation.

St John not claimed by Ebionites.

His last act recorded in St Luke's narrative is a visit to the newly founded Churches of Samaria, in company with St Peter (viii.

His position in the apostolic history.

[1] In the portion of the first book of the Recognitions, which seems to have been taken from the 'Ascents of James,' the sons of Zebedee are introduced with the rest of the Twelve confuting heresies, but the sentiments attributed to them are in no way Ebionite (i. 57). It is this work perhaps to which Epiphanius refers (xxx. 23), for his notice does not imply anything more than a casual introduction of St John's name in their writings. In another passage Epiphanius attributes to the sons of Zebedee the same ascetic practices which distinguished James the Lord's brother (*Haer.* lxxviii. 13); and this account he perhaps derived from some Essene Ebionite source. But I do not know that they ever claimed St John in the same way as they claimed St Peter and St James.

14). He thus stamps with his approval the first movement of the Church in its liberal progress. From the silence of both St Paul and St Luke it may be inferred that he took no very prominent part in the disputes about the Mosaic law. Only at the close of the conferences we find him together with St Peter and St James recognising the authority and work of St Paul, and thus giving another guarantee of his desire to advance the liberties of the Church. This is the only passage where he is mentioned in St Paul's Epistles. Yet it seems probable that though he did not actually participate in the public discussions, his unseen influence was exerted to promote the result. As in the earliest days of the Church, so now we may imagine him ever at St Peter's side, his faithful colleague and wise counsellor, not forward and demonstrative, but most powerful in private, pouring into the receptive heart of the elder Apostle the lessons of his own inward experience, drawn from close personal intercourse and constant spiritual communion with his Lord.

His life in relation to his writings.

At length the hidden fires of his nature burst out into flame. When St Peter and St Paul have ended their labours, the more active career of St John is just beginning. If it had been their task to organize and extend the Church, to remove her barriers and to advance her liberties, it is his special province to build up and complete her theology. The most probable chronology makes his withdrawal from Palestine to Asia Minor coincide very nearly with the martyrdom of these two Apostles, who have guided the Church through her first storms and led her to her earliest victories. This epoch divides his life into two distinct periods: hitherto he has lived as a Jew among Jews; henceforth he will be as a Gentile among Gentiles. The writings of St John in the Canon probably mark the close of each period. The Apocalypse winds up his career in the Church of the Circumcision; the Gospel and the Epistles are the crowning result of a long residence in the heart of Gentile Christendom.

Both the one and the other contrast strongly with the leading features of Ebionite doctrine; and this fact alone would deter the Judaizers from claiming the sanction of a name so revered.

Of all the writings of the New Testament the Apocalypse is

most thoroughly Jewish in its language and imagery. The whole book is saturated with illustrations from the Old Testament. It speaks not the language of Paul, but of Isaiah and Ezekiel and Daniel. Its tone may be well described by an expression borrowed from the book itself; 'the testimony of Jesus is the spirit of prophecy (xix. 10).' The doctrine of Balaam, the whoredoms of Jezebel, the song of Moses, the lion of Judah, the key of David, the great river Euphrates, the great city Babylon, Sodom and Egypt, Gog and Magog, these and similar expressions are but the more striking instances of an imagery with which the Apocalypse teems. Nor are the symbols derived solely from the canonical Scriptures; in the picture of the New Jerusalem the inspired Apostle has borrowed many touches from the creations of rabbinical fancy. Up to this point the Apocalypse is completely Jewish and might have been Ebionite. But the same framing serves only to bring out more strongly the contrast between the pictures themselves. The two distinctive features of Ebionism, its mean estimate of the person of Christ and its extravagant exaltation of the Mosaic law, are opposed alike to the spirit and language of St John. It might have been expected that the beloved disciple, who had leaned on his Master's bosom, would have dwelt with fond preference on the humanity of our Lord: yet in none of the New Testament writings, not even in the Epistles of St Paul, do we find a more express recognition of His divine power and majesty. He is 'the Amen, the faithful and true witness, the beginning (the source) of the creation of God (iii. 14).' 'Blessing, honour, glory, and power' are ascribed not 'to Him that sitteth on the throne' only, but 'to the Lamb for ever and ever (v. 13).' His name is 'the Word of God (xix. 13).' Therefore he claims the titles and attributes of Deity. He declares himself 'the Alpha and Omega, the first and last, the beginning and the end (xxii. 13; comp. i. 8).' He is 'the Lord of lords and the King of kings (xvii. 14, xix. 16).' And so too the Ebionite reverence for the law as still binding has no place in the Apocalypse. The word does not occur from beginning to end, nor is there a single allusion to its ceremonial as an abiding ordinance. The Paschal

The Apocalypse Hebrew in its imagery,

but not Ebionite in doctrine.

The Christ.

The law.

Lamb indeed is ever present to St John's thought; but with him it signifies not the sacrifice offered in every Jewish home year by year, but the Christ who once 'was slain, and hath redeemed us to God by his blood out of every kindred and tongue and people and nation (vii. 9).' All this is very remarkable, since there is every reason to believe that up to this time St John had in practice observed the Jewish law[1]. To him however it was only a national custom

[1] Certain traditions of St John's residence at Ephesus, illustrating his relation to the Mosaic law, deserve notice here. They are given by Polycrates who was himself bishop of Ephesus (Euseb. *H. E.* v. 24). Writing to pope Victor, probably in the last decade of the second century, he mentions that he 'numbers (ἔχων) sixty-five years in the Lord' (whether he refers to the date of his birth or of his conversion, is uncertain, but the former seems more probable), and that he has had seven relations bishops, whose tradition he follows. We are thus carried back to a very early date. The two statements with which we are concerned are these. (1) St John celebrated the Paschal day on the 14th of the month, coinciding with the Jewish passover. It seems to me, as I have said already (see p. 343), that there is no good ground for questioning this tradition. The institution of such an annual celebration by this Apostle derives light from the many references to the Paschal Lamb in the Apocalypse; and in the first instance it would seem most natural to celebrate it on the exact anniversary of the Passover. It is more questionable whether the Roman and other Churches, whose usage has passed into the law of Christendom, had really the apostolic sanction which they vaguely asserted for celebrating it always on the Friday. This usage, if not quite so obvious as the other, was not unnatural and probably was found much more convenient. (2) Polycrates says incidentally of St John that he was 'a priest wearing the mitre and a martyr and teacher (ὃς ἐγενήθη ἱερεὺς τὸ πέταλον πεφορεκὼς καὶ μάρτυς καὶ διδάσκαλος).' The reference in the πέταλον is doubtless to the metal plate on the high-priest's mitre (Exod. xxviii. 36 πέταλον χρυσοῦν καθαρόν, comp. *Protevang.* c. 5 τὸ πέταλον τοῦ ἱερέως); but the meaning of Polycrates is far from clear. He has perhaps mistaken metaphor for matter of fact (see Stanley *Apostolical Age* p. 285); in like manner as the name Theophorus assumed by Ignatius gave rise to the later story that he was the child whom our Lord took in his arms and blessed. I think it probable however that the words as they stand in Polycrates are intended for a metaphor, since the short fragment which contains them has several figurative expressions almost, if not quite, as violent; e.g. μεγάλα στοιχεῖα κεκοίμηται (where στοιχεῖα means 'luminaries,' being used of the heavenly bodies); Μελίτωνα τὸν εὐνοῦχον (probably a metaphor, as Rufinus translates it, 'propter regnum dei eunuchum'; see Matt. xix. 12 and comp. Athenag. *Suppl.* 33, 34, Clem. Alex. *Paed.* iii. 4, p. 269, *Strom.* iii. 1. p. 509 sq); τὸν μικρόν μου ἄνθρωπον ('my insignificance'; comp. Rom. vi. 6 ὁ παλαιὸς ἡμῶν ἄνθρωπος, 2 Cor. iv. 16 ὁ ἔξω ἡμῶν ἄνθρωπος, 1 Pet. iii. 4 ὁ κρυπτὸς τῆς καρδίας ἄνθρωπος). The whole passage is a very rude specimen of the florid 'Asiatic' style, which even in its higher forms Cicero condemns as suited only to the ears of a people wanting in polish and good taste ('minime politae minimeque elegantes,' *Orator*, 25) and which is described by another writer as κομπώδης καὶ φρυαγματίας καὶ κενοῦ γαυριάματος καὶ φιλοτιμίας ἀνωμάλου μεστός, Plut. *Vit. Anton.* 2; see Bernhardy *Griech. Litt.* 1. p. 465. On the other hand it is possible—I think not probable—that St John did wear

and not an universal obligation, only one of the many garbs in which religious worship might clothe itself, and not the essence of religious life. In itself circumcision is nothing, as uncircumcision also is nothing; and therefore he passes it over as if it were not. The distinction between Jew and Gentile has ceased; the middle wall of partition is broken down in Christ. If preserving the Jewish imagery which pervades the book, he records the sealing of twelve thousand from each tribe of Israel, his range of vision expands at once, and he sees before the throne 'a great multitude, which no man could number, of all nations and kindreds and peoples and tongues (vii. 9).' If he denounces the errors of heathen speculation, taking up their own watchword 'knowledge (γνῶσις)' and retorting upon them that they *know* only 'the depths of Satan (ii. 24)[1],' on the other hand he condemns in similar language the bigotry of Jewish prejudice, denouncing the blasphemy of those 'who say they are Jews and are not, but are a synagogue of Satan' (ii. 9; comp. iii. 9).

The Gospel and Epistles contrasted and compared with the Apocalypse.

A lapse of more than thirty years spent in the midst of a Gentile population will explain the contrast of language and imagery between the Apocalypse and the later writings of St John, due allowance being made for the difference of subject[2]. The language and colouring of the Gospel and Epistles are no longer Hebrew; but so far as a Hebrew mind was capable of the transformation, Greek or

this decoration as an emblem of his Christian privileges; nor ought this view to cause any offence, as inconsistent with the spirituality of his character. If in Christ the use of external symbols is nothing, the avoidance of them is nothing also. But whether the statement of Polycrates be metaphor or matter of fact, its significance, as in the case of the Paschal celebration, is to be learnt from the Apostle's own language in the Apocalypse, where not only is great stress laid on the *priesthood* of the believers generally (i. 6, v. 10, xx. 6), but even the special privileges of the *high-priest* are bestowed on the victorious Christian (Rev. ii. 17, as explained by Züllig, Trench, and others: see Stanley l. c. p. 285; comp. Justin *Dial.* 116 ἀρχιερατικὸν τὸ ἀληθινὸν γένος ἐσμὲν τοῦ Θεοῦ, and see *Philippians* p. 252). The expression is a striking example of the lingering power not of Ebionite tenets but of Hebrew imagery.

[1] See above, p. 309, note 3.

[2] Owing to the difference of style, many critics have seen only the alternative of denying the apostolic authorship either of the Apocalypse or of the Gospel and Epistles. The considerations urged in the text seem sufficient to meet the difficulties, which are greatly increased if a late date is assigned to the Apocalypse. Writers of the Tübingen school reject the Gospel and Epistles but accept the Apocalypse. This book alone, if its apostolical authorship is conceded, seems to me to furnish an ample refutation of their peculiar views.

rather Greco-Asiatic. The teaching of these latter writings it will be unnecessary to examine; for all, I believe, will allow their general agreement with the theology of St Paul; and it were a bold criticism which should discover in them any Ebionite tendencies. Only it seems to be often overlooked that the leading doctrinal ideas which they contain are anticipated in the Apocalypse. The passages which I have quoted from the latter relating to the divinity of Christ are a case in point: not only do they ascribe to our Lord the same majesty and power; but the very title 'the Word,' with which both the Gospel and the first Epistle open, is found here, though it occurs nowhere else in the New Testament. On the other hand, if the Apocalypse seems to assign a certain prerogative to the Jews, this is expressed equally in the sayings of the Gospel that Christ 'came to his own (i. 11),' and that 'Salvation is of the Jews (iv. 22),' as it is involved also in St Paul's maxim 'to the Jew first and then to the Gentile.' It is indeed rather a historical fact than a theological dogma. The difference between the earlier and the later writings of St John is not in the fundamental conception of the Gospel, but in the subject and treatment and language. The Apocalypse is not Ebionite, unless the Gospel and Epistles are Ebionite also.

St James holds a local office.

3. St James occupies a position very different from St Peter or St John. If his importance to the brotherhood of Jerusalem was greater than theirs, it was far less to the world at large. In a foregoing essay I have attempted to show that he was not one of the Twelve. This result seems to me to have much more than a critical interest. Only when we have learnt to regard his office as purely local, shall we appreciate the traditional notices of his life or estimate truly his position in the conflict between Jewish and Gentile Christians.

Reasons for his appointment.

A disbeliever in the Lord's mission to the very close of His earthly life, he was convinced, it would seem, by the appearance of the risen Jesus[1]. This interposition marked him out for some special work. Among a people who set a high value on advantages of race

[1] See above, p. 265.

and blood, the Lord's brother would be more likely to win his way than a teacher who would claim no such connexion. In a state of religious feeling where scrupulous attention to outward forms was held to be a condition of favour with God, one who was a strict observer of the law, if not a rigid ascetic, might hope to obtain a hearing which would be denied to men of less austere lives and wider experiences. These considerations would lead to his selection as the ruler of the mother Church. The persecution of Herod which obliged the Twelve to seek safety in flight would naturally be the signal for the appointment of a resident head. At all events it is at this crisis that James appears for the first time with his presbytery in a position though not identical with, yet so far resembling, the 'bishop' of later times, that we may without much violence to language give him this title (Acts xii. 17, xxi. 18).

His allegiance to the law.

As the local representative then of the Church of the Circumcision we must consider him. To one holding this position the law must have worn a very different aspect from that which it wore to St Peter or St John or St Paul. While they were required to become 'all things to all men,' he was required only to be 'a Jew to the Jews.' No troublesome questions of conflicting duties, such as entangled St Peter at Antioch, need perplex him. Under the law he must live and die. His surname of the Just[1] is a witness to his rigid observance of the Mosaic ritual. A remarkable notice in the Acts shows how he identified himself in all external usages with those 'many thousands of Jews which believed and were all zealous of the law (xxi. 20).' And a later tradition, somewhat distorted indeed but perhaps in this one point substantially true, related how by his rigid life and strict integrity he had won the respect of the whole Jewish people[2].

The account of Hegesippus

A strict observer of the law he doubtless was; but whether to this he added a rigorous asceticism, may fairly be questioned. The

[1] In the account of Hegesippus, referred to in the following note, ὁ δίκαιος 'Justus' is used almost as a proper name. Two later bishops of Jerusalem in the early part of the second century also bear the name 'Justus' (Euseb. *H. E.* iv. 5), either in memory of their predecessor or in token of their own rigid lives: compare also Acts i. 23, xviii. 7, Col. iv. 11 (with the note).

[2] Hegesippus in Euseb. *H. E.* ii. 23.

account to which I have just referred, the tradition preserved in Hegesippus, represents him as observing many formalities not enjoined in the Mosaic ritual. 'He was holy,' says the writer, 'from his mother's womb. He drank no wine nor strong drink, neither did he eat flesh. No razor ever touched his head; he did not anoint himself with oil; he did not use the bath. He alone was allowed to enter into the holy place (εἰς τὰ ἅγια). For he wore no wool, but only fine linen. And he would enter into the temple (ναόν) alone, and be found there kneeling on his knees and asking forgiveness for the people, so that his knees grew hard like a camel's knees, because he was ever upon them worshipping God and asking forgiveness for the people.' There is much in this account which cannot be true: the assigning to him a privilege which was confined to the high-priest alone, while it is entangled with the rest of the narrative, is plainly false, and can only have been started when a new generation had grown up which knew nothing of the temple services[1]. Moreover the account of his testimony and death, which follows, not only contradicts the brief contemporary notice of Josephus[2], but is in itself

not trustworthy.

[1] It is perhaps to be explained like the similar account of St John: see above, p. 362, note. Compare Stanley *Apostolical Age* p. 324. Epiphanius (*Haer.* lxxviii. 14) makes the same statement of St James which Polycrates does of St John, πέταλον ἐπὶ τῆς κεφαλῆς ἐφόρεσε.

[2] Josephus (*Antiq.* xx. 9. 1) relates that in the interregnum between the death of Festus and the arrival of Albinus, the high-priest Ananus the younger, who belonged to the sect of the Sadducees (notorious for their severity in judicial matters), considering this a favourable opportunity καθίζει συνέδριον κριτῶν, καὶ παραγαγὼν εἰς αὐτὸ τὸν ἀδελφὸν Ἰησοῦ τοῦ λεγομένου Χριστοῦ, Ἰάκωβος ὄνομα αὐτῷ, καί τινας ἑτέρους, ὡς παρανομησάντων κατηγορίαν ποιησάμενος παρέδωκε λευσθησομένους. This notice is wholly irreconcilable with the account of Hegesippus. Yet it is probable in itself (which the account of Hegesippus is not), and is such as Josephus might be expected to write if he alluded to the matter at all. His stolid silence about Christianity elsewhere cannot be owing to ignorance, for a sect which had been singled out years before he wrote as a mark for imperial vengeance at Rome must have been only too well known in Judæa. On the other hand, if the passage had been a Christian interpolation, the notice of James would have been more laudatory, as is actually the case in the spurious passage of Josephus read by Origen and Eusebius (*H. E.* ii. 23, see above, p. 313, note 2), but not found in existing copies. On these grounds I do not hesitate to prefer the account in Josephus to that of Hegesippus. This is the opinion of Neander (*Planting* I. p. 367, Eng. Trans.), of Ewald (*Geschichte* VI. p. 547), and of some few writers besides (so recently Gerlach *Römische Statthalter etc.* p. 81, 1865): but the majority take the opposite view.

so melodramatic and so full of high improbabilities, that it must throw discredit on the whole context[1].

He was perhaps an ascetic.

We are not therefore justified in laying much stress on this tradition. It is interesting as a phenomenon, but not trustworthy as a history. Still it is possible that James may have been a Nazarite, may have been a strict ascetic. Such a representation perhaps some will view with impatience, as unworthy an Apostle of Christ. But this is unreasonable. Christian devotion does not assume the same

[1] The account is briefly this. Certain of the seven sects being brought by the preaching of James to confess Christ the whole Jewish people are alarmed. To counteract the spread of the new doctrine, the scribes and Pharisees request James, as a man of acknowledged probity, to 'persuade the multitude not to go astray concerning Jesus.' In order that he may do this to more effect, on the day of the Passover they place him on the pinnacle (πτερύγιον) of the temple. Instead of denouncing Jesus however, he preaches Him. Finding their mistake, the scribes and Pharisees throw him down from the height; and as he is not killed by the fall, they stone him. Finally he is despatched by a fuller's club, praying meanwhile for his murderers. The improbability of the narrative will appear in this outline, but it is much increased by the details. The points of resemblance with the portion of the Recognitions conjectured to be taken from the 'Ascents of James' (see above, p. 330) are striking, and recent writers have called attention to these as showing that the narrative of Hegesippus was derived from a similar source (Uhlhorn *Clement.* p. 367, Ritschl p. 226 sq). May we not go a step farther and hazard the conjecture that the story of the martyrdom, to which Hegesippus is indebted, was the grand *finale* of these 'Ascents,' of which the earlier portions are preserved in the Recognitions? The Recognitions record how James with the Twelve refuted the Jewish sects: the account of Hegesippus makes the conversion of certain of these sects the starting-point of the persecution which led to his martyrdom. In the Recognitions James is represented ascending the stairs which led up to the temple and addressing the people from these: in Hegesippus he is placed on the pinnacle of the temple whence he delivers his testimony. In the Recognitions he is thrown down the flight of steps and left as dead by his persecutors, but is taken up alive by the brethren; in Hegesippus he is hurled from the still loftier station, and this time his death is made sure. Thus the narrative of Hegesippus seems to preserve the consummation of his testimony and his sufferings, as treated in this romance, the last of a series of 'Ascents,' the first of these being embodied in the Recognitions.

If Hegesippus, himself no Ebionite, has borrowed these incidents (whether directly or indirectly, we cannot say) from an Ebionite source, he has done no more than Clement of Alexandria did after him (see above, p. 324), than Epiphanius, the scourge of heretics, does repeatedly. The religious romance seems to have been a favourite style of composition with the Essene Ebionites: and in the lack of authentic information relating to the Apostles, Catholic writers eagerly and unsuspiciously gathered incidents from writings of which they repudiated the doctrines. It is worthy of notice that though the *Essenes* are named among the sects in Hegesippus, they are not mentioned in the Recognitions; and that, while the Recognitions lay much stress on baptisms and washings (a cardinal doctrine of Essene Ebionism), this feature entirely disappears in the account of James given by Hegesippus.

outward garb in all persons, and at all times; not the same in James as in Paul; not the same in mediæval as in protestant Christianity. In James, the Lord's brother, if this account be true, we have the prototype of those later saints, whose rigid life and formal devotion elicits, it may be, only the contempt of the world, but of whom nevertheless the world was not and is not worthy.

St James stands apart from the Twelve in the Acts,

But to retrace our steps from this slippery path of tradition to firmer ground. The difference of position between St James and the other Apostles appears plainly in the narrative of the so-called Apostolic council in the Acts. It is Peter who proposes the emancipation of the Gentile converts from the law; James who suggests the restrictive clauses of the decree. It is Peter who echoes St Paul's sentiment that Jew and Gentile alike can hope to be saved only 'by the grace of the Lord Jesus'; James who speaks of Moses having them that preach him and being read in the synagogue every sabbath day. I cannot but regard this appropriateness of sentiment as a subsidiary proof of the authenticity of these speeches recorded by St Luke.

and in the Catholic Epistles.

And the same distinction extends also to their own writings. St Peter and St John, with a larger sphere of action and wider obligations, necessarily took up a neutral position with regard to the law, now carefully observing it at Jerusalem, now relaxing their observance among the Gentile converts. To St James on the other hand, mixing only with those to whom the Mosaic ordinances were the rule of life, the word and the thing have a higher importance. The neutrality of the former is reflected in the silence which pervades their writings, where 'law' is not once mentioned[1]. The respect of the latter appears in his differential use of the term, which he employs almost as a synonyme for 'Gospel[2].'

The Gospel a higher law.

But while so using the term 'law,' he nowhere implies that the Mosaic ritual is identical with or even a necessary part of Chris-

[1] As regards St John this is true only of the Epistles and the Apocalypse: in the Gospel the law is necessarily mentioned by way of narrative. In 1 Joh. iii. 4 it is said significantly, ἡ ἁμαρτία ἐστὶν ἡ ἀνομία. In St Peter neither νόμος nor ἀνομία occurs.

[2] The words εὐαγγέλιον, εὐαγγελίζεσθαι, do not occur in St James.

tianity. On the contrary he distinguishes the new dispensation as the perfect law, the law of liberty (i. 25, ii. 12), thus tacitly implying imperfection and bondage in the old. He assumes indeed that his readers pay allegiance to the Mosaic law (ii. 9, 10, iv. 11), and he accepts this condition without commenting upon it. But the mere ritual has no value in his eyes. When he refers to the Mosaic law, he refers to its moral, not to its ceremonial ordinances (ii. 8—11). The external service of the religionist who puts no moral restraint on himself, who will not exert himself for others, is pronounced deceitful and vain. The external service, the outward garb, the very ritual, of Christianity is a life of purity and love and self-devotion[1]. What its true essence, its inmost spirit, may be, the writer does not say, but leaves this to be inferred.

St James and St Paul.

Thus, though with St Paul the new dispensation is the negation of law, with St James the perfection of law, the ideas underlying these contradictory forms of expression need not be essentially different. And this leads to the consideration of the language held by both Apostles on the subject of faith and works.

Faith and works.

The real significance of St James's language, its true relation to the doctrine of St Paul, is determined by the view taken of the persons to whom the epistle is addressed. If it is intended to counteract any modification or perversion of St Paul's teaching, then there is, though not a plain contradiction, yet at all events a considerable divergency in the mode of dealing with the question by the two Apostles. I say the mode of dealing with the question, for antinomian inferences from his teaching are rebuked with even greater severity by St Paul himself than they are by St James[2]. If on the other hand the epistle is directed against an arrogant and barren orthodoxy, a Pharisaic self-satisfaction, to which the Churches of the Circumcision would be most exposed, then the case is considerably altered. The language of the Epistles to the Romans and Galatians

[1] James i. 26, 27. Coleridge directs attention to the meaning of θρησκεία, and the consequent bearing of the text, in a well-known passage in *Aids to Reflection*, Introd. Aphor. 23. For the signification of θρησκεία both in the New Testament and elsewhere, as the 'cultus exterior,' see Trench *Synon.* § xlviii.

[2] e.g. Rom. vi. 15—23, 1 Cor. vi. 9—20, Gal. v. 13 sq.

at once suggests the former as the true account. But further consideration leads us to question our first rapid inference. Justification and faith seem to have been common terms, Abraham's faith a common example, in the Jewish schools[1]. This fact, if allowed, counteracts the *prima facie* evidence on the other side, and leaves us free to judge from the tenour of the epistle itself. Now, since in this very passage St James mentions as the object of their vaunted faith, not the fundamental fact of the Gospel 'Thou believest that God raised Christ from the dead[2],' but the fundamental axiom of the law 'Thou believest that God is one[3]'; since moreover he elsewhere denounces the mere ritualist, telling him that his ritualism is nothing worth; since lastly the whole tone of the epistle recalls our Lord's denunciations of the scribes and Pharisees, and seems directed against a kindred spirit; it is reasonable to conclude that St James is denouncing not the moral aberrations of the professed disciple of St Paul (for with such he was not likely to be brought into close contact), but the self-complacent orthodoxy of the Pharisaic Christian, who, satisfied with the possession of a pure monotheism and vaunting his descent from Abraham, needed to be reminded not to neglect the still 'weightier matters' of a self-denying love. If this view be correct, the expressions of the two Apostles can hardly be compared, for they are speaking, as it were, a different language. But in either case we may acquiesce in the verdict of a recent able writer, more free than most men both from traditional and from reactionary prejudices, that in the teaching of the two Apostles 'there exists certainly a striking difference in the whole bent of mind, but no opposition of doctrine[4].'

Ebionite misrepresentations of St James explained.

Thus the representation of St James in the canonical Scriptures differs from its Ebionite counterpart as the true portrait from the caricature. The James of the Clementines could not have acquiesced in the apostolic decree, nor could he have held out the right hand of fellowship to St Paul. On the other hand, the Ebionite picture was not drawn entirely from imagination. A scrupulous observer

[1] See above, p. 164.

[2] Rom. x. 9.

[3] ii. 19. Comp. *Clem. Hom.* iii. 6 sq.

[4] Bleek (*Einl. in das N. T.* p. 550), who however considers that St James is writing against perversions of St Paul's teaching.

of the law, perhaps a rigid ascetic, partly from temper and habit, partly from the requirements of his position, he might, without any very direct or conscious falsification, appear to interested partisans of a later age to represent their own tenets, from which he differed less in the external forms of worship than in the vital principles of religion. Moreover during his lifetime he was compromised by those with whom his office associated him. In all revolutionary periods, whether of political or religious history, the leaders of the movement have found themselves unable to control the extravagances of their bigoted and short-sighted followers: and this great crisis of all was certainly not exempt from the common rule. St Paul is constantly checking and rebuking the excesses of those who professed to honour his name and to adopt his teaching: if we cannot state this of St James with equal confidence, it is because the sources of information are scantier.

His relations with the Judaizers.

Of the Judaizers who are denounced in St Paul's Epistles this much is certain; that they exalted the authority of the Apostles of the Circumcision: and that in some instances at least, as members of the mother Church, they had direct relations with James the Lord's brother. But when we attempt to define these relations, we are lost in a maze of conjecture.

Antioch.

The Hebrew Christians whose arrival at Antioch caused the rupture between the Jewish and Gentile converts are related to have 'come from James' (Gal. ii. 12). Did they bear any commission from him? If so, did it relate to independent matters, or to this very question of eating with the Gentiles? It seems most natural to interpret this notice by the parallel case of the Pharisaic brethren, who had before troubled this same Antiochene Church, 'going forth' from the Apostles and insisting on circumcision and the observance of the law, though they 'gave them no orders' (Acts xv. 24). But on the least favourable supposition it amounts to this, that St James, though he had sanctioned the emancipation of the Gentiles from the law, was not prepared to welcome them as Israelites and admit them as such to full communion: that in fact he had not yet overcome scruples which even St Peter had only relinquished after many years and by a special revelation; in this, as in his recognition of Jesus as the Christ, moving more slowly than the Twelve.

Galatia. Turning from Antioch to Galatia, we meet with Judaic teachers who urged circumcision on the Gentile converts and, as the best means of weakening the authority of St Paul, asserted for the Apostles of the Circumcision the exclusive right of dictating to the Church. How great an abuse was thus made of the names of the Three, I trust the foregoing account has shown: yet here again the observance of the law by the Apostles of the Circumcision, especially by St James, would furnish a plausible argument to men who were unscrupulous enough to turn the occasional concessions of St Paul himself to the same account. But we are led to ask, Did these false teachers belong to the mother Church? had they any relation with James? is it possible that they had ever been personal disciples of the Lord Himself? There are some faint indications that such was the case; and, remembering that there was a Judas among the Twelve, we cannot set aside this supposition as impossible.

Corinth. In Corinth again we meet with false teachers of a similar stamp; whose opinions are less marked indeed than those of St Paul's Galatian antagonists, but whose connexion with the mother Church is more clearly indicated. It is doubtless among those who said 'I am of Peter, and I of Christ,' among the latter especially, that we are to seek the counterpart of the Galatian Judaizers[1]. To the latter class St Paul alludes again in the Second Epistle: these must have been the men who 'trusted to themselves that they were *of Christ*' (x. 7), who invaded another's sphere of labour and boasted of work

The two Judaizing parties.

[1] Several writers representing different schools have agreed in denying the existence of a 'Christ party.' Possibly the word 'party' may be too strong to describe what was rather a sentiment than an organization. But if admissible at all, I cannot see how, allowing that there were three parties, the existence of the fourth can be questioned. For (1) the four watchwords are co-ordinated, and there is no indication that ἐγὼ δὲ Χριστοῦ is to be isolated from the others and differently interpreted. (2) The remonstrance immediately following (μεμέρισται ὁ Χριστός) shows that the name of Christ, which ought to be common to all, had been made the badge of a party. (3) In 2 Cor. x. 7 the words εἴ τις πέποιθεν ἑαυτῷ Χριστοῦ εἶναι and the description which follows gain force and definiteness on this supposition. There is in fact more evidence for the existence of a party of Christ than there is of a party of Peter.

which was ready to hand (x. 13—16), who were 'false apostles, crafty workers, transforming themselves into apostles of Christ' (xi. 13), who 'commended themselves' (x. 12, 18), who vaunted their pure Israelite descent (xi. 21—23). It is noteworthy that this party of extreme Judaizers call themselves by the name not of James, but of Christ. This may perhaps be taken as a token that his concessions to Gentile liberty had shaken their confidence in his fidelity to the law. The leaders of this extreme party would appear to have seen Christ in the flesh: hence their watchword 'I am of Christ'; hence also St Paul's counter-claim that 'he was of Christ' also, and his unwilling boast that he had himself had visions and revelations of the Lord in abundance (xii. 1 sq). On the other hand, of the party of Cephas no distinct features are preserved; but the passage itself implies that they differed from the extreme Judaizers, and we may therefore conjecture that they took up a middle position with regard to the law, similar to that which was occupied later by the Nazarenes. In claiming Cephas as the head of their party they had probably neither more nor less ground than their rivals who sheltered themselves under the names of Apollos and of Paul.

Letters of commendation.

Is it to these extreme Judaizers that St Paul alludes when he mentions 'certain persons' as 'needing letters of recommendation to the Corinthians and of recommendation from them' (2 Cor. iii. 1)? If so, by whom were these letters to Corinth given? By some half-Judaic, half-Christian brotherhood of the dispersion? By the mother Church of Jerusalem? By any of the primitive disciples? By James the Lord's brother himself? It is wisest to confess plainly that the facts are too scanty to supply an answer. We may well be content to rest on the broad and direct statements in the Acts and Epistles, which declare the relations between St James and St Paul. A habit of suspicious interpretation, which neglects plain facts and dwells on doubtful allusions, is as unhealthy in theological criticism as in social life, and not more conducive to truth.

Inferences from these notices.

Such incidental notices then, though they throw much light on the practical difficulties and entanglements of his position, reveal nothing or next to nothing of the true principles of St James. Only so long as we picture to ourselves an ideal standard of obedience, where the will of the ruler is the law of the subject, will such notices cause us perplexity. But, whether this be a healthy condition for any society or not, it is very far from representing the state of Christendom in the apostolic ages. If the Church had been a religious machine, if the Apostles had possessed absolute control over its working, if the manifold passions of men had been for once annihilated, if there had been no place for misgiving, prejudice, treachery, hatred, superstition, then the picture would have been very different. But then also the history of the first ages of the Gospel would have had no lessons for us. As it is, we may well take courage from the study. However great may be the theological differences and religious animosities of our own time, they are far surpassed in magnitude by the distractions of an age which, closing our eyes to facts, we are apt to invest with an ideal excellence. In the early Church was fulfilled, in its inward dissensions no less than in its outward sufferings, the Master's sad warning that He came 'not to send peace on earth, but a sword.'

INDEX.

CAMBRIDGE: PRINTED BY C. J. CLAY, M.A. AND SONS, AT THE UNIVERSITY PRESS.

www.ingramcontent.com/pod-product-compliance
Lightning Source LLC
Chambersburg PA
CBHW031412230426
43668CB00007B/281
* 9 7 8 3 7 4 4 6 6 1 1 5 7 *